D1401932

University Casebook Series

PROBLEMS AND MATERIALS

ON

PROFESSIONAL RESPONSIBILITY

By

THOMAS D. MORGAN
S. Chesterfield Oppenheim Professor of Law
The George Washington University
National Law Center

and

RONALD D. ROTUNDA
Albert E. Jenner, Jr., Professor of Law
University of Illinois
College of Law

SIXTH EDITION

Westbury, New York
THE FOUNDATION PRESS, INC.
1995

Library of Congress Cataloging-in-Publication Data

Morgan, Thomas D.
 Problems and materials on professional responsibility / Thomas D.
Morgan, Ronald D. Rotunda. — 6. ed.
   p. cm. — (University casebook series)
 Includes bibliographical references and index.
 ISBN 1–56662–254–9
 1. Legal ethics—United States—Cases. I. Rotunda, Ronald D.
II. Series.
KF306.A4M6 1995
174'.3'0973—dc20   95–12171

TEXT IS PRINTED ON 10% POST CONSUMER RECYCLED PAPER

To Kathryn and Marcia

*

PREFACE

The law of professional responsibility continues to evolve. From concerns about the appearance of impropriety that had lain dormant until Watergate, through the transformation of the profession into a larger, more diverse, more competitive institution, lawyers have found that their status and behavioral norms are not always what they had thought them to be.

In the face of all of this change, experience has confirmed, however, the continued utility of the problem approach in helping students understand these issues. As is sometimes said about law school examinations, "The questions remain the same; only the answers keep changing."

In this edition, we have made a special effort to cite recent cases and readings raising contemporary issues. We have also organized the problems in a way that largely tracks the A.L.I. Restatement of the Law (Third): The Law Governing Lawyers. Even though the Restatement is not in final form, we believe its internal logic will structure the way lawyers will think about ethical issues during the period in which your students will be practicing.

We express our thanks to the authors and publishers cited, in particular, the American Bar Association, for permission to reprint their copyrighted material. We thank Ruth Manint for her assistance in preparation of the manuscript, and Christopher Lentz (J.D., '95), the Stuart N. Greenberger Research Assistant in Legal Ethics, and Daniel Eisele, (LL.M., 1995), for their research assistance. We also thank the many professors and practitioners, in particular, Victor Kramer, Jonathan Rose and Robert Tuttle, who have offered thoughtful comments and suggestions on our materials.

Footnotes to articles are numbered as in the original. No special indication is made when footnotes or other citations have been deleted. We have usually described the positions of authors of major readings using the position held at the time the article was written.

T.D.M.
R.D.R.

Washington, DC
Champaign, IL
March, 1995

*

SUMMARY OF CONTENTS

*

TABLE OF CONTENTS

TABLE OF CASES

Principal cases are in italic type. Non-principal cases are in roman type. References are to Pages.

TABLE OF CASES

TABLE OF OTHER AUTHORITIES

TABLE OF OTHER AUTHORITIES

TABLE OF OTHER AUTHORITIES

TABLE OF OTHER AUTHORITIES

TABLE OF OTHER AUTHORITIES

TABLE OF OTHER AUTHORITIES

TABLE OF OTHER AUTHORITIES

TABLE OF OTHER AUTHORITIES

*

Chapter I

THE LEGAL PROFESSION: BACKGROUND AND FUNDAMENTAL ISSUES

A. Introduction

DOONESBURY by Garry Trudeau

The Doonesbury humor is still biting, but in this case Garry Trudeau proved a poor prophet. The study of professional responsibility has proved to be more than "just another defunct fad." It has survived and prospered and seems likely to continue to do so. At least three reasons may account for the continuing interest.

First, the subject of the course in professional responsibility is the legal profession itself. It has not escaped law students that while they may use the substance of their torts course periodically, they will use the substance of professional responsibility daily. This course is about lawyers as they engage in the practice of law. Whatever the theoretical interest of the subject matter, its practical content is extremely high.

Second, at the time Trudeau produced the Doonesbury cartoon, the ABA Model Code of Professional Responsibility was only five years old. Many people believed that the Code, the product of several years work by a distinguished commission, had resolved all questions that were worth considering.

Almost as soon as significant numbers of people began to look seriously at the Code, however, they realized it had answered many questions badly and left others unresolved altogether. The work of the ABA Commission on Evaluation of Professional Standards, commonly called the Kutak Commission after its chair, the late Robert J. Kutak, produced the ABA Model Rules of Professional Conduct and demonstrated that there were many issues left to debate and discuss.

Third, while work in professional responsibility during the 1970s focused primarily on the legal rules applicable to an attorney's behavior, it has become increasingly clear that "legal ethics" offers an unusually good opportunity to apply the insights of history, sociology, economics and philosophy to fundamental legal questions.

What such study reveals is that, far from being a unitary profession with a long and consistent tradition grounded in fundamental philosophical ideals, the legal profession is a rich, complex, and often perverse mixture of traditions, roles and standards. Understanding the insights and distinctions suggested by history and philosophy will not automatically resolve practical problems, but they may help a lawyer better understand the questions presented and better see relationships between issues that otherwise might be obscured.

B. Development of the American Legal Profession

As of 1995, the United States has about 875,000 practicing lawyers. That is about 2½ times the number in 1970. Roughly 40,000 new lawyers are admitted to the bar each year from ABA accredited schools, and about 15,000 leave the practice annually due to death, retirement, or simply because they don't like the work.[1]

In any event, if present trends continue the bar is likely to have about one million members in the year 2000. Not everyone takes a sanguine view of this development. The growth of the profession led Harvard President Derek Bok, for example, to assert:

> The net result of these trends is a massive diversion of exceptional talent into pursuits that often add little to the growth of the economy, the pursuit of culture, or the enhancement of the human spirit. I cannot press this point too strongly. * * * [T]he supply of exceptional people is limited. Yet far too many of these rare individuals are becoming lawyers at a time when the country cries out for more talented business executives, more enlightened public servants, more inventive engineers, more able high-school principals and teachers.

> * * * A nation's values and problems are mirrored in the ways in which it uses its ablest people. In Japan, a country

1. The most carefully documented statistics on the American legal profession are those in the American Bar Foundation study by Barbara A. Curran, The Lawyer Statistical Report—A Statistical Profile of the U.S. Legal Profession in the 1980s (1985), and Barbara A. Curran & Clara N. Carson, Supplement to the Lawyer Statistical Report: The U.S. Legal Profession in 1988 (1991). More recent data is contained in ABA Task Force on Law Schools and the Profession: Narrowing the Gap, Legal Education and Professional Development—An Educational Continuum (1992) (hereafter ABA Task Force). Even when calculated as carefully as in these studies, of course, the number of lawyers will always be an estimate primarily because of the difficulty in knowing how many licensed lawyers are no longer engaged in a law-related activity.

only half our size, 30 percent more engineers graduate each year than in all the United States. But Japan boasts a total of less than 15,000 lawyers, while American universities graduate 35,-000 *every year.* It would be hard to claim that these differences have no practical consequences. As the Japanese put it, "Engineers make the pie grow larger; lawyers only decide how to carve it up." [2]

――――――

QUESTIONS

1. Do you agree with President Bok's analysis? Apart from any given lawyer's economic interest in slowing the growth of the legal profession, can one objectively say that there are too many lawyers? What standard would you use to make such an assessment? For example, can you say that all persons with a need for a lawyer now get help at prices they can afford?

2. The average American lawyer earns over $100,000 per year.[3] Is such an income level characteristic of a profession that is overcrowded? Does the income data tend to answer President Bok's concerns, or does it tend to reinforce them?

――――――

Whatever one's answers to these questions, it is clear that the legal profession and the role of the lawyer in our society is significantly different today than at most times in the nation's history. The following two excerpts help put our present situation into context.

RICHARD B. MORRIS,* THE LEGAL PROFESSION IN AMERICA ON THE EVE OF THE REVOLUTION, IN HARRY W. JONES, ED., POLITICAL SEPARATION AND LEGAL CONTINUITY
4–11, 18–19 (1976).

* * *

If the Revolutionary era was a legal- and constitution-minded age dominated by lawyers, the period of seventeenth-century settlement was

2. Bok, "A Flawed System": Report to the [Harvard] Board of Overseers, 85 HARVARD Magazine 38, 41 (May-June 1983).

3. There is not good recent data but a number of sources confirm this figure, among them Blodgett, Time and Money: A Look at Today's Lawyer, ABA Journal, Sept. 1, 1986, p. 47. The median income of lawyers was lower—$64,448 in 1986. According to the ABA survey, about 45% of American lawyers in 1986 earned between $35,000 and $75,000 per year. Another

35% earned between $75,000 and $250,000 annually. About 16% earned less than $35,000 per year, and about 4% earned over $250,000. Lawyer salaries, on average, have remained constant or even fallen in recent years. Lissy, American Management Ass'n Compensation and Benefits Review, p. 10 (May 1994).

* The author was Gouverneur Morris Professor of History Emeritus at Columbia University.

the miraculous era of law without lawyers, a time when law was shaped by theologians, politicians, farmers, fishermen, and merchants. This generalization applies to all the colonies settled before the Stuart Restoration, but it is conspicuously appropriate to the Puritan colonies wherein the clergy played an exceptional role in lawmaking and where laymen universally acted as judges. Not a single lawyer came to Plymouth on the *Mayflower*. Massachusetts Bay, settled a decade later, did have some legally-trained men among its first arrivals, but not one among them had then been practicing law in England. The first educated attorney venturing to practice in that colony was Thomas Lechford, whose activities dating from 1637 or thereabouts, were limited, since he was disbarred shortly thereafter for tampering with a jury. While lawyers were not technically prevented from practice, Article XXVI of the Body of Liberties, the initial law code adopted in 1641, while permitting attorneys to plead causes other than their own, disallowed all fees or rewards, thus, for a time at least, withholding inducements to practice as a respectable means of livelihood. Indeed, many of John Cotton's fellow Puritans, both in England and in America at that time, would have agreed with his characterization of lawyers as unconscionable advocates who "bolster out a bad case by quirks of writ and tricks and quillets of law."

Early hostility to the profession of the law was by no means confined to reformist New England. It was manifest as well in the tobacco colonies. A Maryland act of 1674 recited the allegation that the "good people of this Province are much burthened" by lawyers taking and exacting "excessive fees." Curbs continued into the eighteenth century. In 1707, Maryland's legislature set rules for controlling the admission of attorneys on the basis of the alleged "corruption, ignorance and extortion" of several of them and set such ceilings on fees that leading attorneys withdrew in protest from practice for a short time. The limitation on fees continued in force as late as 1729. In Virginia so deep-seated was anti-lawyer prejudice that a statute of 1645 virtually disbarred paid attorneys. Its repeal a decade later failed to end discrimination against the legal profession. In 1657 the court heavily fined a lawyer for appearing in court on behalf of a client, and the situation was not stabilized until 1680, when attorneys were permitted to practice under rigid restrictions and after obtaining a license from the governor.

* * *

Whether the low repute of the lawyers stemmed from their relatively obscure social origins in this early period, from their lack of professionalism, or from their tendency to regard law as a minor part of the multiple enterprises in which they were engaged, their early conduct failed to evoke good will. In short, courts dominated by laymen informed by a few basic lawbooks such as Dalton's *Country Justice*, as in the contemporary English county seats, and litigated by attorneys in fact, who were agents with powers of attorney (including among them numerous wives of absent litigants), provided the substance of justice without the benefit of a professional bar.

* * *

* * * Somewhere between the Stuart Restoration and that systematic imperial machinery set up following the Glorious Revolution, one finds that the socio-economic structure of the colonies underwent a transformation. In the North a merchant-capitalist system was evolving based upon rapidly expanding transatlantic and intercolonial trade. In the South, a plantation economy emerged, based on the production for export of the great staples, tobacco and rice, and spawning a slave-holding and property-conscious society. That emergent business society was less egalitarian than at the time of settlement and determined to protect its interests against a variety of threats—whether from the constrictive trade laws of Parliament, from challenges to land titles, or from depreciating currencies. Everywhere the propertied class now exerted an influence toward security and stability, while the rapid expansion of business and the utilization of more sophisticated instruments in transatlantic trade necessitated a resort to the more technical legal system of the mother country.

Somewhere, then, around 1690 we find the legal profession establishing a foothold in the colonies. While the roster of trained legal specialists expanded dramatically over the next three decades, nonspecialists without professional training were descending on the courts in hordes. A host of parasitic pettifoggers, encouraged by the practice of filing writs by sheriffs and their deputies, easily outnumbered the trained members of the bar. Shoemakers, wigmakers, and masons procured deputations from the sheriffs and stirred up petty and contemptible litigation. It seems almost incredible that the colonial folk of the eighteenth century would manifest a litigious spirit even more intense than their forbears, but the theologian-statesman Cotton Mather was prompted in 1719 to found, in addition to a variety of organizations for effective lobbying and for suppressing vice, a Society of Peacemakers, which aimed to "divert Law-suits" and promote arbitration. If Mather achieved any success, it was not perceptible to the later generation of lawyers which claimed John Adams. Rather did Adams, whose own town attained such notoriety that "as litigious as Braintree" became proverbial, feel impelled to declaim against "the dirty dabblers in the law" who were taking bread out of the mouths of respectable lawyers.

Efforts to limit the legal profession to qualified attorneys mark the entire pre-Revolutionary era, along with enjoining sheriffs and their deputies from filing writs or giving legal advice. Even earlier, in the first few decades of the eighteenth century we find the legal profession asserting its claims to a monopoly over litigation. In New York a bar association has been unearthed as early as 1710, and one scholar insists that it functioned continuously thereafter, certainly in a rather formal sense by the year 1756. In Massachusetts an embryo bar association can be traced back at least to the year 1759. Even John Adams found its meeting "delightful." Aside from affording their members a chance for sociability, such associations, in effect guilds, were concerned about limiting the number of practitioners, restricting clerkships, barring the disqualified and, in later years, proposing legislative reforms.

To a rising and ambitious lawyer like Adams, the restrictive measures that had been taken by the bar of his province did not seem a sufficient deterrent, and he was led to bemoan the threatening number of his juniors seeking admission to practice. "They swarm and multiply," he complained with characteristic exaggeration. Still, the standards that were drawn up in Massachusetts were rather rigid. The Essex County bar in 1769 prescribed three years of clerking before admission to the inferior courts, another two years of practice in the lower courts before being admitted to the Superior Court as an attorney, and another two years more in practice before the Superior Court as a prerequisite to the status of barrister that they were desperately intent on establishing. Not only did they attempt to transplant those distinctions in the legal profession found in contemporary England, but in 1762 they further introduced the pageantry of the common law courts by requiring judges and lawyers to wear austere judicial gowns and wigs, a practice emulated in New York two years later.

In New York also, the lawyers raised the bars. An agreement entered into in 1756 by the "gentlemen of the Law" provided that they would cease taking any clerks for a period of fourteen years, the only exception being that each subscriber could take one of his own sons. Furthermore, at the end of that period, when clerkships were reopened, the lawyers stipulated that clerks must possess college degrees and that attorneys could take only one clerk at a time. The lawyer was to exact a £200 fee from his clerk, who would be required to serve for a minimum of five years. It was this monopolistic agreement which stood in the way of young John Jay's plans to study law. His father, a prosperous New York merchant, considered sending his son to London or Bristol to clerk in a law office there. He found out that in Bristol a five-year clerkship was required and the payment of a fee of from £200 to £300. If there was no alternative, Jay's father even thought of enrolling his son at the Inns of Court. Fortunately for Jay, in January of 1764 the members of the New York City bar relaxed their rules. Under the new agreement, an attorney could take a second clerk, but only after his first clerk had served for three years, thus insuring that no attorney would have more than two clerks at one time. Benjamin Kissam agreed to take John Jay on under these terms, but in fact Kissam had taken Lindley Murray as his clerk only a year before. Strictly speaking, Kissam should have waited until the end of 1764 before admitting another clerk to his office. Somehow these technicalities were waived; no one seems to have protested, and the first Chief Justice of the United States Supreme Court finally won his chance to climb the ladder of the legal profession.

ROBERT STEVENS,** DEMOCRACY AND THE LEGAL
PROFESSION: CAUTIONARY NOTES

3 Learning and the Law 18 (No. 3, 1976).***

Law was not a profession [then] open to the masses, and during the 1780s and 1790s in most states an effort was made to keep it as narrow as possible. Each state except for Virginia—and that for peculiar reasons—retained a period of apprenticeship. This period was reduced if the young lawyer attended college, but there were still only half a dozen colleges in the new states. (For instance, Massachusetts had a five-year apprenticeship at that time, but only three years for Harvard or Yale graduates.)

* * * We still don't know what happened to lawyers [from 1820 to 1860] * * *. But what we can say, categorically, is that if the profession was heavily anglicized until 1820, after 1820 the old English notions of the professions slowly collapsed.

The differences between the American and English systems of legal training were made dramatically evident. In America, there was an obvious decline of formal structures; the bar associations had largely evaporated, as had the apprenticeship system. Legal education in the United States had fallen into a decline. The legal profession was "wide open." Such training as there was in law was almost invariably picked up on the job.

What does appear to have emerged from the impact of these forces is that, by the mid-nineteenth century, the lawyer had a different function in America from his counterpart in England. He became the man who greased the wheels of society—what today might be referred to, depending on one's perspective, as the "leading citizen," "hired gun," or "the multi-purpose social science decision maker." Whichever perspective you have, however, there is no question that the concept of the lawyer and the function he served in America after the Civil War bore little resemblance to his English counterparts.

What happened after 1870, both in the society as a whole and in the legal profession, was a process of institutionalization. It followed the years of Civil War, of rapid growth in population and of westward expansion. It was a time when great corporations were born, when great law firms grew and when universities came of age.

Significantly, the development of legal education—or, more accurately, of the resurgence of law schools—preceded that of the legal profession. Dwight at Columbia in the late 1860s, and Langdell, who became dean of Harvard Law School in 1870, were the two who set the pattern for the kind of legal education which we think of today.

What Langdell did was to take the erratic law training as it was being practiced in the law offices and systematize it. Building on the

** At the time of this article, the author was Provost at Tulane University.

earlier work of Story at Harvard, he completed the process of taking law training out of the law offices and placed it firmly inside the universities. Academic law became respectable, as it never had been under the English system—or during the Jacksonian period.

* * *

Langdell had a vision of academic respectability, and he was remarkably successful as a role model. Other universities began developing law schools, as did various private entrepreneurs. At the same time, under pressure from the ABA, states gradually reintroduced a period of apprenticeship.

Indeed, by 1900 most states had returned to the three-year apprenticeship requirement, and bar exams had begun to reappear in the 1890s. Yet legal education still remained voluntary. "The principle of supply and demand works" remarked the Englishman Bryce upon his visit to Harvard during this time. "No one is obliged to attend these courses to obtain admission and the [bar] examinations are generally too lax to require elaborate preparation. But the instruction is found so valuable, so helpful for professional success, that young men throng the lecture halls, willingly spending two or three years in the scientific study of law, which they might have spent in the chambers of a practicing lawyer."

Basically, anyone who wanted to be a lawyer could hang out his shingle, and there were very few requirements for doing so, except limited apprenticeship in some states. So the vast majority of lawyers at the turn of the century—80 to 90 percent—never saw the inside of a university, whether it was a law school or a college. Most of them had to take a bar exam, but, unlike the situation today, the market was the primary determinant of whether they would be successful.

Meanwhile, Harvard Law School continued to grow and to train the elite lawyers—at least those whose parents had money. In 1900 a young man went to Harvard Law School if he wanted to practice with one of the large Boston or New York firms. But in addition, there were a plethora of other law schools—part-time and full-time, one year, two year and three year—while apprenticeship remained the normal method of entry to the profession.

In the last 70 years, we have seen the apprenticeship method go the way of the dodo and formal, institutionalized legal education become compulsory.

What happened was not really the academic lawyer's fault. It was the American Bar Association's. I don't mean to say that the academic lawyer was entirely innocent in the implementation of this retrograde step, but it was the ABA which was the primary mover in making law school compulsory. It wanted to make law school compulsory because it wanted to contribute to "raising standards."

"Raising standards" is purposely vague. What it meant in this case undoubtedly included concern over the large number of illiterate and dishonest lawyers. A significant number of lawyers in 1900 had not finished high school and heretofore the ABA's effort to raise standards was in part a genuine effort to protect the public.

The developments, however, also represented an effort on the part of many practitioners to restrict numbers. The move was, to some extent, an anticompetitive device, and it was also undoubtedly—although I think that some recent studies overstate this—an effort to discriminate against certain groups. It was an effort to keep blacks and immigrant groups—especially Jews—out of the legal profession.

The first state to make law school compulsory was West Virginia which, in 1928, required one year of law school. It was not difficult to see where these pressures were coming from. West Virginia argued the need to inculcate "The Spirit of American Government." A New York delegate to the ABA put it more bluntly: "The need to have lawyers able to read, write and talk the English language—not Bohemian, not Gaelic, not Yiddish, but English." That was the beginning of compulsory legal education and prior college training in the United States—the debates of the House of Delegates in the 1930s and 1940s make it clear that the same sentiment motivated the ABA when it tried to drive out some law schools—and the depression provided a powerful stimulus to "raising standards."

Gradually, between 1929 and 1942 each state, partly for anticompetitive reasons and partly in a genuine effort to raise standards, followed the lead of West Virginia—and the suggestions of the American Bar Association. In 1920 there had still been a certain flexibility: many law schools only had two-year programs and only two or three law schools required an undergraduate degree. Increasingly, lawyers had gone to law school and most of the leading universities had law schools—but not because they were required to. At that time virtually every state allowed, as an alternative, three years of apprenticeship; and the majority of American lawyers had still not been to law school.

By 1950 attendance at law school was compulsory, and during the 1950s law school entrance requirements included two, and later three years of college. It was all part of the movement to "improve standards," although for reasons both good and bad. Moreover, in the post-Second World War years, the number of lawyers who had attended law school for the first time outran the number who had not.

The transition from compulsory apprenticeship to compulsory legal education was accomplished in three steps. First, law schools had become an alternative to apprenticeship; second, they had gradually driven out apprenticeship, and finally, they had become anxious to tighten standards and cut back on the number of accredited schools, thereby further limiting access to a legal education.

* * *

The question of access to the legal profession, especially for minorities, is directly tied to the accreditation process. For example, when a new, small, low cost law school opens which has a sizable minority student population, is that school serving a minority group or exploiting it? The line between serving and exploiting is an extremely difficult one, but, in effect, there is always an inherent danger in a self-regulating profession to reproduce itself in the same colors and tones.

Changes in the Bar Over the Past Twenty Years

The above articles were written in 1976 at the time of the bicentennial of the nation and the centennial of the founding of the American Bar Association. Few lawyers in 1976 could have predicted the changes in professional life that were about to come.

The profession in 1976 was beginning a rate of growth that has not abated and that so concerned President Bok a few years later. The number of lawyers admitted to the bar in 1975 was 34,930, for example; that was almost double the number admitted in 1970.[4]

The demographics of the legal profession had begun to change as well. Less than 7,000 women were in law school in 1970; the figure rose to over 40,000 by 1980.[5] During the same decade, the number of African–Americans in law school rose from less than 4000 to almost 15,000.[6] The numbers were even higher by the end of the 1980s.[7]

The rules governing the practice of law were likewise on the brink of change. Before 1975, most lawyers adhered to schedules that established minimum levels for their fees for countless services.[8] Lawyers were potentially subject to professional discipline if they allowed their legal talents to be praised in a positive newspaper story.[9]

Further, while some legal practitioners have always been more prominent or successful than others, the profession has probably become even more stratified than before. Professors Heinz and Laumann concluded their landmark study of Chicago lawyers this way:

> [M]uch of the differentiation within the legal profession is secondary to one fundamental distinction—the distinction between lawyers who represent large organizations (corporations, labor unions, or government) and those who represent individuals. The two kinds of law practice are the two hemispheres of the profession. Most lawyers reside exclusively in one hemisphere or the other and seldom, if ever, cross the equator.

4. ABA Task Force at 14.

5. Id. at 18.

6. Id. at 25.

7. By 1991, for example, women constituted 43% of law school students. Curran, Lawyers in Profile, in 5 Researching Law: An American Bar Foundation Update 1, 4 col. 2 (Spring, 1994).

8. The fee schedules were found to violate the antitrust laws in Goldfarb v. Virgi-

nia State Bar, 421 U.S. 773, 95 S.Ct. 2004, 44 L.Ed.2d 572 (1975), discussed in Problem 7, infra.

9. Cf., Belli v. State Bar, 10 Cal.3d 824, 112 Cal.Rptr. 527, 519 P.2d 575 (1974) (lawyer censured for comments in advertisement for scotch in which his legal talent was praised).

Lawyers who serve major corporations and other large organizations differ systematically from those who work for individuals and small businesses whether we look at the social origins of the lawyers, the prestige of the law schools they attended, their social or political values, their networks of friends and professional associates, or several other social variables.[10]

In 1986, the ABA appointed a "Commission on Professionalism". Its report called for the profession's return to a common set of institutional values based on Roscoe Pound's definition of a profession as "a common calling in the spirit of a public service—no less a public service because it may incidentally be a means of livelihood." [11]

As you work your way through these materials, ask yourself whether law indeed is still a profession with a common core. Is it united by any more than a set of regulatory provisions? If there are still core values, do they include the "spirit of a public service." If not, should the lack of such a core be a cause for concern?

In the mid–1990s, of course, the principal concern of lawyers may be which of them will continue to have jobs. Editor Stephen Brill has predicted that large firms may have to lay off as many as one-third of their lawyers.[12] There is reason to believe those concerns may be overstated, but there will unquestionably be increased pressure for the efficient delivery of legal services at ever lower prices.[13]

What will such pressures do to the idea of a unified legal profession? What will it do to lawyers' ability and willingness to deliver pro bono service? Can lawyers' professional standards survive the economic pressures lawyers will face? Will the profession itself survive if its standards do not exceed those of the economic marketplace?

C. The Development of Standards of Professional Conduct

For at least 150 years, American lawyers have tried to describe proper professional behavior. The earliest such standards were statements of moral principles that had no legal effect. Throughout most of the 19th Century, such principles were developed and published by lawyers who were also teaching law.

In 1836, for example, Baltimore lawyer David Hoffman closed his two volume *A Course of Legal Study* with "Fifty Resolutions" to which he urged lawyers to adhere. Those resolutions, in turn, appear to have

---

10. J. Heinz & E. Laumann, Chicago Lawyers: The Social Structure of the Bar, pp. 319–20 (1982).

11. Roscoe Pound, The Lawyer from Antiquity to Modern Times 5 (1953).

12. E.g., Steven Brill, The Coming Crisis: Lopping off a Third, The American Lawyer, June 1993, p. 5; Discussion, Is There 30% Overcapacity?, The American Lawyer, Oct. 1993, p. 7.

13. E.g., Thomas D. Morgan, Economic Reality Facing Twenty–First Century Lawyers, 69 U.Wash.L.Rev. 625 (1994).

been an important influence on the writing of George Sharswood, whose *A Compend of Lectures on the Aims and Duties of the Profession of the Law* was published in Philadelphia in 1854.

Sharswood's standards are usually cited as the source of the Code of Ethics adopted by the State of Alabama in 1887. It was the Alabama Code, in turn, that formed the basis for the American Bar Association's first statement of ethical principles, the Canons of Professional Ethics, published in 1908.

The ABA Canons remained the national professional model for over sixty years, although over that time its original thirty-two Canons were supplemented by fifteen others. You will find the ABA Canons in the Standards Supplement to this book. In many states, however, lawyers were subject to professional discipline for offenses not much more specific than "conduct unbecoming a lawyer."

Thus, in 1969, the ABA adopted its Model Code of Professional Responsibility. That Code, adopted almost universally by state supreme courts around the country, was a set of principles designed to be more specific and more amenable to disciplinary enforcement.

The nine "Canons" in the Code were "axiomatic norms," i.e., general propositions serving as little more than chapter headings for the rest of the text. The "Disciplinary Rules" were "mandatory in character," that is, violations would subject the attorney to discipline up to and including disbarment. The Ethical Considerations, on the other hand, were "aspirational in character" and were said to be an unenforceable but articulate statement of the profession's consensus about proper lawyer behavior.

As mentioned earlier in connection with the Doonesbury cartoon, and as you will see throughout this course, the decade of the 1970s was a period of great ferment in the field of legal ethics. Important Supreme Court cases were handed down and there was vigorous debate about ethical propositions that had to that point been little challenged.

Thus, in 1983, the ABA adopted yet another version of its statement of professional standards. The ABA Model Rules of Professional Conduct are structured in a "Restatement" format. They have black-letter rules that are followed by explanatory "Comments" and notes comparing the Model Rules to the Model Code.[14] The Comments are meant to have authoritative status; the Code Comparison notes do not.

It is important to understand, however, that none of the ABA documents is legally binding on anyone. That is, they are models that must be adopted or rejected by individual state supreme courts before they have any legal effect. As of 1995, over thirty-five states have revised their own rules to follow the Model Rules in substantial part.

---

14. Unlike an actual Restatement, however, the Model Rules offer no examples and illustrative cases.

Others have amended their Model Code to adopt important Model Rules ideas.

Both the ABA Model Rules and the ABA Model Code are contained in the Standards Supplement to this book. In this text, we ask how both the Model Rules and Model Code approach the ethical problems confronting lawyers. Keep in mind, however, that the "Code of Ethics" that will be legally binding on you will be the one adopted by the supreme court of the state or states in which you are licensed.[15] It may or may not correspond exactly to the ABA model from which it is derived.

At least three other sources of authority and advice will also be important to your analysis of problems. First are the decisions of courts, whether in cases seeking discipline of lawyers, civil suits seeking malpractice damages, contempt proceedings, criminal cases, or the like.

In addition, the ABA and state and local bar associations often issue ethics opinions. These are advisory opinions that respond to a specific question or to an assumed state of facts. Courts often cite such opinions as evidence of the law, but they are not formally binding on any lawyer.

Third, in 1987, the American Law Institute began work on the Restatement of the Law (Third), The Law Governing Lawyers.[16] It is expected to be finished sometime before the start of the next millennium. Like other Restatements, this one will not be law, but courts are likely to cite it as reliably describing the law. The topics addressed in the Restatement go beyond subjects of lawyer discipline to cover issues such as lawyer malpractice, liens to secure legal fees, and the like.

D. Some Contributions From Moral Philosophy to the Study of Legal Ethics

Ethics is a traditional field for philosophers. The dilemma for any course such as this one is how to acknowledge philosophical traditions while recognizing that most questions of modern legal ethics are debated in more traditional legal terms. The most helpful approach here seems to be to look at some distinctions that have been important in the philosophical tradition and can also be useful to us.[17]

15. Lawyers licensed in more than one state face problems of potentially conflicting ethical standards. Situations in which disclosure of information is required by some states and prohibited by others are likely to prove particularly difficult. At least in principle, a state supreme court may impose discipline on lawyers it has licensed wherever the conduct takes place. ABA Model Rule 8.5 is the latest attempt to try to deal with this problem.

16. There is no Restatement, First or Second, of The Law Governing Lawyers. This proposed Restatement is called

"Third" because the American Law Institute is now drafting the third wave of Restatements on various subjects. Though we do not normally think of a "third" unless there is a "first" or "second", there are exceptions. Napoleon III was Emperor of France although there was never a Napoleon II who was Emperor.

17. Professor Ted Schneyer appropriately cautions lawyers and law students to discount the insights of moral philosophers when those insights reflect a lack of understanding of the issues actually faced in law practice. See Schneyer, Moral Philosophy's

1. The Ethics of Duty Versus the Ethics of Aspiration

Should the goal of ethical analysis be understood as one of defining a minimum standard below which conduct may not fall, establishing standards of ideal behavior toward which individuals should aim but cannot realistically expect to reach, or should it consist of giving "practical advice" that is somewhere in between?

Professor Lon Fuller suggested a distinction between what he called the "morality of duty" and the "morality of aspiration."

FULLER, THE MORALITY OF LAW
5–6, 9–10 (Rev. Ed. 1969).

The morality of aspiration is most plainly exemplified in Greek philosophy. It is the morality of the Good Life, of excellence, of the fullest realization of human powers. In a morality of aspiration there may be overtones of a notion approaching that of duty. But these overtones are usually muted, as they are in Plato and Aristotle. Those thinkers recognized, of course, that a man might fail to realize his fullest capabilities. As a citizen or as an official, he might be found wanting. But in such a case he was condemned for failure, not for being recreant to duty; for shortcoming, not for wrongdoing. Generally with the Greeks instead of ideas of right and wrong, of moral claim and moral duty, we have rather the conception of proper and fitting conduct, conduct such as beseems a human being functioning at his best.

Where the morality of aspiration starts at the top of human achievement, the morality of duty starts at the bottom. It lays down the basic rules without which an ordered society is impossible, or without which an ordered society directed toward certain specific goals must fail of its mark. It is the morality of the Old Testament and the Ten Commandments. It speaks in terms of "thou shalt not," and, less frequently, of "thou shalt." It does not condemn men for failing to embrace opportunities for the fullest realization of their powers. Instead, it condemns them for failing to respect the basic requirements of social living.

* * *

As we consider the whole range of moral issues, we may conveniently imagine a kind of scale or yardstick which begins at the bottom with the most obvious demands of social living and extends upward to the highest reaches of human aspiration. Somewhere along this scale there is an invisible pointer that marks the dividing line where the pressure of duty leaves off and the challenge of excellence begins. The whole field of moral argument is dominated by a great undeclared war over the location of this pointer. There are those who struggle to push it upward; others work to pull it down. Those whom we regard as being unpleasantly—or at least, inconveniently—moralistic are forever trying to inch the pointer upward so as to expand the area of duty. Instead of inviting us to join them in realizing a pattern of life they consider worthy of human nature, they try to bludgeon us into a belief we are duty bound to embrace this pattern. All of us have probably been subjected to some variation of this technique at one time or another. Too long an exposure to it may leave in the victim a lifelong distaste for the whole notion of moral duty.

––––––

The ABA Model Code of Professional Responsibility was an explicit attempt to create propositions based on the morality of duty. Its Disciplinary Rules are exactly the kinds of minimum standards that can be enforced in disciplinary proceedings. The ABA Model Rules of Professional Conduct continue that approach. Contrast that with the following provision from the ABA Canons of Professional Ethics that the Model Code replaced.

AMERICAN BAR ASSOCIATION, CANONS OF PROFESSIONAL ETHICS, CANON 32 (1908)

The Lawyer's Duty in Its Last Analysis

No client, corporate or individual, however powerful, nor any cause, civil or political, however important, is entitled to receive nor should any lawyer render any service or advice involving disloyalty to the law whose ministers we are, or disrespect of the judicial office, which we are bound to uphold, or corruption of any person or persons exercising a public office or private trust, or deception or betrayal of the public. When rendering any such improper service or advice, the lawyer invites and merits stern and just condemnation. Correspondingly, he advances the honor of his profession and the best interests of his client when he renders service or gives advice tending to impress upon the client and his undertaking exact compliance with the strictest principles of moral law. * * * But above all a lawyer will find his highest honor in a deserved reputation for fidelity to private trust and to public duty, as an honest man and as a patriotic and loyal citizen.[18]

––––––

QUESTIONS

1. Which approach to ethics seems more appropriate? Could a lawyer ever be prosecuted for violating most of former Canon 32? Does that mean that it was inappropriate to include it in a code of conduct for

––––––

18. The sexist language of Canon 32 is jarring to present–day ears, but the terms "he" and "his" did accurately describe the vast majority of members of the bar when Canon 32 was in force.

lawyers? Would lawyers' conduct likely be elevated more by minimum standards or by ethical aspirations?

2. Notice as you look at the ABA Model Code of Professional Responsibility that the Ethical Considerations that it contains are nominally aspirational provisions of the sort described by Fuller. Do the ECs qualify as aspirational in any real sense? Could they be rewritten so as to assert principles that elevate a lawyer's thinking about behavior in particular situations?

3. The ABA Model Rules abandoned the use of separate "Ethical Considerations." Does that make the Model Rules less aspirational than the Model Code? Is the current ABA and state bar concern about "professionalism" a new shorthand for an attempt to revive aspirational standards? Do you agree that restoration of such standards would be desirable?

----

2. Moral People Versus Moral Actions

Is there a difference between what we want a lawyer to do and the kind of person we want a lawyer to be? Should the law demand only that a lawyer comply with applicable rules of professional conduct, or should it be concerned that a lawyer be a person who will seek to act morally in each of life's situations?

Many people assume that personal and professional standards are congruent. That is, if someone has good moral sense, his or her behavior will necessarily comply with professional standards. But professional ethics are not synonymous with moral conduct. It is not "immoral" for a lawyer to form a law partnership with a non-lawyer, for example, but it would violate current professional standards in almost every jurisdiction.

Confusing concepts of personal character and professional conduct has even caused some to assert that legal ethics cannot be taught. If one assumes—and if the assumption were correct—that a law student has largely formed his or her moral character before coming to school, the question would naturally be whether there is anything left to teach in a course such as this one? To the extent one sees differences between personal ethics and professional standards, however, and to the extent that personal moral development continues to occur all through life, there is a lot left to examine in a professional responsibility course.

Furthermore, if the definition of an ethical lawyer consists only of a capacity to follow rules, one might understandably worry about the future of the profession. Real life ethical problems rarely come up in forms that are easily resolvable by simple norms.

Indeed, most important moral choices require a person to make important judgments when no one else is looking. Thus, there must inevitably be a concern for the quality of a lawyer's moral decisionmaking in the countless situations when a lawyer is unlikely to get caught. The source of good decisions in those settings is what we usually call a person's "character".

Psychologist Lawrence Kohlberg is usually credited with identifying six stages of moral development.[19] Adherence to rules such as those imposed on lawyers by state supreme courts is only Kohlberg's first stage and represents no more than the moral development achieved by a small child who knows wrongdoing is associated with punishment.

In the second stage of moral growth, a person basically says "I will be good to you if you are good to me," while in the third stage a person conforms behavior to something he thinks others will approve. Neither is the morality of aspiration, but both forms of moral thought are certainly familiar to lawyers.

Stages four and five of Kohlberg's moral development require conformance of acts to what is required by the social order and the social contract respectively. Stage four requires respect for authority, and would be seen in legal ethics as respect for courts and other legal institutions. Stage five recognizes greater possibilities of change in the social order and is what Kohlberg identifies as the "official" morality of democracy.

Finally, in the sixth and highest stage of moral development a person looks to "universal ethical principles." These principles ultimately must be self-chosen, but they must appeal to "logical comprehensiveness, universality, and consistency."

In Kohlberg's view, a mature person—certainly a mature lawyer—should be engaged in a lifelong effort to identify and conform behavior to universal ethical principles. As is true when dealing with any field of substantive law, of course, lawyers must also conform their behavior to rules applicable to their conduct. Problems such as the ones in this book should help you analyze how lawyers should decide what constitutes appropriate *behavior* in concrete and problematic situations. Ideally, you and other lawyers can conform your conduct *both* to law and to "universal ethical principles."

---

3. Role Ethics Versus Common Ethical Standards

Can a good person be a good lawyer? Can a good lawyer be a good person? Is behavior that would be morally unacceptable for persons in general permitted or even required of persons who have assumed the mantle of attorney? The nature of the debate on these issues is suggested in the following contrasting excerpts:

19. See, e.g., Lawrence Kohlberg, The Philosophy of Moral Development: Moral Stages and the Idea of Justice 17–19 (1981).

WASSERSTROM, LAWYERS AS PROFESSIONALS: SOME MORAL ISSUES
5 Human Rights 1 (1975).

[O]ne central feature of the professions in general and of law in particular is that there is a special, complicated relationship between the professional, and the client or patient. For each of the parties in this relationship, but especially for the professional, the behavior that is involved is to a very significant degree, what I call, role-differentiated behavior. And this is significant because it is the nature of role-differentiated behavior that it often makes it both appropriate and desirable for the person in a particular role to put to one side considerations of various sorts—and especially various moral considerations—that would otherwise be relevant if not decisive. Some illustrations will help to make clear what I mean * * *.

Being a parent is, in probably every human culture, to be involved in role-differentiated behavior. In our own culture, and once again in most, if not all, human cultures, as a parent one is entitled, if not obligated, to prefer the interests of one's own children over those of children generally. * * * In short, the role-differentiated character of the situation alters the relevant moral point of view enormously.

A similar situation is presented by the case of the scientist. For a number of years there has been debate and controversy within the scientific community over the question of whether scientists should participate in the development and elaboration of atomic theory, especially as those theoretical advances could then be translated into development of atomic weapons that would become a part of the arsenal of existing nation states. The dominant view, although it was not the unanimous one, in the scientific community was that the role of the scientist was to expand the limits of human knowledge. Atomic power was a force which had previously not been utilizable by human beings. The job of the scientist was, among other things, to develop ways and means by which that could now be done. And it was simply no part of one's role as a scientist to forego inquiry, or divert one's scientific explorations because of the fact that the fruits of the investigation could be or would be put to improper, immoral, or even catastrophic uses. The moral issues concerning whether and when to develop and use nuclear weapons were to be decided by others; by citizens and statesmen; they were not the concern of the scientist *qua* scientist.

* * *

All of this is significant just because to be a professional is to be enmeshed in role-differentiated behavior of precisely this sort. One's role as a doctor, psychiatrist, or lawyer, alters one's moral universe in a fashion analogous to that described above. Of special significance here is the fact that the professional *qua* professional has a client or patient whose interests must be represented, attended to, or looked after by the professional. And that means that the role of the professional (like that of the parent) is to prefer in a variety of ways the interests of the client or patient over those of individuals generally.

————

POSTEMA, MORAL RESPONSIBILITY IN PROFESSIONAL ETHICS
55 N.Y.U.L.Rev. 63 (1980).

Maintaining a hermetically sealed professional personality promises to minimize internal conflicts, to shift responsibility for professional "knavery" to broader institutional shoulders, and to enable a person to act consistently within each role he assumes. But for this strategy to succeed, the underlying values and concerns of important professional roles, and the characteristic activities they require, must themselves be easily segregated and compartmentalized. However, since there is good reason to doubt they can be easily segregated, [this] strategy risks a dangerous simplification of moral reality. Furthermore, in compartmentalizing moral responses one blocks the cross-fertilization of moral experience necessary for personal and professional growth. * * * I contend that a sense of responsibility and sound practical judgment depend not only on the quality of one's professional training, but also on one's ability to draw on the resources of a broader moral experience. This, in turn, requires that one seek to achieve a fully integrated moral personality. Because this is not possible under the present conception of the lawyer's role, as exemplified by the Code of Professional Responsibility, that conception must be abandoned, to be replaced by a conception that better allows the lawyer to bring his full moral sensibilities to play in his professional role.

————

QUESTIONS

1. Are you convinced that a scientist has no moral responsibility for the uses made of his or her discoveries? Why? Can scientist *A* rest comfortably knowing that if she had not learned how to make nuclear weapons someone else would have? Can lawyer *A* make a comparable argument about the work she does?

2. Is Professor Postema correct that role ethics contemplates a "hermetically sealed professional personality"? On the other hand, does Professor Wasserstrom deal here with the tough issue of how far from ordinary norms role identity might allow one to stray?

————

4. Consequential Versus Deontological Standards

In thinking about universal principles, another distinction philosophers sometimes draw is between whether the ethical analysis is based on achieving a good result (consequentialism) or whether the analysis values given behavior itself (deontological).

The consequential approach is best illustrated for most lawyers by utilitarianism. The utilitarian asks how particular conduct affects people's happiness and well being. If more total well being will be generated by one course of conduct than another, then that course of conduct is morally preferable.

Utilitarianism is not an obviously sound approach; a policy that harmed all African–Americans but benefitted all other racial groups in the United States might be preferred by a utilitarian, for example, because African–Americans constitute a minority of U.S. citizens. Yet lawyers act as utilitarians most of the time in evaluating legal rules. In most substantive fields of law, we look to see how a rule seems to "work" and ask whether people are "better off" as a result of one rule than they would be under some other rule.

Utilitarianism, in turn, can be divided into two categories—act utilitarianism and rule utilitarianism. The first asks which behavior will lead to more happiness or well being in a particular situation. The second, on the other hand, takes the view that there is value in establishing appropriate standards of behavior for particular classes of cases. Thus, one would not ask how best to produce maximum welfare in a unique case, but what principle or course of conduct is most appropriate for a class of similar cases.

Deontological approaches, on the other hand, tend to be based on a set of first principles, such as "responsibility" or "equal rights." Where the first principles come from and how they are to be justified present problems for deontological theories, but for many people the truths either are revealed by religious faith or are obvious. A deontological approach subordinates goals such as maximizing happiness or welfare to such first principles.

Deontological approaches, in turn, can also be subdivided into two categories. The first is based on "duty" and says that there are particular general principles of moral responsibility that can be derived logically and applied universally; "act in a manner that you would have others act toward you" might be an example. A moral person acting from this perspective would say that behavior is right or wrong, without regard to particular effects produced by the behavior in a given situation. A person who says it is God's will that he or she behave in a given manner, for example, would not be impressed by the argument that the consequence of that behavior in a given case would not serve the utilitarian goal of maximizing happiness in the society.

Another important deontological approach is based on "rights," a term with which lawyers are certainly comfortable. This approach would assert, for example, that individuals have certain human rights that lawyers should help preserve and protect. This position sees particular behavior of lawyers as appropriate quite without regard to what the effect would be on the general happiness or well being of the rest of society produced by asserting the rights.

5.   The Ethic of Care

An important alternative line of argument, however, suggests that both adhering to standards of conduct such as those prescribed by the courts and seeking to identify universal moral principles to govern one's behavior may actually reduce the moral quality of a lawyer's actions. Drawing particularly on the insights of feminist writers such as Carol Gilligan,[20] this view stresses enhancing the quality of the *relationship* between the lawyer and "all those affected by a given situation," not on analyzing the inherent propriety of particular conduct of the lawyer.[21]

At minimum, this represents an important change of perspective on legal ethics and suggests, for example, that neutrality and objectivity are simply not possible for lawyers and clients. Even objectively accurate trial testimony may be impossible because witnesses come from different backgrounds and social settings and express themselves in ways different from those in which lawyers and judges often seek to pigeonhole their answers.

Ultimately, this view holds that the governing ethical concept should be the positive personal relationship the lawyer and client have. There will always be conflicts of interest between lawyers and clients; the task must be to manage them in ways that seem to work for both. Clients are often unsure of what they want and lawyers are often unsure what is possible; thus, one cannot always say that either lawyer or client should "control" the relationship. Issues can be best evaluated by a pragmatic assessment of the concrete contexts out of which they arise.

The basic focus of the ethic of care is on the lawyer's acting as a healer who takes a comprehensive view of her situation and seeks to make everyone—not necessarily just her client—better off. That makes it an attractive alternative for many to the rhetoric of individual rights that pervades so much of legal analysis.

Ask yourself, however, whether such an approach will always be helpful to a lawyer faced with tough issues affecting the interests of many people. Might one need some universal principles—perhaps even some rules—to know what values and interests should best be recog-

20. The key book is Carol Gilligan, In a Different Voice: Psychological Theory and Women's Development (1982). Gilligan criticized Kohlberg, for example, because he primarily used male subjects in his empirical work.

21. Among the best descriptions of this approach is Stephen Ellmann, The Ethic of Care as an Ethic for Lawyers, 81 Georgetown L.J. 2665 (1993).

nized and advanced? Without such principles, might a lawyer revert to unexamined prejudices or even to the lawyer's own self–interest in formulating approaches to difficult situations.

6.   Personal Versus Social Ethics

Up to now, we have largely assumed that ethical issues are limited to choices about personal loyalties and integrity. In a larger sense, however, one might include a sense of the lawyer as a political and social actor within the realm of legal ethics.

It surely is appropriate, for example, to think of Thurgood Marshall's choices of how to invest his professional time and talent as "ethical" decisions. Every day, thousands of lawyers make similar ethical choices—for good or ill—about how they try to influence the ways in which legal authority is brought to bear on the allocation of power within society and on political choices the society makes.

Keep these issues in mind as you explore the technical issues of legal ethics. Does a given ethical principle affect who is likely to require legal assistance, obtain it, or both? Are some persons or interests—perhaps those of the poor or powerless—more deserving of legal assistance than others? Should lawyers be compelled to represent persons or interests that would otherwise go unrepresented?

———

This Chapter has introduced a number of fundamental distinctions. Before going on to the next Chapter, the various theoretical approaches may be illustrated by our first problem:

PROBLEM 1

Achieving Justice for the Innocent Client

A lawyer knows that her client is innocent of the murder with which he is charged, but she also knows that the prosecutor has a convincing eyewitness who will not be shaken and who will testify that he saw the client commit the crime. The lawyer knows that she can obtain a forged hotel register from a city several hundred miles away that will "prove" that her client was in the other city at the time of the event; the lawyer firmly believes that she will not be caught if she engages in this fraud. If you were the lawyer, what would you do?

QUESTIONS

1.   How do you instinctively react to this problem? What is the level of maturity of your thinking in terms of Kohlberg's six stages? Are you moved more by a fear of punishment if you get caught falsifying evidence than you are by your desire to "do the right thing?"

2.   Is your choice of what to do affected by your status as a lawyer? That is, would a morally sensitive layperson tend to think differently about the right way to act than you as a lawyer would?

3.   How would a situation-oriented act utilitarian approach this problem? Might he or she argue that the lawyer should obtain the false document and introduce it into evidence?   Could a client's potential execution for a crime we know he did not commit ever be outweighed by any legitimate happiness of others about the client's conviction?

4.   On the other hand, might a rule utilitarian reach the opposite result?   Fraud might seem to serve justice in this case, but reliance on such behavior generally in litigation would tend to reduce the amount of justice done in the world.   Would a regular practice of fraud thus lower confidence in the system and the degree of well being and satisfaction of litigants generally?

5.   What would a deontological philosopher approaching the issue say if she sees problems through the lens of duty?   Might she conclude that the lawyer has a duty not to assist in a lie because lying is immoral? If the result of adhering to such a moral standard might be the sending of an innocent client to the electric chair, should this standard of morality control? [22]

6.   On the other hand, what would a deontological "rights-based" lawyer argue?   Might she say that the client has a right not to be convicted unjustly?   Reasoning from that position, might she argue that she has both the right and obligation to do everything possible on her client's behalf to see that such a conviction does not occur?

7.   Where would the ethics of care lead the lawyer?   Might it lead her to seek a negotiated disposition of the charge?   The problem says the lawyer "knows" the client is innocent, but how can she be sure?   If the source of her knowledge is legally protected against disclosure, as well as embarrassing to her client, should she nevertheless give the information to the prosecutor in an effort to have the charges dropped and obviate the need for fraud?

8.   And how might a socially-conscious lawyer deal with the case? Should it be relevant whether this was a street crime and whether violence is seen to be a serious problem in the city?   What if, instead, the accused had previously been guilty of frequent acts of domestic violence and this victim was his wife?   Would such facts increase or reduce the justification for producing the fraudulent document to save an innocent man?   Should they have any impact at all?

———

One can see from the above problem that simply articulating distinctions highlighted by moral philosophy will not lead to easy answers or

22.   If the client's life were not at stake, should the answer be different?   Would that be because no one is a deontologist in all cases or because opposition to the death penalty can also be a deontological principle?

eliminate the moral dilemmas a lawyer faces in practice. Indeed, knowing some of the philosophical distinctions may make apparently simple questions even harder.

On the other hand, the distinctions should reveal that top of the head responses or even uncritical applications of the text of the Model Rules and Model Code to a problem are also not enough. The distinctions may indeed show that when two people disagree about conclusions in the area of legal ethics, they are often disagreeing about the premises underlying their moral reasoning.

E. A Word on the Organization of this Book

Most of the problems that follow are adapted from actual cases collected from ethics opinions, disciplinary proceedings, news articles, other published sources, and the authors' professional experiences. Of course, all names are hypothetical and all facts have been disguised to protect the persons involved or to make a question more interesting. Yet most of these problems were faced by real people. They should suggest that an attorney in a concrete situation must sometimes act when no course is wholly satisfactory.

They should also suggest that some situations may present professional dilemmas that are not at first apparent. Professor of psychiatry and law Andrew Watson has properly accused law schools of developing analytic barriers to students' reliance on their personal moral reactions to situations.[23] But you will see that lawyers can be disciplined for conduct that may trigger little righteous indignation; developing *sensitivity* to ethical ambiguity is an important objective of these materials.

Few of the problems presented here may be readily answered yes or no. Indeed, as to most you may seem to find yourself adrift on a sea of ambiguity. To help you keep your bearings, each problem is followed by questions designed to get you thinking concretely about the issues raised. Further, with respect to each problem it should be helpful to ask yourself questions such as the following:

    1. Is the conduct in question a violation of one or more standards of the ABA Model Rules or Model Code? What should be the penalty, if any, for the misconduct?

    2. Is the conduct properly subject to criticism even if not inconsistent with the terms of the Model Rules or Model Code? By what standard do you judge the propriety or moral character of the conduct?

23. Watson, The Watergate Lawyer Syndrome: An Educational Deficiency Dis- ease, 26 J. Legal Ed., 441, 442 (1974).

3. Should the lawyer have taken particular action even though the failure to take action would not subject the lawyer to discipline?

4. How could the lawyer have served the client well and still have been professionally responsible?

Another useful way to approach these problems is to recognize that in an important sense, any Model Code of Professional Responsibility or set of Model Rules is an attempt to accommodate at least five interests. The interests are those of (1) lawyers as individuals, (2) lawyers in their relationships with each other, (3) lawyers' responsibilities to their clients, (4) lawyers' responsibilities to non-clients with whom the lawyer deals, and (5) institutions of the legal system through which the lawyer works. Look for these interests as they appear and conflict in particular problems. Is the client's interest always to be furthered above all others? Is the lawyer's personal interest ever given ethical precedence over legitimate public concerns?

Many of the problems include readings that should prove helpful in recognizing and dealing with particularly difficult issues raised in that problem. The readings include cases and some thoughtful articles, as well as ethics opinions from the ABA and state bar associations. Each chapter is also followed by a selected bibliography of articles that should be useful to someone doing further research in the area.

As a supplement to the problems, questions and readings, a separate Standards Supplement has been prepared. That Supplement includes not only the ABA Model Rules of Professional Conduct, ABA Model Code of Professional Responsibility, and ABA Model Code of Judicial Conduct (which has also been adopted by many state Supreme Courts), but also other statutes and guides to professional conduct that have proved relevant or influential in determining the legal profession's standards. You should begin an analysis of each problem by looking at the ABA Model Rules and Model Code, but do not assume that they are the only sources of relevant authority.

Finally, be on your guard against two simplistic approaches that initially may be tempting when you read these problems.

First, it will usually not be enough to say, "I would tell the client to get another lawyer." That may, of course, be a part of the answer in some cases, but it is easier for a law student to turn down a hypothetical client than for a practicing lawyer to insult someone who may be a long-time client and a good friend. Save classroom "resignations" for situations in which you believe you would have the courage and necessity to do so in practice. Do not use withdrawal as a substitute for addressing tough questions.

Second, do more than simply decide that you will always stay "well within" ethical boundaries; in some situations the territory between two ethical frontiers may be very narrow. One of the prime professional obligations of the Model Code, for example, is to "represent [a] client *zealously* within the bounds of the law, which includes Disciplinary Rules and enforceable professional regulations." [24]   The lawyer cannot always merely decide to forego a certain tactic.   The lawyer must serve his or her client *well* and still be professionally responsible.

After you have completed this course you should be in a better position to evaluate the comments expressed at the outset of this Chapter by the Doonesbury characters.   Is a course in Professional Responsibility a naive attempt to teach "right and wrong" to adults with fixed moral views?   More cynically, is it only "trendy lip service to our better selves"?   Or, is the study of professional responsibility based on a recognition that (1) ethical issues are as important to a lawyer as any other aspect of his or her professional life; (2) like any other area of law, the *law* of professional responsibility may be learned; and (3) *ethical* questions present analytic problems as challenging and difficult as any a law student or lawyer will face?

24. Ethical Consideration 7–1, Code of
Professional Responsibility (emphasis added).

SELECTED BIBLIOGRAPHY ON ISSUES IN CHAPTER I

Background About the Legal Profession

R. Abel, American Lawyers (1989).

A.B.A. Young Lawyers Division, The State of the Legal Profession: 1990 (1993).

J. Auerbach, Unequal Justice: Lawyers and Social Change in Modern America (1976).

Berger & Robinson, Woman's Ghetto Within the Legal Profession, 8 Wisconsin Women's L.J. 71 (1992–93).

Bok, A Flawed System, 85 Harvard Magazine 38 (May/June 1983).

M. Cain & C.B. Harrington, Eds., Lawyers in a Postmodern World (1994).

J.E. Carlin, Lawyers' Ethics: A Survey of the New York City Bar (1966).

The Lord Chancellor, Legal Services: A Framework for the Future (1989).

Chon, Multidimensional Lawyering and Professional Responsibility, 43 Syracuse L.Rev. 1137 (1992).

Clark, Why So Many Lawyers? Are They Good or Bad?, 61 Fordham L.Rev. 275 (1992).

Commission of the European Communities, Lawyers in the European Community (1987).

Cross, The First Thing We Do, Let's Kill All the Economists: An Empirical Evaluation of the Effect of Lawyers on the United States Economy and Political System, 70 Texas L.Rev. 645 (1992).

B. Curran, et al., The Lawyer Statistical Report—A Statistical Profile of the U.S. Legal Profession in the 1980s (1985).

B. Curran & C. Carson, Supplement to the Lawyer Statistical Report in 1988 (1991).

Developments in the Law, Lawyers' Responsibilities and Lawyers' Responses, 107 Harvard L.Rev. 1547 (1994).

C. F. Epstein, Women in Law (1981).

Galanter, Predators and Parasites: Lawyer Bashing and Civil Justice, 28 Georgia L.Rev. 633 (1994).

M. A. Glendon, A Nation Under Lawyers: How the Crisis in the Legal Profession is Transforming American Society (1994).

Green, Lawyers Versus the Marketplace, Forbes, Jan. 16, 1984, at 73.

G. Hazard, Ethics in the Practice of Law (1978).

G. Hazard & W. Hodes, The Law of Lawyering (2d Ed.1990).

Hazard, The Future of Legal Ethics, 100 Yale L.J. 1239 (1991).

J. Heinz & E. Leumann, Chicago Lawyers: The Social Structure of the Bar (1982).

Imwinkelried, A Sociological Approach to Legal Ethics, 30 American U.L.Rev. 349 (1981).

M. Kelly, Lives of Lawyers: Journeys in the Organization of Practice (1994).

A. T. Kronman, The Lost Lawyer (1993).

G. P. Lopez, Rebellious Lawyering: One Chicano's Vision of Progressive Law Practice (1992).

Morgan, Economic Reality Facing 21st Century Lawyers, 69 Washington L.Rev. 625 (1994).

R. Nader & M. Green, eds., Verdicts on Lawyers (1976).

Nader, Book Review of Hazard, Ethics in the Practice of Law, 89 Yale L.J. 1442 (1980).

D. Nolan, Readings in the History of the Legal Profession (1980).

Rhode, Ethical Perspectives on Law Practice, 37 Stanford L.Rev. 589 (1985).

Rhode, The Rhetoric of Professional Reform, 45 Maryland L.Rev. 274 (1986).

Rhode, Institutionalizing Ethics, 44 Case Western Reserve L.Rev. 665 (1994).

Smith, Justice and Jurisprudence and the Black Lawyer, 69 Notre Dame L.Rev. 1077 (1994).

Strickland, Yellow Bird's Song: The Message of America's First Native American Attorney, 29 Tulsa L.J. 247 (1993).

Symposium, The Future of the Legal Profession, 44 Case Western Reserve L.Rev. 333 (1994).

Symposium, First Women: The Contribution of American Women to the Law, 28 Valparaiso U.L.Rev. 1161 (1994).

Symposium, The Legal Profession, 20 Law & Society Review 7 (1986).

Formal Standards of Professional Conduct

Abel, Why Does the ABA Promulgate Ethical Rules?, 59 Texas L.Rev. 639 (1981).

Aronson, An Overview of the Law of Professional Responsibility: The Rules of Professional Conduct Annotated & Analyzed, 61 Washington L.Rev. 823 (1986).

Biernat, Why Not Model Rules of Conduct for Law Students, 12 Florida State U.L.Rev. 781 (1985).

Council of the Bars and Law Societies of the European Community, Code of Conduct for Lawyers in the European Community (1988).

Council of Law Society, A Guide to the Professional Conduct of Solicitors (1974).

Fiflis, Risks of Violation of Rules of Professional Responsibility by Reason of the Increased Disparity Among the States, 45 Business Lawyer 1229 (1990).

Finman & Schneyer, The Role of Bar Association Ethics Opinions in Regulating Lawyer Conduct: A Critique of the Work of the ABA Committee on Ethics and Professional Responsibility, 29 U.C.L.A. L.Rev. 67 (1981).

M. Freedman, Understanding Lawyers' Ethics (1990).

Freedman, The Kutak Model Rules v. The American Lawyer's Code of Conduct, 26 Villanova L.Rev. 1165 (1981).

General Council of the Bar, Code of Conduct of the Bar of England and Wales (1990).

Goebel, Professional Responsibility Issues in International Law Practice, 29 American J.Compar.Law 1 (1981).

Hodes, The Code of Professional Responsibility, the Kutak Rules, and the Trial Lawyer's Code: Surprisingly, Three Peas in a Pod, 35 U.Miami L.Rev. 739 (1981).

Koniak, The Law Between the Bar and the State, 70 North Carolina L.Rev. 1389 (1992).

Kutak, The Rules of Professional Conduct in an Era of Change, 29 Emory L.J. 89 (1980).

Luban, The Sources of Legal Ethics: A German–American Comparison of Lawyers' Professional Duties, 48 Rabels Zeitschrift 245 (1984).

Lumbard, Setting Standards: The Courts, the Bar, and the Lawyer's Code of Conduct, 30 Catholic U.L.Rev. 249 (1981).

Morgan, The Evolving Concept of Professional Responsibility, 90 Harvard L.Rev. 703 (1977).

L. R. Paterson & E.E. Cheatham, The Profession of Law (1971).

Patterson, The Function of a Code of Legal Ethics, 35 University of Miami L.Rev. 695 (1981).

Pina, Systems of Ethical Regulation: An International Comparison, 1 Georgetown J.Legal Ethics 797 (1988).

Rhode, Why the ABA Bothers: A Functional Perspective on Professional Codes, 59 Texas L.Rev. 689 (1981).

Schuchman, Ethics and Legal Ethics: The Propriety of the Canons as a Group Moral Code, 37 George Washington L.Rev. 244 (1968).

Terry, An Introduction to the European Community's Legal Ethics Code Part I: An Analysis of the CCBE Code of Conduct, 7 Georgetown J.Legal Ethics 1; Part II, p. 345 (1993).

Teschner, Lawyer Morality, 38 George Washington L.Rev. 789 (1970).

Wilkins, Who Should Regulate Lawyers?, 105 Harvard L.Rev. 799 (1992).

C. Wolfram, Modern Legal Ethics (1986).

Wolfram, The Concept of a Restatement of the Law Governing Lawyers, 1 Georgetown J. Legal Ethics 195 (1987).

Wolfram, Parts and Wholes: The Integrity of the Model Rules, 6 Georgetown J.Legal Ethics 861 (1993).

Zacharias, Specificity in Professional Codes: Theory, Practice, and the Paradigm of Prosecutorial Ethics, 69 Notre Dame L.Rev. 223 (1993).

Professionalism

A.B.A. Commission on Professionalism, "In the Spirit of Public Service": A Blueprint for the Rekindling of Lawyer Professionalism (1986), reprinted in 112 F.R.D. 243–312 (1987).

Association of American Law Schools, Selected Readings on the Legal Profession (1962).

D'Amato & Eberle, Three Models of Legal Ethics, 27 Saint Louis U. L.J. 761 (1983).

Elliston, Ethics, Professionalism and the Practice Of Law, 16 Loyola U.(Chicago) L.J. 529 (1985).

Freeman, The Profession of Law is NOT on the Decline, 96 Dickinson L.Rev. 149 (1992).

Harno, A Letter to Lawyers, 51 Texas Bar J. 146 (Feb.1988) (originally published in 1938).

Hazard, My Station as a Lawyer, 6 Georgia State U.L.Rev. 1 (Fall 1989).

Higginbotham, The Life of Law: Values, Commitment, and Craftsmanship, 100 Harvard L.Rev. 795 (1987).

Keeling, A Prescription for Healing the Crisis in Professionalism: Shifting the Burden of Enforcing Professional Standards of Conduct, 25 Texas Tech L.Rev. (1993).

Leubsdorf, Three Models of Professional Reform, 67 Cornell L.Rev. 1021 (1982).

Mashburn, Professionalism as Class Ideology: Civility Codes and Bar Hierarchy, 28 Valparaiso U.L.Rev. 657 (1994).

Mathews, The Decline of Professionalism: An Historical Perspective, 13 Virginia Bar Ass'n J. 10 (Fall 1987).

McKay, Beyond Professional Responsibility, 10 Capital U.L.Rev. 709 (1981).

McKay, Law, Lawyers, and the Public Interest, 55 U.Cincinnati L.Rev. 351 (1986).

Morgan, The Fall and Rise of Professionalism, 19 U.Richmond L.Rev. 451 (1985).

Penegar, The Five Pillars of Professionalism, 49 U.Pittsburgh L.Rev. 307 (1988).

Powell, Lawyer Professionalism as Ordinary Morality, 35 S.Texas L.Rev. 275 (1994).

Rosenblum, Interactions of Classroom, Law Office, and Marketplace: Bearings on Professionalism, 22 Valparaiso U.L.Rev. 653 (1988).

Rotunda, Lawyers and Professionalism: A Commentary on the Report of the American Bar Association Commission on Professionalism, 18 Loyola U.(Chicago) L.J. 1149 (1987).

Rotunda, Professionals, Pragmatists or Predators?, 75 Illinois Bar J. 420 (Part I); 482 (Part II); 540 (Part III).

Rotunda, The Word "Profession" Is Only a Label—And Not a Very Useful One, 4 Learning and the Law 16 (No. 2, Summer 1977).

J. Sammons, Lawyer Professionalism (1988).

Schneyer, Professionalism as Bar Politics: The Making of the Model Rules of Professional Conduct, 14 Law & Social Inquiry 677 (1989).

Simkins, The Dignity of the Profession, 51 Texas Bar J. 162 (1988) (originally written in the 1920's).

Stanley, Professionalism and Commercialism, 50 Montana L.Rev. 1 (1989).

Symposium, Professionalism, 41 Emory L.J. 403 (1992).

Symposium, The Commercialization of the Legal Profession, 45 S.Carolina L.Rev. 875 (1994).

Symposium, Professionalism in the Practice of Law: Civility and Judicial Ethics in the 1990s, 28 Valparaiso U.L.Rev. 513 (1994).

Moral Philosophy Underlying Legal Ethics

Atkinson, Beyond the New Role Morality for Lawyers, 51 Maryland L.Rev. 583 (1992).

Bean, A Proposal for the Moral Practice of Law, 12 J. Legal Profession 49 (1987).

Cahn, Inconsistent Stories, 81 Georgetown L.J. 2475 (1993).

Eberle, Toward Moral Responsibility in Lawyering: Further Thoughts on the Deontological Model of Legal Ethics 64 St. John's L.Rev. 1 (1989).

Eberle, The Three Foundations of Legal Ethics: Autonomy, Community and Morality, 7 Georgetown J. Legal Ethics 89 (1993).

Elkins, Ethics: Professionalism, Craft, and Failure, 73 Kentucky L.J. 937 (1985).

Elkins, The Examined Life: A Mind in Search of Heart, 30 Amer.J. Jurisprudence 155 (1985).

Ellmann, Lawyering for Justice in a Flawed Democracy, 90 Columbia L.Rev. 116 (1990).

Ellmann, The Ethic of Care as an Ethic for Lawyers, 81 Georgetown L.J. 2665 (1993).

Floyd, Realism, Responsibility and the Good Lawyer: Niebuhrian Perspectives on Legal Ethics, 67 Notre Dame L.Rev. 587 (1992).

Freedman, Legal Ethics and the Suffering Client, 36 Catholic U. L.Rev. 331 (1987).

Gillers, What We Talked About When We Talked About Ethics: A Critical View of the Model Rules, 46 Ohio State L.J. 243 (1985).

Hazard, Communitarian Ethics and Legal Justification, 59 U.Colorado L.Rev. 721 (1988).

Kalish, David Hoffman's Essay on Professional Deportment and the Current Legal Ethics Debate, 61 Nebraska L.Rev. 54 (1982).

Kleinberger, Wanted: An Ethos of Personal Responsibility—Why Codes of Ethics and Schools of Law Don't Make for Ethical Lawyers, 21 Connecticut L.Rev. 365 (1989).

D. Luban, Lawyers and Justice: An Ethical Study (1988).

D. Luban, ed., The Good Lawyer (1983).

Luban, Calming the Hearse Horse: A Philosophical Research Program for Legal Ethics, 40 Maryland L.Rev. 451 (1981).

Luban, Epistemology and Moral Education, 33 J. Legal Education 636 (1983).

Luban, Freedom and Constraint in Legal Ethics: Some MidCourse Corrections To Lawyers and Justice 49 Maryland L.Rev. 424 (1990).

Mashburn, Pragmatism and Paradox: Reinhold Niebuhr's Critical Social Ethics and the Regulation of Lawyers, 6 Georgetown J.Legal Ethics 737 (1993).

Nelson, Moral Ethics, Adversary Justice, and Political Theory: Three Foundations for the Law of Professional Responsibility, 64 Notre Dame L.Rev. 911 (1989).

Noonan, Other People's Morals: The Lawyer's Conscience, 48 Tennessee L.Rev. 227 (1981).

Pearce, Rediscovering the Republican Origins of the Legal Ethics Codes, 6 Georgetown J.Legal Ethics 241 (1992).

Postema, Moral Responsibility in Professional Ethics, 55 New York U.L.Rev. 63 (1980).

Reavley, A Perspective on the Moral Responsibility of Lawyers, 19 Texas Tech L.Rev. 1393 (1988).

Sammons, Meaningful Client Participation: An Essay Toward a Moral Understanding of the Practice of Law, 6 J.Law & Religion 61 (1988).

Schneyer, Moral Philosophy's Standard Misconception of Legal Ethics, 1984 Wisconsin L.Rev. 1529 (1984).

T. L. Shaffer, On Being a Christian and a Lawyer (1981).

T. L. Shaffer & R.F. Cochran, Jr., Lawyers, Clients and Moral Responsibility (1994).

T. L. Shaffer & M.M. Shaffer, American Lawyers and Their Communities: Ethics in the Legal Profession (1991).

Shaffer, Christian Lawyer Stories and American Legal Ethics, 33 Mercer L.Rev. 877 (1982).

Shaffer, Legal Ethics and the Good Client, 36 Catholic U.L.Rev. 319 (1987).

Shaffer, The Legal Ethics of Belonging, 49 Ohio State L.J. 703 (1988).

Shaffer, The Legal Ethics of Radical Individualism, 65 Texas L.Rev. 963 (1987).

Shaffer, The Legal Ethics of the Two Kingdoms, 17 Valparaiso U. L.Rev. 1 (1983).

Shaffer, The Practice of Law as Moral Discourse, 65 Notre Dame Lawyer 231 (1979).

Teachout, Worlds Beyond Theory: Toward the Expression of an Integrative Ethic for Self and Culture, 83 Michigan L.Rev. 849 (1985).

Legal Education

ABA Task Force on Law Schools and the Profession: Narrowing the Gap, Legal Education and Professional Development—An Educational Continuum (1992).

Benjamin, Kaszniak, Sales & Shanfield, The Role of Legal Education in Producing Psychological Distress Among Law Students and Lawyers, 1986 Amer.Bar Foundation Res.J. 225 (1986).

Burger, The Role of the Law School in the Teaching of Legal Ethics and Professional Responsibility, 20 Cleveland State L.Rev. 377 (1980).

Carrington, One Law: The Role of Legal Education in the Opening of the Legal Profession Since 1776, 44 Florida L.Rev. 501 (1992).

Carrington, The Theme of Early American Law Teaching: The Political Ethics of Francis Lieber, 42 J.Legal Education 339 (1992).

Cramton, The Ordinary Religion of the Law School Classroom, 29 J.Legal Education 247 (1978).

Dickinson, Moral Development Theory and Clinical Legal Education: The Development of Professional Identity, 22 U.Western Ontario L.Rev. 183 (1984).

Dubin, The Role of Law School in Balancing a Lawyer's Personal and Professional Life, 10 J.Psychiatry & Law 57 (1982).

Elkins, Moral Discourse and Legalism in Legal Education, 32 J.Legal Education 11 (1982).

Espinoza, Constructing a Professional Ethic: Law School Lessons and Lesions, 4 Berkeley Women's L.J. 215 (1989).

Fischer, The Impact of Legal Education and Practice on the New England Economy (1989).

Freedman, The Professional Responsibility of the Law Professor: Three Neglected Questions, 39 Vanderbilt L.Rev. 275 (1986).

Garth & Martin, Law Schools and the Construction of Competence, 43 J.Legal Education 469 (1993).

Hegland, Moral Dilemmas in Teaching Trial Advocacy, 32 J.Legal Education 69 (1982).

Jewell, Teaching Law Ethically: Is It Possible?, 8 Dalhousie L.J. 474 (1984).

Lesnick, The Integration of Responsibility and Values: Legal Education in an Alternative Consciousness of Lawyering and Law, 10 Nova L.J. 633 (1986).

Nivala, Zen and the Art of Becoming (and Being) a Lawyer, 15 U.Puget Sound L.Rev. 387 (1992).

Redlich, Law Schools as Institutional Teachers of Professional Responsibility, 34 J.Legal Education 215 (1984).

Richards, Moral Theory, the Developmental Psychology of Ethical Autonomy and Professionalism, 31 J.Legal Education 359 (1982).

Rotunda, Learning the Law of Lawyering, 136 U.Pennsylvania L.Rev. 1761 (1988).

Schneyer, Teaching Legal Ethics to Yuppies, 57 Bar Examiner 4 (1988).

Sexton, The Preconditions of Professionalism: Legal Education for the Twenty–First Century, 52 Montana L.Rev. 331 (1991).

Shaffer, Moral Implications and Effects of Legal Education, 34 J.Legal Education 190 (1984).

Smith, Should Lawyers Listen to Philosophers about Legal Ethics?, 9 Law & Philosophy 67 (1990).

Swygert, Striving to Make Great Lawyers—Citizenship and Moral Responsibility: A Jurisprudence for Law Teaching, 30 Boston College L.Rev. 803 (1989).

Symposium on Education in the Professional Responsibilities of the Lawyer, 41 U.Colorado L.Rev. 303 (1968).

Thielens, The Influence of the Law School Experience on the Professional Ethics of Law Students, 21 J.Legal Education 587 (1969).

Tuoni, Teaching Ethical Considerations in the Clinical Setting: Professional, Personal and Systemic, 52 U.Colorado L.Rev. 409 (1981).

Weinstein, On the Teaching of Legal Ethics, 72 Columbia L.Rev. 452 (1972).

Willging & Dunn, The Moral Development of the Law Student: Theory and Data on Legal Education, 31 J.Legal Education 306 (1982).

Woody, Professional Responsibility Training in Law School and Its Philosophical Background, 7 J.Legal Profession 119 (1982).

F. K. Zemans & V. Rosenblum, The Making of a Public Profession (1981).

Chapter II

REGULATION OF THE LEGAL
PROFESSION

As we saw in Chapter I, both entry into the legal profession and the conduct of lawyers once admitted are regulated by the highest court of each state. Although in a few states, the supreme courts have ceded limited authority over lawyers to the state legislatures, in most states, bar governance continues to be the exclusive province of the court.

To exercise their authority, the courts have established admission and disciplinary machinery. While most bar associations are voluntary, some jurisdictions require that lawyers join an official bar organization, which is then called an "integrated" or "unified" bar. The responsibilities of such an official bar association typically include a role in bar admission and enforcement of conduct standards.

In states that have no official bar association, the courts often turn to the voluntary bar for assistance in staffing the disciplinary system. In both cases, the courts often fund the disciplinary system by taxing lawyers in the form of mandatory dues and fees.*

State supreme courts regulate the right to practice law even if the lawyer is solely an office counselor and never appears in court. Federal courts separately regulate admission to practice before them, but a lawyer need not be admitted to a federal court unless he or she will be litigating there. Federal courts usually defer to state admission standards, and admission before a federal court is often close to automatic, but lately some federal judges have been interested in asserting a more active role.

In the problems which follow, consider questions such as:

a. Why do courts regulate admission to the bar and the professional behavior of attorneys? Should they be concerned

---

* The uses to which mandatory bar dues may properly be applied were considered in Keller v. State Bar of California, 496 U.S. 1, 110 S.Ct. 2228, 110 L.Ed.2d 1 (1990). The bar had argued that it was a state agency and that its public responsibilities included taking positions on law-related issues such as abortion and gun control. The Supreme Court held that even an official bar functions more like a labor union than a government office. Thus mandatory dues may only be used to finance activities of common benefit to bar members and as to which there would be a risk of "free riders" if all lawyers were not required to share the burden. The Court said that these activities included recommending bar admission standards, conducting bar discipline, and recommending changes in bar codes of conduct, but not taking positions on broader public questions. See also, The Florida Bar Re: Frankel, 581 So.2d 1294 (Fla.1991).

35

about specific conduct, discerning a lawyer's moral character, or both?

b. What should be the relative roles of the courts, both state and federal, legislatures, bar associations, individual lawyers, and even lay persons in these processes?

c. What is the range of sanctions that lawyers face for a violation of professional standards? Are public sanctions such as disbarment necessarily of more concern to lawyers than private sanctions such as malpractice liability?

PROBLEM 2

Character and Fitness in Admission to the Bar

You have been in practice for a few years in the city where you went to law school. Gerry Smith, a third year law student, has come to you for help. "I have been accused of cheating on the final exam in my advanced tax class," he tells you. "I did it. I had not had time to study, and I wanted to get a good grade. The exam proctor will testify that he thought he saw me cheat, but I have denied everything. I'm afraid of what this could do to my chances of being admitted to the bar. Please help me."

In addition, Smith has told you, "I changed my name when I was a senior in college. My name then was Patrick Saville. Under that name, I was convicted of a misdemeanor for possession of marijuana. Do I have to report something like that? Will the bar ever catch me?"

You are an old friend of the law school dean. The dean has offered not to charge Smith and force him to a hearing on the charge of cheating if Smith agrees to accept an failing grade in the course. He can make up the course in summer school (for which he will have to pay tuition), and that will let him graduate in time to take the bar with the rest of his class. The dean also offers to agree not to disclose the incident to the character and fitness committee of the bar. Smith is happy to be able to get off so lightly.

QUESTIONS

1. **Every American jurisdiction requires that applicants for admission to the bar have the necessary "character and fitness" to practice law. What do states mean when they say that a lawyer must be of "good moral character"?**

a. Should Gerald Smith's cheating in law school be sufficient to deny him admission to the bar? Should one be equally concerned about the subsequent denial of guilt as about the original act of cheating? Can one say, on the other hand, that "denying guilt" is a major part of a lawyer's stock in trade?

b. Should Smith/Saville's drug conviction be conclusive evidence of a lack of "character and fitness"? Would your answer be different if he had been convicted of a drug-related felony? [1]

c. If a practicing lawyer in your state would not be suspended or disbarred for a charge of marijuana possession, does that mean that Smith must be allowed to be admitted to practice? Hallinan v. Committee of Bar Examiners, 65 Cal.2d 447, 55 Cal.Rptr. 228, 421 P.2d 76 (1966), said the test for discipline and bar admission is the same, namely whether the individual "is a fit and proper person to be permitted to practice law". Do you agree that it should be no easier to deny a person a license than to take a license away?

d. Does cheating constitute conduct involving "dishonesty, fraud, deceit, or misrepresentation" within the meaning of Model Rule 8.4(c) and DR 1–102(A)(4) of the Model Code? Should marijuana possession be held to be "a criminal act that reflects adversely on the lawyer's honesty, trustworthiness, or fitness as a lawyer in other respects"? See Model Rule 8.4(b) and Comment 1 thereto.

e. Should dishonesty in the handling of money disqualify a student from bar admission? In re Mustafa, 631 A.2d 45 (D.C.App.1993), involved the chief justice of a law school's moot court program who was found to have embezzled over $2000 from the moot court account to pay emergency expenses of his sister. The money was repaid and the school fully supported his bar admission, but only a year had passed since the misconduct, so the court denied admission. See also, Application of Majorek, 508 N.W.2d 275 (1993), denying admission of an applicant who was found to have embezzled $300 of law student association funds and shoplifted a pack of cigarettes among other offenses.

Why might these kinds of offenses be of particular concern to bar admission authorities? Are lawyers frequently entrusted with the handling of client funds? [2]

f. Should an applicant to the bar be denied admission for borrowing money for his education and then filing for bankruptcy three days before law school graduation? Does such action show a lack of sensitivity to his "moral responsibility to his creditors * * * [and] a lack of the moral values" required of a lawyer? Some states have held that it does, while acknowledging the applicants' legal right to file bankruptcy. [3]

---

1. Current practice in most states does not automatically deny bar admission to convicted felons. See, e.g., In re Polin, 630 A.2d 1140 (D.C.App.1993) (applicant admitted after serving time for conspiracy to distribute cocaine).

2. Frasher v. West Virginia Board of Law Examiners, 408 S.E.2d 675 (W.Va. 1991), even held that a record of three DUI convictions was enough to deny an applicant admission to the bar. The result initially seems harsh, but it represents an important part of a continuing struggle with the problem of lawyer alcoholism that we will see again in Problem 3.

3. Florida Bd. of Bar Examiners v. G.W.L., 364 So.2d 454 (Fla.1978); In re Gahan, 279 N.W.2d 826 (Minn.1979); Application of Taylor, 293 Or. 285, 647 P.2d 462 (1982). But see Matter of Anonymous, 74 N.Y.2d 938, 550 N.Y.S.2d 270, 549 N.E.2d 472 (1989).

g. Why do we have a requirement that lawyers demonstrate they have sufficient character and fitness to practice law? Professor Deborah Rhode summarizes the requirement's traditional purposes this way:

> The first is shielding clients from potential abuses, such as misrepresentation, misappropriation of funds, or betrayal of confidences. * * * A second concern involves safeguarding the administration of justice from those who might subvert it through subornation of perjury, misrepresentation, bribery, or the like.
>
> * * * [A] less frequently articulated rationale for character screening rests on the bar's own interest in maintaining a professional community and public image. * * * An overriding objective of any organized profession is to enhance its members' social standing, and the bar is scarcely an exception.[4]

Do Smith's cheating and marijuana conviction raise any of those concerns?

h. Should there be a statute of limitations on how long prior incidents can affect current bar admission decisions? See, e.g., Hallinan v. Committee of Bar Examiners, supra, finding "adolescent misbehavior" not sufficient to disqualify the applicant.[5] Would you want to know how old Smith–Saville was at the time of the alleged college incidents before you turned him in? Is it your business to ask, or is the seeking of such information up to others? Compare Rule 8.1 of the Model Rules with EC 1–3 and DR 1–101(B) of the Model Code.

2. How candid should you advise Smith to be in his bar application?

a. It is often said that an applicant is more likely to be denied admission for covering up his or her past than for what that past contains. In Attorney Grievance Comm'n v. Myers, 635 A.2d 1315 (Md.1994), for example, a lawyer was disbarred for lying on his bar application about the number of traffic tickets he had even though the driving record itself would not have justified denial of admission. Cf. Rule 8.1 and DR 1–101. Is such an approach by admission authorities reasonable? Is it likely to be inevitable?

b. In re Zbiegien, 433 N.W.2d 871 (Minn.1988), on the other hand, involved a bar applicant who admitted he had plagiarized several pages of a paper in a products liability seminar, but said that he had been under great stress because of work pressures and injuries that his wife had suffered. Petitioner was given an "F" in the course but permitted to graduate. He reported the incident in his application for admission to

---

4. Rhode, Moral Character as a Professional Credential, 94 Yale L.J. 491, 508–10 (1985).

5. An interesting analogy can be drawn to the problem of an attorney's reinstatement after disbarment. As a general rule, almost no matter how serious the original offense, the attorney may be reinstated upon a showing of rehabilitation and present fitness. See, e.g., In re Hiss, 368 Mass. 447, 333 N.E.2d 429 (1975); In re Wigoda, 77 Ill.2d 154, 32 Ill.Dec. 341, 395 N.E.2d 571 (1979).

the bar, and while the Court held that a single incident of misconduct could be the basis for denial of bar admission, the applicant had been punished for the misconduct and now showed remorse, so he was admitted to the bar.

c.   But compare, Application of Taylor, 293 Or. 285, 647 P.2d 462 (1982), where the applicant had been arrested for shoplifting; the charges were later dismissed by the trial court when the defendant denied he had intended to steal the item. Before the bar committee, however, the applicant made a clean breast of things and admitted that he really had had an intent to steal. Rather than commend his current honesty, the committee denied him admission for his misleading testimony in the criminal case. Are you troubled by this result? Relieved that the dishonesty came out in time? What is its message to bar applicants about how safe it is to be completely candid?

d.   How much may a state supreme court lawfully ask a candidate for bar admission? May it inquire into the applicant's beliefs? Her membership in clubs or political organizations? Look at the questions asked in the Character portion of a widely-used bar application set forth in the Readings to this Problem. Do you think the questions are limited to what is necessary to get information properly relevant to the admission decision? Are any questions unconstitutional?[6]

e.   May bar examiners ask applicants whether they have been treated for a mental illness? Is such an illness a "disability" within the meaning of the Americans with Disabilities Act. A number of suits challenging such questions have been filed[7] and the ABA adopted a resolution at its August 1994 Annual Meeting noting that questions about mental health treatment could discourage prospective lawyers from getting needed help. It urged states to limit inquiry to "specific, targeted questions about the applicant's behavior, conduct or any current impairment of the applicant's ability to practice law." Do Questions 27, 28 & 29 in the Character questionaire in the Readings to this problem meet those standards?

---

6. Important constitutional cases on bar admissions include, Konigsberg v. State Bar, 353 U.S. 252, 77 S.Ct. 722, 1 L.Ed.2d 810 (1957) (Konigsberg I); Schware v. Board of Bar Examiners, 353 U.S. 232, 77 S.Ct. 752, 1 L.Ed.2d 796 (1957) (one cannot be denied admission merely because he is a member of the communist party); Konigsberg v. State Bar (Konigsberg II), 366 U.S. 36, 81 S.Ct. 997, 6 L.Ed.2d 105 (1961) (the Bar can refuse admission because applicant obstructs the investigation—e.g., refuses to say whether he is or is not a knowing member of the Communist Party); In re Anastaplo, 366 U.S. 82, 81 S.Ct. 978, 6 L.Ed.2d 135 (1961); Baird v. State Bar of Arizona, 401 U.S. 1, 91 S.Ct. 702, 27 L.Ed.2d 639 (1971) (applicant may not be denied bar admission for failure to state whether she has ever been a member of an organization that "advocates overthrow of the United States by force or violence"); Application of Stolar, 401 U.S. 23, 91 S.Ct. 713, 24 L.Ed.2d 657 (1971); Law Students Civil Rights Research Council, Inc. v. Wadmond, 401 U.S. 154, 91 S.Ct. 720, 27 L.Ed.2d 749 (1971) (one can be refused admission if, with scienter, he is a knowing member of the Communist Party with intent to further its illegal goals). See generally, 4 R. Rotunda & J. Nowak, Treatise on Constitutional Law: Substance and Procedure § 20.44 (2d Ed.1992). J. Nowak & R. Rotunda, Constitutional Law § 16.44 (5th ed.1995).

7. E.g., Ellen S. v. Florida Board of Bar Examiners, 859 F.Supp. 1489 (S.D.Fla. 1994).

f. Suppose that your state were considering a policy of fingerprinting all applicants for admission to the bar, a procedure that might tend to expose people who had tried to change their identity. Would you support such a procedure? Should lawyers have to submit to procedures such as fingerprinting that are not required of the public generally? [8]

3. What are your own obligations to the bar admission authorities in connection with Smith's application?

a. Must you report what Smith admitted to you about his guilt in the cheating case? Is your answer the same under Rule 8.1 as it was under EC 1–3 and DR 1–101?

b. Must you report what you know about Smith's change of name and past criminal record? Look at Rule 8.1(b) and EC 1–3.

c. What should be the obligation of law schools and their deans in cooperating with investigations conducted by bar admission officials? Was it proper for the law school to enter into a "plea bargain" with Smith under which Smith agreed to accept a law school sanction for cheating and the school agreed not to report the matter to the bar? You might want to think again about this question after reading the *Himmel* case in Problem 3.[9]

4. What standards of knowledge and ability are appropriate to require for admission to the bar?

a. Should applicants be required to pass a bar examination after they have already completed a three year legal education? [10] Why or why not? Should a uniform test be used nationwide? Should it have a uniform passing score?

b. What should the test examine? Would it be possible to develop a reliable test of the practical ability to serve a client instead of solely the

8. In Cantor v. Supreme Court of Pennsylvania, 353 F.Supp. 1307 (E.D.Pa.1973), affirmed without opinion 487 F.2d 1394 (3d Cir.1973), the court upheld as constitutional and not violating any right of privacy a state requirement that lawyers provide their social security number to the Court Administrator. By way of dictum the court approved a fingerprinting requirement and rejected a host of other constitutional challenges to Pennsylvania's disciplinary system. When Georgia instituted a policy of fingerprinting applicants, 100 applicants reportedly withdrew their applications. 53 Bar Examiner 20 (Aug. 1984).

9. Law schools' reluctance to get involved may be partly explained by fear of a case like Rothman v. Emory University, 828 F.Supp. 537 (N.D.Ill.1993). There, a law school dean had submitted a critical letter about an applicant to the Board of Law Examiners reporting the applicant's "chronic hostility" toward other students and the faculty. The applicant was admitted to the Bar, but he sued the law school alleging that his demeanor was the result of "chronic epilepsy" and thus that the negative report constituted a violation of the Americans with Disabilities Act. Although the negative report to the Bar was absolutely privileged as a matter of state libel law, the Court said that reports to the Bar about most students are positive and thus that such reports are "services" and "privileges" that may not be denied on the basis of an applicant's disability. The Court refused to dismiss the ADA claim.

10. California has an additional "baby bar" requirement for students at unaccredited law schools. At the end of their first year, such students must pass the special examination or not receive credit for further law study. The requirement has been upheld against a charge that it invidiously discriminates between students at accredited and unaccredited schools. Lupert v. California State Bar, 761 F.2d 1325 (9th Cir. 1985).

applicant's legal knowledge? [11]

c. Should the taking of particular law school courses—skills courses, for example—be a prerequisite to becoming a lawyer? [12]

d. Should an applicant have an unlimited number of chances to take the bar examination? Is a failure to provide such opportunities unfair to individuals or groups? See Jones v. Board of Comm'rs of Alabama State Bar, 737 F.2d 996 (11th Cir.1984), upholding a five-time limit to take the bar over a thoughtful dissent.

e. The American with Disabilities Act is beginning to have an important effect on the bar exam process itself.

D'Amico v. New York State Board of Law Examiners, 813 F.Supp. 217 (W.D.N.Y.1993), involved an applicant who was near-sighted and suffered visual fatigue when reading for extended periods. She was given a separate testing room, extra light, a large print exam, and 50% more time than other applicants but she still failed the exam. In this decision, the federal court ordered the state to give her four days to complete the exam that other applicants were required to complete in two days.

In re Rubenstein, 637 A.2d 1131 (Del.1994), involved an applicant who had failed the bar exam three times. Only then was she diagnosed as learning disabled. She passed the essay portion of the exam on her fourth try after being given an extra hour for each three hour block of essays and in this decision she was granted 50% more time than other students to take the Multistate portion of the exam. The effort to give disabled persons appropriate accommodation is one everyone can applaud, but if these cases are any indication, bar examiners are likely to find it increasingly hard to know exactly what accommodation is required.

f. Should bar examiners be subject to damage suits filed by unsuccessful bar applicants? Might such potential liability make the examiners more careful? Might it make volunteer examiners hard to recruit? Hoover v. Ronwin, 466 U.S. 558, 104 S.Ct. 1989, 80 L.Ed.2d 590 (1984), granted at least antitrust immunity to examiners acting pursuant to delegation from their state's supreme court.

11. California has tried to develop such a "performance test". See, e.g., Performance Testing: A Valuable New Dimension or a Waste of Time and Money?, The Bar Examiner, November 1983, p. 12.

12. Cf. Rule 13 of the Rules on Admission to the Bar of Indiana (1975), requiring 14 specific courses totalling at least 54 semester hours of a student's law study. South Carolina Supreme Court Rule 5A mandates courses in 14 specific fields for admission to the bar. Both states include Professional Responsibility as one of the required courses. Cf. Report of the Task Force on Law Schools and the Profession: Narrowing the Gap, "Legal Education and Professional Development—An Educational Continuum" (1992). This Report, by a distinguished Commission chaired by former ABA President Robert MacCrate, eschews a regulatory objective, but its suggestion that law schools produce lawyers with specific "skills and values" will almost certainly be used in some states to justify performance testing of applicants or their having taken specific skills courses.

5.   Should a state be able to create additional requirements for admission to its bar?

a.   Should a state be able to limit bar admission to the state's own residents? What legitimate state interests would such a requirement arguably serve? This formerly common requirement was struck down by the Supreme Court on the ground that it violated the Privileges and Immunities clause. Supreme Court of New Hampshire v. Piper, 470 U.S. 274, 105 S.Ct. 1272, 84 L.Ed.2d 205 (1985).

b.   May a state require bar applicants to be U.S. citizens? In re Griffiths, 413 U.S. 717, 93 S.Ct. 2851, 37 L.Ed.2d 910 (1973), held that such a requirement denies aliens the Fourteenth Amendment guarantee of equal protection of the law.

c.   Should admission to the bar of one state guarantee admission to the bar of another? Many states automatically admit experienced lawyers who are licensed in other states if the state of licensure will reciprocally do the same for the first state's lawyers. These states require an examination, however, of lawyers from states that do not grant reciprocity or grant it only on certain conditions. So far, challenges to the constitutionality of such reciprocity requirements have been upheld. E.g., Schumacher v. Nix, 965 F.2d 1262 (3d Cir.1992) (first state required everyone to take bar examination); Matter of Saretsky, 506 N.W.2d 151 (Wis.1993) (first state required that out–of–state lawyers maintain a local office; thus, second state could impose same requirement).

d.   Supreme Court of Virginia v. Friedman, 487 U.S. 59, 108 S.Ct. 2260, 101 L.Ed.2d 56 (1988), on the other hand, involved a Maryland resident who challenged a Virginia requirement that in order to be admitted to the Virginia bar "on motion", i.e., without taking the bar exam, a lawyer had to be a resident of Virginia. The State argued that because the nonresident could be admitted by passing the bar examination, there was no denial of her right to become a member of the Virginia bar. The Supreme Court held that making nonresidents take an additional test went to a matter of "fundamental concern" and that this distinction also violated the Privileges and Immunities Clause. Chief Justice Rehnquist and Justice Scalia dissented.[13]

e.   Should the right of an out-of-state lawyer to be admitted to the bar differ from her right to appear pro hac vice, i.e. in a single case? Appearance pro hac vice is usually routinely permitted and in some civil rights cases has even been held to be required. E.g. Sanders v. Russell, 401 F.2d 241 (5th Cir.1968) (court invalidates restrictive district court

---

13. See also, Barnard v. Thorstenn, 489 U.S. 546, 109 S.Ct. 1294, 103 L.Ed.2d 559 (1989) (same result with respect to a one-year residency with an intent-to-remain rule imposed by the Virgin Islands bar). Cf. Frazier v. Heebe, 482 U.S. 641, 107 S.Ct. 2607, 96 L.Ed.2d 557 (1987) (striking down local rule requiring Louisiana residency for admission to practice in the Federal District Court for the Eastern District of Louisiana).

rule limiting pro hac vice appearance by out of state lawyers as applied to non-fee generating civil rights cases).[14]

6. Should different standards exist for admission to federal courts than to the state courts?

As a practical matter, admission to the highest court of a state will ordinarily be sufficient to qualify for admission to the federal courts of that state. However, some courts have tried to justify different rules for federal litigators. See Brown v. McGarr, 583 F.Supp. 734 (N.D.Ill.1984) (upholding special rules for membership in a federal trial bar).

READINGS

NATIONAL CONFERENCE OF BAR EXAMINERS
Request For Preparation Of A Character Report

* * *

PERSONAL INFORMATION

Name

Social Security Number

List below all the other names or surnames you have used or been known by and describe when, how, and why your name was changed (e.g., marriage or divorce). If a change was made in a judicial or naturalization proceeding, enclose an exact and complete copy of the order or other evidence of change with the application.

Sex

Date of birth

Place of birth (City, State, Country)

Area codes and telephone numbers where you can be reached during the next six months:

Mailing address(es) for the next six months:

2. Circle the name of every jurisdiction to which you have previously been admitted [to the bar]. Make certain that you complete question 10 for each jurisdiction indicated.

---

14. As to whether concerns about the lawyer's possible "courtroom demeanor" permit denial of a pro hac vice appearance, compare In re Evans II, 524 F.2d 1004 (5th Cir.1975), with In re Admission of Lumumba, 526 F.Supp. 163 (S.D.N.Y.1981). Ordinarily, a lawyer is entitled to a hearing before revocation of the right to appear pro hac vice; see Kirkland v. National Mortgage Network, Inc., 884 F.2d 1367 (11th Cir.1989). The Circuits are split on whether revocation of pro haec vice status is an appealable final order. See, e.g., United States v. Dickstein, 971 F.2d 446 (10th Cir. 1992) (order unappealable); Cox, Denver Attorney Battles 10th Circuit, National Law Journal, April 25, 1994, p. A–6 (lawyer sanctioned for seeking to test *Dickstein* rule).

3.   Of what country are you a citizen?

If you are not a citizen of the United States, what is your immigration status?

4.   Indicate below whether you have ever been a member of the armed forces of the United States, its reserve components or the National Guard * * *.

* * *

c.   While a member of the armed forces of the United States: Did you receive an honorable discharge?   (If yes, enclose a copy of Report of Separation DD Form 214).   Were you ever court-martialed?   Were you ever awarded non-judicial punishment?   (Art.15 UCMJ) Were you allowed to resign in lieu of court-martial?   Were you administratively discharged?   [If the answer to any of these is yes,] * * * on a separate sheet of paper provide a narrative explanation of the circumstances surrounding the occurrence.

5.   List every permanent and temporary residence in which you have lived during the last ten years or since you were first admitted to the bar in any state (whichever period of time is longer).   List addresses in reverse chronological order starting with your current address.

EDUCATIONAL INFORMATION

6.   List the names of the colleges and universities other than law schools you attended, their location (including the name of the campus if the school had more than one), the dates attended, and the degree received.   * * *

7.   List below the names of all the law schools you attended, their location (including the name of the campus if the school had more than one), the dates attended, and the degree received.   * * *

* * *

9.   Have you ever been dropped, suspended, warned, placed on scholastic or disciplinary probation, expelled or requested to resign or allowed to resign in lieu of discipline from any school above the elementary school level, college or university, or otherwise subjected to discipline by any such school or institution or requested or advised by any such school or institution to discontinue your studies therein?   If yes, on a separate sheet of paper provide a brief narrative explanation of the circumstances surrounding each occurrence.

ADMISSION INFORMATION

10.   List every state or foreign country to which you have ever submitted an application to be admitted by examination (even if the application was subsequently withdrawn), motion or diploma privilege, or to be reinstated to the bar. For each application, indicate the nature of the application (examination, comity, etc.) and date it was submitted and its ultimate disposition; i.e., admitted to the bar, withdrew application, or

not admitted. Provide a brief narrative explanation of the circumstances surrounding the reason for any withdrawals of applications or failures to be admitted (other than those due to failing the examination).

* * *

LEGAL AND OTHER EMPLOYMENT

12.   Have you ever held judicial office?   [If yes, give period of service and reason for termination.]

13.   List every job you have held since you were twenty-one years of age beginning with your current job. Please include self-employment, clerkships, temporary or part-time employment and military service. Account for any period of time when you were unemployed.

14.   Complete one copy of FORM 10 for each job listed in question 13. Make as many additional copies of FORM 10 as you need to describe each job or change of location.   Your application will be processed only after you provide all the information requested on FORM 10 for each job.

15.   Have you ever applied for (or applied for and then withdrew an application) or held a license for a business, trade, or profession, other than as an attorney at law, the procurement of which required proof of good character and/or examination (e.g., certified public accountant, patent practitioner, or real estate broker)?

CHARACTER AND FITNESS INFORMATION

16.   A.   Have you ever been denied a business, trade, or professional license (e.g., CPA, real estate broker, physician, patent practitioner)?

B.   Have you ever had a business, trade or professional license revoked? If yes, please explain.

C.   Have you ever permitted a business, trade or professional license to expire?   If yes, please explain.

17.   Have you ever been disqualified from practicing law?

Name and address of authority in possession of the records regarding the disqualification:

18.   A.   Have you ever been disbarred, suspended, censured, or otherwise reprimanded or disqualified as an attorney, as a member of another profession, or as a holder of public office?

B.   To the best of your knowledge, have there ever been or are there now any charges, complaints, or grievances (formal or informal) pending concerning your conduct as an attorney, as a member of any other profession, or as a holder of public office?

C.   If you answered yes to either A or B, state the date of each occurrence and the name and address of the authority in possession of the records regarding the matter and provide a brief narrative explanation of the circumstances surrounding each matter.

19.   Has any surety on any bond on which you were the principal been required to pay any money on your behalf? If yes, complete FORM 11.

20.   Have there ever been or are there now pending any civil actions or have any judgments been filed against you? If yes, complete FORM 12. Attach a copy of the pleadings and final disposition.

21.   Have you ever had a complaint filed against you in any civil, criminal or administrative forum, alleging fraud, deceit, misrepresentation, forgery or legal malpractice? If yes, complete FORM 12 and attach copies of the pleadings, allegations, and judgments.

22.   Have you ever filed a petition for bankruptcy? If yes, complete FORM 13.

23.   Have you ever, either as an adult or a juvenile, been cited, arrested, charged or convicted for any violation of any law (except minor parking violations)? NOTE: Alcohol or drug related offenses are not considered to be minor. If yes, complete FORM 14 and attach a copy of the arresting officer's report, complaint, indictment, trial disposition, sentence and appeal, if any.

24.   On FORM 14A, list any moving traffic violations incurred during the past ten years.

25.   Have you ever had a credit card revoked? If yes, complete FORM 15.

26.   A. Do you have any debts, including student loans, which are more than 90 days past due? If yes, give names and addresses of the creditor(s), the account number(s), the nature of the debt(s), and reason for arrearage.

B.   Have you ever defaulted on any student loan? If yes, on a separate sheet of paper give the name and address of the creditor or the guaranteeing agency to whom the loan was sold or assigned, the loan account number, the amount owed and the steps taken to make the account current.

27.   Within the past five years, have you been diagnosed with or have you been treated for bi-polar disorder, schizophrenia, paranoia, or any other psychotic disorder?

28.   a. Do you currently have any condition or impairment (including, but not limited to, substance abuse, alcohol abuse, or a mental, emotional, or nervous disorder or condition) which in any way currently affects, or if untreated could affect, your ability to practice law in a competent and professional manner?

b.   If your answer to Question 28(a) is affirmative, are the limitations or impairments caused by your mental health condition or substance abuse problem reduced or ameliorated because you receive ongoing treatment (with or without medication) or because you participate in a monitoring program?

If your answer to Question 28(b) is affirmative, describe the condition or problem and any treatment or monitoring program on Forms 16 and 17.

As used in Question 28, "currently" means recently enough so that the condition could reasonably have an impact on your ability to function as a lawyer.

29. Within the past five years, have you ever raised the issue of consumption of drugs or alcohol or the issue of a mental, emotional, nervous, or behavioral disorder or condition as a defense, mitigation, or explanation for your actions in the course of any administrative or judicial proceeding or investigation; any inquiry or other proceeding; or any proposed termination by an educational institution, employer, government agency, professional organization, or licensing authority?

If you answered yes, to 27, 28 or 29, complete FORMS 16 and 17. Make as many copies of FORMS 16 and 17 as you need to describe the event.

PERSONAL AND PROFESSIONAL REFERENCES

30. State the names and addresses of three references in every locality where you have practiced. If you have not practiced previously or if you have practiced less than one year, provide the names and addresses of three references in each locality in which you have lived during the past 15 years. References should be persons with whom you are personally acquainted and preferably not your former or present employers or law partners. Do not list anyone as a reference who is related to you by blood or marriage.

31. Give the names and addresses of three attorneys who know you and who are not related to you by blood or marriage. The attorneys listed here must be different from those listed under question 30.

32. Give the names and addresses of two clients who are not related to you by blood or marriage. If you have not had any clients, substitute the names of two law professors or other attorneys. The persons listed here must be different from those listed under questions 30 and 31.

33. Insert three original notarized copies of the Authorization and Release Form.

* * *

Execute Three Original Copies

AUTHORIZATION AND RELEASE

I, (Name), born at (City), (State), (Country), on (Date), having filed an application for admission to the bar of (Jurisdiction), hereby apply for a character report and consent to have an investigation made as to my moral character, professional reputation and fitness for the practice of law and such other information as may be received, all of which will be reported only to the admitting authority. I agree to give any further information which may be required concerning my past record. I understand that the contents of my character report are confidential.

I also authorize and request every person, firm, company, corporation, governmental agency, law enforcement agency, court, association or institution having control of any documents, records or other information pertaining to me, to furnish to the National Conference of Bar Examiners any such information, including documents, records, bar association files regarding charges or complaints filed against me, including any complaints erased by law, whether formal or informal, pending or closed, or any other pertinent data; and to permit the National Conference of Bar Examiners or any of its agents or representatives to inspect and make copies of such documents, records or other information. The records, however, will not include any information with respect to a juvenile offense.

I authorize the National Personnel Records Center, in St. Louis, MO or other custodian of my military record to release to the National Conference of Bar Examiners information or photocopies from my military personnel and related medical records, or only the following information/records: [This could include a photocopy of my DD Form 214, Report of Separation.]

I hereby release, discharge and exonerate the National Conference of Bar Examiners, its agents and representatives, the admission agency of the above jurisdiction, its agents and representatives, and any person so furnishing information from any and all liability of every nature and kind arising out of the furnishing or inspection of such documents, records, and other information or the investigation made by the National Conference of Bar Examiners or by the admission agency.

I have read the foregoing document and have answered all questions fully and frankly. The answers are complete and true of my own knowledge.

* * *

FORM 10/ DESCRIPTION OF EMPLOYMENT [To be used with Question 13]

Position held   From Mo/Yr   To Mo/Yr

Employer

Employer's address at time of employment:

Type of business

Reason for leaving

If you are self-employed, or if firm is now out of business, please provide name, address and telephone number of a verifying reference.

* * *

FORM 12/ RECORD OF CIVIL ACTIONS [To be used with questions 20 and 21]

Complete title of action

Court file number

Full name(s) and address(es) of plaintiff(s) and attorney(s)

Full name(s) and address(es) of defendant(s) and attorney(s)

Name and complete address of court involved:

Trial date

Date of final disposition

Disposition

If the disposition resulted in a judgment, has the judgment been satisfied?

If yes, give the date the judgment was satisfied

If no, what amount is still owing and why?

Attach a copy of the pleadings, allegations and/or judgments.

* * *

FORM 13/ RECORD OF BANKRUPTCY OR INSOLVENCY [To be used with Question 22]

Date bankruptcy filed

Complete title of action

Court file number

Name and complete address of court involved

Names and addresses of major creditors

Brief description of circumstances surrounding filing petition for bankruptcy

Date of final disposition

Disposition

Were any adversary proceedings instituted?

Were there any allegations of fraud?

Were any debts not discharged? If yes, list them on a separate sheet of paper.

Attach a schedule of indebtedness, the petition for bankruptcy, and discharge from bankruptcy order.

* * *

FORM 14/ RECORD OF CRIMINAL CASES [To be used with Question 23]

Date of incident (or time period involved)

Location

Title of complaint or indictment

Criminal Number

Brief description of incident

Name and complete address of court involved:

Names and address of law enforcement agency involved:

Date first heard

Charge(s) at time of arrest

Charge(s) at time of trial

Date of final disposition

Final disposition

Attach a copy of the arresting officer's report, complaint, indictment, trial disposition, sentence and appeal, if any.

* * *

FORM 15/ CREDIT CARD OR CHARGE ACCOUNT REVOCATIONS
[To be used with Question 25]

Name and address of charge account or credit card that was revoked:

Account number of charge account or credit card

Date revoked

Amount due at the time of revocation

Payment was made to:

If the credit card was issued by a bank, * * * have you made any payment on the outstanding balance? If so, identify * * * [to whom it was made].

Brief description of circumstances surrounding the revocation

* * *

FORM 16/ AUTHORIZATION TO RELEASE MEDICAL RECORDS [To be used with Questions 27, 28, and 29]

Upon presentation of the original or a photocopy of this signed authorization,

I (Applicant's Name) authorize (Name, Address of Institution or Doctor) to provide information, including copies of records, concerning advice, care or treatment provided to me without limitation relating to mental illness, use of drugs or alcohol to representatives of the National Conference of Bar Examiners who are involved in conducting an investigation into my moral character, professional reputation and fitness for the practice of law. I understand that any such information as may be received will be reported only to the admitting authority.

I hereby release, discharge and exonerate the National Conference of Bar Examiners, its agent and representatives, the admission agency, its agents and representatives and [anyone] * * * so furnishing information from any and all liability of every nature and kind arising out of the furnishing or inspection of such documents, records and other information or the investigation made by the National Conference of Bar Examiners or the admitting authority.

* * *

FORM 17/ DESCRIPTION OF MENTAL, EMOTIONAL, NERVOUS DISORDERS OR CHEMICAL DEPENDENCY [To be used with Questions 27, 28, and 29]

Date of treatment: From Mo/Yr   To Mo/Yr

Name of attending physician

Describe completely the diagnosis and treatment

Please include dates, location of the hospital, outpatient clinic, or institution, type of problem, and name and address of the attending physician, hospital or institution.

PROBLEM 3

The Disabled Lawyer and the Problem of Neglect

Morris Andrews has been watching his contemporary and good friend Harold Black slowly lose his battle with a drinking problem. Andrews knows from long association that Black was once an able lawyer but that a series of personal crises have stimulated a case of alcoholism that has greatly reduced his effectiveness. In a recent case, Andrews' client had a less-than-even chance of winning, but won easily because Black seemed simply unable to represent his own client effectively.

Andrews resolved to go to Black and encourage him to withdraw from practice until he had gotten himself together. Black took the suggestion as an officious insult. "I represent my clients better than you do," Black said. "At least I don't take on more work than I can handle. You never finish anything. All your cases are on the back burner and you only appear in court to get continuances. I lay off the bottle when I have a big case, and as for that recent one when you beat me, you were just lucky."

Andrews did not consider Black's outburst wholly responsive to the main issue, but he did have to admit that Black was right about his caseload. Indeed, Andrews made a mental note to settle some of his minor cases so as to spend more time on the rest. But he was still left uncertain about what, if anything, to do about Black.

QUESTIONS

1. Has Harold Black or Morris Andrews done anything for which professional discipline might be imposed?

a. Notice that in a state that has adopted the ABA Model Rules, professional discipline is imposed for violations of Rule 8.4; in Model Code states, the corresponding provision is DR 1–102. These provisions then incorporate by reference the other Model Rules and Disciplinary Rules, respectively.

b. If a lawyer is licensed in two or more states and their disciplinary rules differ, which state's law should be used to judge a lawyer's conduct? Look at Model Rule 8.5, adopted by the ABA House of Delegates in August 1993. Basically, any state in which the lawyer is licensed may try a disciplinary case for conduct wherever it occurs. The law to be applied, however, must be that of the state in which the lawyer "principally practices", unless the "predominant effect" of the lawyer's conduct is clearly in another state, in which case that state's law governs.

2. Have Andrews and Black represented their clients "competently" within the meaning of Model Rule 1.1 and DR 6–101(A)?

a. In taking on more work than he can handle expeditiously and effectively, has Morris Andrews "neglected" his clients' work?

ABA Informal Opinion 1273, November 20, 1973, asserted that:

"Neglect involves indifference and a consistent failure to carry out the obligations which the lawyer has assumed to his client or a conscious disregard for the responsibility owed to the client. * * * Neglect usually involves more than a single act or omission. Neglect cannot be found if the acts or omissions complained of were inadvertent or the result of an error of judgment made in good faith."

Is the standard set by that definition appropriate for interpreting DR 6–101(A)(3)? Is it consistent with the concerns of clients as revealed in the Marks & Cathcart article in the Readings to this problem? May Andrews rely on Opinion 1273 to continue with business as usual? Has Opinion 1273 been effectively superseded by Model Rule 1.3's requirement that lawyers act with "reasonable diligence"?

b. Incompetence, negligence and neglect have been pursued in lawyer discipline proceedings as violation of Model Rules 1.1 & 1.3 and DR 6–101(A). In re Wolfram, 847 P.2d 94 (Ariz.1993), for example, imposed an 18–month suspension from practice on a lawyer whose acts of neglect constituted providing inadequate assistance of counsel in a criminal case.

c. Does use of the discipline process to pursue Andrews and Black seem desirable? Are they "bad people"? Indeed, is Andrews' problem that too many people have found him to be a very good lawyer? As a practical matter, does Andrews have the luxury of determining the amount of work in the office at any one time? Might turning a client away today cause that client (and perhaps a friend of that client) not to come back tomorrow?

d. What should be the purposes and functions of the lawyer discipline process? Should they only be to punish dishonesty or other "serious" wrongdoing? Should the purposes of the process include responding to what clients see to be problems with their lawyers, even if the concerns seem minor to lawyers themselves? Do the Steele &

Nimmer article in the Readings to this Problem help in your thinking about these questions?

3. What other kinds of conduct should subject a lawyer to professional discipline?

a. Violation of a specific Disciplinary Rule or Model Rule subjects a lawyer to discipline pursuant to DR 1–102(A)(1) & (2) and Model Rule 8.4(a), respectively. However, both DR 1–102(A) and Model Rule 8.4 have other important provisions.

b. Notice that DR 1–102(A)(3) forbade engaging in "illegal conduct involving moral turpitude"; the comparable provision of Model Rule 8.4(b) now prohibits committing "a criminal act that reflects adversely on the lawyer's honesty, trustworthiness or fitness as a lawyer in other respects." Some of the conduct sanctioned under such rules borders on the unbelievable.

In re Bloom, 44 Cal.3d 128, 241 Cal.Rptr. 726, 745 P.2d 61 (1987), for example, was a case in which a lawyer apparently got deeply involved in his client's illegal sale of explosives to Libya. He leased a plane for his client, and filed false documents with the U.S. Customs Service. His defense was that his client told him that the sale was a top secret government operation and that to seek to verify that fact would violate national security. The lawyer's good-faith-belief defense was found not credible.

Attorney Grievance Commission v. Protokowicz, 619 A.2d 100 (Md. App.1993), was even more bizarre. A divorce lawyer was convicted of helping his former client break into the home of the client's estranged wife. When a feline resident of the home came into the kitchen, the lawyer put it into the microwave oven. You can guess the rest. For cooking the cat, the lawyer was suspended from practice for not less than a year.

c. Model Rule 8.4(c) tracks DR 1–102(A)(4); both prohibit a lawyer's engaging "in conduct involving dishonesty, fraud, deceit or misrepresentation," whether or not while acting as a lawyer.

In re Fornari, 599 N.Y.S.2d 545 (App.Div.1993), for example, suspended a lawyer for one year for filing fraudulent documents in making a claim with his homeowner's insurer. He submitted bills for work other than that caused by a storm, for example, and altered the figures on other bills, allegedly to speed up payment he legally was due.

In re Scruggs, 475 N.W.2d 160 (Wis.1991), saw the lawyer suspended for resume fraud. He had taken another student's transcript and inserted his own name and biographical information on it. He also said he had attended American University when he had actually attended American Technological University. Do you agree that these kinds of misrepresentation should cost a lawyer his or her license? Why or why not? [15]

---

15. See also In re Lamberis, 93 Ill.2d 222, 66 Ill.Dec. 623, 443 N.E.2d 549 (1982) (discipline imposed for lawyer's plagiarism in work on an LL.M. degree); In re Lamb,

d. Should an attorney be subject to professional discipline for behavior not in his or her capacity as an attorney? What might lead state supreme courts to sanction lawyer misconduct regardless of when it occurs?

The ABA has noted that:

> "The provisions of DR 1–102(A)(3) and (4) are not limited to a lawyer's conduct while he is acting in his professional capacity as a lawyer. They are applicable to all conduct of the nature specified in those provisions without regard to the capacity in which the lawyer may be acting.
>
> "In regulating a lawyer's nonprofessional as well as professional conduct, the Code of Professional Responsibility charted no new course. It is recognized generally that lawyers are subject to discipline for improper conduct in connection with business activities, individual or personal activities, and activities as a judicial, governmental or public official." ABA Formal Opinion 336 (1974) (footnotes omitted).

Do the Model Rules take the same approach? Look at Rule 8.4 and the Comments thereto.

In re "X", 577 A.2d 139 (N.J.1990), involved a lawyer disbarred after pleading guilty to extensive and willful sexual abuse of his three young daughters. He clearly deserved the maximum criminal penalty for his conduct, but the record spoke of his unquestioned legal competence and public service. Did his conduct so involve "moral turpitude" that he should be denied the right to practice law as well? Would you reach the same result under both the Model Code and the Model Rules?

In Matter of Rowe, 604 N.E.2d 728 (N.Y.1992), the lawyer had killed his wife and three children but had been found not guilty by reason of mental disease. He was now cured and wanted to resume practice. The court, however, would not let him. It justified disbarment primarily on grounds of public perception. It would "undermine public confidence in the bar" to have a killer practicing law, regardless of his lack of legal responsibility for the acts. Do you agree? Is concern about the bar's public image a sufficient basis on which to deny an otherwise qualified person the right to practice law?

e. The Model Rule 8.4(d) and DR 1–102(A)(5) prohibitions of "conduct that is prejudicial to the administration of justice" are less often invoked, probably because most such conduct violates other specific Model Rules or DRs. Crawford County Bar Ass'n v. Nicholson, 613 N.E.2d 1025 (Ohio 1993), however, illustrated a situation where a general rule was helpful. There, the lawyer was suspended for 6 months for making a gesture with his middle finger to a judge and making gratuitous comments of a sexual nature to court employees.

49 Cal.3d 239, 260 Cal.Rptr. 856, 776 P.2d 765 (Calif. 1989) (lawyer disbarred for 5 years for taking bar exam for her husband).

f. If Harold Black were to assert his privilege against self-incrimination in a discipline proceeding against him, could that assertion itself be held to be "prejudicial to the administration of justice" and thus a basis for discipline? See Spevack v. Klein, 385 U.S. 511, 87 S.Ct. 625, 17 L.Ed.2d 574 (1967), holding that a state may not disbar an attorney for taking the fifth amendment. But see, In re Schwarz, 51 Ill.2d 334, 282 N.E.2d 689 (1972), cert. denied 409 U.S. 1047, 93 S.Ct. 527, 34 L.Ed.2d 499 (1972), where the court held that if an attorney is granted use immunity in a criminal case, the state may use the information so acquired in a later lawyer discipline proceeding because discipline proceedings are not criminal matters.[16]

4. What should be the relevance, if any, of Harold Black's alcoholism in deciding whether he should be subject to professional discipline? Should it be a factor in mitigation or aggravation?

a. Should a lawyer be disciplined for past behavior over which he or she lacked real control? Is it proper to impose discipline to prevent future misconduct arising from a condition such as alcoholism? If so, does it follow that all lawyers should have to pass psychological stability tests before admission to practice so as to increase the public's protection? Cf. Dershowitz, Preventive Disbarment: The Numbers Are Against It, 58 A.B.A.J. 815 (1972).

b. There is evidence suggesting that the problem of drug and alcohol abuse may be significant. A State of Washington study, for example, reported that 18% of all lawyers and 25% of those in practice over 20 years have a problem with drugs or alcohol. See Wall Street Journal, Nov. 30, 1991.

In addition, a study by the Association of American Law Schools Special Committee on Problems of Substance Abuse in the Law Schools, 44 J.Legal Educ. 35, 41 (1994), found that nearly ⅔ of law students admitted using at least one illegal drug during their lifetime. Over 20% had used marijuana, and nearly 5% had used cocaine during the previous year.

c. Rule 23 of the ABA Model Rules for Lawyer Disciplinary Enforcement (1989) provides for placing lawyers on an indefinite period of "disability inactive status" in case of their mental or physical incapacity.

---

16. See also, In re Daley, 549 F.2d 469 (7th Cir.1977), cert. denied 434 U.S. 829, 98 S.Ct. 110, 54 L.Ed.2d 89 (1977), where Daley been compelled to testify before a Special Grand Jury under an order of immunity that also purported to protect Daley against use of his testimony "in conjunction with any professional disciplinary proceeding or disbarment." The Illinois Attorney Registration and Discipline Commission had not been party to the negotiations as to the immunity order and the Court of Appeals held that while bar discipline proceedings were called "quasi-criminal" in In re Ruffalo, 390 U.S. 544, 88 S.Ct. 1222, 20 L.Ed.2d 117 (1968), for purposes of requiring fair notice of the charges, the label ought not be extended to the grant of immunity. The attempt to extend immunity beyond the scope of the federal statute was ineffective, and the testimony could be used in the discipline proceeding. Accord, Anonymous Attorneys v. Bar Ass'n of Erie County, 41 N.Y.2d 506, 393 N.Y.S.2d 961, 362 N.E.2d 592 (1977).

Proceedings are to be conducted in the manner of a discipline case, but they are to be confidential. Provisions are made to notify clients and the public if a lawyer is placed on disability status.

Is such a procedure and disposition too severe for a condition or illness such as alcoholism? Is it necessary for protection of the public and more humane than disbarment? Is it necessary to have the leverage of tough sanctions, if only as a threat to coerce the lawyer into getting help? [17]

d. In re Kelley, 801 P.2d 1126 (Cal.1990), involved a lawyer who was brought into the discipline system after her second conviction for drunk driving. Nominally, this was because she had violated the probation imposed in the first drunk driving case, but it also seems to have been part of California's effort to identify lawyers with an alcohol problem *before* they injure a client. Her professional discipline in this case consisted primarily of three years probation on condition that she abstain from alcohol.

Three justices were troubled at what could become an arbitrary use of discipline to coerce behavior that only *might* get worse. Indeed, might sanctions imposed to try to prevent harm rather than punish actual conduct constitute a violation of the Americans with Disabilities Act? Recall the relation of that legislation to bar admission issues discussed in Problem 2.

e. On the other hand, alcoholism has sometimes been cited in mitigation of the sanction for lawyer misconduct. In Matter of Walker, 254 N.W.2d 452 (S.D.1977), for example, there was proof that alcoholism had been the causative factor in the lawyer's conduct. Proof the lawyer was now a recovering alcoholic, although not excusing the misconduct, led the court to allow the lawyer to keep his license. Cf. Petition of Johnson, 322 N.W.2d 616 (Minn.1982) (suggests criteria for when proof of recovery should lead to such a result).

Other mental illnesses have also been cited in mitigation of lawyer discipline. In Conduct of Loew, 292 Or. 806, 642 P.2d 1171 (1982), for example, the lawyer's defense was that he was a victim of "burn-out syndrome." His psychiatrist testified that professionals commonly take on too much work and then psychologically evade it by "procrastination and self-denial." Should this be a good defense? Would recognition of such a defense give adequate protection to clients? Here, the court was sufficiently impressed by the defense that it did not disbar the lawyer, although it did suspend him for 30 days.

5. Do Anderson and Black have a duty to report each other to the lawyer disciplinary authorities in their state? Look at Model Rule 8.3 and DR 1–103.

---

17. The impaired attorney has been one of the particular concerns of the American Bar Association in the last few years, and Model Rule 8.3 was amended in August 1991 to provide that lawyers need not report to discipline authorities any information they learn as part of a lawyers' assistance program (often called an "L.A.P.") designed to help lawyer–abusers recover from addiction.

a. How sure must the lawyer be before making a charge to disciplinary authorities? Doe v. Federal Grievance Committee, 847 F.2d 57 (2d Cir.1988), considered the concept of degrees of certainty in the context of DR 7–102(B)(2) which requires reporting information "clearly establishing" that someone has committed fraud on tribunal. The court held a lawyer must have "actual knowledge" before a failure to report is actionable under that rule.

b. Should the standard for reporting to bar or judicial discipline authorities be different than the standard for making a disclosure under DR 7–102(B)(2)? Look at EC 1–4. Does the advice in EC 1–3 to report and then let the authorities determine whether to take action apply here as well? See Comment 1 to Rule 8.3.

c. Is there a cost to overreporting? Might reporting become vindictive or a tactical ploy in litigation? Is that at least part of the message of Comment 3 to Rule 8.3? Would it be better to have Black and Andrews call each other's law partners and have their firms impose informal sanctions?

d. Might Andrews' knowledge about Black be "privileged"? Would Andrews' client want it known that he won largely because Black was an alcoholic? Is that the kind of information Rule 1.6 was meant to protect? [18] Should the concept of privilege be read broadly or narrowly for this purpose?

e. Do you agree with how narrowly the term "privilege" is read in In re Himmel, set forth as a Reading to this Problem? The *Himmel* court's construction of "privilege" is inconsistent with that used in ABA Formal Opinion 341 (1975), which said that "privilege" covered all information learned by a lawyer in the course of representation, i.e. both "confidences" and "secrets".

The court in *Himmel* says that "a lawyer may not choose to circumvent the rules by simply asserting that his client asked him to do so." Was that a fair statement of lawyer Himmel's position? Assuming that some information was indeed confidential, would not the lawyer have needed the client's permission to disclose the information?

Should *Himmel* be limited to its facts? The case arguably involved selling out the public interest for a potentially increased recovery and attorney's fee. Does the Illinois court seem to place any such limit on its holding?

By contrast, In re Ethics Advisory Panel Opinion, 627 A.2d 317 (R.I.1993), is a careful discussion of the tension between the duty to preserve client confidences and the duty to report misconduct by other lawyers. The Court concludes that a lawyer requires client consent to report another lawyer's misconduct that he learned about from a client.

---

18. You will learn more about the protection of confidential information in Problem 6.

f. Is there a particular time at which the lawyer is obliged to report? Must the lawyer do so immediately upon hearing the relevant facts? Would waiting tend to give a lawyer a better understanding of the facts before reporting?

If there is a civil or criminal action pending involving the same conduct, should the lawyer wait until that action is completed? Would that allow the disciplinary authorities to work with a complete record and avoid duplicative investigation? Would you want to know whether the disciplinary commission follows a practice of "abatement", i.e., of suspending its own action on the case until other proceedings are completed?

Would waiting tend to avoid the complaint's being used as leverage in the underlying case? Cf. DR 7–105. See ABA Formal Opinion 94–383 (July 5, 1994), expressing just such a concern about the threat to file a discipline charge to get an advantage in a civil case and urging the postponing of reporting until the conclusion of the civil case. Do you agree? Might the dynamics work the other way? Would the coercive power of the charge exist *before* reporting and be dissipated thereafter? [19]

g. If a judge were to observe Black's impaired state or Andrews' inability to keep up with his caseload, would the judge's obligation to report be any different than that of a lawyer? May a judge assume that an attorney will report all misconduct in a case? Might lawyers in turn rely on the judge? Look at Canon 3D(2) of the ABA Code of Judicial Conduct (1990).

h. Does a complainant have a personal right to have his or her complaint actively pursued by disciplinary authorities? In Doyle v. Oklahoma Bar Ass'n, 998 F.2d 1559 (10th Cir.1993), the court found the claim of such a right was frivolous.

6. What alternatives to disbarment or suspension should be available to the disciplinary authority?

a. It has been argued that the Court should be given "corrective (not punitive) jurisdiction over a single act of negligent performance." "Punishment" includes reprimand, suspension, or disbarment. Corrective actions might include counseling a lawyer to reduce his case load, not to accept cases in certain areas, and to establish new office procedures. Manson, Helping Lawyers Who Need Help, 9 ALI–ABA CLE Review, Feb. 10, 1978, at 6.

b. In several cases that the Securities and Exchange Commission has brought against lawyers, the SEC has agreed to a settlement in which the law firms agree to adopt special firm policies and procedures designed to avoid future misconduct. E.g., SEC v. National Student

---

19. Cf. ABA Formal Opinion 94–384 (July 5, 1994), advising that a lawyer who is made the subject of a disciplinary charge filed by the opponent in connection with a pending case is not required to withdraw from representation of the client in that case.

Marketing Corp., CCH [1977–78 Transfer Binder] Fed.Sec.L.Rep. ¶ 96,-027 (D.D.C. May 2, 1977).

c.   Should an lawyer be permitted to resign from a state bar when charged with a disciplinable offense? Should an admission of guilt be a prerequisite to resignation? Why or why not? Is it important to know how easy it is for an attorney who has resigned to apply for readmission to the bar? [20]

7.   What sanctions should be imposed on Andrews and Black for the conduct described in this problem?

a.   In 1986, the ABA House of Delegates approved the "Standards for Imposing Lawyer Sanctions." Various courts have referred to these new Standards for guidance.[21] The Standards propose that a court, in imposing a sanction after a finding of lawyer misconduct, should consider four factors:

(a) the duty violated;

(b) the lawyer's mental state; and

(c) the actual or potential injury caused by the lawyer's misconduct; and

(d) the existence of aggravating or mitigating factors.

If a lawyer "engages in a pattern of neglect with respect to client matters and causes serious or potentially serious injury to a client," the Standards state that disbarment is generally appropriate. Standard 4.41(c).

If the lawyer's pattern or neglect causes injury or potential injury that is not serious, the Standards recommend suspension. Standard 4.42(b).

If the lawyer is merely negligent, does not act with reasonable diligence, and causes injury or potential injury to a client, the Standards recommend only a reprimand. Standard 4.43.

If such a lawyer causes little or no actual or potential injury, the Standards recommend admonition. Standard 4.44. A reprimand is a public censure and an admonition is private.

A lawyer's physical or mental disability or impairment are to be mitigating factors, while aggravating factors include the lawyer's refusal to acknowledge the wrongful nature of his conduct, the vulnerability of the victim, the lawyer's substantial experience in the practice of law, and his or her indifference to making restitution. Standards 9.22, 9.32.

In addition to the sanctions of disbarment, suspension, reprimand, admonition, or probation (which allows the lawyer to practice law under specified conditions), the Standards allow "restitution, assessment of

20. Cf. Court Rejects a Nixon Bid to Resign from State Bar, N.Y.Times, Sept. 20, 1975, p. 1, col. 2.

21. Alaska was the first state to officially adopt them. See, Disciplinary Matter Involving Buckalew, 731 P.2d 48 (Alaska 1986).

costs, limitation upon practice, appointment of a receiver, requirement that the lawyer take the bar examination or professional responsibility examination, requirement that the lawyer attend continuing education courses," or other sanctions that the disciplinary authority may deem appropriate. Standard 2.8.

How would these Standards suggest one should sanction Harold Black? Would Morris Andrews get the same sanction?

b. Is there any reason to impose professional sanctions only on individual lawyers? Should law firms be subject to sanctions as well? Might imposition of sanctions on law firms create a better incentive for firms to police their own policies and the practices of their individual members? See Schneyer, Professional Discipline for Law Firms, 77 Cornell L.Rev. 1 (1991).

8. If disciplinary charges are brought against a lawyer, should the general public be allowed to attend the disciplinary hearing?

a. The ABA has proposed that upon the filing and service of formal charges the proceedings should be public except for: "(a) deliberations of the hearing committee, board or court; and (b) information with respect to which the hearing committee has issued a protective order." ABA Model Rules for Lawyer Disciplinary Enforcement, Rule 16(B).

b. There has been no rush to open proceedings to the public. Opponents of openness "say their biggest fear is the specter of sensationalist newspaper publicity about a flimsy allegation of misconduct. If the allegation ultimately is disproved, they are convinced, then news of the vindication would be banished to the back pages of the paper, doing little to offset the stigma of the original publicity." Proponents "say they see no reason for protecting lawyers' privacy in disciplinary proceedings when no similar protective measures exist for laymen charged with crime." [22]

c. What should be the make-up of bar discipline panels? Consider the following:

> "[T]he National Organization of Bar Counsel [has] recommended that there be nonlawyer members in the disciplinary process at all levels in all jurisdictions. * * * That in turn should speed the day when disciplinary agencies tackle incompetence as an ethical failing." Woytash, It's Time To Do Something about Lawyer Competence, 64 A.B.A.J. 308 (1978).

The ABA Model Rules for Lawyer Disciplinary Enforcement (1989) provide for ⅓ public members on both the hearing panels and disciplinary board. Do you agree with this approach? Does it represent a decline in self-regulation by the bar?

---

22. Moya, The Doors Stay Shut on Discipline, Nat'l L.J., Dec. 8, 1980, at pp. 1, 11   and 12.

d.   In August 1991, the ABA adopted most of the recommendations in the report of the McKay Commission. The recommendations include giving the agency power to order mandatory fee arbitration, lawyer practice assistance, and substance abuse counseling. The recommendations also include: an expedited system of alternative dispute resolution for minor misconduct, so as to make the disciplinary agency a one–stop destination for clients who have problems with their lawyers; random audits of lawyer accounts; and the establishment of a national system of records of discipline offenses, while retaining the present state judicial control of discipline.

9.   Should state standards for professional discipline apply in the federal courts sitting in that state as well?

a.   In Kolibash v. Committee on Legal Ethics of the West Virginia Bar, 872 F.2d 571 (4th Cir.1989), an Assistant U.S. Attorney participated on the Government's side in a case in which he had formerly represented the defendant before the grand jury. The state bar initiated disciplinary proceedings against him, and he petitioned to remove the proceedings to federal court. The court upheld the removal as consistent with the general concern that federal officers not be subject to harassment by state officials, however justified any particular proceeding might be.

b.   In addition, United States v. Walsh, 699 F.Supp. 469 (D.N.J. 1988), considered New Jersey amendments to Model Rule 1.11 on disqualification of former government lawyers. The court held that, pursuant to local court rule, the Model Rules as adopted by the ABA were made controlling in that federal court, not the Rules as adopted by the state in which the court is located.

c.   We will see this issue again in connection with federal prosecutors who have asserted they are not bound by state ethics rules restricting ex parte contact with represented defendants, an issue we will look at more directly in Problem 19.

READINGS

MARKS AND CATHCART,* DISCIPLINE WITHIN THE LEGAL PROFESSION: IS IT SELF–REGULATION
1974 U.Illinois Law Forum 193, 195–217 (1974).

The Association of the Bar of the City of New York, which handles the disciplinary functions in the First Department of New York State, publishes the most detailed (and probably the most accurate) classifica-

---

* F. Raymond Marks and Darlene Cathcart, at the time they wrote this article, were attorneys with the American Bar Foundation. Although the specific data is now 25 years old, the patterns of enforcement do not seem to have changed significantly in the interim.

tion of complaints. For the year ending April 30, 1970, the report of the Association's Grievance Committee gave the distribution of complaints shown in Table I. Of the 966 complaints in the First Department which, in the judgment of the intake screeners, stated a prima facie allegation that came within the jurisdiction of the disciplinary agency, 524 (54.6 per cent) involved "neglect." Other jurisdictions studied show similarly high percentages of prima facie complaints of neglect.

Table I

CLASSIFICATION OF COMPLAINTS, ASSOCIATION OF THE BAR OF THE CITY OF NEW YORK, YEAR ENDING APRIL 30, 1970

1.	Offenses Against Clients			
	a.	Conversion	32	
	b.	Overreaching	36	
	c.	Neglect	524	
	d.	Misinforming	16	
	e.	Conflict of interest	13	
	f.	Fraud	12	
	g.	Other	80	713
2.	Direct Offenses Against Colleagues			
	a.	Personal relationships	4	
	b.	Agreements	13	
	c.	By-passing other attorney	10	
	d.	Other	4	31
3.	Indirect Offenses Against Colleagues			
	a.	Solicitation	7	
	b.	Advertising	7	14
4.	Direct Offenses Against the Administration of Justice			
	a.	Improper influence	8	
	b.	Other	7	15
5.	Indirect Offenses Against the Administration of Justice			
	a.	Fraudulent representation	12	
	b.	False swearing	7	
	c.	Actions in bad faith—abuse of process	41	
	d.	Violations of Court Rules	2	
	e.	Concealing of evidence	1	
	f.	Other	26	89
6.	Other Professional Misconduct			
	a.	Derelictions	18	
	b.	Lack of cooperation	7	
	c.	Other	16	41
7.	Non-Professional Misconduct			
	a.	Financial irresponsibility	19	
	b.	Fraud	11	
	c.	Other	38	68

8A	Crime		
	a. Larceny	6	
	b. Forgery	1	
	c. Perjury	2	
	d. Bribery	5	
	e. Income tax evasion, failure to file	3	
	f. Other	4	21
8B	Minor Offenses		
	a. Miscellaneous (disorderly conduct, violation of Administrative Code, etc.)	4	4
	SUBTOTAL, CATEGORIES 1 to 8B		996
9.	Complaints Against Attorneys Outside Committee's Jurisdiction	15	
10.	Complaints Which Set Forth No Unethical Behavior		
	a. Advice—Requests for legal advice or assistance	164	
	b. Minor fee disputes	174	
	c. Minor disagreements in personal business transactions	51	
	d. Minor disagreements not attributable to misconduct	181	
	e. Other	148	720
TOTAL ALL CATEGORIES			2,031

Fee disagreements constitute another major grievance. But as a general rule, fee disputes fall outside disciplinary agency jurisdiction. When a fee dispute raises issues of fraud or overreaching, however, the disciplinary agency may have jurisdiction (see Table I, Categories 1b and 1f). One bar counsel even suggested that if one could consider as "fee disputes" all complaints in which the client felt "short-changed," fee disputes would account for 75 per cent of his docket. This system of classification would, of course, include what others have called "neglect": a lawyer accepts money and fails to act promptly or even fails to act at all.

Disciplinary Action on Complaints

In the year ending April 30, 1970, 1,716 complaints were filed in the First Department of New York against attorneys within its jurisdiction. The Grievance Committee determined that 996 of the complaints set forth prima facie cases of misconduct. After investigation, 144 resulted in letters of admonition. In addition, three attorneys admitted their guilt and were permitted to surrender their licenses with prejudice against any right to be reinstated automatically. Only 41 lawyers, some of whom faced multiple charges, were brought before the hearing committee on formal charges representing 66 complaints. The results of these hearings were:

Prosecution in the courts recommended	19
Formally admonished	15
Dismissed	5

Pending $\frac{2}{41}$

Thus, in one of the best administered discipline systems, 213 complaints, or about 12 per cent of all complaints, resulted in admonition, resignation, or recommendation of suspension or disbarment. Considerably less than 1 per cent of the 30,000 lawyers in the First Department were disciplined in any way.

* * *

Given the small percentage of complaints resulting in discipline, what types of cases lead to suspension or disbarment? Remember that a large proportion of client complaints center on neglect and fee disputes. But fee disputes and cases of neglect or other negligence rarely result in either suspension or disbarment. Indeed, few of the less stringent sanctions are even applied to these types of complaints.

Most agencies do not treat neglect or other negligence as within their jurisdiction, unless it is gross negligence. If a neglect or negligence case is taken, it may be treated as a "breakdown of communication" that can be handled by a phone call or letter to the attorney asking him to explain the situation to the client. Even in the jurisdictions that do handle negligence complaints, complainants may be viewed as "probably mistaken" because "the client doesn't really understand what he wants."

While some jurisdictions will arbitrate fee disputes, none generally consider fee disputes to be matters that deserve the attention of grievance committees.

* * *

In sum, most disciplinary agencies decline to take jurisdiction in the types of cases with which most complainants are concerned—neglect, other negligence, and fee disputes. They devote a large amount of their time to screening out these complaints and to an informal handling of those complaints they classify as a "misunderstanding" or "lack of communication." A diversionary process is involved: rather than formal acceptance of jurisdiction and official recognition of the problems of competence, neglect, other negligence, and fee disputes, informal adjustment is relied on. * * *

When we look at the types of cases that reach the formal hearing stage and that may result in serious discipline, generally we find the list dominated by conversion, bribery, fraud, conviction of a felony, income tax evasion, and solicitation. The largest number of discipline adjudications and those that receive the severest sanctions involve conversion; yet this is the least frequent type of complaint. One must keep in mind that conversion is usually covered by the criminal law under theft and embezzlement provisions and by a wide range of civil remedies. What specific function (or utility), then, do bar procedures and sanctions have

when applied to conduct already covered by the criminal and civil law?
* * *

————

ERIC H. STEELE AND RAYMOND T. NIMMER,* LAWYERS, CLIENTS AND PROFESSIONAL REGULATION
1976 A.B.F.Res.J. 917, 999–1014.

The current policy goals of professional self-regulation may be expressed analytically in terms of three functions: (1) to identify and remove from the profession all seriously deviant members (the "cleansing" function), (2) to deter normative deviance and maximize compliance with norms among attorneys (the deterrence function), and (3) to maintain a level of response to deviance sufficient to forestall public dissatisfaction (the public image function).

The cleansing function assumes an archaic view that deviance results solely from, and can be defined in terms of, innate characteristics of the individual whose conduct is in question, that is, basic deficiencies of character. Under this view it is assumed that the function of the disciplinary system is simply to identify those inherently "unfit" attorneys and remove them from the profession. How many attorneys must be removed before the profession will have been "cleansed" is the subject of much debate.

* * *

The deterrence rationale is both more traditional and more tenable. However, the entire field of deterrence remains empirically obscure and any discussion of it must proceed cautiously. Its basic concept is the utilitarian notion that threatened or actual imposition of sanctions for deviant conduct will encourage individuals to conform to operative norms. Presumably, the deterrent effect is determined by the probability that a sanction will be imposed and by the seriousness of the sanction. As probability or seriousness increases, the effect on the deviant conduct should also increase.

The proposition about probability of enforcement makes apparent the weakness of present professional regulation. A precondition to the imposition of a sanction is that the alleged deviance be brought to the attention of the enforcement system. The reporting process in the context of lawyer misconduct is inexact and incomplete. The main sources of information are the reports of victimized clients. Peer review is ineffective, despite the ethical obligation of attorneys to report the misconduct of fellow professionals.

The primary responsibility for identifying lawyer deviance falls on the client, who does not expect to encounter such problems with his attorney. In attempting to resolve their problems, the clients inter-

* Research Attorneys, American Bar Foundation.

viewed in our study felt powerless. They had no conception of what response would be effective and as a result they usually did nothing. Business clients exhibited no greater tendency to report attorney misconduct to the disciplinary system, though they were more resourceful in responding to their problems. But their response was to minimize costs rather than to seek regulatory control. The result of nonreporting is the insulation of the lawyer from disciplinary agency scrutiny even when the lawyer's conduct has injured the client.

* * *

The final function of self-regulation concerns public image. A disciplinary system with public image as its only concern would avoid publicity. When responding to public unrest about attorney conduct, it would tend to act only in highly publicized cases, communicating the image that few members of the profession are deviants. Such a pure focus on image would, of course, not be an acceptable posture. More typically, concern over public image motivates sincere attempts to strengthen disciplinary enforcement in cases of serious lawyer deviance in the belief that this will get at the root causes of public dissatisfaction. This posture, which pervades the Clark Report, is also troublesome, for it too fixes all but exclusively on extreme lawyer deviance, which, as our data show, accounts for only a small portion of client complaints.

A. Models of Social Control

The overriding problem of professional discipline lies in the assumption that regulatory activity must focus primarily on lawyer deviance, leading to dissonance between client complaints and formal agency policy. Client complaints suggest a need for a quite different response, both preventive and remedial. The policy implications of our research lead us to deal not only with the objectives of professional regulation, but also with three alternative models of regulation: (1) deviance control, (2) administrative supervision, and (3) dispute management. Each rests on a different view of the problem to be addressed.

* * *

1. *Deviance Control*

The deviance control model is epitomized by the criminal justice system. It focuses on the normative character of an individual's behavior. * * * The product of such a system is a series of decisions that label persons deviants and impose on them collateral consequences, usually punishment or treatment.

* * *

Behavior control strategies are uniquely geared toward behavior that is consciously elected. * * * Thus deviance control cannot deal effectively with the emerging concern with attorney competence, since competence is a status, not an act. A norm that all attorneys be competent to perform legal services is not susceptible to a deviance control approach, although deviance control *can* prescribe and seek compliance with a course of conduct enhancing competence or a requirement that an attorney reasonably evaluate his competence before accepting a proffered contract. * * *

* * *

2. *Administrative Supervision*

The deviance model makes normative judgments and labels individuals as deviants. In contrast, a chief characteristic of administrative supervision is that it seeks to act preventively. The administrative model functions with reference to the behavior of an individual or organization as a whole. * * *

* * *

The administrative model is most clearly relevant to lawyer competence. A basic aspect of a licensing system is the assurance that every licensee has the basic skills necessary to perform those services for which he is engaged. Traditionally, legal skills have been assumed to exist once a lawyer has been admitted to the bar, but the frequency of client complaints about quality of performance suggests that the assumption is not justified.

Incompetence, however, must be distinguished from negligence. Competence refers to the possession of requisite skills and not to the adequacy of their application. A competent attorney can be negligent and render inadequate services. Competence involves not questions of attentiveness, care, and motivation in particular cases but rather the underlying ability to perform.

* * *

3. *Dispute Management*

* * *

* * * Most client-lawyer disputes arise not out of attorney deviance or incompetence but out of the failure of the parties to express and reconcile their mutual expectations. Such contractual disputes are often summarily dismissed by the profession as "mere misunderstandings" or "lack of communication," but these categories reflect a deviance perspective instead of recognition of the typical vagueness and nonmutuality of the legal service contract. The typical contract for legal services would, in fact, be unacceptable to most people when contracting for any other type of goods or services. Standardization of expectations, obligations and forms of expression, and routinization of legal tasks are complex but ultimately unavoidable regulatory tasks. An administrative approach is necessary for the achievement of these objectives.

The second level involves the traditional dispute management perspective of adjudicating or resolving disputes over contract terms and performance. While the general record of professional involvement in dispute settlement systems for lawyer-client contracts is poor, several existing and emerging response systems indicate the diverse formats that might be employed. The first is the client security fund. These funds are based on the principle of indemnification or bonding such as has long existed for bank couriers and cashiers. While client security funds represent a potentially dispute-oriented or remedial response, in practice they have been tightly constrained by the deviance perspective. As currently structured, they are (even where separately administered) almost totally constrained by the standards and actions of the disciplinary system and provide compensation for only the narrow segment of losses caused by intentionally dishonest lawyers (e.g., defalcations and misappropriations of funds). Typically, compensation is available only after the claim has been fully processed through the disciplinary system, misconduct officially found, and a sanction officially imposed.

* * *

The second development, more clearly exhibiting the dispute management model, is the arbitration of fee disputes. These programs are unambiguously dispute-oriented but to date they have been applied only to the narrow range of disputes where the client explicitly defines the grievance as a dispute over the amount of the lawyer's fee. As we have seen, while explicit fee disputes constitute a large portion of clients' complaints, many complaints involve issues of quality, efficiency, promptness, and effectiveness. These are not presently subject to arbitration. Such issues are complaints about the service itself. Once the fee is submitted to arbitration, of course, questions about the type and quality of the services can be addressed in determining the appropriate fee. But such questions cannot themselves now be arbitrated.

* * *

IN RE JAMES H. HIMMEL
Supreme Court of Illinois, 1988.
125 Ill.2d 531, 127 Ill.Dec. 708, 533 N.E.2d 790.

Justice STAMOS delivered the opinion of the court:

This is a disciplinary proceeding against respondent, James H. Himmel. * * *

* * *

In October 1978, Tammy Forsberg was injured in a motorcycle accident. In June 1980, she retained John R. Casey to represent her in any personal injury or property damage claim resulting from the accident. Sometime in 1981, Casey negotiated a settlement of $35,000 on Forsberg's behalf. Pursuant to an agreement between Forsberg and Casey, one-third on any monies received would be paid to Casey as his attorney fee.

In March 1981, Casey received the $35,000 settlement check, endorsed it, and deposited the check into his client trust fund account. Subsequently, Casey converted the funds.

Between 1981 and 1983, Forsberg unsuccessfully attempted to collect her $23,233.34 share of the settlement proceeds. In March 1983, Forsberg retained respondent to collect her money and agreed to pay him one-third of any funds recovered above $23,233.34.

Respondent investigated the matter and discovered that Casey had misappropriated the settlement funds. In April 1983, respondent drafted an agreement in which Casey would pay Forsberg $75,000 in settlement of any claim she might have against him for the misappropriated funds. By the terms of the agreement, Forsberg agreed not to initiate any criminal, civil, or attorney disciplinary action against Casey. This agreement was executed on April 11, 1983. Respondent stood to gain $17,000 or more if Casey honored the agreement. On February 1985, respondent filed suit against Casey for breaching the agreement, and a $100,000 judgment was entered against Casey. If Casey had satisfied the judgment, respondent's share would have been approximately $25,588.

The complaint stated that at no time did respondent inform the Commission of Casey's misconduct. According to the Administrator, respondent's first contact with the Commission was in response to the Commission's inquiry regarding the lawsuit against Casey.

In April 1985, the Administrator filed a petition to have Casey suspended from practicing law because of his conversion of client funds and his conduct, including moral turpitude in matters unrelated to Forsberg's claim. Casey was subsequently disbarred on consent on November 5, 1985.

A hearing on the complaint against the present respondent was held before the Hearing Board of the Commission on June 3, 1986. In its report, the Hearing Board noted that the evidence was not in dispute. The evidence supported the allegations in the complaint and provided additional facts as follows.

Before retaining respondent, Forsberg collected $5,000 from Casey. After being retained, respondent made inquiries regarding Casey's conversion, contacting the insurance company that issued the settlement check, its attorney, Forsberg, her mother, her fiance and Casey. Forsberg told respondent that she simply wanted her money back and specifically instructed respondent to take no other action. Because of respondent's efforts, Forsberg collected another $10,400 from Casey. Respondent received no fee in this case.

The Hearing Board found that respondent received unprivileged information that Casey converted Forsberg's funds, and that respondent failed to relate the information to the Commission in violation of Rule 1–103(a) of the Code. The Hearing Board noted, however, that respondent had been practicing law for 11 years, had no prior record of any complaints, obtained as good a result as could be expected in the case, and requested no fee for recovering the $23,233.34. Accordingly, the Hearing Board recommended a private reprimand.

Upon the Administrator's exceptions to the Hearing Board's recommendation, the Review Board reviewed the matter. The Review Board's report stated that the client had contacted the Commission prior to retaining respondent and, therefore, the Commission did have knowledge of the alleged misconduct. Further, the Review Board noted that respondent respected the client's wishes regarding not pursuing a claim with the Commission. Accordingly the Review Board recommended that the complaint be dismissed.

* * *

We begin our analysis by examining whether a client's complaint of attorney misconduct to the Commission can be a defense to an attorney's failure to report the same misconduct. Respondent offers no authority for such a defense and our research has disclosed none. Common sense would dictate that if a lawyer has a duty under the Code, the actions of a client would not relieve the attorney of his own duty. Accordingly, while the parties dispute whether or not respondent's client informed the Commission, that question is irrelevant to our inquiry in this case. We have held that the canons of ethics in the Code constitute a safe guide for professional conduct, and attorneys may be disciplined for not observing them. * * *

As to respondent's argument that he did not report Casey's misconduct because his client directed him not to do so, we again note respondent's failure to suggest any legal support for such a defense. A lawyer, as an officer of the court, is duty-bound to uphold the rules in the Code. * * * A lawyer may not choose to circumvent the rules by simply asserting that his client asked him to do so.

* * *

* * * [I]f the present respondent's conduct did violate the rule on reporting misconduct, imposition of discipline for such a breach of duty is mandated.

The question whether the information that respondent possessed was protected by the attorney-client privilege, and thus exempt for the reporting rule, requires application of this court's definition of the privilege. We have stated that "(1) [w]here legal advice of any kind is sought (2) from a professional legal advisor in his capacity as such, (3) the communications relating to that purpose, (4) made in confidence (5) by the client, (6) are at his instance permanently protected (7) from disclosure by himself or by the legal adviser, (8) except the protection be waived." We agree with the Administrator's argument that the communication regarding Casey's conduct does not meet this definition. The record does not suggest that his information was communicated by Forsberg to the respondent in confidence. We have held that information voluntarily disclosed by a client to an attorney, in the presence of third parties who are not agents of the client or attorney, is not privileged information. In this case, Forsberg discussed the matter with respondent at various times while her mother and her fiance were present.   Consequently, unless the mother and fiance were agents of respondent's client, the information communicated was not privileged. Moreover, we have also stated that matters intended by a client for disclosure by the client's attorney to third parties, who are not agents of either the client or the attorney, are not privileged.   The record shows that respondent, with Forsberg's consent, discussed Casey's conversion of her funds with the insurance company involved, the insurance company's lawyer, and with Casey himself.   Thus, * * * the information was not privileged.

Though respondent repeatedly asserts that his failure to report was motivated not by financial gain but by the request of his client, we do not deem such an argument relevant in this case.   This court has stated that discipline may be appropriate even if no dishonest motive for the misconduct exists.   * * *

* * * We conclude then, that respondent possessed unprivileged knowledge of Casey's conversion of client funds, which is illegal conduct involving moral turpitude, and that respondent failed in his duty to report such misconduct to the Commission.   Because no defense exists, we agree with the Hearing Board's finding that respondent has violated Rule 1–103(a) and must be disciplined.

The third issue concerns the appropriate quantum of discipline to be imposed on this case.   The Administrator cites to the purposes of attorney discipline, which include maintaining the integrity of the legal profession and safeguarding the administration of justice.   * * * The Administrator also argues that both respondent and his client behaved in contravention of the Criminal Code's prohibition against compounding a crime by agreeing with Casey not to report him, in exchange for settlement funds.

In his defense, respondent reiterates his argument that he was not motivated by desire for financial gain.   * * * According to respondent, his failure to report was a "judgment call" which resulted positively in Forsberg's regaining some of her funds from Casey.

In evaluating the proper quantum of discipline to impose, we note that it is this court's responsibilities to determine appropriate sanctions in attorney disciplinary cases.   * * *

* * * Both respondent and his client stood to gain financially by agreeing not to prosecute or report Casey for conversion.   According to the settlement agreement, respondent would have received $17,000 or more as his fees.   If Casey has satisfied the judgment entered against him for failure to honor the settlement agreement, respondent would have collected approximately $25,588.

We have held that fairness dictates consideration of mitigating factors in disciplinary cases.   Therefore, we do consider the fact that Forsberg recovered $10,400 through respondent's services, that respondent has practiced law for 11 years with no record of complaints, and that he requested no fee for minimum collection of Forsberg's funds.

However, these consideration do not outweigh the serious nature of respondent's failure to report Casey, the resulting interference with the Commission's investigation of Casey, and respondent's ill advised choice to settle with Casey rather than report his misconduct.

Accordingly, it is ordered that respondent be suspended from the practice of law for one year.

———

PROBLEM 4

Regulating Lawyers Outside of the Formal Disciplinary System

Sarah Field is a young lawyer with a great future. She has attracted several clients with a wide range of interests and problems. Her outstanding record before juries is the envy of the local bar. Sometimes, however, she is not as careful as she might be.

Field is active in local politics. At a party picnic, an acquaintance of hers, Mary Moore, took her aside and told Field, "My doctor really messed me up two years ago. He performed supposedly minor surgery but cut the wrong things and now I can never have children." Field put her arm around Mary and said, "That's terrible. I know how to handle doctors like that. Leave everything to me." When Field got back to her office, she wrote a nasty letter to the doctor demanding that he "fully compensate my client." By return mail, she received a settlement offer of $25,000. Mary, the client, said she was delighted and Field was impressed at how intimidated the doctor seemed to be by her letter. Field did not have Mary examined by an independent physician. Had she done so, both would have learned that Mary's injuries were much worse than she believed. Field recommended that Mary accept the settlement, which she did. Now, Mary has learned the full extent of her injuries, and she realizes how inadequate her settlement really was.

Field does very little tax work. One of her wealthy clients heard that income can be made taxable to her children, instead of herself, by the use of certain trusts. She asked Field to see that the trusts were properly prepared. Field researched the problem as well as her small office library would permit and discussed the issues over coffee with a CPA from down the hall. The client later learned that Field's handiwork was not good enough to accomplish her objectives, and a large tax deficiency was assessed. "Don't blame me," Field said defensively, "If you wanted tax advice you should have called a specialist. I told you I was not positive of the tax consequences."

In yet another incident, this time a criminal trial in which she was appointed counsel, Field had gone on a vacation and failed to appear when the case was called. The case was reset for the following morning. Field's office reached her and she quickly returned. The next day, although she was physically present for the trial, she was not prepared and did a terrible job. The client was convicted and sentenced to a long prison term.

QUESTIONS

1. What standards should apply in a malpractice action? Would Field be guilty of malpractice in any of these incidents? All of them?

a. Professional discipline issues were considered in Problem 3. Here we look at additional sanctions that lawyers may face. Basically, a malpractice action seeks damages against a lawyer for a wrong characterized in any of three ways—as a tort committed by the lawyer against the client, as a breach of the contract the client made for the lawyer's services, or as a breach of fiduciary duties owed by the lawyer to the client. Sometimes all of these theories will work equally well; sometimes the theory matters, as when determining the relevant statute of limitations.

b. To what standard of performance should a lawyer be held? A treatise on lawyer malpractice says: "[T]he attorney should [be required to] exercise the skill and knowledge ordinarily possessed by attorneys under similar circumstances." 1 R. Mallen & J. Smith, Legal Malpractice 857 (3rd Ed.1989). Has Sarah Field satisfied that standard in these situations?

c. Look at the statistics on lawyer malpractice included as a Reading to this Problem. Are you surprised by the fields of law that generate the most malpractice claims? Are you surprised by the level of experience of the lawyers charged?

d. Lawyers sometimes try to comfort themselves by citing Lucas v. Hamm, 56 Cal.2d 583, 15 Cal.Rptr. 821, 364 P.2d 685 (1961). It said the rule against perpetuities is so difficult that violation of it is not inevitably malpractice. Horne v. Peckham, 97 Cal.App. 3d 404, 158 Cal.Rptr. 714 (3d Dist.1979), however, made clear that the *Lucas* situation was unusual. "An attorney's obligation is not satisfied by simply determining that the law on a particular subject is doubtful or debatable [because] an attorney has a duty to *avoid* involving his client in murky areas of law if research reveals alternative courses of conduct. At least he should inform his client of uncertainties and let the client make the decision." 97 Cal.App.3d at 415, 158 Cal.Rptr. at 721.

e. Woodruff v. Tomlin, 616 F.2d 924 (6th Cir.1980) (en banc), cert. denied 449 U.S. 888, 101 S.Ct. 246, 66 L.Ed.2d 114 (1980), cited what is sometimes called the "barrister's rule" that there is no malpractice liability for an honest exercise of professional judgment. However, even *Woodruff* holds that while the decision whether to call a particular person as a witness is normally a tactical decision involving one's professional judgment, the same does not apply to an attorney's decision not to interview a potentially material witness brought to the attention of an attorney by his client. Without interviewing the witness, the lawyer has no basis on which to make a judgment about the witness' importance, so the failure to interview may be found to be malpractice.

2. How should those principles apply in this case?

a. Should Field be guilty of malpractice for recommending the settlement with the doctor that the client later believes was inadequate? Lowman v. Karp, 476 N.W.2d 428 (Mich.App.1991), Ziegelheim v. Apollo, 607 A.2d 1298 (N.J.1992), and Grayson v. Wofsey, Rosen, Kweskin & Kuriansky, 646 A.2d 195 (Conn.1994), all hold that recommending an inadequate settlement may indeed constitute malpractice.

In Muhammad v. Strassburger, McKenna, Messer, Shilobod and Gutnick, 587 A.2d 1346 (Pa.1991), however, the court held that while a settlement did not completely bar a later action for malpractice, the action would only lie if the client proved that her lawyer had fraudulently induced her to settle as opposed to negligently giving her inadequate information.

Which rule makes more sense? Might the Pennsylvania rule be justified by a concern that settlements often represent less than the party might have gotten at trial? Might it also reflect a desire to have settlements be the end of litigation, not the start of another round of it? However, would the Pennsylvania rule adequately protect the client in this Problem?

b. Should Field have been obliged to refer the tax case to a specialist? In Horne v. Peckham, supra, the client had asked Attorney to draft a Clifford Trust in order to shelter income from federal taxes. Attorney testified that he told the client: "I had no knowledge of tax matters. I had no expertise in tax matters; that if somebody else could figure out what needed to be done, I could draft the documents." Attorney consulted with the client's accountant and a two volume set of American Jurisprudence on federal taxation. When the trust failed to qualify for favorable tax treatment the client sued and the jury awarded damages of $64,983.31. The appellate court affirmed the judgment and upheld a jury instruction that it "is the duty of an attorney who is a general practitioner to refer his client to a specialist or recommend the assistance of a specialist if under the circumstances a reasonably careful and skillful practitioner would do so." If Attorney did not refer the case or seek a specialist's help, it was his duty to have the knowledge and skill possessed and used by specialists in the same locality and under the same circumstances.

Do you agree? Does such a rule simply encourage making legal services more expensive? [1]

c. Should a malpractice action be available against a lawyer who mishandles a criminal case? Should it matter whether the lawyer was appointed or retained?

---

1. See Battle v. Thornton, 646 A.2d 315 (D.C.App.1994), holding that in a jurisdiction that does not certify specialties, the malpractice standard is the ordinary lawyer, not persons who concentrate their practice in a given area of the law and usually handle a given kind of case.

Compare Ferri v. Ackerman, 444 U.S. 193, 100 S.Ct. 402, 62 L.Ed.2d 355 (1979) (federal law does not require immunity of appointed counsel in federal case from state malpractice claim), with Polk County v. Dodson, 454 U.S. 312, 102 S.Ct. 445, 70 L.Ed.2d 509 (1981) (state public defender does not act "under color of state law" so as to be liable for malpractice under 42 U.S.C.A. § 1983). See also, Mossow v. United States, 987 F.2d 1365 (8th Cir.1993) (government can be sued for malpractice of military lawyer).

On the other hand, Dziubak v. Mott, 503 N.W.2d 771 (Minn.1993), held that a public defender is immune from suit by a dissatisfied client. Public defenders may not turn down cases, the Court reasoned, and the public treasury cannot afford to defend malpractice cases. Moreover, immunity may encourage private lawyers to accept court appointments.

Shaw v. Dept. of Administration, 861 P.2d 566 (Alaska 1993), permitted a suit against a public defender but went on to consider the burden of proof and admissible evidence in such a case. The Court held the defendant's actual guilt or innocence is relevant to whether damages should be awarded; wrongdoers should not be rewarded by recoveries from their lawyers. Contrary to the majority rule in such cases, however, the Court refused to place on criminal defendants the burden of proving innocence; the lawyer must raise actual guilt as an affirmative defense. Proof need only be by a preponderance of the evidence, however, and the lawyer is not limited to using proof of guilt that would have been admissible in a criminal trial. Given the threat of such evidence coming out, one wonders whether there are likely to be many suits brought by unhappy criminal clients.

3. How is the trier of fact to know what skill and knowledge would ordinarily be employed by a lawyer in the circumstances presented by the case?

a. A malpractice plaintiff must ordinarily present expert testimony unless the matter under investigation is so simple or the lack of skill so obvious as to be within the range of ordinary experience of laypeople. This rule applies even in a bench trial because the standard of care must be presented on the record with a chance for cross examination rather than left to the subjective standard of the judge. E.g., Lentino v. Fringe Employee Plans, Inc., 611 F.2d 474 (3d Cir.1979).[2]

b. The more controversial question has been whether Field's possible violation of the standards set forth in the Model Code and Model Rules are something the trier of fact may consider in a malpractice setting. What do the Model Rules' Scope provision and the Model Code's Preliminary Statement say about the issue? Do you believe those disclaimers should control a court's decision whether to let a jury hear about the possible violation of professional standards?

2. The lawyer expert need not be licensed to practice in the state, at least when the malpractice claim is based on a federal cause of action. The fact that the expert is not licensed to practice in the state goes to the weight rather than the admissibility of the evidence. Walker v. Bangs, 601 P.2d 1279 (Wash.1979).

c. Some courts have allowed expert witnesses to cite the Model Code and Model Rules as authoritative evidence of the professional standards applicable in a situation. E.g., Woodruff v. Tomlin, 616 F.2d 924 (6th Cir.1980) (en banc), cert. denied 449 U.S. 888, 101 S.Ct. 246, 66 L.Ed.2d 114 (1980) (Model Code is "some evidence of the standards required of lawyers"); Mirabito v. Liccardo, 5 Cal.Rptr.2d 571 (Cal.App. 1992) (disciplinary standards may be the subject of experts' testimony and cited to the jury); Mayol v. Summers, Watson & Kimpel, 585 N.E.2d 1176 (Ill.App.1992) (rules may be treated as analogous to a statute).

In Hizey v. Carpenter, 830 P.2d 646 (Wash.1992), on the other hand, the court came out the other way. Violating a disciplinary rule is not enough to show malpractice, the Court said. Indeed, the language of the rule may not even form the basis of a jury instruction. See also, Lazy Seven Coal Sales, Inc. v. Stone & Hinds, P.C., 813 S.W.2d 400 (Tenn. 1991); Mergler v. Crystal Properties Associates, Ltd., 583 N.Y.S.2d 229 (App.Div.1992).

Maritrans GP, Inc. v. Pepper, Hamilton & Scheetz, 602 A.2d 1277 (Pa.1992), came at the issue yet another way. The Pennsylvania Supreme Court held that the fact that the lawyer's acts violate a state ethics rule does not *preclude* a finding of malpractice. A rule may state a principle of fiduciary duty, for example, and that principle will be enforced in the malpractice case even if the rule embodying it is not itself enforced.

4. May a lawyer be liable for professional malpractice to persons other than the lawyer's client?

a. Liability to non-clients has been a controversial and evolving area of lawyer liability, but Restatement of the Law (Third), The Law Governing Lawyers, Tentative Draft No. 7 (1994), Section 73, suggests three relatively clear situations in which liability may be found.

i. A lawyer may be liable to a prospective client for revealing confidential information communicated to the lawyer or, for example, if the lawyer fails to tell the prospective client that the statute of limitations on his claim will soon run out. E.g., Miller v. Metzinger, 91 Cal.App.3d 31, 154 Cal.Rptr. 22 (1979).

ii. Further, a lawyer may be liable to beneficiaries named in a client's will if, due to the lawyer's negligence, the will does not carry out the testator's intention. See, e.g., Mieras v. DeBona, 516 N.W.2d 154 (Mich.App.1994); Lucas v. Hamm, 56 Cal.2d 583, 15 Cal.Rptr. 821, 364 P.2d 685 (1961).

iii. In addition, a lawyer may be liable to a non–client to whom the lawyer expressly assumes an obligation to investigate facts and accurately report them to the non-client. See, e.g., Greycas, Inc. v. Proud, 826 F.2d 1560 (7th Cir.1987), cert. denied 484 U.S. 1043 (1988) (lawyer who agreed to investigate state of client's title to property being posted as security for loan held liable to the lender when failed to investigate and inaccurately reported the state of the client's title).[3]

b. More controversially, the Tentative Draft of the Restatement suggests that a lawyer who aids a trustee or similar fiduciary to breach an obligation to the intended beneficiary of the fiduciary's duty may be liable to that beneficiary, e.g., Fickett v. Superior Court, 558 P.2d 988 (Ariz.App.1976). Watch for this issue of liability to third parties throughout the remainder of these materials.

5. What sanctions should be imposed for a lawyer's professional malpractice?

a. Should Field be able to defend the malpractice claims by showing that the clients did not have a very strong case anyway? Should Mary have the burden to prove that she would have recovered substantial damages? This so-called "suit-within-a-suit" requirement has traditionally been a required part of a malpractice case and can have a major impact on damages, even if liability is clear. See, e.g., Pickens, Barns & Abernathy v. Heasley, 328 N.W.2d 524 (Iowa 1983); Smith v. Lewis, 13 Cal.3d 349, 118 Cal.Rptr. 621, 530 P.2d 589 (1975).

b. Should the sanctions include possible punitive damages? Patrick v. Ronald Williams, P.A., 402 S.E.2d 452 (N.C.App.1991), held that a lawyer may be sued for punitive damages for gross negligence. The lawyer was found to have failed to estimate the value of his clients' claim, to tell the clients about an offer of settlement, to tell them judgment had been entered until six months had passed, and to have lost their rights under the uninsured motorist provisions of their insurance policy by failing to appeal a trial court order. Those facts were extreme, but even the specter of exposure to punitive damages in a world that is often hostile to lawyers is sobering.

c. Campagnola v. Mulholland, Minion & Roe, 555 N.E.2d 611 (N.Y.1990), added yet a different wrinkle. Because the lawyer did not comply with the policy provisions, the client lost her $100,000 uninsured motorist coverage. The lawyer asserted that this sum should be reduced by the portion of the judgment she would have had to pay as the lawyer's contingent fee. In a sharply divided 4–3 decision, the New York Court of Appeals said her contract to pay fees was not part of the measure of what she had lost; more realistically, Judge Kaye wrote in a concurring opinion that this malpractice case would require the plaintiff to pay fees, so not deducting anything from the damages was necessary to make her whole.

---

3. In some states, this theory of liability to non–clients is significantly qualified by the requirement of privity between lawyer and client to maintain a malpractice action. The privity limitation, in turn, is derived from Ultramares v. Touche, 174 N.E. 441 (N.Y.1932), in which Judge Cardozo had feared giving professionals unlimited liability to investors who relied on their opinions. Compare, e.g., Security Pacific Business Credit, Inc. v. Peat Marwick Main & Co., 597 N.E.2d 1080 (N.Y.1992) (continuing to follow *Ultramares*), with Vereins–Und Westbank, AG v. Carter, 691 F.Supp. 704 (S.D.N.Y.1988) (holding lawyer liable on opinion letter).

6. In the future, in order to reduce her malpractice liability should Field add to her retainer agreement a clause pursuant to which the client waives any malpractice claims against Field except for gross negligence?

a. Does Model Rule 1.8(h) allow the client to enter into such an arrangement? Should it do so? Suppose that, in return, Field would charge the client less per hour than a specialist. A client has a right to buy a Yugo instead of a Cadillac; should the client have the right to buy a lower quality of legal services? Compare DR 6–102 of the Model Code.

b. Does a lawyer have a duty to tell a client about his or her own malpractice in the client's case? See, e.g., Matter of Tallon, 86 A.D.2d 897, 447 N.Y.S.2d 50 (1982) (lawyer must inform the client, withdraw, and advise the client to get independent legal advice about whether or not to sue). Cf., ABA Model Rule 1.8(h), and California Rules of Professional Conduct, Rule 3–400 (lawyer may not settle malpractice claim with lawyer's client without advising in writing that client get independent representation).

c. Is there any duty to tell a client about a former lawyer's malpractice? Suppose one learned in the course of representing a client that a former lawyer had missed a statute of limitations and thus forfeited the client's right to file a suit? Should there be a tacit understanding among lawyers that we will not speak negatively about a fellow professional? Might a lawyer properly be accused of barratry, i.e. stirring up litigation, if the prior malpractice were mentioned? Should we take exactly the opposite view? See, e.g., the Wolkin article contained in the Readings to this problem.

7. What sanctions might Field expect for missing the first trial date? Even if her client does not sue for malpractice, should she have other concerns?

a. See, e.g., In re Yengo, 84 N.J. 111, 417 A.2d 533 (1980), cert.denied 449 U.S. 1124, 101 S.Ct. 941, 67 L.Ed.2d 110 (1981). The trial judge had emphasized to the defense attorneys the need for regular attendance, and that before any tardiness or absence the attorney should secure her prior approval. After an attorney failed to appear for several days of trial, the judge tried to reach the attorney by phone. The judge talked to the attorney's daughter who said that he was in Bermuda on vacation. When the attorney finally appeared before the judge he explained that he was in Bermuda on business and had no opportunity to obtain the judge's prior approval. The judge summarily held the attorney in contempt and fined him $500. The state supreme court affirmed.[4]

b. Might there be other financial sanctions as well? Could Field properly bill the client for the time she spends getting the default

---

4. See also, Matter of Mix, 901 F.2d 1431 (7th Cir.1990) (lawyer censured for seemingly doing as little as he could get away with in appeal on behalf of appointed client).

judgment reopened, for example? Contrast Esser v. A.H. Robins Co., Inc., 537 F.Supp. 197 (D.Minn.1982), in which the court claimed an inherent judicial power to deny fees to a firm that should have known it was ethically disqualified to take a matter, with United States v. Vague, 697 F.2d 805 (7th Cir.1983), denying that the courts have such power.

c. Should the criminal defendant be able to cite Field's poor representation as a basis of reversing the conviction?

The leading case on "ineffective assistance of counsel" is Strickland v. Washington, 466 U.S. 668, 104 S.Ct. 2052, 80 L.Ed.2d 674 (1984). To justify a reversal, Field's acts or omissions would have to be found to be "outside the wide range of professionally competent assistance" and the ineffectiveness must have caused "actual prejudice". "It is not enough for the defendant to show that the errors had some conceivable effect on the outcome of the proceedings." 466 U.S. at 691, 104 S.Ct. at 2067.

In Frazer v. United States, 18 F.3d 778 (9th Cir.1994), on the other hand, the defendant was charged with bank robbery. He waived his right to a jury trial and was convicted based on stipulated facts. The defendant alleged the lawyer had called him a racially-derogatory name and warned that if he insisted on going to trial the lawyer would promise to be "very ineffective." The Court found that from such statements, prejudice could be presumed. Although the issues were not before the Court, one would think the lawyer also could be subject to professional discipline and possibly malpractice liability.

8. In addition to malpractice and contempt sanctions, lawyers face other legal remedies and bases for liability that you will want to watch for in other problems in these materials.

a. Lawyers may find themselves charged as accomplices of their clients, for example. See, e.g., United States v. Morris, 988 F.2d 1335 (4th Cir.1993) (lawyer charged with conspiracy to distribute drugs based in part on real estate work he did in closing purchase of a house where crack cocaine was manufactured).

b. In addition, clients may be excused from the obligation to pay fees to a lawyer who breaches a fiduciary duty to the client. E.g., Jeffry v. Pounds, 136 Cal.Rptr. 373 (Cal.App. 1977) (midway through the client's case, the lawyer filed a divorce case against him on behalf of the client's wife).

c. Further, a court may void transactions made in violation of the lawyer's professional obligations. E.g., Abstract & Title Corp. of Florida v. Cochran, 414 So.2d 284 (Fla.App.1982) (lawyer's right of first refusal on client's property set aside); Spaulding v. Zimmerman, 116 N.W.2d 704 (Minn.1962) (tort settlement with minor set aside where lawyer for defendant did not disclose what he knew of the seriousness of plaintiff's injury).

d. Paulemon v. Tobin, 30 F.3d 307 (2d Cir.1994), held that a lawyer's act of writing to the lawyer for a debtor saying that he will file suit if a debt is not paid makes the lawyer a "debt collector" subject to terms and sanctions of the federal Fair Debt Collection Act. Jenkins v. Heintz, 25 F.3d 536 (7th Cir.1994), similarly found that lawyers "regularly engaged for profit in collection of debts allegedly owed by consumers" were subject to the Act. Certiorari was granted in the latter case sub nom. Heintz v. Jenkins, ___ U.S. ___, 115 S.Ct. 416, 130 L.Ed.2d 332 (1994).

9. Are there broader or more general ways in which lawyers can and should increase their overall professional competence and care.

a. Is compulsory Continuing Legal Education the answer? Several states have adopted or are considering it and lawyers are actually losing their licenses for failure to attend class, e.g. In re Yamagiwa, 650 P.2d 203 (Wash.1982).

b. What do you think of Paul Wolkin's proposal set forth as a Reading to this problem? Should lawyers have a duty to report poor quality performance just as they have a duty to report misconduct? Would such a requirement likely be obeyed any more than the present one is? Mr. Wolkin's proposal is far from wholly theoretical. A Peer Review Pilot Project has long been under development by the ABA Standing Committee on Professional Discipline.

READINGS

CHARACTERISTICS OF LEGAL MALPRACTICE: REPORT OF THE NATIONAL LEGAL MALPRACTICE DATA CENTER (1989) *

Table 1
Area of Law Relating to Claim

Plaintiff Personal Injury	25%
Real Estate	23%
Collection & Bankruptcy	11%
Family Law	8%
Estate, Trust & Probate	7%
Other	26%

* The National Legal Malpractice Data Center was created by the ABA to gather reports from the major malpractice insurance carriers and help understand the nature of the malpractice problem. The data, covering 29,227 cases during the years 1981–85, is only summarized in these tables. The report itself is much more detailed.

Table 3
Type of Alleged Error

Failure to Calendar Properly	11%
Failure to Know/Apply Law	9%
Failure to Get Client Consent	9%
Inadequate Discovery	9%
Wrong Choice of Procedure	8%
Failure to Know Deadlines	7%
Other	47%

Table 13
Claims by Years Admitted to Practice

Over 10 Years	66%
4 to 10 Years	30%
Under 4 Years	4%

PAUL A. WOLKIN,** A BETTER WAY TO
KEEP LAWYERS COMPETENT
61 A.B.A. Journal 574 (1975).

Bar associations are racing to institute mandatory continuing legal education programs. * * * This may be a time to * * * search for an alternative, less sweeping in its impact and likely to be more efficacious in attaining the goal of enhancing professional competence.

* * *

The principal justification advanced for mandatory continuing legal education is the urgent need for the bar to meet the challenge of advancing the competency of its members. * * *

The overriding question persists, however, whether it will be met by requiring all lawyers to attend a certain number of hours of continuing legal education, year in and year out, under any of the systems now being structured or prescribed.

Few will dispute that mere attendance at continuing legal education courses will not necessarily enhance competence. Presence is not evidence of learning. Attendance may be passive or active. What is heard in the classroom, without advance preparation, classroom participation, review, and application, is unlikely to be retained. Under the proposed or adopted systems, the number of hours of attendance being prescribed is so minimal that it is difficult to perceive any long-lasting benefits related to enhancing competence. Two or three half-days of course attendance a year or at the end of a year meets the standards. The subject matter of a program may or may not bear any relation to the particular needs of the lawyer. There are no testing procedures for trying to determine how much has been acquired in the way of addition-

** Director, ALI–ABA Committee on Continuing Professional Education.

al knowledge or techniques. Self-serving statements of attendance suffice as evidence of fulfillment of requirements.

* * *

What may likely come about is that ten or fifteen hours a year of required professional education for all will entail big business for some continuing legal education entities, rote programming for others, and an exercise in frustration for most. Mandatory continuing legal education is not likely to facilitate significant educational programming for those who will undertake it. The result may well be a deterioration in the quality of courses now available in many states.

* * *

Let us hypothesize one possible alternative founded on the character of the practice of law and the structural organization of the profession. The alternative must be able to surmount the defects of mandatory continuing legal education proposals. A major criticism of these proposals is the failure to discriminate among lawyers in terms of their relative competence and to relate mandated education to indicated needs.

As the profession is now structured for practice purposes, significant segments are self-policing in respect to the competence of its members. Many law firms are mindful of the level of competence of their partners and associates. Those who fail to meet standards of competence are severed from the firm. Comparable policies and practices prevail in substantial corporate legal offices, in many governmental agencies, in law faculties, in legal aid or public defender offices, and in community legal service groups. Learned legal societies, bar association sections and committees, continuing legal education agencies, law reviews and bar publications, and discriminating lawbook publishers, are, among other agencies, not likely to tolerate professional incompetence. In combination, all of these outlets for professional fulfillment operate implicitly to certify professional competence. They encompass, as a rule, lawyers who are competent to serve their clients—practitioners who practice law as members of a learned profession. The need for compulsory education is not here.

The manner in which the profession functions can reveal where the need exists. Performance by lawyers is subject to observance by others. The observer may be a client, an opposing party, other counsel, a judge, a court clerk, a governmental employee, a bank officer, a title clerk. Each of these is in a position to see a lawyer's performance, and many of them are able to recognize incompetence.

Observance of what a lawyer does and how well he does it could be the basis for a bar-operated monitoring system of professional competence. The system would presuppose the observer's reporting the incompetent rendition of services to a designated agency of the bar for appropriate investigation and remedial action. * * *

The bar agency would be specially designated to perform, with respect to complaints and charges of incompetence, the same function that a professional responsibility committee serves with respect to professional misconduct under the code. It might well be a subcommittee of an over-all grievance committee with jurisdiction limited to matters of competence.

The agency would be empowered to investigate complaints of incompetence, to determine whether there was a basis for them, to determine the extent and character of the lack of competence, and to prescribe and require fulfillment of remedial measures. These might include a defined educational program and proof of its successful completion. Proof might entail examination to determine whether competence has been enhanced. The right to practice might be withheld, fully or partly, during the period of fulfillment of the remedial program. Restoration of the license to full practice would be conditioned on meeting the requirements prescribed.

SELECTED BIBLIOGRAPHY ON ISSUES IN CHAPTER II

Problem 2

Aultman, Moral Character and Professional Regulation, 8 Georgetown J.Legal Ethics 103 (1994).

Bickley, The Effect of Financial Irresponsibility on Admission to the Bar, 8 Journal of the Legal Profession 171 (1983).

Brennan, Defining Moral Character and Fitness, 58 The Bar Examiner 24 (1989).

Copeland, Admission and Reinstatement of Felons to the Bar: West Virginia and the General Rule, 91 West Virginia Law Rev. 451 (1988).

Elliston, Character and Fitness Tests: An Ethical Perspective, 51 The Bar Examiner 8 (1982).

Garber, Moral Character: Inquiries Without Character, 57 The Bar Examiner 13 (May 1988).

Kaslow, Moral, Emotional and Physical Fitness for the Bar: Pondering (seeming) Imponderables, 51 The Bar Examiner 38 (1982).

McChrystal, A Structural Analysis of the Good Moral Character Requirement for Bar Admission, 60 Notre Dame L.Rev. 67 (1984).

Morrissey, The Origins and Objectives of the MPRE, 50 The Bar Examiner 24 (1981).

Report of the AALS Special Committee on Problems of Substance Abuse in the Law Schools, 44 Journal of Legal Education 35 (1994).

Rhode, Moral Character as a Professional Credential, 94 Yale Law Journal 491 (1985).

Rogers, The ADA, Title VII, and the Bar Examination: The Nature and Extent of the ADA's Coverage of Bar Examinations and an Analysis of the Applicability of Title VII to Such Tests, 36 Howard L.J. 1 (1993).

Scanlon, Ethics and Law School Admission, 32 Catholic Lawyer 150 (1988).

Problem 3

Benjamin, Reciprocal Discipline: An Approach to Lawyer Discipline, 31 Howard L.J. 299 (1988).

Benjamin, Sales & Darling, Comprehensive Lawyer Assistance Programs: Justification and Model, 16 Law & Psych.Rev. 113 (1992).

Black, Attorney Discipline for "Offensive Personality" in California, 31 Hastings L.J. 1097 (1980).

Calais, Ethical Violations Resulting from Excessive Workloads in Legal Aid Offices: Who Should Bear the Responsibility for Preventing Them?, 16 Loyola U.(Chicago) L.J. 589 (1985).

Crawford, Would You Tell a Lawyer He or She's a Drunk?, 14 Canadian Lawyer 5 (March 1990).

Devlin, The Development of Lawyer Disciplinary Procedures in the United States, 7 Georgetown J.Legal Ethics 911 (1994).

Finman & Schneyer, The Role of Bar Association Ethics Opinions in Regulating Lawyer Conduct: A Critique of the Work of the ABA Committee on Ethics and Professional Responsibility, 29 U.C.L.A. L.Rev. 67 (1981).

Garth, Rethinking the Legal Profession's Approach to Collective Self–Improvement: Competence and the Consumer Perspective, 1983 Wisconsin L.Rev. 639.

Green, *Doe v. Grievance Committee*: On the Interpretation of Ethical Rules, 55 Brooklyn L.Rev. 485 (1989).

Hackett, Misappropriation of Clients' Funds: Is Disbarment Always Justified?, 12 J.Legal Profession 75 (1987).

Kavanaugh, Performance Evaluation, Education & Testing: Alternatives to Punishment in Professional Regulation, 30 U.Miami L.Rev. 953 (1976).

Kramer, The Appearance of Impropriety Under Canon 9: A Study of the Federal Judicial Process Applied to Lawyers, 65 Minnesota L.Rev. 243 (1981).

Levy, The Judge's Role in the Enforcement of Ethics—Fear and Learning in the Profession, 22 Santa Clara L.Rev. 95 (1982).

Manson, Observations From an Ethical Perspective on Fitness, Insanity and Confidentiality, 27 McGill Law Journal 196 (1982).

Martyn, Lawyer Competence and Lawyer Discipline: Beyond the Bar?, 69 Georgetown L.J. 705 (1981).

McKay, Competence and the Professionally Responsible Lawyer, 29 Emory Law Journal 971 (1980).

Note, Professional Discipline of Solicitors in England, 75 Mich.L.Rev. 1732 (1977).

O'Brien, Multistate Practice and Conflicting Ethical Obligations, 16 Seton Hall L.Rev. 678 (1986).

O'Keefe, The Cocaine Addicted Lawyer and the Disciplinary System, 5 St.Thomas L.Rev. 217 (1992).

Olsson, Reporting Peer Misconduct: Lip Service to Ethical Standards is Not Enough, 31 Arizona Law Rev. 657 (1989).

Outcault & Peterson, Lawyer Discipline and Professional Standards in California: Progress and Problems, 24 Hastings L.J. 675 (1973).

Podgor, Criminal Misconduct: Ethical Rule Usage Leads to Regulation of the Legal Profession, 61 Temple Law Rev. 1323 (1988).

Powell, Professional Divestiture: The Cession of Responsibility for Lawyer Discipline, 1986 A.B.F. Research J. 31.

Powell, Open Doors, Open Arms, and Substantially Open Records: Consumerism Takes Hold in the Legal Profession, 28 Valparaiso U. L. Rev. 709 (1994).

Pregenzer, Substance Abuse Within the Legal Profession: A Symptom of a Greater Malaise, 7 Notre Dame J.L.Ethics & Public Policy 305 (1993).

Rotunda, The Lawyer's Duty to Report Another Lawyer's Unethical Violations in the Wake of *Himmel*, 1988 U. Ill. L. Rev. 977.

Rotunda, The Case Against Permanent Disbarment, 5 The Professional Lawyer 22 (A.B.A., Feb.1994).

Spaeth, To What Extent can a Disciplinary Code Assure the Competence of Lawyers?, 61 Temple L.Rev. 1211 (1988).

Steele & Nimmer, Lawyers, Clients & Professional Regulation, 1976 Amer. Bar Foundation Res.J. 917.

Terrell, When a Lawyer Needs a Lawyer: Representing Respondents in Disciplinary Actions, 29 South Texas Law Rev. 371 (1988).

Thode, Duty of Lawyers and Judges to Report Other Lawyers' Breaches of the Standards of the Legal Profession, 1976 Utah L.Rev. 95 (1976).

Tucker, Disbarment and the Supreme Court of the United States, 37 Fed. B.J. 37 (1978).

Problem 4

Benjamin, The Rules of Professional Conduct: Basis for Civil Liability of Attorneys, 39 U.Florida L.Rev. 777 (1987).

Blair, Trial Lawyer Incompetence: What the Studies Suggest About the Problem, the Causes and the Cures, 11 Capital U.L.Rev. 419 (1982).

Bowman, Lawyer Liability to Non–Clients, 97 Dickinson L.Rev. 267 (1993).

Dranoff, Attorney Professional Responsibility: Competence Through Malpractice Liability, 77 Northwestern U.L.Rev. 633 (1982).

Hoover, The Model Rules of Professional Conduct and Lawyer Malpractice Actions: The Gap Between Code and Common Law Narrows, 22 New England L.Rev. 595 (1988).

Johnston, Legal Malpractice in Estate Planning—Perilous Times Ahead for the Practitioner, 67 Iowa L.Rev. 629 (1982).

R. Mallen & J. Smith, Legal Malpractice (3d ed. 1989).

Melinda, Privity Requirement for Attorney Liability to Nonclients, 4 St. John's J.Legal Commentary 321 (1989).

Moore, Expanding Duties of Attorneys to "Non-Clients": Reconceptualizing the Attorney-Client Relationship in Entity Representation and Other Inherently Ambiguous Situations, 45 S.Carolina L.Rev. 659 (1994).

Munneke & Loscalzo, The Lawyer's Duty to Keep Clients Informed: Establishing a Standard of Care in Professional Liability Actions, 9 Pace L.Rev. 391 (1989).

Peters, Nord & Woodson, An Empirical Analysis of the Medical and Legal Professions' Experiences and Perceptions of Medical and Legal Malpractice, 19 U.Michigan J.Law Reform 601 (1986).

Pfennigstorf, Type and Causes of Lawyers' Professional Liability Claims: The Search for Facts, 1980 Amer.Bar Foundation Res.J. 253.

Symposium, Professional Liability, 37 Mercer L.Rev. 559 (1986).

CHAPTER III

FUNDAMENTALS OF THE LAWYER–CLIENT RELATIONSHIP

The legal relation between lawyer and client is *sui generis*. It is made up, however, of familiar elements—agency law, contracts, and requirements of the ABA Model Code and Model Rules.

Perhaps the lawyer-client relation may best be seen as a mixture of status and contract. That is, some elements of the relationship are the subject of a contract between lawyer and client that is basically like any other service contract. Other obligations, however, are inherent in the status of a lawyer as a fiduciary and are not entirely subject to amendment by lawyer and client.

Throughout this chapter, ask yourself which matters should be limited only by issues of informed consent of the client and which require a more absolute and general prohibition. Think about questions such as the following:

a. How is the lawyer-client relationship formed? At what point do preliminary discussions produce enforceable obligations?

b. What is a lawyer required/authorized to do on behalf of a client? May lawyer and client define and limit the scope and objectives of the representation? What are the lawyer's rights and obligations if they fail to do so?

c. What legal protection is afforded to communications between lawyer and client? What obligations does that protection impose on the lawyer?

d. What is the impact of the financial relation between lawyer and client on the lawyer's obligations? May the lawyer refuse to provide legal services until the fee is paid, for example? Should the lawyer's obligation to protect confidential information of the client be suspended in a fee dispute?

e. What are the lawyer's obligations to protect client property in the lawyer's possession? Should failure to keep accurate financial records be grounds for the lawyer's disbarment?

———

PROBLEM 5

The Relation of Lawyer and Client

You are a lawyer in a private firm. Morris Cannell, an elderly man whom you had never met before, came to you complaining about the handling of his investment account by a local broker. Cannell told you that the broker invested over $200,000 of Cannell's pension money in speculative stocks and the account's value has now been reduced to less than $20,000. Cannell claimed that the broker engaged in a great deal of buying and selling of stocks, with the result that the broker made a lot in commissions while the client sold when the stocks were low and purchased when they were high. Cannell told you in no uncertain terms, "I want you to throw the book at my broker. He showed me no mercy and I don't want you to show any to him."

The more you talked to Cannell, the more you concluded that he is unsophisticated in financial matters. Further, his mind seemed to wander during your discussions, and you believe he may lack even average mental ability.

In researching the problem before deciding whether to take the case, you developed several arguments. You planned to argue that the broker engaged in illegal churning (excessive buying and selling), and that he violated federal rules relating to an investor's suitability (what stocks are suitable to meet a given investor's objectives, here safety and income). With respect to both arguments you planned to focus on Cannell's lack of sophistication and ability, and thus his reliance on the broker.

When you told Cannell the results of your analysis, however, he was angry and wanted you to do more. "He must have a license," Cannell said. "Do everything you can to get him suspended. See what you can do to tie up his bank accounts." The statute of limitations was about to run on all state and federal claims and you told Cannell you would only represent him if you would be required to raise no more than the churning and suitability issues. You refused to seek suspension of the broker's license or to try to harass him financially. Cannell reluctantly agreed and signed your retainer agreement.

You entered an appearance as Cannell's attorney and filed suit on his behalf. Now, however, after several months, you have grown tired of dealing with Cannell and want to withdraw from the case.

QUESTIONS

1. How is the lawyer-client relation formed? Was there a magic moment when Cannell became your client?

a. Did you have any obligation to accept Cannell as your client? Look at EC 2–26. Is there a comparable provision in the Model Rules?

b. Was Cannell your client during the time you were researching his possible claims? Who should bear the risk of ambiguity about whether the lawyer-client relation has been formed?

Consider Togstad v. Vesely, Otto, Miller & Keefe, 291 N.W.2d 686 (Minn.1980). Mrs. Togstad consulted an attorney about a possible medical malpractice claim. The attorney said he did not believe she had a case but that he would "discuss this with his partner." No fee was charged and Mrs. Togstad waited a full year before talking to another attorney. By then the statute of limitations had run. The first law firm was held liable to the Togstads for $649,500. The curbstone advice the lawyer had given Mrs. Togstad about her lack of a case was both inaccurate and inadequate. At minimum, the lawyer should have told Mrs. Togstad about the statute of limitations.

In DeVaux v. American Home Assurance Co., 387 Mass. 814, 444 N.E.2d 355 (1983), an attorney/client relation was found to have been formed at the time the client wrote the firm asking for help. The fact that the lawyer's secretary misfiled the letter so that no attorney ever saw it did not change the result. Does that help clarify whether the test is whether the lawyer believed the relation had been formed or whether a reasonable client would so conclude?

What do these cases suggest about the need for attorneys to tighten up their office procedures? Extensive suggestions for "engagement letters," file control and the like, may be found in R. Mallen & J. Smith, Legal Malpractice, Chap. 2 (3d Ed.1989).

c.   In the period during which you were deciding whether to accept Cannell as your client, did you have any duties to him? First, as you will see later, at minimum you had a duty to respect the confidentiality of what you learned about his case. Second, as the *Togstad* case reveals, you had a duty to be sure that any advice you did give him was sound.

2.   Were you within your rights in refusing to take the case unless Cannell agreed to limit the issues you would raise in the representation?

a.   Look at Model Rule 1.2(c). Was there a comparable provision in the Model Code? Is a limitation on the issues to be raised the same thing as a limitation on the "objectives of the representation"? Look at Comment 4 to Rule 1.2. Are "objectives" of the representation the same as the "scope of services to be provided by the lawyer"?

b.   Was your client's anger at the broker something you should have given greater weight in decisions about how to pursue the case? Alternatively, suppose you believed that your client's claim had some merit, but that the main reason the client wanted to sue was to retaliate for wrongs he believed had been done to him; could you properly have taken the case without getting the agreement you did to limit the issues raised? Compare Model Rule 3.1 and Comment 2 with DR 2–109(A)(1) and DR 7–102(A)(1).[1]

1. We will see this issue again in Problem 26 when we consider possible limits on the proper zeal of a prosecutor. Cf. Bill Johnson's Restaurants, Inc. v. NLRB, 461 U.S. 731, 742–43, 103 S.Ct. 2161, 76 L.Ed.2d 277 (1983) (In light of "the First Amendment right of access to the courts," the "filing and prosecution of a well-found-

c. In Nichols v. Keller, 19 Cal.Rptr.2d 601 (Cal.App.1993), the lawyer was found not to have given the client a factual basis for knowing the limits being placed on the scope of the representation. Nichols was a construction worker hit in the head by a piece of steel while on the job. He signed a retainer asking the lawyer to file a worker's compensation on his behalf. Later, Nichols learned he could have filed a third-party claim as well, and he sued the lawyer for not telling him. The Court held that when a lawyer takes on a case, the client may not know the range of remedies that is possible. It is not enough to present a retainer agreement for the worker's compensation case without discussing with the client what other remedies may be possible and either bringing those actions too or advising the client that he may get other counsel to do so.

d. Were you wise to reach the agreement to limit the issues you would assert at the outset of the representation, as opposed to later? Does Rule 1.2(c) answer the question? Typically, an agreement between lawyer and client made after representation has begun may be avoided by the client unless both the substance of the agreement and the manner of reaching it are shown by the lawyer to have been fair and reasonable to the client. See, e.g., Terzis v. Estate of Whalen, 489 A.2d 608 (N.H.1985) (attempt to revise fee agreement).

3. In the course of the representation, what issues are for the lawyer to decide and what issues are reserved to the client?

a. Do you have to get permission from your client to say what you plan to say in the pleading about his mental ability? Look at Model Rule 2.1 and EC 7–11 and 7–12.

Assume that you explain the pleading to Cannell and he says, "I'm paying you to represent me; I don't want you to say that." Your firm has a reputation as a tough litigator, and you are reluctant to abandon your best argument. May you, notwithstanding client objection, make the argument? Is Canon 4 relevant? Model Rule 1.2(a)? Are DR 7–101 and EC 7–1, 7–7, and 7–8 helpful?

b. Suppose the client wants you to make an argument that you believe is a loser. Suppose he has a theory that the broker's firm had registered its name incorrectly. You explain the weakness of that argument, but the client insists that you use it anyway. Must you? May you? See Model Rule 3.1; DR 7–102(A)(2). Is there *any* proposition for which no "good faith argument" for "modification or reversal of existing law" can be made? Compare the much stricter requirements of Federal Rule 11, discussed in Problem 23, infra.

c. What values are really at stake in the question of who controls the litigation? Do you agree with the commentator who argued: "Unless the client chooses to delegate decision-making authority to the lawyer, the client should be presumed to have control over all aspects of his case. * * * [Client control increases] the moral force and acceptabil-

---

ed lawsuit may not be enjoined as an unfair labor practice, even if it would not have been commenced but for plaintiff's desire to retaliate against the defendant for exercising rights protected by the [National Labor Relations] Act.")

ity of the decisions made by the system, in that each party has had the opportunity 'to choose his strategy, plot his fate, and rise or fall by his own choices.' * * * When the lawyer, as a representative, acts without authority, he violates the clients integrity by presenting the client falsely to others." [2] If all key decisions have to be made by the client, what is the professional role of the lawyer?

    d.   Should the client be able to control your decisions about trial strategy? How about your decisions to show common courtesy? Suppose that after you file your suit, defense counsel asks you for a short delay to allow him extra time to file an answer. Must you check with the client before you agree to the delay? May the client forbid you to grant any delays on the ground that he is anxious to move the case along? How about on the ground that he is so angry at the broker that he does not want to give any quarter? Look at Model Rule 1.3 & Comments 1 & 2; DR 7–101(A)(1) & EC 7–38.

    e.   Suppose this client had been investing the $200,000 as trustee for his grandchildren. Would that change your obligation to follow the client's directions? Suppose the client asked you to settle the case on terms that would enrich him, the trustee, but not benefit the trust?

    Does the client's authority to direct you depend in part on restrictions the law imposes on the client's conduct of which you are aware? If you accept direction the client does not have legal authority to give, should you be liable to the party to whom the client owed the duties? As you will see later in Problem 22, many lawyers paid substantial sums in damages to the receiver of their savings and loan clients for accepting direction from officers of those clients to do things the officers were not authorized by law to have the clients do. E.g., F.D.I.C. v. Mmahat, 907 F.2d 546 (5th Cir.1990); F.D.I.C. v. O'Melveny & Myers, 969 F.2d 744 (9th Cir.1992), rev'd on other grounds sub nom. O'Melveny & Myers v. F.D.I.C., ___ U.S. ___, 114 S.Ct. 2048, 129 L.Ed.2d 67 (1994).

    4.   Should any of your duties in this problem turn on what seem to be your client's deficiencies in mental ability?

    a.   Look at EC 7–12 and Rule 1.14. When should you conclude that your client is "disabled"? Are you really competent to tell? See ABA Informal Opinion 89–1530 (1989)(lawyer may consult with client's doctor even though client has not consented and is not mentally competent enough to do so). Should you be held to be guilty of malpractice if you treat your client as sovereign when he really is impaired?

    b.   If your client is indeed incompetent, did he have the capacity to retain you? Can he consent to your continuing to act as counsel? Does such a client have the capacity to fire you? Look at Model Rule 1.16, Comment 6. Might a client have the capacity to make the decisions to

---

    2.   Spiegel, Lawyering and Client Decision–Making: Informed Consent and the Legal Professional, 128 U.Pa.L.Rev. 41, 73–76 (1979). See also Spiegel, The New Model Rules of Professional Conduct: Lawyer–Client Decision–Making and the Role of Rules in Structuring Lawyer–Client Dialogue, 1980 A.B.F.Res.J. 1003.

retain and terminate you without having the capacity to make all decisions about the objectives and conduct of the litigation?

c. May or must you seek to have a guardian appointed to act on an apparently incompetent client's behalf? Suppose the client objects to having a guardian? See Model Rule 1.14, Comment 3 & 5. May you testify at the client's competency hearing? In doing so, should you be permitted to reveal what the client told you in confidence? What if the incoherence of those confidential conversations is your best evidence of the client's need of a guardian's assistance?

Matter of M.R., 638 A.2d 1274 (N.J.1994), is a particularly interesting case raising these impaired client issues. M.R. is a 21–year old woman with Down's syndrome who is clearly not capable of managing her day-to-day affairs. Her father and mother each wanted to be her guardian; M.R. wanted to live with her father. A lawyer for M.R. was appointed by the Court. The Court concluded that the lawyer is not to decide for himself what is best for M.R.; that would be the function of a guardian. The lawyer is to advocate what M.R. wants, short of things "patently absurd or that pose an undue risk of harm to the client."

d. If there were grounds to believe that your client in a criminal case were mentally ill, would you have an obligation to plead him not guilty by reason of insanity (assuming the local jurisdiction allowed such a defense) even though the resulting civil commitment would be longer than the imprisonment for the crime?

Overholser v. Lynch, 288 F.2d 388 (D.C.Cir.1961), was a disturbing case on this question. There, the majority upheld a municipal court decision not allowing a defendant charged with two violations of the D.C. bad check law to plead guilty. The trial judge found Lynch not guilty by reason of insanity and ordered him committed to St. Elizabeth's Hospital. The D.C. Circuit held:

> "The cases * * * establish almost a positive duty on the part of the trial judge not to impose a criminal sentence on a mentally ill person. * * * Appellee argues that the plea of guilty had been carefully considered by competent counsel and by appellee, who had been judicially declared competent to stand trial and to assist in his own defense. We think that, for the reasons stated above, this decision was one which appellee and his counsel did not have an absolute right to make." Id. at 393.

The Supreme Court reversed on other grounds but appeared not to reject the above reasoning. Lynch v. Overholser, 369 U.S. 705, 719, 82 S.Ct. 1063, 1072, 8 L.Ed.2d 211 (1962). After the Supreme Court decision, Lynch remained at St. Elizabeth's without hope of any early release; there he committed suicide.[3]

---

3. See Arens, Due Process and the Rights of the Mentally Ill, 13 Catholic U.L.Rev. 3, 37–38 (1964). In People v. Gauze, 15 Cal.3d 709, 125 Cal.Rptr. 773, 542 P.2d 1365 (1975), on the other hand, the California Supreme Court held that nei-

e. Convicted killer Gary Gilmore is reported to have said that he "had to" die for a crime he had committed two centuries ago in England, and that he would still be in existence after his death. His attorneys thought that Gilmore's references to eighteenth century England would have made a difference to psychiatrists if they had heard it. The lawyers said, "we feel duty bound to go ahead with the appeal." Gilmore sent a letter to the attorneys saying: "butt out" and "you're fired." The attorneys then filed a notice of appeal in their own names saying that it was "in the best interest" of Gilmore, who was eventually executed.[4]

Were the lawyers right to ignore the client's call for his own death? One commentator has argued: "If the client expresses ends which, due to imprudence or excessive moralism, seem self-destructive, it is the lawyer's job to question the client's competence where it may need questioning * * *. When, on the other hand, the client is able to make his or her ends plausible to the lawyer, the check which he means to provide must give way."[5] Do you agree? Should the client have to convince the lawyer before the lawyer has to give the client his own way?

g. People v. Bloom, set forth as a Reading to this Problem, presents these issues in a particularly poignant form. Do you agree with the Court that a respect for the defendant's dignity required that he be permitted to ask the jury for death? Would a court similarly be required to enjoin efforts to prevent the defendant's attempt to commit suicide? Does the Court in *Bloom* seem to have believed simply that a defendant must be bound by what he elected to do so that he cannot later rely upon his own ineptitude as a basis for reversal of his conviction?

5. May the lawyer withdraw when the client becomes a pain in the neck?

a. Compare DR 2–110(C) with Model Rule 1.16(b). Is one rule more permissive than the other? Must one of the six conditions listed be present before a lawyer may withdraw under DR 2–110(C)? Is the same true under Rule 1.16(b)?

b. Which rule do you prefer? Is there any reason that a lawyer should not be permitted to withdraw from representation at any time, so long as no material interests of the client are affected? Should withdrawal be seen to be a breach of the lawyer's duty of loyalty to the client unless the lawyer has a good reason?

c. Smith v. R.J. Reynolds, 630 A.2d 820 (N.J.App.1993), raised important issues about withdrawal, especially the Rule 1.16(b)(5) right to withdraw because of an "unreasonable financial burden on the lawyer". A firm had agreed to charge a contingent fee to represent a smoker in a damage claim against R.J. Reynolds. As the case went on, however, the firm decided it was going to cost more to try than the

ther defense counsel nor the court may compel a defendant to present an insanity defense, no matter how justified by the apparent facts.

4. N. Mailer, The Executioner's Song 490, 513–14 (1979).

5. Luban, Paternalism and the Legal Profession, 1981 Wisconsin L.Rev. 454, 493.

firm's fee would be and thus it wanted to withdraw. The trial judge relied on Haines v. Liggett Group, 814 F.Supp. 414 (D.N.J.1993), to say the firm had made a deal with the client and had to live with it. This Court says, however, that if the litigation had been paid for at hourly rates, all would agree the time had come to call it quits. Because the client has no incentive to so conclude when a contingent fee is involved, the Court must make the assessment that Rule 1.16(b)(5) contemplates. Do you agree?

d. Should the client similarly be limited in his or her right to fire the lawyer? Traditionally, a client is said to have the right to dismiss the lawyer at any time and to have only a duty to pay for work done to that time. See, e.g., Model Rule 1.16, Comment 4. Why should a client have more right than a lawyer to terminate what, after all, is otherwise a binding contract between them?

PEOPLE v. BLOOM

Supreme Court of California, 1989.
48 Cal.3d 1194, 259 Cal.Rptr. 669, 774 P.2d 698.

KAUFMAN, Justice.

Defendant Robert M. Bloom, Jr., appeals from a judgment imposing the death penalty following his conviction of three counts of first degree murder * * *.

* * *

IV. PENALTY PHASE FACTS

A. *Motion for Self–Representation.*

On December 5, 1983, following the return of the guilt phase verdicts, defendant requested that he be allowed to represent himself (to "go pro. per.," as defendant phrased it) for the penalty phase, with his attorney to remain as "cocounsel." Defendant stated that he did not want to put on a defense, that it would be "counterproductive" to do so because he did not "intend spending the rest of [his] natural life in some institution," and that if granted self-representation he would help the prosecution obtain a death verdict and would address the jury and "seek the death penalty." Defense counsel stated that if allowed to remain in control of the case he would be willing to inform the jury of defendant's preference for a death verdict and defendant's reasons therefor, but defendant said he wanted to address the jury personally and noted that he could "always take the stand." The court recessed until the following day to consider the request.

When proceedings resumed, on December 6, defendant affirmed that it was still his wish to represent himself with his attorney as "cocounsel." The court found that defendant possessed sufficient intellect to understand the proceedings, to read and write, and to address the court, and the jury. The court further found that defendant understood the gravity of the situation. Defendant's attorney stated that defendant had instructed him to take no affirmative action regarding witnesses for the penalty phase, although defendant himself intended to call "witnesses which would aid the prosecution in obtaining the death penalty." Defendant affirmed that this was correct. The attorney stated that if the motion was granted he would advise defendant on proper procedures and on how to address any requests to the court. The trial court told defendant he was "making an enormous mistake" but acknowledged "there are few things more personal to an individual than the decisions you are making right now."

* * *

C. *The Closing Arguments and Verdict.*

The prosecutor urged imposition of the death penalty, based on the charged offenses, the aggravating circumstances, defendant's lack of remorse, and defendant's failure to proffer any mitigating evidence.

Defendant then addressed the jury, also urging it to impose the death penalty. Defendant explained that he deserved to die because one who takes a life should die for it, and that he wanted to die. Although defendant stated there were no mitigating circumstances, he did refer to evidence at the guilt phase regarding his abuse at the hands of Bloom, Sr., stating that "Every man on the jury, if you knew the facts on [*sic*]my life, you'd kill him too."

The jury imposed a death sentence.

D. *Subsequent Events.*

* * *

During the psychiatric evaluations defendant admitted he had sought the death penalty not for purposes of ending his life but to expedite his appeal to this court. According to one of the examining psychiatrists, defendant said, in an apparent reference to the automatic appeal in death penalty cases, that he was "confident that the State Supreme Court will overturn [his case], and the sooner it goes up there the sooner he has a chance of being acquitted or having the ruling overturned."

* * *

V. PENALTY PHASE ISSUES

A. *Failure to Offer Mitigating Evidence—Denial of Effective Counsel.*

Defendant contends that the failure to present mitigating evidence at the penalty phase, in conjunction with his own request to the jury for a death verdict, deprived him of his right to effective assistance of counsel and offended the state's interest in ensuring the reliability of capital penalty determinations.

* * *

The issue presented, then, is whether a trial court in a capital case abuses its discretion by granting a competent defendant's midtrial motion for self-representation, when the motion is made for the announced purpose of seeking a verdict of death.

This court's opinions have been sensitive to the basic Sixth Amendment values found controlling in [Faretta v. California, 422 U.S. 806, 95 S.Ct. 2525, 45 L.Ed.2d 562 (1975)]. On numerous occasions we have "recognized the need to respect the defendant's personal choice on the most 'fundamental' decisions in a criminal case."

Given the importance which the decisions of both this court and the United States Supreme Court have attached to an accused's ability to control his or her own destiny and to make fundamental decisions affecting trial of the action, and given this court's recognition that it is not irrational to prefer the death penalty to life imprisonment without parole, it would be incongruous to hold that a trial court lacked power to grant a midtrial motion for self-representation in a capital case merely because the accused stated an intention to seek a death verdict. While we do not suggest that trial courts must or even should grant such midtrial motions, we do not find the trial court's ruling on the motion in this case to be violative of defendant's rights or contrary to any fundamental public policy.

* * *

A defendant may challenge the grant of a motion for self-representation on the basis that the record fails to show that the defendant was made aware of the risks of self-representation.

* * *

The trial court in this case gave few specific warnings or advisements regarding the risks of self-representation, but in the unusual situation facing the court an elaborate catalog of dangers and pitfalls was unnecessary. As the trial court observed, defendant would be assisting rather than opposing the prosecutor and not only appreciated the risk of a death verdict but actively sought it. The record reveals, and the trial court found, that defendant possessed sufficient intellect to understand the proceedings and to address the court and the jury. Defendant was aware of the possible penalty verdicts on each count, and was advised by the trial court that his decision was "an enormous mistake." Defendant acknowledged that the prosecutor had practiced law longer than defendant had been alive and thus would be a skilled opponent. The record therefore establishes that defendant was sufficiently aware of the dangers and disadvantages of self-representation and made his decision with open eyes.

* * *

MOSK, Justice, dissenting

* * *

Manifestly, the penalty phase of a capital trial in this state is an adversary process. "The very premise of our adversary system of criminal justice is that partisan advocacy on both side of a case will best promote the ultimate objective" of punishment in accordance with deserts. Thus, the trial court errs when it permits a defendant to try to subvert the adversary process and undermine its reliability indirectly through counsel.

PROBLEM 6

The Duty of Confidentiality

Your long-time client, John Carter, came to your office to tell you that he expected to be sued by the person who bought his house. He had told the buyer that the house had a dry basement. Although the basement had never flooded in the five years he had lived there, Carter had been told by a prior owner that the basement regularly flooded after a heavy rain. There was such a rain this year, and the buyer's furniture suffered major damage.

Shortly before his death, you were able to interview the prior owner of the house, who told you what he had told Carter about the tendency to flood. You have notes of that interview in which you comment on the former owner's likely credibility at trial. In addition, while at a party at a friend's home, Carter's banker let slip that Carter is in bad financial condition. You mentally filed that away as important to your settlement posture in case Carter is sued.

The buyer has now filed suit against Carter. You have been subpoenaed by the buyer to give a discovery deposition in the case. You expect to be asked what Carter told you about whether his house tended to flood.[1] You have also been asked to produce your notes of the statement of the prior owner. Someone else has asked you informally if the rumors that Carter has suffered financial reverses are true.

QUESTIONS

1. Are any of the above pieces of information protected by the attorney-client privilege? Which ones?

a. Professor Wigmore summarized the basic rule governing the application of the attorney-client privilege as follows:

"(1) where legal advice of any kind is sought (2) from a professional legal adviser in his capacity as such, (3) the commu-

---

1. At this point, you may assume that you will not be called as a witness at trial. The rules relating to a lawyer who can be expected to be a witness in a case are examined in Problem 25.

nications relating to that purpose, (4) made in confidence (5) by the client, (6) are at his instance permanently protected (7) from disclosure by himself or by the legal adviser, (8) except the protection be waived." 8 Wigmore, Evidence, § 2292 at 554 (McNaughton rev. 1961) (footnote omitted; emphasis in original omitted).

The attorney-client privilege is governed by statute in many states, but for the most part the statutes are merely declaratory of the common law rule. 8 Wigmore, supra, § 2292 at 556–57.

b.   Tentative Draft No. 1 of the American Law Institute's Restatement of the Law (Third), The Law Governing Lawyers (1988), § 118, reduces Wigmore's eight categories to four.

"Except as provided elsewhere in this Chapter, neither a lawyer, the lawyer's client, nor any other person shall be compelled to give testimony or otherwise produce evidence concerning:

"(1) A communication

"(2) Made between privileged persons

"(3) In confidence

"(4) For the purpose of obtaining or providing legal assistance for the client."

c.   Under these definitions of the privilege, may you be compelled to reveal what the client admitted to you about what he knew about the basement? Consider as well the materials on the privilege which are included as Readings to this Problem.

d.   Do you reach the same answer with respect to the client's own obligation to tell what happened? Does the fact that he discussed the facts with a lawyer protect Carter from being forced to testify as to what he knew about the tendency to flood?

e.   Why do we protect against disclosure, communications with a lawyer that were solely designed to help the client avoid the consequences of his wrongful conduct? Is Wigmore persuasive:

"In order to promote freedom of consultation of legal advisers by clients, the apprehension of compelled disclosure by the legal advisers must be removed; hence the law must prohibit such disclosure except on the client's consent." 8 Wigmore, supra § 2291 at 545.

Because the exercise of this privilege conflicts with the search for truth, commentators and the courts have long held that the privilege "ought to be strictly confined within the narrowest possible limits consistent with the logic of its principle." 8 Wigmore, supra § 2291, at 554.

f.   Suppose the client had not yet sold the house when he told you that he intended to make a false statement to buyers about the tendency of the basement to flood? Wigmore said the privilege does not extend to conversations in furtherance of an intended, unlawful end. Such an end may be either a crime or any "deliberate plan to defy the law and oust another person of his rights, whatever the precise nature of those rights may be." 8 Wigmore § 2298, at 577. The traditional common law view requires that the communication be in furtherance of a crime or *fraud* before the privilege is ruled lost. See proposed Federal Rule of Evidence 503(d)(1), set forth as a Reading to this Problem.

g. In this problem, would the attorney-client privilege prevent the lawyer from being deposed or testifying about the statement by the former owner or the revelation by the banker? Although lawyers often cite the "privilege" when they mean some other doctrine, the attorney-client privilege would not protect either the statement or the revelation against disclosure. If the lawyer is not to be questioned about them by the client's opponent, it must be on the basis of some other principle.

2. Should attorney-client privilege rules be any different when the client is a corporation?

a. Remember that corporations do not have the Fifth Amendment right not to incriminate themselves that individuals have. McPhaul v. United States, 364 U.S. 372, 81 S.Ct. 138, 5 L.Ed.2d 136 (1960). Does it follow that the law should not protect corporations' communications with their lawyers against disclosure? Do the privilege against self-incrimination and the attorney-client privilege in fact have completely different histories and purposes?

b. Look at the *Upjohn* case which is set forth as a Reading to this Problem. Do you agree with the Court's concern that corporations have the ability to get legal advice in order to help them comply with the law? Does the complexity of many modern corporate organizations mean that, without protection of the privilege, it would be impossible for management to try to verify compliance with the law as Upjohn tried to do? Is it likely instead that corporations would conduct compliance audits whether or not there was a privilege simply because failing to comply with the law could subject them to massive liability? [2]

c. Spectrum Systems International Corp. v. Chemical Bank, 575 N.Y.S.2d 809 (N.Y.1991), is a more recent version of *Upjohn*. The bank had retained a New York law firm to investigate possible fraud by bank employees and vendors. Spectrum was a vendor identified as possibly overcharging the bank and *it* wanted to see the law firm's report. The Court held the report privileged and denied discovery.

d. Samaritan Foundation v. Goodfarb, 862 P.2d 870 (Ariz.1993), was an unusually careful effort to limit the individuals whose statements would be protected by the corporate attorney-client privilege. A parale-

---

2. Some courts have recognized a related "self-evaluative" privilege protecting internal reports done by non-lawyers. See, e.g., Bredice v. Doctors Hospital, Inc., 50 F.R.D. 249 (D.D.C.1970), aff'd 479 F.2d 920 (D.C.Cir.1973). But as suggested in Federal Trade Commission v. TRW, Inc., 628 F.2d 207 (D.C.Cir.1980), the concept has met with limited success in the courts.

gal had interviewed operating room personnel in preparation for defense of a medical malpractice case, and the plaintiff wanted summaries of the interviews. The Court refused to rely on either the control group test (requiring that the interviewee be part of senior management) or the subject matter test (requiring only that the interview concern the subject matter of the case) and instead asked whether the interviews were conducted "to assist the lawyer in assessing or responding to the legal consequences of [the employee's own] conduct for the corporate client." The Court ordered the notes disclosed because, although the personnel were witnesses to the acts alleged to be negligent, their own acts were not alleged to be negligent.[3]

3.   Is any information here protected by the work product immunity?

a.   Restatement of the Law (Third): The Law Governing Lawyers, § 136 (Tent.Draft No.5, 1992), says that material is protected as work product if:

(a) The material records or reflects litigation investigation or analysis * * *,

(b) The material was prepared by or for a party or a party's representative, including a party's lawyer, consultant, surety, indemnitor, insurer, or agent; and

(c) The material was prepared in anticipation of litigation, that is, it was prepared for litigation then in progress or its preparation was primarily motivated by the prospect of future litigation.

b.   Work product immunity is the legacy of Hickman v. Taylor, 329 U.S. 495, 67 S.Ct. 385, 91 L.Ed. 451 (1947). Construing the proper scope of discovery, the Court wrote: "Not even the most liberal of discovery theories can justify unwarranted inquiries into the files and the mental impressions of an attorney." 329 U.S. at 510, 67 S.Ct. at 393. The Court went on to say that where one side had information other than mental impressions that was "essential to the preparation of [the other side's] case", it could be discovered "and production might be justified where the witnesses are no longer available or can be reached only with difficulty." *Id.*, at 511, 67 S.Ct. at 394. The doctrine is now embodied in Federal Rules of Civil Procedure, Rule 26(b)(3).

c.   Is there any protected work product described in this problem? What about the interview with the former owner? Did you conduct the interview with him in anticipation of litigation? This particular lawsuit?

d.   Should the fact that the former owner is now dead mean that the notes that you took may be discovered? See Federal Rule 26(b)(3)

---

3. See also, In re Six Grand Jury Witnesses, 979 F.2d 939 (2d Cir.1992), where the client company was accused of fraud in pricing a government contract. The outside lawyer hired to conduct the defense directed key employees who had worked on the contract to investigate and analyze the facts. When those employees were called before the grand jury, they claimed what they knew was now privileged. The Court disagreed and ordered them to testify.

which requires a "showing that the party seeking discovery has substantial need of the materials in preparation of the party's case and that the party is unable without undue hardship to obtain the substantial equivalent of the material by other means." See also, Admiral Insurance Co. v. United States Dist. Ct. (King Ranch Properties), 881 F.2d 1486 (9th Cir.1989) (unavailability of information from corporate executives by deposition does not justify forcing their own counsel to turn it over).

e.   Should it matter whether the notes of the discussion with the now-deceased former owner are considered ordinary or opinion work product? Look again at the language of Hickman v. Taylor quoted above and at the Court's analysis in *Upjohn*. If you make sure to comment in your notes about the witness' credibility, will it make the notes absolutely immune from discovery?

4. Is the information you learned at the party about the client's financial health protected against disclosure?

a.   Is the information covered by either the attorney-client privilege or the work product immunity? Why not? Even if not so protected, the information may be something that the lawyer must keep confidential unless ordered by a court to disclose it.

b.   Look at DR 4–101(A). Is the information a "confidence" of the client? Is it a "secret"? Would it tend to embarrass the client? Was it learned as part of the "professional relationship"?

c.   Look at Model Rule 1.6. Does this qualify as information "relating to the representation"? Remember that you have said yourself that the information may affect your settlement posture.

d.   What does it mean to say that the information is protected against disclosure by these rules? Does it mean any more than that the lawyer may not volunteer the information? Is there any doubt that, if a Court orders the lawyer to reveal the comment overheard at the party, the lawyer must do so?

5. How may the privilege or other legal protection of the information against disclosure be lost?

a.   Suppose the client tells a trusted friend about your discussions of what the former owner had told the client. If the client, by mistake or otherwise, tells outsiders the substance of your confidential conversations with him, his privilege as to those conversations is lost for all time. Furthermore, you can be asked about those conversations as well. See, e.g., Connecticut Mutual Life Ins. Co. v. Shields, 18 F.R.D. 448, 451 (S.D.N.Y.1955). Query? May a lawyer properly assert the privilege knowing that it has been thus lost but hoping that the other side does not know of the disclosure?

b.   May you reveal privileged information if it is useful to do so in settlement negotiations? Look at Model Rule 1.6(a). Typically, such a revelation will result in waiver of the privilege. See, e.g., United States v. Martin, 773 F.2d 579 (4th Cir.1985) (attempt to settle tax case). Further, if a lawyer reveals some privileged information, typically the privilege will be lost at least for all information needed to put the privileged material into context. See, e.g., United States v. Woodall, 438 F.2d 1317 (5th Cir.1970) (en banc); but see In re von Bulow, 828 F.2d 94 (2d Cir.1987) (waiver no broader than privileged material actually disclosed in book by defense counsel Alan Dershowitz because the disclosures were not made in court).

c. Some authorities strictly construe the requirement that the communication be intended to be kept confidential. For example, Illinois State Bar Opinion 90–7 (11/26/90), advised that if a communication is capable of being overheard, even though not intended to be, the privilege can be lost. The committee opined that talking with a client over a cordless telephone such as a car phone might forfeit the privilege because such conversations can be overheard by someone with a radio receiver. A lawyer is not required to ask whether the client is using a cordless or mobile phone, the opinion said, but if it sounds like the client may be doing so, the lawyer is to warn that the privilege may be lost. See also, New York State Bar Assoc. Opinion 641 (2/16/93) (lawyers obeying recycling laws must take precautions to know how papers with client confidences are disposed of); Granada Corp. v. Honorable First Court of Appeals, 844 S.W.2d 223 (Tex.1992) (even inadvertent disclosure of documents waives privilege).

d. Should the privilege be lost as to later private litigation if a company voluntarily turns documents over to a government agency in an effort to settle an enforcement proceeding? See, e.g., Salomon Brothers Treasury Litigation v. Steinhardt Partners L.P., 9 F.3d 230 (2d Cir. 1993), holding the privilege was indeed lost.

e. Suppose the client has been sued jointly with another person. May they discuss the facts with a common attorney or with each other's attorney? What would be the effect of such discussions on the privilege? Ordinarily, defendants with a common interest may hold such joint discussions, but if they then have a falling out, there is, in a subsequent controversy between the two clients, no attorney-client privilege regarding the substance of the conversations. 8 Wigmore, supra § 2312, at 604.

6. The confidentiality rules have yet other exceptions.

a. Suppose there are multiple interests involved, e.g., suppose shareholders of a corporate client need the information for a derivative suit. May corporate officers keep the information from them? See Garner v. Wolfinbarger, 430 F.2d 1093 (5th Cir.1970), cert. denied sub nom. Garner v. First American Life Ins. Co., 401 U.S. 974, 91 S.Ct. 1191, 28 L.Ed.2d 323 (1971) (shareholders may have access to attorney-corporate communications in order to prosecute a derivative suit).

b. Suppose the opponent believed that you had known about the tendency to flood before Carter's house was sold. Could you be joined as a defendant? Would this then force (permit) you to reveal privileged material? See DR 4–101(C)(4) and Model Rule 1.6(b)(2).

c. May a lawyer reveal confidential client information in order to coerce the client into paying the lawyer's fee? Again, look at DR 4–101(C)(4) and Model Rule 1.6(b)(2). How much disclosure should those provisions be construed to permit?

d. If Carter were now to die, would your duty to protect the confidentiality of his statements die with him? Matter of John Doe Grand Jury Investigation, 562 N.E.2d 69 (Mass 1990), gave the usual answer on some tough facts. The case involved whether the late Charles Stuart had been responsible for the deaths of Carol and Christopher Stuart. Charles Stuart had talked with his lawyer for two hours on the day before his death, and the prosecutor guessed that he had admitted the crime to the lawyer. If so, the state could both stop looking for a suspect for the murders and be sure not to charge someone else for them. The Court held, however, that the privilege did not end with Charles' death and no amount of interest in knowing the truth could justify making the lawyer testify. Do you agree?

e. Suppose a corporation "dies", i.e., goes into receivership or bankruptcy. May the successor management waive the privilege to learn what their predecessors told the lawyers? See, e.g., Linde Thomson Langworthy Kohn & Van Dyke, P.C. v. Resolution Trust Corporation, 5 F.3d 1508 (D.C.Cir.1993), where a law firm refused to turn over to the RTC (1) the work that it did for a failed savings and loan and (2) communications with the law firm's liability carrier. The Court ordered disclosure. The work done for the client is relevant to the RTC effort to recover sums owed the client, the Court said, and the communications with the insurer were neither privileged nor attorney work product.

READINGS

APPENDIX TO THE HEARINGS OF THE SELECT COMMITTEE ON PRESIDENTIAL CAMPAIGN ACTIVITIES

93d Cong., 1st & 2d Sess., Part I, at 119 (June 28, 1974).

MEMORANDUM OF LAW

Attorney–Client Privilege

* * *

III. *Some Guidelines Governing the Scope of the Attorney–Client Privilege*

(A) The first requirement of the attorney-client privilege is that *legal* advice must be sought. See generally, 8 Wigmore, supra § 2296, at 566. Thus, communications with an attorney seeking, e.g., his business advice is not within the privilege. United States v. Vehicular Parking, Ltd., 52 F.Supp. 751, 753–54 (D.Del.1943). However, where the client generally seeks legal advice, the existence of nonlegal, incidental communications between them does not result in loss of the privilege. United States v. United Shoe Machinery Corp., 89 F.Supp. 357, 359 (D.Mass. 1950) (Wyzanski, J.). Accord, McCormick, supra § 88, at 179–80.

(B) A client may not claim the privilege if the communication was in furtherance of a criminal or fraudulent transaction. Wigmore states that the privilege does not attach where the advice is sought for a knowingly unlawful end; it is, however, not necessary, in order to determine that the privilege is invalid, to conclude that the attorney actually became a participant in the client's intended wrong. E.g., A.B. Dick Co. v. Marr, 95 F.Supp. 83, 102 (S.D.N.Y.1950) (Medina, J.); In re Sawyer's Petition, 229 F.2d 805, 808–09 (7th Cir.1956) (a client's communication to his attorney in pursuit of a criminal or fraudulent act yet to be performed is not privileged in any judicial proceeding). 8 Wigmore, supra, § 2298, at 573, 577.

* * *

In order to determine if the legal advice was tainted and is thus not within the privilege the test is as follows:

"Where there is some evidence of crime or fraud apart from the communications with the attorney, and there have been transactions with him, *let the burden be on the attorney to satisfy the court* (apart from the jury) that the transaction has to his best belief *not been wrongful, before the claim of privilege is allowed.*" Wigmore, supra, § 2299, at 578 (emphasis in original).

See also, Pollock v. United States, 202 F.2d 281, 286 (5th Cir.1953), cert. denied, 345 U.S. 993 (1953):

"[W]here the party is being tried for a crime in furtherance of which the communication to the attorney was made and evidence has been introduced giving color to the charge, it is well settled that the communication is no longer privileged. [Citations omitted.]"

In short, it is not necessary that the court make a finding that the client's purpose was in fact criminal: if there is some evidence giving color to the charge, the privilege must yield. In determining whether the client had an unlawful purpose in consulting with an lawyer it is the client's guilty intention that is controlling; the good faith or lack thereof of the lawyer is irrelevant. McCormick, supra § 95, at 200. Evidence of the client's wrongful intent may be circumstantial. Id. at n. 51, citing Sawyer v. Stanley, 241 Ala. 39, 1 So.2d 21 (1941).

(C) If a client tells the attorney about the contents of a preexisting document the attorney may not ordinarily be forced to testify about such conversations, even though the client may be compelled to testify as to the contents of documents as well as required to produce them. Wigmore, supra § 2308. However, if the communications were part of an attempt by the client to avoid production of the document's contents, the privilege does not apply. Id. at 596. It is also generally true that information regarding the existence, execution or place of custody of a document is ordinarily not within the privilege. Wigmore, supra § 2309.

Communications about documents should be distinguished from the documents themselves. A document never acquires any privileged character by virtue of being passed from a client to his attorney, and thus client documents in the possession of an attorney are subject to subpoena. Falsone v. United States, 205 F.2d 734, 739 (5th Cir.1953); McCormick, supra § 89, at 185.

(D) The purpose of the attorney-client privilege is to protect *confidential* communications. Communications to a lawyer not intended to be confidential are not protected. E.g., United States v. Tellier, 255 F.2d 441 (2d Cir.1958); see generally, 8 Wigmore, supra § 2311, at 600. Thus, communications to an attorney in the presence of a third person who is not the agent of either the attorney or client are not privileged. 8 Wigmore, supra, at 601–02. If the client intends that the lawyer reveal the conversations to third persons there is no privilege. E.g., United States v. Tellier, 255 F.2d 441 (2d Cir.1958) (attorney's advice to client not privileged where client expected attorney to prepare letter to third person setting forth client's position). Wilcox v. United States, 231 F.2d 384 (10th Cir.1956) cert. denied, 351 U.S. 943 (1956) (client's private instructions to attorney that at preliminary hearing he should propound certain questions to witnesses not privileged).

* * *

(H) The client may voluntarily waive the attorney-client privilege. If he does so, the attorney must testify since the privilege belongs only to the client, not to the attorney. See 8 Wigmore, § 2327. A client may also be found to have waived the privilege if he makes a partial disclosure. Having revealed a portion of his communications, he may not withhold the remainder. 8 Wigmore, supra § 2327, at 636; McCormick, supra § 93.

(I) Under traditional common law, the attorney-client privilege protects the relationship between a lawyer and his *private* client and does not extend to communications to an attorney representing the Government or Governmental officials regarding their official duties. McCormick, supra, § 88, at 181. There are several reasons for limiting the privilege to the private client and his private lawyer. In the Government there is not so much an attorney-client relationship as an employee-employer relationship, which serves to provide the necessary degree of confidentiality for the employer. More importantly, the employer is not the actual client of the Government lawyer. It is the people who not only pay the Government lawyer's salary but who are supposed to be the beneficiaries of his legal work and his true client. Thus, the Government lawyer, unlike a private one, may take an oath to uphold the Constitution and laws thereunder. The Code of Professional Responsibility also applies differently to a Government lawyer, for his duty is to the public at large and not to a narrow client interest. See, e.g., A.B.A. Code of Professional Responsibility, DR 7–103. Finally, in the executive branch of Government, any necessary confidentiality is provided by Executive Privilege. When that privilege is waived, the only privilege of confidentiality that the Executive has is waived. However, some recent cases have extended the privilege to cover lawyers for a government. E.g., Connecticut Mutual Life Ins. Co. v. Shields, 18 F.R.D. 448, 450–51 (S.D.N.Y.1955) (without stating its reasons the court states that lawyers for the Bellevue Bridge Commission are covered by the privilege insofar as the Commissioners' communications were only with their lawyers). Proposed Federal Rule 503(a)(1), if enacted, would change the traditional law and apply the privilege to attorneys for governmental bodies. See 56 F.R.D. at 237.

* * *

PROPOSED FEDERAL RULE 503

Rule 503. Lawyer–Client Privilege*

(a) Definitions. As used in this rule:

(1) A "client" is a person, public officer, or corporation, association, or other organization or entity, either public or private, who is rendered professional legal services by a lawyer, or who consults a lawyer with a view to obtaining professional legal services from him.

(2) A "lawyer" is a person authorized, or reasonably believed by the client to be authorized, to practice law in any state or nation.

(3) A "representative of the lawyer" is one employed to assist the lawyer in the rendition of professional legal services.

(4) A communication is "confidential" if not intended to be disclosed to third persons other than those to whom disclosure is in furtherance of the rendition of professional legal services to the client or those reasonably necessary for the transmission of the communication.

(b) General Rule of Privilege. A client has a privilege to refuse to disclose and to prevent any other person from disclosing confidential communications made for the purpose of facilitating the rendition of professional legal services to the client, (1) between himself or his representative and his lawyer or his lawyer's representative, or (2) between his lawyer and the lawyer's representative, or (3) by him or his lawyer to a lawyer representing another in a matter of common interest,

---

* When the Federal Rules of Evidence were approved by Congress, none of the 13 rules dealing with privileges, including Proposed Rule 503 were enacted, see Fed. Rules of Evidence, Pub.L. 93–595 (Jan. 2, 1975). The reasons for nonenactment did not reflect on the merits of Proposed Rule 503, which is, in general, a fair summary of the law of most states.

or (4) between representatives of the client or between the client and a representative of the client, or (5) between lawyers representing the client.

(c) Who May Claim the Privilege. The privilege may be claimed by the client, his guardian or conservator, the personal representative of a deceased client, or the successor, trustee, or similar representative of a corporation, association, or other organization, whether or not in existence. The person who was the lawyer at the time of the communication may claim the privilege but only on behalf of the client. His authority to do so is presumed in the absence of evidence to the contrary.

(d) Exceptions. There is no privilege under this rule:

(1) Furtherance of crime or fraud. If the services of the lawyer were sought or obtained to enable or aid anyone to commit or plan to commit what the client knew or reasonably should have known to be a crime or fraud; or

(2) Claimants through same deceased client. As to a communication relevant to an issue between parties who claim through the same deceased client, regardless of whether the claims are by testate or intestate succession or by *inter vivos* transactions; or

(3) Breach of duty by lawyer or client. As to a communication relevant to an issue of breach of duty by the lawyer to his client or by the client to his lawyer; or

(4) Document attested by lawyer. As to a communication relevant to an issue concerning an attested document to which the lawyer is an attesting witness; or

(5) Joint clients. As to a communication relevant to a matter of common interest between two or more clients if the communication was made by any of them to a lawyer retained or consulted in common, when offered in an action between any of the clients.

PROPOSED FEDERAL RULE 511

Rule 511. Waiver of Privilege by Voluntary Disclosure

A person upon whom these rules confer a privilege against disclosure of the confidential matter or communication waives the privilege if he or his predecessor while holder of the privilege voluntarily discloses or consents to disclosure of any significant part of the matter or communication. This rule does not apply if the disclosure is itself a privileged communication.

UPJOHN CO. v. UNITED STATES

United States Supreme Court, 1981.
449 U.S. 383, 101 S.Ct. 677, 66 L.Ed.2d 584.

JUSTICE REHNQUIST delivered the opinion of the Court.

We granted certiorari in this case to address important questions concerning the scope of the attorney-client privilege in the corporate context and the applicability of the work-product doctrine in proceedings to enforce tax summonses.

* * *

I

Petitioner Upjohn Co. manufactures and sells pharmaceuticals here and abroad. In January 1976 independent accountants conducting an audit of one of Upjohn's foreign subsidiaries discovered that the subsidiary made payments to or for the benefit of foreign government officials in order to secure government business. The accountants so informed petitioner Mr. Gerald Thomas, Upjohn's Vice President, Secretary and General Counsel. * * * He consulted with outside counsel and R.T. Parfet, Jr., Upjohn's Chairman of the Board. It was decided that the company would conduct an internal investigation of what were termed "questionable payments." As part of this investigation the attorneys prepared a letter containing a questionnaire which was sent to "All Foreign General and Area Managers" over the Chairman's signature. * * * The letter indicated that the Chairman had asked Thomas, identified as "the company's General Counsel," "to conduct an investigation for the purpose of determining the nature and magnitude of any payments made by the Upjohn Company or any of its subsidiaries to any employee or official of a foreign government." The questionnaire sought detailed information concerning such payments. Managers were instructed to treat the investigation as "highly confidential" and not to discuss it with anyone other than Upjohn employees who might be helpful in providing the requested information. Responses were to be sent directly to Thomas. Thomas and outside counsel also interviewed the recipients of the questionnaire and some 33 other Upjohn officers or employees as part of the investigation.

On March 26, 1976, the company voluntarily submitted a preliminary report to the Securities and Exchange Commission on Form 8–K disclosing certain questionable payments. A copy of the report was simultaneously submitted to the Internal Revenue Service, which immediately began an investigation to determine the tax consequences of the payments. Special agents conducting the investigation were given lists by Upjohn of all those interviewed and all who had responded to the questionnaire. On November 23, 1976, the Service issued a summons pursuant to 26 U.S.C.A. § 7602 demanding production of:

"All files relative to the investigation conducted under the supervision of Gerald Thomas to identify payments to employees of foreign governments * * *."

The company declined to produce the documents specified in the second paragraph on the grounds that they were protected from disclosure by the attorney-client privilege and constituted the work product of attorneys prepared in anticipation of litigation.

* * *

II

Federal Rule of Evidence 501 provides that "the privilege of a witness ... shall be governed by the principles of the common law as they may be interpreted by the courts of the United States in light of reason and experience." The attorney-client privilege is the oldest of the privileges for confidential communications known to the common law. 8 J. Wigmore, Evidence § 2290 (McNaughton rev. 1961). Its purpose is to encourage full and frank communication between attorneys and their clients and thereby promote broader public interests in the observance of law and administration of justice. The privilege recognizes that sound legal advice or advocacy serves public ends and that such advice or advocacy depends upon the lawyer's being fully informed by the client. * * * [T]his Court has assumed that the privilege applies when the client is a corporation and the Government does not contest the general proposition.

The Court of Appeals, however, considered the application of the privilege in the corporate context to present a "different problem," since the client was an inanimate entity and "only the senior management, guiding and integrating the several operations, ... can be said to possess an identity analogous to the corporation as a whole." * * * Such a view, we think, overlooks the fact that the privilege exists to protect not only the giving of professional advice to those who can act on it but also the giving of information to the lawyer to enable him to give sound and informed advice. The first step in the resolution of any legal problem is ascertaining the factual background and sifting through the facts with an eye to the legally relevant. * * *

* * * Middle-level—and indeed lower-level—employees can, by actions within the scope of their employment, embroil the corporation in serious legal difficulties, and it is only natural that these employees would have the relevant information needed by corporate counsel if he is adequately to advise the client with respect to such actual or potential difficulties. * * *

* * *

The narrow scope given the attorney-client privilege by the court below not only makes it difficult for corporate attorneys to formulate sound advice when their client is faced with a specific legal problem but also threatens to limit the valuable efforts of corporate counsel to ensure their client's compliance with the law. * * *

The communications at issue were made by Upjohn employees to counsel for Upjohn acting as such, at the direction of corporate superiors in order to secure legal advice from counsel. * * * Information, not available from upper-echelon management, was needed to supply a basis for legal advice concerning compliance with securities and tax laws, foreign laws, currency regulations, duties to shareholders, and potential litigation in each of these areas. The communications concerned matters within the scope of the employees' corporate duties, and the employees themselves were sufficiently aware that they were being questioned in order that the corporation could obtain legal advice. * * * Consistent with the underlying purposes of the attorney-client privilege, these communications must be protected against compelled disclosure.

The Court of Appeals declined to extend the attorney-client privilege beyond the limits of the control group test for fear that doing so would entail severe burdens on discovery and create a broad "zone of silence" over corporate affairs. Application of the attorney-client privilege to communications such as those involved here, however, puts the adversary in no worse position that if the communications had never taken place. The privilege only protects disclosure of communications; it does not protect disclosure of the underlying facts by those who communicated with the attorney. * * * Here the Government was free to question the employees who communicated with Thomas and outside counsel. Upjohn has provided the IRS with a list of such employees, and the IRS has already interviewed some 25 of them. While it would probably be more convenient for the Government to secure the results of petitioner's internal investigation by simply subpoenaing the questionnaires and notes taken by petitioner's attorneys, such considerations of convenience do not overcome the policies served by the attorney-client privilege. * * *

Needless to say, we decide only the case before us, and do not undertake to draft a set of rules which should govern challenges to investigatory subpoenas. Any such approach would violate the spirit of Federal Rule of Evidence 501. * * *

III

Our decision that the communications by Upjohn employees to counsel are covered by the attorney-client privilege disposes of the case so far as the responses to the questionnaires and any notes reflecting responses to interview questions are concerned. The summons reaches further, however, and Thomas has testified that his notes and memoranda of interviews go beyond recording responses to his questions. To the extent that the material subject to the summons is not protected by the attorney-client privilege as disclosing communications between an employee and counsel, we must reach the ruling by the Court of Appeals that the work-product doctrine does not apply to summonses issued under 26 U.S.C.A. § 7602.

The Government concedes, wisely, that the Court of Appeals erred and that the work-product doctrine does apply to IRS summonses. This doctrine was announced by the Court over 30 years ago in Hickman v. Taylor, 329 U.S. 495 (1947). In that case the Court rejected "an attempt, without purported necessity or justification, to secure written statements, private memoranda and personal recollections prepared or formed by an adverse party's counsel in the course of his legal duties." *Id.*, at 510. The Court noted that "it is essential that a lawyer work with a certain degree of privacy" and reasoned that if discovery of the material sought were permitted

> "much of what is now put down in writing would remain unwritten. An attorney's thoughts, heretofore inviolate, would not be his own. Inefficiency, unfairness and sharp practices would inevitably develop in the giving of legal advice and in the preparation of cases for trial. The effect on the legal profession would be demoralizing. And the interests of the clients and the cause of justice would be poorly served." Id., at 511.

The "strong public policy" underlying the work-product doctrine * * * has been substantially incorporated in Federal Rule of Civil Procedure 26(b)(3).

* * * While conceding the applicability of the work-product doctrine, the Government asserts that it has made a sufficient showing of necessity to overcome its protections. The Magistrate apparently so found. The Government relies on the following language in *Hickman*:

> "We do not mean to say that all written materials obtained or prepared by an adversary's counsel with an eye toward litigation are necessarily free from discovery in all cases. Where relevant and nonprivileged facts remain hidden in an attorney's file and where production of those facts is essential to the preparation of one's case, discovery may properly be had * * *. And production might be justified where the witnesses are no longer available or can be reached only with difficulty." 329 U.S., at 511.

The Government stresses that interviewees are scattered across the globe and that Upjohn has forbidden its employees to answer questions it considers irrelevant. The above-quoted language from *Hickman*, however, did not apply to "oral statements made by witnesses ... whether presently in the form of [the attorney's] mental impressions or memoranda." Id., at 512. * * * Forcing an attorney to disclose notes and memoranda of witnesses' oral statements is particularly disfavored because it tends to reveal the attorney's mental processes.

Rule 26 accords special protection to work product revealing the attorney's mental processes. The Rule permits disclosure of documents and tangible things constituting attorney work product upon a showing of substantial need and inability to obtain the equivalent without undue hardship. This was the standard applied by the Magistrate. Rule 26 goes on, however, to state that "[i]n ordering discovery of such materials when the required showing has been made, the court shall protect against disclosure of mental impressions, conclusions, opinions or legal theories of an attorney or other representative of a party concerning the litigation." Although this language does not specifically refer to memoranda based on oral statements of witnesses, the *Hickman* court stressed the danger that compelled disclosure of such memoranda would reveal the attorney's mental processes. It is clear that this is the sort of material the draftsmen of the Rule had in mind as deserving special protection.

* * *

While we are not prepared at this juncture to say that such material is always protected by the work-product rule, we think a far stronger showing of necessity and unavailability by other means than was made by the Government or applied by the Magistrate in this case would be necessary to compel disclosure. Since the Court of Appeals thought that the work-product protection was never applicable in an enforcement proceeding such as this, and since the Magistrate whose recommendations the District Court adopted applied too lenient a standard of protection, we think the best procedure with respect to this aspect of the case would be to reverse the judgment of the Court of Appeals for the Sixth Circuit and remand the case to it for such further proceedings in connection with the work-product claim as are consistent with this opinion.

Accordingly, the judgment of the Court of Appeals is reversed, and the case remanded for further proceedings.

It is so ordered.

———

PROBLEM 7

Setting Legal Fees

A well-known local psychiatrist has a contract claim for about $100,000 against a local firm. The matter appears to be of average complexity. She has brought her case to attorney Paul T. Novak. "I'll take your case," Novak says. "My fee will be only 44 per cent of the amount recovered." Shocked, the psychiatrist says that she has never heard of even psychiatrists charging such high fees. "One-third is average," Novak tells her. "I am giving you a bargain. I am only charging you one-third more than the going rate and I am at least twice as good as the average lawyer."

Novak also has been asked to be counsel for the executor of the estate of Hiram Paulsen, late of Novak's city. Paulsen died in a nursing home with few personal effects and an estate consisting of unimproved land worth $50,000 which he had owned in joint tenancy with his daughter, $150,000 in corporate securities held by his broker and $50,-000 in life insurance payable to his daughter. The daughter was executor and sole beneficiary. Novak took all proper steps to settle the estate, including payment of taxes. He sent a bill for $15,000. "Lawyers in this town have charged 6 per cent as long as I can remember," he said. "If word got around I was shaving the price, think what that would do to my reputation."

Novak also has agreed to represent a plaintiff in a personal injury suit for a "discount" contingent fee of one-third of the amount recovered. The other side has offered, before Novak begins work, to pay his client $15,000. Based on what he knows about the case, Novak believes the actual damages that a jury would award would be more like $60,000, but it would take him about 200 hours of work to recover that amount, and, of course, the client might possibly not recover anything at all. Novak has concluded that it is best to recommend to the client that he accept the $15,000 immediately so that Novak can pocket a $5,000 fee with little effort and go on to the next case.

QUESTIONS

1. When should a fee agreement between lawyer and client be reached? Should it be required to be in writing?

a. Compare Rule 1.5(b) and EC 2–19. Is there sound reason for making the timing and form of fee agreements a matter for professional discipline? Why does Rule 1.5(c) take a mandatory approach in the case of a contingent fee but not in any other case?

b. May the lawyer's fees be increased during the course of the representation? Severson & Werson v. Bolinger, 235 Cal.App.3d 1569, 1 Cal.Rptr.2d 531 (1991), ruled that the issue turns on the understanding of a reasonable client. The firm's standard contract said the client would pay the firm's "regular hourly rates" and the client had been told orally what those rates were. The court held that under these circumstances, the firm could not increase the rates it charged the client "without notice". The Court left open the option of giving notice of an increase and then imposing it if the client did not object.

But what if the client objects? Should a client have a right to insist that a lawyer's rates be frozen for the many years it may take to complete a matter? Remember that, as discussed in Problem 5, a lawyer and client may revise their agreement as to scope of work and fees after the representation has begun, but at that point the lawyer assumes a greater burden of showing the agreement to be fair and reasonable.

2. What makes a fee "clearly excessive"? Is that test different than a "reasonable" fee? Do the criteria specified in Rule 1.5(a) and DR 2–106 answer those questions for you?

a. Is the fee Novak proposes to charge the psychiatrist excessive? See, e.g., Matter of Hanna, 294 S.C. 56, 362 S.E.2d 632 (1987) (charging 40% to collect the no-fault benefits under the client's auto policy found excessive). Should a fee negotiated at arms length between the lawyer and a competent adult ever be held to violate this standard? [1] Are there important reasons for limiting freedom of contract in this way? What are the reasons?

b. May a lawyer properly consider the client's ability to pay in setting a "reasonable" fee? Would it be improper not to do so? Does this mean that wealthy clients may be charged an otherwise "unreasonable" fee in order to subsidize work done without compensation?

c. Should the trial judge be permitted to raise the issue whether an excessive fee is being charged by counsel? United States v. Vague, 697 F.2d 805 (7th Cir.1983), gave the usual answer, holding that the judge may refer the matter to disciplinary authorities but may not himself decide an issue which he "is neither asked nor required to resolve."

See also, Gagnon v. Shoblom, 565 N.E.2d 775 (Mass.1991). There, a truck driver severely injured the plaintiff when he crashed into the plaintiff's trailer. The plaintiff signed a 33% contingent fee agreement and after extensive discovery, there was a settlement for $2.9 million. The trial judge thought a fee of $975,000 was too large for the case, and, although the plaintiff had not complained, the judge lowered the fee to $695,000. The Massachusetts Supreme Court held that a trial judge has no general authority to lower a fee on his own motion.

United States v. Strawser, 800 F.2d 704 (7th Cir.1986), cert.denied sub nom. Anderson v. United States, 480 U.S. 906, 107 S.Ct. 1350, 94 L.Ed.2d 521 (1987), on the other hand, involved a situation where the criminal defendant's payment of an excessive fee in Case 1 meant that the defendant was indigent and needed appointed counsel in Case 2. On those facts, the court said, it was proper to order part of the excessive fee in Case 1 refunded.

3. Should it be proper to charge a fee expressed as a flat percentage of the sum involved as Novak has proposed for the Paulsen estate?

a. May the "fee customarily charged in the locality" any longer be considered in setting fees? Is that the message of Goldfarb v. Virginia State Bar, included as a Reading for this Problem?

b. Even if there is no formal fee schedule, is pricing as a percentage of the amount involved in a case inherently likely to lead to uniform rates if many lawyers are like Novak and are concerned that lowering their rates will adversely affect their reputation? On the other hand, do uniform rates necessarily connote illegal pricing fixing?

---

1. Rule 4–200(B)(11), of the Rules of Professional Conduct of the State Bar of California, provides that, among the factors that may be considered in determining the reasonableness of the fee is the "informed consent of the client to the fee agreement."

4. May Novak properly claim a $5,000 fee in the personal injury suit if the case is settled before he begins work? [2]

a. Is it enough to say that Novak needs to make a few big fees, as here, to make up for the losing cases on which he realizes nothing? Look at Judge Grady's argument in the Readings to this Problem. Do you agree with Judge Grady?

b. One court has established and enforced a schedule of maximum fees in contingent fee cases. The schedule provides for 50% on the first thousand dollars recovered, 40% on the next two thousand, 35% on the next twenty-two thousand and 25% thereafter. An attorney's fee at or below these sums is conclusively deemed "reasonable." Any sum in excess of these figures is by definition "unconscionable" unless approved by the court.[3] Would you favor such an approach?

Even if not applied generally, would such a schedule of fees be a partial solution to the so-called "medical malpractice crisis"? Some state legislatures have thought so. See, e.g., Bernier v. Burris, 113 Ill.2d 219, 100 Ill.Dec. 585, 497 N.E.2d 763 (1986), upholding the constitutionality of such a plan.

c. American Home Assurance Co. v. Golomb, 606 N.E.2d 793 (Ill.App.1992), illustrates one way to guarantee that lawyers will not charge illegal fees. A lawyer in a medical malpractice case had his clients sign an agreement purporting to pay a contingent fee of 40% and to "hold the lawyer harmless" from any reduction of fees required by an Illinois statute limiting fees in such cases. The Court held the fee contract void and denied the lawyer all fees for the representation, even on a quantum meruit basis.

d. Suppose personal injury lawyers were required to ask the defendant to make an offer of settlement very early. If the offer were accepted, the plaintiff's lawyer would have to bill based on hours worked and the total fee could be no more than 10% of the recovery. If the initial offer were rejected, the contingent fee could be charged on only so much of the ultimate recovery as exceeded the initial offer.

Would you favor such a plan? What would Judge Grady likely think of it? What would it do to the dynamics of settlement negotiations? Would it tend to reduce the number of lawyers who would serve injured clients? Would it tend to reduce the amount of lawyer advertising as the expected return to the lawyer from getting each new client in the office was decreased? See Lester Brickman, Michael Horowitz & Jeffrey O'Connell, Rethinking Contingency Fees (1994).

---

2. In this connection, see Committee on Legal Ethics v. Gallaher, 376 S.E.2d 346 (W.Va.1988) (50% contingent fee excessive for recovering personal injury damages where the lawyer advised acceptance of the first real offer the insurance company made).

3. See Gair v. Peck, 6 N.Y.2d 97, 188 N.Y.S.2d 491, 160 N.E.2d 43 (1959), cert. denied 361 U.S. 374, 80 S.Ct. 401, 4 L.Ed.2d 380 (1960). A good discussion of the genesis of this plan may be found in F. MacKinnon, Contingent Fees for Legal Services: A Study of Professional Economics and Responsibilities 159–67 (1964).

5. Should a contingent fee be used if the client can afford to pay an hourly rate?

a. In England, the contingent fee is considered inherently unethical as a violation of the rule against champerty and maintenance (an agreement to carry on a lawsuit in exchange for a promise of a share in the expected recovery).[4] Should the same be true in this country?

b. The contingent fee is sometimes called a "poor-man's fee." However, might a wealthy client prefer a contingent fee in some cases? Must the lawyer give the client an option how to pay? Look at Rule 1.5. Does it continue EC 2–20's counsel on these issues?

c. The Chicago Council of Lawyers has suggested "that the contingent fee 'problem' is a symptom, rather than a cause of a much wider problem—the unequal access to the courts for the poor and near poor."[5] Thus, the Council favors dealing with that "wider problem." Do you agree? In what ways might a system of prepaid legal insurance, for example, radically change the calculation as to the proper time to charge a contingent fee? Would that be a change for the better? Should this affect the bar's position on prepaid insurance?[6]

6. Are there be kinds of cases in which a contingent fee should not be proper?

a. Should a contingent fee be improper in a criminal case? Why? Look at Rule 1.5(d) and DR 2–106(C). Winkler v. Keane, 7 F.3d 304 (2d Cir.1993), considered whether the fact a contingent fee was charged in a criminal case should be per se grounds for reversal of the conviction. The defendant was accused of killing his father. The fee agreement provided that if the defendant were acquitted and thus able to inherit from his father, the lawyer would get an extra $25,000. The New York Court of Appeals had accepted the defendant's contention that the basis for prohibiting contingent fees in criminal cases is the law's concern that such a fee arrangement might discourage the lawyer from encouraging the client to plead guilty in an appropriate case, seek a charge on a lesser included offense, or the like. The Court had held in People v. Winkler, 523 N.E.2d 485 (N.Y.1988), however, that while charging the contingent fee might be grounds for professional discipline of the lawyer, it was not per se grounds for reversal. For that, actual prejudice to the defendant must be shown. In this case, it found, there was no actual prejudice, and the Second Circuit agreed.

b. May a contingent fee be charged in a domestic relations case? Compare Rule 1.5(d) and EC 2–20. Licciardi v. Collins, 180 Ill.App.3d 1051, 129 Ill.Dec. 790, 536 N.E.2d 840 (1989), examined use of a contingent fee for obtaining a property settlement in a marriage dissolution proceeding. Although the lawyer characterized the fee as one for

---

4. F. MacKinnon, supra n. 3, at 37–38.

5. Chicago Council of Lawyers, Report on Code of Professional Responsibility 20 (1972).

6. Issues relating to prepaid legal insurance will be taken up in Problem 37 of these materials.

enforcing a letter agreement between the parties, the court held it was unenforceable and that its use was a basis for denying the lawyer any fee at all. Do you agree? Are the reasons for prohibiting the contingent fee in these cases the same as in criminal cases? [7]

c. Should contingent fee arrangements for defense counsel in civil cases be permitted?

Wunschel Law Firm, P. C. v. Clabaugh, 291 N.W.2d 331 (Iowa 1980), was a defamation action. The defendant agreed with defense counsel that the law firm would defend him for a fee that would be one-third of the difference between the prayer in the petition and the amount actually awarded. Defendant was offered the alternative of paying an hourly fee of $50. The court held that such a contingent defense fee is void and unenforceable as a matter of public policy. The court reasoned that such a fee would be based on "pure speculation" because "it provides for determination of the fee by factors having no logical relationship to the value of the services." Do you agree?

In Formal Opinion 93–373 (1993), the ABA Standing Committee on Ethics and Professional Responsibility expressly rejected that view and held that contingent fees for defense counsel in civil cases do not violate the Model Rules provided that the amount saved is "reasonably ascertainable", the total amount of the fee is reasonable, and the client's consent to the arrangement was "fully informed".

d. Has the time come for something like contingent fees in corporate transactions? Should counsel in takeover fights receive a "premium" if they successfully complete or defeat the takeover attempt, for example? Should counsel for an entertainer take a percentage of the value of contracts negotiated?

Do such fee arrangements bring a lawyer dangerously close to engaging in "business"? Is that something about which we should be concerned? Does the practice sound better if the lawyer calls it "value billing" and consistently sets the fee on the basis of how much the client has benefitted from the lawyer's efforts? See, e.g., Symposium, Legal Billing: Seeking Alternatives to the Hourly Rate, Judicature, Jan.– Feb.1994, pp. 186–202.

7. Does the presence of DR 5–103(A)(2) in Canon 5 on conflict of interest suggest that contingent fees have attributes of an inherent conflict of interest?

a. Are hourly fees similarly subject to abuse? May a lawyer charge Client A for the hour spent flying to a meeting, for example, and charge Client B for the same hour spent reading Client B's file on the airplane?

---

7. Connecticut Bar Ethics Opinion 87–17 (1988), on the other hand, takes the position that a lawyer may take a contingent fee in a action to partition ownership of a house owned by an unmarried couple. The rule against charging a contingent fee in domestic relations matters is said not to apply where the couple is not married. Do you agree? In a time when unmarried relationships are common, might one ask whether the policies behind the rule, e.g., not discouraging parties from reconciling, should apply to such cases too?

The practice of hourly rate billing is full of such issues, and ABA Formal Opinion 93–379 (December 6, 1993) addressed them as follows:

" * * * [I]t is helpful to consider these questions, not from the perspective of what a client could be forced to pay, but rather from the perspective of what the lawyer actually earned. A lawyer who spends four hours of time on behalf of three clients has not earned twelve billable hours. A lawyer who flies for six hours for one client, while working for five hours on behalf of another, has not earned eleven billable hours. A lawyer who is able to reuse old work product has not re-earned the hours previously billed and compensated when the work product was first generated. * * *

* * *

" * * * *[If] it turns out that the lawyer is particularly efficient in accomplishing a given result, it nonetheless will not be permissible to charge the client for more hours than were actually expended on the matter. * * * [T]he economies associated with the result must inure to the benefit of the client, not give rise to an opportunity to bill a client for phantom hours."

When invited to extend a similar analysis to contingent fees, however, the ABA Standing Committee on Ethics and Professional Responsibility said only that "the charging of a contingent fee * * * does not violate ethical standards as long as the fee is appropriate in the circumstances and reasonable in amount, and as long as the client has been fully advised of the availability of alternative fee arrangements." ABA Formal Opinion 94–389 (Dec. 5, 1994).

b. Might one argue that any fee arrangement presents an inherent conflict of interest because it creates an way for an unscrupulous lawyer to put his or her interest ahead of the client's? Indeed, might the process of agreeing upon a fee itself be inherently "unethical" because it is the one time in the lawyer-client relationship that the lawyer and client are adversaries?

c. Obviously, if lawyers are to remain in business, the law cannot declare charging and setting fees to be inherently improper. However, can the problems be minimized? Might fees best be set as some combination of fixed fee for routine services, hourly rate where complexity of the case is hard to predict, and a contingent element where intensity of the lawyer's efforts may make a difference? See, e.g., Clermont & Currivan, Improving on the Contingent Fee, 63 Cornell L.Rev. 529 (1978).

READINGS

GOLDFARB v. VIRGINIA STATE BAR

Supreme Court of the United States, 1975.
421 U.S. 773, 95 S.Ct. 2004, 44 L.Ed.2d 572.

Chief Justice BURGER delivered the opinion of the Court.

* * *

I

In 1971 petitioners, husband and wife, contracted to buy a home in Fairfax County, Virginia. The financing agency required them to secure title insurance; this required a title examination, and only a member of the Virginia State Bar could legally perform that service. Petitioners therefore contacted a lawyer who quoted them the precise fee suggested in a minimum fee schedule published by respondent Fairfax County Bar Association; the lawyer told them that it was his policy to keep his charges in line with the minimum fee schedule which provided for a fee of 1% of the value of the property involved. Petitioners then tried to find a lawyer who would examine the title for less than the fee fixed by the schedule. They sent letters to 36 other Fairfax County lawyers requesting their fees. Nineteen replied, and none indicated that he would charge less than the rate fixed by the schedule; several stated that they knew of no attorney who would do so.

The fee schedule the lawyers referred to is a list of recommended minimum prices for common legal services. Respondent Fairfax County Bar Association published the fee schedule although, as a purely voluntary association of attorneys, the County Bar has no formal power to enforce it. Enforcement has been provided by respondent Virginia State Bar which is the administrative agency through which the Virginia Supreme Court regulates the practice of law in that State; membership in the State Bar is required in order to practice in Virginia. Although the State Bar has never taken formal disciplinary action to compel adherence to any fee schedule, it has published reports condoning fee schedules, and has issued two ethical opinions indicating fee schedules cannot be ignored. The most recent opinion states that "evidence that an attorney *habitually* charges less than the suggested minimum fee schedule adopted by his local bar association raises a presumption that such lawyer is guilty of misconduct * * *."

Because petitioners could not find a lawyer willing to charge a fee lower than the schedule dictated they had their title examined by the lawyer they had first contacted. They then brought this class action against the State Bar and the County Bar alleging that the operation of the minimum fee schedule, as applied to fees for legal services relating to residential real estate transactions, constitutes price fixing in violation of

§ 1 of the Sherman Act. Petitioners sought both injunctive relief and damages.

* * *

II

* * *

A purely advisory fee schedule issued to provide guidelines, or an exchange of price information without a showing of an actual restraint on trade, would present us with a different question. The record here, however, reveals a situation quite different from what would occur under a purely advisory fee schedule. Here a fixed, rigid price floor arose from respondents' activities * * * and no lawyer asked for additional information in order to set an individualized fee. The price information disseminated did not concern past standards, but rather minimum fees to be charged in future transactions, and those minimum rates were increased over time. The fee schedule was enforced through the prospect of professional discipline from the State Bar, and the desire of attorneys to comply with announced professional norms; the motivation to conform was reinforced by the assurance that other lawyers would not compete by underbidding. * * *

* * *

The County Bar argues that Congress never intended to include the learned professions within the terms "trade or commerce" in § 1 of the Sherman Act, and therefore, the sale of professional services is exempt from the Act. * * * Also, the County Bar maintains that competition is inconsistent with the practice of a profession because enhancing profit is not the goal of professional activities; the goal is to provide services necessary to the community. That, indeed, is the classic basis traditionally advanced to distinguish professions from trades, businesses, and other occupations, but it loses some of its force when used to support the fee control activities involved here.

* * * We cannot find support for the proposition that Congress intended any such sweeping exclusion. The nature of an occupation, standing alone, does not provide sanctuary from the Sherman Act, nor is the public service aspect of professional practice controlling in determining whether § 1 includes professions. Congress intended to strike as broadly as it could in § 1 of the Sherman Act, and to read into it so wide an exemption as that urged on us would be at odds with that purpose.

* * * Whatever else it may be, the examination of a land title is a service; the exchange of such a service for money is "commerce" in the most common usage of that word. It is no disparagement of the practice of law as a profession to acknowledge that it has this business aspect [17]
* * *.

---

17. The fact that a restraint operates upon a profession as distinguished from a business is, of course, relevant in determining whether that particular restraint vio-

In Parker v. Brown, 317 U.S. 341, 63 S.Ct. 307, 87 L.Ed. 315 (1943), the Court held that an anticompetitive marketing program "which derived its authority and efficacy from the legislative command of the state" was not a violation of the Sherman Act because the Act was intended to regulate private practices and not to prohibit a State from imposing a restraint as an act of government. Respondent State Bar and respondent County Bar both seek to avail themselves of this so-called state action exemption.

* * * Here we need not inquire further into the state action question because it cannot fairly be said that the State of Virginia through its Supreme Court Rules required the anticompetitive activities of either respondent. * * * It is not enough that, as the County Bar puts it, anticompetitive conduct is "prompted" by state action; rather, anticompetitive activities must be compelled by direction of the State acting as a sovereign.

* * *

III

We recognize that the States have a compelling interest in the practice of professions within their boundaries, and that as part of their power to protect the public health, safety, and other valid interests they have broad power to establish standards for licensing practitioners and regulating the practice of professions. * * * The interest of the States in regulating lawyers is especially great since lawyers are essential to the primary governmental function of administering justice, and have historically been "officers of the courts." In holding that certain anticompetitive conduct by lawyers is within the reach of the Sherman Act we intend no diminution of the authority of the State to regulate its professions.

* * *

---

lates the Sherman Act. It would be unrealistic to view the practice of professions as interchangeable with other business activities, and automatically to apply to the professions antitrust concepts which originated in other areas. The public service aspect, and other features of the professions, may require that a particular practice, which could properly be viewed as a violation of the Sherman Act in another context, be treated differently. We intimate no view on any other situation than the one with which we are confronted today.

JOHN F. GRADY,* SOME ETHICAL QUESTIONS
ABOUT PERCENTAGE FEES
2 Litigation 20 (Summer, 1976).**

* * *

I propose to analyze the typical automobile accident case. Let me emphasize that I am not referring to a complicated, multi-party type of case, but to the common case involving two cars or a car and a pedestrian. I choose this kind of case because it accounts for the vast majority of personal injury claims. * * *

I think it should take a competent lawyer no more than 15 hours to prepare this type of case for trial. * * *

The trial itself should not take more than two to two and one-half days, assuming it is a jury trial. Including time for preparation of jury instructions and any additional legal research, the trial should take no more than 15 hours of the lawyer's time. The usual breakdown would be about ten hours in court and five hours spent before and after court sessions at the office, including any time required for post-trial motions.

* * *

Let us assume that the lawyer has taken the case on a one-third contingent basis, which is typical. If plaintiff's injury was not very serious—assume he sustained soft tissue injuries with modest special damages—we might have a verdict of $4,500. This would certainly be in the low range of cases that would be thought worth trying to a jury verdict. On such a verdict, the lawyer would receive a fee of $1,500, which, divided by his 30 hours of effort, results in compensation at the rate of $50 per hour. * * * A $3,000 verdict would result in a fee of $33 per hour, an amount that would not be satisfactory compensation, but that would probably cover the lawyer's overhead.

Consider what happens as we go up the scale. A $15,000 verdict results in a $5,000 fee, which, divided by 30 hours, comes to $166 per hour. On a $45,000 verdict, the $15,000 fee compensates the attorney at a rate of $500 per hour.

What causes me to question the propriety of the ever-increasing fee in proportion to the size of the verdict is this: there is little, if any, relationship between the efforts of the lawyer and the size of the verdict, once we assume a verdict in favor of the plaintiff. The size of the verdict is determined by the nature and extent of the plaintiff's injury and resulting damages. Conceding that some lawyers are more brilliant and more eloquent than others, we flatter ourselves unduly if we think the performance of counsel is a large factor in the size of the verdict. Juries award money to compensate for injuries, and, as a general rule, the worse the injury the larger the verdict. To illustrate the point, the identical collision can cause a whiplash injury or result in an amputation of a leg. No more work is required to develop the medical aspects of an amputation case than is involved in a whiplash case. In fact, considering the skepticism that many people have about soft tissue injuries, the

---

* The author, a former trial lawyer, is United States District Judge for the Northern District of Illinois.

amputation case will probably take less persuasive ability. But even though the same amount of work is involved, the whiplash verdict might be $4,500, for a fee of $50 per hour, while the amputation verdict might be $200,000, providing a fee of more than $6,000 per hour.

* * *

Another fortuitous circumstance affecting the fee is the number of claimants the lawyer represents in a particular case. Assume that a father, mother and two children are struck at an intersection and all of them sustain injuries. The liability evidence is the same for all. Frequently, they will have the same doctor, who simply brings four sets of records to court instead of one. His testimony takes longer, and I admit that there is some additional work required of the lawyer. However, in the typical case of four plaintiffs, the additional work is not at all proportionate to the additional fees the lawyer will realize when he charges each of the plaintiffs the same percentage, which—make no mistake about it—is what he ordinarily does.

* * *

Neither is there any appreciable difference in the amount of work each side must do in preparing and trying the case. Sometimes the defense lawyer actually does more work, since he has an insurance company to satisfy and frequently has to spend time writing formal reports to the company. In general, however, he will spend the same 30 hours in preparing and trying the simple accident case that the plaintiff's attorney will spend.

Assume the verdict comes in at $45,000. The plaintiff's attorney would receive a fee of $15,000 for his 30 hours of work. The attorney retained by the insurance company invariably charges on a time basis, with perhaps some allowance made for a good result. In the Chicago area, very few insurance defense attorneys charge more than $50 an hour for time prior to trial or more than $500 a day for trial. These ceilings exist because there is intense competition for insurance company business, and the companies know what they have to pay to engage competent counsel. In other words, on the defense side we have the two factors that are usually lacking on the plaintiff's side: a sophisticated client and price competition among the available attorneys. The result is that, for the case involving the $45,000 verdict, a defense attorney would probably receive a maximum fee of $2,500 (15 hours trial preparation at $50 an hour, plus three days on trial at $500 a day). So, for trying the same case, the plaintiff's attorney receives a fee that is more than six times that received by the defense attorney.

* * *

Thus far, I have been raising questions about the propriety of the fees charged in cases tried to verdict. As we all know, however, very few personal injury cases are actually tried to verdict. Roughly 90 percent of the cases filed are settled before trial commences. Thus, in 90 percent of the simple accident cases, the lawyer will spend no more than 15 hours of his time. The ethical questions presented in the settled cases are, I think, even more serious than those presented by the cases which are tried. In the case of the $45,000 settlement, for example, how can a $15,000 fee be justified? Such a fee amounts to $1,000 an hour, assuming the lawyer has completed his trial preparation and settles just as the trial is about to start. But it might not happen that way. The case may be settled before suit is even filed, or shortly after it is filed, or midway through discovery. In any of those situations (and, again, confining ourselves to the simple automobile accident case), the lawyer will spend less than 15 hours.

* * *

* * * Surely there is much to be said for providing a means to permit indigent persons to engage counsel to press meritorious suits. There is no doubt that the contingent fee has made possible many suits that could not otherwise have been brought. But while one may approve the basic concept of contingent fees—and I do—one can still question how the concept is applied. The problem, it seems to me, is that we have regarded the "one-third contingent fee" arrangement as applicable to all cases involving personal injuries, without paying enough attention to the facts of the particular case and the needs of the particular client. * * *

* * *

The vast majority of personal injury cases involve no uncertainty that the lawyer is going to be paid something. The only question is how much. Thus, the question is whether a mere uncertainty about the amount of compensation justifies a lawyer taking a large percentage of the recovery, such as one-third or one-fourth. Assume, for instance, the good liability case where the admitted special damages exceed the policy limit and the defendant has no assets worth pursuing. The only uncertainty here is whether the case will be settled for the full policy limit or at a discount of, say, 10 percent. The company may hold back payment for a vexatious length of time, but the case will never be tried because the company does not want to spend money on a loser and, in addition, cannot risk being held liable for an excess verdict on a negligence or bad faith theory. Such situations occur frequently and they usually involve policy limits of $10,000. How can a lawyer justify a fee of $3,300 or even $2,500 in such a situation? I submit that he cannot but I know that such fees are routinely charged.

One sometimes hears the argument that the attorney is entitled to collect his "third" in easy cases to make up for all the "losers" he handles. This explanation does not withstand analysis. Putting aside for a moment the question of whether one client can properly be surcharged to compensate for the deficiencies in another client's case, the fact of the matter is that there just are not very many "losers." As we have seen, at least 95 percent of the total claims handled by lawyers are settled before trial, and many of these settlements involve very little work on the part of the lawyer.

I think the answer is an almost total abandonment of our present fee system in personal injury cases. It is a rare case that fits what has become the "standard" one-third fee arrangement. For every case in which a one-third fee is justified, there are dozens where that amount is excessive by any standard of reasonableness.

* * *

I think we must start determining our fee charges in personal injury cases on the same basis we determine fees in any other kind of litigation. We cannot continue with the unthinking assumption that every injured plaintiff should be charged one-third, or even that he is necessarily charged on a percentage basis at all.

Specifically, I think the lawyer must consider at least these three questions in each case:

    1. Is there a genuine and substantial question on liability, or is the only real question the amount of damages?

    2. Is the case likely to be settled or tried to verdict?

    3. Is the amount of the recovery likely to be small or large—for example, is it a soft tissue injury or does it involve the death of the family breadwinner?

Until the lawyer knows the answers to these questions, he has insufficient basis for determining whether a percentage fee is proper and, if proper, what percentage would be fair.

————

PROBLEM 8

Limits on Techniques for Collecting a Fee

Elizabeth Jackson is a well-known and very busy litigator. The Atlas Brothers Co. (ABC) has retained her to defend a lawsuit filed against them by a former employee. The complaint was filed 28 days ago and a state statute provides that all allegations will be deemed admitted if an answer is not filed within 30 days. Jackson has had the case for the past 18 days but has done nothing toward the preparation of an answer. When called about the status of the case, she tells ABC that unless $75,000 is paid immediately, she will not file the answer on time. The President of ABC has had experience in dealing with lawyers in the past. He believes that $75,000 is likely to be a high fee even if the case has to go to trial, and it is a very high fee indeed if the matter can be settled. However because he believes himself effectively coerced into either paying the fee or losing the case by default, he has sent Jackson the check for $75,000.

In yet another matter, Jackson represents a local business person in a dispute over title to real estate. She anticipates a hard time collecting her fee. She demanded payment in advance but the client would not agree to that. Now she proposes to take a security interest in the real estate that is the subject of the suit, or perhaps an interest-bearing promissory note in advance payment.

Finally, in a recent suit to recover a valuable ring that had been wrongfully withheld, a jury awarded Jackson's client the ring and $100,000 punitive damages. The fee contract between Jackson and her client provided that Jackson would get 40% of all punitive damages. "That was because we thought the punitive damages would be low," the client complained after the verdict was announced. "On a big recovery such as this, 40% is unfair," the client said. "I'll pay you 25% and not a penny more." The defendant in the case satisfied the judgment by giving Jackson the ring and a check for $100,000 payable to Jackson. Jackson promptly deposited the full amount of the check in her client trust account and put the ring on her finger. She told Baker, "Until we get this fee dispute worked out, I'm not giving you a nickel."

QUESTIONS

1. Should Jackson be subject to discipline for her handling of the ABC matter?

a. Are a lawyer's right to be paid and the lawyer's obligation to render professional services competently independent of each other? That is, may a lawyer withhold services or render them less well as a device to stimulate payment? State v. Mayes, 216 Kan. 38, 531 P.2d 102 (1975), disbarred a lawyer for doing so. Cf. Estate of Hash v. Henderson, 109 Ariz. 174, 507 P.2d 99 (1973) (lawyer died leaving 200 divorce decrees in his desk drawer that he had left unfiled pending payment of fees).

b. In the absence of agreement, what rights should a lawyer have if the client terminates the relationship the day before trial, for example, or under other circumstances where significant time has been invested but no results achieved on which to calculate a contingent or percentage fee? The usual rule is to permit the first lawyer a quantum meruit recovery; in the case of a contingent fee, the first lawyer can usually recover only if the second lawyer wins the case, i.e. if the plaintiff ultimately prevails. E.g. Plaza Shoe Store Inc. v. Hermel, Inc., 636 S.W.2d 53 (Mo.1982) (en banc).

c. Would Jackson thus be well advised to collect her fees in advance? May a lawyer charge a client a "nonrefundable retainer", for example? That is, may the lawyer say that the fee is payable before any work is begun and is not refundable even if the work turns out to take little time or if the client later fires the lawyer?

Non–refundable fees were held to be invalid in Matter of Cooperman, 633 N.E.2d 1069 (N.Y.1994). What Cooperman did was basically say, "Once I enter an appearance in this case, even if you fire me, I will not have to return any part of the fee." In at least three cases, he was fired by clients before doing much work, and he had been warned by the bar to return part of the fee in such cases. Non-refundable fees violate the fiduciary relationship between lawyer and client, the Court of Appeals agreed, and they inhibit the client's right to terminate the lawyer. Thus, the Court affirmed the lawyer's two-year suspension from practice.[1]

Do you agree that the issue is that simple? Suppose a lawyer incurs real opportunity costs by taking a case? What if the client tells the lawyer he wants her to set aside the month of May to try a matter. She agrees to do so for a "non-refundable" fee of $25,000, her typical monthly billing, and turns down work she would otherwise do in May. On April 30, the client fires the lawyer. Is it clear the lawyer should not be able to keep all or most of the fee? See In re Gastineau, 857 P.2d 136 (Ore.1993), holding that non-refundable flat-fee contracts are not per se improper, but they result in a prohibited unreasonable fee where the lawyer does not do the necessary legal work.

d. Should Jackson ever be able to turn to the Court for help in seeing that the client pays the fee in advance?

Journalist Martin Mayer writes that:

" * * * criminal practice is the one branch of the law where lawyers collect their fees in advance. Not long ago, an older New York lawyer with little experience in the criminal courts had a client who had been picked up in another county for drunk driving, and for whom a conviction at precisely this moment would be extremely inconvenient. He wanted a postponement, but knew of no excuse a judge would have to accept, so he consulted with the young assistant district attorney who would be on duty that day. The DA heard the reason for the postponement, which was a good one, and said. 'That's all right. You just tell the judge that you haven't been able to get hold of your witness, Mr. Green.' "

"But I don't have any witness, Mr. Green."

The DA looked incredulously at the older lawyer's white hairs and said, "Don't you *know*? It means you haven't been paid. Any judge will give you an adjournment on that."

In Washington, D.C., these matters are handled with greater formality: a lawyer still waiting for his fee comes into court and

---

1. The point of this rule is suggested by Federal Savings & Loan Insurance Corp. v. Angell, Holmes & Lea, 838 F.2d 395 (9th Cir.1988), cert.denied sub nom. Van Voorhis & Skaggs v. FSLIC, 488 U.S. 848, 109 S.Ct. 127, 102 L.Ed.2d 100 (1988). Counsel for a savings and loan was paid a large fee which purported to be nonrefundable. Three weeks later, the client was put into receivership. The FSLIC fired the lawyer and asked for return of the retainer. The court here held that a client is always free to fire its lawyer. Thus the firm had to return all but a reasonable fee for work done before termination.

demands an adjournment "pursuant to Rule I of this Court." [2] Should a Judge assist an attorney to collect a fee in this way? Is it only professional courtesy to do so? Is there anything else the judge might do to assist the lawyer other than grant a delay? What is the professionally responsible way for both lawyer and judge to handle this situation?

2. Would it be proper for Jackson to take a security interest in the property whose title is at issue in the second paragraph of this problem?

a. Do Model Rule 1.8(j) and DR 5–103(A) answer the question? Do they seem to recognize any exceptions? Should they do so?

b. Opinion 95 of the District of Columbia Bar (1988), argues that a lawyer who prosecutes a patent application may not take an interest in the patent as security for payment of the fee. Because a patent application is technically "litigation", the arrangement would necessarily constitute taking an interest in the subject matter of litigation prohibited by DR 5–103(A) and Model Rule 1.8(j). Why isn't this arrangement a permissible contingent fee allowed by DR 5–103(A)(2) and Model Rule 1.8(j)(2)?

c. Hawk v. State Bar of California, 45 Cal.3d 589, 247 Cal.Rptr. 599, 754 P.2d 1096 (1988), says that when a lawyer takes an interest in property of the client as security for payment of the lawyer's fee, the arrangement is a business transaction with the client subject to DR 5–104(A) and Model Rule 1.8(a). This implies that in some cases the arrangement could properly be entered into as a way of helping the client afford necessary legal services. If the lawyer ignores the conflict of interest concerns and does not comply with the safeguards of the cited rules, however, he or she will be subject to discipline, here a four year suspension. Do you agree with this approach?

d. Where the recovery is in the form of an annuity payable over the client's life, should the lawyer be entitled to an immediate cash payment of the negotiated percentage of the present cash value of the annuity? Must the client send the lawyer a check for a share of her recovery each month for the rest of her life? Sayble v. Feinman, 76 Cal.App.3d 509, 142 Cal.Rptr. 895 (1978), held that when the employment contract, without further elaboration, gave the attorney a percentage recovery, the lawyer could not compel a lump-sum payment. Accord, Cardenas v. Ramsey County and Special Care Associates, 322 N.W.2d 191 (Minn. 1982). Are such results necessary to prevent a lawyer's overreaching the client? Does the approach give a lawyer a prohibited "interest" in the recovery? Assuming better drafting, would it be conscionable to structure the retainer agreement so as to give the lawyers their money "off the top"?

3. Did Jackson violate Model Rule 1.15 or DR 9–102 by her handling of the ring and settlement check when the client disputed the amount of fee due?

---

2. M. Mayer, The Lawyers 161–62 (1967) (emphasis in original).

a. Where did Jackson go wrong? Was it proper for her to deposit the $100,000 check into her trust account? Was it proper for her to wear the ring? Why or why not?

b. When the client asked for his money, should she have paid him the full $75,000 that the client thought was due? Would it have been proper for Jackson to pay only what Jackson thought was due? Does your answer depend on whether you believe the client had a valid claim to have the fee reduced?

c. How must an attorney keep his or her office accounts? May all funds go into a single checking account, regardless of to whom the funds belong? Is it important that each client's funds go into a separate account or only that individual records be kept? [3]

The California and New York rules found in the Standards Supplement are good examples of much more detailed provisions than the ABA has heretofore provided. Their basic purpose is to require the lawyer to establish records that an auditor can then review. In February 1993, the ABA House of Delegates adopted a "Model Financial Recordkeeping Rule" much like the state rules. Its status is a bit unclear; it has not been formally made a part of the Model Rules.

d. Should an attorney's trust account be subject to random audits, i.e. "spot checks"? In February 1992, the ABA House of Delegates approved the McKay Commission's proposals for disciplinary reform that called for random audits.

Traditional doctrine requires that there be "probable cause to believe that the accounts have not been properly maintained * * *." Do you believe audits might be conducted without probable cause to believe a *particular* lawyer to be in violation of the legal requirements? Some lawyers have tried to resist audit of their trust accounts, citing attorney-client privilege or their own expectation of privacy. Those defenses have generally not prevailed. E.g. In re Kennedy, 442 A.2d 79 (Del.1982) (spot check system); Doyle v. State Bar of California, 32 Cal.3d 12, 184 Cal.Rptr. 720, 648 P.2d 942 (1982) (subpoena system).[4]

e. Should a lawyer also be subject to discipline for the dishonesty of office staff or associated lawyers?

Office of Disciplinary Counsel v. Ball, 618 N.E.2d 159 (Ohio 1993), involved a lawyer who gave responsibility for most of his probate practice to his secretary. She took in money and wrote checks on his trust accounts. Ultimately, she got behind and diverted funds from some accounts to others. The lawyer said he knew nothing about this. If

---

3. One lawyer who did not maintain separate accounts successfully claimed that overdraft protection on his personal account was sufficient to protect clients against conversion of their funds. In re Rosin, 156 Ill.2d 202, 620 N.E.2d 368 (1993). Do you agree with this reasoning? Most courts would not.

4. Even where the audit determines that the lawyer has stolen from his or her law firm instead of a client, disbarment of the lawyer may follow. See, e.g., In re Siegel, 627 A.2d 156 (N.J.1993). See also, In re Busby, 855 P.2d 156 (Ore.1993), where the lawyer was suspended for four months for lying to his firm about the fees he was paid and pocketing the difference.

that were true, the Court said, the lawyer failed in his duty of supervision. He was suspended from practice for 6 months.

Duggins v. Guardianship of Washington, 632 So.2d 420 (Miss.1993), involved a lawyer retained to pursue a medical malpractice action on behalf of a child. He associated himself with a second lawyer who was actually to try the case. The second lawyer ultimately settled the case without telling the client or Duggins, and ran off with most of the money. The question was Duggins' liability to the clients. The Court held that under these circumstances, the lawyers were partners or joint venturers with respect to the case. Thus, Duggins was liable for all damage caused by the second lawyer, plus punitive damages, even though he had no moral culpability for what had occurred. Do you agree with taking such a strict liability approach to the problem?

f. Suppose there had been no affirmative dishonesty. Suppose a check payable to one of the clients was sent to Sharp's office as an offer of settlement of a claim. The client could not be found, and Sharp thought the offer fair, so Sharp endorsed the client's name on the check and deposited the proceeds in his trust account. Now the client has returned and accused Sharp of forgery. Does a lawyer have a right to cash a check for the benefit of the client? Should a lawyer be able to assume the client will want his or her lawyer to protect the client's interest? See, e.g., Sampson v. State Bar, 12 Cal.3d 70, 115 Cal.Rptr. 43, 524 P.2d 139 (1974) (endorsement of clients' names to checks without authorization of clients, accepting false acknowledgments and failing to secure clients' authorization for payment of settlement funds to doctor may properly be the subject of disciplinary action).

4. Does it similarly violate Model Rule 1.15 and DR 9–102 for a lawyer to keep the client's papers in the lawyer's possession until the fee is paid?

a. In many states,[5] an attorney has a "retaining lien" which permits exactly that. A "retaining lien" gives the lawyer a possessory interest in the client's papers and funds in the attorney's possession.[6] If the attorney loses possession of the papers, he loses the lien.

b. Should the lawyer be able to enforce a retaining lien where new counsel for a murder defendant needs the files to prepare for trial? People v. Altvater, 78 Misc.2d 24, 355 N.Y.S.2d 736 (1974), held that the first lawyer could retain the originals but had to let the second lawyer make copies. See also Pomerantz v. Schandler, 704 F.2d 681, 683 (2d Cir.1983) (per curiam) (exception to attorney's lien, in court's discretion, when client has urgent need for papers to defend criminal case and lacks the means to pay the lawyer's fee; otherwise the "attorney's lien cannot

---

5. California is an important exception. See Academy of California Optometrists, Inc. v. Superior Court, 51 Cal.App.3d 999, 124 Cal.Rptr. 668 (1975).

6. The retaining lien does not apply to property given to the lawyer for safekeeping. See Akers v. Akers, 233 Minn. 133, 46 N.W.2d 87 (1951).

be disregarded merely because the pressure it is supposed to exert becomes effective").[7]

c.   In addition, most states give the attorney a "charging lien" that is non-possessory but gives the lawyer a right to have any recovery in the case applied to payment of his or her fees. The attorney must give notice to the person paying the judgment or settlement. Once such notice is given, the person paying the judgment or settlement is liable for the attorney's fees if that person pays the entire judgment or settlement directly to the attorney's client.

d.   Should a lawyer thus be able to demand that a settlement check be made out solely to him so as to be able to enforce his charging lien? See Hafter v. Farkas, 498 F.2d 587 (2d Cir.1974), holding no, but permitting the check to be made out to *both* lawyer and client.

e.   Similarly, a lawyer may not take excess funds deposited by the client for payment of court reporter charges and apply them to payment of the lawyer's unpaid fees. See State ex rel. Oklahoma Bar Ass'n v. Cummings, 863 P.2d 1164 (Okl.1993).

5.   Should a lawyer be limited in his or her ability to sue to collect a fee? Would there be any reason for such a limitation?

a.   ABA Formal Opinion 250 (1943) upheld suits against clients, but without enthusiasm. Do you agree with the committee that "Ours is a learned profession, not a mere money-getting trade"? Does it follow that "suits to collect fees should be avoided"? See EC 2–23.

b.   Is the lawyer bound by the obligation to preserve client confidences and secrets in establishing the elements of the lawyer's claim? What principle, if any, would justify sacrificing confidentiality in favor of the lawyer's personal interest? Compare DR 4–101(C)(4) and Rule 1.6(b)(2). May the lawyer use the threat of revealing client confidences to "encourage" the client's payment?

c.   Should a fee dispute between attorney and client be subject to arbitration? Mandatory arbitration at the request of the client?

Anderson v. Elliott, 555 A.2d 1042 (Me.1989), cert. denied 493 U.S. 978, 110 S.Ct. 504, 107 L.Ed.2d 507 (1989), upheld the Maine requirement that lawyers submit to client-initiated mandatory arbitration of fee claims. The lawyer had argued that arbitration denied him his constitutional right to a jury trial, but the court held that the right must be read in the context of the court's supervisory power over attorneys. See also, Devine, Mandatory Arbitration of Attorney–Client Fee Disputes: A Concept Whose Time Has Come, 14 U.Toledo L.Rev. 1205 (1983).

7. Resolution Trust Corporation v. Elman, 949 F.2d 624 (2d Cir.1991), considered lawyers use of retaining liens when the banks they had represented failed. The lawyers simply held on to all the files in the banks' cases in an attempt to move to the head of the line for payment. That will not work, the Court held. To collect their fees in such cases, lawyers must file their claims with the Resolution Trust Corporation like every other creditor. See also F.D.I.C. v. Shain, Schaffer & Rafanello, 944 F.2d 129 (3d Cir.1991).

In Guralnick v. New Jersey Supreme Court, 747 F.Supp. 1109 (D.N.J.1990), aff'd 961 F.2d 209 (3d Cir.1992), lawyers argued that a New Jersey system of fee arbitration that only a client may initiate unconstitutionally denied them due process, violated their Thirteenth Amendment rights and violated the antitrust laws as well. In a thoughtful opinion, the Court rejected all such challenges. A set of "Model Rules for Fee Arbitration" was adopted by the ABA House of Delegates in February 1995.

d. Should a lawyer's retainer agreement be able to specify that non–fee complaints the client has about the lawyer must be submitted to arbitration as well? In Haynes v. Kuder, 591 A.2d 1286 (D.C.App. 1991), the lawyer had included such a mandatory arbitration clause in his retainer agreement. The court even upheld its application to a malpractice action against the lawyer.

California State Bar Standing Committee on Professional Responsibility and Conduct, Formal Opinion 1989–116, similarly concluded that public policy favors arbitration and that a lawyer dealing with a new client has no fiduciary obligation that would prohibit using such a clause in the retainer. Because arbitration goes to remedy and not liability, the committee reasoned, it does not constitute limiting liability for malpractice. When dealing with an existing client, however, the committee said that the lawyer has a fiduciary duty to fully explain the provision and its legal consequences.

e. May a lawyer charge interest or a "late payment penalty" on overdue accounts? May a lawyer accept Master Card in payment of his fees and simply leave all collection problems up to the credit card company? Both charging interest and accepting credit cards were upheld in ABA Formal Opinion 338 (November 16, 1974), that limits the use of credit cards in six ways, including: "A lawyer shall not encourage participation in the plan, but his position must be that he accepts the plan as a convenience for clients who desire it; and the lawyer may not because of his participation increase his fee for legal services rendered the client."

6. Suppose the lawyer who had converted client funds were now judgment proof? What remedies, if any, might you pursue on the client's behalf?

a. The bar of England and Wales, and the bar of Victoria, Australia, have both made malpractice insurance for lawyers compulsory in order to increase bargaining power with the insurance carrier and to provide coverage for all practicing lawyers regardless of their track record. Should the American bar similarly require compulsory insurance and, in effect, forbid self-insurance? [8]

---

8. Ogrinz v. James, 309 Md. 381, 524 A.2d 77 (1987), upheld the taxation of lawyers to create a malpractice insurance company for members of the bar. The Maryland legislature found that malpractice rates were skyrocketing for lawyers and found a public purpose in creating an entity that would help guarantee that all lawyers were covered.

b. Should the bar establish a Client Security Fund to reimburse clients victimized by their attorneys?[9] Should all members of the bar be assessed to provide the corpus of such a fund? Should the existence of the fund be kept quiet so as to prevent the lawyers' assessments from becoming as high as doctors' malpractice premiums? See EC 9–7.

---

9. See, e.g., Bryan, The Clients' Security Fund Ten Years Later, 55 A.B.A.J. 757 (1969); M.T. Bloom, The Trouble With Lawyers 1–35 (1969). Beard v. North Carolina State Bar, 320 N.C. 126, 357 S.E.2d 694 (1987), has upheld a system by which the state Supreme Court requires each lawyer to pay $50 each year into the client security fund. See also, Clients' Security Fund of State v. Grandeau, 72 N.Y.2d 62, 530 N.Y.S.2d 775, 526 N.E.2d 270 (1988) (upholds suit by New York Fund against the partner of defaulting lawyer on a theory of vicarious liability).

SELECTED BIBLIOGRAPHY ON ISSUES IN CHAPTER III

Problem 5

Allegretti, Shooting Elephants, Serving Clients: An Essay on George Orwell and the Lawyer–Client Relationship, 27 Creighton L.Rev. 1 (1993–94).

Devine, The Ethics of Representing the Disabled Client: Does Model Rule 1.14 Adequately Resolve the Best Interests–Advocacy Dilemma?, 49 Missouri L.Rev. 493 (1984).

Marcus, For a Lawyers' Boycott of South Africa: Ethics and Choice of Client, 4 Yale Law & Policy Rev. 504 (1986).

Maute, Allocation of Decisionmaking Authority Under the Model Rules of Professional Conduct, 17 U.C. Davis L.Rev. 1049 (1984).

McCants, Recognizing and Dealing with Professional Responsibility Issues Arising in Initial Legal Consultations, 18 Creighton L.Rev. 1461 (1985).

Patterson, An Inquiry Into the Nature of Legal Ethics: The Relevance and Role of the Client, 1 Georgetown J.Legal Ethics 43 (1987).

Patterson, Legal Ethics and the Lawyer's Duty of Loyalty, 29 Emory L.J. 909 (1980).

D. Rosenthal, Lawyer and Client: Who's in Charge? (1975).

Rosenwald, Death Wish: What Washington Courts Should Do When a Capital Defendant Wants to Die, 68 Washington L.Rev. 735 (1993).

Schneyer, Limited Tenure for Lawyers and the Structure of Lawyer–Client Relations: A Critique of the Lawyer's Proposed Right to Sue for Wrongful Discharge, 59 Nebraska L.Rev. 11 (1980).

Spiegel, The New Model Rules of Professional Conduct: Lawyer–Client Decision Making and the Role of Rules in Structuring the Lawyer–Client Dialogue, 1980 A.B.F. Research J. 1003.

Symposium, Ethics Issues in Representing Older Clients, 72 Fordham L. Rev. 961 (1994).

Underwood, Taking and Pursuing a Case: Some Observations Regarding "Legal Ethics' and Attorney Accountability", 74 Kentucky L.J. 173 (1986).

Woodruff, Withdrawal of Counsel in Criminal Cases, 5 J.Legal Profession 243 (1980).

Problem 6

ABA Tort and Insurance Practice Section, The Attorney–Client Privilege Under Siege (1989).

Alexander, The Corporate Attorney–Client Privilege: A Study of the Participants, 63 St. John's L.Rev. 191 (1989).

Crystal, Confidentiality Under the Model Rules of Professional Conduct, 30 U.Kansas L.Rev. 215 (1982).

Hacker & Rotunda, Waiver of Attorney Client Privilege, 2 Corporation L.Rev. 250 (1979).

Harding, Waiver: A Comprehensive Analysis of a Consequence of Inadvertently Producing Documents Protected by the Attorney–Client Privilege, 42 Catholic L.Rev. 465 (1993).

Hazard, An Historical Perspective on the Attorney–Client Privilege, 66 California L.Rev. 1061 (1978).

Hood, The Attorney–Client Privilege and a Revised Rule 1.6: Permitting Limited Disclosure After the Death of the Client, 7 Georgetown J.Legal Ethics 741 (1994).

Landesman, Confidentiality and the Lawyer–Client Relationship, 1980 Utah L.Rev. 765.

LoCascio, Reassessing Attorney–Client Privileged Legal Advice in Patent Litigation, 69 Notre Dame L.Rev. 1203 (1994).

Lynn, Restricting Attorney Speech About Matters of Recent Employment, 24 Arizona L.Rev. 531 (1982).

Marcus, The Perils of Privilege: Waiver and the Litigator, 84 Michigan L.Rev. 1605 (1986).

Moore, Limits to Attorney–Client Confidentiality: A "Philosophically Informed" and Comparative Approach to Legal and Medical Ethics, 36 Case Western Reserve L.Rev. 177 (1986).

Note, The Attorney–Client Privilege After Attorney Disclosure, 78 Michigan L.Rev. 927 (1980).

Note, Attorney–Client Privilege—Contempt: The Dilemma in Nondisclosure of Possibly Privileged Information, 45 Washington L.Rev. 181 (1970).

Note, Attorney–Client Privilege in Multiple Party Situations, 8 Columbia J.Law & Social Problems 179 (1972).

Note, Attorney–Client Privilege in the EEC: The Perspective of International Corporate Counsel, 20 International Lawyer 677 (1986).

Note, Attorney–Client Privilege: The Remedy of Contempt, 1968 Wisconsin L.Rev. 1192 (1968).

Note, Confidential Communications in Student Legal Clinics, 1972 Law & Social Order 668 (1972).

Note, The Constitutional Right to Confidentiality, 51 George Washington L.Rev. 133 (1982).

Note, Corporate Disclosure and Limited Waiver of the Attorney–Client Privilege, 50 George Washington L.Rev. 812 (1982).

Note, Law Clerk's Duty of Confidentiality, 129 U.Pennsylvania L.Rev. 1230 (1981).

Note, Preservation of Confidences and Secrets—Consideration of Time, 7 J.Legal Profession 213 (1982).

Note, "Secrets" on the Public Record?, 6 J.Legal Profession 357 (1981).

Parness, The Presence of Family Members and Others During Attorney–Client Communications: Himmel's Other Dilemma, 25 Loyola U. (Chicago) L.J. 481 (1994).

Popkin, Client–Lawyer Confidentiality, 59 Texas L.Rev. 755 (1981).

Powell & Link, The Sense of a Client: Confidentiality Issues in Representing the Elderly, 72 Fordham L.Rev. 1197 (1994).

Rotunda, The Notice of Withdrawal and the New Model Rules of Professional Conduct: Blowing the Whistle and Waiving the Red Flag, 63 Oregon L.Rev. 455 (1984).

Silbert, The Crime–Fraud Exception to the Attorney–Client Privilege and Work–Product doctrine, the Lawyer's Obligations to Disclosure, and the Lawyer's Response to Accusation of Wrongful Conduct, 23 American Criminal L.Rev. 351 (1986).

Thornburg, Sanctifying Secrecy: The Mythology of the Corporate Attorney–Client Privilege, 69 Notre Dame L.Rev. 157 (1993).

Waits, Opinion Work Product: A Critical Analysis of Current Law and a New Analytical Framework, 73 Oregon L.Rev. 385 (1994).

Problem 7

Arledge, Contingent Fees, 6 Ottawa L.Rev. 374 (1974).

Aronson, Attorney–Client Fee Arrangements: Regulation and Review (Fed.Judicial Center 1980).

Branca & Steinberg, Attorney Fee Schedules and Legal Advertising: Implications of Goldfarb, 24 U.C.L.A. L.Rev. 475 (1977).

Brickman, Contingent Fees Without Contingencies: *Hamlet* Without the Prince of Denmark?, 37 U.C.L.A. L.Rev. 29 (1989).

Brickman, Setting the Fee When the Client Discharges a Contingent Fee Attorney, 41 Emory L.J. 367 (1992).

Brickman & Cunningham, Nonrefundable Retainers Revisited, 72 N.Carolina L.Rev. 1 (1993).

Clermont & Currivan, Improving on the Contingent Fee, 63 Cornell L.Rev 529 (1978).

Dana & Spier, Expertise and Contingent Fees: The Role of Asymmetric Information in Attorney Compensation, 9 J.Law, Econ. & Organ. 349 (1993).

Dimitriou, The Individual Practitioner and Commercialism in the Legal Profession: How Can the Individual Survive?, 45 S.Carolina L.Rev. 965 (1994).

Green, From Here to Attorney's Fees: Certainly, Efficiency, and Fairness in the Journey to the Appellate Courts, 69 Cornell L.Rev. 207 (1984).

Kritzler, et al., The Impact of Fee Arrangement on Lawyer Effort, 19 Law & Society Rev. 251 (1985).

F. B. MacKinnon, Contingent Fees for Legal Services (1964).

Lerman, Lying to Clients, 138 U.Pennsylvania L. Rev. 659 (1990).

Lubet, The Rush to Remedies: Some Conceptual Questions About Nonrefundable Retainers, 73 N.Carolina L.Rev. 271 (1994).

Miceli, Do Contingent Fees Promote Excessive Litigation?, 23 J.Legal Studies 211 (1994).

Morgan, Where Do We Go From Here with Fee Schedules?, 50 A.B.A.J. 1403 (1973).

Note, Contingent Fee Contracts: Validity, Controls and Enforceability, 47 Iowa L.Rev. 942 (1962).

R.C. Reed, Ed., Win–Win Billing Strategies: Alternatives that Satisfy Your Clients and You (1992).

Rhein, Judicial Regulation of Contingent Fee Contracts, 48 J.Air Law and Commerce 151 (1982).

Schwartz & Mitchell, An Economic Analysis of the Contingent Fee in Personal Injury Litigation, 22 Stanford L.Rev. 1125 (1970).

See, An Alternative to the Contingent Fee, 1984 Utah L.Rev. 485.

Symposium, Attorney's Fees, 1984 Utah L.Rev. 533.

Whitfield, Where the Wind Blows: Fee Shifting in Domestic Relations Cases, 14 Florida State U.L.Rev. 811 (1987).

Problem 8

Brickman, Attorney–Client Fee Arbitration: A Dissenting View, 1990 Utah L.Rev. 277.

Brickman & Cunningham, Nonrefundable Retainers: Impermissible Under Fiduciary, Statutory and Contract Law, 57 Fordham L.Rev. 149 (1988).

Brickman, The Advance Fee Payment Dilemma: Should Payments be Deposited to the Client Trust Account or to the General Office Account?, 10 Cardozo L.Rev. 647 (1989).

Conn, Attorney Misappropriation of Client Funds, 27 Howard L.J. 1597 (1984).

Dubin, The Retaining Lien: An Ethical Trap for the Unwary Lawyer, 63 Michigan Bar J. 257 (1984).

Johnson & Long, Lawyer, Thou Shall Not Steal, 36 Rutgers L.Rev. 454 (1984).

Rau, Resolving Disputes Over Attorneys' Fees: The Role of ADR, 46 S.M.U. L.Rev. 2005 (1993).

Smith, The Realities of Collecting Legal Fees, 24 Res Gestae 432 (1980).

Windscheffel, Ethical and Legal Issues Related to a Lawyer's Retention of Client's Property and Documents, 57 J.Kansas Bar Ass'n 25 (1988).

Chapter IV

THE REQUIREMENT OF LOYALTY
TO THE CLIENT

————

The Biblical injunction that no person can serve two inconsistent masters applies with full force in the Model Code and Model Rules. For a lawyer, the "master" possibly conflicting with the client's interest may be the lawyer's own self-interest, that of another client, a previous client, a third party, or possibly even an abstract idea.

Each client of a lawyer expects full loyalty, yet it is as usual for a lawyer to represent many clients as for a doctor to treat many patients. In some cases, indeed, several persons may believe they want a common attorney. Moreover, the attorney's partners will be representing other clients and thus extending the possible conflicts.

The economics of the situation normally do not cause a lawyer to be overly broad in defining conflicts: firms usually do not like to turn away business and clients may believe they are saving money when they do not have to pay two fees. Yet the law of legal ethics sets limits beyond which attorneys may not go without client consent. In the problems that follow, consider questions such as:

  a. How should the lawyer recognize, anticipate, and avoid conflicts or potential conflicts of interest?

  b. When do a lawyer's personal interests, as opposed to those of clients, make his or her zealous representation subject to question?

  c. Do the ethics rules on conflict of interest ever serve to increase lawyers' fees when the clients might properly choose to save the cost of the extra lawyer?

  d. If a lawyer determines that she is in a conflict situation, how should she deal with it? Is it enough to obtain consent of all the affected persons? When must the lawyer refuse to take the case? When must she withdraw?

  e. To what extent do conflict of interest rules represent ends in themselves, and to what extent do they further objectives such as the obligation to preserve client confidences?

————

PROBLEM 9

Representing Multiple Parties Dealing With Each Other

Mr. and Mrs. Wilson have been married for 12 years. They have children ages 10, 8, and 6. They both consider that their marriage has not been going well for the past four years, and while they consider each other friends, they no longer wish to remain married. They have come to attorney Wayne Green's office and have asked Green to help them secure a divorce.

The Wilsons tell Green they have agreed that Mr. Wilson will be the custodial parent of the 8-year-old son and Mrs. Wilson will be custodial parent of the two daughters. Each will have liberal rights of contact with the children living with the other. Mrs. Wilson wants $1000 a month child support, and Mr. Wilson considers that a bargain.

Neither of the Wilsons wants a separate attorney called into the case because of the added expense. "We both trust you," they say. "Why create problems when there aren't any now?"

QUESTIONS

1. May Green take the case? What problems should he foresee in helping two people accomplish what they see as an amicable dissolution of an unwanted legal relationship?

a. Are the interests of Mr. and Mrs. Wilson in conflict? Look at DR 5–105. What analytic process does that rule require Green to go through here? Do you believe that the problems contemplated by DR 5–105(A) are presented here?

b. Compare Model Rules 1.7 and 1.8. Is their analytic process any different? What do they require Green to consider?

c. What concerns underlie the rules governing conflicts of interest? Do EC 5–14 & 5–15 give you any help? Do the concerns principally relate to the protection of client confidences? The actual ability of the lawyer to exercise independent judgment? The appearance of disloyalty?

d. Is there a problem of confidences here? Is the problem instead related to the ability of Wayne Green to push hard for one client at the expense of the other? If Mr. Wilson is willing to pay $1000 a month, for example, should Green, on behalf of Mrs. Wilson, ask for $1500?

2. Is the simple answer to all conflicts problems that the clients may waive the conflict? How should Mr. and Mrs. Wilson effectuate their consent to joint representation?

a. What kind of information should Green provide the Wilsons about the advantages and disadvantages of waiver? Is the potential saving in cost the only advantage? What disadvantages should he stress? Do you suppose Green will be telling the Wilsons something they do not already know?

b.   Can Green ever be wholly be free of self-interest as he explains the clients' option to waive the conflict?   See EC 5–16.   One district court asserted that consent "cannot be presumed to be fully informed when it is procured without the advice of a lawyer who has no conflict of interest." Aetna Casualty & Surety Co. v. United States, 438 F.Supp. 886, 888 (W.D.N.C.1977).

Is that realistic?   The Fourth Circuit reversed, finding "no authority or reason to support the theory that the consent to multiple representation under the Rule can be effective only upon the advice of an independent attorney. * * * "   570 F.2d 1197, 1201–02 (4th Cir.1978), cert.denied 439 U.S. 821, 99 S.Ct. 87, 58 L.Ed.2d 113 (1978).   Which result reflects the better rule?   Why?   Compare ABA Defense Function Standard 4–3.5 in the Standards Supplement.

c.   Should the Model Code and Model Rules require that any waiver be in writing?   California is one state that has such a rule.   See Rule 5–102 of the California Rules of Professional Conduct set forth in the Standards Supplement.   Might the better practice even for lawyers in other states be to discuss conflicts in their retainer letters so as to be able to prove later that the advice about advantages and disadvantages was given?

d.   For how long should a conflicts waiver be effective?   Suppose that in the course of the representation, the lawyer learns facts that make the conflict more severe than first appeared.   Must a new waiver be obtained?

3.   Are there some conflicts that the clients may not waive? What might make a conflict nonconsentable?

a.   Are DR 5–105(C) and Model Rule 1.7 consistent on this point? Does it appear that the Wilsons could waive the potential conflict here?

b.   Should it be relevant that Green in the past has represented Mr. Wilson, who retained him on some business matters, but that he has never before represented Mrs. Wilson?   What if Green had represented Mr. Wilson often? [1]

c.   May a lawyer represent both the biological and adoptive parents in a private adoption?   Would having just one lawyer more likely

---

1.   Consider an Opinion of the Committee on Legal Ethics of the Los Angeles Bar Association, Opinion No. 207 (July 10, 1953), reprinted in 29 L.A.Bar Ass'n Bull. 137 (Feb. 1953).   For about 7 years an attorney represented primarily the husband but on occasions both the husband and the wife in income tax and other matters. When the couple was seeking a divorce, which might be bitterly contested, the wife asked this same attorney to represent her. The Bar Association advised that even with the husband's consent, there was a conflict of interest because: (1) "Even assuming that an effort at full disclosure has been made, it appears unlikely that the husband can fully contemplate, or that the attorney can fully disclose to the husband, all of the possible detriment to the husband of having his former attorney as the husband's adversary in a bitterly contested divorce action." (2) "It may be impossible for the attorney to represent the wife and yet keep the secrets and confidences of the husband * * *," and (3) "The attorney * * * should therefore avoid the suspicion of collusion which might result from the fact that he who has been the husband's attorney appears as attorney for the wife."

promote a nondivisive carrying out of the parties' intent? What about a biological parent's possible right to revoke consent? Because it is easy to foresee that an effort to revoke consent might occur, ABA Informal Opinion 87–1523 (1987) says that the situation presents an unwaivable conflict.[2]

d.   In Fiandaca v. Cunningham, 827 F.2d 825 (1st Cir.1987), the New Hampshire Legal Assistance (NHLA) represented women prison inmates who claimed that their prison facilities were overcrowded. The state offered to move some of the female inmates to another facility that was currently used as a hospital by mentally retarded citizens whom NHLA represented in another case challenging conditions at that facility. The NHLA rejected the state's offer because the mentally retarded clients would be adversely affected if the hospital were converted into a women's prison. The court held that it was error for the trial court to certify NHLA as class counsel; when a lawyer must decline a settlement offer in one case in order to benefit the lawyer's clients in another case, there is a fatal conflict of interest requiring NHLA's disqualification from continuing to act for the women prisoners.

e.   In Baldasarre v. Butler, 625 A.2d 458 (N.J.1993), the lawyer represented the sellers in a real estate transaction, all the while knowing that the buyer, his other client, had arranged immediately to sell the property to someone else at a large profit. Needless to say, the first sellers believed their lawyer should have told them that the ultimate buyer wanted the property and should have helped the first seller get the higher price. The New Jersey Supreme Court believed there was no way the lawyer could have acted loyally to both clients in such a situation and held that a lawyer may not represent both buyer and seller in a commercial real estate deal, even with the consent of both.

f.   Hyden v. Law Firm of McCormick, Forbes, Caraway & Tabor, 848 P.2d 1086 (N.M.App.1993), presented a similar problem. The firm represented both the buyer and seller in a sale of an automobile dealership. The buyer asked the lawyer to include warranties of the business' financial statements in the sales agreement. The seller didn't like that, so the lawyer said he would have it changed. The requirement was not entirely removed, the books were found to be misleading in a later suit, and the sale price was lowered by the court. The seller accused the lawyer of malpractice in not protecting its interest. Summary judgment for the client was denied, but the basic force of his argument based on the lawyer's conflict was not in doubt.

g.   Finally, In re Cohen, 853 P.2d 286 (Ore.1993), is an example of how a relatively simple situation can quickly become a conflict. The husband was accused of beating the wife's daughter; the husband faced criminal charges and both parents faced the possibility the child would be taken from them. The lawyer agreed to represent the husband in the

2. Similarly, New York State Bar Opinion 584 (1987) says that the same lawyer may not represent both the surrogate mother and the intermediary arranging a surrogacy contract (even assuming that the arrangement is otherwise legal).

criminal case and both parents in the custody matter. Later, the wife called the lawyer and told him the husband was not going to counselling. A presentence report was to the same effect and said the wife was often calling the police about the husband. The wife said she still wanted to be jointly represented with him, however, and to "act as a team." In imposing discipline on the lawyer, the Court found that he had neither adequately explained the potential conflict at the outset nor dealt with the actual conflict later.

4. Assume now that the parties who have come to Green are three individuals who wish to set up a close corporation. He has met none of them before. May Green represent all of them?

a. Should professional standards more readily allow the attorney to act for all the parties in this non-litigation setting than in a matter such as a divorce? Compare Model Rules 1.7 and 2.2 with EC 5–15 and EC 5–20.

b. Would it be proper for Green to introduce previously unrelated clients of his to each other and to suggest that one invest in the other's business? What problems with such matchmaking can you foresee? Cf. De La Maria v. Powell, Goldstein, Frazer & Murphy, 612 F.Supp. 1507 (N.D.Ga.1985).

c. In the corporate counseling situation, should one think of the lawyer as not representing any of the individuals but rather representing the corporate entity? If the lawyer represents the corporation and one of the individuals develops a conflict with the other parties that the individual does not want to waive, may the lawyer continue to represent the entity? Compare Rule 1.13(a) with EC 5–18.

d. If the differing interests become too hard to reconcile in the course of the representation, may simply Green drop one of the clients and continue to represent the other? Compare Model Rules 1.7(b) and 2.2(c). Should the law impose an absolute bar? See Griva v. Davison, 637 A.2d 830 (D.C.App.1994), holding that it was proper to represent partners, with the consent of each, in establishing a partnership. However, it was improper then to help two of the individual partners take steps to frustrate the veto power held by a dissident partner.

5. Are conflicts issues presented when Mr. and Mrs. Wilson, instead of seeking a divorce, come in for estate planning advice.

a. A recent ABA report poses the issue as follows:

"From an ethical standpoint, the risk is that, in counseling the couple as a unit for tax and planning purposes, neither individual will receive the representation a single individual might receive under the same circumstances. Yet family needs, tax incentives, and the very nature of marriage often make separate counseling unnecessary, and indeed, inappropriate."

Report of the Special Study Committee on Professional Responsibility, Comments and Recommendations on the Lawyer's Duties in Representing Husband and Wife, 28 Real Property, Probate and Trust Journal 765, 770 (1994).

b. Conceding both aspects of that observation, is a lawyer obliged to obtain a conflicts waiver before beginning estate planning for the couple? May one properly "view the couple as unified in goals and interests until shown otherwise"? Id. at 779.

c. What are the lawyer's obligations with respect to confidential information disclosed by either spouse? May the lawyer tell the wife about the husband's illegitimate child whom he wants to remember in his will, for example? Does your answer depend on whether the wife is leaving all her property to her husband in the expectation he is doing the same for her?

d. Might it be best for a lawyer to let the couple decide at the outset whether the representation will be "joint", i.e., where all information will be shared and all decisions will serve the interdependent interests of the couple, or "separate", i.e., the couple will be treated as independent persons and confidential information of each will not be shared? Id. at 771–72.

e. If confronted with the choice between "joint" and "separate" representation, which option do you believe most couples would choose, at least when they were together in the lawyer's office? What should the lawyer do if, the day after both wills are signed, the wife comes back to the lawyer's office and says, "I want to change my will and don't want my husband to know"?

6. Are the ethics rules too quick to find conflicts? Are they too willing to find costs to conflicted representation but not eager enough to achieve a noncontentious resolution of disputes?

a. In spite of the problems associated with Mr. and Mrs. Wilson using the same lawyer for their divorce, might it nonetheless be reasonable for them to desire that arrangement? Is cost a relevant consideration? Is the desire for noncontentious resolution of the matter a legitimate concern?

b. Evaluate the following analysis of simultaneous representation of conflicting interests in a nonlitigation context.

"1. *Simultaneous Representation of Conflicting Interests.* A lawyer certainly cannot sit at both counsel tables in contested litigation. However by no means all legal problems involve going to court, and when they do not, having more than one lawyer to accomplish the parties' objectives may be an unnecessary and wasteful luxury. Individuals entering upon a contractual relationship, for example, might find it significantly less expensive and less disruptive to hire a single lawyer to draft a contract incorporating the business consensus of both sides than to have two lawyers, each trying to exact the marginal pound of flesh for his client. So, too, in many cases of uncontested divorce, the presence of combatant lawyers may reopen wounds better left closed and exacerbate problems rather than solve them.

"The response to this argument from many lawyers is that a situation which appears nonlitigious at the moment may develop into a contested situation in the future. This is not an unreasonable concern and may appear to go in part to the interest of the client. But having two lawyers from the outset in every case is expensive insurance against the unknown. Moreover, in many situations where things go badly, both sides can simply bring in separate counsel. The only person hurt by such a procedure would be the first lawyer who will now represent neither party. That the lawyer might not like this result is understandable. That his unhappiness should rise to the level of an ethical precept is less clear.

"The Code simply does not allow the client to choose how he wishes to deal with the risk of possible litigation. The lawyer may refuse to represent two clients even if both want joint representation. Indeed he or she apparently must do so unless the adequacy of such representation is 'obvious'—a standard which is both so strict and so ambiguous that in avoiding multiple representation the lawyer can never be wrong. Nothing in the Code requires—or even permits—the lawyer to suggest dual representation as an option or to take account of the savings to the client which might result. But while clients may be put to unnecessary expense in some cases, the interests of the legal community as a whole are always served: the effect of the rule is to maximize the number of lawyers in transactions while relieving them of responsibility to identify those cases likely to develop into adversary conflicts."[3]

Do you agree?

7. What remedies should be available when a lawyer is found to have been involved in a conflict of interest?

a. Should professional discipline be the only remedy?

b. If either or both of the clients is disadvantaged by the conflict, should a malpractice remedy be available?

c. Should a court order the lawyer disqualified from representing any or all of the clients in the matter?

d. Might the lawyer be denied all fees for the representation as a sanction for breach of the lawyer's fiduciary duty?

3. Morgan, The Evolving Concept of Professional Responsibility, 90 Harvard L.Rev. 702, 727–28 (1977). Copyright © 1977 by the Harvard Law Review Association.

e. Should these remedies be exclusive, or should all be available simultaneously in appropriate cases? [4]

8. Would Green avoid the conflict problem by representing Mr. Wilson and having his law partner represent Mrs. Wilson?

Look at Model Rule 1.10(a) and DR 5–105(D). What concerns or assumptions about attorney behavior underlie them? The concept of imputed disqualification is well settled and should be presumed throughout most of the course. We explore some problems of applying the concept later, primarily in Problem 15.

———

READINGS

———

EXCERPTS FROM THE RESTATEMENT OF THE LAW, THIRD, THE LAW GOVERNING LAWYERS
(Tent. Draft No. 4, April 10, 1991) *

§ 201. Basic Prohibition of Conflict of Interest

Unless all affected clients consent to the representation under the limitations and conditions provided in § 202, a lawyer may not represent a client if the representation would constitute a conflict of interest. A conflict of interest exists if there is substantial risk that the lawyer's representation of the client would be materially and adversely affected by the lawyer's own interests or by the lawyer's duties to another current client, to a former client, or to a third person.

§ 202. Client Consent to a Conflict of Interest

(1) A lawyer may represent a client notwithstanding a conflict of interest prohibited by § 201 if each affected client gives informed consent to the lawyer's representation. Informed consent requires that the client have adequate information about the risks and advantages of such representation to that client.

(2) Notwithstanding each affected client's consent, a lawyer may not represent a client if:

    (a) The lawyer represents an opposing party in the same litigation;

---

4. The California courts have noted that it frequently occurs in negotiations between husband and wife for settlement of property matters that one attorney serves both parties. While the courts have stated that it is much better in fairness to both parties that each be represented by counsel, the fact that one party is unrepresented does not compel the court to set aside the property settlement or divorce decree. See, e.g., Couser v. Couser, 125 Cal.App.2d 475, 477, 270 P.2d 496, 497 (1954).

(b) One or more the clients is legally incapable of giving consent; or

(c) Special circumstances render it unlikely that the lawyer will be able to provide adequate representation to one or more of the clients.

Reporter's Note to § 209, *Comment c:*

The question of representing opposing clients in hearings on uncontested marital dissolution has arisen frequently. Some courts have permitted use of only one lawyer in some of those situations. While the divorce proceeding is still a nominally contested litigation in most jurisdictions, in some remedial contexts, courts will confirm a negotiated property settlement where both parties consented to the simultaneous representation and the settlement appears fair. * * *

PROBLEM 10

The Duty of Loyalty

You represent the First National Bank in its commercial lending work. A large mortgage loan was made by the bank to International Bolts Co., a parts manufacturer, for construction of a new plant. The loan has now gone into default, and you have been directed by the bank to commence foreclosure proceedings.

International Bolts has occasionally hired you over the last few years to write opinion letters on labor law matters. You do not now happen to be drafting any opinion for that company. You have never represented International Bolts in connection with this loan, but when you mention to the President of International Bolts that you will soon be handling the foreclosure of his plant, he is personally offended. "I really would not like you to be the one that does that to us," he says, "after all we've been through together."

Meanwhile, a neighbor has consulted you with respect to a "prepayment penalty" in the residential mortgage loan he has with the Second National Bank. Second National is not one of your clients, and you agree with the neighbor that "prepayment penalties" seem not to be in consumers' best interests. Thus, as a favor to your neighbor, you have agreed to file a declaratory judgment action challenging the validity of such agreements under state and federal law.

You have informed the Second National Bank of the impending suit, and you have now received a call from the President of your client, the First National Bank. "I've heard about your proposed law suit against the Second National Bank. We do not want the law of prepayment penalties changed," the President tells you. "You owe it to us to withdraw from representing the plaintiff in the pending suit."

QUESTIONS

1. How should you respond to the request by the President of International Bolts that you not represent the First National Bank in the foreclosure proceeding?

a. Is the question simply one of keeping good relations with a sometimes client? Does International Bolts have a right to keep you out of the case? Look at Cinema 5, Limited v. Cinerama, Inc., included as a Reading to this Problem. Do you think the rule applied in that case is too harsh?

b. What is the basis of the concern that prevents a lawyer from taking a case contrary to the interest of a present client? Is it the problem of protecting each client's confidences? Was there any serious concern about confidences leaking in *Cinema 5*?

Would the protection of confidential client information explain a case like Zuck v. Alabama, 588 F.2d 436 (5th Cir.1979), where a law firm represented a defendant in a criminal case but also represented the prosecutor sued in his personal capacity in an unrelated civil matter. The court held that this constituted an actual conflict of interest rendering the criminal trial unfair in the absence of the criminal defendant's knowing and intelligent waiver.

c. What more than confidentiality may be of concern to the courts in these cases? In Grievance Committee v. Rottner, 152 Conn. 59, 203 A.2d 82 (1964), a law firm accepted an assault and battery case for O'Brien and against Twible. At the same time, it was representing Twible in a collection matter against someone else. The cases were not at all related but the court explained:

> "When a client engages the services of a lawyer in a given piece of business he is entitled to feel that, until that business is finally disposed of in some manner, he has the undivided loyalty of the one upon whom he looks as his advocate and his champion. If, as in this case, he is sued and his home attached by his own attorney, who is representing him in another matter, all feeling of loyalty is necessarily destroyed, and the profession is exposed to the charge that it is interested only in money."

Do you agree that this loyalty is what most clients expect? Might the expectations of personal loyalty felt by individual clients differ from the normal expectations of corporate clients?

d. Compare People v. Crawford Distributing Co., Inc., 65 Ill.App.3d 790, 22 Ill.Dec. 525, 382 N.E.2d 1223 (4th Dist.1978). Beer distributors convicted of fixing prices claimed on appeal that the convictions were tainted because the defendants were represented by lawyers in a firm in which at least one member was a special assistant attorney general for non-antitrust civil proceedings. The majority found no conflict. "If such a [person] whose authority does not include criminal cases takes on the representation of a person charged in a criminal proceeding in which the Attorney General is involved, that attorney is not placed in a position * * * where he might have to cross-examine and impeach his own clients. Neither is he placed in a position * * * where his civil clients stand to gain by the conviction of the individual he represents in the criminal case. The special Assistant Attorney General for limited civil types of cases owes no duty to the Attorney General in criminal matters." The dissent argued, however, "It is most doubtful that an attorney retained by a private client to do tax work * * * could properly undertake to sue that client in a personal injury case. The fact that an appointee is retained for a special category of practice does not alter the nature of an attorney-client relationship which establishes the commitment of the attorney to the interests of that client."

   2. It is well established that a lawyer may not represent someone in litigation against a present client without both parties' consent.[1] **See Rule 1.7(a) and Comment 7. But is International Bolts a present client?**

   a. At this very moment you are not doing any legal work for International Bolts. The company may never call again. Should it nevertheless have the right to prevent you from representing another client adverse to its interests?

   In IBM v. Levin, 579 F.2d 271, 281 (3d Cir.1978), IBM sought to disqualify law firm "CBM" for representing a client in a suit against IBM. The trial court disqualified CBM and the court of appeals affirmed. The trial "court found as a fact that at all relevant times CBM had an on-going attorney-client relationship with both IBM and the plaintiffs. This assessment of the relationship seems entirely reasonable to us. Although CBM had no specific assignment from IBM on hand on the day that [CBM filed] the antitrust complaint [against IBM] and even though CBM performed services for IBM on a fee for services basis rather than pursuant to a retainer arrangement, the pattern of repeated retainers, both before and after the filing of the complaint, supports the finding of a continuous relationship."

   Should a law firm be able to avoid the inference of continued representation by writing a letter to each client terminating the relationship at the end of a given matter? Why do you suppose firms are loath to do that? Is the approach in IBM v. Levin simply recognizing a relationship the firm hopes the client believes still exists?

   b. Should every wholly-owned subsidiary of a present client similarly be considered to be a client of the lawyer?

---

   1. In re Dresser Industries, 972 F.2d 540 (5th Cir.1992), holds that the principle against filing suit for one client against another present client is a national standard that federal courts must use in ruling on disqualification motions, even in the face of contrary state law.

Stratagem Development Corp. v. Heron International N.V., 756 F.Supp. 789 (S.D.N.Y.1991), found the law of New York to be that a lawyer has the same duty of loyalty to a wholly-owned subsidiary as to the parent corporation. Thus, a firm could not cease representation of the subsidiary (i.e., drop the client like a "hot potato") in order to file an unrelated action against the parent.[2]

Image Technical Services v. Eastman Kodak Co., 820 F.Supp. 1212 (N.D.Calif.1993), showed how far this rule can reach. The law firm had participated in a Supreme Court antitrust case against Kodak that had now been remanded for trial. It was discovered that the Hong Kong office of the law firm represented a division of Kodak with respect to sales of an unrelated product in China. Division managers had orally consented to the representation against Kodak, but the corporate general counsel had not been consulted. The Court disqualified the law firm from all further participation in the case.

c. Should a lawyer for a group of business partners be deemed the lawyer for each of them individually? The courts have split on the issue, but in those states where partnerships are considered separate "entities" instead of "aggregates" of the individual partners, the Courts have tended to say no. See, e.g., Greate Bay Hotel & Casino, Inc. v. Atlantic City, 624 A.2d 102 (N.J.Super.1993) (lawyer for business trust represents entity and thus is not barred from suing a trust member in an unrelated matter); Responsible Citizens v. Superior Court (Askins), 20 Cal.Rptr.2d 756 (Cal.App.1993) (lawyer who represents partnership may sue individual partner in unrelated proceeding).

d. Should a lawyer for a trade association be considered to be the lawyer for all of the association's members? In Westinghouse Electric Co. v. Kerr–McGee Corp., 580 F.2d 1311 (7th Cir.1978), cert. denied 439 U.S. 955, 99 S.Ct. 353, 58 L.Ed.2d 346 (1978), Kirkland & Ellis filed an antitrust action on behalf of its client, Westinghouse, against various corporations alleging price fixing violations in the uranium industry. Meanwhile the American Petroleum Institute ("AmPI") had retained Kirkland to oppose legislative proposals introduced in Congress to cause energy companies to divest uranium companies that they owned. On the same day that Kirkland's Chicago office filed the antitrust suit, Kirkland's Washington, D.C. office, representing AmPI, released a report which developed the opposite thesis and took an affirmative position on the subject of existing competition in the oil-uranium industry. AmPI was not a defendant in the antitrust suit, but three *members* of AmPI were defendants.

It turned out that individual members of AmPI had given Kirkland & Ellis' Washington office confidential information on their uranium assets in order to aid the firm in opposing the threatened legislation. The General Counsel of AmPI had promised the AmPI members that the

2. See also, Teradyne, Inc. v. Hewlett–Packard Co., 20 U.S.P.Q.2d (BNA) 1143, 1991 WL 239940 (N.D.Cal.1991) (law firm that represented only the pension plan and subsidiary of a company prohibited from filing suit against the company).

information would be held confidential. The Seventh Circuit held that "the attorney is held to obligations to the client which go far beyond those of an agent and beyond the principles of agency * * *. * * * [AmPI members] each entertained a reasonable belief that it was submitting confidential information regarding its involvement in the uranium industry to a law firm which had solicited the information upon a representation that the firm was acting in the undivided interest of each company." 580 F.2d at 1321.

Do you agree? Should *Westinghouse* be read to say any more than that when information is supplied on a promise of confidentiality, a court will see that the promise is honored? [3]

3. If you find that conflicts develop between two clients, may you simply "fire" one of the clients and continue to represent the other?

a. In Pennwalt Corp. v. Plough, Inc., 85 F.R.D. 264 (D.Del.1980), the law firm had been counsel for *A* for many years. In 1978, the firm defended *B* against antitrust charges. In 1979, *C* acquired *B*. Also in 1979, the law firm filed suit against *C* on behalf of its longtime client *A*. Upon learning that it represented *B* in one case, and simultaneously represented *A* against *B* 's parent, the firm sought to withdraw from representation of *B*. After the court granted that motion, *C* moved to disqualify the firm from the second case. The court agreed that counsel may not eliminate a conflict "merely by choosing to represent the more favored client and withdrawing its representation of the other." However, in this case the firm's conflict was inadvertent and it was highly unlikely that as of the date of the law firm's representation there was any misuse of confidential information or adverse effect on its exercise of independent judgment; disqualification was not required. See also, Tipton v. Canadian Imperial Bank of Commerce, 872 F.2d 1491 (11th Cir.1989) (law firm permitted to "fire" one client in order to avoid a conflict).

b. But see, Picker International, Inc. v. Varian Associates, Inc., 670 F.Supp. 1363 (N.D. Ohio 1987), affirmed 869 F.2d 578 (Fed.Cir.1989). A large national law firm merged with a firm in another city, and when the client lists were compared, it turned out that the merging firms represented clients who were opponents in current litigation. The merged firm was suing *B* on behalf of *A* (a long-time client of the acquiring firm), while representing *B* (the acquired firm's client) on various other matters. The firm sought to withdraw from representation of *B*, and to continue to represent the long time client of the big firm. The court held that the firm could not do that without consent of all affected

---

3. Cf. ABA Formal Opinion 92–365 (1992), asserting that a law firm that represents a trade association ordinarily may file an unrelated action against a member of the association with whom the lawyer has formed no attorney-client relationship unless the representation would impair the lawyer's representation of the association itself. This result is consistent with the view that *Westinghouse* is a case about enforcing promises of confidentiality, not giving client-like status to members of associations.

clients. Failing consent, the new firm must withdraw from *all* representation of all parties in the case of *A v. B.*

c. Notice that at the end of *Cinema 5*, the Second Circuit noted that Attorney Fleischmann offered to withdraw from representation of Cinerama in the Western District actions, but Cinerama refused and pressed forward on its disqualification motion. The court did not treat Cinerama's refusal as a waiver of its conflict claim. Why not? We know that at least part of the basis of the disqualification is a breach of the fiduciary duty of loyalty; if the fiduciary "fired" Cinerama (i.e., withdrew from further representation), would the fiduciary be seeking to profit from his breach of loyalty?

d. In Gould Inc. v. Mitsui Mining & Smelting Co., 738 F.Supp. 1121 (N.D.Ohio 1990), the Jones, Day firm was representing Gould in suing various defendants who had allegedly misappropriated Gould trade secrets. One of these defendants was Pechiney. In 1989, Pechiney acquired IG Technologies (IGT), a company Jones, Day represented in an unrelated matter. Thus, Jones, Day found itself in a conflict between Gould and IGT's parent. In response to a motion to disqualify Jones, Day from representing Gould against Pechiney, the court reasoned that, because of the "explosion of merger activity by corporations during the past fifteen years" it is appropriate to adopt a "less mechanical approach" and "balanc[e] the various interests." In this case, there was "no demonstration that Pechiney has been prejudiced by the law firm's representation of Gould." Further, disqualification would cost Gould a great deal of time and money, and significantly delay progress in this case. Finally, "the conflict was created by Pechiney's acquisition of IGT several years after the instant case was commenced, not by an affirmative act of Jones, Day." However, the court held, the conflict "must not endure." Hence, the law firm had to discontinue its representation of either Gould or IGT, and erect a screening device around the lawyers who did work for the party whom the firm dropped.[4]

e. Should clients be able to waive the protection of this rule and agree at the outset of the representation that if a conflict later arises the lawyer may represent one of them against the other? Should law firms make a waiver of such conflicts part of the boilerplate in their retainer agreements? ABA Formal Opinion 93–372 (April 16, 1993) expresses caution:

> "[O]ne principle seems certain: no lawyer can rely with ethical certainty on a prospective waiver of objection to future adverse representations simply because the client has executed a written document to that effect. No lawyer should assume without more, the "coast is clear" for undertaking any and all future conflicting engagements that come within the general terms of the waiver document. Even though one might think that the very purpose of a prospective waiver is to eliminate the need to return to the client to secure a 'present' second waiver

---

4. You will see more about "screening" in Problems 15 & 16, infra.

when what was once an inchoate matter ripens into an immediate conflict, there is no doubt that in many cases that is what will be ethically required."

4. What duty of loyalty, if any, do you have here not to take a legal position on prepayment penalties that is inconsistent with the interest of a regular client like the First National Bank?

a. Is there a technical, legal conflict of interest that would obligate you not to take this case? May you assert a legal position in one case that—if accepted by the court—may conflict with the legal position of another client in a different case? Compare DR 5–105 with Rule 1.7(b).

b. We know that lawyers often take inconsistent legal positions in the *same* case. A lawyer for an alleged debtor pleads, for example, "My client did not borrow the money (it was a gift), but even if he did borrow it, he already has repaid the debt." Is the problem of inconsistency *between* cases different?

c. Does the answer turn on whether contrary interpretations of fact or of law are involved? May you represent Client Y in one case arguing that facts justify a finding of negligence, but defend Client Z in another case on similar facts saying that the facts show due care?

d. Your banking client may not like what you are doing for the consumer in this problem, and it may therefore be bad for future business, but do the Model Rules or Model Code now forbid your representation of the consumer? Does Comment 9 to Rule 1.7 (under "Conflicts in Litigation") merely elaborate on Rule 1.7 itself, or does it go beyond [5]

e. Should it matter whether your inconsistent positions are taken before the same court? What if your law firm takes inconsistent positions in different forums? ABA Formal Opinion 93–377 (October 16, 1993) cast doubt on the trial/appellate court distinction in Comment 9 of Rule 1.7 and analyzed the so-called "positional conflicts" issue as follows:

> "[I]f the two matters are being litigated in the same jurisdiction, and there is a substantial risk that the law firm's representation of one client will create a legal precedent, even if not binding, which is likely materially to undercut the legal position being urged on behalf of the other client, the lawyer should either refuse to accept the second representation or (if otherwise permissible) withdraw from the first, unless both clients consent after full disclosure of the potential ramifications of the lawyer continuing to handle both matters.

* * *

5. Notice that Rule 1.7(b) of the Washington, D.C., Rules of Professional Conduct, contained in the Standards Supplement, deals specifically and restrictively with positional conflicts. The special interest Washington firms have in this issue seems to come largely from the amount of lobbying such firms do.

"[Even if the matters are being litigated in different juris-dictions,] if the lawyer concludes that the issue is of such importance and that its determination in one case is likely to have a significant impact on its determination in the second case, thus impairing the lawyer's effectiveness—or if the lawyer concludes that, because of the dual representation, there will be an inclination by the firm either to 'soft pedal' the issue or to alter the firm's arguments on behalf of one or both clients, thus again impairing the lawyer's effectiveness—the lawyer should not accept the second representation."

By contrast, California State Bar Standing Committee on Professional Responsibility and Conduct, Formal Opinion No. 1989–108 (1989), says that "To devise a rule that could be applied uniformly to 'issues conflicts' threatens the ability of lawyers to carry out their roles in the legal system." In what sense would that be true?

With which of these analyses do you agree?

5. Would it be unethical to refuse to take your neighbor's case against the Second National Bank out of a fear that your regular clients would be offended at your doing so? Cf. EC 2–28 and 8–1.

a. If you want to take this case and in fact do so, must you warn your neighbor that one of your best clients is opposed to your attacking the prepayment penalty? Even if no technical conflict of interest exists, why might the neighbor consider this information relevant?

b. Could your banking client force you out of the case indirectly? Could it insist that, although it is not now a party, it wants you to file an amicus brief on its behalf? If you agreed and withdrew from representing your neighbor, could your neighbor force you to withdraw from the case altogether? Of course you could ask your regular client, the First National Bank, to relieve you of any further obligations to represent it in paying matters, but that would make your pro bono activities on behalf of your neighbor a lot more costly.

c. May you, instead of taking your neighbor's case, write a law review article attacking the legality of prepayment penalties even though your established clients would refuse to embrace this position? Compare EC 7–17 and 8–4, with Model Rule 6.4.

d. Suppose that you are a member of the ABA Section of Corporation Banking and Business Law. The Section has asked you to draft a proposed Model Law governing prepayment penalties. May you ethically draft the section so as to further the interest of your regular clients? May you ethically draft the section any other way? Should you be required to make known your biases? To whom?

6. May you take a position on behalf of one client because it helps another client?

a. Suppose that you also represent the Consumer Association for the People (CAP) on a pro bono basis; CAP opposes regulations prohibiting prepayment penalties because it believes such regulation will raise the cost of credit to unacceptable levels. CAP instructs you to lobby against certain regulatory proposals. *Must* you inform CAP that you also represent the First National Bank who will be pleased by CAP's position? Look at Rule 6.4. *May* you represent CAP without the First National Bank's consent?

b. Assume that you fully inform the CAP and the First National Bank of your representation of each. Must you also voluntarily disclose to the regulatory agency that in representing CAP you also further the interests of the First National Bank? Look at Model Rule 3.9, DR 7–106(B)(2) and EC 7–15. May you state that you represent "CAP and another client whose name is privileged"?

c. Should your conclusion as to disclosure of all of your clients differ if you were involved in litigation challenging the regulations in court? Consider DR 7–106(B)(2). Is it reasonable to argue that a court's decision is supposed to be based on the law, not on its favorable feelings toward the plaintiff, and thus that the First National Bank's interest in the litigation should be irrelevant to the court?

d. If you were testifying in a legislative hearing, would you have to disclose the dual representation? Does the Model Code draw a distinction between courts and administrative or legislative tribunals for this purpose? Should it? Does Model Rule 3.3 adopt the requirements of DR 7–106(B)(2)?

7. Does Model Rule 6.3 impose different obligations if you are a member of a legal service organization's board of directors while remaining in private practice?

a. May you agree to defend the First National Bank in a suit brought by the legal services organization's indigent client? Suppose the client alleges that the First National Bank has promoted practices that support "red-lining," a racially motivated refusal to lend mortgage money. In light of A.B.A. Formal Opinion 345 (July 12, 1979), in the Readings to this Problem, how should you react to the news that the legal services organization is planning to sue your client? May you seek to dissuade the staff lawyer from handling the case for the plaintiff? If you do represent the First National Bank, must you first resign from the Board of the legal services agency?[6]

b. John Erlenborn, a former member of Congress, was appointed by the President to the Board of the Legal Services Corporation ("LSC"). He was also a partner in a major law firm that represented growers in disputes over farm workers' conditions; the farm workers were often

---

6. For an opinion reaching a conclusion opposite to A.B.A. Formal Opinion 345, see N.Y. State Bar Ass'n Committee on Professional Ethics, Opinion 489 (Aug. 7, 1978).

represented by LSC-funded lawyers. The American Farm Bureau Federation, a private lobbying group representing agricultural interests, began a campaign to persuade the firm's agricultural clients (the Farm Bureau was not one of the firm's clients) to object to what the Farm Bureau characterized as Erlenborn's conflict of interest, i.e., he took positions as an LSC board member that the Farm Bureau claimed were harmful to farm interests.

Erlenborn offered to recuse himself from any decisions of the LSC board that directly involved reform legislation that the Farm Bureau supported, or that involved agricultural activities that could have an impact on his firm's clients, but the Farm Bureau's objections (including its objection to Erlenborn's proposed congressional testimony on the reform legislation) continued until Erlenborn resigned from the LSC board. The ABA President-elect said that there was no conflict of interests that required Erlenborn's resignation.[7] Do you agree? Was Erlenborn ethically required to resign from the LSC board, or was he simply bending over backwards to please some firm clients?

8. Would it be better for a lawyer to avoid cultivating outside interests that might interfere with his or her legal practice? Would the losses in terms of public leadership be more significant than the private gains?

a. Paul Cravath of the New York bar encouraged outside *non-*business activities in his firm:

> * * * Cravath himself gave much time to charitable, educational and artistic activities. He wanted his partners and associates to have such interests, and believed that the few who allowed work to pre-empt all their energies were harming themselves and the firm. * * * [8] Do you agree?

b. An important development of the 1960s and 70s was for lawyers to be active in *pro bono* activities along with their private practice.[9] Some have suggested that the "public spirit" has waned as economic conditions have made jobs and clients harder to get. Do the conflicts rules themselves impose opportunity costs (i.e., business that cannot be accepted because of the conflict rules), and make it too expensive for a lawyer to take pro bono cases?

---

7. Kornhauser, Sowing Client Discord, Reaping Political Fallout, 13 Legal Times of Washington 1, 15–16 (June 25, 1990).

8. R.T. Swaine, 2 The Cravath Firm and Its Predecessors 9 (1948). The views set forth in this extract may or may not represent the views of the Cravath firm today.

9. See, e.g., Berman & Cohn, Bargaining for Justice: The Law Student's Challenge to Law Firms, 5 Harv.Civ.Rts.—Civ. Lib.L.Rev. 16 (1970).

READINGS

CINEMA 5, LIMITED v. CINERAMA, INC.
United States Court of Appeals, Second Circuit, 1976.
528 F.2d 1384.

Before MOORE, FEINBERG and VAN GRAAFEILAND, Circuit Judges.

VAN GRAAFEILAND, Circuit Judge. This appeal from an order granting defendants' motion to disqualify plaintiff's counsel presents a somewhat unusual set of facts. Counsel has been disqualified from further representation of plaintiff because a partner in this New York City law firm is also a partner in a Buffalo firm which is presently representing the defendant Cinerama, Inc. in other litigation of a somewhat similar nature. Although we agree with the district court that there was no actual wrongdoing and intend no criticism of the lawyers involved, we find no abuse of the district court's discretion, and so affirm.

There is little or no dispute as to the facts, most of them having been stipulated. Attorney Manly Fleischmann is a partner in Jaeckle, Fleischmann and Mugel of Buffalo and in Webster, Sheffield, Fleischmann, Hitchcock and Brookfield of New York City. He divides his time between the two offices. Cinerama is a distributor of motion pictures and the operator of several large theater chains. In January 1972 the Jaeckle firm was retained to represent Cinerama and several other defendants in an action brought in the United States District Court for the Western District of New York. Plaintiffs in that suit are local upstate theater operators who allege anti-trust violations resulting from discriminatory and monopolistic licensing and distribution of motion pictures in the Rochester area. A similar action involving allegedly illegal distribution in the Buffalo area was commenced in March 1974, and the Jaeckle office represents the interests of Cinerama in this action also. Both suits are presently pending in the Western District.

The instant action, brought in the Southern District of New York in August 1974, alleges a conspiracy among the defendants to acquire control of plaintiff corporation through stock acquisitions, with the intention of creating a monopoly and restraining competition in New York City's first-run motion picture theater market. Judge Brieant found that there was sufficient relationship between the two law firms and the two controversies to inhibit future confidential communications between Cinerama and its attorneys and that disqualification was required to avoid even the appearance of professional impropriety, citing as authority our decision in General Motors Corp. v. City of New York, 501 F.2d 639 (2d Cir.1974).

Appellant's counsel strongly dispute these findings. They say that they should not be disqualified unless the relationship between the controversies is substantial, and they contend there is nothing substantial in the relationship between an upstate New York conspiracy to deprive local theater operators of access to films and an attempted corporate take-over in New York City.

The "substantial relationship" test is indeed the one that we have customarily applied in determining whether a lawyer may accept employment against a former client. * * * However, in this case, suit is not against a former client, but an existing one. One firm in which attorney Fleischmann is a partner is suing an actively represented client of another firm in which attorney Fleischmann is a partner. The propriety of this conduct must be measured not so much against the similarities in litigation, as against the duty of undivided loyalty which an attorney owes to each of his clients.

A lawyer's duty to his client is that of a fiduciary or trustee. * * * When Cinerama retained Mr. Fleischmann as its attorney in the Western District litigation, it was entitled to feel that at least until that litigation was at an end, it had his undivided loyalty as its advocate and champion, * * * and could rely upon his "undivided allegiance and faithful, devoted service." * * * Because "no man can serve two masters", Matthew 6:24; * * * it had the right to expect also that he would "accept no retainer to do anything that might be adverse to his client's interests." * * * Needless to say, when Mr. Fleischmann and his New York City partners undertook to represent Cinema 5, Ltd., they owed it the same fiduciary duty of undivided loyalty and allegiance.

Ethical Considerations 5–1 and 5–14 of the American Bar Association's Code of Professional Responsibility provide that the professional judgment of a lawyer must be exercised solely for the benefit of his client, free of compromising influences and loyalties, and this precludes his acceptance of employment that will adversely affect his judgment or dilute his loyalty. The Code has been adopted by the New York State Bar Association, and its canons are recognized by both Federal and State Courts as appropriate guidelines for the professional conduct of New York lawyers.

Under the Code, the lawyer who would sue his own client, asserting in justification the lack of "substantial relationship" between the litigation and the work he has undertaken to perform for that client, is leaning on a slender reed indeed. Putting it as mildly as we can, we think it would be questionable conduct for an attorney to participate in any lawsuit against his own client without the knowledge and consent of all concerned. * * *

Whether such adverse representation, without more, requires disqualification in every case, is a matter we need not now decide. We do hold, however, that the "substantial relationship" test does not set a sufficiently high standard by which the necessity for disqualification should be determined. That test may properly be applied only where the representation of a former client has been terminated and the parameters of such relationship have been fixed. Where the relationship is a continuing one, adverse representation is prima facie improper, * * * and the attorney must be prepared to show, at the very least, that there will be no actual or *apparent* conflict in loyalties or diminution in the vigor of his representation. We think that appellants have failed to meet this heavy burden and that, so long as Mr. Fleischmann and his Buffalo partners continue to represent Cinerama, he and his New York City

partners should not represent Cinema 5, Ltd. in this litigation. * * *
[T]he record shows that after learning of the conflict which had developed, the Jaeckle firm, through Mr. Fleischmann, offered to withdraw its representation of Cinerama in the Western District actions. However, that offer was not accepted, and Mr. Fleischmann continued, albeit reluctantly, to have one foot in each camp.

Under the circumstances, Judge Brieant's order of disqualification cannot be construed as an abuse of his discretion. We therefore affirm.

A.B.A. FORMAL OPINION 345 (RECONSIDERATION OF INFORMAL OPINION 1395)

(July 12, 1979).*

* * *

The question addressed in Informal Opinion 1395 was whether it was ethical for attorney-members of the Board of Directors of a legal services program ("Program" hereafter) to represent clients under circumstances where the opposing party was already represented by the staff attorneys of the Program. To fully consider the issue, we deem it best to broaden the inquiry by examining not only the narrow question posed, but also the situation where suit is brought on behalf of a client by a Board member or lawyer in the Board member's firm against an individual who comes to the Program to defend the case. In that circumstance, must the staff lawyer disqualify himself? Must both sets of lawyers disqualify themselves?

The result in Informal Opinion 1395 (to the effect that a member of a Board of Directors of a Program could not ethically represent a party where the opposing party was represented by a Program attorney) was reached by relying on Disciplinary Rules 5–101(A) and 5–105. * * *

The Committee, upon due reflection, has concluded that these provisions would not be violated necessarily by the representation by the Board member or his firm of a client involved in litigation with a Program client. The Program staff lawyers are the lawyers for the client. Accordingly, the lawyer-Board member does not have a lawyer-client relationship with the Program client so the problem is not one of a lawyer representing clients with conflicting interests.

The Board is required by our prior opinions, the Code, and by its own rules to insulate the staff from any influence, whatsoever, attempted by the Board or any member thereof with respect to individual cases. The Board's role is restricted solely to establishment of broad policy for the Program, and not the management of or the direct participation in Program client representation. The Committee in Formal Opinion 334,

* Excerpted, with permission, from Recent Ethics Opinions, as updated 1981, copyright American Bar Association.

stressed the ethical duty of Board members to use their positions to set broad policy guidelines for priorities based on consideration of client community need for legal services and the resources available to the Program. * * *

Having said all this, the Committee does not concur that there is no problem in a Board member's representation of a client adverse to a Program client. Depending upon the nature of the case, the circumstances of the clients or otherwise, one counsel or the other may feel unexpectedly self-restrained from representation of the client in the fullest sense. From the clients' side it should not be overlooked that clients in the poverty group, particularly, may tend to be submissive and to acquiesce in the representation—feeling that they have no choice, but at the same time feeling concerned that they may not be getting independent representation. The real possibility of an appearance of impropriety, even though no actual impropriety may exist, is also troubling to the Committee.

Accordingly, it is important that the Board and clients on both sides be made aware of the Board member's role and the fact that he or a lawyer in his firm is representing a client opposing a Program client. The clients and counsel on both sides must feel comfortable that in the particular circumstances neither client will be deprived of independent and uninhibited representation. Lawyers on both sides must be sensitive and alert to these possibilities and, if, in the course of the representation, it becomes apparent that independent representation is not being afforded on both sides or one or the other of the clients perceives that it is not afforded, no matter what the reality, then the lawyers should assist in change of counsel for one or both clients.

In those situations where the firm of a Board member is large enough to provide lawyers other than the Board member to represent clients who are in dispute with clients of the Program, this is preferable to having the Board member directly involved in the representation. In such situations, the Committee urges that the Board member's firm provide screening procedures such as those suggested in Formal Opinion 342 so that the Board member has no knowledge and no access to knowledge concerning the particular litigated matter. * * *

Because of the extreme value of having active practitioners who are litigators themselves (or who have partners who are) serve as Board members, the Committee does not wish to raise artificial barriers to their participation on Program Boards by forcing them to choose between service on a Board and representation of their clients. It should be noted that in some smaller communities it is impossible to secure qualified lawyer-members for Boards who would not be involved from time to time representing clients opposing persons represented by Program staff lawyers. Recognizing the need for qualified lawyer-Board members, Program staff lawyers should not seek unfairly to gain advantage for their clients by disqualification of the Board member or his firm. To the extent that the Program can make available to its clients competent volunteer legal counsel in these situations, Program clients can be offered an alternative. On the other side, a Board member should be sensitive to the possible problems posed by such relationships and should be quick to disqualify himself and his firm in proper cases.

On balance, the Committee concludes that the compelling need for resources, not the least of which is strong interest in legal services and participation on Program Boards by active practitioners, to provide legal services for the indigent outweighs the risk of any possible appearances of impropriety in those cases where adequate representation is provided by Board members (or members of their firms) for one side and Program staff attorneys for the other. * * *

PROBLEM 11

Conflict of Interest in Criminal Litigation

Barbara Bentley regularly represents Bitter Creek, Inc, the defendant in a case charging price fixing, a criminal violation of the federal antitrust laws. Chuck Carson, manager of the widget division at Bitter Creek is accused of conspiring with Mary Morton, his counterpart at Widgetech, Inc., a major competitor. In Bentley's first interview with Carson, Carson told Bentley he was unrepresented and asked her to represent him. Carson told Bentley that Mary Morton also needed a lawyer and thought it would be best if Bentley would represent her as well. Widgetech, Inc., has in–house counsel and Bentley already has been meeting with him to share information and develop a joint defense.

Bentley confirmed Morton's interest in retaining her and she has now entered an appearance on behalf of Bitter Creek, Carson and Morton. The United States Attorney is interested in demonstrating his commitment to consumers because he plans to run for Governor next year. Thus, he is determined to obtain convictions, although he does not care who takes the fall. He proposes to Bentley that she get Carson and Morton to plead guilty to charges for which he will recommend no jail time. In exchange, he will drop the felony charge against Bitter Creek. Because this will reduce the chance of subsequent treble damage actions against the corporation, Bentley finds the proposal attractive. She recommends that Carson and Morton accept it, accurately telling them that if they were found guilty after a trial, their sentences could be more severe.

QUESTIONS

1. Should a single lawyer be able to represent two or more co-defendants in a criminal case?

a. For federal criminal cases like the one in this problem, Rule 44(c), Federal Rules of Criminal Procedure provides:

"(c) JOINT REPRESENTATION. Whenever two or more defendants have been jointly charged pursuant to Rule 8(b) or have been joined for trial pursuant to Rule 13, and are represented by the same retained or assigned counsel or by retained or assigned counsel who are associated in the practice of law, the court shall promptly inquire with respect to such joint representation and shall personally advise each defendant of his right to the effective assistance of counsel, including separate representation. Unless it appears that there is good cause to believe no conflict of interest is likely to arise, the court shall take such measures as may be appropriate to protect each defendant's right to counsel."

b. Should state trial courts be required to make a similar inquiry? Holloway v. Arkansas, 435 U.S. 475, 98 S.Ct. 1173, 55 L.Ed.2d 426 (1978), held that a state criminal conviction must be reversed if a trial judge requires joint representation in a criminal case after a defendant's timely objection. The joint representation is presumed prejudicial. "Joint representation of conflicting interests is suspect because of what it tends to prevent the attorney from doing."

In *Holloway*, the joint representation may have precluded defense counsel "from exploring possible plea negotiations and the possibility of an agreement to testify for the prosecution, provided a lesser charge or a favorable sentencing recommendation would be acceptable. [A] conflict may also prevent an attorney from challenging the admission of evidence prejudicial to one client but perhaps favorable to another, or from arguing at the sentencing hearing the relative involvement and culpability of his clients in order to minimize the culpability of one by emphasizing that of another." [1]

c. Was Bentley's independent judgment on behalf of each client compromised here? Notice that the federal rules requires the Court to "take such measures as may be appropriate to protect each defendant's right to counsel." What kind of inquiry should the judge conduct in this case to assure the effective assistance of counsel for Carson and Morton?

2. Should the prosecution have standing to "protect" defendants from such multiple representation?

a. Deputy Assistant Attorney General Joe Sims once announced that the Antitrust Division would aggressively seek to stop such multiple

---

1. Contrast Burger v. Kemp, 483 U.S. 776, 107 S.Ct. 3114, 97 L.Ed.2d 638 (1987). One lawyer represented one defendant and the lawyer's partner represented the co-defendant in a separate proceeding. The Court (5 to 4) explained that *Holloway* had rejected a per se approach and required a showing that the conflict had an adverse effect on the lawyer's performance; the Court would presume prejudice "only if the defendant demonstrates that counsel 'actively represented conflicting interests' and that 'an actual conflict of interest adversely affected his lawyer's performance.' " Here, the two partners did talk about trial strategy, but there were separate trials, reducing any incentive of one lawyer to change tactics for the benefit of the other client. There was no argument that any conflict prevented counsel from negotiating a plea bargain because the prosecutor refused to bargain. And, even if there was an actual conflict of interest, the majority concluded that it did not harm the lawyer's advocacy.

representation by seeking relief from the court having supervisory power over the grand jury. "[T]hese conflicts—where both the corporation and potentially culpable employees are represented by a single counsel—are so inherently serious that there should be a presumption against such multiple representation during a criminal investigation." He continued

"the target corporation all too often sees its best interest served by keeping witnesses in 'friendly' hands and limiting the cooperation of its employees. Such an attitude will inevitably lead to bad advice for the individual if he does not have independent counsel. [M]erely informing the employee of the existence of the potential conflict and seeking a waiver from him [does not] satisfactorily deal with this problem. For example, it is frequently in the interest of one or more low level employees in a corporation to seek immunity by offering evidence against higher level employees or the corporation itself. In this situation, even if there has been a waiver, it is impossible for a single lawyer to give each of his clients effective legal representation." [2]

Mr. Sims was writing about facts close to the ones in this Problem. Do you agree with him? What if it is in fact in the best interests of all defendants to keep each other in "friendly" hands rather than risk the chance that one of the parties will plead guilty and implicate the others? Do public policy and professional responsibility forbid, or require, the attorney to seek knowing waivers of the conflicts and participate in a "We're all in this together" arrangement? See ABA Standards Relating to the Defense Function, § 4–3.5(b), in the Standards Supplement.

b. In Wheat v. United States, 486 U.S. 153, 108 S.Ct. 1692, 100 L.Ed.2d 140 (1988), the Supreme Court (5 to 4) held that the district court was within its discretion in rejecting defendant's waiver of his right to conflict-free counsel and by refusing to permit defendant's proposed substitution of attorneys. Two days before trial, defendant asked to be represented by the lawyer who was representing others charged in a series of cases against an alleged drug conspiracy. The government objected on the grounds that defendants in some cases would be witnesses in others. If the same lawyer represented them all, he would be restricted in his cross-examination of his clients when they were witnesses and would lay the predicate for a later claim of ineffective assistance of counsel. [3]

The Court upheld the district court's power to limit the joint representation: "Federal courts have an independent interest in ensuring that criminal trials are conducted within the ethical standards of the profession and that legal proceedings appear fair to all who observe

2. Bureau of Nat'l Affairs, Antitrust & Trade Reg.Rptr., No. 819, June 23, 1977, at p. A–13.

3. See also, Burden v. Zant, ___ U.S. ___, 114 S.Ct. 654, 126 L.Ed.2d 611 (1994), a very brief opinion remanding for factual findings to see if pretrial counsel's representation of a prosecution witness who had been granted immunity created an actual conflict affecting the result.

them. Both the American Bar Association's Model Code of Professional Responsibility and its Model Rules of Professional Conduct * * * impose limitations on multiple representation of clients. DR 5–105(C); Rule 1.7. Not only the interest of a criminal defendant but the institutional interest in the rendition of just verdicts in criminal cases may be jeopardized by unregulated multiple representation. * * * The District Court must recognize a presumption in favor of petitioner's counsel of choice, but that presumption may be overcome not only by a demonstration of actual conflict but by a showing of a serious potential for conflict."

c.   United States v. LoCascio, 6 F.3d 924 (2d Cir.1993), involved the prosecution of John Gotti. Bruce Cutler had very effectively represented Gotti in previous criminal trials. The Government did not want him to do so again. This time, he had been caught on tapes of conversations with Gotti that the Government intended to introduce at trial to show the planning of illegal acts. Thus, even if Cutler would not be called to testify, he was said to be in a position analogous to an "unsworn witness" who would be forced to defend his own conduct before the jury.[4] Further, Cutler had once represented a Gotti associate, Michael Coiro, who had now turned government witness. He would thus be impaired in cross-examining Coiro. Over Gotti's objection, the Court intervened to "protect" Gotti from Mr. Cutler's conflicts. The Second Circuit affirmed. Do you suppose Mr. Gotti was grateful for the court's concern for his welfare?

3.   Do items of information shared in multi-lawyer conferences or conferences with multiple defendants constitute "confidences" or "secrets" of the client(s)?

a.   Assume that the Widgetech lawyer has told Bentley things that he would not tell the prosecutor. Does Bentley need his permission before she uses the information to try to get a better deal for Bitter Creek, Carson and Morton? Is a secret still secret once it is told to others? Cf. Rule 1.9(b).

Schmitt v. Emery, 211 Minn. 547, 554, 2 N.W.2d 413, 417 (1942), held that if an attorney furnishes a copy of a document entrusted to him by his client to an attorney who is engaged in maintaining substantially the same cause on behalf of other parties in the same litigation, even without an express understanding that the recipient shall not communicate the contents thereof to others, the "recipient of the copy stands

4. In a related line of cases, the court will disqualify a lawyer who represents a client in a criminal case and is also personally a target of the investigation. United States v. Fulton, 5 F.3d 605 (2d Cir.1993), was a prosecution for importation of heroin where one lawyer represented four co–defendants. One of the defendants had told the DEA that the lawyer was himself personally involved in the heroin sales. The U.S. Attorney informed the Court, and the Second Circuit held that where a defense lawyer is accused of being involved in the same or closely related criminal conduct, the conflict is per se unwaivable and that continued representation constitutes ineffective assistance of counsel. See also, United States v. Salinas, 618 F.2d 1092 (5th Cir.1980) (per curiam), cert. denied 449 U.S. 961, 101 S.Ct. 374, 66 L.Ed.2d 228 (1980).

under the same restraints arising from the privileged character of the document as the counsel who furnished it, and consequently he has no right, and cannot be compelled, to produce or disclose it contents [by oral testimony]."

See also, Hunydee v. United States, 355 F.2d 183 (9th Cir.1965). At a joint conference attended by two defendants (husband and wife) and their separate attorneys, the husband agreed to plead guilty of income tax evasion and "take the blame." But he went to trial, and the Government, over objection, had the wife and her attorney testify to what was said at this joint conference. The court held that it was error to admit the testimony. The joint conference was privileged to the extent it concerned a common issue and was intended to facilitate representation in possible subsequent proceedings.

b. McCormick, on the other hand, qualified that principle:

"When two or more persons, each having an interest in some problem or situation, jointly consult an attorney, their confidential communications with the attorney, though known to each other, will of course be privileged in a controversy of either or both of the clients with the outside world, that is, with parties claiming adversely to both or either of those within the original charmed circle. But it will often happen that the two original clients will fall out among themselves and become engaged in a controversy in which the communications at their joint consultation with the lawyer may be vitally material. In such a controversy it is clear that the privilege is inapplicable." [5]

c. The Commentary to Proposed (but not enacted) Rule 503 of the Federal Rules of Evidence was also cautious. It said that in the "joint defense" or "pooled information" situation, the "better view" is not that one of the various clients "could prevent another from disclosing what the other had himself said," but rather that "if all resist disclosure, none will occur."

d. Does all this suggest that the decision of multiple defendants to adopt a common defense is not risk free? Cf. Note, The Attorney–Client Privilege in Multiple Party Situations, 8 Columbia J.Law & Social Problems 179, 180–81 (1972) (survey of lawyers indicating a lack of awareness as to when the attorney-client privilege will apply to multi-lawyer exchanges of information in joint conferences).

4. Of what relevance is it that the prosecutor in this problem is highly motivated to get convictions that will tend to further his political ambitions?

a. Could a prosecutor's personal motives ever constitute a conflict of interest with his or her duties as a public prosecutor? In most cases, will they instead reinforce the incentive to perform the public duties?

5. McCormick on Evidence (E. Cleary,   ted).
3d ed. 1984), § 91, at 219 (footnote omit-

Look at ABA Standards, The Prosecution Function § 3–1.3 and 3–3.9, in the Standards Supplement.

b.   In People v. Superior Court (Greer), 19 Cal.3d 255, 137 Cal. Rptr. 476, 561 P.2d 1164 (1977), the Court upheld the decision of the trial court to disqualify the district attorney from prosecuting a murder case.   The unusual conflict was based on the fact that the victim's mother was employed in the office of the prosecutor.   Moreover, the mother was scheduled to be a material witness for the prosecution, and if the defendant were convicted, the mother would stand to gain custody of her grandchild.   Evidence surrounding the arrest of the criminal defendant suggested that the arrest had been used to aid the victim's mother in gaining such custody.   The Court concluded that a "district attorney may thus prosecute vigorously, but both the accused and the public have a legitimate expectation that his zeal, as reflected in his tactics at trial, will be born of objective and impartial consideration of each individual case."   137 Cal.Rptr. at 484, 561 P.2d at 1172.[6]

c.   Young v. United States ex rel. Vuitton et Fils S.A., 481 U.S. 787, 107 S.Ct. 2124, 95 L.Ed.2d 740 (1987), was an important Supreme Court case on prosecutor conflict of interest.   The District Court had issued an injunction against violation of Vuitton's trademark.   When it was learned that defendants were violating the trademark, Vuitton's counsel asked the District Court to appoint him as special prosecutor to bring a charge of criminal contempt against defendants.   The court did so.   The Supreme Court reversed the contempt conviction (5 to 4), holding that such a case constitutes an actual conflict of interest because the special prosecutor also represented the private party who would be the beneficiary of the court order allegedly violated.   While the trial court has inherent authority to appoint someone to enforce its order, the matter must be referred first to the public prosecutor.   If he refused to prosecute, the court should appoint someone not connected to the civil plaintiff.   Only in that way can the court avoid the "potential for private interest to influence the discharge of public duty".[7]

d.   In re Complaint of Rook, 276 Or. 695, 556 P.2d 1351 (1976) (per curiam), involved a state district attorney accused of refusing to plea bargain with 15 criminal defendants on the same basis as previously offered to another criminal defendant so long as the 15 were represented by either of two attorneys.   After the two attorneys withdrew as counsel and another attorney represented the 15, the district attorney allowed the 15 to accept the plea bargain that he had earlier offered the other

---

6. The subsequent California statute modifying the standard for prosecutor disqualification was explained and construed in People v. Conner, 34 Cal.3d 141, 193 Cal.Rptr. 148, 666 P.2d 5 (1983).

7. Federal Trade Commission v. American National Cellular, 868 F.2d 315 (9th Cir.1989), considered what effect *Vuitton* should have on the FTC practice of having its attorneys act as special prosecutors to punish TRO violations in its cases.   The court found *Vuitton* not controlling where a government lawyer rather than a private attorney was acting as special prosecutor. Appearances are important, however, the court said.   The U.S. Attorney's office should be in control of the contempt matter, although it may then delegate prosecution to the agency attorney.

defendant. When the district attorney was asked to explain his position, he is reported to have said that one of the unacceptable defense attorneys was involved in "organized crime" and that he was upset with the other for saying "bad things" about him. The state Supreme Court publicly reprimanded the district attorney. The court found a violation of DR 1–102(A)(5), based on a state statute which provided, inter alia, that "[s]imilarly situated defendants should be afforded equal plea bargaining opportunities;" and a finding that the accused was motivated in his conduct not only by frustration but also by "animosity and a desire to punish" supported the finding of a violation of DR 7–102(A)(1).

e.   People ex rel. Clancy v. Superior Court (Ebel), 39 Cal.3d 740, 218 Cal.Rptr. 24, 705 P.2d 347 (1985), cert.denied 475 U.S. 1121, 106 S.Ct. 1638, 90 L.Ed.2d 184 (1986), examined the incentives created by "privatization" of prosecutorial services. A city had hired a private attorney to bring abatement proceedings against an adult book store. The fee arrangement with the lawyer provided that his fee would double if he won the case. The court cited EC 7–13, and pointed to the "prosecutor's duty of neutrality" which stems from the fact that "he is a representative of the sovereign" and "has the vast power of the government available to him." Giving the prosecutor a contingent fee compromised the duty of fairness and neutrality inherent in the role of prosecutor, the Court said, and the private attorney was disqualified. Do you agree with this result? Should DR 2–106(C) and Model Rule 1.5(d)(2) now be revised so that they are not limited to the case of "a contingent fee for representing a *defendant* in a criminal case"? (emphasis added).

5. To what extent, if any, may either the prosecutor or defense attorney personally and financially benefit from the publicity surrounding a major trial?

a.   Is any ethical restriction placed on a prosecutor who wishes to write a book on his or her legal adventures? Should the prosecutor wait until after leaving office to write it? Might the possibility of future royalties improperly influence conduct of the prosecutor while in office? Compare DR 5–104(B) and Rule 1.8(d).

b.   May a criminal defense lawyer write a book about his trials, or a particular case he defended?

People v. Corona, 80 Cal.App.3d 684, 720, 145 Cal.Rptr. 894, 915 (1st Dist.1978), held that by entering into a literary rights contract with the accused prior to trial, he "was forced to choose between his own pocketbook and the best interests of his client, the accused." The lawyer's financial stake in the literary rights encouraged him to insist on a lengthy and sensational trial, rather than invoke various defenses which might abort or change the nature of the trial.

Compare United States v. Hearst, 638 F.2d 1190, 1193–95 (9th Cir.1980), where a hearing was ordered in which Hearst would be required to show that the conflict in fact affected the lawyer's judgment whether to seek a continuance and a change of venue, and whether to have the defendant testify. It would not be necessary, however, for her to show that the conflict actually changed the result in the case.

c. Should a client be able to waive the protection of Rule 1.8(d) and DR 5–104(B)? The California Supreme Court in Maxwell v. Superior Court of Los Angeles County, 30 Cal.3d 606, 180 Cal.Rptr. 177, 639 P.2d 248 (1982), allowed waiver by relying on California Rule 5–101 allowing lawyers to enter into business relations adverse to a client if the client consents. The defendant, charged with capital crimes, signed a contract with his attorneys in which the attorneys promised to act competently but also warned the defendant of the possible conflicts and prejudice which the publication agreement would create: "It declares that counsel may wish to (1) create damaging publicity to enhance exploitation value, (2) avoid mental defenses because, if successful, they might suggest petitioner's incapacity to make the contract, and (3) see him convicted and even sentenced to death for publicity value." The court did not require disqualification of defense counsel but it also did not deny the possibility of later discipline of the attorney.

Do you agree with this result? Is the purpose of the publication rights rule only to protect the defendant? Is there also a systemic interest in seeing that defendants get a fair trial? If the latter interest is relevant, should it be improper for a court to accept the defendant's "waiver" of the conflict?

d. May a criminal defense lawyer secure literary rights *after* the conclusion of the legal matter? See ABA Defense Function Standard § 4–3.4, in the Standards Supplement. Why should this distinction be drawn? Might publication of a lawyer's memoirs waive the attorney-client privilege of the clients regardless of when the contract is made? See, e.g., In re von Bulow, 828 F.2d 94 (2d Cir.1987) (privilege waived as to matters specifically revealed in book; thus, those facts can be used against the client in later civil litigation; no waiver as to broader subject matter surrounding the facts disclosed).

PROBLEM 12

Conflicts Between Client Interests and the Lawyer's Personal Interest

Attorney Joan Doe went to high school with James Johnson, a local engineer. Johnson asked Doe to help him set up a small business. He had very little money, and the capital he had raised from a few local investors was not enough to pay much of a legal fee. Johnson asked if he could pay the fee over an extended period of time, with interest. Instead, Doe suggested that Johnson pay her by giving her 10 percent of the stock in the new corporation as payment for all work necessary to establish it and carry it through the first year. Doe thought the business looked like a good, relatively cheap investment opportunity, and after Johnson agreed to the arrangement, Doe drafted the articles of incorporation, by-laws and a shareholders' agreement.

Johnson's company is now doing very well. Doe has learned from him that the company will be building a new plant in an industrial park near town. The plans for the industrial park are a secret to all but a few people, and Doe realizes that property in proximity to the park is likely to increase in value. She knows of such a nearby parcel that is for sale, and, after concluding that Johnson probably does not plan to buy it, she has now done so.

After his company had made its first million dollars, Johnson was thrilled. "Joan", he said, "you have been my lawyer these three years and I could not have succeeded without you. Please draw up the papers to transfer the title to my 1994 Mercedes Benz to yourself." The car is worth $75,000. Doe is stunned and does not know how to reply to Johnson's generous request.

QUESTIONS

1. Is any real or potential ethical problem presented by Doe's accepting payment from Johnson in the form of stock?

a. Was it proper for Doe to suggest that she be paid in stock rather than in cash? Compare Rule 1.8(a) with DR 5–104(A) and EC 5–3. Look also at Committee on Professional Ethics v. Mershon, in the Readings to this Problem. Is the court's approach in *Mershon* tougher than you might have expected?

b. May Doe ethically write into the Articles of Incorporation or By–Laws a requirement that the corporation pay a minimum proportion of its profits in dividends each year? If the corporation later fails to pay dividends, would there be any ethical problem in her suing the corporation to have the dividends paid?

c. If Doe obtains the stock from Johnson, would it be proper for her to invest some of her other funds in a competing company so as to "hedge her bets"? See, e.g., Morgan v. North Coast Cable Co., 586 N.E.2d 88 (Ohio 1992), where the lawyer had apparently previously represented the opponent and had obtained a limited partnership interest in it, perhaps as part of the fee. The lawyer obtained waivers of the former-client conflict, but the opponent/defendant wanted to prevent the lawyer from representing the current client on the grounds that the lawyer was also a limited partner in the opponent. The Court held that this concern was not grounds for disqualification, but the lawyer must be sure that the current client consents to his continuing representation of it under these circumstances.

d. What are the lawyer's obligations if she gets a job offer from someone with interests adverse to those of her client? In its Opinion 1991–1 (April 30, 1991), the Association of the Bar of the City of New York said that if the lawyer believes that the offer will cloud the lawyer's judgment, he or she must withdraw. Even if the lawyer believes there will be no effect on his or her judgment, the lawyer must tell the client of the offer and get consent to continuing the representation. Absent consent, the lawyer must withdraw.

The opinion seems clearly correct in principle (see Model Rule 1.12(b) on judges' law clerks), but the practical impact on our mobile lawyer population could be profound. Will it be evidence of malpractice not to have disclosed the offer, for example, if the client does not like the result in the case? Will the partners of the lawyer also be liable for malpractice even though the lawyer had not told them of the negotiations and they had no way to compel disclosure?

2. May Doe, without Johnson's consent, invest in the parcel near the industrial park?

a. Is the only proper question whether or not Johnson's interests are adversely affected? Notice that the ABA Canons of Professional Ethics (1908), Canon 11 and 37, in the Standards Supplement, prohibited the lawyer from using secret or confidential client information, even if the lawyer did not reveal this information to third parties and even if the client did not suffer detriment. See, e.g., Healy v. Gray, 184 Iowa 111, 119, 168 N.W. 222, 225 (1918).

b. Compare Rule 1.8(b) with DR 4–101(B)(3). Why did the Model Code take the position it did? Do you agree with the change made by the Model Rules?

c. A lawyer is an agent of the client; the client is the principal. The typical agency rule is that an agent may not use secret information of a principal without securing the principal's consent. See, A.L.I., Restatement (Second) Agency, § 388, Comment *c* :

> "[If] a corporation has decided to operate an enterprise at a place where land values will be increased because of such operation, a corporate officer who takes advantage of his special knowledge to buy land in the vicinity is accountable for the profits he makes, even though such purchases have no adverse effect upon the enterprise."

d. A.L.I. Restatement of the Law, Third, The Law Governing Lawyers (Tent. Draft No. 3, 1990), § 111(1) provides, on the other hand, that a lawyer "shall not use or disclose confidential client information * * * about a client if there is a reasonable likelihood that doing so will adversely affect a material interest of the client or if the client has directed that the lawyer not use or disclose it." Otherwise, the lawyer may use client secrets for the lawyer's personal benefit. Comment 3 explains:

> "Section 111(1) prohibits a lawyer against using or disclosing confidential client information solely for the lawyer's personal enrichment, if doing so may result in financial harm, disadvantage in a present or future legal representation, or any other prejudice to a client. Subject to that limitation, and so long as otherwise legal, a lawyer may use confidential client

information in market transactions for the lawyer's own enrichment, as for the purpose of purchasing publicly traded shares of stock in a corporate client, so long as a careful and disinterested assessment of any possible risk to the client reveals that doing so creates no risk of prejudice to the client."

What do you think of proposed Restatement § 111(1)? Can the lawyer who plans such trading be in a position to engage in a "careful and disinterested assessment"? Why should the Restatement draft put the burden on the client to specifically direct the lawyer not to use the client's secret information? Would it be preferable to place the burden on the lawyer to ask the client's permission to use client secrets? Compare DR 4–101(B)(3).

Comment 3—unlike proposed § 111(1) itself—states that the lawyer's use of inside information must be "otherwise legal." Should that restriction be in the black letter? If a lawyer engages in illegal insider trading in a client's stock, and the trading does not hurt the client, is the lawyer immune from professional discipline?

3. What limits exist on Doe's accepting unsolicited gifts from happy clients?

a. Does the answer turn on the size of the gift? If the client insists, must Doe prepare the transfer documents? Are Model Rule 1.8(c) and ECs 5–5 & 5–6 consistent on this issue?

b. In re Barrick, 87 Ill.2d 233, 57 Ill.Dec. 725, 429 N.E.2d 842 (1981), was unusual in that the court did not discipline an attorney who wrote himself into the client's will. A widow had told her business manager that she wanted to leave her attorney a lifetime annuity amounting to his annual retainer ($12,000 per year). The manager relayed this information to the attorney, who advised her to select another lawyer to draft the will. The widow objected; she said that she did not want others to know her business. She was "adamant." The attorney drafted the new will as requested, eventually received the legacy, and the Attorney Registration and Disciplinary Commission brought disciplinary proceedings.

The state Supreme Court upheld the lawyer's conduct in the special circumstances of this case: "[A]lthough undue influence might [be] presumed, the evidence established that there was none. There was no overreaching by the respondent. On the contrary, he urged his client to employ another attorney until she would hear no more about it. Exactly how far to press the point was a matter of judgment, and we will not snipe at the respondent's."

c. Suppose that in our problem, Johnson had gone to separate counsel as the Model Code and Model Rules direct. What could such counsel have properly done? Is arm twisting or coercion by the regular lawyer all we should worry about? Is true undue influence by that lawyer something that will be likely to be overcome by having a new lawyer draft the document?

4. Why does the law regulate lawyers' business dealings with their clients?

a. The principal fear is that the lawyer will not give the client the detached judgment of the client's plans that the lawyer might otherwise give. Beery v. State Bar of California, 43 Cal.3d 802, 239 Cal.Rptr. 121, 739 P.2d 1289 (1987), illustrates the problem. A lawyer had represented a client in a personal injury suit and had been asked to write his will. The client wanted advice on what to do with his settlement and the lawyer advised him to invest it in a satellite venture that the lawyer told the client was a "good investment." The lawyer did not tell the client that the venture was in trouble, that it could borrow no money commercially, and that the lawyer was a principal in the venture. The client trusted the lawyer, invested, and lost $35,000. The court, rejecting the argument that the nondisclosures were technical or minor, suspended the lawyer from practice.

See also, Matter of Pappas, 159 Ariz. 516, 768 P.2d 1161 (1988), where the CPA/lawyer was marketing tax shelters to people he said he considered accounting clients. He became general partner in one of the deals that went bad. The court held that the business transactions violated DR 5–104(A), rejected the argument that he was not acting as a lawyer in the transactions, and suspended him from practice for five years.

b. Not all business transactions between lawyer and client necessarily lead to professional discipline, however, and the client is not always the victim. In re Kirsh, 973 F.2d 1454 (9th Cir.1992), involved a lawyer's loan to his client and close friend. The lawyer knew the friend was in financial trouble, loaned him $40,000, and took real property as security. He took the client's word that the title was good. It was not, the client took bankruptcy, and the lawyer alleged that he had been defrauded and thus that the debt should not be discharged. While lawyers ordinarily should not engage in business transactions with clients, the Court said, the purpose of that rule is to protect clients against overreaching; here the terms of the loan were fair and the lawyer was the victim. But, the Court found, there was no fraud because the lawyer could not reasonably rely on the client's representation about the title. Lawyers know how to determine the state of title, and a failure to do so cannot support a claim of reliance on the fraud.

c. In re Blackwelder, 615 N.E.2d 106 (Ind.1993), provides a warning to lawyers who realize they have committed malpractice. The clients sought to reopen a default judgment entered against them, but the lawyer missed the filing deadline for doing so, and he proposed to handle their bankruptcy free in exchange for a release from malpractice liability. The Court found that the clients had not been advised in writing to get independent counsel before signing the malpractice release and publicly reprimanded the lawyer. See Model Rule 1.8(h) and DR 6–102(A).

5. Suppose that Johnson and Doe now fall in love. Should the law prohibit an intimate relationship between lawyer and client?

a. ABA Formal Opinion 92–364 (1992) tackled this issue. It concentrated on (1) potential abuse of the fiduciary relationship between the lawyer and a vulnerable client, (2) loss of emotional distance from the client required for good professional judgment, (3) potential conflicts of interest between lawyer and client, and (4) confusion between what communications were made in a professional relationship and which were personal. The Opinion concludes:

> "[B]ecause of the danger of impairment to the lawyer's representation associated with a sexual relationship between lawyers and client, the lawyer would be well advised to refrain from such a relationship. If such a sexual relationship occurs and the impairment is not avoided, the lawyer will have violated ethical obligations to the client.

*   *   *

> "The client's consent to sexual relations alone will rarely be sufficient to eliminate this danger. In many cases, the client's ability to give meaningful consent is vitiated by the lawyer's potential undue influence and/or the emotional vulnerability of the client."

b. How do those considerations apply here. Is James Johnson, the client, likely weak or vulnerable, for example? Are Joan Doe's possible loss of emotional distance, potential conflicts of interest, and possible compromise of confidentiality of communications, however, all likely to be concerns?

c. Reported cases suggest why the problem is one the law should address.

Drucker's Case, 577 A.2d 1198 (N.H.1990), involved a lawyer who knew his client was under psychiatric care and emotionally fragile. The lawyer initiated, then ended their affair, but the client had fallen in love with him and her husband found her diary describing her feelings, thus making her divorce more tense. The Court found that the lawyer had taken advantage of his client and suspended him for two years.

In re Lewis, 415 S.E.2d 173 (Ga.1992), involved a lawyer who had a sexual relationship with the client while representing her in a child custody proceeding. The court noted that not only were issues of differential power and impaired judgment presented, but the fact of the relationship could affect whether the mother got custody of the children. Three justices voted for disbarment but the lawyer was only suspended, perhaps because lawyer and client had been lovers before the professional relationship began.

Suppressed v. Suppressed, 565 N.E.2d 101 (Ill.App.1990), involved a divorce client who testified that her lawyer twice took her to an apartment where he had her inhale something that disoriented her and then had sexual relations with her. She filed a discipline charge, but the Illinois ARDC did not take the conduct seriously and dismissed the matter. Here, an action alleging breach of fiduciary duty was also dismissed. The court reasoned that a lawyer's fiduciary obligation to a client is not to make sex a quid pro quo; this client felt coerced into sex, but that was not enough. Further, the client only suffered emotional harm, not "quantifiable" injury. Are you shocked by this result?

In Tante v. Herring, 264 Ga. 694 (1994), on the other hand, a woman consulted a lawyer for help in collecting a social security disability claim. The lawyer helped her get a favorable award, but when he learned of the woman's impaired emotional and mental functioning, he persuaded her to have an affair with him. He infected her with two strains of venereal disease and she in turn infected her husband. Both husband and wife were permitted to recover from the lawyer for breach of fiduciary duty. The lawyer was also suspended from practice for 18 months. In re Tante, 264 Ga. 692 (1994).

d. What should be the content of professional rules on this subject? The California Rules are good examples of efforts in this area. Look at California Rule 3–120 and California Business & Professions Code § 6106.9 in the Standards Supplement.

Note first that the California Rules only deal with intercourse or intimate touching. That may not be the only offensive conduct. In re Heilprin, 482 N.W.2d 908 (Wis.1992), disbarred the lawyer for asking women clients "sexually explicit and suggestive * * * questions". He had earlier been suspended after exposing himself to clients. The case suggests that conduct well short of physical contact can and probably should raise discipline issues.

Next, the California rules deal only with quid pro quo and intimidation-based advances by lawyers. Often, lawyers are much more sophisticated at playing on a client's vulnerability. A per se rule against relationships, however, strikes many as too extreme.

Third, the California rule has exceptions for family relationships, relationships that predated the representation, and relationships with a lawyer in the firm who is not personally representing the client.

The future of such rules is something to continue to watch. It is not that there is only one side to the problem; the courts have been worried about false accusations, and about unlimited liability for emotional distress. But the question of our professional accountability for how we treat our clients—particularly when they are vulnerable to over-reaching—should be basic to legal ethics.

READINGS

COMMITTEE ON PROFESSIONAL ETHICS
AND CONDUCT v. MERSHON

Supreme Court of Iowa, 1982.
316 N.W.2d 895.

McCORMICK, Justice.

This case involves review of a Grievance Commission report recommending that respondent be reprimanded for alleged ethical violations arising from a business transaction with a client. Because we find respondent's conduct violated the principle in DR 5–104(A), we adopt the recommendation.

From our de novo review of the record, we find the facts as follows. Respondent is a Cedar Falls attorney. He began to do tax and property work for Leonard O. Miller, a farmer, in 1951. Miller owned 100 acres of farmland adjacent to a country club near the city. In 1969, when he was 68, Miller became interested in developing the land for residential purposes. He employed a landscape architect and R.O. Schenk, of Schenk Engineering Company, to prepare a preliminary plat and market study.

When the preliminary work was completed, Miller brought Schenk to meet with respondent to discuss the project. Miller wished to proceed with the development but did not have sufficient funds to pay engineering costs. Schenk suggested that the three men form a corporation to which Miller would contribute the land, Schenk would contribute engineering services, and respondent would contribute legal services. They agreed the land was worth approximately $400 an acre. Schenk estimated engineering costs at $400 an acre, and he said legal costs were usually one half that amount.

After several conferences in early 1970, the three men formed a corporation, Union Township Development, Inc. Subsequently Miller conveyed the farmland to the corporation at a capitalized value of $12,500 and received 400 shares of stock. Schenk gave the corporation a $12,500 promissory note and also received 400 shares of stock. Respondent gave the corporation a $6,250 promissory note and received 200 shares of stock. The promissory notes were interest free and due at the discretion of the corporation. They were to represent the services to be rendered by Schenk and respondent.

Development plans were premised on the corporation's ability to obtain financing on the security of the farmland. As it turned out, the corporation was unable to borrow money unless the three individuals would guarantee the obligation personally. They refused to do so and financing was never obtained.

The trio met at least annually to discuss the development, but when Miller died on December 31, 1978, at the age of 77, the project was still at a stalemate. Respondent believed the parties had an oral agreement that if development did not occur he and Schenk would relinquish their interests in the corporation to Miller. Three days after Miller's death, he transferred his stock to the corporation. He asked Schenk to do the same thing, but Schenk refused, denying any obligation to do so.

Respondent was nominated in Miller's will as executor of his estate. He served in that capacity until Miller's two daughters expressed dissatisfaction with his role in Miller's conveyance of the farmland to the corporation. He then resigned as executor. Consistent with his view, he showed Miller as owner of all corporate stock in the preliminary probate inventory. The farmland was appraised at $4,000 an acre.

Although respondent had expended $900 in out-of-pocket expenses for the corporation and performed legal services worth more than $6,000, he did not intend to seek payment. Schenk, however, maintained at the time of the grievance hearing that he still owned one half of the outstanding stock of the corporation.

The determinative question in our review is whether this evidence establishes a violation of the principle in DR 5–104(A), which provides:

> A lawyer shall not enter into a business transaction with a client if they have differing interests therein and if the client expects the lawyer to exercise his professional judgment therein for the protection of the client, unless the client has consented after full disclosure.

* * *

In order to establish a violation of DR 5–104(A) it is necessary to show that the lawyer and client had differing interests in the transaction, that the client expected the lawyer to exercise his professional judgment for the protection of the client, and that the client consented to the transaction without full disclosure.

* * *

* * * Miller and Mershon plainly had differing interests in at least two aspects of the transaction. One was the issue of giving respondent a present interest in the corporation in anticipation of future legal services. The fee agreement was made during the existence of the attorney-client relationship and thus was subject to the general principles governing attorney-client transactions. Because respondent's fee was tied to the amount of his stock in the corporation, he and Miller had differing interests concerning the extent of respondent's stock ownership. Another differing interest involved making respondent a debtor of the corporation to assure that the services would be performed. Because Miller's interest was aligned wholly with the corporation, he and respondent had differing interests with respect to respondent's promissory note.

No dispute exists that Miller relied on respondent to exercise his professional judgment to protect him. One respect in which respondent did so was in preparing a written agreement to assure that Miller was reimbursed from the first profits of the corporation for the preincorporation expenses of preliminary studies. This, however, was the only agreement of the parties that was reduced to writing.

The fighting issue before the Commission was whether respondent made full disclosure to Miller within the meaning of the Canon before Miller entered the transaction. If full disclosure means only that respondent made Miller fully aware of the nature and terms of the transaction, this requirement was satisfied. Nothing was hidden from Miller, and he was an active participant in the transaction. Full disclosure, however, means more than this.

> Because of the fiduciary relationship which exists, the attorney has the burden of showing that the transaction "was in all respects fairly and equitably conducted; that he fully and faithfully discharged all his duties to his client, not only by refraining from any misrepresentation or concealment of any material fact, but by active diligence to see that his client was fully informed of the nature and effect of the transaction proposed and of his own rights and interests in the subject matter involved, and by seeing to it that his client either has independent advice in the matter or else receives from the attorney such advice as the latter would have been expected to give had the transaction been one between his client and a stranger."

Goldman v. Kane, 3 Mass.App. 336, 341, 329 N.E.2d 770, 773 (1975) (citations omitted). See Matter of Sedor, 73 Wis.2d 629, 639, 693, 245 N.W.2d 895, 901 (1976) ("an informed consent requires disclosure which details not only the attorney's adverse interest, but also the effect it will have on the exercise of his professional judgment.").

Respondent acknowledges he did not suggest to Miller that he obtain independent advice. The record does not show he otherwise gave Miller the kind of advice Miller should have had if the transaction were with a stranger. * * * Respondent let Schenk estimate the value of his legal services and thus the extent of respondent's stock ownership without any investigation to determine whether the estimate was accurate. Nor did he suggest to Miller that he make such investigation. If Schenk's estimate was generous, the effect may have been to chill respondent's scrutiny of the benchmark for the valuation, which was Schenk's valuation of his own services. Furthermore there was no discussion or investigation concerning the reasonableness or wisdom of tying respondent's fee for future services to a present twenty percent interest in the corporation. * * *

Nothing was done to assure that Miller would get his farm back if either Schenk or respondent did not perform or if the development should not be undertaken. Nothing was done to protect Miller or his estate in the event of the death of any of the parties. The promissory notes could hardly have been on more favorable terms to the debtors. The record does not show whether Miller was informed of the difficulty the corporation might have in enforcing respondent's obligation. So far as the record shows, Miller was not told of any possible effect of respondent's differing interests on the exercise of his professional judgment.

The Commission found respondent is forthright and honest and gained no profit from the transaction. The record confirms this finding. As the Commission also found, however, a violation of DR 5–104(A) was nevertheless established. Respondent had three alternatives when the Schenk proposal was first made. The safest and perhaps best course would have been to refuse to participate personally in the transaction. Alternatively, he could have recommended that Miller obtain independent advice. Finally, if Miller refused to seek independent advice or respondent did not recommend he do so, he could have made the least desirable choice. He could have attempted to meet the high standard of disclosure outlined in this opinion.

Having chosen to enter the transaction without recommending that Miller obtain independent advice, respondent was obliged to make full disclosure. Because the record does not show full disclosure was made before Miller consented to the transaction, a violation of DR 5–104(A) has been established. This is true even though respondent did not act dishonestly or make a profit on the transaction.

In accordance with the Commission recommendation, we reprimand him for the violation.

ATTORNEY REPRIMANDED.

PROBLEM 13

Representing the Insured and the Insurer

Terry Tenant is the son-in-law of Larry Landlord. Tenant rented an apartment in one of Landlord's apartment complexes. Landlord has a liability insurance policy with the All–Mutual Company covering all accidents in the apartment complex up to $100,000. One cold evening in January 1993, Tenant injured himself when he slipped on some ice just outside the main entrance. Landlord saw the accident and rushed to help Tenant, but Tenant said that he would "be all right." Thus, Landlord did not report the accident to All–Mutual. Unknown to Landlord, Tenant took several weeks off from work claiming back injuries. In June 1993, Tenant sued Landlord, his father-in-law, for $175,000 for his alleged pain and suffering and expenses in connection with the resulting back injury.

All–Mutual's liability insurance policy has several standard clauses. First, a "Notice of Accident" clause requires the insured to notify the carrier promptly of any accident for which it will expect coverage; failure to so notify is said to be a waiver of coverage. Second, the policy requires All–Mutual to provide and pay for a lawyer to defend the insured from any claim arising under the policy and to pay any claim within the monetary limits of the policy. Third, the policy requires the insured to cooperate with All–Mutual in defending against any claims.

After Tenant filed suit, Landlord notified All–Mutual, and All–Mutual retained Sara Henderson to investigate and prepare the defense. All–Mutual also wrote Landlord that it "was not waiving any defenses under the policy." Henderson interviewed Landlord and Tenant but was unable to find any other witnesses who had a clear recollection of the accident. Landlord's and Tenant's version of the events were almost identical and very favorable to Tenant. Henderson, on the other hand, has wondered how Tenant could be so careful and suffer such severe injuries, and yet have an immediate reaction that he would "be all right." Moreover, because Landlord and his son-in-law seem to be on good terms, she has wondered why Tenant neither told Landlord of the alleged "serious complications" nor, at least prior to filing, that Tenant was going to bring a lawsuit.

Tenant has offered to settle for $50,000, and Landlord has told Henderson that he would prefer All–Mutual's agreeing to that amount rather than going to trial and placing Landlord at risk for the $75,000 in excess of policy coverage.

Henderson believes that Landlord's failure to notify All–Mutual about the accident at the time it happened has so hampered factual development of the case that All–Mutual should deny coverage under its prompt notice clause. She has not told either Landlord or All–Mutual of her opinion. She also believes that Landlord is not cooperating, although she also has not said this to Landlord or All–Mutual either. During one interview Landlord told Henderson: "Just between you and me, my son-in-law and I remain the best of friends, but I wouldn't want All–Mutual to know that."

Henderson has communicated Tenant's settlement offer to both Landlord and All–Mutual. All–Mutual has asked for her advice on whether it should accept the offer.

QUESTIONS

1. Whom does Henderson represent in a case like this? Does she represent All–Mutual, the insurance company that hired her? Does she represent Landlord, the insured? Does she represent both?

a. Take a look at Model Rule 1.8(f), DR 5–107(A) & (B) and EC 5–17. Do they apply to this situation? Is this properly a third-party-payment case? That is, does Henderson represent the insured, and is the insurer simply someone contractually obligated to pay the lawyer's fee?

b. Is it instead better to think of this case as one in which the lawyer jointly represents the insurer and the insured? See Model Rule 1.7(b) and DR 5–105(B) & (C).

c. Why is it important to identify whom Henderson represents? Might how we characterize her relationships with Henderson and All–Mutual affect her duty to protect confidential information of each? Might it affect how consent to the representation is to be obtained and from whom, and to whom the lawyer's duty of loyalty is owed? Regardless of how we identify who the client is, however, might Henderson owe some duties even to non–clients in a case like this?

2. Here, All–Mutual is providing a defense for the insured under a "reservation of rights", i.e., it has said that it is not waiving any defenses it may have under the policy against bearing the ultimate liability. What is the effect of All–Mutual's position on Henderson's duties to Landlord?

a. Traditionally, the insurer's duty to defend and its duty to pay a damage award are separate duties. That is, a policy may provide coverage of defense costs even though the company would have a valid defense against paying the ultimate judgment.

b. Because defense of the plaintiff's claim and the gathering of evidence as to policy coverage tend to go on simultaneously for some period, the usual rule is that two different lawyers must be involved, i.e., one to give the insurer an opinion on policy defenses or policy coverage and one to defend the insured.

In Allstate Insurance Co. v. Keller, 149 N.E.2d 482 (Ill.App.1958), for example, the attorneys assigned to represent the insured deposed the insured to gather evidence that he was not the driver of the vehicle at the time of the accident. They did not explain to the insured that the purpose of the deposition was to strengthen the insurer's claim of lack of coverage. The court agreed that the insured's initial false statements that he was the driver were a breach of the cooperation clause, but it held the defense was waived. After the insured's assigned attorneys "became aware of a conflict of interest between their client, the defendant [insured], and their employer, the plaintiff [insurer]," they had to disclose "this information or its significance" to the insured. Failure to deal with this conflict in a way that assured the insured had loyal, independent representation, resulted in loss of the policy defense.

Similarly, in Employers Casualty Company v. Tilley, 496 S.W.2d 552 (Tex.1973), the insured had claimed that his failure to report an accident promptly, as the policy required, was because he had not known about it until he was sued. A lawyer was assigned to defend him, pursuant to a reservation of the company's rights. All the while he was preparing the defense, however, the lawyer was apparently also gathering evidence of just when Tilley or his employees first knew of the accident. "An attorney employed by an insurer to represent the insured simply cannot take up the cudgels of the insurer against the insured," the Court said. The insured was found to have been prejudiced by the lawyer's dual role, so the insurer was "estopped as a matter of law" from asserting its policy defense.

3.   What obligation does Henderson owe Landlord to protect the confidentiality of his statements to her?

a.   Take a look at Parsons v. Continental National American Group, used as a Reading to this Problem. What does it say about Henderson's duty of confidentiality in a case like this? Are you persuaded by the way it describes the proper object of the attorney's loyalty?

b.   Then, what should Henderson tell All–Mutual with respect to the prompt notice clause? Would it constitute disloyalty to the insured to report to the company that five months passed between the accident and the insured's report? Would that be information the company would already know if they had looked at the insured's report?

c.   How about reporting the "I wouldn't want All–Mutual to know" comment to the company? Would such a report constitute a breach of Henderson's duty of confidentiality? Would a failure to report it constitute participation in possible fraud by the insured?

d.   Suppose that when Landlord gets on the witness stand, he tells a story more favorable to Tenant then he had told Henderson earlier. May Henderson seek to impeach Landlord's story? Montanez v. Irizarry–Rodriguez, 641 A.2d 1079 (N.J.App.1994), hold that she may not do so.

e.   Do your conclusions about the obligation of confidentiality with regard to coverage-sensitive or policy-defense issues extend to keeping the insurance company generally informed about the progress of a case? Remember that all information "relating to the representation" is protected by Model Rule 1.6, but the insured has a contractual duty to cooperate with the insurer. Is there a distinction between the disclosure of "innocent" information under a duty of cooperation and the non–disclosure of more sensitive information?

f.   If Henderson obtains "sensitive" information, from whatever source, should she simply withdraw from the representation under Rule 1.16 or DR 2–110? Could she do so without signalling to the company that there was a possible policy or coverage defense? Would such signalling be appropriate? Cf. Rule 1.6, Comments 14 & 15. In a case like this, should Henderson treat possible policy defenses as someone else's problem?

g.   Does it trouble you that Henderson's decision what to do in these situations might be motivated in part by her desire to be employed by the insurance company in the next case? No matter what the courts say about who the client is in situations like this, is it realistic to presume that the attorney faces no conflict of loyalties? Concern about this conflict has led some courts to say an insured himself must be entitled to select the lawyer who will represent him (at the insurer's expense) on the liability issues when the insurer has raised a policy defense. See, e.g., CHI of Alaska, Inc. v. Employers Reinsurance Corp., 844 P.2d 1113 (Alaska 1993).

4. How should Henderson react to the settlement offer? Does EC 5–17 offer concrete guidance on the question?

a.   Do you see the conflict of interest? The insured would normally want to settle any case at a figure within policy limits because that will assure he will not have to bear liability in excess of those limits; the insurer, on the other hand, faced with an offer for the full amount of the policy, has relatively little to lose by going to trial.

b.   In such cases, as a matter of substantive law in many states, if the insurance company rejects a reasonable offer within policy limits, it must bear any sum—even in excess of policy limits—that the Court ultimately awards. E.g., Crisci v. Security Insurance Co., 66 Cal.2d 425, 429, 58 Cal.Rptr. 13, 16, 426 P.2d 173, 176 (1967) ("when 'there is great risk of a recovery beyond the policy limits so that the most reasonable manner of disposing of the claim is a settlement which can be made within those limits, a consideration in good faith of the insured's interest requires the insurer to settle the claim.' ").

c.   Lysick v. Walcom, 65 Cal.Rptr. 406 (Cal.App.1968), was a case in which the lawyer somehow found himself holding the bag. The insurer was prepared to concede liability and initially authorized the lawyer to settle for up to $9500, policy limits being $10,000. The plaintiff proposed to settle for $12,500, and the estate of the insured had expressed a willingness to contribute $2,500 over the policy limits. However, because the lawyer lacked the authority to pay full policy limits and was hesitant about seeking more authority from the insurer, he failed to tell the insured's estate about the offer. Nor did he tell the insured's estate when he rejected the offer on its behalf. The action went to trial and resulted in a judgment in favor of plaintiff for $225,000. The Court held:

> "[When the attorney for the insured] became aware of a conflict of interest between his two clients concerning the settlement offer made by plaintiffs[,] [h]e could have then terminated his relationship to the estate, but chose to continue to act as attorney for both clients. Accordingly, by so continuing to act, he impliedly agreed to use such skill, prudence and diligence in the representation of the estate as lawyers of ordinary skill and capacity commonly possess in the performance of like tasks. Moreover, since he was representing two parties with divergent interests, insofar as the settlement of the case was concerned, defendant labored under the duty of disclosing all facts and circumstances which, in the judgment of a lawyer of ordinary skill and capacity, were necessary to enable each of his clients to make free and intelligent decisions regarding the subject matter of the representation. * * *
>
> " * * * By continuing to act as counsel for the estate, while entertaining the belief that his primary obligation in the matter of settlement was to the insurer, defendant violated the legal

and ethical concepts which delineated his duties to the estate."
65 Cal.Rptr. at 416.

The Court concluded that, assuming proximate cause, the attorney would be personally liable for the amount of the judgment in excess of policy limits. Is the implication, then, that Henderson should advise acceptance of this settlement? Does she inevitably have a prohibited personal stake in whatever she recommends?

   d. What should the lawyer do if the insurer wants to settle but the insured does not? Normally, it is standard insurance law that an "insurance company is free to exercise its own judgment as to whether to enter into a settlement. It can, therefore, absent an express policy provision to the contrary, settle a case despite the insured's request that it not do so." [8] Cf. Mitchum v. Hudgens, 533 So.2d 194 (Ala.1988) (the insurance contract may give the insurer the right to settle a malpractice case within the policy limits, even over the objection of the insured). See also, Feliberty v. Damon, 527 N.E.2d 261 (N.Y.1988).

   Professional malpractice policies, however, are sometimes written differently than the garden variety automobile policy. The professional wants to protect her reputation and avoid any implication that she was incompetent. Thus the insured may want the insurer to fight, not settle. Consequently "[p]rofessional liability policies usually contain a *settlement clause* permitting the insured to refuse to consent to a settlement, and expressly limiting the insurer's liability in the event of a subsequent excess judgment." [9] What should the lawyer do with a settlement offer when representing a professional under such an arrangement?

   Suppose there is no such clause; must the lawyer nevertheless get the insured's permission to settle? Must the lawyer inform the insured about the offer of settlement even if the insured has no veto power? The Illinois Supreme Court said yes in Rogers v. Robson, Masters, Ryan, Brumund and Belom, 407 N.E.2d 47 (Ill.1980). Plaintiff was a doctor who had an insurance policy that provided that the insurer did *not* have to secure the written consent of the insured before the insurer made settlement of any claim or suit. The doctor was sued for medical malpractice and the lawyers assigned by the insurer to defend the case negotiated a settlement with the victim. The insurer accepted the settlement, paid $1250, and the lawyers effected dismissal of the action. The doctor had "repeatedly informed" one of the law partners that he would not consent to settlement and the doctor was never advised that the insurer intended to settle. The Illinois Supreme Court held that these facts gave rise to a cause of action. Saying that the doctor and the insurance company were both the lawyers' clients, the court said that the doctor—

---

8. A. Windt, Insurance Claims and Disputes; Representation of Insurance Companies and Insureds 191 (1982).

9. Id. at 191 n. 22.

"was entitled to a full disclosure of the intent to settle the litigation without his consent and contrary to his express instructions. Defendants' duty to make such disclosure stemmed from their attorney-client relationship with plaintiff and was not affected by the extent of the insurer's authority to settle without plaintiff's consent. * * * Nor need we reach the question whether plaintiff can prove damages which are the proximate result of the breach of the duty to make a full disclosure of the conflict between the defendants' two clients."

Do you agree with this analysis? What is the "conflict between the defendants' two clients" in a case like this?

5.   Who should have the right to define the appropriate level of effort by the lawyer when the insurer is paying for the defense?

a.   Suppose the insurance company faces a maximum liability of $10,000 under the policy. Litigation costs could well be that much or more, in addition to the amount of the liability. In order to reduce the cost of litigation, may the insurer direct the lawyer to take no more than, say, two depositions in the case?

b.   Look at Model Rule 1.8(f) and DR 5–107(B). Do they forbid the lawyer to honor such a direction by the insurer? Do you agree with the principle underlying those rules? Is a prohibition against accepting direction by others something that is generally in the interest of clients rather than in the interest of lawyers? Does such a prohibition serve the interest of insureds in cases such as the one in this problem?

c.   If the foreseeable liability is within policy limits, is there any reason that the insurance company should not be permitted to specify litigation tactics? If it were willing to pay the full amount of the claim, could it decide to put on no defense at all? Does the *Rogers* case, above, suggest that lawyers can never be wholly confident they can ignore the insured's non–economic interest in vigorously fighting a claim?

d.   Should the lawyer be concerned about potential malpractice liability to the insurer, the insured, or both, if the lawyer accedes to the company's limited-effort demand? Should the lawyer simply ask the insurer and insured to waive in advance any right to sue for any malpractice that results from adhering to the insurance company's direction? Be careful! What about DR 6–102 and Rule 1.8(h)? Does Rule 1.2(c) save the day for the lawyer? Which "client's" consent would the lawyer have to obtain?

6.   What implication would follow from a finding that the insurance company is a second client of the lawyer instead of simply a third party paying the bills?

a.   If the insurance company and insured were equal co-clients, would the lawyer ordinarily be barred from sharing the confidential information of one with the other?

    b.   Would the lawyer be obligated to get the consent of *both* to any settlement proposal? See Model Rule 1.8(g) and DR 5–106.

    c.   Are the problems of obtaining consent different depending on whether the insurance company is characterized as a client? Must the lawyer explain the advantages and disadvantages of the lawyer's representation of the insured for which the insurer will pay? Must the lawyer list all payments received or anticipated from the insurance company over the past year, for example? Does the lawyer need consent from the insurance company as well? May the lawyer assume that the insurance policy, which both parties signed when insurance was obtained, constitutes whatever consent is necessary to waive whatever conflicts of interest are presented?

    7.   Are the issues in this problem unique to cases involving insurance companies and insureds?

    a.   If parents pay a lawyer to represent their child accused of a hit and run accident, for example, should the analysis of whom the lawyer represents equally apply? Must the lawyer explain to the child the advantages and disadvantages of having the parents pay the bill? Must the lawyer secure the child's consent before disclosing information to the parents?

    b.   Suppose a corporation pays an attorney to represent a member of the board of directors. Should the corporation be able to specify the effort that should be put into the defense? Does it matter whether the corporation has agreed to indemnify the director for any judgment rendered against the director in the case?

    c.   Or think about the lawyer who is paid by a legal aid office to represent an indigent client. Might such a lawyer face issues very similar to those in this problem? What should the lawyer do about verifying the client's eligibility for free assistance, for example? Should the legal aid lawyer and the insurance defense lawyer resolve such questions in exactly the same way? What differences might there be?

READINGS

PARSONS v. CONTINENTAL NATIONAL AMERICAN GROUP

Supreme Court of Arizona, 1976.
113 Ariz. 223, 550 P.2d 94.

    * * * We are asked to determine whether an insurance carrier in a garnishment action is estopped from denying coverage under its policy when its defense in that action is based upon confidential information obtained by the carrier's attorney from an insured as a result of representing him in the original tort action.

Appellant, Michael Smithey, age 14, brutally assaulted his neighbors, appellants Ruth, Dawn and Gail Parsons, on the night of March 26, 1967.

During April, 1967 Frank Candelaria, CNA claims representative, began an investigation of the incident. On June 6, 1967 he wrote to Howard Watt the private counsel retained by the Smitheys advising him that CNA was "now in the final stages of our investigation," and to contact the Parsons' attorney to ascertain what type of settlement they would accept. Watt did contact the Parsons' attorney and requested that a formal demand settlement be tendered and the medical bills be forwarded to Candelaria. On August 11, 1967 Candelaria wrote a detailed letter to his company on his investigation of Michael's background in regards to his school experiences. He concluded the letter with the following:

"In view of this information gathered and in discussion with the boy's father's attorney, Mr. Howard Watts, and with the boy's parents, I am reasonably convinced that the boy was not in control of his senses at the time of this incident.

"It is, therefore, my suggestion that, and unless instructed otherwise, I will proceed to commence settlement negotiations with the claimant's attorney so that this matter may be disposed of as soon as possible."

Prior to the following dates: August 15, 1967, August 28, 1967, and October 23, 1967, Candelaria tried to settle with the Parsons for the medical expenses and was unsuccessful.

On October 13, 1967, the Parsons filed a complaint alleging that Michael Smithey assaulted the Parsons and that Michael's parents were negligent in their failure to restrain Michael and obtain the necessary medical and psychological attention for him. At the time that the Parsons filed suit they tendered a demand settlement offer of $22,500 which was refused by CNA as "completely unrealistic."

CNA's retained counsel undertook the Smithey's defense and also continued to communicate with CNA and advised [it] on November 10, 1967:

"I have secured a rather complete and confidential file on the minor insured who is now in the Paso Robles School for Boys, a maximum-security institution with facilities for psychiatric treatment, and he will be kept there indefinitely and certainly for at least six months * * *.

"The above referred-to confidential file shows that the boy is fully aware of his acts and that he knew what he was doing was wrong. It follows, therefore, that the assault he committed on claimants can only be a deliberate act on his part."

After CNA had been so advised they sent a reservation of rights letter to the Smitheys stating that the insurance company, as a courtesy to the insureds, would investigate and defend the Parsons' claim, but would do so without waiving any of the rights under the policy. The letter further stated that it was possible the act involved might be found to be an intentional act, and that the policy specifically excludes liability for bodily injury caused by an intentional act. This letter was addressed only to the parents and not to Michael.

In preparing for trial the CNA attorney retained to undertake the defense of the Smitheys interviewed Michael and received a narrative statement from him in regard to the events of March 26, 1967, and then wrote to CNA: "His own story makes it obvious that his acts were willful and criminal."

CNA also requested an evaluation of the tort case and the same attorney advised CNA: "Assuming liability and coverage, the injury is worth the full amount of the policy or $25,000.00."

On the issue of liability the trial court directed a verdict for Michael's parents on the grounds that there was no evidence of the parents being negligent. This Court affirmed, * * *. On the question of Michael's liability the trial court granted plaintiff's motion for a directed verdict after the defense presented no evidence and there was no opposition to the motion. Judgment was entered against Michael in the amount of $50,000.

The Parsons then garnished CNA, and moved for a guardian ad litem to be appointed for Michael which was granted by the trial court. On November 23, 1970 appellee Parsons offered to settle with CNA in the amount of its policy limits, $25,000. This offer was not accepted.

CNA successfully defended the garnishment action by claiming that the intentional act exclusion applied. The same law firm and attorney that had previously represented Michael represented the carrier in the garnishment action.

Appellants contend that CNA should be estopped to deny coverage and have waived the intentional act exclusion because the company took advantage of the fiduciary relationship between its agent (the attorney) and Michael Smithey. We agree.

The attorneys, retained by CNA, represented Michael Smithey at the personal liability trial, and, as a result, obtained privileged and confidential information from Michael's confidential file at the Paso Robles School for Boys, during the discovery process and, more importantly, from the attorney-client relationship. Both the A.B.A. Committee on Ethics and Professional Responsibility and the State Bar of Arizona, Committee on Rules of Professional Conduct have held that an attorney that represented the insured at the request of the insurer owes undivided fidelity to the insured, and, therefore, may not reveal any information or conclusions derived therefrom to the insurer that may be detrimental to the insured in any subsequent action. * * *

* * *

The attorney in the instant case should have notified CNA that he could no longer represent them when he obtained any information (as a result of his attorney-client relationship with Michael) that could possibly be detrimental to Michael's interests under the coverage of the policy.

The attorney representing Michael Smithey in the personal injury suit instituted by the Parsons had to be sure at all times that the fact he was compensated by the insurance company did not "adversely affect his judgment on behalf of or dilute his loyalty to [his] client, [Michael Smithey]". Ethical Consideration 5–14. Where an attorney is representing the insured in a personal injury suit, and, at the same time advising the insurer on the question of liability under the policy it is difficult to see how that attorney could give individual loyalty to the insured-client. "The standards of the legal profession require undeviating fidelity of the lawyer to his client. No exceptions can be tolerated." Van Dyke v. White, 55 Wash.2d 601, 349 P.2d 430 (1960). This standard is in accord with Ethical Consideration 5–1.

* * *

The attorney in the present case continued to act as Michael's attorney while he was actively working against Michael's interests. When an attorney who is an insurance company's agent uses the confidential relationship between an attorney and a client to gather information so as to deny the insured coverage under the policy in the garnishment proceeding we hold that such conduct constitutes a waiver of any policy defense, and is so contrary to public policy that the insurance company is estopped as a matter of law from disclaiming liability under an exclusionary clause in the policy. Employers Casualty Company v. Tilley, 496 S.W.2d 552 (Tex.1973). In the *Tilley* case the Texas Supreme Court also noted that such conduct on the part of an attorney and insurance carrier has been the subject of litigation in other jurisdictions especially in regards to the situation where an attorney representing the carrier does not fully and completely disclose to the insured the specific conflict of interest involved.

* * *

Appellee urges that the personal liability matter was defended under a reservation of rights agreement and this agreement had the effect of allowing the insurance company to investigate and defend the claim and still not waive any defenses. We hold that the reservation of rights agreement is not material to this case because the same attorney was representing conflicting clients. * * *

Appellee further urges that if the appellants are entitled to a judgment against the appellee insurance company the only judgment they are entitled to is in the amount of coverage $25,000.00. We do not agree. The evidence shows that the insurance company was advised by their legal counsel that if they were liable the injury was "worth the full amount of the policy." The evidence further shows that CNA could have settled the Parsons' claim against Michael Smithey well within the policy limits and refused to do so on the basis that the settlement was "completely unrealistic." It is clear from the record that the carrier failed to enter into good faith settlement negotiations. * * * In the instant case the further fact that the carrier believed there was no coverage under the policy and so refused to give any consideration to the proposed settlements did not absolve them from liability for the entire judgment entered against the insured. * * *

PROBLEM 14

The Lawyer and Her Former Client

Martha Heath has a wide reputation for her success handling medical malpractice cases for plaintiffs. She is in great demand and is rightly feared by doctor defendants.

Recently, Linda Parker came to Heath with a claim against Dr. Charles Abraham. Heath investigated the facts, found they seemed sound, and proceeded to go to work on the matter. Until she had worked on the matter for about 90 days, Heath had not recalled that about five years earlier she had represented Dr. Abraham in the routine adoption of his wife's children.

Heath might have forgotten Dr. Abraham but he had not forgotten her. "How could you of all people—my own lawyer—sue me?" he said. More to the point, he had his malpractice defense counsel move to disqualify Martha Heath from handling Parker's claim.

QUESTIONS

1. Do you find anything in the Model Code of Professional Responsibility directly covering the propriety of Heath's action?

a. If your answer is no, don't panic. This much litigated issue was virtually ignored by the Model Code. The rules that have developed are almost completely a product of case law incorporated into the Code by inference from Canons 4 and 9.

b. Judge Weinfeld developed the basic test in the leading case of T.C. Theatre Corp. v. Warner Brothers Pictures, Inc., 113 F.Supp. 265, 268–69 (S.D.N.Y.1953):

" * * * I hold that the former client need show no more than that matters embraced within the pending suit wherein his former attorney appears on behalf of his adversary are *substantially related* to the matters or cause of action wherein the attorney previously represented him, the former client. The Court will assume that during the course of the former representation confidences were disclosed to the attorney bearing on the subject matter of the representation. It will not inquire into their nature and extent. Only in this manner can the lawyer's duty of absolute fidelity be enforced and the spirit of the rule relating to privileged communications be maintained." (emphasis added).

c. The Model Rules now incorporate Judge Weinfeld's test in Rule 1.9(a). Do the Comments to Rule 1.9 stress only the objective of protecting client confidences? Are there additional concerns underlying this rule?

2. What's makes something a "matter" for purposes of Rule 1.9?

a. Look again at Judge Weinfeld's statement of the principle? Are "matters" limited to "causes of action"? If they were, would Judge Weinfeld have used the terms in the disjunctive?

b. Do Comments 1 & 2 to Rule 1.9 help you determine whether "matters" cover more than lawsuits? Would a lawyer be barred from seeking to rescind a contract drafted for a former client if the term "matter" were not to be construed broadly?

c. Take a look at Rule 1.11(d). The definition there relates to former government lawyers, but is it a useful definition to apply in Rule 1.9 as well?

3. When are matters the "same or substantially related"?

a. Assume that Dr. Abraham had hired Heath to represent him in defense of a suit that International Surgical Supply had filed against him. Heath filed an appearance and received an additional 10 days to answer the complaint. Assume that, two days later, Dr. Abraham and Heath had a falling out, the doctor hired new counsel, and Heath had no more to do with the case. Why should Heath not be able to accept employment by Surgical Supply in the *same* matter? What interest is protected by a rule prohibiting such representation? Would it matter if the doctor conceded that Heath learned no material confidential information in the short time she had represented him?

b. Wood's Case, 634 A.2d 1340 (N.H.1993), was a particularly tough application of the "same case" rule. It involved a lawyer who had begun to help a developer get zoning changes to build a new mall. It then turned out that the mall abutted Wood's own property, so his firm withdrew as counsel. Wood then gave an interview to the newspaper and otherwise publicly opposed the mall. The Court found that Wood had represented the developer in the same matter, so the only question was whether in presenting his own views and serving his own interests he was representing "another client". The Court found the purposes of the former client rule required such a construction of Rule 1.9 and publicly censured Wood.

c. Are the medical malpractice and adoption matters discussed in this problem "substantially related"? Are the legal issues in the two cases likely to be the same? If they were, should the cases be held to be substantially related even though the factual issues are different? See, e.g., Government of India v. Cook Industries, Inc., 569 F.2d 737 (2d Cir.1978).

d. Suppose the factual issues are closely related, but the problem of confidentiality is not presented. Allegaert v. Perot, 565 F.2d 246 (2d Cir.1977), for example, was a bankruptcy case. Law Firm had earlier represented a joint venture consisting of Company *A* and Company *B*. Company *B* is now bankrupt. Law Firm wants to represent Company *A* in the bankruptcy proceeding and the trustee for Company *B* is opposed. Law Firm was obviously closely involved with the factual issues relating to the joint venture, the court held, but there was no reasonable expectation that the facts it learned would be kept confidential from Company *A*. Thus the "substantial relation" test was not met. "[B]efore the substantial relationship test is even implicated, it must be shown that the attorney was in a position where he *could* have received information which his former client might reasonably have assumed the attorney would withhold from his present client." 565 F.2d at 250 (emphasis in original). Would the same result be reached under the Model Rules?

e. Rosenfeld Construction Co. v. Superior Court, 286 Cal.Rptr. 609 (Cal.App.1991), involved a suit against a contractor whom the plaintiff's law firm had previously represented in defense of a claim. In determining whether the cases were substantially related, the court mandated the trial court to apply the factors articulated in H.F. Ahmanson & Co. v. Salomon Bros. Inc., 280 Cal.Rptr. 614 (Cal.App.1991), which were (1) the factual similarity of the cases, (2) their legal similarity, and (3) the extent of the lawyer's involvement in the cases. The court specifically found the fact that firm members testified that they did not presently remember anything about the prior representation was *not* a relevant factor.[1]

4. To the extent confidentiality is the controlling issue, what kinds of confidential information should be disqualifying? Would one expect to learn secrets in an adoption case, for example, that would be useful to Heath in the malpractice action?

a. Suppose Heath knows no crucial secrets (e.g. that Abraham operates while intoxicated), but she does have general impressions of Abraham's personality and specific knowledge of his financial situation.

Consider Chugach Electric Association v. United States District Court, 370 F.2d 441 (9th Cir.1966), cert.denied 389 U.S. 820, 88 S.Ct. 40, 19 L.Ed.2d 71 (1967). There, an attorney was general counsel and later consultant to Chugach. The Board of Directors of the Company was divided on many issues and when a minority of the Board gained control and became a majority, the attorney resigned. The attorney later

---

1. See also, In re American Airlines, Inc., 972 F.2d 605 (5th Cir.1992) (Vinson & Elkins disqualified from taking an antitrust case on behalf of Northwest Airlines against American Airlines, a client V & E had represented in earlier antitrust matters).

represented the trustee in bankruptcy of a coal company and sued Chugach claiming an antitrust conspiracy because of alleged agreements and overt acts occurring after the attorney severed any connection with Chugach. The Court disqualified the attorney. "The problem here is not limited to the question whether [the attorney] was connected with petitioner as its counsel at the time agreements were reached and overt acts taken, but includes the question whether, as attorney, he was in a position to acquire knowledge casting light on the purpose of later acts and agreements. * * * A likelihood here exists which cannot be disregarded that [the attorney's] knowledge of private matters gained in confidence would provide him with greater insight and understanding of the significance of subsequent events in an antitrust context and offer a promising source of discovery." Id. at 443.

Similarly, in Kaselaan & D'Angelo Associates v. D'Angelo, 144 F.R.D. 235 (D.N.J.1992), Lawyer had represented Plaintiff in several cases alleging employees had misappropriated confidential information and breached restrictive covenants in the employment contract. Now, he represented a terminated employee against Plaintiff in a similar case, but one on which he had not worked. The Court held that Lawyer had learned so much about how Plaintiff handled cases of this type that disqualification was required.[2]

But see, Unified Sewerage Agency v. Jelco Inc., 646 F.2d 1339 (9th Cir.1981), refusing to disqualify a law firm even though it had earlier gained "information and insights from Jelco about such things as Jelco's institutional attitudes towards negotiation and settlement and Jelco's method of doing business." The law firm did "not have access to any specific information that would help [it] prevail against Jelco (other than general information concerning the personality of a client, which is always helpful in later suits against that client)." The court also found that the party seeking disqualification had earlier consented and thus waived its rights.

b. Should Dr. Abraham's discomfort alone be sufficient to say that Heath may not represent the malpractice plaintiff? Recall Problem 10. What do the courts say about the lawyer's obligation not to sue a *present* client, even in an unrelated matter? Is there any reason the rule as to former clients should be more lenient?

c. Assume Heath had not represented the present opponent in the prior case, but rather a co-defendant. She represented *B* in a criminal case, for example, and now files a civil suit on behalf of *A* against *B* 's co-defendant *C* arising out of the same facts. Does Rule 1.9 apply? Should Heath be disqualified? See Wilson P. Abraham Const. Corp. v. Armco Steel Corp., 559 F.2d 250 (5th Cir.1977), and Kevlik v. Goldstein, 724

2. See also, Ullrich v. Hearst Corp., 809 F.Supp. 229 (S.D.N.Y.1992). There, a lawyer who had handled employment discrimination cases for a company for 20 years started bringing such cases against the company. Although he had not worked on *these* cases for his former employer, Judge Laval found the likelihood of abuse of confidential insights too great to allow the lawyer to continue.

F.2d 844 (1st Cir.1984), holding that the lawyer must be disqualified because of the shared confidences in such a common defense.

d.   In State ex rel. McClanahan v. Hamilton, 430 S.E.2d 569 (W.Va. 1993), the prosecutor faced a former client charged with crime.   While in private practice, the prosecutor had represented the defendant in a divorce case in which she alleged her husband beat her.   The couple later reconciled, but now the wife was charged with malicious assault on her husband.   The Court held the prosecutor was disqualified from handling the prosecution.   In the divorce case, the wife revealed information relevant to a "battered spouse" defense she might use here; there thus would be a danger that what the prosecutor knew would be used against her.

e.   Stepak v. Addison, 20 F.3d 398 (11th Cir.1994), further extended the implications of the rule.   A derivative action had been filed against the directors and officers of the Southern Company, a large electric utility.   The suit alleged that insiders had engaged in illegal acts involving spare parts, concealing facts, and political contributions.   The acts had been the subject of SEC, IRS and criminal investigations in which the law firm had represented some of the officers and directors. Now, the firm investigated the shareholders' claims and advised the outside directors that the corporation should not file suit.   The Court set the conclusion of the outside directors aside;   the law firm had a conflict because of its prior representation of the officers.   The firm's prior representation limited its current investigation and its inability to be candid with the outside directors tainted the directors' business judgment.

5.   May you ever take the other side of a case in which one of the parties has talked to you and decided to retain another lawyer?

a.   Remember that communications are privileged when you interview a prospective client and EC 4–1 requires a lawyer to protect the confidences and secrets of one who has "sought to employ him."   See also, Proposed Federal Rule of Evidence 503(a)(1) and Model Rule 1.6.

b.   Preliminary interviews thus may impose a real opportunity cost on lawyers to the extent that they preclude them from taking other cases.   Clients, it is said, realize this and some of them conduct "beauty contests" among law firms in an effort to preclude those firms who are not selected from proceeding against them.   At its best, such a contest allows a prospective client to make an informed choice about which firm to retain.   However, an unscrupulous prospective client might also plant confidential information in the minds of law firms not chosen.   This would allow the prospective client to try later to disqualify those firms from representing any of their other clients in matters against the prospective client.

The problem may be particularly acute for law firms that specialize in a narrow range of legal problems and develop a national reputation that enables them to attract corporate clients from around the country.

Assume, for example, that a firm has a national reputation for representing takeover targets or raiders. A corporate officer *deliberately* telephones the firm to discuss possible representation in a takeover attempt but without any real intent to hire the firm. Should the call disqualify the firm from representing the target in the takeover attempt?

c. ABA Formal Opinion 90–358 (1990) agrees that protection of confidential information of prospective clients is an important value to protect, and it suggests steps a firm should take to minimize the risk of future disqualification. The steps include limiting information obtained at the initial interview to that necessary to check for conflicts, possibly obtaining waivers of confidentiality of disclosures at the initial interview, and screening persons who receive confidential information at the interview from participation in any subsequent proceedings against the former prospective client.

d. Section 213, Comment g(i), of the Restatement of the Law, Third, the Law Governing Lawyers, Tentative Draft No. 4 (1991), offers similar counsel. It suggests, however, that even if the lawyer obtains confidential information from the former prospective client in the course of the initial interview, as long as the information is not "extensive and sensitive," the lawyer is not barred by reason of having that information from representing the lawyer's other clients who might benefit from use of the information. That is, the lawyer will be trusted not to use it. It remains to be see if the courts will adopt this position that arguably reads a large exception into Model Rule 1.9.

6. Suppose it is a non-lawyer who switches sides?

a. In re Complex Asbestos Litigation, 283 Cal.Rptr. 732 (Cal.App. 1991), upheld the disqualification of a law firm representing plaintiffs in asbestos claims because it had hired a paralegal who had worked for one of the defense firms on similar asbestos cases. The danger of misuse of defense confidences was too great given the fact that the non–lawyer had not been screened from participation in asbestos matters.

b. Allen v. Academic Games Leagues of America, Inc., 831 F.Supp. 785 (C.D.Cal.1993), was a suit for trademark and copyright infringement brought by a maker of educational games. Wright had been a competitor while a law student, had served on the plaintiff's advisory committee, and had even tried to help settle this lawsuit. Once he became a lawyer, he went to work for the firm that represented the defendant and participated actively in that defense. Because Wright had been a law student at the earlier time, the plaintiff was not his "former client", the Court held, but Wright had a duty to protect the plaintiff's confidential information. To prevent a violation of that duty, his law firm was disqualified from continuing to represent the defendant.

c. It doesn't help avoid disqualification to call a former lawyer a non-lawyer.

Ackerman v. National Property Analysts, Inc., 1993 WL 258679 (S.D.N.Y.1993), involved an attempt to avoid the bite of Rule 1.9 by having the former lawyer act as a "consultant" to the opposing law firm. An in-house lawyer who had drafted private placement memoranda for a company became a Deep Throat for the law firm that sued the company for fraud. The Court found the lawyer's argument that he was not now acting as an attorney for the plaintiffs to be unavailing and it disqualified the law firm that had relied on the violation of confidences.

American Motors Corp. v. Huffstutler, 575 N.E.2d 116 (Ohio 1991), involved a former lawyer who had worked on defense of product liability cases for Jeep and who now decided to hire himself out as a non–lawyer "expert" to work with lawyers bringing claims against his former employer. Because of all the confidential information he had, he too was enjoined from doing so.

State ex rel. Creighton University v. Hickman, 512 N.W.2d 374 (Neb.1994), involved a woman who had worked for the law firm representing the defendant during law school and later as a lawyer. Indeed, she had worked on this very case. Later, she was disbarred and went to work for an agency that placed people to work in litigation support. The law firm representing the plaintiff used her as a paralegal in this case, in ignorance of her prior involvement in the case. The Court held that a "bright line" test was required, and, in order to protect Defendant's confidential information, the Court disqualified Plaintiff's law firm in spite of the fact that it had been misled about her prior history.

7. Should there be ethical standards concerning when to file motions to disqualify?

a. Conflicts of interest between present and former clients are redressed, not primarily in disciplinary actions, but largely by courts during litigation. One of the major issues raised for the judicial process by the former client problem was once the proliferation of motions to disqualify one's opponent. Attorneys had an incentive to disqualify their opponent's lawyer; the motion, if granted, burdened the adversary by delaying the litigation and by increasing the opponent's legal expenses because the new lawyers had to familiarize themselves with the case. See, e.g., International Electronics Corp. v. Flanzer, 527 F.2d 1288, 1289 (2d Cir.1975): "We have been met recently with a number of appeals on matters involving the disqualification of lawyer-opponents. * * * Such moves and countermoves by adversaries appear to have become common tools of the litigation process."

b. Should a lawyer be reluctant to try to disqualify a colleague if the motion has only a slight chance of success? See Model Rule 1.7, Comment 15 ("Conflict Charged by Opposing Party"). In determining whether to move to disqualify an attorney, should a lawyer take into account the resulting advantages of delay to the client? Does Rule 3.2 answer the question? Is it relevant that the motion implies a fellow lawyer is "unethical"? Should the test for moving to disqualify a lawyer be more strict than the test used to determine whether to sue a medical doctor for malpractice?

c. Should the courts allow interlocutory appeals of trial court decisions refusing to disqualify an attorney? The Supreme Court resolved the issue for federal courts by holding that denials of disqualification motions in civil cases are *not* appealable final decisions under 28 U.S.C.A. § 1291. Firestone Tire & Rubber Co. v. Risjord, 449 U.S. 368, 101 S.Ct. 669, 66 L.Ed.2d 571 (1981). Likewise, the granting of a disqualification motion in a criminal case is not immediately appealable. Flanagan v. United States, 465 U.S. 259, 104 S.Ct. 1051, 79 L.Ed.2d 288 (1984). The same result has been reached with respect to the grant of a motion to disqualify in a civil case, Richardson–Merrell, Inc. v. Koller, 472 U.S. 424, 105 S.Ct. 2757, 86 L.Ed.2d 340 (1985), and the denial of a motion to disqualify in a criminal case, United States v. White, 743 F.2d 488 (7th Cir.1984).

Recently, however, a few courts of appeal have agreed to review lower court decisions when the losing party has sought a writ of mandamus. E.g., In re American Airlines, Inc., 972 F.2d 605 (5th Cir.1992); Matter of Sandahl, 980 F.2d 1118 (7th Cir.1992). The Seventh Circuit concluded that mandamus is appropriate if the trial judge applied an incorrect legal rule; it continues to defer to the trial judge on questions of fact. Do you think the law/fact distinction is likely to be easily applied in disqualification cases?

d. Should a judge ignore conflicts of interest that taint the litigation and leave sanctions for unethical conduct up to the state's discipline system? SWS Financial Fund A v. Salomon Brothers Inc., 790 F.Supp. 1392 (N.D.Ill.1992), held that disqualification is not always required. The law firm had filed suit against the defendant for alleged violation of commodities regulations and the antitrust laws. The defendant was found to be a current client of the firm with respect to issues of compliance with commodities trading regulations. In spite of this, the court denied the defendant's motion to disqualify the firm. Judge Duff said that he wanted to avoid creating an incentive for companies to give several law firms small pieces of business so as to disqualify them later, although there was no evidence that had happened in this case. Do you share the judge's concern? Should big law firms be treated in such cases as if they were defenseless victims?

8. If Dr. Abraham's motion were granted and Heath were disqualified, should substituted counsel have access to Heath's work product?

a. In First Wisconsin Mortgage Trust v. First Wisconsin Corp., 584 F.2d 201 (7th Cir.1978) (en banc), the majority held that there is no per se rule against subsequent counsel's use of work product developed by disqualified counsel. Thus, unless there is evidence of "improper advantage" having been secured, "such as the use of confidential information", it is an abuse of discretion for the trial court to prevent the turning over of the work product. The work product at issue in that case was an analysis of loan files conducted by a team of 15 lawyers for more than a year prior to the ultimate disqualification of the firm. The majority thought the loan file summaries to be "the result of routine lawyer work of a type which any competent lawyer, by spending the substantial time which would be required, could accomplish just as well as did [the disqualified counsel]." Accord, IBM Corp. v. Levin, 579 F.2d 271 (3d Cir.1978).

b.   The dissent in *First Wisconsin* accused the majority of "attempting to draw fine ethical lines based upon the specific content of the objectionable material," an approach "which has been repeatedly condemned.   * * * [T]he majority further compounds its error by intimating that once the defendants have disclaimed the use of confidential information, the former client is the one who must point to the confidences used in the work." *In camera* inspection of the work product, the dissenters argued, would be "both unworkable and a dangerous departure from long-accepted ethical guidelines."   584 F.2d at 211–13 (emphasis in original.)

Who had the better of the argument in *First Wisconsin*? Who really won the case? Would you expect the new law firm to take advantage of the opportunity to get the work product? Might doing so simply get it mired down in litigation over whether the work product was based on confidential information?

———

PROBLEM 15

Imputed Disqualification

Charles & Burls (C & B) is a prestigious, 200–person Wall Street firm with a national clientele. It represents World Wide Container Corp. in many matters, one of which is a suit by National Gasket Co. against World Wide for contribution in a products liability case. The case is to be tried in New Orleans, and C & B is cooperating with Willis & Xeres (W & X), the law firm that World Wide uses as local counsel in New Orleans.

Willis of W & X is the only lawyer actively working on the case. His only role is to file papers, motions, and other pleadings forwarded to him by C & B. National Gasket has now moved to disqualify both C & B and W & X from acting as World Wide's lawyers because Xeres (while he had been in a solo practice before forming W & X) had represented National Gasket in various product liability matters arising out of the same facts that led to the present suit. Xeres learned confidential information that, if disclosed, would be useful to World Wide's defense of the present suit. C & B has never represented National Gasket.

QUESTIONS

1. May Willis continue to represent World Wide? Look at Model Rules 1.10(a) & (b) and DR 5–105(D).

a. We know from Problem 14 that Xeres could not represent World Wide because of his previous representation of National Gasket in a matter substantially related to the present matter. What reasons justify a sweeping disqualification of everyone in Xeres' firm?

b. Should disqualification turn on whether Willis has learned any relevant confidences from Xeres? [1] Could Xeres properly disclose any such confidences to Willis, whether or not the firm was involved in this lawsuit?

2. To how many persons and firms involved in defense of the case, should the imputation of conflicts extend?

a. If the court disqualifies the firm of W & X and all of its partners and associates, will disqualification also extend to the firm of C & B? What reasons would justify such a result? Is the result required by Model Rule 1.10(a), Comment 1? Are W & X and C & B "affiliated" firms within the meaning of DR 5–105(D)?

b. If Xeres' confidential knowledge about National Gasket is imputed to Sandra Jones, an associate at W & X, but Jones then leaves to join a second firm, is that firm also disqualified? Consider American Can Co. v. Citrus Feed Co., 436 F.2d 1125, 1129 (5th Cir.1971). The court noted that: "All authorities agree that all members of a partnership are barred from participating in a case from which one partner is disqualified. * * * [O]nce a partner is thus vicariously disqualified for a particular case, the subsequent dissolution of the partnership cannot cure his ineligibility to act as counsel in that case. * * * However, new partners of a vicariously disqualified partner, to whom knowledge has been imputed during a former partnership, are not necessarily disqualified: they need show only that the vicariously disqualified partner's knowledge was imputed, not actual." The court was concerned that "imputation and consequent disqualification could continue *ad infinitum*," and that such a result is not needed "to maintain public confidence in the bar."

Do you agree with this analysis? Is it consistent with Model Rule 1.9(b)? Should the logic of the imputed disqualification rule yield to policy considerations such as those the court cites?

---

1. Cf., W.E. Bassett Co. v. H.C. Cook Co., 201 F.Supp. 821 (D.Conn.1961), aff'd per curiam 302 F.2d 268 (2d Cir.1962). There, lawyer X had represented the plaintiff in a lengthy case. X then joined a firm—one member of which had once represented and advised a corporate defendant on some important issues in the same controversy. It was agreed in X's new firm that X would continue to represent the plaintiff corporation in the litigation but without any participation by X's new partners. Nor did X's partnership or any present partner of the firm share in any fees paid for services rendered by X. But when the district court learned of this state of affairs, it *sua sponte* held a hearing on the disqualification of X. While the court found X's partners and X "made every effort to comply with Canons 6 and 37 [of the 1908 ABA Canons of Ethics as amended] as they honestly interpreted them," still, the circumstances created "will inevitably lead to suspicion and distrust in them in the minds of the defendants and the opportunity for misunderstanding on the part of the public. * * *" 201 F.Supp. at 825. Thus, the court required X to cease all further participation in the case.

c. Now suppose Xeres resigns from the firm of W & X. Will Willis still be disqualified from representing World Wide? What factual determination does Rule 1.10(b) require be made? Who should have the burden of proof on the question of what information was disclosed by Xeres before he left the firm? Would a hearing on that question ever consist of more than testimony about who told what to whom at W & X, testimony that the other side could neither challenge nor rebut?

These issues are illustrated by Novo Terapeutisk Laboratorium A/S v. Baxter Travenol Laboratories, Inc., 607 F.2d 186 (7th Cir.1979) (en banc). During July 1976, while at the Hume law firm, Cook spent 2¼ hours reviewing legal authorities and conferring with Baxter attorneys, during which time he received confidential information relating to a patent infringement matter. In December, 1976, Cook left the Hume firm and took the Baxter account with him. In February, 1977, plaintiff Novo filed a patent infringement action (substantially related to the July conference) against Baxter, and in August, 1977, the Hume firm filed an appearance on behalf of Novo. The court readily agreed that on these facts Cook could not represent Novo, but that was not the issue; Cook was at a new firm and was still counsel for Baxter. The question was whether Cook's disqualification should be imputed to the other members of the Hume firm. "It is reasonable to presume that members of a law firm freely share their client's confidences with one another," but the circumstances of this case demonstrated that such a presumption need not be irrebuttable. Since Cook received the confidences, "he is in a position to know exactly what confidences he may have shared with others in his firm." He said he did not share any and the remaining members of the Hume firm submitted affidavits confirming that they did not receive any confidential information from Cook. The court thus refused to disqualify the Hume firm.

d. Should the extent of imputation depend in part on how large a part the disqualified lawyer played in the matter? In Silver Chrysler Plymouth, Inc. v. Chrysler Motors Corp., 518 F.2d 751 (2d Cir.1975), the court considered whether an attorney was disqualified from representing an automobile dealer by reason of once having been an associate in the firm that represented the manufacturer. At that firm, he conceded he had worked on Chrysler matters. The court concluded, however, that the "cases and the Canons on which they are based are intended to protect the confidences of former clients when an attorney has been in a position to learn them." Id. at 757. The court held that the attorney had rebutted the presumption that he had received significant confidential material when he was associated with the 80–member firm. The attorney's involvement

> "was, at most, limited to brief, informal discussions on a procedural matter or research on a specific point of law. * * * [W]e do not believe that there is any basis for distinguishing between partners and associates on the basis of title alone—both are members of the bar and bound by the same Code of Professional Responsibility. But there is reason to differentiate for disquali-

fication purposes between lawyers who become heavily involved in the facts of a particular matter and those who enter briefly on the periphery for a limited and specific purpose related solely to legal questions. In large firms at least, the former are normally the more seasoned lawyers and the latter the more junior." Id. at 756–57.

While purporting not to make a distinction between partners and associates, is the *Silver* case in effect making such a distinction? While neither the Model Rules not the Model Code distinguish between partners and associates, should they? Would a bright line test be appropriate?

    e. In deciding these cases, should courts give weight to the fact that lawyers' movement from a position at one firm to a position at another is very common these days?

City of Cleveland v. Cleveland Electric Illuminating Co., 440 F.Supp. 193, 211 (N.D.Ohio 1976), aff'd without published opinion 573 F.2d 1310 (6th Cir.1977), noted: "Imputing to an attorney in the private practice all confidential information obtained, or presumed to have been obtained, by other members of his law firm may severely limit the scope of the private attorney's future career and the effective operation of his firm, as well as the individual's right to legal counsel of choice." [2]

What do you think of this analysis? Court of Appeals opinions following *Silver Chrysler Plymouth* include Gas–A–Tron of Arizona v. Union Oil Co. of California, 534 F.2d 1322 (9th Cir.1976) (per curiam), cert. denied 429 U.S. 861, 97 S.Ct. 164, 50 L.Ed.2d 139 (1976), and Schloetter v. Railoc of Indiana, Inc., 546 F.2d 706 (7th Cir.1976). In the latter, the court suggested:

> "a different result in *Gas–A–Tron* or *Silver Chrysler* might have severely restricted mobility within the legal profession. For law firms would be understandably reluctant to hire a young lawyer who had previously worked at a large firm if it were to mean full automatic disqualification from any case involving a party represented by the young lawyer's former employer."

Id. at 712 n. 11. But see Reardon v. Marlayne, 416 A.2d 852, 860 (N.J.1980) ("problems in the job market and mobility are not solved by loosening ethical standards required of the profession.").

---

2. The Court also asserted a narrow, but now rarely followed test. "The * * * rule in the private practice of law should therefore limit the imputation of confidential disclosures, actual or presumed, to only those lawyers practicing in the attorney's area of concentration. Absent direct proof to the contrary, the attorney would not be deemed to have shared confidential information relating to matters and services exclusively within the sphere of representation of another department or section of his firm. This * * * rule is more acutely dramatized in the large, departmentalized law firm characteristically more prevalent in an era of evolving legal specialization." Should such a rule be taken more seriously than most courts have done?

3. How should courts approach the question of imputation outside the traditional law firm setting?

a. Should the same strict imputation be required if two parties are both clients of a legal aid office? Put another way, if one legal aid lawyer represents the plaintiff, may another represent the defendant? It has been suggested that, unlike a private law firm, a "government-financed organization of lawyers does not receive any compensation directly from its clients; therefore, a legal aid attorney has no economic interest in a client represented by a colleague in the same office." In addition, the "attorneys in a legal aid service are not associated for the practice of law in the same sense that private law firm members are associated. Legal aid operates solely as a nonprofit, public benefit organization." [3]

Do you agree that these considerations should be controlling? What problems does the existence of an association between legal aid attorneys raise? Are the problems insuperable? Cf. ABA Informal Opinion 1309 (1975) (agency can take case on side opposite to that of its funding source); but see Flores v. Flores, 598 P.2d 893 (Alaska 1979) (state must supply private counsel to one party where agency's internal procedures are inadequate to guarantee confidentiality to both).

b. Does the same logic apply to dual representation by a Public Defender's Office? The Chief Public Defender of a state asked the ABA Standing Committee on Ethics and Professional Responsibility whether the Public Defender Department could represent two criminal defendants in the same case with conflicting interests. Public Defender office in City 1 had 16 lawyers and Public Defender office in City 2 had 5 lawyers. The Committee ruled that there was a conflict. If one public defender in City 1 is disqualified, then all those in City 1 are disqualified; and since the Public Defender Department is "subject to the common control" of the Chief Public Defender, both offices in City 1 and City 2 are disqualified. The Committee offered no reason and merely cited DR 5–105(D). ABA Informal Opinion 1418 (1978).

Accord, Commonwealth v. Westbrook, 484 Pa. 534, 400 A.2d 160 (1979) (members of public defender's office are members of the "same firm" for conflict of interest purposes). Do you agree that this should be true? Why or why not?

c. How about imputation within a prosecutor's office?

State ex rel. Eidson v. Edwards, 793 S.W.2d 1 (Tex.Crim.App.1990), considered whether an entire prosecutor's office should be disqualified because a new assistant prosecutor had previously represented the defendant. Indeed, he had interviewed the defendant, potential witnesses, and acted as lead defense counsel at the preliminary hearing. The court held, however, that prosecutors' offices are different from private law firms. The former defense lawyer obviously could not try the case, but his disqualification would not be imputed to the office.

---

3. Note, Professional Responsibility—Conflicts of Interest Between Legal Aid Lawyers, 37 Mo.L.Rev. 346, 349 (1972).

Turbin v. Arizona Superior Court, 797 P.2d 734 (Ariz.App.1990) reached exactly the opposite result. There, too, the lawyer had interviewed the defendant and witnesses and had negotiated with the prosecutor before withdrawing and joining the prosecutor's staff. There, too, it was conceded he discussed the case with no one while at the prosecutor's office, but this Court believed that the appearance of impropriety required that the whole office be disqualified when the lawyer had been this involved in the defendant's representation.

With which of these cases do you agree?

d. Where do military legal offices fit into this analysis? Except in cases of military necessity, the ABA Standing Committee on Ethics and Professional Responsibility has concluded that "representation of opposing sides by lawyers working in the same military office and sharing common secretarial and filing facilities should be avoided." ABA Informal Opinion 1474 (1982) (citing Formal Opinion 343 and Informal Opinion 1309).

e. What problems are these opinions driving at? May private lawyers who share office space but not fees take opposing sides of a case? Yes, said ABA Informal Opinion 1486 (1982), if the lawyers "exercise reasonable care" to protect confidences of the clients. In addition, the lawyers "should" get client consent. Do you agree? Is "reasonable care" to protect confidential information enough? If so, why is client consent required?

4. Assuming Willis & Xeres may not represent World Wide in the case brought by National Gasket, may W & X suggest that World Wide go to the firm across the street in which Xeres' wife practices?

a. Would it be relevant that a member of the firm across the street (but not necessarily the one who would handle the case W & X has referred) is Xeres' spouse? How about Xeres' brother? See ABA Formal Opinion 340 (September 23, 1975), excerpted as a Reading to this Problem.

b. Does Rule 1.8(i) reach the same result as Formal Opinion 340? Is the prohibition in Rule 1.8(i) imputed to the firm of each spouse? See Rule 1.10(a).

c. Suppose that, instead of being spouses, the opposing lawyers had gone to dinner and to the movies together several times. They had not informed their clients of this relationship. Should they have done so and sought client consent to continue their representation of the parties? Would it affect your answer if one lawyer were the public prosecutor and one a criminal defense lawyer? See People v. Jackson, 167 Cal.App.3d 829, 213 Cal.Rptr. 521 (3d Dist.1985), setting aside the defendant's conviction because counsel failed to disclose the fact of their dating.

5. Suppose it is not a lawyer with confidential information who changes firms but a non-lawyer such as the lawyer's secretary.

a.   Should the secretary's knowledge about the former boss' cases be imputed to the new employer?   Herron v. Jones, 637 S.W.2d 569 (Ark.1982), holds that there need be no imputation so long as the secretary was "walled off" from work on the case for the new firm.

b.   Suppose, instead, it was a law student who had worked on a case for Firm A between her first and second years in law school but worked for opposing counsel, Firm B, the next summer.   Should that disqualify Firm B from continuing in the case?   Should the student also have to be screened from participation in the matter?   Would strict rules in this area tend to decimate the law placement market?   Again, should that concern be relevant where "ethics" are at stake?

c.   What if the person working with the firm was a consultant (such as a law professor) who had worked on a series of cases for the firm, but was not a member or regular employee of the firm?   Should the knowledge or other reason for disqualification of the law professor be imputed to the entire law firm?   Should any of the firm's knowledge or bases for its disqualification travel with the professor if she consults with a different firm on another matter?   Should it make a difference whether the law professor is listed as "of counsel" on the law firm's letterhead? [4]

d.   What about "law-temporaries," a relatively recent phenomenon?   A "temporary lawyer" is a lawyer engaged by a law firm for a limited period of time, either directly or through a placement agency.   The temporary may work on a single matter or on several different matters. He or she may simultaneously work on other matters for other firms. Firms typically hire temporaries to meet short–term staffing needs or to supply special expertise on a particular matter.   Should they be treated as any other lawyers for purposes of imputing disqualification?

ABA Formal Opinion 88–356 (1988) considered issues related to temporary lawyers and said that Rules 1.7 and 1.9 govern.   For example, a temporary lawyer, under Rule 1.7, may not personally work simultaneously on matters for clients of different firms if the representation of

---

4.   An "of counsel" designation is normally used to indicate that the person will assist in the legal matter but is not a partner attorney or an associate/employee in the firm.   See ABA Opinion 90–357 (May 10, 1990), which states in part that the use of the tile "of counsel" on letterheads, law lists, professional cards, notices, office signs and the like is "a holding out to the world at large about some general and continuing relationship between the lawyers and the law firms in question.   A different use of the same term occurs when a lawyer (or firm) is designated as of counsel in filings in a particular case: in such circumstances there is no general holding out as to a continuing relationship, or as to a relationship that applies to anything but the individual case."   A lawyer may be "of coun-

sel" to more than one firm, and a firm may be "of counsel" to another firm.   The Opinion concluded:

"There can be no doubt that an of counsel lawyer (or firm) is 'associated in' and has an 'association with' the firm (or firms) to which the lawyer is of counsel, for purposes of both the general imputation of disqualification pursuant to Rule 1.10 of the Model Rules and the imputation of disqualifications resulting from former government service under Rules 1.11(a) and 1.12(c); and is a lawyer *in* the firm for purposes of Rule 3.7(b), regarding the circumstances in which, when a lawyer is to be a witness in a proceeding, the lawyer's colleague may nonetheless represent the client in that proceeding."

each is directly adverse to each other. But are temporary lawyers "associated" in a firm for purposes of the *imputed* disqualification sections of Rule 1.10? The Opinion concluded that the answer must be determined by a functional analysis of the facts and circumstances involved.

> "Ultimately, whether a temporary lawyer is treated as being 'associated with a firm' while working on a matter for the firm depends on whether the nature of the relationship is such that the temporary lawyer has access to information relating to the representation of firm clients other than the client on whose matters the lawyer is working and the consequent risk of improper disclosure or misuse of information relating to representation of other clients of the firm."

What do these examples suggest to you about the general duty of a law firm to supervise the handling of confidential information by its employees? Look again at Rules 5.1 & 5.3 and DR 4–101(D).

6. Can any of these problems of imputation be solved by "screening" one lawyer in a firm from participation in a matter?

a. What might such screening entail? If the opponent raises a legal challenge to the sufficiency of the screen, how will a judge be able to rule on its effectiveness unless the judge is told what it is that is supposed to remain confidential? If the judge is told, the confidentiality is lost. If the judge is told the information *in camera*, can the other party effectively reply unless it too is informed of what the judge was told?

b. Do the Model Rules seem to permit screening of a lawyer who has moved from one private firm to another? See Rule 1.10, Comment 5. Do you agree with the policy reasons expressed in that Comment? Is it important to have a bright line test? Does prohibiting a screen eliminate the problem of determining if the screen is sufficiently opaque?

c. For many years courts rejected any notion that a law firm could build a screen or "Chinese Wall" around someone disqualified on the basis of knowing significant confidential information that would traditionally be imputed to other lawyers in the firm. See, e.g., Fund of Funds, Ltd. v. Arthur Andersen & Co., 567 F.2d 225, 229 n. 10 (2d Cir.1977). As one commentator has explained, imputed disqualification based on a irrebuttable presumption of shared confidential information "is required by three realities of life in the modern law firm."

> "First is the relative informality of information exchange within most law firms [because] people tend to specialize their work within firms and tend to consult others in the firm who can give them necessary help on areas outside their expertise.

> "Second is the powerful economic incentive to use information that will help the firm win a case on behalf of a current client. * * * Indeed, a highly-regarded American Bar Foundation study of Chicago lawyers suggests that the fear of losing

clients creates the single most important pressure to engage in less-than-clearly ethical behavior today.

"Third and perhaps most important is the fact that no one outside a firm—indeed often leadership inside a firm—can ever be sure what has transpired behind the law firm's closed doors."

The proper question, therefore, is "not whether one can screen the disqualified lawyer from contact with others in the firm—but whether the lawyer realistically should be said to have received enough of the former client's information that the court's protection is required." [5]

d.   Some cases, however, have suggested that screening of lawyers may be permissible.

In Schiessle v. Stephens, 717 F.2d 417 (7th Cir.1983), Attorney MK, while a partner in the Antonow firm, had been in charge of representing one of the defendants in the *Schiessle* litigation. MK had discussed the case with his defendant/client and was involved in strategy sessions. MK then left the Antonow firm and became a partner in the Ross firm, which was co–counsel for the plaintiff. The Seventh Circuit concluded that a substantial relationship existed between the matters. The court concluded that MK was "actually privy" to and shared confidential information involving the case while at the Antonow firm. Evidence that would rebut this presumption of shared confidences "must 'clearly and effectively' demonstrate that the attorney had no knowledge of the information, confidences and/or secrets related by the client in the prior representation."

Because there was no effective rebuttal of the presumption of the shared confidences with respect to the prior representation, the trial court was required to determine whether a "specific institutional mechanism" had been implemented to insulate effectively against confidential information flowing from the "infected" attorney to any other member of his present firm.

"Such a determination can be based on objective and verifiable evidence presented to the trial court and must be made on a case-by-case basis. Factors appropriate for consideration by the trial court might include, but are not limited to, the size and structural divisions of the law firm involved, the likelihood of contact between the 'infected' attorney and the specific attorneys responsible for the present representation, the existence of rules which prevent the 'infected' attorney from access to the present litigation or which prevent him from sharing in the fees derived from such litigation."

The Court found the screening in this case ineffective and upheld the disqualification.

---

5. Morgan, Screening the Disqualified Lawyer: The Wrong Solution to the Wrong Problem, 10 U. Ark. at Little Rock L. J.37, 48 (1987–88).

Nemours Foundation v. Gilbane, Aetna, Federal Insurance Co., 632 F.Supp. 418 (D.Del.1986), upheld the use of screening and refused to disqualify Lawyer, who had been an associate at Firm A that represented Client. At the direction of lead counsel, Lawyer had prepared books of documents for use in a "mini-trial" to be conducted as part of settlement negotiations. After the mini-trial, Lawyer was hired by Firm B, the firm that represented Opponent in the litigation, to work on completely different matters. Lawyer was totally "screened" from the litigation between Client and Opponent. No one at Firm B could talk to Lawyer about the case, and Lawyer was permitted to see no files. Firm A moved to disqualify Firm B. Citing what it saw as the policies underlying Rule 1.6, the court held that the "cone of silence" created around Lawyer by Firm B was sufficient to avoid disqualification. Lawyer had been an associate at Firm A and had not been intimately involved in the case. The court refused to adopt a per se rule, reasoning that, "Attorney mobility, especially among young associates, would be severely restricted if a per se rule against a 'cone of silence' were adopted."

In Manning v. Waring, Cox, James, Sklar and Allen, 849 F.2d 222 (6th Cir.1988), bondholders had sued the underwriter ("Bank") when a bond issue went into default. Bond counsel ("Counsel") was named a third party defendant. "Lawyer" had been a chief attorney for Bank in its defense of the bondholders' case and in Bank's action over against Counsel. Then the law firm representing Counsel hired Lawyer for work not in the litigation side of that firm's practice. The court, again anxious not to impede lawyer mobility, remanded for factual findings but held that imputed disqualification can be avoided if the law firm bears the burden of showing "objective and verifiable evidence" of effective screening. Factors such as the "size and structural divisions" of the firm, "rules" that prevent the "infected" lawyer from having access to files in the case, and whether the infected attorney will share in fees from the case all should be considered by the lower court.

And in Cromley v. Lockport Board of Education, 17 F.3d 1059 (7th Cir.1994), a lawyer in the firm representing a teacher who alleged she had been denied administrative positions moved to the firm representing the school board. The Court found the same matter was involved and asked whether the presumption of shared confidences had been rebutted (citing Schiessle v. Stephens). The Court found an effective screening procedure had been established at the time the lawyer was hired, and the screen denied the lawyer access to the relevant files (which were kept in a different city). It admonished the lawyer not to discuss the case, and denied him any share in the fees derived from the case.

What do you think? Have these courts brought realism to the world of imputed disqualification? Have they unwisely created uncertainty about a rule that was previously clear? [6]

---

6. Other recent cases have been more restrictive. State ex rel. Freezer Services, Inc. v. Mullen, 458 N.W.2d 245 (Neb.1990), for example, involved a merger of the law firm representing the plaintiff with the firm representing the defendant. The new firm

e. Restatement of the Law (Third), The Law Governing Lawyers, Tentative Draft No. 4 (1991), Section 204(2), reflects substantial lobbying efforts, primarily by large law firms seeking the wide availability of screening. The proposed Restatement takes the Model Rules position with respect to screening in most cases, but adopts a *Silver Chrysler* or *Nemours* exception. It provides that screening is available, but only with respect to former clients and then only when:

(a) The confidential client information * * * is not likely to be significant in the later case;

(b) Adequate screening measures are in effect to eliminate involvement by the personally-prohibited lawyer in the representation; and

(c) Timely and adequate notice of screening has been provided to all affected clients.

What do you think of these standards? Do they appropriately balance the competing interests? It remains to be see whether the Restatement's formulation of the rule will now be adopted by the courts, either in the course of litigation or by amending court rules.

READINGS

ABA FORMAL OPINION 340 (SEPTEMBER 23, 1975)

Where both husband and wife are lawyers but they are not practicing in association with one another, may they or their firms represent differing interests?

This question, in varying forms, has been presented to this Committee with some frequency recently. Some firms apparently have been reluctant to employ one spouse-lawyer where that person's husband or wife is, or may soon be, practicing with another firm in the same city or area. On the other hand, some law schools have expressed disapproval of the practice by some firms in their hiring practices of attaching grave importance to the fact that the law student under consideration is married to a lawyer or a law student. Some law firms are concerned whether a law firm is disqualified, by reason of its employment of one spouse, to represent a client opposing an interest represented by another law firm that employs the husband or wife of the inquiring firm's

wished to continue to represent the defendant and to screen the lawyer who had handled the plaintiff's case. The court held the firm must be disqualified. "When a lawyer who has been 'intimately involved' with one side of a case joins the firm on the other side, no amount of screening can give the first client a secure feeling that its confidential information will be safe." Courts also rejected screening as a remedy in Lansing–Delaware Water District v. Oak Lane Park, Inc., 808 P.2d 1369 (Kan.1991); United States v. Davis, 780 F.Supp. 21 (D.D.C.1991); and Henriksen v. Great American Savings & Loan, 11 Cal.App.4th 109 (1992).

associate. Some of the circumstances bearing on this question include whether the fee of either firm is contingent, whether the disputed matter is one of negotiation or litigation, and whether the married lawyer in question will or will not actually be working on the particular matter. Another variation of the problem is the situation in which a governmental agency, such as a district attorney or an attorney general, is the employer of either the husband or the wife, and the spouse is associated with a law firm in the same community.

The problem undoubtedly will arise with increasing frequency and in different settings, for it is a fact of modern society that women are entering the profession in increasing numbers and that increasing numbers of these women are married to lawyers. Clearly, today it is not uncommon for husband and wife lawyers to be practicing in different offices in the same city, and the current enrollment of women in law schools indicates that women lawyers will constitute a greater percentage of the bar in the future than now.

It is not necessarily improper for husband-and-wife lawyers who are practicing in different offices or firms to represent differing interests. No disciplinary rule expressly requires a lawyer to decline employment if a husband, wife, son, daughter, brother, father, or other close relative represents the opposing party in negotiation or litigation. Likewise, it is not necessarily improper for a law firm having a married partner or associate to represent clients whose interests are opposed to those of other clients represented by another law firm with which the married lawyer's spouse is associated as a lawyer.

A lawyer whose husband or wife is also a lawyer must, like every other lawyer, obey all disciplinary rules, for the disciplinary rules apply to all lawyers without distinction as to marital status. We cannot assume that a lawyer who is married to another lawyer necessarily will violate any particular disciplinary rule, such as those that protect a client's confidences, that proscribe neglect of a client's interest, and that forbid representation of differing interests. Yet it also must be recognized that the relationship of husband and wife is so close that the possibility of an inadvertent breach of a confidence or the unavoidable receipt of information concerning the client by the spouse other than the one who represents the client (for example, information contained in a telephoned message left for the lawyer at home) is substantial. Because of the closeness of the husband-and-wife relationship, a lawyer who is married to a lawyer must be particularly careful to observe the suggestions and requirements of EC 4–1, EC 4–5, EC 5–1, EC 5–2, EC 5–3, EC 5–7, DR 4–101, and DR 5–101.

Even though the representation by husband and wife of opposing parties is not a violation of any disciplinary rule, the possibility of a violation of DR 5–101, in particular, is real and must be carefully considered in each instance. If the interest of one of the marriage partners as attorney for an opposing party creates a financial or personal interest that reasonably might affect the ability of a lawyer to represent fully his or her client with undivided loyalty and free exercise of professional judgment, the employment must be declined. We cannot assume, however, that certain facts, such as a fee being contingent or varying according to results obtained, necessarily will involve a violation of DR 5–101(A). In some instances the interest of one spouse in the other's income resulting from a particular fee may be such that professional judgment may be affected, while in other situations it may not be; the existence of such interest is a fact determination to be made in each individual case. Wherever one spouse is disqualified under DR 5–101(A), the entire firm is disqualified under DR 5–105(D).

In any event, the advice contained in EC 5–3 and EC 5–16 is apropos; the lawyer should advise the client of all circumstances that might cause one to question the undivided loyalty of the law firm and let the client make the decision as to its employment. If the client prefers not to employ a law firm containing a lawyer whose spouse is associated with a firm representing an opposing party, that decision should be respected.

The views expressed in this opinion are consistent with the views expressed by other committees in regard to the close relationships of opposing lawyers. For example, it has been held that a father and son may represent opposite sides in litigation: See Opinion 19 (January 23, 1963), Professional Ethics Committee of the Kansas Bar Association; Opinion 48, Missouri Advisory Opinions. In its Opinion No. 170 (1970), the New Jersey Advisory Committee on Professional Ethics held it is not improper for a lawyer to represent an indigent when the lawyer's brother is employed by the prosecutor's office.[7]

Accordingly, we conclude that a law firm employing a lawyer whose spouse is a lawyer associated with another local law firm need not fear consistent or mandatory disqualification when the two firms represent opposing interests; yet it is both proper and necessary for the firm always to be sensitive to both the possibility of disqualification and the wishes of its clients.* Marriage partners who are lawyers must guard carefully at all times against inadvertent violations of their professional responsibilities arising by reason of the marital relationship.

———

PROBLEM 16

Special Problems of Government Lawyers

Harold Smithers was a commissioner with the Federal Trade Commission for several years until 10 months ago when his term expired.

7. But see Opinion No. 288 (1974) of the New Jersey Advisory Committee on Professional Ethics holding that a "wife should not be permitted to practice criminal defense law in New Jersey while her husband is" a deputy attorney general assigned to the Appellate Section of the Division of Criminal Justice.

* Ed. Note: Accord, Blumenfeld v. Borenstein, 247 Ga. 406, 276 S.E.2d 607 (1981).

Prior to his appointment as a commissioner he had spent about 15 years—over half of his professional life—on the staff of the F.T.C.

Smithers retired from the Government at the end of his term and became a partner in the well-respected firm of Able & Baker in Washington, D.C. Smithers became familiar with Able & Baker because it engages in a great deal of F.T.C. work and has a reputation for excellence. In fact, for the last year, the firm has been representing the subject of a major investigation before the F.T.C. Although he disagreed with the strategy that Able & Baker was using in that case, he carefully avoided discussing that case while he was quietly negotiating with Able & Baker about his future employment at the firm.

Now that Smithers has moved to Able & Baker, P.D. Quick, Chief Executive Officer of Quick, Inc., has come from California to seek Able & Baker's help. The Commission staff has threatened to file an action in United States District Court seeking a preliminary injunction pending institution of a proceeding before the Commission alleging consumer fraud by Quick, Inc. The fraud is minor, but Quick is personally worried about it and wants to end the matter as soon as possible.

Neither Quick nor Quick, Inc., had ever before consulted with Able & Baker about this matter. P.D. Quick, during his initial conference with Smithers, mentioned in passing that the reason he decided to come to Able & Baker was because Smithers was there and a recent article about Smithers in Forbes Magazine (published as he was leaving the F.T.C.) said that Smithers had been one of the most influential and hardworking members in the history of the Commission. The article quoted one F.T.C. staff member who said that "even today when Smithers calls me on the phone, I instinctively straighten my tie and call him 'Sir!' "

The actual drafting of papers to be filed with the Commission staff will be handled by another partner of Able & Baker, but Smithers has been asked by the client and the active partner to give "a topside look" at the client's problems and to sign the important papers that will be filed with the Commission. Smithers also has agreed to call several staff members and a current commissioner or two who "owe their jobs to me." This last remark was made in an off-hand way in the presence of P.D. Quick who appeared pleased.

QUESTIONS

1. While Able & Baker had not previously been counsel to P.D. Quick or his corporation, is it important whether the F.T.C. had Quick or Quick, Inc. under investigation while Smithers was a Commissioner or staff member?

a. It is important to realize that all government employees (and former government employees), including lawyers, are often subject to special ethics legislation. In this case, because Smithers is a former *federal* official, he is subject to the limitations of 18 U.S.C.A. § 207 in the Standards Supplement. In addition, because Smithers is a lawyer, he is subject to Model Rule 1.11(a) and DR 9–101(B).

b. Suppose Smithers had participated in the vote to begin the investigation of Quick, Inc. that led to the present action. What limits, if any, would there be on what he could do for Quick today? Be sure to look at 18 U.S.C.A. § 207(a)(i), as well as the Model Rules and Model Code. What sanction would Smithers face if he violated the federal statute? [1]

c. Is there any statute of limitations on the bar to subsequent representation of a private party in such a case? If Smithers had personally worked on a case 15 years ago, for example, early in his career at the F.T.C., would he now be free to work on the matter in private practice?

d. What if the investigation had been going on at the staff level while Smithers was a Commissioner but Smithers had no direct responsibility for it other than in the sense that all F.T.C. staff "work for" the Commission? Do Model Rule 1.11 and DR 9–101(B) deal with this question at all? How about 18 U.S.C.A. § 207(a)(ii)?

e. Now assume the matter came to the Commission the week after Smithers left the agency. Does that mean that there are no limits on his ability to contact his friends there? Look at 18 U.S.C.A. § 207(c). What purpose is served by such a one-year "cooling-off" provision?

United States v. Nofziger, 878 F.2d 442 (D.C.Cir.1989), reversed the conviction of President Reagan's assistant, Lynn Nofziger, who had been convicted under 18 U.S.C.A. § 207(c). On behalf of clients of his lobbying firm, he had sent a letter to Edwin Meese, then Counselor to the President, urging that the Army be encouraged to give a contract to Wedtech, a minority-owned firm in the South Bronx. He also sent a copy of a letter to a Meese deputy urging use of civilian crews on noncombatant Navy ships. Finally, he met with National Security Council staff members to urge continued production on the A–10 aircraft for which Congress had cut off funds. Nofziger alleged that the Government had not proved that he knew these were issues in which the agencies he had contacted already had a "direct and substantial interest." Judges Buckley and Williams found such a knowledge requirement arguably in the statute and concluded that where there is ambiguity in a criminal statute the defendant should prevail. Judge Edwards in dissent argued there was no ambiguity.

---

1. Looking at the other direction of the revolving door, what must the lawyer consider when he or she enters government service? Must a government official recuse herself every time something comes up involving a former private client? See Rule 1.11(c)(1), and Formal Opinion 342, in the Readings to this Problem.

2. Should the former government lawyer be disqualified only when he or she wants to take a case opposed to the government's earlier position?

a. Remember that Model Rule 1.9 only prohibits representation that is "materially adverse" to the former client. Is Rule 1.11 so limited? Consider especially Rule 1.11(b). How about DR 9–101(B)?

b. Rule 1.11(b), Comment 4 is basically derived from General Motors Corp. v. City of New York, 501 F.2d 639 (2d Cir.1974), rev'g 60 F.R.D. 393 (S.D.N.Y.1973). While a lawyer for the U.S. Government in 1956, *L* filed and signed an antitrust complaint against General Motors. He had had substantial responsibility for the preparation of that suit. Subsequently, in 1972, while he was in private practice he agreed to represent New York City in another, similar antitrust claim on a contingent fee basis. The court disqualified the lawyer. It concluded that his prior responsibility for the case was "substantial;" that his contingent fee arrangement with the City constituted private employment; that the City's antitrust suit was sufficiently similar to the federal case so as to constitute the same "matter" for purposes of DR 9–101(B); that it was irrelevant that the lawyer had not "switched sides" but had continued to litigate against G.M.; and that the lawyer's representation of the City would constitute the "appearance of impropriety." Why? What reasons might forbid a lawyer who has left government from taking a case that *furthers* the government's objectives? [2]

c. Under present law, should a military reservist lawyer be permitted to accept as clients, ex-soldiers whom he first represented while on active duty? A thorough analysis upholding the practice may be found in Woods v. Covington County Bank, 537 F.2d 804 (5th Cir.1976).

3. Did Smithers do anything wrong when he was negotiating for employment prior to his retirement from the F.T.C.?

a. How may a lawyer in government service look for a job on the outside? May he or she contact firms that regularly deal with the lawyer's agency? See Rule 1.11(c)(2). Might those be the principal firms that would find the lawyer's experience valuable?

b. Would it have been ethical for Smithers to have encouraged the publication of the Forbes article? How about to have aided it such as by allowing himself to be interviewed? Does the public have such an interest in knowing about persons like Smithers that for Smithers to refuse to provide information about himself might itself be wrong?

c. Smithers mentioned that several commissioners "owe their jobs to me." Assuming that this statement is factually correct and well known, what is the comment trying to imply? Are Model Rule 8.4(e) and DR 9–101(C) implicated by the comment?

2. Cf. Armstrong v. McAlpin, 625 F.2d 433 (2d Cir.1980) (en banc), vac'd 449 U.S. 1106, 101 S.Ct. 911, 66 L.Ed.2d 835 (1981), where the court assumes this construction of DR 9–101(B) but accepts the screening approach of ABA Formal Opinion 342, set forth as a Reading to this Problem.

**4.   Should it be wrong for a lawyer who has built up exper-
tise in an area of law by decades of hard work to benefit from
his reputation by using access to governmental officials?**

a.   Even if in the process of taking a "topside look" at P.D. Quick's
problems with the F.T.C., Smithers makes no improper overtures to the
F.T.C. staff or commissioners, has Smithers acted responsibly?   With
good judgment?   Consider P.D. Quick's view of the situation.   Why
would Quick travel all the way from California to hire Smithers when
there are plenty of good lawyers in California?[3]

b.   Should Smithers' attempt to influence the F.T.C. on behalf of
P.D. Quick be considered to be improper?   Not everyone could telephone
an F.T.C. commissioner and expect to talk to her personally, but Smithers (and others like him) can.   Is that kind of access unethical per se?
Does any judgment of it depend on what is said during the ex parte
communication?

c.   Would it be unrealistic to require people like Smithers never to
use the access they obtained while working for the government?   President Truman is said to have—

> "had strong feelings about using one's official position, *past or
> present*, for gain.   He was extremely fond of General Omar
> Bradley, the fellow Missourian who at one time during Mr.
> Truman's administration was Chief of Staff.   After Bradley
> retired, he took a job as chairman of the board of the Bulova
> Watch Company, and one day in discussing General Bradley Mr.
> Truman said, 'I hold it against him, taking that job.   They
> weren't hiring him; what they thought they were doing was
> buying some influence in the Pentagon, and I don't care at all
> for that sort of thing, and I can't understand how General
> Bradley could bring himself to do it.'   Being an admirer of
> General Bradley, I said, no doubt apologetically, 'He probably
> felt he needed the money.'   And Mr. Truman said, 'Nobody ever
> needs money that bad.' "[4]

d.   When President Kennedy appointed Arthur Goldberg to the
Cabinet as Secretary of Labor, Goldberg promised never to practice labor
law again, although that field of law had been his specialty.   Goldberg
always kept that promise.   Would such a prophylactic rule—preventing a
former governmental employee from using the benefits of his former
position while in private practice—tend to discourage many good persons
from entering government service?[5]

e.   What should be the rule if the attorney developed special access
without having been in government service?   Consider the following:

3.   Cf. Wall St. J., May 16, 1975, at 1,
col. 5:

> "Legal stars with good connections are
> sought out by companies under S.E.C.
> investigation for payoffs abroad.   Former
> Defense Secretary Clark Clifford repre-
> sents Phillips Petroleum Co.; former
> S.E.C. Chairman Manuel Cohen repre-
> sents Northrop Corp.   Former State De-

partment advisor John J. McCloy heads a
Gulf Oil Corp. committee investigating
Gulf's slush funds."

4.   M. Miller, Plain Speaking: An Oral
Biography of Harry S. Truman (1974) at
201–02, n. † (emphasis added).

5.   See generally A.B.A. Formal Opinion
342 (November 24, 1975), infra.

"[Reuben B. Robertson III is a Washington lawyer who represents a client] interested in aviation. So he made it his business to cultivate the acquaintance of Stephen Alterman, chief enforcement attorney at the Civil Aeronautics Board. 'Quite frankly,' says Mr. Alterman, 'a relationship has developed between Reuben and me. We're in constant contact.'

"Maybe the Robertson–Alterman connection ought to be investigated by one of those muckraking public interest outfits—say, the Aviation Consumer Action Project, the Ralph Nader affiliate that had prodded several CAB investigations into airline practices.

"That's not about to happen, though. You see, Reuben Robertson *is* the Aviation Consumer Action Project." [6]

Are the ethical principles different when your client is the "public interest"?

5. To change our problem somewhat, assume that Smithers is a retired U.S. Senator who had been chairman of a subcommittee charged with oversight of the F.T.C.

a. Suppose P.D. Quick wanted Smithers to persuade his old subcommittee to approve a proposed law that would permit a practice being investigated by the F.T.C. Would former-Senator Smithers be under the same ethical restraints as ex-Commissioner Smithers? Take a look at 18 U.S.C.A. § 207(e)(1). Why should the scope and duration of the rules differ depending on the branch of government in which the former official served?

b. If former-Senator Smithers had been joined at Able & Baker by the Chief Counsel of the Senate subcommittee, would the Chief Counsel have been subject to the same limitations? See 18 U.S.C.A. § 207(e)(3).

6. Assume that you are a state legislator in addition to being a practicing lawyer.

a. Your state, like many states, allows legislators to continue to practice law. Because you are familiar with the problems of the First Savings Bank, which is also one of your constituents, you decide that you will introduce a bill in the state legislature to cut back the powers of your state Credit Regulatory Commission so that this Commission may not investigate alleged inappropriate credit behavior of banks such as red-lining. Is there anything wrong with introducing such a bill if you do not charge First Savings Bank for this service? [7] See DR 8–101 ("Action as a Public Official").

---

6. Schorr, Vox Populi, Public Interest Units Gain More Influence with Federal Agencies, The Wall Street Journal, July 15, 1975, at 1, col. 1.

7. On the Federal level, consider Office of Disciplinary Counsel v. Eilberg, 497 Pa. 388, 441 A.2d 1193 (1982), where a law-

yer/Congressman was suspended for violating 18 U.S.C.A. § 203(a), a federal law prohibiting a member of Congress from receiving compensation for representing a client before a federal agency. The lawyer had set up a "dual practice," i.e., the lawyer's law partners set up a separate entity to

b.   Assume that recently, in arguing a case before the state supreme court, you pointed out that the court ought not change a common law rule because the legislature had considered the matter and refused to enact a statute which had the same result. You had introduced the bill in question after being retained in the case; then, it was referred to your committee where you arranged to have it killed. Leaving aside the question whether the legislature can create legislative history by refusing to pass a law, was it professionally responsible for you a legislator to try to create legislative history to help a private client who is also your constituent?

c.   Would it be proper for you to "create" the legislative history if you believe that it correctly reflects the legislature's view? Notice that the Model Rules have nothing that corresponds exactly to DR 8–101. Rules 1.11(c) and 8.4(e),(f) are the closest that the Model Rules come to it. Was it a good idea for the Model Rules not to copy the Model Code on this issue?

7.   Do the statutory ethics provisions prohibit all activity by Smithers within his own law firm in the case involving Quick, Inc.?

a.   May Smithers talk to Mr. Quick, for example, about what the F.T.C. is likely to do? May he give tactical advice to his partners who are handling the Quick matter? Does the federal statute inhibit what Smithers may do within the law firm?

b.   The legislative history of 18 U.S.C.A. § 207 shows that Congress meant to have questions about attribution of disqualification within a law firm, or any right of the government to waive the disqualification, to be governed by the Bar's own rules of ethics.[8]

c.   Look at ABA Formal Opinion 342, set forth in the Readings to this Problem. Do you agree that application of the usual rules of imputation of disqualification within a firm would "actually thwart the policy considerations underlying DR 9–101(B)"? See also Armstrong v. McAlpin, 625 F.2d 433 (2d Cir.1980) (en banc), vac'd 449 U.S. 1106, 101 S.Ct. 911, 66 L.Ed.2d 835 (1981).

d.   Are you confident that the required screening devices will work? What danger of "breaches in the Wall" might you see? Can a partner in a firm be totally screened from at least indirect "participation in the fees" from a case?

e.   Should the government be able to waive a disqualification? Who should be authorized to issue the waiver? Should there be extensive

receive compensation for representing clients before federal agencies. But the lawyer/Congressman encouraged prospective clients to hire the "other" firm to represent the clients, and, in one case (apparently because of an accounting error) he received a portion of the profits from the representation before a federal agency. The Court said that it need not rule on the ethics of the "dual practice" law firm, but said it is ethically "dubious", even though it does not technically violate section 18 U.S.C.A. § 203(a).

8. Morgan, Appropriate Limits on Participation by a Former Agency Official in Matters Before an Agency, 1980 Duke L.J. 1, 11.

notice requirements, as suggested by Monroe Freedman in the Readings to this Problem, or should the lesser requirements of Rule 1.11(a)(2) be sufficient?

READINGS

ABA FORMAL OPINION 342 (NOVEMBER 24, 1975)

Following the 1974 amendment of DR 5–105(D), which extended every disqualification of an individual lawyer in a firm to all affiliated lawyers, the interpretation and application of DR 9–101(B) have been increasingly of concern to many government agencies as well as to many former government lawyers now in private practice. DR 9–101(B) is based upon former ABA Canon 36, but its standard or test is different. Our task is to interpret DR 9–101(B) in light of its history and in consideration of its underlying purposes and policies.

* * * A lawyer violates DR 4–101(B) only by knowingly revealing a confidence or secret of a client or using a confidence or secret improperly as specified in the rule. Nevertheless, many authorities have held that as a procedural matter a lawyer is disqualified to represent a party in litigation if he formerly represented an adverse party in a matter substantially related to the pending litigation. Even though DR 4–101(B) is not breached by the mere act of accepting present employment against a former client involving a matter substantially related to the former employment, the procedural disqualification protects the former client in advance of and against a possible future violation of DR 4–101(B).

* * * The rules also forbid a lawyer to switch sides even in situations where the exercise of the lawyer's professional judgment on behalf of a present client will not be affected.[8]

* * *

DR 9–101(B) appears under the maxim of Canon 9, "A Lawyer Should Avoid Even the Appearance of Professional Impropriety." It is obvious, however, that the "appearance of professional impropriety" is not a standard, test or element embodied in DR 9–101(B). DR 9–101(B) is located under Canon 9 because the "appearance of professional impropriety" is a policy consideration supporting the existence of the Disciplinary Rule. The appearance of evil is only one of the underlying

---

8. The prohibition against switching sides where the exercise of the lawyer's professional judgment on behalf of a client will not be affected is somewhat obscure. The prohibition is found in DR 5–105(A) and (B), forbidding the acceptance or retention of employment involving the represen-tation of "differing interest," which is defined as every interest "that will adversely affect either the judgment or the loyalty of a lawyer to a client. * * * "Definitions (1). Generally, see E. F. Hutton & Co. v. Brown, 305 F.Supp. 371 (S.D.Tex.1969).

considerations, however, and is probably not the most important reason for the creation and existence of the rule itself.

The policy considerations underlying DR 9–101(B) have been thought to be the following: the treachery of switching sides; the safeguarding of confidential governmental information from future use against the government; the need to discourage government lawyers from handling particular assignments in such a way as to encourage their own future employment in regard to those particular matters after leaving government service; and the professional benefit derived from avoiding the appearance of evil.

There are, however, weighty policy considerations in support of the view that a special disciplinary rule relating only to former government lawyers should not broadly limit the lawyer's employment after he leaves government service. Some of the underlying considerations favoring a construction of the rule in a manner not to restrict unduly the lawyer's future employment are the following: the ability of government to recruit young professionals and competent lawyers should not be interfered with by imposition of harsh restraints upon future practice nor should too great a sacrifice be demanded of the lawyers willing to enter government service; the rule serves no worthwhile public interest if it becomes a mere tool enabling a litigant to improve his prospects by depriving his opponent of competent counsel; and the rule should not be permitted to interfere needlessly with the right of litigants to obtain competent counsel of their own choosing, particularly in specialized areas requiring special, technical training and experience.

DR 9–101(B) itself, while presumably drafted in the light of the above policy considerations, does not embody any of them as a test. The issue of fact to be determined in a disciplinary action is whether the lawyer has accepted "private employment" in a "matter" in which he had "substantial responsibility" while he was a "public employee." Interpretation apparently is needed in regard to each of the quoted words or phrases, and each should be interpreted so as to be consistent, insofar as possible, with the underlying policy considerations discussed above.[17]

As used in DR 9–101(B), "private employment" refers to employment as a private practitioner. If one underlying consideration is to

---

17. Perhaps the least helpful of the seven policy considerations mentioned above is that of avoiding the appearance of impropriety. This consideration appears in the heading of Canon 9 and is developed more fully in EC 9–2 and 9–3, thereby giving guidance to lawyers when making decisions of conscience in regard to their professional responsibility. Thus, "avoiding the appearance of evil" is relevant to our task of interpreting DR 9–101(B), even though it is not relevant when a grievance committee or court is determining whether a violation of the standard of DR 9–101(B) has in fact occurred. It is fortunate that "avoiding even the appearance of professional impropriety" was not made an element of the disciplinary rule, for it is too vague a phrase to be useful (see McKay, An Administrative Code of Ethics: Principles and Implementation, 47 ABA J. 890, 894 (1961)), and lawyers will differ as to what constitutes the appearance of evil (see Silver Chrysler Plymouth, Inc. v. Chrysler Motors Corp., 370 F.Supp. 581 (E.D.N.Y.1973), affirmed 518 F.2d 751 (2d Cir.1975)).

For the same reasons, the concept is of limited assistance as an underlying policy consideration. If "appearance of professional impropriety" had been included as

avoid the situation where government lawyers may be tempted to handle assignments so as to encourage their own future employment in regard to those matters, the danger is that a lawyer may attempt to derive undue financial benefit from fees in connection with subsequent employment, and not that he may change from one salaried government position to another. The balancing consideration supporting our construction is that government agencies should not be unduly hampered in recruiting lawyers presently employed by other government bodies.[18]

Although a precise definition of "matter" as used in the Disciplinary Rule is difficult to formulate, the term seems to contemplate a discrete and isolatable transaction or set of transactions between identifiable parties. Perhaps the scope of the term "matter" may be indicated by examples. The same lawsuit or litigation is the same matter. The same issue of fact involving the same parties and the same situation or conduct is the same matter. By contrast, work as a government employee in drafting, enforcing or interpreting government or agency procedures, regulations, or laws, or in briefing abstract principles of law, does not disqualify the lawyer under DR 9–101(B) from subsequent private employment involving the same regulations, procedures, or points of law; the same "matter" is not involved because there is lacking the discrete, identifiable transactions or conduct involving a particular situation and specific parties.[21]

* * *

The element of DR 9–101(B) most difficult to interpret in light of the underlying considerations, pro and con, is that of "substantial responsibility."

* * *

an element in the disciplinary rule, it is likely that the determination of whether particular conduct violated the rule would have degenerated from the determination of the fact issues specified by the rule into a determination on an instinctive, *ad hoc* or even *ad hominem* basis.

18. This position is not in conflict with General Motors Corp. v. City of New York, 501 F.2d 639 (2d Cir.1974). In that case it appears that the lawyer for the municipality was privately retained, and the appellate court held that this employment constituted "private employment" within the meaning of DR 9–101(B).

21. "Many a lawyer who has served with the government has an advantage when he enters private practice because he has acquired a working knowledge of the department in which he was employed, has learned the procedures, the governing substantive and statutory law and is to a greater or lesser degree an expert in the field in which he was engaged. Certainly this is perfectly proper and ethical. Were it not so, it would be a distinct deterrent to lawyers ever to accept employment with the government. This is distinguishable, however, from a situation where, in addition, a former government lawyer is employed and is expected to bring with him and into the proceedings a personal knowledge of a particular matter", the latter being thought to be within the proscription of former Canon 36. Allied Realty of St. Paul v. Exchange National Bank of Chicago, 283 F.Supp. 464 (D.Minn.1968), affirmed 408 F.2d 1099 (8th Cir.1969). See also B. Manning, Federal Conflict of Interest Law 204 (1964).

A contrary interpretation would unduly interfere with the opportunity of a former lawyer to use his expert technical legal skills, and the prospect of such unnecessary limitations on future practice probably would unreasonably hinder the recruiting efforts of various local, state and federal governmental agencies and bodies.

As used in DR 9–101(B), "substantial responsibility" envisages a much closer and more direct relationship than that of a mere perfunctory approval or disapproval of the matter in question. It contemplates a responsibility requiring the official to become personally involved to an important, material degree, in the investigative or deliberative processes regarding the transactions or facts in question. Thus, being the chief official in some vast office or organization does not *ipso facto* give that government official or employee the "substantial responsibility" contemplated by the rule in regard to all the minutiae of facts lodged within that office. Yet it is not necessary that the public employee or official shall have personally and in a substantial manner investigated or passed upon the particular matter, for it is sufficient that he had such a heavy responsibility for the matter in question that it is unlikely he did not become personally and substantially involved in the investigative or deliberate processes regarding that matter. With a responsibility so strong and compelling that he probably became involved in the investigative or decisional processes, a lawyer upon leaving the government service should not represent another in regard to that matter. To do so would be akin to switching sides, might jeopardize confidential government information, and gives the appearance of professional impropriety in that accepting subsequent employment regarding that same matter creates a suspicion that the lawyer conducted his governmental work in a way to facilitate his own future employment in that matter.

The element of "substantial responsibility" as so construed should not unduly hinder the government in recruiting lawyers to its ranks nor interfere needlessly with the right of litigants to employ technically skilled and trained former government lawyers to represent them.

The last factual element of DR 9–101(B) deserving explanation is that of "public employee." It is significant that the word lawyer was not used instead of employee. Accordingly, the intent clearly was for DR 9–101(B) to be applicable to the lawyer whose former public or governmental employment was in any capacity and without regard to whether it involved work normally handled by lawyers.

The extension by DR 5–105(D) of disqualification to all affiliated lawyers is to prevent circumvention by a lawyer of the Disciplinary Rules. Past government employment creates an unusual situation in which inflexible application of DR 5–105(D) would actually thwart the policy considerations underlying DR 9–101(B).

When the Disciplinary Rules of Canons 4 and 5 mandate the disqualification of a government lawyer who has come from private practice, his governmental department or division cannot practicably be rendered incapable of handling even the specific matter. Clearly, if DR 5–105(D) were so construed, the government's ability to function would be unreasonably impaired. Necessity dictates that government action not be hampered by such a construction of DR 5–105(D). The relationships among lawyers within a government agency are different from those among partners and associates of a law firm. The salaried government employee does not have the financial interest in the success of departmental representation that is inherent in private practice. This important difference in the adversary posture of the government lawyer is recognized by Canon 7: the duty of the public prosecutor to seek justice, not merely to convict, and the duty of all government lawyers to seek just results rather than the result desired by a client. The channeling of advocacy toward a just result as opposed to vindication of a particular claim lessens the temptation to circumvent the disciplinary rules through the action of associates. Accordingly, we construe DR 5–105(D) to be inapplicable to other government lawyers associated with a particular government lawyer who is himself disqualified by reason of DR 4–101, DR 5–105, DR 9–101(B), or similar Disciplinary Rules. Although vicarious disqualification of a government department is not necessary or wise, the individual lawyer should be screened from any direct or indirect participation in the matter, and discussion with his colleagues concerning the relevant transaction or set of transactions is prohibited by those rules.

Likewise, DR 9–101(B)'s command of refusal of employment by an individual lawyer does not necessarily activate DR 5–105(D)'s extension of that disqualification. The purposes of limiting the mandate to matters in which the former public employee had a substantial responsibility are to inhibit government recruitment as little as possible and enhance the opportunity for all litigants to obtain competent counsel of their own choosing, particularly in specialized areas. An inflexible extension of disqualification throughout an entire firm would thwart those purposes. So long as the individual lawyer is held to be disqualified and is screened from any direct or indirect participation in the matter, the problem of his switching sides is not present; by contrast, an inflexible extension of disqualification throughout the firm often would result in real hardship to a client if complete withdrawal of representation was mandated, because substantial work may have been completed regarding specific litigation prior to the time the government employee joined the partnership, or the client may have relied in the past on representation by the firm.

All of the policies underlying DR 9–101(B), including the principles of Canons 4 and 5, can be realized by a less stringent application of DR 5–105(D). The purposes, as embodied in DR 9–101(B), of discouraging government lawyers from handling particular assignments in such a way as to encourage their own future employment in regard to those particular matters after leaving government service, and of avoiding the appearance of impropriety, can be accomplished by holding that DR 5–105(D) applies to the firm and partners and associates of a disqualified lawyer who has not been screened, to the satisfaction of the government agency concerned, from participation in the work and compensation of the firm on any matter over which as a public employee he had substantial responsibility. Applying DR 5–105(D) to this limited extent accomplishes the goal of destroying any incentive of the employee to handle his government work so as to affect his future employment. Only allegiance to form over substance would justify blanket application of DR 5–105(D) in a manner that thwarts and distorts the policy considerations behind DR 9–101(B).

Our conclusion is further supported by the fact that DR 5–105(C) allows the multiple representation that is generally forbidden by DR 5–105(A) and (B), where all clients consent after full disclosure of the possible effect of such representation. DR 5–105(A) and (B) deals, of course, with much more egregious contingencies than those covered by DR 9–101(B). It is unthinkable that the drafters of the Code of Professional Responsibility intended to permit the one afforded protection by DR 5–105(A) and (B) to waive that protection without also permitting the one protected by DR 9–101(B) to waive that less-needed protection. Accordingly, it is our opinion that whenever the government agency is satisfied that the screening measures will effectively isolate the individual lawyer from participating in the particular matter and sharing in the fees attributable to it, and that there is no appearance of significant impropriety affecting the interests of the government, the government may waive the disqualification of the firm under DR 5–105(D). In the event of such waiver, and provided the firm also makes its own independent determination as to the absence of particular circumstances creating a significant appearance of impropriety, the result will be that the firm is not in violation of DR 5–105(D) by accepting or continuing the representation in question.

Although this opinion has dealt explicitly and at length with the interpretation and application of DR 9–101(B), it is not amiss to point out that, on the ethical rather than the disciplinary level of professional responsibility, each lawyer should advise a potential client of any circumstances that might cause a question to be raised concerning the propriety of his undertaking the employment and should also resolve all doubts against the acceptance of questionable employment. See EC 5–105 and EC 5–16.

––––––––

MONROE H. FREEDMAN,* FOR A NEW RULE

[T]here is virtual unanimity that when a lawyer has had substantial responsibility for a particular matter while in governmental service, that lawyer should be disqualified subsequently from opposing the government on behalf of a private client in the same matter.

There is also fairly general agreement on the well-established principle of imputed disqualification—that is, when a lawyer is disqualified from a particular matter, that lawyer's partners and associates were similarly disqualified. For example, the former assistant attorney gener-

* Professor of Law, Hofstra Law School.   A.B.A.J. 724–25 (1977). This article originally appeared at 63

al for the Office of Legal Counsel, Antonin Scalia, has written that the "long recognized" rule of imputed disqualification is not at issue—indeed, the government, he has said, "strenuously supports it." In the context of the former government employee, that means that when an individual lawyer is disqualified because he or she had substantial responsibility for a particular matter while in governmental service, then a partner or associate of that lawyer—that is, one who shares daily conversation and annual profits with that lawyer—must be disqualified also.

The ultimate and proper focus of the debate, therefore, is on the question of whether the imputed disqualification of partners and associates should be open to waiver in some cases. The basis of a waiver would be a determination by the governmental agency involved that the individual disqualified attorney has been "screened" from any participation in the case. There are three major objections to the screening-waiver device, however, and none of them has been answered successfully in the lengthy debates thus far.

The first is that no workable standards have ever been suggested. * * *

The second unanswered objection relates to the virtual impossibility of policing violations of screening once a waiver has been given. * * *

Finally, the screening-waiver device seriously compounds the initial conflict of interest. Agency lawyers who are called on to grant or deny a waiver on behalf of a former colleague's firm have a personal incentive to be generous in granting the waiver, because they will themselves be making similar requests for waivers when they leave governmental service. * * *

The principal argument in favor of permitting a screening-waiver device is expediency based on speculation. Without the support of a single specific illustration, the charge is made that the government will find it impossible to employ competent lawyers if the screening-waiver exception is rejected. As observed by former American Bar Association president Chesterfield Smith, however, that contention is "pure hogwash." For one thing, if concern over the denial of waivers will result in the unemployability of former government lawyers, then that problem will prevail as long as there is any significant risk that waivers will be denied in particular cases. That is, unless the waiver device is a sham, and waivers are to be granted as a matter of course whenever requested, the asserted risks of hiring former government employees will still discourage law firms from employing them.

In fact, however, not a single specific instance has been given of a government employee who would be rendered unemployable by application of the proposed standard * * *. Unquestionably, a particular lawyer might have to forgo employment in a particular law firm—Lawyer A, say, might not be able to return to Firm C and B—but that is hardly the catastrophe that has been conjured up by the opponents of the ethical rule.

The revolving door between governmental service and private practice has been identified as the cause of low morale among government lawyers. Ironically, Calvin J. Collier, chairman of the Federal Trade Commission, contended that the committee's proposed opinion would impair professionalism in his agency. A recent study revealed, however, that the F.T.C. in fact is suffering from a critically high turnover rate and low morale among its attorneys. The reason given for that unhealthy situation is that too many lawyers are using the agency as a steppingstone to jobs outside of government. In short, slowing down the revolving door could well lead to higher morale and a higher degree of dedication and efficiency in governmental service.

* * *

It isn't surprising that the drafters [of a D.C. Bar proposal] found it impossible to articulate adequate standards for screening the disqualified attorney from others in the firm, but the draft provision of a waiver exception represents a distinct advance over the present practice in two important respects. First, any waiver must be in writing, must state clearly the basis for the decision, and must be made public. Second, the waiver must be reviewed and approved by a judge or by another official independent of the agency or department representing the government in the matter.

Those two provisions would provide some minimal assurance that the public interest would be protected in cases of conflict of interests of former government attorneys. Even so, I consider them inadequate to the task because of the absence of standards and the impossibility of policing, and I continue to oppose [any possibility of waiver].

SELECTED BIBLIOGRAPHY ON ISSUES IN CHAPTER IV

Problem 9

Aronson, Conflict of Interest, 52 Washington L.Rev. 807 (1977).

Batt, The Family Unit as Client: A Means to Address the Ethical Dilemmas Confronting Elder Law Attorneys, 6 Georgetown J.Legal Ethics 319 (1992).

Collett, And the Two Shall Become One ... Until the Lawyers Are Done, 7 Notre Dame J.L., Ethics & Public Policy 101 (1993).

Collett, Disclosure, Discretion, or Deception: The Estate Planner's Ethical Dilemma From a Unilateral Confidence, 28 Real Property, Probate and Trust Journal 683 (1994).

Collett, The Ethics of Intergenerational Representation, 62 Fordham L.Rev. 1453 (1994).

Cutler, Conflicts of Interest, 30 Emory L.J. 1015 (1981).

Dam, Class Actions: Efficiency, Compensation, Deterrence, and Conflict of Interest, 4 J.Legal Studies 47 (1975).

Dobris, Ethical Problems for Lawyers Upon Trust Terminations: Conflicts of Interest, 38 U.Miami L.Rev. 1 (1983).

Drinker, Problems of Professional Ethics in Matrimonial Litigation, 66 Harvard L.Rev. 443 (1953).

Dzienkowski, Lawyers as Intermediaries, 1992 U.Illinois L.Rev. 741 (1992).

Elias, Multiple Representation in Shareholder Derivative Suits: A Case–by–Case Approach, 16 Loyola University (Chicago) L.J. 613 (1985).

Epstein, The Legal Regulation of Lawyers' Conflicts of Interest, 60 Fordham L.Rev. 579 (1992).

Flickinger, Surrogate Motherhood: The Attorney's Legal and Ethical Dilemma, 11 Capital U.L.Rev. 593 (Spring 1982).

Frank, The Legal Ethics of Louis D. Brandeis, 17 Stanford L.Rev. 683 (1965).

Hacker & Rotunda, Attorney Conflicts of Interest, 2 Corporation L.Rev. 345 (1979).

Hacker & Rotunda, Standing, Waiver, Laches, and Appealability in Attorney Disqualification Cases, 3 Corporation L.Rev. 82 (1980).

Hilker, It's a Family Affair: Ethical Problems for Estate Planners, The Professional Lawyer 81 (Symposium Issue 1993).

Hobbs, Facilitative Ethics in Divorce Mediation: A Law and Process Approach, 22 U.Richmond L.Rev. 325 (1988).

House, Conflict of Interests When Representing a Beneficiary and the Trustee, 6 J.Legal Profession 309 (1981).

Kramer, The Appearance of Impropriety Under Canon 9: A Study of the Federal Judicial Process Applied to Lawyers, 65 Minnesota L.Rev. 243 (1981).

Moore, Conflicts of Interest in the Simultaneous Representation of Multiple Clients: A Proposed Solution to the Current Confusion and Controversy, 61 Texas L.Rev. 211 (1982).

Note, Developments in the Law: Conflicts of Interest in the Legal Profession, 94 Harvard L.Rev. 1244 (1981).

Note, The Lawyer as Mediator: Inherent Conflict of Interest?, 32 U.C.L.A. L.Rev. 986 (1985).

O'Dea, The Lawyer–Client Relationship Reconsidered: Methods for Avoiding Conflicts of Interest, Malpractice Liability, and Disqualification, 48 George Washington L.Rev. 693 (1980).

Parley, Post–Marital Agreements, 8 J.Am.Acad.Matrimonial Lawyers 125 (1992).

Patterson, Legal Ethics and the Lawyer's Duty of Loyalty, 29 Emory L.J. 909 (1980).

Pearce, Family Values and Legal Ethics: Competing Approaches to Conflicts in Representing Spouses, 62 Fordham L.Rev. 1253 (1994).

Rapoport, Turning and Turning in the Widening Gyre: The Problem of Potential Conflicts of Interest in Bankruptcy, 26 Connecticut L.Rev. 913 (1994).

Rhode, Class Conflicts in Class Actions, 34 Stanford L.Rev. 1183 (1982).

Saffold–Heyward, Outside the Courtroom: Conflicts of Interests in Nonlitigious Situations, 37 Washington & Lee L.Rev. 161 (1980).

Sato, The Mediator–Lawyer: Implications for the Practice of Law and One Argument for Professional Responsibility Guidance—a Proposal For Some Ethical Considerations, 34 U.C.L.A. L.Rev. 507 (1986).

Problem 10

Breger, Disqualification for Conflicts of Interest and the Legal Aid Attorney, 62 Boston U.L.J. 1115 (1982).

Hansen, Dual Representation in Unrelated Matters Permitted with Client Consent When Firm can Protect Clients' Best Interest, 60 Washington U.L.Q. 1155 (1982).

Problem 11

Covy, The Right to Counsel of One's Choice: Joint Representation of Criminal Defendants, 58 Notre Dame Lawyer 793 (1983).

Green, Her Brother's Keeper: The Prosecutor's Responsibility When Defense Counsel Has a Potential Conflict of Interest, 16 American J.Criminal L. 323 (1989).

Green, "Through a Glass, Darkly": How the Court Sees Motions to Disqualify Criminal Defense Lawyers, 89 Columbia L.Rev. 1201 (1989).

Heim, Conflicts of Interest in the Representation of Multiple Criminal Defendants: Clarifying Cuyler v. Sullivan, 70 Georgetown L.J. 1527 (1982).

Larsen, When Constitutional Rights Clash: The Duty of the Trial Judge in Cases Involving Multiple Representation of Criminal Defendants, 19 Valparaiso U.L.Rev. 649 (1985).

Margolin & Coliver, Pretrial Disqualification of Criminal Defense Counsel, 20 American Criminal L.Rev. 227 (1982).

Tague, Multiple Representation of Targets and Witnesses During a Grand Jury Investigation, 17 American Criminal L.Rev. 301 (1980).

Problem 12

Bainbridge, Insider Trading Under the Restatement of the Law Governing Lawyers, 19 J.Corporation Law 1 (1993).

Brill, Sex and the Client: Ten Reasons to Say "No!", 33 Santa Clara L.Rev. 651 (1993).

Comment, Settlement Offers Conditioned upon Waiver of Attorney's Fees: Policy, Legal, and Ethical Considerations, 131 U.Pennsylvania L.Rev. 793 (1983).

Davis & Grimaldi, Sexual Confusion: Attorney–Client Sex and the Need for a Clear Ethical Rule, 7 Notre Dame J. L. Ethics & Public Policy 57 (1993).

DeBroff & Stacy, Lawyers as Lovers: How Far Should Ethical Restrictions on Dating or Married Attorneys Extend, 1 Georgetown J.Legal Ethics 433 (1987).

deFuria, A Matter of Ethics Ignored: The Attorney—Draftsman as Testamentary Fiduciary, 36 U.Kansas L.Rev. 275 (1988).

Forell, Oregon's "Hands–off" Rule: Ethical and Liability Issues Presented by Attorney–Client Sexual Contact, 29 Willamette L.Rev. 711 (1993).

Livingston, When Libido Subverts Credo: Regulation of Attorney–Client Sexual Relations, 62 Fordham L.Rev. 5 (1993).

Maltz, Lawyer–Client Business Transactions: Caveat Counselor, 3 Georgetown J.Legal Ethics 291 (1989).

McGovern, Undue Influence and Professional Responsibility, 28 Real Property, Probate and Trust J. 643 (1994).

Note, Ethical Treatment of Attorneys' Personal Conflicts of Interest, 66 S.California L.Rev. 881 (1993).

Problem 13

Berch & Berch, Will the Real Counsel for the Insured Please Rise?, 19 Arizona State L.Rev. 27 (1987).

Bowdre, Conflicts of Interest Between Insurer and Insured: Ethical Traps for the Unsuspecting Defense Counsel, 17 American J.Trial Advocacy 101 (1993).

Galiher, Conflicts and Problems of the Workers' Compensation Attorney in Representing the Employer and Insurer Before Federal and State Boards, 48 Insurance Counsel J. 140 (1981).

Hurwitz, Conflicts and Other Problems of the Attorney Engaged in the Practice of Property Insurance, 48 Insurance Counsel J. 138 (1981).

Morris, Conflicts of Interest in Defending Under Liability Insurance Policies: A Proposed Solution, 1981 Utah L.Rev. 457 (1981).

Reschly, Attorney Malpractice—Wrongful Settlement by the Insured's and Insurer's Joint Defense Attorney, 45 Missouri L.Rev. 739 (1980).

Riopelle, When May an Insurer Fire Counsel Hired to Represent the Insured?, 7 Georgetown J.Legal Ethics 247 (1993).

Silver, Does Insurance Defense Counsel Represent the Company or the Insured?, 72 Texas L.Rev. 1583 (1994).

Problem 14

Freilich, Disqualification of Counsel: Is it an Appropriate Response in Public Interest Litigation?, 13 Urban Lawyer (1981).

Goldberg, The Former Client's Disqualification Gambit: A Bad Move in Pursuit of an Ethical Anomaly, 72 Minnesota L.Rev. 227 (1987).

Greene, Everybody's Doing It—But Who Should Be? Standing to Make a Disqualification Motion Based on an Attorney's Representation of a Client with Interests Adverse to Those of a Former Client, 6 U.Puget Sound L.Rev. 205 (1983).

Lindgren, Toward a New Standard of Attorney Disqualification, 1982 A.B.F. Research J. 419.

Morgan, Conflicts of Interests and the Former Client in the Model Rules of Professional Conduct, 1982 A.B.F.Research J. 993.

Note, Prospective Waiver of the Right to Disqualify Counsel for Conflicts of Interest, 79 Michigan L.Rev. 1074 (1981).

Note, The Ethics of Moving to Disqualify Opposing Counsel for Conflict of Interest, 1979 Duke L.J. 1310.

Riger, Disqualifying Counsel in Corporate Representation—Eroding Standards in Changing Times, 34 U.Miami L.Rev. 995 (1980).

Temple, Subsequent Representation and the Model Rules of Professional Conduct: An Evaluation of Rules 1.9 and 1.10, 1984 Arizona State L.J. 161.

Problem 15

Bellinger, Vicarious Disqualification of Prosecuting Attorneys: California Courts Examine the Consequences and Possible Alternatives, 3 Whittier L.Rev. 211 (1981).

Comment, The Chinese Wall Defense to Law–Firm Disqualification, 128 U.Pennsylvania L.Rev. 677 (1980).

Cross, Ethical Issues Facing Lawyer–Spouses and Their Employers, 34 Vanderbilt L.Rev. 1435 (1981).

Grishaw, Access to the Work Product of a Disqualified Attorney, 1 Wisconsin L.Rev. 105 (1980).

Martyn, Visions of the Eternal Law Firm: The Future of Law Firm Screens, 45 S. Carolina L.Rev. 937 (1994).

Morgan, Screening the Disqualified Lawyer: The Wrong Solution to the Wrong Problem, 10 U.Arkansas (Little Rock) L.J. 37 (1987).

Note, Access to the Disqualified Attorney's Work Product: A Plea for a Strict Prophylactic Rule, 52 U.Colorado L.Rev. 465 (1981).

Note, Attorney Disqualification and Work Product Availability: A Proposed Analysis, 47 Missouri L.Rev. 763 (1982).

Note, The Availability of the Work Product of a Disqualified Attorney: What Standard?, 127 U.Pennsylvania. L.Rev. 1607 (1979).

Note, The Chinese Wall Defense to Law Firm Disqualification, 128 U.Pennsylvania. L.Rev. 677 (1980).

Rives–Hendricks, Ethical Concerns of Lawyers Who Are Related by Kinship or Marriage, 60 Oregon L.Rev. 399 (1981).

Ross, Rebuttable Presumptions in Vicarious Disqualification Cases: Can the Appearance of Impropriety Be Rebutted?, 29 De Paul L.Rev. 1077 (1980).

Problem 16

Belt, Conflict of Interests Involving Private Practitioners Representing Cities and Counties, 6 J.Legal Profession 251 (1981).

Paul Douglas, Ethics in Government (The Godkin Lectures at Harvard University, 1952).

Freed, Ethical Considerations for the Justice Department When it Switches Sides During Litigation, 7 U. Puget Sound L.Rev. 405 (1984).

Goulden, The Super–Lawyers: The Small and Powerful World of the Great Washington Law Firms (1972).

Hammersmith, Firm Disqualification and the Former Government Attorney, 42 Ohio State L.J. 579 (1981).

Horsky, The Washington Lawyer (1952).

Lampert, Disqualification of Counsel: Adverse Interests and Revolving Doors, 81 Columbia L.Rev. 199 (1981).

Mance, Toward a New Ethical Standard Regulating the Private Practice of Former Government Lawyers, 13 Golden Gate U.L. Rev. 433 (1983).

McLaren, The Future of the Chinese Wall Defense to Vicarious Disqualification of a Former Government Attorney's Law Firm, 38 Washington & Lee L.Rev. 151 (1981).

Merrick, Government Services and the Chinese Wall: An Accommodation Founded on Practicality, 52 U.Colorado L.Rev. 499 (1981).

Morgan, Appropriate Limits on Participation by a Former Agency Official in Matters Before an Agency, 1980 Duke L.J. 1 (1980).

Mundheim, Conflict of Interest and the Former Government Employee: Rethinking the Revolving Door, 14 Creighton L.Rev. 707 (1981).

Note, Professional Ethics in Government Side–Switching, 96 Harvard L.Rev. 1914 (1983).

Note, Firm Disqualification and the Former Government Attorney, 42 Ohio St.L.J. 579 (1981).

Note, The Law Clerk's Duty of Confidentiality, 129 U.Pennsylvania L.Rev. 1230 (1981).

Note, Conflicts of Interest in Inspector General, Justice Department, and Special Prosecutor Investigations of Agency Heads, 35 Stanford L.Rev. 975 (1983).

Rotunda, Ethical Problems in Federal Agency Hiring of Private Attorneys, 1 Georgetown J.Legal Ethics 84 (1987).

Chapter V

ADVISING CLIENTS

A news story reported a class discussion in a business school:

"What should your role as a manager be when a subordinate comes to you reporting a product safety defect?" [Professor James Wilson of the University of Pittsburgh] asks. "Is your primary motivation to make a good widget or a good profit?"

"I'd get another opinion," ventures one candidate for a master's in business administration.*

The lawyer for this widget producer should not be surprised if the manager comes to her for the other opinion. What should the lawyer say? Shouldn't legal ethics be at least as high as business ethics?

Lawyers usually spend more time counseling and trying to stay out of court than they do trying cases. As you concern yourself with the lawyer's obligations in giving advice to clients, consider questions such as these:

a. What is the standard for determining the best interest of the client? Is the client by definition the best judge of his or her interest? Does the lawyer have a right—an obligation—to offer an opinion about what course of action would be in the client's best interest?

b. What special questions are presented when the client is not an individual? When the client is a corporation, for example, who really speaks for the client? Is it the Board of Directors? The managers? The common stockholders? If the client is the fictional corporate entity, what does that mean when the flesh and blood persons are at odds and the lawyer is in the middle?

c. Does a lawyer ever owe obligations to persons or entities other than the client? Does the lawyer owe the same obligation to a third party that the client owes to that party? May the lawyer voluntarily assume an obligation to report accurate information on which third parties may rely? Why might a lawyer do so even where the report might not reflect entirely favorably on the lawyer's client?

d. Does a lawyer have a right—an obligation—to warn third parties about potential wrongdoing by the lawyer's client? On what theory

_____
* Zonana, Bribery and Slush Spur Ethics Courses at Business Schools: Would You Have Gone Along With Equity Funding Deal? Many Students Say Yes, Wall Street J., July 8, 1975, p. 1, col. 4.

would such a right or obligation rest? Should the lawyer with knowledge of potential wrongdoing have a different right or obligation of disclosure than a non-lawyer would have?

PROBLEM 17

The Lawyer as Adviser

Marilyn Anderson came to you for legal help. "They have taken away my children," she told you bitterly. "I have a right to them, don't I? I am a good mother, but the welfare department has put my babies in a foster home."

You were moved by Mrs. Anderson's sincerity and agreed to take the case. In the course of your subsequent investigation, however, you discovered that Mrs. Anderson had not told you all the facts. The children, Mary, age 7, and Billy, age 3, were removed from the home based on a finding of both neglect and abuse. Social workers at Mary's school became suspicious when the little girl appeared bruised and malnourished after several days' absence. The social workers' questioning of Mary revealed that Mrs. Anderson sometimes hit the children and sent them to bed hungry. Mrs. Anderson also often left the home for hours at a time leaving no adult to care for them.

But that was only the beginning of the story. Mrs. Anderson herself told you that her husband, John, has frequent violent episodes during which Mrs. Anderson sometimes leaves the house and the children because she literally fears for her life. John has a job, but he is paid in cash and the family cannot rely on how much will be left in the pay envelope after he gets home. Mrs. Anderson had been employed as a hospital aide before Mary was born, but she has enjoyed staying home with her children.

A particular irritant in the Andersons' relationship has been the situation of Mrs. Anderson's mother. She is alert and lives in her own house, but she is lonely. Marilyn wants to invite her to come to live with the family, but whenever she suggests it, John flies into a violent rage.

You wonder whether or not Marilyn Anderson should win the upcoming custody hearing. Although you sympathize with her situation, you hesitate to use all the skill and resources at your command to overwhelm the overworked counsel for the Department of Children and Family Services. If you do restore custody to Mrs. Anderson, you worry about the children's future.[1]

1. This problem is adapted with permission from one discussed in M.T. Bloom (ed.), Lawyers, Clients & Ethics (Council on Legal Education for Professional Responsibility, Inc. 1974) 1–5.

QUESTIONS

1. How should you see your role on behalf of Marilyn Anderson in this case?

a.   Is Marilyn Anderson buying only your expertise in the law and your toughness as an advocate, or is she also buying your broadly-based experience and judgment?   In 1952, the ABA and the Association of American Law Schools established a Joint Conference on Professional Responsibility.   Its report concluded, inter alia:

> "The most effective realization of the law's aims often takes place in the attorney's office, where litigation is forestalled by anticipating its outcome, where the lawyer's quiet counsel takes the place of public force.   Contrary to popular belief, the compliance with the law thus brought about is not generally lip serving and narrow, for by reminding him of its long-run costs the lawyer often deters his client from a course of conduct technically permissible under existing law, though inconsistent with its underlying spirit and purpose.
>
> "Although the lawyer serves the administration of justice indispensably both as an advocate and as office counselor, the demands imposed on him by these two roles must be sharply distinguished.   * * *   [R]esolution of doubts in one direction [in favor of the client] becomes inappropriate when the lawyer acts as counselor.   * * * "[2]

What does this report mean?   Is its message self-righteous and naive?   Isn't a client entitled to a lawyer who makes a pit bull seem docile?

Is the report instead saying something important that is not often heard?   Does it capture an important reality about how lawyers best serve their clients' interests?

b.   Is there a difference between Marilyn Anderson's short-term and long-term interests?   Which should be more important to you as you decide how to proceed yourself and what to advise her to do?

c.   Is the interest of your client the only relevant interest?   Might a lawyer ever properly consider the interests of others, including the public interest, in rendering advice?   In his address at the laying of the cornerstone of the American Bar Center in 1954, Justice Robert Jackson said:

> "We believe in an independent Bar, free not only from government control, but intellectually independent of client control.   In the client-and-attorney relation the client is not a master, the lawyer is not a mere hired hand—he is an officer of

---

2. Professional Responsibility: Report   1161 (1958).
of the Joint Conference, 44 A.B.A.J. 1159,

the court, with a duty of independent judgment in the performance of his professional service and under a duty to serve all sorts and conditions of men." [3]

Do you agree? Should lawyers be "intellectually independent of client control"? If a lawyer acts with "independence," is the client getting what it properly thinks it is paying for? Putting aside his rhetorical excess, is Justice Jackson really saying that no client is an island and no client's act should be seen as without consequences that a lawyer must consider in giving sound advice?

2. What can you as a lawyer do to help Mrs. Anderson?

a. Are you confident that you know what the dynamics of this family really are? How do you know that Mary told the social workers the truth about her mother's hitting her? How do you know that the social workers accurately reported what Mary said? How do you know that Marilyn's account of her husband's conduct is reliable?

b. How should you as a lawyer go about determining the facts you need to know? Are you obliged to accept what your client tells you as true? Should you assume that most new clients will lie to you about things that embarrass them, at least until they come to trust you? Look at the article by Professor Cahn used as a Reading to this Problem. Do you agree that almost all events are likely to be reported in "inconsistent stories?"

c. What skills do you bring to the handling of this case? Is your law school training preparing you to be a social worker? Are you confident of your skills as a family therapist? May you simply say that you will limit your practice to giving legal advice and not worry about the context in which the client's legal problem arises? Is that a cop-out; can you deal effectively with the legal problems without at least addressing the context?

d. What issues in this problem can you as a lawyer effectively address? Might you get a restraining order against John Anderson's domestic violence, for example? Might you get an order requiring that a regular part of his pay be sent to a bank account to which only Mary would have access? In short, rather than becoming overwhelmed with what you don't know and can't fix, might you concentrate your efforts on steps that only deal with part of the problem but that are steps only a lawyer may take?

3. Are there limits on the advice a lawyer may give? Should a lawyer be permitted to give advice to a client knowing that the client will use the advice to commit a crime or fraud or to try to avoid punishment for doing so?

a. Look at Rule 1.2(d) & Comments 6 & 7, and DR 7–102(A)(7). Is there any doubt about the basic rule?

---

3. Jackson, The American Bar Center: A Testimony to Our Faith in the Rule of Law, 40 A.B.A.J. 19, 21 (1954).

b. FDIC v. Mmahat, 907 F.2d 546 (5th Cir.1990), involved a lawyer who had been general counsel of a savings and loan association for over 20 years. Indeed, he served as chairman of the Board of Directors of the institution for six of those years. When the Garn–St Germain Act of 1982 allowed S & Ls to lend more freely, he did so. Even if a loan would violate the FHLBB's "loans to one borrower" regulations, the lawyer said it was all right to make the loan. Should such advice be seen to be professionally proper? The judgment recovered by the FDIC against the lawyer who gave the advice was $35 million.[4]

c. Suppose you are the tax lawyer for a married couple, both of whom are employed. Suppose the tax laws cause them to pay $2,000 more per tax year on their joint income than if they were single and filing separate returns. Assume that I.R.S. enforcement practice allows a couple who has been divorced and does not intend to remarry to file as single people, even though they continue to live together. Should you— must you—recommend or at least advise the couple of their substantial potential tax savings?[5] Does it make any difference whether it is a crime under state law for unmarried couples to live together? What if the state law is virtually never enforced?

d. On the other hand, suppose a client has been charged with murder and asks the lawyer which South American countries have no extradition treaties with the United States? Must the lawyer ask the client for his passport and hold it lest the client try to flee? Should the lawyer offer the information, even if not asked, as a way of providing the client full service? Must the lawyer refuse to answer the question?

4. Applying the above principles to this case, what creative ways can you see to deal with Marilyn Anderson's family situation?

a. Think back to Marilyn's mother. What would you think of having Marilyn and the children move in with her? She could watch the children while Marilyn went back to work. In exchange, Marilyn would make sure her mother was in good health; she could start proceedings to divorce John and request child support. Do you have some better ideas?

b. Assume that Marilyn's mother owns her house and a few stocks but has no other source of income. If she were to become ill, the house could be seized to reimburse Medicaid authorities for her care. What would you think of encouraging her to give her house to Marilyn? Assume that, as long as she did not make clear she had given her house to a relative, Marilyn's mother could also qualify for welfare because she would be without assets and unable to work. She might then even pay part of her benefits to Marilyn as "rent".

4. As usual in such cases, even though Mmahat had been the only lawyer in the firm involved, all lawyers in the firm were liable for his acts. To the chagrin of the lawyers, however, because the cause of the losses was found to be Mmahat's dishonesty, the firm's malpractice carrier was excused from liability by the terms of its policy. The lawyers apparently had to come up with the money themselves.

5. This fact situation was suggested by Professor Harry Krause and is dealt with more elaborately in his casebook on Family Law.

Would it be appropriate for you to suggest this approach to Marilyn's mother and offer to draft the documents necessary to transfer the property to Marilyn?[6] Would it be important for you to have Marilyn promise to care for her mother or otherwise show some consideration for the transfer?

c. If you as the lawyer fail to give this advice, will you be violating the Model Rule 1.1 and Canon 6 obligation to act "competently"? Will you be committing professional malpractice? If you *do* give the advice, will you be violating Model Rule 1.2(d) and DR 7–102(A)(7)? Which rules should control? Cf. ABA Defense Function Standard 4–3.7.

d. Even if you thought you could avoid being charged with welfare fraud, would you be uncomfortable manipulating ownership of assets in this way? Would you be uncomfortable moving ownership of assets to or from a parent corporation and its subsidiaries? What is the difference, if any, when flesh–and–blood people are involved?

5. Should the lawyer's bottom line simply be that the lawyer will do what the client directs, regardless of the wisdom of the action?

a. Massachusetts Bar Association Ethics Opinion 93–6 (1993) involved a lawyer's representation of a 13-year-old client whose mother had been determined to be unfit to care for her. The lawyer and other professionals in the case agreed with that determination, but the child wanted to return to the home. This ethics opinion says the lawyer's duty in such a case is to advocate for the child's wishes so long as the child is not incompetent. The fact that a client wants to do something the lawyer believes is highly unwise is not, in itself, proof of incompetence. Do you agree? Should lawyers have to take orders from children who are not even mature enough to make a binding contract?

b. In re Pressly, 628 A.2d 927 (Vt.1993), involved a client who had a restraining order against her husband and custody of the children, subject to the husband's visitation rights. Later, she told the lawyer she wanted the husband to have only supervised visitation. When asked why, she said she thought he had sexually abused their daughter but she explicitly told the lawyer not to tell her husband of her suspicions. When the lawyer told opposing counsel the wife wanted supervised visitation, however, opposing counsel asked why. It put the lawyer in an awkward position; the lawyer could not ask for supervised visitation—which his client clearly wanted—without at least impliedly raising the sexual abuse issue. The lawyer confirmed that abuse was suspected, and opposing counsel, of course, told the husband. The wife was furious at her lawyer, and the Court said the lawyer's confirmation that abuse was suspected—contrary to the express direction not to reveal it—justified a public reprimand of the lawyer.

---

6. Lest you think this proposal is hypothetical, the ethics of "asset management" of elderly clients is an every day issue faced by "elder law" attorneys around the nation. See, e.g., Hobbs & Hobbs, The Ethical Management of Assets for Elder Clients: A Context, Role, and Law Approach, 62 Fordham L.Rev. 1411 (1994).

c. How would you have responded to opposing counsel's question in *Pressly*? Was the lawyer's mistake accepting the client's original direction without discussion or qualification? A client can always fire her lawyer, of course, so the client necessarily has the last word. Might the lawyer best take the client's direction as the beginning of a conversation with the client, however, rather than as an order to be carried out blindly?

6. Now, focusing directly on the custody matter. If Marilyn Anderson has rejected your advice and you have concluded that she should lose the custody hearing for the good of the child, what may and what should you do?

a. The California Business and Professional Code provides that it is a lawyer's duty:

"Never to reject, for any consideration personal to himself, the cause of the defenseless or the oppressed." § 6068(h).

Does this section apply to a lawyer for Marilyn Anderson? Is she the one who is oppressed and defenseless, or is it her children?

b. Is your duty different now that you have agreed to take the case and are considering withdrawal than it would have been had you not yet decided whether to represent Mrs. Anderson? Compare Rule 1.16 with DR 2–109 & 2–110. You may also want to look back at the material in Problem 5.

c. Should you be concerned that your conclusions may reflect lawyers' arrogant self–confidence that we are always right? Boswell once reported that Dr. Johnson's solution to supporting a cause he knew to be bad was:

"Sir, you do not know it to be good or bad till the Judge determines it. I have said that you are to state facts fairly; so that your thinking, or what you call knowing, a cause to be bad, must be from reasoning, must be from supposing your arguments to be weak and inclusive. But, Sir, that is not enough. An argument which does not convince yourself, may convince the Judge to whom you urge it: and if it does convince him, why, then, Sir, you are wrong and he is right." [7]

Do you agree, or was Johnson engaged in ethical sophistry?

d. Suppose that at the custody hearing the social worker from the Department of Children and Family Services appears without counsel. You are still representing Mrs. Anderson and, of course, Mrs. Anderson's children are unrepresented by counsel. May you suggest that counsel be appointed for each of the children even though you surmise that if that suggestion is implemented, your chances of winning will be substantially lessened? Do you have an ethical obligation to Mrs. Anderson to oppose appointment of such counsel? Look at Model Rule 4.3 and DR 7–104(A)(2). If counsel were appointed, would that lessen your own

7. 2 Boswell, The Life of Johnson, 47 (Hill Edition 1887).

ethical burden and allow you to use all the tricks in your bag on Mrs. Anderson's behalf?

e. Suppose that the law requires all persons to report every case of suspected child abuse. Should that law apply to lawyers? Is there any reason that it should not?

READINGS

NAOMI R. CAHN,[8] INCONSISTENT STORIES
81 Georgetown L.J. 2475 (1993)

A woman, Darlene Adams, has come into my office, saying that she wants to leave the man she has been living with because he has beaten her up. In the initial interview, she states that the most recent time this happened was yesterday, when she was leaving the apartment with a female friend to go out to the movies. Mr. Ponds pleaded with her not to go; when she refused, he called her a whore and threatened to call Child Protective Services. He then slapped her face and pulled out a clump of hair. Her face stung for several hours, and her scalp still hurt when she came to see me. In the past, he had fractured her jaw, although she had not gone to the doctor for fear of having the violence found out. Mr. Ponds has also threatened to "get" her if she ever had another boyfriend. She and Mr. Ponds have one child, Ben, age two. Both she and Mr. Ponds have provided financially for Ben, although she has been the parent primarily responsible for feeding and changing the child. She wants Mr. Ponds to leave the apartment and to stay away from her; she also wants custody of their child.

At the interview, I take a picture of the bald spot on her head. Ms. Adams then tells me that the friend with whom she was going to the movies came with her to my office and would be happy to talk to me about what happened. When I interview the friend, Ms. Campbell, she tells me that she and Ms. Adams had talked to each other earlier in the day, and that Ms. Adams had told her that the situation at home was tense. When Ms. Campbell came over, the two of them decided to go to a movie, taking along young Ben. As they were leaving, Ms. Adams walked past Mr. Ponds, who then reached out towards her head. After Ms. Adams pulled away from him, he was left holding some hair. The friend did not see Mr. Ponds slap Ms. Adams. When I ask Ms. Campbell about Ben, she tells me that both parents love him and take care of him. At this time, I do not explore with either Ms. Adams or her friend whether the latter would be interested in testifying at any court proceed-

---

8. Naomi R. Cahn is Associate Professor of Law at the National Law Center, The George Washington University. She wrote this article while a Clinical Professor in the Georgetown Legal Clinics.

ing. I begin to prepare the papers and I ask Ms. Adams to return in two days, so that she can review and sign them.

Two days later, Ms. Adams calls to say that she has decided not to go through with any legal action. Mr. Ponds has told her that he loves her, and has been especially nice to her. He has promised never to hit her again and to turn over to her all of the money that he earns as a night watchman. She says that she really has not hurt her all that much, and that he really is a good father to Ben. After some talking, she agrees to think about pursuing a legal action, at least for the purposes of getting an order that prevents him from molesting or assaulting her in the future.

This is a composite story. I frequently had clients "drop out" because they decided to reconcile with their boyfriends (or for some other reason), and my students and I were often faced with the problem of what to say within the appropriate boundaries of our legal role.

I have recognized, after reflection on these experiences * * * the following layers of inconsistent stories: the two different stories my client tells on different days, the discrepancies between my client's perceptions and those of her witness, the differences between what my client wants and what I think she needs, and the variation between my client's desire to stay and the oft-asked question, "Why doesn't she leave?" Underlying these different stories include the stories my client tells me and what she tells herself. Once we file the papers, there will be another set of inconsistent stories: differences between my client's language and "courtroom" language, dissimilarities between my client's story and her desired remedies, which differ from the judge's story and stock of remedies, which further differ from the definitions of what her "case" actually is. I now turn to a focus on the inconsistencies among some of the outsider narratives contained within her story.

A. MS. ADAMS'S TWO (OR MORE) DIFFERENT STORIES

My client has already told me two different stories. When she first came to see me, she told me how hurt—physically and emotionally—she felt from Mr. Ponds's violence and she implied that Mr. Ponds was not a good parent; yet, when she called back, she told me that he had not harmed her very much at any time in the past and that he was a good father. Both times, she sounded rather tentative. The differences between the two stories are, on the surface, a matter of a few days passing, together with his promise not to hurt her. And there may be nothing more.

Nonetheless, I suspect that there is more to her story than she has told me. I do not have access to what she is thinking about herself, her case, or him. She only tells me a limited portion of what the "true" story is to her, and so I must construct my own story based on this inherently partial account. I guess that she has either minimized the pain, convinced herself to believe him, feared leaving, or decided she has nowhere else to go and no resources. Or, she may not think of herself as a "battered woman" who needs help; then again, she may merely feel relieved that she has contacted a lawyer and now knows her legal options.

Another level of complexity emerges from the situation in which she lives. She may be acting based on expectations of her culture. It may be that it is contrary to her religion to seek legal help, or that she is expected to tolerate some abuse, or that she cannot reveal the abuse lest she be condemned by family and friends for staying.

In addition to any of these possible explanations, my client is also fighting against more general expectations that ask why she stayed— why she did not leave before. Battered women are judged for staying with their batterers; yet, it is more dangerous for them once they leave. Somewhere between these two conflicting stories are the actions that she must take, the story that she must construct for herself.

B. MS. ADAMS'S AND HER FRIEND'S STORIES

On a simpler level, there are the customary minor conflicts between the stories of a client and her witness. Ms. Adams claims that Mr. Ponds slapped her, hard, on her face; but her friend did not see or hear the slap. From her language, it is unclear whether the friend denies that the slap could have occurred or whether she believes it might have happened, without her being aware of it at the time. Ms. Campbell also praised Mr. Ponds' parenting abilities, while Ms. Adams minimized his caretaking. It may be that the inconsistencies can be easily explained: the slap occurred but the friend was not paying attention to Ms. Adams when it happened because she was watching the child, or the friend was deaf in one ear, or she was seeking not to testify. Alternatively, it may be that the slap never occurred and, for some reason, Ms. Adams was trying to augment the violence that had occurred. (In that case, how do I ask my client about this?)

At a trial, we could attempt to mask the slight differences. Ms. Adams could testify to what happened to her, and the friend would testify to what she saw. A careful opposing counsel might hear the inconsistencies, and question the friend about the slap; the friend could say that she was busy, she was scared, or give some other reason for not knowing about the slap. Alternatively, we could not call the friend as a witness, thereby presenting only our client's story.

Given the possible reasons for the friend not knowing about the slap, I must ask myself whether it is something I should worry about at all. Aren't minor inconsistencies a part of every set of stories?

C. MS. ADAMS' AND HER LAWYER'S STORIES

My story of what happened to my client is informed by my own expectations. I hope that women will leave abusive relationships and will not be bought off by promises of no future harm, and I trust in my ability to know when a woman seems ready to leave. I also strongly believe that domestic violence is bad for children, and that she should

leave, if only for the sake of Ben. It thus makes me angry and
frustrated to have a client who, notwithstanding severe past abuse, has
decided to return to her abuser. Perhaps in our initial interview I
conveyed my feelings and judgments about abusive relationships to her,
and she felt defensive and angry at me.

As a feminist, I recognize that women are not free to "choose"
whether, and when, to leave an abuser. The economic constraints on
such a decision are serious: if the abuser is the primary economic
provider in the household, then leaving him leaves her with little means
of support. And, the social implications of leaving may be equally
severe, especially because many batterers have systematically cut off
their partners from friends and other family members. If there are
children, then she may fear that he will seek custody and take them
away from her. Or, she may still love him—the abuse does not make all
of the positive emotions disappear. Finally, I have talked with enough
battered women (friends and clients) to know about the anguish of
leaving.

Although she has not actually left her abuser, it is important for me
to remember that my client did take one step towards leaving. She did
seek help, and we discussed her legal options. If the abuse recurs, then
she might decide to take further action. Nonetheless, I still want her to
leave her abuser. I feel quite possessive and protective towards her,
even though I want her to take responsibility for her decision. Her
second story, then, conflicts with my story of what she should do.

D. MS. ADAMS'S AND HER BOYFRIEND'S STORIES

Finally, there will be a conflict, I assume, between what my client
says and what her boyfriend would say at trial (or during pre-trial
investigations). Although the respondents in our cases sometimes admit
that they have hit their partners, or that they have committed some
lesser form of abuse, they more typically deny that they have committed
the abuse, or claim that they acted only in self-defense. Consequently,
when they proffer their side of the story at trial, we have the most
classic form of inconsistent legal stories—those between opposing parties. While her story will include the abuse, his story will not * * *.

As someone trained (in law school) to see different sides of the same
story, I can somewhat understand his side of the story. He may not
remember what happened. He may, in his own mind, simply have tried
to restrain her from leaving and, because he did not intend to hurt her,
he believes he did not actually hurt her. He may view a certain level of
violence as ordinary, rather than defining it as abuse. Alternatively, he
may be confused and scared by the encounter with the legal system.
Understanding that he will not go to jail because this is a civil proceeding requires a sophisticated knowledge of the legal system. Of course, I
do not really know what he thinks about the violence. I can only
speculate about what his story will be based on my own experiences

representing victims of domestic violence, my talks with abusers and the psychologists who treat them, and the structure of the legal system.

E. CONFLICTING OUTSIDERS' STORIES

The four sets of inconsistent stories explored above emerge from different overlaps of outsider groups. My client is a poor, white woman; her friend is a poor, black woman; the man is a poor black man; and I am a middle-class white female lawyer. We are all insiders within certain cultures and outsiders to others. For example, I am an outsider to the culture in which my client lives. My legal training makes me both an insider and an outsider. I have access to the courtroom and to legal reasoning. I am part of that system. On the other hand, as a lawyer who is a woman, I am part of a group that, until recently, has been excluded from the legal profession, and is still underrepresented in the senior ranks of judges and law firms. Moreover, female lawyers often face hostility and sexism from opposing counsel or judges, so in many ways I am an outsider to the traditional legal system. In another sense, * * * all of the stories are inside and consistent * * *.

* * *

So what about these inconsistent stories? The issues of whose story is told and of how the story will be related are complex. A lawyer envisions several tellings of the story; the client envisions several tellings as well. Each has (in)complete information about what will happen within the legal system, and about what "actually happened." Different approaches by lawyers and clients and a more fluid ethical system will allow for some better attorney-client relationships and some better retellings. Some stories will also "seem" truer than others. But the conflicts will remain, conflicts between stories within the same "case," conflicts over what constitutes the "case," and conflicts between and within outsider groups seeking to tell their own stories. Narrative theories provide some help in their encouragement of listening to divergent stories, but they provide conflicting criteria on why and how to evaluate these stories. So long as we have a legal system that values consistent stories, we must confront, and challenge, the possibility of constructing a true story of a case. Examining how inconsistent stories are left out of traditional legal ethics makes visible their presence and their significance, and provides an opportunity to accept and use them.

———

PROBLEM 18

Advising the Business Corporation

You have long been are outside counsel to Sleepware, Inc., a clothing manufacturer. The company makes a line of children's pajamas that is a big seller. Recent tests have shown, however, that the pajama fabric can catch fire if a match is held against it for a few seconds.

The Vice President of Sleepware wants to keep selling the pajamas. Regulations of the Consumer Product Safety Commission prohibit sale of products known to cause burns to children but the Vice President believes that the CPSC is unlikely to recognize the potential injuries the pajamas will cause.

Further, the Vice President points out that although children wearing pajamas sometimes play with matches, experts he has consulted say that not more than one in 50,000 children would hold the matches on their pajamas long enough for it to catch fire. The experts admit that if the pajamas burn, the child's injuries could be expected to be severe, but a management consulting firm has estimated that civil damages would not exceed $250,000 per victim. Sleepware sells 200,000 of these pajamas each year, the Vice President tells you proudly, and it makes a profit of $2,000,000 on this product. Thus, even under a worst-case scenario, he has calculated that it will be $1 million more profitable to sell the pajamas than not to sell them.

You have not been asked for advice about whether to market this product; you only learned about the flammability while working on an unrelated matter. Indeed, the Vice President is annoyed that you have raised the issue with him. "The President will retire soon," he tells you, "and I am his natural successor. My enemies in the company would love to embarrass me with this."

QUESTIONS

1. To whom do you as outside counsel to Sleepware owe your primary loyalty?

a. Are your clients the corporate managers such as the Vice President of Sleepware to whom most of your advice is given? Are your real clients the large shareholders? Shareholders generally? The company's directors? Employees, present and future? Consumers who will buy the company's products and perhaps be injured by them?

b. Compare EC 5–18 and Rule 1.13(a). Do they describe the client in exactly the same way? What do they mean when they say a lawyer represents the "entity"? Does that mean a lawyer's loyalty must be to a "thing" rather than to people?

c. Might the idea that lawyer represents an "entity" be best understood by seeing the entity as the core objectives and purposes shared by people who have invested in and managed the corporation? Those people have many different private interests, of course, but the lawyer for the corporation not only does not represent those private interests, he or she must often see that they are subordinated to the common purposes.

d. One commentator has argued that the board of directors has the last word in defining the goals of the corporate client and it is to the board that the lawyer should look for guidance. "That answer is certainly the one suggested by most corporate laws. * * * If the view is taken that the board of directors *cannot* be accepted as representing the corporation * * * then we are indeed in a difficult position * * *." [1] Do you agree that the answer is that simple?

2. What steps are you required to take in this situation? Is the Vice President's instruction to drop the matter something you may accept as final?

a. Look at Model Rule 1.13(b). There was no corresponding provision in the Model Code, but do you suppose Rule 1.13(b) also provides appropriate guidance for lawyers in states that have not yet adopted the Model Rules?

b. Is the sale of the pajamas "a violation of a legal obligation to the organization"? Is it "a violation of law which reasonably might be imputed to the organization"? Is it "likely to result in substantial injury to the organization"?

c. On the "substantial injury" issue, is the Vice President's judgment the only relevant one? Are his "experts'" estimates of the rate of injury and the management consultant's estimate of the likely jury award convincing to you? Indeed, is reevaluation of critical factual assumptions such as these often one of the most helpful services a lawyer can perform for a client?

d. Assuming the Vice President will not reconsider and does not want a second opinion, is this a matter you would take to the President of Sleepware? If the President tells you to take the issue no farther, should you accept that as a binding directive? Can you answer that question without knowing the reasons for the President's direction?

e. If you now take the matter to Sleepware's Board of Directors, what will be your appropriate role? Must you be an advocate against the continued sale of the product? Is such advocacy an appropriate role for outside counsel? Whatever happened to the idea that the client is the principal and the lawyer only the agent?

3. If your advice to discontinue sales of the pajamas is ignored by the Board of Directors, may or must you report the client to the shareholders, or the Consumer Product Safety Commission, or another public agency?

a. If Sleepware's Board fails to act, may you go over its head and communicate directly with the public shareholders about the wisdom of continued sales of the product? Look at Rule 1.13 (b) and (c). Do they prohibit disclosure? Indeed, do they say anything about disclosure at all? [2] Is Rule 1.13(c) too absolute and insensitive to the complexity of the issues presented?

1. Lorne, The Corporate and Securities Adviser, The Public Interest, and Professional Ethics, 76 Michigan L.Rev. 425, 436–37 (1978) (emphasis in original). See also id. at 477–79.

2. But look at draft Model Rules 1.6 and 1.13 as proposed by the Kutak Commission and reprinted as footnotes to the respective rules in the Standards Supplement. Were the Model Rules as adopted intended to change the lawyer's right or obligation to

b. Consider DR 4–101(C)(3). Under that provision, *must* a lawyer reveal confidences? ABA Opinion 314 (1965) indicated that a lawyer must disclose even the confidences of his clients if "the facts in the attorney's possession indicate beyond reasonable doubt that a crime will be committed." Does the text of DR 4–101(C)(3) support that interpretation? Should violation of a CPSC regulation be treated as the equivalent of a crime? Cf. ABA Defense Function Standard 4–3.7(d).

c. Assume that selling pajamas in violation of the CPSC regulation is a misdemeanor. Look at Model Rule 1.6(b)(1). Does it permit disclosure here? How "likely" does the lawyer have to believe it is that the death and serious bodily harm will occur? How "imminent" must the injury be?

d. Assume that Rule 1.6(b)(1) permits disclosure in this case. Should it be read to require disclosure? Model Rules, Scope ¶ 8 advises: "The lawyer's exercise of discretion to disclose information under Rule 1.6 should not be subject to examination." But see State v. Hansen, 862 P.2d 117 (Wash.1993), where the lawyer had gotten a call from a prospective client, recently out of prison, who said of the participants in his criminal trial, "I am going to get a gun and blow them all away, the prosecutor, the judge and the public defender." The lawyer did not take the case but he did call the prosecutor, who called the judge, who called the police. The prospective client was convicted of intimidating a judge and claimed that the remarks for which he was convicted had been privileged. Not surprisingly, the Court found that the comments were within the crime-fraud exception to the privilege. And, the Court went on, lawyers have a *duty*, as officers of the Court, to warn of "true threats to harm members of the judiciary communicated to them by clients or by third parties."

e. Even if a lawyer is not subject to discipline for failure to disclose Sleepware's misdemeanor, would the lawyer be liable in civil damages to consumers for failure to disclose? Might there be a message for lawyers in Tarasoff v. Regents of the University of California, 17 Cal.3d 425, 131 Cal.Rptr. 14, 551 P.2d 334 (1976), vacating 13 Cal.3d 177, 118 Cal.Rptr. 129, 529 P.2d 553 (1974)? There, a psychotherapist knew of a planned murder and did not warn the victim. The court held that a cause of action in tort existed. "When a therapist determines, or pursuant to the standards of the profession should determine, that his patient presents a serious danger of violence to another, he incurs an obligation to use reasonable care to protect the intended victim against such danger. The discharge of this duty may require the therapist to take one or more of various steps, depending upon the nature of the case. Thus it may call for him to warn the intended victim or others likely to apprise the victim of the danger, to notify the police, or to take whatever other steps are

disclose from that which had existed under the Code? Were the Model Rules intended to make disclosure *less* permissive? Securities lawyers were the segment of the bar most concerned about the original Kutak proposals. That may help your understanding of how broadly or narrowly to read the present form of Rules 1.6 and 1.13 in cases like the one in this problem.

reasonably necessary under the circumstances." 17 Cal.3d at 431, 131 Cal.Rptr. at 20, 551 P.2d at 340.[3]

4. If you fail to take appropriate action in this matter, may you be held liable to the shareholders individually for losses suffered by the corporation?

a. Issues analogous to those raised by this problem have been on the front pages in recent years as law firms have been sued for arguably not giving sufficiently tough advice to prevent the failure of their savings and loan clients.

FDIC v. O'Melveny & Meyers, 969 F.2d 744 (9th Cir.1992), rev'd on other grounds sub nom. O'Melveny & Myers v. FDIC, ___ U.S. ___, 114 S.Ct. 2048, 129 L.Ed.2d 67 (1994), for example, was a suit against a law firm that had helped a bank create real estate syndications that were sold to large investors. The firm wrote much of the private placement memorandum and purported to do a due diligence review of the relevant facts. Much of the success of the deal depended on the financial health of the bank. The bank's auditors had said the bank had little or no net worth, but the law firm apparently did not talk to them. The investors did not bring the lawsuit; they had complained earlier and the FDIC had given them their money back. Thus the suit here was a claim by the bank's receiver to recover funds it had to repay the investors. The law firm argued that the client had deceived it and that the firm did not have to protect the client against its own wrong. The court rejected such a bright line test. "It is an attorney's duty to protect the client in every possible way," the court said. "No California cases advise us of an exception to the general rule that a lawyer has to act competently to avoid public harm when he learns that his is a dishonest client."[4]

FDIC v. Clark, 978 F.2d 1541 (10th Cir.1992), gave lawyers even more reason for concern. The law firm had represented the bank in many matters since its opening. Unknown to the law firm, several bank officers initiated a "heist money scheme" in which they used $2 million

3. N.Y. State Bar Committee Professional Ethics Opinion No. 486 (June 26, 1978), took the position that, although New York no longer treats suicide as a crime, "an announced intention to commit suicide is to be treated in a manner similar to that which would obtain in the case of proposed criminal conduct under DR 4–101(C)(3)" because of our "deep concern for the preservation of human life." However, in light of the "permissive character of the exception created by DR 4–101(C)(3), there may be circumstances when a lawyer can properly elect to remain silent. For example, a client of apparently sound mind may disclose that he is contemplating suicide to avoid a lengthy, painful, and expensive terminal illness." Do you agree? Should the right to die be considered a constitutional right? Should survivors of the deceased have an action against the lawyer for a failure to act?

4. The Supreme Court decision in the case, ___ U.S. ___, 114 S.Ct. 2048, 129 L.Ed.2d 67 (1994), was largely an anticlimax. The firm said that the F.D.I.C. itself should be deemed to know what company management knew, and thus that the law firm had nothing to discover or "inform" anyone about. The F.D.I.C. tried the case on the theory that federal law, not state law, governed the question of what knowledge would be imputed to it. In its opinion, the Supreme Court said there is no general federal common law and no statute that creates a federal rule of decision on the question of what management knowledge should be imputed to the F.D.I.C. Thus, the case was remanded for decision of that point under state law.

in bank money to buy $9 million in stolen money. To do this, they created loan files to non-existent borrowers and forged checks on non–existent accounts. Ultimately, they were caught, but the FDIC argued that the lawyers were slow to act when they first heard the charges. The bank officers had told the lawyers that it was all a misunderstanding and not to worry about it. The law firm so advised the bank's board without making an investigation of its own. The court, citing *O'Melveny & Meyers*, affirmed that inaction under these circumstances is a sufficient basis for imposing liability. A lawyer may not simply rely on a client's officers assertions about their own lack of wrongdoing.

Given these cases, would you feel comfortable simply taking the Vice President's assurance that selling the pajamas raised no issues worth examining further? [5]

b. Some cases find that the theory that lawyers represent the entity serves to insulate lawyers from suits by individual shareholders.

TJD Dissolution Corp. v. Savoie Supply Co., 460 N.W.2d 59 (Minn. App.1990), for example, was a malpractice action in which a corporate shareholder sued the corporation's lawyer for losses the shareholder personally suffered in a deal that the lawyer had worked out for a buyout of the corporation by other shareholders. The shareholder argued that the lawyer owed a duty of fairness to each shareholder, but the court said no: the lawyer clearly represented the corporation and had advised the shareholder to get separate counsel. The lawyer did not owe the shareholder any duty individually. See also, Skarbrevik v. Cohen, England & Whitefield, 282 Cal.Rptr. 627 (Cal.App.1991).

Waggoner v. Snow, Becker, Kroll, Klaris & Krauss, 991 F.2d 1501 (9th Cir.1993), was a particularly interesting case dealing with corporate counsel's dealings with the major shareholder. When the company was in financial trouble, Waggoner, the CEO and major shareholder, agreed to sign guarantees in exchange for voting control of the corporation. Corporate counsel said that could be arranged, drew up the papers and had Waggoner sign them. Later, the Board fired Waggoner, and he tried to remove them using what he thought was his voting control. It turned out, however, that corporate counsel had not successfully delivered the

---

5. But see, FDIC v. Ferguson, 982 F.2d 404 (10th Cir.1991), holding that the proportion of the loss for which the lawyer can be held liable can be reduced by extent of the contributory acts of the bank client's officials. Cf. Reves v. Ernst & Young, __ U.S. __, 113 S.Ct. 1163, 122 L.Ed.2d 525 (1993), holding that for purposes of RICO liability, professionals such as lawyers may not he sued unless they actually took part in the management of the client. See also, F.D.I.C. v. Shrader & York, 991 F.2d 216 (5th Cir.1993), where the question was when the F.D.I.C. had knowledge of possible malpractice claims against the lawyers based on conflicts of interest. The case holds that because the F.D.I.C. stands in the shoes of the entity for other purposes, it should be deemed to know of the acts whenever the savings and loan management knew of them. Because that was typically several years before the F.D.I.C. became receiver of the institutions, many potential cases against the lawyers will be barred by the statute of limitations. See also, O'Melveny & Myers v. F.D.I.C., __ U.S. __, 114 S.Ct. 2048, 129 L.Ed.2d 67 (1994) (state law governs attribution of officers' knowledge to the institution and the receiver); F.D.I.C. v. Cocke, 7 F.3d 396 (4th Cir.1993) (statute of limitations in suits against lawyers for savings and loan associations is a matter of state law).

powers to Waggoner, so Waggoner both lost his job and remained liable on the guarantees. He sued the corporate counsel for malpractice. The Court found that corporate counsel had not assumed any personal duties to Waggoner and denied Waggoner all recovery.[6]

5. Assume that you represent Sleepware, Inc. in negotiating with the CPSC over how strict the new regulations on flammable pajamas should be. Quite apart from your legal obligations, would you feel comfortable helping Sleepware to continue to sell its pajamas?

a. The question whether a lawyer may pursue a legally-sound but unjust case often seems not to trouble lawyers today. Our instincts seem to be to look to positive law, not natural law. But for many, the problem of what causes to champion has been one of the fundamental moral issues facing the legal profession.

b. David Hoffman, the Baltimore lawyer who in 1836 was one of the first to organize and espouse legal ethics principles, for example, considered the situation of the client who owes a just debt, suit to collect which is barred by the Statute of Limitations. His conclusion would surprise many modern lawyers.

> "I will never plead the Statute of Limitations, when based on the *mere efflux of time;* for if my client is conscious he owes the debt; and has no other defence than the *legal bar*, he shall never make me a partner in his knavery." [7]

Is that idea archaic? Would a lawyer who lived out his own morality in this way have to answer in malpractice to his client?

6. Should the same principle apply in partnerships, i.e., should a lawyer who purports only to represent the partnership have civil liability to individual partners or should liability run only to the partnership as an entity?

Hopper v. Frank, 16 F.3d 92 (5th Cir. 1994), states that, normally, the lawyer-client relationship is only with the partnership, not the partners personally. The Court quoted with approval, ABA Formal Ethics Opinion 91–361 (1991): "[A] lawyer who represents a partnership represents the entity rather than the individual partners unless the specific circumstances show otherwise. * * * This analysis may include such factors as whether the lawyer affirmatively assumed a duty of representation to the individual partner, * * * whether the lawyer had represented an individual partner before undertaking to represent the partnership, and whether there was evidence of reliance by the individual partner on the lawyer as his or her separate counsel * * *."

Arpadi v. First MSP Corporation, 628 N.E.2d 1335 (Ohio 1994), however, held that under Ohio law (1) a lawyer for a partnership represents the partners, not the entity, so each partner has a right of action, and (2) a lawyer may not assist one partner to breach the fiduciary duty owed to another partner so there may be liability on that theory as well.

ABA Formal Opinion 94–380 (1994) raised the "who is the client" issue as to whether a lawyer for a fiduciary owes duties to the intended beneficiary of the fiduciary's actions. The opinion says that the Model Rules adopt the majority view that the lawyer's duties run only to the fiduciary, not the beneficiary. Comment 13 to Model Rule 1.7, of course, acknowledges that the duty is different in some states, and lawyers should make clear to fiduciary clients just what the lawyer's obligations are.

7. D. Hoffman, A Course of Legal Study 754 (2d Ed.1846).

c. Move on to George Sharswood, whose lectures laid the groundwork for the Alabama Code of Ethics of 1887, and in 1908, for the American Bar Association Canons of Ethics.

> Counsel * * * have an undoubted right, and are duty bound, to refuse to be concerned for a plaintiff in the legal pursuit of a demand which offends his sense of what is just and right. The courts are open to the party in person to prosecute his own claim, and plead his own cause; and although * * * he ought to examine and be well satisfied before he refuses to a suitor the benefit of his professional skill and learning, yet * * * it would be on his part an immoral act to afford that assistance, when his conscience told him that the client was aiming to perpetrate a wrong through the means of some advantage the law may have afforded him.[8]

Is that shocking to you? Does a lawyer bear a moral responsibility for accepting an unjust cause? Is Sharswood right that it is only acceptance of plaintiffs' cases to which that responsibility attaches (because defendants don't have a choice whether or not to be sued)? Compare EC 7–9, EC 7–17 and Rule 1.2(b).

d. Make the issue even more contemporary. Compare the views of Professors Monroe Freedman and Michael Tigar in the Readings to this Problem. Would you have represented John Demjanjuk?

6. Would it be proper for you to be both a director of and lawyer for this client? Could you use your Board position to advocate business policies about which it is hard for a mere lawyer to get a hearing?

a. In 1993, 78 of the largest 250 industrial companies had an attorney on their board, a number that had dropped slightly from 1988, when 83 of these companies had a lawyer-director. The Attorneys' Liability Assurance Society (ALAS), one of the largest insurance carriers for law firm malpractice, discourages lawyers from serving on the boards of public companies and excludes from malpractice coverage those attorneys who hold major board positions, such as Chairman or Vice Chairman.[9]

b. Paul Cravath believed:

"that in *most* cases the client is best advised by a lawyer who maintains an objective point of view and that such objectivity may be impeded by any financial interest in the clients' business or any participation in its management. Accordingly, he made it the policy of the firm that neither its partners nor its associates should hold equity securities of any client, or serve as a director of a corporate client, or have a financial interest,

8. G. Sharswood, Professional Ethics 33–35 (1854).

9. Stevens, Lawyers are Finding Corporate Board Seats More Uncomfortable, Wall Street J., Dec. 31, 1993, at 12, col. 1 (midwest ed.).

direct or indirect, in any transaction in which the firm was acting as counsel. Occasionally, more frequently in recent years, clients have insisted upon exceptions permitting partners to occupy directorships and own qualifying equity securities, but the exceptions have been few." [10]

c. Consider Lefkowitz, The Attorney–Client Relationship and the Corporation, 26 Record of the Association of the Bar of the City of New York 697 (No.8, Nov.1971):

"Let me give you some examples of the everyday problems.
* * *

"The most difficult situation arises when an attorney is himself a witness to events involving a corporation in which he has a financial interest as a stockholder-director as well as being counsel. His questioning is continually interrupted by assertions of privilege because of the attorney-client relationship. Once again all parties must wade through a morass to determine whether the privilege is being misused.

"Another set of problems exists when an attorney is called upon to advise a client as to the client's exercise of his privilege against self-incrimination. Sometimes it is apparent that the business dealings of the attorney involved were perhaps more incriminating than the acts of his client involving the same set of circumstances. How can such an attorney be expected to impartially advise his client as to the wisdom of the exercise of the privilege against self-incrimination, when the attorney's own incrimination may possibly be involved? * * *

"The attorney in such position potentially may be involved in the conflict of interest that may emerge within his mind when he weighs advice. For that task, he wears two hats. He is a businessman quite often with a personal business stake in the decisions of the company. However, he is more than likely to be called on for legal advice by the company. Can it not be said that determinations made by such an attorney, when asked for legal advice, are necessarily colored by the personal interest which he has as a substantial stockholder, option-owner, salaried official, or otherwise? To put it more simply, the question is whether we should permit the continuing growth of such conflicts in the practice of law by which the lawyer-confidant merges with the interested businessman."

d. Notice that the Model Rules' guidance on this issue is only a reference in Comment 14 to Rule 1.7. Does it adequately guide a lawyer in a case like the one posed by this problem? Does it give inadequate recognition to the good a lawyer could potentially do as a director?

10. R.T. Swaine, The Cravath Firm and Its Predecessors: 1819–1948, vol. II, at 9–10 (1948) (emphasis added). Note: The views set out here may or may not represent the views of the firm today.

7. Does your answer to any of these questions depend on whether the lawyer is outside counsel or employed by the corporation?

a. One author has written that a lawyer sometimes chooses the life of "salaried employment" in a corporate law department because he may be "just happier in a job where someone else has the ultimate responsibility." And—unlike a private practice—the salaried lawyer's job has "aspects of dependence." [11]

In reply, another commentator defended the professionalism of house counsel and contended that "a lawyer is a lawyer whether he charges fees or receives a salary. A salary corrupts no more than does a fee. * * * " [12] Who is correct?

b. In connection with the possible differences in pressures bearing on in-house and outside counsel consider the following:

"Do we ask too much of inside counsel? Should the Code of Professional Responsibility draw distinctions between the independence of judgment expected of outside counsel and the independence of judgment expected of inside counsel? * * * For example, the law could require that the responsibility of inside counsel be normally satisfied by reporting to outside counsel and accepting his judgment as to the proper course of action in close cases and ambiguous situations. By expecting too much of inside counsel we may receive nothing. By requiring less we are more likely to obtain all that we can realistically require. Yet we ought not, by relaxing rules, to encourage wrong behavior. We should continue to require in-house counsel to be responsible for the exercise of independent judgment. However, in close or ambiguous situations, in-house counsel ought not to be satisfied with relying solely on its own judgments. In-house counsel should be required particularly in these close cases to inform outside counsel who is subject to different pressures, and then rely on the latter's advice.

* * *

"One should not overdraw the differences between outside and inside counsel. The associate of a law firm is also subject to similar pressures because disagreement with the ethical judgment of his partners could require withdrawal from the firm. The Code does not provide in such instances for a discreet withdrawal from a particular matter any more than it provides for discreet withdrawal on the part of in-house counsel. Even a large firm may be under economic pressures because a large percentage of its business may come from a very few corporate clients. While this line, which distinguishes the differing pres-

---

11. Hanaway, Corporate Law Department—A New Look, 17 Business Lawyer 595, 599 (April, 1962).

12. Davis, Corporate Law Department—A New Look at the "New Look," 18 Business Lawyer 569, 570 (January, 1963).

sures on in-house and outside counsel may not be a bright one, it still provides a useful starting point." [13]

c.   We may well expect the use of inside counsel to increase because of the rising legal fees charged by outside corporate counsel.   For example, the Chairman of the Board of I.B.M. once said that its general counsel "is the only department head to whom we've given an unlimited budget—and he's already exceeded it."   Many corporations, in an effort to cut costs, push for settlements, try to use arbitrators, and expand their inside corporate legal staff.   The average hourly costs of work of inside counsel has been said to be approximately half that of outside counsel.   Ryan, Costly Counsel, Wall St.J., April 13, 1978, at 1, col. 1. (midwest ed.).   See also, Wall St.J., April 26, 1984, at 1, col. 6 (midwest ed.) (for a major bank, inside legal costs average less than $100 an hour compared with outside bills of up to $250 an hour).

d.   Whatever the reasons, the number of inside counsel is large.   In 1980, for example, the number of lawyers employed as such by private industry was 54,626, or just over 10% of the 542,205 lawyers in the country.   That was a 40% increase from 39,000 such lawyers in 1970. Roughly one-third worked in offices of 3 or less, one-third in offices from 4 lawyers to 50, and one-third in offices of over 50 lawyers.   See Curran, et al., The Lawyer Statistical Report 19–21 (1985).

e.   One of the major functions of the corporate general counsel, of course, is the selection and supervision of outside counsel.   How might that affect the freedom felt by outside counsel to tell the officers of the corporation what they might not want to hear?   Might the growing alternative of going inside, and possibly getting an answer more support- ive of what management wants to do, tend to make outside firms less "independent"?   This argument is made persuasively in J. Heinz & E. Laumann, Chicago Lawyers: The Social Structure of the Bar 365–373 (1982).

f.   In re Oracle Securities Litigation, 829 F.Supp. 1176 (N.D.Cal. 1993), involved both a class action and a derivative suit.   The Court considered the class action settlement fair to those who bought or sold the stock.   The question was whether the Board had the requisite independence to settle the derivative action; the proposed settlement released the directors and paid the lawyers but seemed to do little for the current shareholders.   For our purposes, the principal issue was the Court's concern that the Board's legal advice about the settlement had come from in–house counsel.   In-house lawyers have to live with man- agement, the Court suggested, and thus cannot give independent judg- ment.   Do you think that is a fair assessment of in–house counsel generally?   Does it make sense to always require expensive independent assessments of what will sometimes be meritless suits?

g.   By contrast, in Bell Atlantic Corp. v. Bolger, 2 F.3d 1304 (3d Cir.1993), the Court went so far as to approve a settlement where a

13. Rotunda, Law, Lawyers, and Man- agers, in C. Walton, ed., The Ethics of Cor- porate Conduct 127, 135–36 (American As- sembly 1977).

single law firm represented both the corporation and the directors in a derivative action alleging that the directors were guilty of mismanagement, but not fraud. It takes evidence of conscious wrongdoing, the Court suggested, to make separate representation mandatory. Does this case go too far the other way? See Model Rule 1.13, Comments 11 & 12.

8. Today, of course, large corporations are often composed of several divisions and subsidiaries. Who is the lawyer's client in those situations?

a. Suppose, for example, that Sleepware produces hats through an existing subsidiary. It wants to acquire a new firm in the same industry, but to do so it must divest itself of the present sub. Is it clear whose interests Consolidated's corporate counsel must represent in structuring the sale of the subsidiary firm? Would it matter to you whether the subsidiary was wholly-owned or whether it still had other shareholders as well? See, e.g., F.T.C. v. Exxon Corp., 636 F.2d 1336 (D.C.Cir.1980) (separate counsel required for divested subsidiary because former parent might structure sale so as to see that it did not survive as a viable competitor).

b. Could you as Sleepware's general counsel be named a director of a firm being acquired? Again, does it depend upon whether the subsidiary will be wholly-owned? Might the service as director be proper if the subsidiary has independent outside counsel?

c. A major problem has arisen in recent years when a corporate subsidiary is a regulated entity that arguably has duties to interests other than those of the parent. Lincoln Savings, for example, was a wholly–owned subsidiary of ACC, the holding company that Charles Keating used to make other investments. The government asserted that lawyers for Lincoln could not accept direction from ACC's officers, at least once Lincoln was in financial trouble, even though ACC would bear the entire loss of equity from its failure. The point was that the FDIC's funds were exposed as well.[14]

9. Are questions of the duties of corporate counsel properly the subject of outside regulation at all?

Would it be better to provide simply that a corporate resolution should state a policy on where counsel's loyalties are to lie? Then, stock prices set in the open market would reward firms that made investors feel they were well represented and punish those who did not? This approach was proposed by the Roscoe Pound–American Trial Lawyers Foundation in § 2.5 of The American Lawyer's Code of Conduct found in the Standards Supplement. Do you agree with the position? Why or why not?

---

14. An excerpt from the *ACC/Lincoln* litigation concerning the liability of the Jones Day firm is set out as a Reading to Problem 22, *infra*.

READINGS

MONROE FREEDMAN, MUST YOU BE
THE DEVIL'S ADVOCATE? [15]

Legal Times, August 23, 1993

Item. A lawyer at New York's Sullivan & Cromwell recently turned down a court appointment to represent Mahmoud Abou–Halima, who is charged with involvement in the car-bombing of the World Trade Center. A Sullivan & Cromwell partner explained to The Wall Street Journal that the firm did not want to dedicate its resources to the case, because the bombing was "such a heinous crime" and because the defendant is "so personally objectionable." The partner added that Abou–Halima is "anti-Semitic in the most dangerous way." And the firm was also concerned about adverse reactions from some of its current clients.

Item. Michael Tigar, a professor at Texas Law School, recently argued in a federal appeals court that John Demjanjuk should be allowed to return to the United States when he leaves Israel. The Israeli Supreme Court has reversed Demjanjuk's conviction for participating in the mass murder of Jews in the gas chambers of Treblinka. The court was won over by compelling evidence that Demjanjuk has an alibi. Because he had been engaged in the mass murder of Jews at other Nazi camps, Demjanjuk couldn't possibly have been a guard at Treblinka.

Was Sullivan & Cromwell right to refuse to defend Abou–Halima? Was Tigar right to represent Demjanjuk? And what do the rules of ethics say about it?

Before answering those questions, we should recall the ethical obligations that a lawyer assumes by agreeing to represent a client. Under the traditional view, a lawyer is bound to represent a client zealously, using all reasonable means to achieve the client's lawful objectives. Some academics would like to do away with the ethic of zeal and substitute a more "communitarian" approach, while some practitioners favor a more paternalistic role of the lawyer. In short, these critics would replace democratic equality under law with the elitist discretion of lawyers. But the traditional view, which recognizes the client as a free person in a free society, is still the dominant ideal among American lawyers, as it has been for well over a century.

That does not mean that lawyers should disregard moral concerns in representing clients. On the contrary, if a lawyer believes that what the client proposes is immoral or even simply imprudent, the client is entitled to the lawyer's judgment and counsel. But "[in] the final

---

15. Reprinted with permission of *Legal Times*. Copyright © 1993. Monroe Freedman is the Howard Lichtenstein Distinguished Professor of Legal Ethics at Hofstra University Law School.

analysis ... the lawyer should always remember that the decision whether to forgo legally available objectives or methods because of non-legal factors is ultimately for the client and not for himself." American Bar Association Model Code of Professional Responsibility, EC 7–8.

Thus, a lawyer's decision to represent a client may commit that lawyer to zealously furthering the interests of one whom the lawyer or others in the community believe to be morally repugnant. For that reason, the question of whether to represent a particular client can present the lawyer with an important moral decision—a decision for which the lawyer can properly be held morally accountable, in the sense of being under a burden of public justification.

That would not be so if each lawyer were ethically bound to represent every client seeking the lawyer's services. If there were no choice, there would be no responsibility. Under both rule and practice, however, lawyers have always been free to choose whether to represent particular clients. Ethical Consideration 2–27 of the ABA Model Code does urge lawyers not to decline representation because a client or a cause is unpopular, but EC 2–26 says flatly that a lawyer has "no obligation" to take on every person who wants to become her client. And the Comment to Rule 6.2 of the ABA Model Rules of Professional Conduct says similarly that a lawyer ordinarily is "not obliged to accept a client whose character or cause the lawyer regards as repugnant."

Thus, Sullivan & Cromwell violated no ethical rule in declining to defend Mahmoud Abou–Halima. Indeed, on the facts as reported, the firm would have acted unethically if it had taken the case. Under Disciplinary Rule 5–101 of the ABA Model Code, which is controlling in New York, a lawyer has a conflict of interest if the exercise of her professional judgment on behalf of her client "reasonably may be affected" by her own personal or business interests.

And that is precisely the position of the lawyers at Sullivan & Cromwell who find the potential client so personally objectionable that they don't think the partnership should put its resources into the case, who find the crime so heinous that they don't want to be associated with its defense, and who are worried about how other clients and potential clients will view the representation. Certainly those powerful concerns may reasonably be expected to affect the zeal with which those lawyers would represent that client.

What then about Michael Tigar's representation of John Demjanjuk?

I said earlier that a lawyer's decision to represent a client is a decision for which the lawyer is morally accountable. But I must confess that this has not always been my position. At one time I argued that it is wrong to criticize a lawyer for choosing to represent a particular client or cause. If lawyers were to be vilified for accepting unpopular clients or causes, I said, then those individuals who are most in need of representation might find it impossible to obtain counsel.

But I was mistaken. Lawyers have always been vilified for taking unpopular cases, even by other lawyers and judges, and lawyers have nevertheless been found to represent the most heinous of clients. In the face of the harshest invective, lawyers have represented "The Meanest Man in New York" (whom I represented) and even Nazis, to advocate their right to march in Skokie, Ill.

What ultimately changed my mind on the issue of moral accountability was a debate I participated in about 25 years ago. It was sparked by the picketing of D.C.'s Wilmer, Cutler, & Pickering by a group of law students led by Ralph Nader. The demonstrators were protesting the firm's representation of General Motors in an air-pollution case. I took the position that the protesters were wrong to criticize a firm for its choice of clients.

My opponent argued that it was entirely proper for the demonstrators to challenge lawyers at the firm to ask themselves: "Is this really the kind of client to which I want to dedicate my training, my knowledge, and my skills as a lawyer? Did I go to law school to help a client that harms other human beings by polluting the atmosphere with poisonous gases?"

Although I didn't realize it for some time, my opponent won the debate in the most decisive way—by converting me to his position. The issue is not whether General Motors should be represented. Of course they should, and there will always be someone who will do it. The real issue for each of us is: Should I be the one to represent this client, and if so, why?

And so I now ask my victorious opponent in that long-ago debate: Mike Tigar, is John Demjanjuk the kind of client to whom you want to dedicate your training, your knowledge, and your extraordinary skills as a lawyer? Did you go to law school to help a client who has committed mass murder of other human beings with poisonous gases? Of course, someone should, and will, represent him. But why you, old friend?

MICHAEL E. TIGAR, SETTING THE RECORD STRAIGHT ON THE DEFENSE OF JOHN DEMJANJUK [16]

Legal Times, September 6, 1993

All of Monroe Freedman's statements about me in this newspaper are wrong, except two: We are—or were—old friends. And I do represent John Demjanjuk.

* * *

Professor Freedman is wrong about the Israeli Supreme Court decision and about the American judicial decisions that caused Demjanjuk to linger in a death cell for years, for a crime he did not commit.

---

16. Reprinted with permission of *Legal Times*. Copyright © 1993. Michael E. Tigar holds the Joseph D. Jamail Centennial Chair in Law at the University of Texas School of Law. The reported case, providing a richer factual background, is Demjanjuk v. Petrovsky, 10 F.3d 338 (6th Cir.), cert.denied sub nom. Rison v. Demjanjuk, ___ U.S. ___, 115 S.Ct. 295, 130 L.Ed.2d 205 (1994).

John Demjanjuk was extradited to Israel to stand trial as "Ivan the Terrible" of Treblinka, one of the worst mass murderers of the Holocaust. It turned out that crucial exculpatory evidence—that someone named Ivan Marchenko, not Demjanjuk, was Ivan the Terrible—was withheld from the defense. That evidence was not an "alibi"; it had to do with tragically mistaken identification and the U.S. government's failure to live up to its obligations of candor to its adversary and to the courts.

Freedman is wrong about what the Israeli Supreme Court did once it found doubt that Demjanjuk was Ivan. That court did not, as Freedman asserts, hold that Demjanjuk was guilty of other crimes. The Israeli court did consider whether Demjanjuk should be convicted as having served at other Nazi death camps, but found that Demjanjuk never had a fair opportunity to rebut evidence of service at other camps.

In 1981, a U.S. district judge found that Demjanjuk should be denaturalized. The judge found that Demjanjuk was Ivan the Terrible, a decision that is now universally conceded to have been wrong. There is powerful evidence that government lawyers suppressed evidence that would have shown that decision to have been wrong when made.

The U.S. judge also considered the question of whether Demjanjuk served at other camps. The judge found that, since Demjanjuk was Ivan and denied being Ivan, he probably should not be believed when he denied other culpable conduct at other camps. Thus, the judge's decision, now argued by the government as barring judicial review of Demjanjuk's right to enter the United States, was taken in the shadow of these now-discredited allegations.

Those are the facts. I represent Mr. Demjanjuk pro bono, along with the federal public defender, in an American judicial proceeding. The proceeding will, we hope, vacate earlier judgments against Demjanjuk and leave the government free—if it wishes—to bring and try fairly its allegations that John Demjanjuk served at death camps. If, as Professor Freedman says, there is evidence of such service, which Mr. Demjanjuk has denied, my client is entitled to a fair trial where that evidence can be tested.

* * *

We must remember the Holocaust, and we should pursue and punish it perpetrators. We dishonor that memory and besmirch the pursuit if we fail to accord those accused of Holocaust crimes the same measure of legality and due process that we would give to anyone accused of wrongdoing. Precisely because a charge of culpable participation in the Holocaust is so damning, the method of judging whether such a charge is true should be above reproach.

So much for the factual difficulties in which Professor Freedman finds himself. Let us turn to his analysis of the ethical issues.

Professor Freedman begins by lauding a major law firm for refusing a court appointment to represent an unpopular indigent defendant. The firm doesn't like the client, doesn't like the fact that he is accused of a "heinous crime," and is afraid that its other clients will object. OK, says Freedman, those are good reasons for the law firm to refuse.

Let us all hurry to the library, and rewrite To Kill a Mockingbird. Atticus Finch is not a hero after all. He should have thought more of maintaining his law practice and refused to represent someone charged with a heinous—and possibly racially motivated—crime. Clarence Darrow should have stayed with the railroad, instead of taking on those Commie unionists as clients. The lawyers who lost their licenses for daring to represent the colonial newspaper editor John Peter Zenger for the heinous crime of seditious libel were chumps. And John Hancock, that notorious tax evader, had no right to have John Adams as his counsel.

Maybe Sullivan & Cromwell has the right to refuse a court appointment, and maybe it should have that right. I have represented plenty of unpopular folks in my 25 years at the bar and have always stood up to the task of telling my paying clients that they just have to understand a lawyer's responsibility in such matters, or they should take their business elsewhere.

From praise of Sullivan & Cromwell, Professor Freedman then makes a giant leap. He invents a new rule of legal ethics. Based on the supposed right to refuse a court appointment, we are told that every lawyer must bear "a burden of public justification" for representing someone accused of odious crimes. There is no rule of professional responsibility that so provides, and several rules cut directly against his assertions.

If Atticus Finch decides to represent an indigent defendant, Freedman will require him not only to incur the obloquy of his friends and clients, but to undertake a public defense of his ethical right to accept the case.

To put lawyers under such a burden of public justification undermines the right to representation of unpopular defendants. It invites the kind of demagoguery that we are now seeing in the attacks on lawyers for defendants in capital cases. It even invites the kinds of unwarranted attacks on zealous advocacy that have often been directed—and quite unjustly—at Professor Freedman.

I undertook the pro bono representation of John Demjanjuk in the 6th Circuit after a thorough review of the facts and law. I can no more be under a duty to make a public accounting of why I took this case than I can be under a duty to open up the files of all my cases to public view.

Professor Freedman does not end matters by inventing a pernicious rule. He also claims to remember what he calls a "debate" of 25 years ago. We did, in fact, meet on a stage at the George Washington University law school some 23 years ago. I did not make the statement he attributes to me.

I did say then, and still believe, that lawyers have a responsibility to their own conscience for the kinds of clients they choose to represent and the positions they choose to advance. The lawyers who have upheld that principle, from Sir Thomas More to Lord Brougham to Clarence Darrow, are rightly celebrated.

Having misquoted me, Freedman (who is still at this point in his diatribe calling me his "friend") wonders why I would choose to use my talent for John Demjanjuk, instead of letting some other lawyer do it. I am not sure what alternative scenario he sees being played out here. Maybe he thinks I should represent some of Sullivan & Cromwell's clients instead.

I have answered that question for myself, and it is insulting for Professor Freedman to suggest that I am faithless to my principles. When the most powerful country on earth gangs up on an individual citizen, falsely accuses him of being the most heinous mass murderer of the Holocaust, and systematically withholds evidence that would prove him guiltless of that charge, there is something dramatically wrong. When that man is held in the most degrading conditions in a death cell based on those false accusations, the wrong is intensified. When the government that did wrong denies all accountability, the judicial branch should provide a remedy. I have spent a good many years of my professional life litigating such issues. I am proud to be doing so again.

MONROE FREEDMAN, THE MORALITY OF LAWYERING

Legal Times, September 20, 1993 [17]

* * *

My question to Tigar relates to one of the most fundamental issues of lawyers' ethics and the nature of the lawyer's role. That issue is frequently posed by asking whether one can be a good person and a good lawyer at the same time. Or whether the lawyer forfeits her conscience when she represents a client. Or whether the lawyer is nothing more than a hired gun. Essentially, these questions ask whether the lawyer, in her role as a lawyer, is a moral being. There are three answers to that question:

* The amoral lawyer. One answer has been dubbed "the standard conception." It holds that the lawyer has no moral responsibility whatsoever for representing a particular client or for the lawful means used or the ends achieved for the client. Critics have accurately pointed out that under the standard conception, the lawyer's role is at best an amoral one and is sometimes flat-out immoral.

* Moral control of the client. A second answer insists that the lawyer's role is indeed a moral one. It begins by agreeing with the

17. Reprinted with permission of *Legal Times*. Copyright © 1993.

standard conception that the lawyer's choice of client it not subject to moral scrutiny. But it holds that the lawyer can impose his moral views on the client by controlling both the goals pursued and the means used during the representation.

According to this view, the lawyer can properly stop the client from using lawful means to achieve lawful goals. For example, the lawyer, having taken the case and having induced the client to rely upon her, can later threaten to withdraw from the representation—even where this would cause material harm to the client—if the client does not submit to what the lawyer deems to be the moral or prudent course. * * *

* Choice of client as a moral decision. The third answer also insists that the lawyer's role is a moral one. It begins by agreeing with the standard conception that the client is entitled to make the important decisions about the client's goals and the lawful means used to pursue those goals. But this answer recognizes that the lawyer has the broadest power—ethically and in practice—to decide which clients to represent. And it insists that the lawyer's decision to accept or to reject a particular client is a moral decision. Moreover, that decision is one for which the lawyer can properly be held morally accountable.

Although critics have erroneously, and repeatedly, identified me with the standard conception, I have consistently advocated the third answer for 17 years. It is refreshing, therefore, to be criticized at last for what I believe, rather than for what I don't believe.

* * *

It is no surprise that Tigar, in response to my question, has come through with a powerful, persuasive explanation—a moral explanation—of his decision to represent John Demjanjuk.

First, he notes that the memory of the Holocaust should not be dishonored by denying even its perpetrators the fullest measure of legality. One lesson of the Holocaust is that the vast powers of government must constantly be subjected to the most exacting scrutiny in order to guard against their abuse.

Further, Tigar refers to "powerful evidence" that lawyers in the Department of Justice suppressed evidence that would have shown that Demjanjuk should not have been extradited on charges of being Ivan the Terrible. (Note that these government lawyers have not been found guilty after trial by jury, but that Tigar nevertheless—and properly—finds enough evidence of their guilt to justify his personal moral decision.) This kind of corruption of justice is an intolerable threat to American ideals, regardless of one's opinion of the accused.

And Tigar concludes: "When the government that did wrong denies all accountability, the judicial branch should provide a remedy. I have spent a good many years of my professional life litigating such issues. I am proud to be doing so again."

Thus, Tigar's moral response to my question illuminates a crucial issue of enormous public importance about what lawyers do and why they do it. And it illustrates why I am proud to call Mike Tigar my friend.

––––––

PROBLEM 19

Contact With Represented and Unrepresented Parties

Speedy Corp. has a fleet of trucks and couriers to deliver packages throughout the city. The company has made a standing offer to return the shipper's fee for any package not delivered within one hour. There is reason to believe that this policy causes Speedy's drivers and couriers to take dangerous chances.

One rainy Tuesday, President Mary Speedy was standing across the street from the company headquarters. Barry Winters, an employee in the accounting department of Speedy Corp. happened to be standing beside her. Just then, a Speedy delivery truck came out of the headquarters building at a high rate of speed. It hit an elderly man, causing him serious injuries.

Before filing the complaint, Louis Shabazz, lawyer for the injured man, interviewed Barry Winters and the truck driver and took their statements about how the accident happened. Barbara Bentley, lawyer for Speedy Corp., was not told of those interviews or invited to be present. Now, Shabazz has called Mary Speedy and asked to interview her as well; Speedy, in turn, has called Bentley who has told Speedy to decline to be interviewed in any setting other than a formal deposition.

Bentley herself now wants to investigate to find out what the facts surrounding the accident are. She wants to prepare for litigation and to formulate recommendations for possible changes of the one-hour guarantee. Indeed, she fears a grand jury may be convened to determine whether Speedy's guarantee of one-hour service might support a charge of criminal negligence. Bentley wants to talk to present and former employees of Speedy, both officers and nonofficers, who might know how the policy has affected safety. Shabazz, of course, would like to talk to the same people.

QUESTIONS

1. Was it proper for Shabazz to interview Winters and the truck driver about how the accident occurred?

a. Must a lawyer have permission of opposing counsel to interview all eyewitnesses to an accident? How about all company employees? Is there anyone in this problem whom Shabazz could not properly interview without Bentley's consent?

b. What do Model Rule 4.2 and DR 7–104(A)(1) say about this issue? Was Winters a "party" to the accident? Should his status as an employee of Speedy Corp., in itself, bring Winters within the coverage of these "no contact" rules? Look at Comment 2 to Model Rule 4.2.

c. In Niesig v. Team I, 76 N.Y.2d 363, 559 N.Y.S.2d 493, 558 N.E.2d 1030 (1990), a personal injury lawyer for a plaintiff wished to interview a corporate defendant's employees who had witnessed an accident. The court noted that when a corporation is a party to a lawsuit, the incorporeal entity is the only "party." However, a corporation only acts through natural persons, and unless one or more of these employees is also sued, the corporation would have no protection under DR 7–104(A)(1) or Rule 4.2. The court noted that there should be a public policy of reducing litigation costs by allowing plaintiffs to use informal, off the record, private interviews rather than costly depositions or interviews attended by the adversary counsel. And, it said, the corporation has ample opportunity to interview its own employees, gather facts, and counsel them so that they do not make improvident disclosures.

The court thus concluded that "parties" for purposes of DR 7–104(A)(1) should include (1) only corporate employees whose acts or omissions in the matter under inquiry are binding on the corporation (that is, who are the corporation's alter egos), (2) employees whose acts or omissions are imputed to the corporation for purposes of its liability, or (3) employees implementing the advice of counsel.[18] All other employees may be interviewed informally. Thus, "parties" do not include former employees.

The case represents a good statement of the general rule. In this problem, whom could Shabazz properly interview without Bentley's permission or advance knowledge?

d. In re Opinion 668 of Advisory Committee on Professional Ethics, 633 A.2d 959 (N.J.1993)(per curiam), sent the issues back for further study but as an interim matter concluded that Rule 4.2 barred interviews with both present and former employees in the company control group. Notice to the corporation, but not permission, was also required to talk to present or former "employees whose conduct, in and of itself, establishes the organization's liability." Do you agree that the range of prohibited contacts should be extended?

---

18. State ex rel. Charleston Area Medical Center v. Zakaib, 190 W.Va. 186, 437 S.E.2d 759 (W.Va.1993), reviewed an order allowing plaintiff's counsel to interview all present and former employees of a medical center in a malpractice action. The Court adopted the majority view that Rule 4.2 does not bar interviews with former employees of an opponent. It was more permissive than usual, however, on interviews with present employees, only barring interviews with present employees "who are responsible for implementing the advice of the corporation's lawyer."

2. Does the rule against contact with a represented party make sense to you? Whom does the rule seek to protect and against what?

a. Is the concern that a persuasive lawyer will negotiate a settlement disadvantageous to the represented party without that party's realizing what is going on?

b. Is the concern that the opposing lawyer will interfere with the party's attorney-client relationship by undermining the party's faith in the party's own lawyer?

c. May the rule be based in part on the desire of some lawyers that they be able to control their clients, i.e., that the clients not be able to work things out without their lawyer's help? Might it even reflect the concern of lawyers who want to be sure they spend the maximum number of billable hours being involved in the pre–trial process?

d. How do these concerns apply to the facts of this problem? Other than perhaps Mary Speedy, is there anyone whom Shabazz should be prevented from interviewing without Bentley's permission?

e. What limits are there on how Shabazz may conduct his interviews of Winters and others? May he take potential witnesses to lunch, for example, and seek to develop a good rapport with them so that they will be more forthcoming in their conversations with him? May he imply that he is conducting an investigation on behalf of a government traffic safety agency, i.e., must he say that he represents the witnesses' employer's potential opponent in litigation? Remember Model Rule 8.4(c) and DR 1–102(A)(4).

3. May represented clients talk to each other without going through their lawyers?

a. State Bar of California, Formal Opinion 1993–131 (1993), gives the standard answer that the clients *may* talk; indeed, it says that failure to encourage such talks may forfeit opportunities to terminate disputes short of trial. The opinion also says the lawyers for each client may advise the clients before they get together, but the communications must be those of the clients, not the lawyers acting through the lawyers' "scripts" for them.

b. ABA Formal Opinion 92–362 (1992), states that a lawyer who has made an offer to opposing counsel may not call the opposing party to see if the offer has been communicated. The lawyer may, however, advise her client that he may talk to the opposing party directly to see if that party received the offer.

c. Why do we draw these distinctions? Are lawyers really more likely to be guilty of overreaching than business people are? Should the law encourage lawyers to do their overreaching through agents?

4. What will be Bentley's duty, if any, to Speedy Corp.'s officers and employees when she questions them herself?

a. Should she take a "we're all in this together" approach? Should she advise the truck driver, for example, to obtain his own counsel? How about the Vice President in charge of the truck maintenance facility? The Board members who approved the on-time delivery guarantee?

b. Should she become the lawyer for each of the corporate officers, directors and employees personally? At minimum, would that make them all "represented persons" and invoke the protection of Rule 4.2? Cf. Model Rule 1.13(d).

c. W.T. Grant Co. v. Haines, 531 F.2d 671 (2d Cir.1976), involved a corporation's antitrust action against one of its former employees and others. The employee moved to disqualify the corporation's law firm, alleging it had violated DR 7–104(A) when corporate attorneys had earlier interviewed the employee. When this interview took place, counsel correctly identified the character and nature of their representation, but did not disclose that earlier that morning a lawsuit had been filed naming the employee as a defendant. Counsel told the employee that candid answers might clear his name and secured the employee's authorization to examine his taxes, credit cards, etc. The court found no violation of DR 7–104(A)(1) because the employee was not yet represented by counsel and corporate counsel had accurately said whom they represented. See also, Rule 4.2, 4.3. The employee was said to be sophisticated, "neither a callow youth nor a befuddled widow." As for DR 7–104(A)(2) on not giving advice to unrepresented persons with interests opposed to the client's, the court said that the question was "close," but that even assuming a violation, disqualification of counsel was inappropriate because defense counsel failed to establish that the questioned behavior tainted the trial. The Court said that the appropriate forum was the Grievance Committee of the bar association.[19]

d. On the problem of the employees being misled by corporate counsel, see the dictum in Diversified Industries, Inc. v. Meredith, 572 F.2d 596, 611 n.5 (8th Cir.1977)(en banc):

> "We need not address at this time the situation where an employee's confidential communications to the corporation's counsel may reveal potential liability of the employee. Ordinarily, the privilege belongs to the corporation and an employee cannot himself claim the attorney-client privilege and prevent disclosure of communications between himself and the corporation's counsel if the corporation has waived the privilege. In re Grand Jury Proceedings, Detroit, Michigan, August, 434 F.Supp. 648 (E.D.Mich.1977). However, circumstances may reveal that the employee sought legal advice from the corporation's counsel for himself or that counsel acted as a joint attorney. Under such circumstances, he may have a privilege. See generally, 8 Wigmore, Evidence § 2312 (McNaughton rev. 1961)."

19. Compare Wilson P. Abraham Construction Corp. v. Armco Steel Corp., 559 F.2d 250 (5th Cir.1977) (per curiam) (case remanded to determine whether confidential communications were being used against the former co-defendant).

If Bentley is interviewing a witness who is an employee of her corporate client—but who is not her client—and the witness starts giving incriminating information that is helpful to Bentley's corporate client, must Bentley give *Miranda* warnings? See Defense Function Standard 4–4.3(c). Compare Model Rules 1.13(d),(e); 4.3. What should Bentley do?

5. Now suppose the police interview the same group of company employees.

a. Should the police be considered to be the agents of the prosecuting attorney for purposes of Model Rule 4.2 and DR 7–104(A)(1) when they conduct such questioning? Must the prosecutor take responsibility for requiring the police—whom we may assume are not lawyers—to follow the Model Rules and the ABA Standards Relating to the Prosecution Function in states that have adopted those guidelines? See ABA Prosecution Function Standards, §§ 3–2.6 & 2.7, in the Standards Supplement.

b. Consider United States v. Thomas, 474 F.2d 110 (10th Cir.1973), cert. denied 412 U.S. 932, 93 S.Ct. 2758, 37 L.Ed.2d 160 (1973). In *Thomas,* the court held that, even though the defendant had waived his *Miranda* rights:

> "[O]nce a criminal defendant has either retained an attorney or had an attorney appointed for him by the court, any statement obtained by interview from such defendant may not be offered in evidence unless the accused's attorney was notified of the interview which produced the statement and was given a reasonable opportunity to be present. To hold otherwise we think would be to overlook conduct which violated both the letter and the spirit of the canons of ethics. This is not something which the defendant alone can waive.

> "A violation of the canon of ethics as here concerned need not be remedied by a reversal of the case wherein it is violated. This does not necessarily present a constitutional question, but this is an ethical and administrative one relating to attorneys practicing before the United States courts. * * * The enforcement officials are agents of the prosecuting party, and in the event use is made of information secured by interviews of the nature which here took place, short of its introduction in evidence, the problem will be dealt with in the proper case." 474 F.2d at 112.

c. Should the *Thomas* analysis be applied in a typical state system where the state's attorney, usually a county officer, has no direct control over the police, headed by the Chief of Police, an official who is usually is responsible to the Mayor or City Council. Should this problem be recognized by the Code? Even before Formal Opinion 95 (May 3, 1933), the ABA Committee had said:

"The law officer is, of course, responsible for the acts of those in his department who are under his supervision and control. Opinion 85. * * *

"It would be unavailing to contend that the police officers or detectives are not under the supervision and control of the law officer, but rather are under the supervision and control of the municipality."

Do you agree? Is this Opinion realistic today?

d. In State v. Richmond, 114 Ariz. 186, 560 P.2d 41 (1976), cert. denied 433 U.S. 915, 97 S.Ct. 2988, 53 L.Ed.2d 1101 (1977), the Court said that DR 7–104 and EC 7–8 "are generally assumed to be for the purpose of affording civil litigants some of the protection which the Constitution guarantees to criminal defendants * * *. As long as law enforcement officers comply with the requirement of the Constitution in pursuit of their investigation, an incriminating statement which is freely and voluntarily given is admissible." There was no allegation that the police officers, who interrogated the defendant without his counsel, acted with the knowledge of the county attorney or staff.

Do you agree? Should the ethical restrictions on dealing with represented parties only be relevant in civil cases? Is the Court saying that the Constitution represents the maximum limits that may be placed on prosecutorial misconduct? Is it saying that if any other limits are imposed, the only remedy is that of professional discipline, i.e., that the exclusionary rule is not to be invoked? [20]

e. United States v. Ryans, 903 F.2d 731 (10th Cir.1990), involved the secret recording of the conversation between the target of an investigation, known to be represented by his regular lawyer, and a cooperating witness at a time prior to indictment. The court did not itself suppress the evidence obtained but reported that "it is now well settled that DR 7–104(A)(1) applies to criminal as well as civil litigation", and that it applies to agents of public prosecutors " 'when they act as the alter ego of the prosecuting attorneys.' " *Id.,* at 735. Three circuits, the 5th, 7th and 10th have said that the principle applies to pre-indictment interviews when the defendant is in custody. United States v. Hammad, 846 F.2d 854 (2d Cir.1988), has applied DR 7–104 to noncustodial, pre-indictment investigations as well, but even that case refused to require exclusion of the evidence obtained.

If a disciplinary rule should be enforced at all, why shouldn't it be enforced at the trial? Does experience with the conflict of interest rules

20. Cf. Nai Cheng Chen v. INS, 537 F.2d 566, 568–69 (1st Cir.1976), where the court refused to exclude evidence obtained from an interview for which there had been a failure to provide notice to counsel. The court noted that the immigration proceeding was not criminal, and that Immigration Service investigators are "authorized by law" to interrogate aliens or suspected aliens, thus coming within the exception to DR 7–104(A)(1). 537 F.2d at 569 & n. 7. However, the court said, it would be "better practice" to give such notice.

suggest that such direct enforcement would convert disciplinary rules into mere trial tactics?

f. In United States v. Ofshe, 817 F.2d 1508 (11th Cir.1987), the defendant faced drug charges. He retained one lawyer to prepare for trial and another (Glass) to negotiate with the government about a plea. The latter simultaneously found himself accused in Chicago's "Operation Greylord" corruption cases, and he wanted to do what he could to win favorable treatment for himself. Chicago Assistant U.S. Attorney (and well-known author) Scott Turow had Glass wear a body bug to his meeting with Ofshe, his Florida client. Agents monitoring the tape "were given very strict guidelines to instruct Glass not to violate any attorney-client privilege"; instead, Ofshe and Glass discussed other criminal plans.

Ofshe argued that this use of defense counsel as informer justified dismissing the indictment against him. The court held that, absent prejudice, the remedy is not warranted. Not only was no useful information developed by the bug, but the Florida U.S. Attorney's office was given none of what was developed. Finally, although Glass did not provide effective assistance of counsel to Ofshe, his co-counsel did, so there was no harm done. What do you think of this analysis? Should a prosecutor ever be able to use a suspect's lawyer as an informant? Does this practice make Barbara Bentley, by comparison, look like a saint?

g. A continuing source of tension in this area, of course, has been the so-called "Thornburgh Memorandum". It purports to authorize ex parte contacts by Justice Department lawyers with targets of criminal investigations who are known to have counsel but who have not yet been arrested or charged and thus arguably are not opposing "parties".

Attorney General Janet Reno withdrew this Memorandum, but then promulgated a rule that does not dramatically change the government's position or theory. See, Communications with Represented Persons, 38 Code of Federal Regulations, Part 77 (1994). In the comments accompanying this rule, the Attorney General emphasized that the Department of Justice "has long maintained, and continues to maintain, that it has authority to exempt its attorneys from the application of DR 7–104 and Model Rule 4.2 and their state counterparts." 59 Fed. Register 39910, 39911 (Aug. 4, 1994).

38 C.F.R. § 77.5 is a short statement providing, in general, that, unless "otherwise authorized by law," a government attorney may not communicate with a represented party "who the attorney for the government knows is represented by an attorney" if this representation concerns "the subject matter of the representation," unless the lawyer consents.

A much lengthier provision, § 77.6, follows, listing various exceptions. For example, there is an exception for discovery by legal process (such as during a grand jury testimony); or when the "represented party initiates the communication directly with the attorney for the government or through an intermediary" and the party knowingly waives his or her right and a federal judge or magistrate concludes that the waiver is knowing and voluntary; or when there is a waiver of *Miranda* rights at the time of arrest; or when there is an investigation of "additional, different or ongoing crimes or civil violations," including "undercover or covert" operations; or when the government attorney believes in "good faith" that the communication is necessary to prevent against the "risk of injury or death" to any person.

In § 77.11 the Attorney General assumes "exclusive enforcement" power; this section specifically excludes all private remedies of civil or criminal defendants. Section 77.12 provides that this new rule "is intended to preempt and supersede the application of state laws and rules and local federal court rules to the extent that they relate to contacts by attorneys for the government" and their agents. Neither state or federal courts or disciplinary boards may impose sanctions unless the Attorney General first determines that there was a willful, intentional, deliberate violation of these federal rules. See also, 59 Fed. Reg. 39910, 39927.

h. United States v. Lopez, 4 F.3d 1455 (9th Cir.1993), is a particularly interesting example of these issues. Lopez was charged with a drug offense and feared his children were being abused while he was in prison. He wanted to discuss cooperation with the government. However, his lawyer, Barry Tarlow, had a reputation for refusing to negotiate cooperation. Thus, Lopez tried to deal with the government directly. The District Court held that—even where the defendant initiated the contact—it was so improper for the U.S. Attorney's office to talk to him in the absence of his lawyer that the indictment must be dismissed. The Ninth Circuit opinion was contemptuous of the Thornburgh memorandum and critical of the U.S. Attorney, but it concluded that dismissing the indictment went too far. In a concurring opinion, Judge Fletcher opined that Tarlow's unwillingness to negotiate on Lopez' behalf had been a big part of the problem and thus his conduct should have been criticized by the Court as well.

How would you have decided this case? Do criminal defendants sometimes need protection from their own lawyers? Should it ever be improper for a prosecutor to talk with a defendant who voluntarily seeks such a meeting?

PROBLEM 20

The Ethics of Negotiation

James Young, age 19, was in a traffic accident. The driver of the other car suffered personal injuries and has paid medical bills of $18,000. There was $7,000 in property damage to the other car. Young was unhurt, but his car suffered $5,000 damage.

At the scene of the accident, the investigating officer charged Young with drunk driving. Young denied it and told the officer that he had had nothing alcoholic to drink the entire day. He has told you, however, that he had three large drinks within an hour of the accident. By chance, the arresting officer had failed to bring along his kit to test for blood alcohol, so there is no scientific evidence on that issue.

Young's criminal trial is coming up next week. Conviction of drunk driving would probably mean that Young would pay a large fine and lose his driving privileges for a year. You have plea negotiations scheduled with the prosecutor this afternoon. Settlement discussions about the potential civil claims are also expected soon.

QUESTIONS

1. May you assert in negotiations about this case that Young had nothing alcoholic to drink on the day of the accident? Remember, that is the story that he has told everyone but you.

a. Could you let Young so testify in the upcoming criminal trial? As you will see in Problem 28, the answer is clearly no.

b. May your negotiating position in the civil and criminal cases be that your client was not intoxicated at the time of the accident? Is that something that you *know* is untrue? May you assert that neither the police nor the plaintiff can prove that he was intoxicated? Are those two statements different as a practical matter? Are they—should they be— different as a matter of ethics?

c. May you tell your adversary that your client will testify that the other car was traveling at an excessive rate of speed and "came out of nowhere" to cause the accident? You know that your client really does not remember the accident very well, but you hope that the other side may factor into its own estimate of the worth of the case the risk that that would be your client's story.

d. The late Federal Judge Alvin B. Rubin took a strong stand on the issue of honesty in negotiations:

> " * * * Most lawyers say it would be improper to prepare a false document to deceive an adversary or to make a factual statement known to be untrue with the intention of deceiving him. * * *

> "Interesting answers are obtained [, however,] if lawyers are asked whether it is proper to make false statements that concern negotiating strategy rather than the facts in litigation. Counsel for a plaintiff appears quite comfortable in stating, when representing a plaintiff, 'My client won't take a penny less than $25,000,' when in fact he knows that the client will happily settle for less; counsel for the defendant appears to have no qualms in representing that he has no authority to settle, or that a given figure exceeds his authority, when these are untrue statements. Many say that, as a matter of strategy, when they

attend a pre-trial conference with a judge known to press settlements, they disclaim any settlement authority both to the judge and adversary although in fact they do have settlement instructions; estimable members of the bar support the thesis that a lawyer may not misrepresent a fact in controversy but may misrepresent matters that pertain to his authority or negotiating strategy because this is expected by the adversary.

"To most practitioners it appears that anything sanctioned by the rules of the game is appropriate. From this point of view, negotiations are merely, as the social scientists have viewed it, a form of game; observance of the expected rules, not professional ethics, is the guiding precept. But gamesmanship is not ethics." [1]

e. Consider a largely opposing view. Professor James J. White writes of the "paradoxical nature of the negotiator's responsibility":

"On the one hand the negotiator must be fair and truthful; on the other he must mislead his opponent. Like the poker player, a negotiator hopes that his opponent will overestimate the value of his hand. Like the poker player, in a variety of ways he must facilitate his opponent's inaccurate assessment. The critical difference between those who are successful negotiators and those who are not lies in this capacity both to mislead and not to be misled." [2]

2. Are all lies created equal? Might some lies be tolerated, some even encouraged, while other lies are forbidden?

a. What about misrepresenting one's attitude? Is it proper to fake anger during negotiations, for example? Is it proper to delay making or responding to an offer so as not to let the other side get the sense that your client is in a hurry to dispose of the case by settlement? Does the duty to bargain in good faith prohibit such behavior?

b. May a lawyer lie about the client's alternatives? Might the lawyer arrange for a "telephone call" in the middle of the negotiation, for example, so that she can leave the room and pretend to have received a better offer? May the lawyer say she has to "seek permission from the client to go any higher" when in fact the client has already approved the suggested settlement figure as within the attorney's discretion?

c. May the lawyer lie about where John was going on the day of the accident? May he say John was going to church services when he really was going to shoot pool? Is the issue of where he was going "material" to the legal issues in the case? Would it be disloyal to the client to suggest he is other than a choir boy?

1. Rubin, A Causerie on Lawyers' Ethics in Negotiation, 35 Louisiana L.Rev. 577, 585–86 (1975).

2. White, Machiavelli and the Bar: Ethical Limits on Lying in Negotiation, 1980 A.B.F. Research J. 926, 927.

d. Is any distinction between deception in a trial versus deception in negotiation supported by Model Rules 4.1 and 8.4(c)? How about DR 1–102(A)(4) or DR 7–102(A)(5)? Should a distinction be drawn?

3. Is the obligation to be truthful higher for lawyers than for non-lawyers?

a. Look closely at Model Rule 4.1 and its Comments. Does it prohibit any more than "false" statements of "material" fact? If a non-lawyer makes a false statement of material fact, wouldn't the non-lawyer be guilty of fraud?

b. If a statement would not constitute the tort of fraud or intentional misrepresentation, would it violate either Model Rule 4.1 or DR 7–102(A)(5)? Look especially at Model Rule 4.1, Comment 2. Put another way, is there any statement for which the lawyer would be subject to professional discipline but not liability for damages?

c. Restatement of the Law (Third): The Law Governing Lawyers § 153 (Preliminary Draft No. 10, 1994) suggests that Model Rule 4.1 imposes no greater obligation on lawyers than on persons generally. Do you agree that the law should ask no more of lawyers?

d. On the other hand, might it be fair to say that because people are more on their guard when dealing with a lawyer for someone else, the obligation of a lawyer to tell the truth should be less?

4. Is deception and withholding of information inevitably good negotiating strategy?

a. Is negotiation inevitably a zero–sum game in which anything one side receives is at the expense of the other? Suppose Ann has a candy bar and Bill has a pen. Ann needs something with which to write and Bill is hungry. Will Ann and Bill each be better off trying to figure out how to trick the other out of what the other has? Might the first to acknowledge the possibility of a fair trade improve the lot of both of them?

b. Some students of negotiating strategy have used computer simulations to explore numerous approaches to negotiation and have evaluated them in terms of benefits to each negotiator. One successful strategy is known as tit-for-tat.[3] You, as a negotiator, break the process down into a series of small "deals", not just one large one. As to the first deal, you begin by being open and honest in your negotiating. If your opposing number responds in the same way, you reward him by again being open and honest. If he ever deceives you or takes advantage of your honesty, however, you punish him by non–cooperative behavior as to the next issue. The point is that neither side needs to trust the other or sacrifice its own interests. It simply turns out to be better for all sides to make honesty and cooperation pay.

c. Even assuming that is true, however, is every negotiating situation one that has multiple steps? Is every situation one that both sides

3. See Robert Axelrod, The Evolution of Cooperation (1984).

can win? Might even negotiations that "increase the size of the pie" have a stage in which the pie gets divided? At that stage, what would good negotiators do? Might they be expected to agree on a solution that mimics the situation in which one party gets to cut the pie and the other chooses the first piece? [4]

5. What should be the legal limits on what you as a lawyer must affirmatively disclose in negotiation? May you simply say it is the responsibility of the other side to ask, not your responsibility to volunteer information?

a. In Virzi v. Grand Trunk Warehouse and Cold Storage Co., 571 F.Supp. 507 (E.D.Mich.1983), plaintiff's attorney failed to inform opposing counsel and the court, prior to the settlement, of the plaintiff's death. Plaintiff had died from causes unrelated to the lawsuit, and at no time did defendant's attorney ask plaintiff's attorney if plaintiff was still alive and available for trial. The court relied on DR 7–102(A)(3), (5), EC 7–27; Model Rules 3.3 & 4.1, and on Judge Rubin's article, to set aside the settlement. Zealous representation "does not justify a withholding of essential information, such as the death of the client, when the settlement of the case is based largely upon the defense attorney's assessment of the impact the plaintiff would make upon a jury because of his appearance at depositions. Plaintiff's attorney clearly had a duty to disclose the death of his client both to the Court and to opposing counsel prior to negotiating the final agreement." 571 F.Supp. at 512. Do you agree?

b. Virginia State Bar Opinion 952 (1987), in contrast, questioned whether the lawyer must disclose the fact that the lawyer's client had died. The Opinion said that no such disclosure is required unless opposing counsel directly inquires about the state of the client's health. The Opinion does not explain whether an answer such as, "He's out of pain," would be an adequately candid response to such a question. Should each round of settlement discussions have to begin with questions by each side designed to trigger this kind of disclosure? Would a general obligation on lawyers to disclose relevant changed circumstances be a better approach?

c. Kath v. Western Media, Inc., 684 P.2d 98 (Wyo.1984), was a complex case that involved several individuals and a corporation, all of whom had been represented by a single lawyer in an earlier proceeding. The former co-defendants were now suing each other and part of the question related to the role their attorney had played in the prior action. The former attorney had given a deposition in which he purported not to have known that some of the co-defendants planned to sue the others

---

4. Many observers remain unconvinced that honesty is the best policy if the only measure is to be "profit and effectiveness." See, e.g., Wetlaufer, The Ethics of Lying in Negotiations, 75 Iowa L. Rev. 1219, 1230 (1990): "In those bargaining situations which are at least in part distributive, a category which includes virtually all negotiations, lying is a coherent and often effective strategy." Professor Wetlaufer argues that "lying in negotiations is instrumentally effective and that most such lies are ethically impermissible." Id. at 1221.

after his conclusion of the first case. Later, however, counsel for those persons benefited by the failure of the prior lawyer to tell the truth, learned of that lawyer's deception. The question was whether, in the course of settling the current case, the new lawyer was obliged to disclose what he knew of the lies in the prior lawyer's deposition. Citing DR 7–102(A)(3), EC 7–27, Model Rule 3.3(a)(2), and Judge Rubin's article, the court held that the lawyer did have a "duty of candor and fairness to disclose [the deception] to opposing counsel and the court." The settlement was set aside and the case reopened.

d. Cresswell v. Sullivan & Cromwell, 668 F.Supp. 166 (S.D.N.Y. 1987), accepted the view that an opponent may sue a law firm for fraud where the firm failed to disclose material facts during discovery proceedings in a now-settled case. The plaintiff must show that the failure to disclose led to a settlement which was less favorable to it than the parties otherwise would have negotiated, but the allegation of fraud need not be raised under Rule 60(b) which would presumably require the party to tender back the settlement and reopen the case on the merits.

Does this approach appeal to your sense of justice? Might a cheap, unilateral opportunity to reopen a settlement undercut the finality of settlements generally and make the soundness of this decision less clear?

e. ABA Formal Opinion 94–387 (September 26, 1994) narrowly interprets the duty to disclose. It ruled that a lawyer has "no ethical duty to inform an opposing party in negotiations that the statute of limitations has run on her client's claim; to the contrary, it would violate Rule 1.3 and 1.6 to reveal such information without the client's consent." However, the lawyer must "be careful not to make any affirmative misrepresentations about the facts showing that the claim is time-barred, or suggest that she plans to do something to enforce the claim (e.g., file suit) that she has no intention of doing. See Rule 4.1."

According to this opinion, there is also no violation of Rule 3.1 (no frivolous suits) and Rule 3.3 (candor to tribunal) to file a time–barred claim in court "so long as this does not violate the law of the relevant jurisdiction," such as would be the case if the limitations defect were jurisdictional. Normally, the Opinion noted, the statute of limitations is an affirmative defense that the opposing party must assert. Finally, there is no basis in the ethical rules to hold a government lawyer to a higher or different standard.

Richard McFarlain filed a dissent. He regarded this Opinion much "as Julia Child would regard a fly in her soup;" it is "too much to swallow." In his view, Rule 8.4(c), prohibiting deceit, prohibits all lawyers from engaging in this activity. In particular, the "worst part of this opinion is its theory that government lawyers do not owe a greater duty to the public than other lawyers, particularly the pettifogger described in this opinion."

6. Should the rules about negotiation be different in criminal cases?

a. Does a defense lawyer have an obligation to consider plea bargaining and so advise the client? See ABA Defense Function Standard § 4–6.1(b). Does a prosecutor have a comparable duty to try to negotiate a plea bargain? See generally ABA Standards, The Prosecution Function, §§ 3–4.1 to 3–4.3.

b. How candid should a prosecutor have to be about the strength of the evidence? In People v. Jones, 44 N.Y.2d 76, 404 N.Y.S.2d 85, 375 N.E.2d 41 (1978), cert. denied 439 U.S. 846, 99 S.Ct. 145, 58 L.Ed.2d 148 (1978), the court held that the defendant was not denied due process when the District Attorney did not disclose during plea negotiations that the complaining witness had died. Under Brady v. Maryland, 373 U.S. 83, 83 S.Ct. 1194, 10 L.Ed.2d 215 (1963), the prosecutor is under a constitutional duty to respond to defendant's request that he disclose material evidence favorable to the accused, either as to guilt or punishment. The death of the state's critical witness did not fit within *Brady,* the court reasoned, because it affected whether the case could be proved, not whether there was exculpatory evidence. Nor was the ABA Standard Relating to the Prosecution Function 4.1(c) violated because the prosecutor made no affirmative misrepresentation. There is no constitutional or ethical duty to disclose, the court held, at least where defendant has not protested his innocence. Do you agree?

c. Compare Fambo v. Smith, 433 F.Supp. 590 (W.D.N.Y.1977), aff'd 565 F.2d 233 (2d Cir.1977), where the court again refused to disturb a guilty plea. It held that the prosecutor *did* have a duty to disclose to Defendant, who was charged with possession of explosives, that the dynamite (which formed the basis of one of the counts) had been destroyed prior to Defendant's arrest (and replaced with sawdust). However the court then found that under the circumstances the error was harmless and the defendant's plea bargain was fair and reasonable.

d. Should Model Rule 3.8(d), DR 7–103(B) or EC 7–13 change the result in either of these cases? Do these provisions merely incorporate the *Brady* rule?

e. In the plea-bargaining negotiations with the prosecutor, may criminal defense counsel assert that he or she "knows" the client is innocent. Is the case for stretching the truth stronger in criminal defense work? Why? Is it because potential sanctions are more severe than in most civil litigation? Is it because "everyone expects" counsel for criminal defendants to be dishonest?

7. Is it a mistake to think of negotiation as a single type of phenomenon?

a. Consider again the insights of Professor White:

"One who conceives of negotiation as an alternative to a lawsuit has only scratched the surface. Negotiation is also the process by which one deals with the opposing side in war, with terrorists, with labor or management in a labor agreement, with buyers and sellers of goods, services, and real estate, with lessors, with governmental agencies, and with one's clients, acquaintances, and family. * * * Surely society would tolerate and indeed expect different forms of behavior on the one hand from one assigned to negotiate with terrorists and on the other from one who is negotiating with the citizens on behalf of a government agency. * * * Performance that is standard in one negotiating arena may be gauche, conceivably unethical, in another." [5]

b. Do you agree with Professor White? Would you have a right to mislead management in a labor negotiation about your union client's willingness to strike? Might you even have a *duty* to mislead a hostage-taker about whether he will be granted amnesty if he lets his hostages go? What ethical values lead you to your conclusions?

c. ABA Formal Opinion 314 (1965) considered the lawyer's obligation in settling a tax claim with the I.R.S.:

"Negotiation and settlement procedures of the tax system do not carry with them the guarantee that a correct tax result necessarily occurs. The latter happens, if at all, solely by reason of chance in settlement of tax controversies just as it might happen with regard to other civil disputes. In the absence of either judicial determination or of a hypothetical exchange of files by adversaries, counsel will always urge in aid of settlement of a controversy the strong points of his case and minimize the weak; this is in keeping with Canon 15 [of the ABA Canons of Ethics of 1908, as amended], which does require 'warm zeal' on behalf of the client. Nor does the absolute duty not to make false assertions of fact require the disclosure of weaknesses in the client's case and in no event does it require the disclosure of his confidences, unless the facts in the attorney's possession indicate beyond reasonable doubt that a crime will be committed. A wrong, or indeed sometimes an unjust, tax result in the settlement of a controversy is not a crime."

Do you agree? Are these insights peculiar to negotiations with the I.R.S.? Do they represent a realistic understanding of many kinds of negotiations?

8. Would the lawyer have a greater duty when making representations on behalf of a financial institution client in the course of its review by a federal agency?

Matter of Peter M. Fishbein * * * and Kaye, Scholer, Fierman, Hays & Handler, OTS AP–92–19 (1992), is the case that attracted many lawyers' attention to these issues. Briefly, Lincoln Savings' semi-annual routine regulatory examination in 1986 turned up signs that the institution was in trouble. The regulators wanted more information and

---

5. White, Machiavelli and the Bar: Ethical Limits on Lying in Negotiation, 1980   A.B.F. Research J. 926, 927.

Charles Keating allegedly knew the future of his organization was at stake. He hired Kaye, Scholer to protect him from the regulators and Peter Fishbein, a litigator, took over the defense. Fishbein allegedly treated the situation as adversary litigation, resisted document requests, and did not volunteer negative information. OTS charged that Kaye, Scholer had thus become the alter ego of the client. Lincoln was obliged to make information available, OTS argued, so the law firm could not assume that the secrecy that would be proper in litigation was proper in this situation. The regulations required disclosure to protect third parties (such as the depositors). If Lincoln Savings had to disclose this information pursuant to regulation, Lincoln's lawyers had no privilege to refuse to disclose. After a "freeze" of the law firm's assets, Kaye Scholer agreed to pay the government $42 million.

What would you have done if you were in Mr. Fishbein's position? At the very least, can we say that lawyers should not assume they can do things for their clients that the clients could not legally do themselves.[6]

PROBLEM 21

The Lawyer as Evaluator

Luther Klose is president of the Klose Corporation, a privately-held family enterprise. All of the stockholders are also officers of the corporation and receive benefits from the corporation both in the form of dividends and in the form of salary. In order to keep the overall tax liability at a minimum, the shareholders would prefer that as much money as possible be paid as salary that is deductible to the corporation, rather than as dividends that are not. Mr. Klose would like you, the corporation's outside attorney, to write him an opinion letter explaining that a new salary schedule to be inaugurated by the company properly represents greater responsibilities of the shareholder officers and thus is bona fide and not adopted with intent to circumvent the tax laws.

Klose Corporation is also seeking a large loan from the local bank. Given the Klose Corporation's local reputation for taking aggressive tax positions, the bank wants to be aware of any foreseen tax difficulties that might materially affect the Klose Corporation's ability to repay its loan. Mr. Klose, at the suggestion of the bank, has asked you to write a letter giving your legal opinion that all of the major tax deductions that the Klose Corporation took in the last three years are reasonable under the tax laws and that, if the Internal Revenue Service disallows any of these major deductions, the taxpayer is likely to prevail in litigation.

In addition, the bank has asked for information on "all other legal problems that might materially affect the Klose Corporation". You know that Klose Corporation has sold a large stock of defective goods,

---

6. A portion of judicial opinion on the alleged role of the Jones Day firm in this situation is set forth as a Reading to Problem 22, infra.

but no customer has yet discovered the defects. When the defects are discovered it may be difficult to trace them back to your client, but if the tracing is made, the company may be liable for up to half its net worth in damages.

QUESTIONS

1. Does Mr. Klose have a right to "purchase" the opinion letter from you? What are your obligations to be sure your conclusion is legally justified?

a. Does your duty of loyalty require you to do what Mr. Klose has asked? Even if you might support his argument in a litigation context, must you personally conclude that Klose's salaries are reasonable before you give him your legal "opinion"? Compare EC 7–5, Rule 1.2(d) and Rule 4.1(b).

b. To what extent, if any, must you "audit" the client to assure yourself that the duties of the officers are in fact as your opinion will assume them to be? Look at ABA Formal Opinion 335 (1974), set forth as a Reading to this problem. What does it tell us about the obligations of a securities lawyer before he or she signs an opinion letter? Does this ethics opinion impose a higher standard on attorneys than do the Model Rules and Model Code? Does it provide good counsel to *any* attorney asked to sign an opinion?

c. Consider ABA Formal Opinion 314 (1965), dealing with the lawyer's duty of candor in dealing with the I.R.S.:

"The Internal Revenue Service is neither a true tribunal, nor even a quasi-judicial institution. * * * [F]ew will contend that the service provides any truly dispassionate and unbiased consideration to the taxpayer. * * *

* * *

"[A] lawyer who is asked to advise his client in the course of the preparation of the client's tax returns may freely urge the statement of positions most favorable to the client just as long as there is reasonable basis for those positions. Thus where the lawyer believes there is a reasonable basis for a position that a particular transaction does not result in taxable income, or that certain expenditures are properly deductible as expenses, the lawyer has no duty to advise that riders be attached to the client's tax return explaining the circumstances surrounding the transaction or the expenditures."

d. On the other hand, in describing the lawyer's duties in connection with the issue of a tax shelter opinion, ABA Formal Opinion 346 (1982), also set forth as a Reading to this problem, says bluntly:

"The lawyer who accepts as true the facts which the promoter tells him, when the lawyer should know that a further inquiry would disclose that these facts are untrue, * * * gives a false opinion. * * * We equate the minimum extent of the knowledge required for the lawyer's conduct to have violated these disciplinary rules with the knowledge required to sustain a Rule 10b–5 recovery, see Ernst & Ernst v. Hochfelder, 425 U.S. 185 (1976), rather than the lesser negligence standard."

"But even if the lawyer lacks the knowledge required to sustain a recovery under the *Hochfelder* standard, the lawyer's conduct nevertheless may involve gross incompetence, or indifference, inadequate preparation under the circumstances, and consistent failure to perform obligations to the client. If so, the lawyer will have violated DR 6–101(A). A.B.A. Informal Opinion 1273 (1973)."

e. Would you let a client purchase your ratification of its officials' *good* judgment in the guise of a legal opinion? For example, suppose the client wants to pay a claim to engender goodwill or for more general positive reasons, but also wants to nip in the bud a shareholder suit second guessing its judgment. May you tell the client that certain legal considerations require it to pay the claim when in fact your real reason for the conclusion is based on nonlegal considerations? Assume that you need not lie about the state of the law and need only be less than candid about your primary motivation. Medical doctors, some people claim, are sometimes justified in lying to their patients. May juris doctors ever lie to the clients for the clients' own good?

2. Suppose you conclude and say in your opinion letter that the ultimate tax liability will depend to a great extent on the intent of the taxpayer. May you help Klose "manufacture" intent?

a. Does your answer depend on whether you personally believe that Klose has the proper legal intent and you are merely helping him preserve and articulate it? See EC 7–6.

b. How may you properly counsel creation of proof of intent? May you prepare minutes of meetings that never occurred in which the participants recite their intent? Does it matter whether these minutes are eventually approved ("ratified") by the participants?

c. One might argue that the lawyer is not justified in "drawing a misleading minute" in order to develop intent for tax consideration, but that "having made the decision in his own mind that the action the client proposes is justified under the law, he is entitled to set out in the minutes the considerations that led him to that conclusion, and when he has done that he probably has gone as far as he can." [7] Do you agree?

7. Business Planning and Professional Responsibility—Problem 1, 8 The Practical Lawyer 18, 33 (Jan.1962).

3. May your opinion fail to discuss relevant facts that you know are inconsistent with your client's position on the tax questions?

a. With respect to what must be disclosed on a tax return, one tax practitioner reports that:

> "The consensus of opinion appears to be that the smaller the amount involved and the greater the likelihood that the taxpayer will ultimately prevail, the less is the obligation to disclose the weakness. On the other hand, where the amount involved is large and the taxpayer's ultimate chance of success substantially less than even, most Bostonians feel some disclosure is required. Rarely however, will the disclosure be a large red flag. Usually it will be a relatively inconspicuous reference to a fact—just enough to preclude any claim of fraud, but not enough to stimulate further inquiry by any but the most astute of agents." [8]

Do you think this position is morally defensible? Is it a practical compromise based on how likely one is to face sanctions if caught defending an indefensible position?

b. The ABA modified Formal Opinion 314 in Formal Opinion 85–352 (1985). The ABA Standing Committee on Ethics and Professional Responsibility reported that it was "informed that the standard of 'reasonable basis' [to support a position] has been construed by many lawyers to support the use of any colorable claim on a tax return to justify exploitation of the lottery of the tax return audit selection process."

To correct the record, the Standing Committee offered this guidance: "[A] lawyer may advise reporting a position on a return even where the lawyer believes the position probably will not prevail, there is no 'substantial authority' in support of the position, and there will be no disclosure of the position in the return. However, the position to be asserted must be one which the lawyer in good faith believes is warranted in existing law or can be supported by a good faith argument for an extension, modification or reversal of existing law. This requires that there is some realistic possibility of success if the matter is litigated."

Does that help? Now is your responsibility clear?

4. Look at Model Rule 2.3. Did it add something not in the Model Code? Was it an important addition? Do you suppose lawyers were "evaluators" even before adoption of the Rule?

a. In connection with the bank loan described in this problem, what does Rule 2.3 require of you? Must you "consult" with the client before agreeing to give the opinion, for example; is the fact the client asked you to do it enough? What circumstances would ever make you

---

8. Corneel, Ethical Guidelines for Tax Practice, 28 Tax.L.Rev. 1, 10 (1972) (footnote omitted). Mr. Corneel, in addition to his own research and experience, relied in this article on a survey of Boston lawyers and practitioners engaged in tax practice.   Reprinted by permission from the "Tax Law Review" Volume 28, Number 1, Fall, 1972, Copyright 1972 Warren Gorham & Lamont, Inc., 210 South St., Boston, Mass. All Rights Reserved.

conclude that the evaluation was incompatible with other aspects of your relationship with the client?

b. Assume that the independent auditors of the Klose Corporation have also asked you about evaluating various legal claims that have been or are likely to be asserted against Klose Corporation. What are your responsibilities in replying? See the Note on the ABA's Statement of Policy Regarding Lawyers' Responses to Auditor's Request for Information, excerpted in the Readings to this problem. See also, Rule 2.3, Comment 6. Cf. Matter of Carter and Johnson, [1981] CCH Federal Securities Law Reports ¶ 82,847 (Feb. 28, 1981) (attorney discipline proceeding).

c. Must you disclose, in your opinion letter to the bank, the possible litigation regarding the product defect, in light of the ABA's Statement of Policy Regarding Lawyer's Responses to Auditors' Requests for Information? Is the bank's inquiry any different than an auditor's inquiry?

5. Does the attorney-client privilege apply when one is conducting an internal investigation, some results of which may be available to others?

a. Look again at Upjohn Co. v. United States, 449 U.S. 383, 101 S.Ct. 677, 66 L.Ed.2d 584 (1981), used as a Reading in Problem 6. The corporation's general counsel had begun an internal investigation of possible illegal payments to foreign government officials. Company lawyers talked to numerous officers, managers and employees throughout the company's world-wide operations. They did *not* intend these findings to be later disclosed outside the company. The I.R.S. conducted a parallel investigation of the payments and issued a summons to the company to produce the notes taken of the general counsel's interviews. The lower courts ordered the notes produced on the ground that they were of conversations with people outside the corporate "control group" and thus were not protected by the attorney-client privilege. The Supreme Court reversed:

"The narrow scope given the attorney-client privilege by the court below not only makes it difficult for corporate attorneys to formulate sound advice when their client is faced with a specific legal problem but also threatens to limit the valuable efforts of corporate counsel to ensure their client's compliance with the law. * * *"

The protection that will be granted to communications with inside and outside corporate counsel appears to be broad in cases where no public disclosure is planned, but the result may be different where the lawyer's conclusions are intended to be made available outside of the corporation.

b. If the opinion of one corporation's lawyer discusses what she learned in talks with lawyers from separate corporate entities, should the privilege be considered waived? Ordinarily the answer would be yes, but the results of a lawyer's investigation may often be shared with others within a corporate "family" without a waiver being the result. See, e.g., State ex rel. Syntex Agri–Business, Inc. v. Adolf, 700 S.W.2d 886 (Mo.App.1985).

c. Who may waive the corporate attorney-client privilege? Ordinarily, the officers or directors may do so, but suppose the corporation is in bankruptcy. May the trustee in bankruptcy waive the privilege in the face of former management's opposition to having their discussions revealed? The Supreme Court has held that such a waiver by the trustee is proper and effective. Commodity Futures Trading Commission v. Weintraub, 471 U.S. 343, 105 S.Ct. 1986, 85 L.Ed.2d 372 (1985).

6. Does a lawyer assume special duties when acting as counsel for an issuer of securities?

a. While he was a SEC Commissioner, A. A. Sommer noted:

"[T]he registration statement has always been a lawyer's document and with very, very rare exceptions the attorney has been the field marshal who coordinated the activities of others engaged in the registration process, wrote (or at least rewrote) most of the statement, made the judgments with regard to the inclusion or exclusion of information on the grounds of materiality, compliance with registration form requirements, necessities of avoiding omission of disclosure necessary to make those matters stated not misleading.

* * *

"[T]he professional judgment of the attorney is often the 'passkey' to securities transactions. * * * If he judges that certain information must be included in a registration statement, it gets included (unless the client seeks other counsel or the attorney crumbles under the weight of client pressure); if he concludes it need not be included, it doesn't get included. * * *

"I would suggest that in securities matters (other than those where advocacy is clearly proper) the attorney will have to function in a manner more akin to that of the auditor than to that of the advocate. * * * "

Sommer, Emerging Responsibilities of the Securities Lawyer, [1973–1974 Transfer Binder] Fed.Sec.L.Rep. ¶ 79,631 (Jan., 1974).

b. Do you agree with Mr. Sommer that—at least as to documents the lawyer bears primary responsibility for preparing for disclosure to third parties—the lawyer should act as an auditor rather than an advocate? May the securities lawyer accept all of her client's representations about matters to be disclosed, or must she independently investigate the client? Look at ABA Formal Opinions 335 and 346, referenced above and set forth as Readings to this Problem.

c. In SEC v. Frank, 388 F.2d 486 (2d Cir.1968), the defendant, an attorney, appealed from a district court's temporary injunction ordering him to refrain from "drafting or causing to be drafted any offering circular, prospectus or other document or writing containing any untrue statements of material facts, or omissions to state material facts necessary in order to make the statements made in the light of the circumstances under which they were made, not misleading, concerning Nylo–Thane Plastics Corp.'s principal product, a chemical additive ingredient purportedly designed to reduce the time required in curing rubber * * *." The court, per Friendly, J., in reversing and ordering an evidentiary hearing, stated:

"Although Frank makes much of this being the first instance in which the Commission has obtained an injunction against an attorney for participation in the preparation of an allegedly misleading offering circular or prospectus, we find this unimpressive. As this court said in United States v. Benjamin, 328 F.2d 854, 863 (2 Cir.), cert. denied 377 U.S. 953, 84 S.Ct. 1631, 12 L.Ed.2d 497 (1964), 'In our complex society the accountant's certificate and the lawyer's opinion can be instruments for inflicting pecuniary loss more potent than the chisel or the crowbar.' A lawyer has no privilege to assist in circulating a statement with regard to securities which he knows to be false simply because his client has furnished it to him. At the other extreme it would be unreasonable to hold a lawyer who was putting his client's description of a chemical process into understandable English to be guilty of fraud simply because of his failure to detect discrepancies between their description and technical reports available to him in a physical sense but beyond his ability to understand. The instant case lies between these extremes. The SEC's position is that Frank had been furnished with information which even a non-expert would recognize as showing the falsity of many of the representations * * *, notably those implying extensive and satisfactory testing at factories and indicating that all had gone passing well at the test by the Army Laboratories. If this is so, the Commission would be entitled to prevail; a lawyer, no more than others, can escape liability for fraud by closing his eyes to what he saw and could readily understand. Whether the fraud sections of the securities laws go beyond this and require a lawyer passing on an offering circular to run down possible infirmities in his client's story of which he has been put on notice, and if so what efforts are required of him, is a closer question on which it is important that the court be seized of the precise facts, including the extent, as the SEC claimed with respect to Frank, to which his role went beyond a lawyer's normal one, Compare Securities Act of 1933, § 11(a)." 388 F.2d at 488–89.

d. Should the SEC and other federal agencies be obliged to respect the confidentiality requirements of the Model Code of Professional

Responsibility and the Model Rules? Is there any reason that the desire to protect the public against securities fraud should require a compromise of lawyers' ethical standards when the desire to protect the public against, say, rapists does not? Given the existence of Model Rule 2.3, is it fair to say that the SEC position stated above is consistent with the Model Rules and the Model Code?

7. To whom might the lawyer be liable for an inaccurate report on the company's financial picture?

a. In Greycas, Inc. v. Proud, 826 F.2d 1560 (7th Cir.1987), cert. denied 484 U.S. 1043, 108 S.Ct. 775, 98 L.Ed.2d 862 (1988), Judge Posner analyzed the basis for finding a cause of action when a lawyer has negligently performed the role of evaluator. A borrower sought to raise money from a finance company on the strength of a security interest in certain farm assets. The lender agreed to put up the money if the borrower would supply the borrower's lawyer's opinion that the borrower had unencumbered title to the assets. The lawyer (who was the borrower's brother-in-law) wrote a letter asserting that he had examined whether there were prior security interests in the property and that there were none. In fact, the lawyer had made no such inquiry, the assets were encumbered, and when the borrower defaulted the lender was left with no security.

Under these circumstances, the court held, the lawyer was liable to the finance company for the amount of the loan. The lawyer argued that he owed no duty to someone not his client. The court agreed with that general proposition, and indeed called it "an undesirable novelty to hold that every bit of sharp dealing by a lawyer gives rise to prima facie tort liability to the opposing party in the lawsuit or negotiation." Here, however, the court said, the lawyer supplied information to the lender knowing that it was to be relied upon by the lender. Whether the suit was treated as one for negligent misrepresentation or professional malpractice, it stated a cause of action and the lawyer was liable.[9]

b. Petrillo v. Bachenberg, 623 A.2d 272 (N.J.Super.1993), certification granted 636 A.2d 523 (N.J.1993), involved whether the seller of land misled a potential buyer as to suitability of the land for a septic system. Percolation tests had been done by the seller, most of which said it was unsuitable. The seller's lawyer, however, handed the buyer what appeared to be a single report showing two positive tests. The lawyer said he had no obligation to the buyer to expand on the document his client had prepared and to give a more complete account of the tests; the Court said that the lawyer knew the buyers would rely on the misleading document, so the damage claim against the lawyer was sent back for a new trial.

c. In Crossland Savings FSB v. Rockwood Insurance Co., 692 F.Supp. 1510 (S.D.N.Y.1988), however, Judge Leval came down the other

9. Accord, Vanguard Production Inc. v. Martin, 894 F.2d 375 (10th Cir.1990) (title opinion used in selling oil & gas leases); Vereins–Und Westbank, AG v. Carter, 691 F.Supp. 704 (S.D.N.Y.1988) (lawyer's letter to support issuance of surety bond).

way. His reading of New York law was that it still is based on Judge Cardozo's opinion in Ultramares Corp. v. Touche, 255 N.Y. 170, 174 N.E. 441 (1931). The fear of "indefinite expansion of liability for honest blunders, as for example, where a lawyer certified his opinion as to the validity of a municipal bond" has led the New York courts to be reluctant to extend liability beyond the immediate client. You will find that this "privity" rule applies in an important minority of states. Which approach to liability makes more sense to you?

d. Central Bank of Denver, N.A. v. First Interstate Bank of Denver, N.A., ___ U.S. ___, 114 S.Ct. 1439, 128 L.Ed.2d 119 (1994), limited lawyers' financial exposure in another important area, this time under § 10(b) of the Securities Exchange Act of 1934. Municipal bonds issued in 1986 to finance public improvements related to a residential and commercial project near Colorado Springs required that the appraised value of the land exceed 160% of the amount of the bonds. Central Bank was the indenture trustee; it delayed getting an independent 1988 appraisal, allegedly thinking it might show land values had been declining. When the bonds went into default, the issuer and underwriter were alleged to be primarily liable under § 10(b), but Central Bank was alleged to be secondarily liable for aiding and abetting the violation. The Supreme Court held that there is no "aiding and abetting" liability under § 10(b). Because many lawyers, accountants, and other professionals would be sued under such an "aiding and abetting" theory, the decision appears to have limited this form of exposure.

e. Geaslen v. Berkson, Gorov & Levin, Ltd., 613 N.E.2d 702 (Ill. 1993), involved the sale of a business. The buyer was to give the seller stock in the buyer's business and the buyer's lawyer wrote an opinion letter to the seller stating that the lawyer had "no reason to believe that any representation or warranty or Purchaser contained in the Agreement [was] untrue or misleading in any material respect." In fact, the buyer soon looted the business and went bankrupt; the seller then sued the buyer's lawyer on the allegedly false opinion. The Court agreed that the buyer's lawyer owed a duty to the seller to use due care in preparation of the opinion; the lawyer did not, however, have a fiduciary duty to the seller.

f. Because such large amounts of potential liability turn on the interpretation of particular language in what have come to be called "third party opinions", i.e., opinions to be relied upon by persons other than the lawyer's client, several bar association groups have developed standard definitions for the usual representations that lawyers make. These definitions are collected and analyzed in Scott FitzGibbon and Donald W. Glazer, Legal Opinions: What Opinions in Financial Transactions Say and What They Mean (1992).

g. Might professional discipline be preferable to malpractice liability as a way to enforce Rule 2.3? On the other hand, is discipline likely to be as great a deterrent for most lawyers as malpractice liability would be? Further, are violations of Rule 2.3 unusually likely to cause financial losses to recipients of the erroneous information?

———

READINGS

———

ABA FORMAL OPINION 335 (FEBRUARY 2, 1974).

Release # 5168 of the Securities and Exchange Commission (SEC) under the Securities Act of 1933 (Release # 9239 under the Securities Exchange Act of 1934) was published on July 7, 1971. It set forth certain basic standards of conduct required of broker-dealers to meet their responsibilities in connection with sales of unregistered securities. In a footnote to the next-to-last paragraph of the Release, dealing with the obligation of a broker-dealer to review the surrounding facts and obtain the opinion of competent disinterested counsel concerning the legality of sales, it [said]:

> In this regard, the Commission has stated that "if an attorney furnishes an opinion based solely on hypothetical facts which he has made no effort to verify, and if he knows that his opinion will be relied upon as the basis for a substantial distribution of unregistered securities, a serious question arises as to the propriety of his professional conduct."

The Commission's repetition of this language led to inquiries of this Committee * * *.

* * *

Where an exemption is claimed it has been common for the principals to rely on opinions of attorneys who recite the facts, and then say that on the basis of such facts the transaction is entitled to the exemption.

It is, of course, important that the lawyer competently and carefully consider what facts are relevant to the giving of the requested opinion and make a reasonable inquiry to obtain such of those facts as are not within his personal knowledge. Depending upon the circumstances, the lawyer may or may not need to go beyond directing questions to his client and checking the answers by reviewing such appropriate documents as are available.

Before going into more detail on the matter of the extent of any required further inquiry, we should point out the importance of avoiding mistakes in communication between the client and the lawyer. In cases turning upon whether or not registration of securities is required, the facts are likely to be important and a lack of proper communication between the client and the lawyer could cause grave difficulties. Therefore, before a lawyer signs an opinion based on facts furnished by his client, he should take reasonable steps to make sure that the client understands exactly what facts he has requested and that he accurately understands what the client has told him.

We turn now to the precise question presented, namely, the circumstances under which, and the extent to which, a lawyer should verify or supplement the facts presented to him as the basis for such an opinion.

In any event, the lawyer should, in the first instance, make inquiry of his client as to the relevant facts and receive answers. If any of the alleged facts, or the alleged facts taken as a whole, are incomplete in a material respect; or are suspect; or are inconsistent; or either on their face or on the basis of other known facts are open to question, the lawyer should make further inquiry. The extent of this inquiry will depend in each case upon the circumstances; for example, it would be less where the lawyer's past relationship with the client is sufficient to give him a basis for trusting the client's probity than where the client has recently engaged the lawyer, and less where the lawyer's inquiries are answered fully than when there appears a reluctance to disclose information.

Where the lawyer concludes that further inquiry of a reasonable nature would not give him sufficient confidence as to all the relevant facts, or for any other reason he does not make the appropriate further inquiries, he should refuse to give an opinion. However, assuming that the alleged facts are not incomplete in a material respect, or suspect, or in any way inherently inconsistent, or on their face or on the basis of other known facts open to question, the lawyer may properly assume that the facts as related to him by his client, and checked by him by reviewing such appropriate documents as are available, are accurate.

Preliminarily, we state two examples as a means of defining the extremes of the problem in giving an opinion to a security holder who wishes to sell securities to the public without registration. On the one extreme, if a lawyer is asked to issue an opinion concerning a modest amount of a widely traded security by a responsible client, whose lack of relationship to the issuer is well known to the lawyer, he may ordinarily proceed to issue the opinion with considerable confidence. On the other extreme, if he is asked to prepare an opinion letter covering a substantial block of a little known security, where the client (be it selling shareholder or broker) appears reluctant to disclose exactly where the securities came from or where the surrounding circumstances raise a question as to whether or not the ostensible sellers may be merely intermediaries for controlling persons or statutory underwriters, then searching inquiry is called for.

As a further example, suppose that a broker client requests a legal opinion that a proposed sale of shares of X Company would comply with Rule 144, and thus be exempt from registration, and supplies the lawyer with a statement of the facts that allegedly would support such an opinion and a copy of Form 144 proposed to be filed, if any. Assuming that the broker is known to the lawyer to be of good repute, that the lawyer has read the proposed or executed Form 144, if any, and that the alleged facts do not require further inquiry for any of the reasons stated above, the lawyer may properly give the opinion. If on the other hand the alleged facts do require further inquiries for any of the reasons stated above, the lawyer should either make such inquiries until satisfied or refuse to give an opinion if he concludes that reasonable inquiry would still not satisfy him. It is difficult to state a formula for determining how far a lawyer must go to satisfy the requirement that he make a reasonable effort to verify particular facts in such a case. However, it would seem that, for example, the verification from the issuer or its counsel of the number of shares of the class outstanding and the verification (perhaps through financial journals) of the relevant trading volume, an attempt (by checking through a quotation service and/or the relevant "pink" quotation sheets) to determine whether or not the broker is making solicitations of offers to buy the securities, and the inspection of a written statement from the issuer of the securities that it has complied with the reporting requirements mentioned in Rule 144 should normally be sufficient where verification is indicated.

Another example would be where a corporate client requests an opinion as to whether a proposed transaction would be within the private offering exemption furnished by Section 4(2) of the Securities Act of 1933. In this situation, the lawyer should obtain from the client information, preferably in writing, from which the lawyer may reach the legal conclusion that the exemption is (or is not) available. Here again, the lawyer may properly rely upon the information furnished by a client well known to him, assuming that it is not inconsistent, suspect, otherwise open to question, or incomplete in a material respect.

If the lawyer has some reason to believe that one or more of the statements of fact furnished him as a basis for the opinion may not be correct, he should make a determination as to whether to refuse to give an opinion or whether to attempt to verify one or more of the relevant facts. This matter was discussed in connection with the example dealing with Rule 144. If he does determine that he will proceed, he should decide on the extent of verification in the light of the particular situation. If, for example, the lawyer has any reason to doubt the reliability of the information relevant to whether the offerees have the requisite sophistication to meet the standard applicable to the Section 4(2) exemption, he should reasonably satisfy himself that the client correctly understands the concept of "sophistication" and he might appropriately obtain from his client further information on each offeree and his background in order to determine that each was sufficiently "sophisticated" to be able to fend for himself and did not need the protection of a registration statement. Where information which may be relevant to a determination of whether or not the exemption provided by Section 4(2) is available may be quite difficult, if not impossible, to verify, it might in fact be necessary to rely completely on the client, but this necessity does not decrease the lawyer's ultimate responsibility to exercise his independent judgment in determining whether the client had a reasonable basis for its determination that each client was sufficiently "sophisticated" and whether, in view of all the facts developed, the Section 4(2) exemption is available. If the lawyer considers that there is any material deficiency in that information, he should simply refuse to give an opinion on the subject.

A properly drafted opinion will recite clearly the sources of the attorney's knowledge of the facts. Where verification is otherwise called for, an attorney should make appropriate verification and should not rely on the use of such phrases as "based upon the facts as you have given them to me" or "apart from what you have told me, I have not inquired as to the facts."

The essence of this opinion, the scope of which has been set forth in the third paragraph, supra, is that, while a lawyer should make adequate preparation including inquiry into the relevant facts that is consistent with the above guidelines, and while he should not accept as true that which he should not reasonably believe to be true, he does not have the responsibility to "audit" the affairs of his client or to assume, without reasonable cause, that a client's statement of the facts cannot be relied upon.

The steps reasonably required of the lawyer in making his investigation must be commensurate with the circumstances under which he is called upon to render the opinion, but he must bear in mind that his responsibility is to render to the client his considered, independent opinion whether, having made at least inquiries such as those suggested by the above guidelines, the claimed exemption is or is not available under the law. While the responsibility of the lawyer is to his client, he must not be oblivious of the extent to which others may be affected if he is derelict in fulfilling that responsibility. A good lawyer is a conscientious lawyer who strives to fulfill, not only the obligations imposed by the Code's Disciplinary Rules, but also the higher responsibilities contained in the Code's Ethical Considerations.

A.B.A. FORMAL OPINION 346 (JANUARY 29, 1982)

An opinion by a lawyer analyzing the tax effects of a tax shelter investment is frequently of substantial importance in a tax shelter offering.[1] The promoter of the offering may depend upon the recommendations of the lawyer in structuring the venture and often publishes the opinion with the offering materials or uses the lawyer's name in connection with sales promotion efforts. The offerees may be expected to rely upon the tax shelter opinion in determining whether to invest in

1. A "tax shelter," as the term is used in this opinion, is an investment which has as a significant feature for federal income or excise tax purposes either or both of the following attributes: (1) deductions in excess of income from the investment being available in any year to reduce income from other sources in that year, and (2) credits in excess of the tax attributable to the income from the investment being available in any year to offset taxes on income from other sources in that year.

the venture. It is often uneconomic for the individual offeree to pay for
a separate tax analysis of the offering because of the relatively small sum
each offeree may invest.

* * *

A false opinion is one which ignores or minimizes serious legal risks
or misstates the facts or the law, knowingly or through gross incompetence. The lawyer who gives a false opinion, including one which is
intentionally or recklessly misleading, violates the disciplinary rules of
the Model Code of Professional Responsibility. * * *

The lawyer who accepts as true the facts which the promoter tells
him, when the lawyer should know that a further inquiry would disclose
that these facts are untrue, also gives a false opinion. * * * We equate
the minimum extent of the knowledge required for the lawyer's conduct
to have violated these disciplinary rules with the knowledge required to
sustain a Rule 10b–5 recovery, see Ernst & Ernst v. Hochfelder, 425 U.S.
185 (1976), rather than the lesser negligence standard.

But even if the lawyer lacks the knowledge required to sustain a
recovery under the *Hochfelder* standard, the lawyer's conduct nevertheless may involve gross incompetence, or indifference, inadequate preparation under the circumstances, and consistent failure to perform obligations to the client. If so, the lawyer will have violated DR 6–101(A).
A.B.A. Informal Opinion 1273 (1973).

* * * Because third parties may rely on the advice of the lawyer
who gives a tax shelter opinion, the principles announced in A.B.A.
Formal Opinion 314 have little, if any, applicability.

The lawyer should establish the terms of the relationship with the
offeror-client at the time the lawyer is engaged to work on the tax
shelter offering. This includes making it clear that the lawyer requires
from the client a full disclosure of the structure and intended operations
of the venture and complete access to all relevant information.

A.B.A. Formal Opinion 335 (1974) establishes guidelines which a
lawyer should follow when furnishing an assumed facts opinion in
connection with the sale of unregistered securities. The same guidelines
describe the extent to which a lawyer should verify the facts presented to
him as the basis for a tax shelter opinion.

* * *

For instance, where essential underlying information, such as an
appraisal or financial projection, makes little common sense, or where
the reputation or expertise of the person who has prepared the appraisal
or projection is dubious, further inquiry clearly is required. Indeed,
failure to make further inquiry may result in a false opinion. If further
inquiry reveals that the appraisal or projection is reasonably well supported and complete, the lawyer is justified in relying upon the material
facts which the underlying information supports.

* * *

A "material" tax issue for purposes of this opinion is any income or excise tax issue relating to the tax shelter that would have a significant effect in sheltering from federal taxes income from other sources by providing deductions in excess of the income from the tax shelter investment in any year or tax credits which will offset tax liabilities in excess of the tax attributable to the tax shelter investment in any year.
* * *

The lawyer should satisfy himself that either he or another competent professional has considered all material tax issues. In addition, the tax shelter opinion should fully and fairly address each material tax issue respecting which there is a reasonable possibility that the Internal Revenue Service will challenge the tax effect proposed in the offering materials.

* * * If, as a result of review of the written advice of another professional or otherwise, the lawyer believes that there is a reasonable possibility that the Internal Revenue Service will challenge the proposed tax effect respecting any material tax issue considered by the other professional, and the issue is not fully addressed in the offering materials, the lawyer has ethical responsibilities to so advise the client and the other professional and to refuse to provide an opinion unless the matter is addressed adequately in the offering materials. The lawyer also should assure that his own opinion identifies clearly its limited nature, if the lawyer is not retained to consider all of the material tax issues.

Since the term "opinion" connotes a lawyer's conclusion as to the likely outcome of an issue if challenged and litigated, the lawyer should, if possible, state the lawyer's opinion of the probable outcome on the merits of each material tax issue. However, if the lawyer determines in good faith that it is not possible to make a judgment as to the outcome of a material tax issue, the lawyer should so state and give the reasons for this conclusion.

A tax shelter opinion may question the validity of a revenue ruling or the reasoning in a lower court opinion which the lawyer believes is wrong. But there also must be a complete explanation to the offerees, including what position the service is likely to take on the issue and a summary of why this position is considered to be wrong. The opinion also should set forth the risks of an adversarial proceeding if one is likely to occur.

* * *

The committee does not accept the view that it is always ethically improper to issue an opinion which concludes that the significant tax benefits in the aggregate probably will not be realized. However, full disclosure requires that the negative conclusion be clearly stated and prominently noted in the offering materials.

* * *

In all cases, the lawyer who issues a tax shelter opinion, especially an opinion which does not contain a prediction of a favorable outcome, should assure that the offerees will not be misled as a result of mischaracterizations of the extent of the opinion in the offering materials or in connection with sales promotion efforts. In addition, the lawyer always should review the offering materials to assure that the standards set forth in this opinion are met and that the offering materials, taken as a whole, make it clear that the lawyer's opinion is not a prediction of a favorable outcome of the tax issues concerning which no favorable prediction is made. The risks and uncertainties of the tax issues should be referred to in a summary statement at the very outset of the opinion or the tax aspects or tax risks section of the offering materials.

If the lawyer disagrees with the client over the extent of disclosure made in the offering materials or over other matters necessary to satisfy the lawyer's ethical responsibilities as expressed in this opinion, and the disagreement cannot be resolved, the lawyer should withdraw from the employment and not issue an opinion.

NOTE ON THE ABA'S STATEMENT OF POLICY REGARDING LAWYERS' RESPONSES TO AUDITORS' REQUESTS FOR INFORMATION

As courts began to hold accountants liable in damage actions if they did not maintain independence from and verify the representations of the corporate clients whose books were being audited, the auditors sought "comfort" from the corporation's lawyers. The auditors asked the lawyers to verify the corporation's contingent liabilities.

"When the legal profession became fully aware of the implications of such requests for information regarding contingent liabilities, the die was cast. By then the accounting profession had come to view responses to these inquiries as essential to an audit, and a failure to receive the appropriate response was viewed as a limitation on the scope of the audit, necessitating a disclaimer of opinion or, depending on the circumstances, other qualification, which could render the financial statements effectively unaudited. That, in turn, had a serious impact on the client—which often was required to pay its auditors and its attorneys to debate the question—since it was required to file audited financial statements under the 1934 Act or, in the case of any new registration of securities, the 1933 Act.

"For a number of reasons, however, the lawyers could not readily submit to such an inquiry. First, the lawyer has the ethical obligation * * * to 'Preserve the Confidences and Secrets of a Client.' Accompanying that ethical obligation is the legal obligation, imposed under slightly varying conditions, to maintain the attorney-client privilege. While each of those barriers to disclosure might technically be overcome by the client's consent, there was significant doubt about whether consent coerced in this fashion could be valid, particularly when—as was usually the case—the client was not fully cognizant that such disclosure might destroy the confidentiality privilege for all purposes. Moreover, most law firms, and in particular the larger ones, reasonably feared liability for a failure to recognize the full consequences of facts coming to the attention of their lawyers in a context other than request by the client for advice. For example, a lawyer involved in litigating one case might easily become aware, through discovery, of facts that could constitute the basis for another action by a different party against the client.

"Finally, of course—and to this difficulty clients were most sensitive—disclosure of a contingent liability could often lead to removal of its contingent aspect. While a publicly held company might properly be required to disclose some potential liabilities to existing or potential shareholders, the analysis of whether or not disclosure was, in fact, required could often be a close question of judgment. Since it was obviously not in the interest of all shareholders to increase the claim's potential by disclosure, lawyers were understandably reluctant to substitute their judgment for that of their clients. And since the lawyers themselves received no economic benefit from nondisclosure, ran no risk from disclosure, but did run a risk in nondisclosure, one could reasonably expect that a disclosure decision made by lawyers would have an overly conservative bias not necessarily in the public interest." [1]

The ABA and the American Institute of Certified Public Accountants reached a compromise and both groups issued coordinated statements.[2] The ABA Statement of Policy Regarding Lawyers' Responses to Auditors' Requests for Information, 31 Business Lawyer 1709 (1976), first distinguished between "litigation which is pending or which a third party has manifested to the client a present intention to commence," and "other contingencies of a legal nature or having legal aspects."

1. Lorne, The Corporate and Securities Adviser, The Public Interest, and Professional Ethics, 76 Mich.L.Rev. 425, 448–49 (1978) (footnote omitted).

2. The American Institute of Certified Public Accountants (AICPA), which is the principal organization of practicing accountants, issued Statement on Auditing Standards (SAS) No. 12, Inquiry of a Client's Lawyer Concerning Litigation, Claims and Assessments (1976), which coordinates with the ABA Statement of Policy Regarding Lawyers' Responses to Auditors' Requests

for Information * * * [an edited version of which] is reprinted here.

While Chairman of the Securities and Exchange Commission, Roderick M. Hills called this ABA/AICPA compromise "a major step forward," Wall St.J., Jan. 8, 1976, at 6, col. 3 (midwest ed.), others have thought the compromise "as resting, in the final analysis, upon a mutual abdication of purported responsibilities. As such it is only a matter of time before its frailty is exposed." Lorne, supra n. 1, at 449–50 (1978).

As to the first category, "unquestionably the lawyer representing the client in a litigation matter may be the best source for a description of the claim or claims asserted, the client's position (e.g. denial, contest, etc.) and the client's possible exposure in the litigation. * * * " As to the second category, the Statement found that "it is not in the public interest for the lawyer to be required to respond to general inquiries from auditors concerning possible claims."

Paragraph (3) of the Statement stated that the lawyer's response to the auditors request for disclosure of the loss contingencies of the client may be limited "to items which are considered individually or collectively material to the presentation of the client's financial statements."

Paragraph (5) then provided:

"(5) *Loss Contingencies. When properly requested by the client,*[3] it is appropriate for the lawyer to furnish to the auditor information concerning the following matters if the lawyer has been engaged by the client to represent or advise the client professionally with respect thereto and he has devoted substantive attention to them in the form of legal representation or consultation:

(a) *overtly threatened or pending litigation*, whether or not specified by the client;

(b) *a contractually assumed obligation* which the client has specifically identified and upon which the client has specifically requested, in the inquiry letter or a supplement thereto, comment to the auditor;

(c) *an unasserted possible claim or assessment* which the client has specifically identified and upon which the client has specifically requested, in the inquiry letter or a supplement thereto, comment to the auditor.

With respect to clause (a), overtly threatened litigation means that a potential claimant has manifested to the client an awareness of and present intention to assert a possible claim or assessment unless the likelihood of litigation (or of settlement when litigation would normally be avoided) is considered remote. With respect to clause (c), where there has been no manifestation by a potential claimant of an awareness of and present intention to assert a possible claim or assessment, * * * the client should request the lawyer to furnish information to the auditor only if the client has determined that it is probable that a possible claim will be asserted, that there is a reasonable possibility that the outcome (assuming such assertion) will be unfavorable, and that the resulting liability would be material to the financial condition of the client. Examples of such situations might (depending in each case upon the particular circumstances) include the following: (i) a catastrophe, accident

3. Emphasis added.

or other similar physical occurrence in which the client's involvement is open and notorious, or (ii) an investigation by a government agency where enforcement proceedings have been instituted or where the likelihood that they will not be instituted is remote, under circumstances where assertion of one or more private claims for redress would normally be expected, or (iii) a public disclosure by the client acknowledging (and thus focusing attention upon) the existence of one or more probable claims arising out of an event or circumstance. * * *

"The information that lawyers may properly give to the auditor concerning the foregoing matters would include (to the extent appropriate) an identification of the proceedings or matter, the stage of proceedings, the claim(s) asserted, and the position taken by the client.

"In view of the inherent uncertainties the lawyer should normally refrain from expressing judgments as to outcome except in those relatively few clear cases where it appears to the lawyer that an unfavorable outcome is either 'probable' or 'remote;' for purposes of any such judgment it is appropriate to use the following meanings:

      (i) **probable**—an unfavorable outcome for the client is probable if the prospects of the claimant not succeeding are judged to be extremely doubtful and the prospects for success by the client in its defense are judged to be slight.

      (ii) **remote**—an unfavorable outcome is remote if the prospects for the client not succeeding in its defense are judged to be extremely doubtful and the prospects of success by the claimant are judged to be slight. * * * No inference should be drawn, from the absence of such a judgment, that the client will not prevail.

"The lawyer also may be asked to estimate, in dollar terms, the potential amount of loss or range of loss in the event that an unfavorable outcome is not viewed to be 'remote.' In such a case, the amount or range of potential loss will normally be an inherently impossible to ascertain, with any degree of certainty, as the outcome of the litigation. Therefore, it is appropriate for the lawyer to provide an estimate of the amount or range of potential loss (if the outcome should be unfavorable) only if he believes that the probability of inaccuracy of the estimate of the amount or range of potential loss is slight. * * * The lawyer should not be asked, nor need the lawyer undertake, to furnish information to the auditor concerning loss contingencies except as contemplated by this Paragraph 5."

Paragraph (6) provided that the lawyer may not "knowingly" participate in any violation by his client "of the disclosure requirements of the securities laws" and that "[i]ndependent of the scope of his response to the auditor's request for information" the "lawyer also may be required under the Code of Professional Responsibility to resign his engagement if his advice concerning disclosures is disregarded by the client." While the lawyer is under a duty to consult with the client concerning the question of disclosure, there is no requirement that the attorney inform the auditor.

PROBLEM 22

Obligations When the Client May Be Engaged in Fraud

International Energy, Inc., a publicly held company listed on the New York Stock Exchange, is about to borrow a large sum of money from a bank. The company, in order to induce the bank to lend the money, has given the bank glowing reports about its prospects.

The strength of the company has been based on its reputation for vigorous research, which thus far has resulted in a series of patents for energy saving devices. The new product, production of which will be financed by the loan, will be another patented device. All of the reports that the company has showed the bank suggest glowing prospects for performance of the device. The company's auditors have issued a report showing International Energy to be in outstanding financial health. The current draft of your firm's opinion letter indicates no knowledge of material facts inconsistent with that optimism.

You had lunch today with your good friend, the head of the research and development section of International Energy, Inc. "A great company is in real trouble," he told you. "When our former president retired, a sense of integrity retired as well." Your friend and his scientist colleagues have great concern that the new product described in the documents given the bank has not been sufficiently tested and that its reliability and performance have been overrated.

In addition, the engineer told you that the production facility for the new product was recently purchased from a shell corporation owned by the company's new president. He said the price paid by the company was outrageously high. The auditors did not catch the problem and thus their audit did not footnote the fact that the purchase was from a corporate officer. As a result, the balance sheet of the corporation looks significantly better than it would if the facility were carried at its true value.

Finally, the engineer also told you that he is dying of cancer. He has not yet told most of his friends and would like the information kept confidential. Throughout his tenure with the company, his reputation as a creative engineer has been such that investors pay a premium for the company's stock.

QUESTIONS

1. Has your lunch given you indigestion? May you tell the bank what the head of research and development has told you? May you fail to do so?

a. SEC v. National Student Marketing Corp., 457 F.Supp. 682 (D.D.C.1978), was an SEC proceeding challenging the behavior of lawyers and others in a situation involving a failure to disclose. A merger of National Student Marketing Corp. with Interstate National Corporation was immediately followed by the sale of newly acquired NSMC stock by former Interstate principals.

> "These transactions are alleged to have occurred despite the prior receipt by the defendants of information which revealed that NSMC's interim financial statements, used in securing shareholder approval of the merger and available to the public generally, were grossly inaccurate and failed to show the true condition of the corporation. The information was included in a comfort letter prepared by NSMC's accountants."

The court concluded that each of the defendants violated the securities laws. When information is "obvious[ly]" material, "the attorneys' responsibilities to their corporate client required them to take steps to ensure that the information should be disclosed to the shareholders. However, it is unnecessary to determine the precise extent of their obligations here, since it is undisputed that they took no steps whatsoever to delay the closing pending disclosure to and resolicitation of the Interstate shareholders. But, at the very least, they [the lawyers] were required to speak out at the closing concerning the obvious materiality of the information and the concomitant requirement that the merger not be closed until the adjustments were disclosed and approval of the merger was again obtained from the Interstate shareholders. Their silence was not only a breach of this duty to speak, but in addition lent the appearance of legitimacy to the closing. The combination of these factors clearly provided substantial assistance to the closing of the merger." Id. at 713.

b. SEC v. Universal Major Industries Corp., 546 F.2d 1044 (2d Cir.1976), cert. denied 434 U.S. 834, 98 S.Ct. 120, 54 L.Ed.2d 95 (1977), held that an attorney violated Section 5 of the Securities and Exchange Act of 1933, 15 U.S.C.A. § 77e, by aiding and abetting his client's selling of unregistered stock. The lawyer advised UMI that the stock could be sold as a private offering exempt from registration only under certain conditions. When UMI failed to comply with the conditions, the lawyer instructed the client to do so. UMI hired a second lawyer to process the registration, but he never did. Later, the Continental Transfer Corporation required an opinion letter from the first lawyer stating that various stock transfers were legal. The first lawyer sent a letter stating that he had no opinion, but "I rely on the opinion of [the second lawyer] * * *."

He enclosed that opinion which said: "In view of the fact that the debentures and the underlying stock into which they are convertible were, in our opinion, sold in transactions violative of Section 5 of the Securities Act of 1933, as amended (as well as the Trust Indenture Act) the conversions at this time, as proposed, would not constitute additional violations of the Act."

This second lawyer's opinion was wrong, and the district court found that the first lawyer knew or should have known it. The District Court rejected the first lawyer's "obvious attempt to avoid a personal commitment in these letters," and the Court of Appeals accepted this finding. The District Court enjoined the lawyer from future violations of the Act, and the Court of Appeals affirmed.

c. Can these cases be dismissed as decided under the federal securities laws? Do they state more general principles about what a lawyer faced with fraud must do?

2. If the client will not disclose what the lawyer believes should be disclosed, is it enough for the lawyer to withdraw from the representation? May (must) the lawyer do more?

a. In Meyerhofer v. Empire Fire & Marine Insurance Co., 497 F.2d 1190 (2d Cir.1974), cert. denied 419 U.S. 998, 95 S.Ct. 314, 42 L.Ed.2d 272 (1974), a lawyer working on a registration statement expressed concern to the partners in his firm that the company's statement failed to disclose adequately certain features of the compensation arrangements between the company and the law firm, as well as other matters. After the lawyer insisted on a full and complete disclosure and the partners disagreed, he resigned from the firm. That same day he appeared before the SEC and placed before it the relevant information on the nondisclosure.

Later, another law firm sued on behalf of the purchasers of the common stock alleging that the registration statement and prospectus were materially false and misleading. One of the named defendants was the lawyer who had gone to the SEC. After consulting his own attorney and a Special Counsel to the SEC's Division of Enforcement, the lawyer, in an attempt to defend himself, gave the plaintiffs' firm a copy of the affidavit with exhibits that he had earlier given to the SEC. The other defendants, relying on Canons 4 and 9, moved to disqualify the plaintiffs' lawyers and to enjoin the lawyer from disclosing any relevant information claimed to be confidential. The district court granted the motions but the Second Circuit reversed, relying on the right of permissive disclosure in DR 4–101(C)(4).

b. With the lawyer's approach in *Meyerhofer*, contrast the following:

"When outside corporate counsel give advice that management rejects, what is counsel's duty? Must they inform the outside directors? If the advice is that the Corporation has a duty to disclose a past or continuing offense to investors or to the authorities, or to terminate a practice that may violate the law, we think they must. If the outside directors decline to act, should outside counsel resign? We think they should. Is mere resignation sufficient, or must they also inform the authorities about a past or continuing offense? If the continuing act or omission is a criminal offense, the CPR [Code of Professional Responsibility] says they have a right if not a duty to disclose, but I think this is outmoded and unrealistic in at least one important current context. The Code was written to fit the lawyer whose human client tells him of an intent to commit a bodily assault. It does not appear to fit the lawyer who advises a corporate client that it is committing a continuing but unchallenged violation of an environmental or other regulation backed by criminal penalties, where the client decides not to desist because compliance is beyond the state of the art or beyond the client's resources, or even because the cost of correction is greater than the potential fine if detected. The lawyer has a clear duty to advise the client that the continuing violation should be terminated and perhaps even to resign if it is not terminated. But it would severely limit the willingness of companies to seek legal advice about complex compliance issues if the lawyer has the right to inform the authorities that his advice has been rejected.

* * *

"In my own view, a law firm's willingness to carry its advice to the highest corporate level and to resign if all else fails is a more potent enforcement weapon than the threat that the firm may inform. Directors will rarely act contrary to firm legal advice, and they will certainly think again if their lawyers show a willingness to resign when their advice is declined. They will think again not only because of the potential public consequences if the resignation becomes generally known, but also because most managements genuinely respect the judgment and character of their counsel, and are bound to be impressed by the courage and conviction that a decision to resign involves. Unhappily, resignation on principle went out of style in public life a long time ago. But in the private relationships between corporations and their lawyers, it is a potential that should always be preserved." Cutler, The Role of the Private Law Firm, 33 Bus.Law. 1549, 1556–57 (Mar.1978).

c. Compare Elam, The Role of a Lawyer Isn't to Police Clients, USA Today, Feb. 15, 1983, at 10A, with Rotunda, id. Elam states:

"It's a fallacy to make the lawyer a watchman or policeman over his client; that would be a mortal blow to the traditional attorney-client privilege. The true function of a lawyer is to counsel a client on proper conduct. A lawyer cannot give sound and informed advice unless the lawyer obtains *all* the facts.

The client must be able to feel free to communicate all of the facts without fear of disclosure. * * * Attempting to make lawyers the self-appointed consciences of their corporate clients has the same inherent evil—of discouraging the free exchange of information."

Rotunda answers:

"[It should be the law] that the lawyer 'may reveal' client information in order to prevent the client from committing a criminal or fraudulent act likely to result in 'substantial' financial injury to another, or to rectify the consequences of the client's criminal or fraudulent act, where the lawyer's services had been used to further the scheme. [It is wrong to] discipline—and even disbar—a lawyer who would speak out to prevent the fraud. * * * Client confidentiality is important, to be sure, when the client has confessed *past crimes*. But what public policy justifies allowing the client to misuse his lawyer in order to commit *future crimes*? [Ethical rules] allow a lawyer to breach his client's confidences if necessary to collect a fee. If lawyers can breach confidentiality to protect themselves, they should have the same right to protect the public."

d. See also draft Rule 1.6(b)(1), (2), and draft Rule 1.13(c), both proposed by the Kutak Commission and reprinted as footnotes to Rules 1.6 and 1.13 in the Standards Supplement. In Report of the Trustee Concerning Fraud and Other Misconduct in the Management of * * * O.P.M. Leasing Service, Inc., Reorganization No. 81–B–10533 (BRL) (April 25, 1983), the Trustee condemned the ABA House of Delegates for rejecting draft Rule 1.6: "[T]he ABA House of Delegates, the organization's policy-making body, rejected the proposed rule and voted instead for a rule that would make it unethical for lawyers to divulge client secrets in order to protect third parties from an ongoing fraud. * * * The Trustee considers the ABA's action outrageous and irresponsible. The Trustee hopes that the ABA will reconsider the issue and that state bar authorities will reject the rule in favor of one that goes at least as far as the proposed rule in permitting lawyers to prevent their clients from committing future frauds and from using lawyers as instruments in fraudulent schemes." Id. at 422.

e. Most of the above opinions were written before the Model Rules and Comments 14, 15 & 16 to Rule 1.6 were adopted. May you (must you) now send a notice of withdrawal to others with whom you have dealt in the matter saying, e.g., "I have withdrawn from this matter for ethical reasons"? Would you be "flying a red flag" and thus prejudicing your client's interests? Do the Comments permit, or require, a form of "disclosure" about which the Rule itself is silent?

3. Does the right or obligation to withdraw or disclose depend on the kind of transaction and what role the lawyer is playing in the transaction?

a. We have assumed in most of this problem that your firm would be rendering an opinion that would be given to the bank. In it, you would at least opine that the appropriate corporate resolutions had been adopted and powers granted. In many typical transactions, you might also opine that you know of no material facts that have been misstated or omitted from the documents that the bank has received. If that is to be your role here, what should you do now that you have had your lunch with the chief engineer?

b. Suppose your firm is doing work with the Department of Energy to get the new device approved for sale. Suppose further that if the DOE had the device tested at an independent laboratory it would be likely to find the device unreliable and thus ruin the likelihood of the loan being made. May you argue before the Department of Energy that it should not require outside testing? May you help the company "create" some records of outside tests that would increase the likelihood that DOE would agree? Take a look at *In re American Continental Corporation*, in the Readings to this Problem. It suggests how at least one Court thought about such issues.

c. Suppose, instead, that you give advice to the company about how to structure the financing transaction but that you do not render an opinion? May you assume that therefore the bank will not rely on anything you did? Does that mean you need do nothing to correct misstatements?

The SEC seems to be resurrecting some of its old positions on these questions. Consider its settlement with senior executives of Salomon Brothers in connection with alleged illegal bids at auctions of Treasury bills. Although the Salomon general counsel was not formally charged, the SEC report of the settlement made clear that the agency would not consider such an in-house lawyer a mere bystander. Instead, the lawyer would have a duty to "take appropriate action." See, e.g., Legal Times, Dec. 14, 1992, p. 14.

d. Assume that all you do is pass document prepared by the client on to the investors? If you know that the documents are materially inaccurate, are you liable for making a false representation to the investors? In Schatz v. Rosenberg, 943 F.2d 485 (4th Cir.1991), the client was obliged to give the sellers of a business a current financial statement. His prior statement had been accurate, but the new one concealed serious financial losses. The lawyer did not prepare the statement but he delivered it to the sellers, allegedly knowing it was fraudulent. The Fourth Circuit held that the lawyer was not liable; he had only "papered the deal" and acted as a "scrivener." Thus, he had no duty to the sellers.

Do you agree? Isn't handing over a fraudulent statement itself an act aiding and abetting the client's fraud? Could the driver of the get away car in a bank robbery argue that he was outside the bank all the time and thus not a participant in the crime?

4.   Suppose the lawyer only discovers the misinformation after the loan has closed.   Does the lawyer's duty change?

a.   ABA Formal Opinion 92–366 (Aug. 8, 1992) was part of the continuing effort to define what a lawyer may disclose consistent with Model Rule 1.6.   The opinion assumes that a lawyer for a small manufacturing firm has given an opinion that its client's accounts receivable represent legal obligations of the purchasers of the goods.   Now, the lawyer finds that many of the accounts are fictional and that the client is in financial trouble.   The opinion says that under Model Rule 1.6, the lawyer *must* withdraw from all future dealings involving this loan, and *must* disavow the prior opinion.   Otherwise, the lawyer would be "assisting" the client to get future extensions of credit, for example.   The opinion was controversial, and there was a vigorous dissent.

b.   A.B.A. Formal Opinion 93–375 (1993), dealt with a lawyer's obligation to disclose adverse information in the context of a bank examination.   The opinion says that the lawyer may not lie to the bank examiners but the lawyer is not affirmatively obliged to warn about problems at the bank or otherwise reveal client confidences.   If the lawyer reasonably believes the bank is engaged in fraud, however, the lawyer *must* take steps to avoid assisting it to do so, including, in some cases, withdrawing from the representation.

5.   Where do all these principles lead you in your analysis of this problem?

a.   Would the possibly unreliable character of the product raise withdrawal or disclosure obligations?   Do you really *know* that it is unreliable?   Might your friend, the engineer, just be depressed?

b.   Must you somehow communicate accurate financial information to the bank?   How would you do it?   Could you go to the auditors and ask them to look into your new information, for example?

c.   Might you similarly disclose the serious illness of the company's scientific star?   Is he entitled to endure his serious illness with some dignity and peace?   Are such values entitled to any weight at all where significant money is at stake?

6.   Are the issues regarding "whistle blowing" by a government lawyer comparable to the issues involved in a corporate context?   Why or why not?

a.   Is the client of a government lawyer his department?   Is it the President or Governor?   Is it the "public interest"?

b.   Does Canon 4 impose an obligation of confidentiality on government lawyers comparable to that imposed on private lawyers?   What is the effect of Model Rules 1.6 and 1.13?

c.   To whom should the government lawyer turn with her information about dishonesty in government?   Her superiors?   A crusading Congressman?   The Department of Justice?   The news media?

d. Would it be preferable for the government lawyer to resign and publicly attack the alleged wrongdoing? Consider Dam, The Special Responsibility of Lawyers in the Executive Branch, 55 Chicago Bar Record 4 (Special Centennial Issue, 1974):

"I have pointed to the great tradition of this country of members of the bar entering the Government for limited periods; surely we should not make Government an even more hazardous occupation than it inevitably is. By the same token, many law schools emphasize public service as a natural part of a lawyer's career. Many schools have begun to enrich their curricula by courses designed with the future public servant specifically in mind. In my view, this emphasis on public service is not only desirable but indispensable in a period when government has not only the power but increasingly the legislative obligation to run the economy, dictate social conditions, and reach into the private lives of millions through welfare, health, and other social programs.

"All of that said, it is unquestionably a prime lesson of Watergate that ethical standards in Washington are miserably low. The bar can make a contribution by raising ethical standards for lawyers, and perhaps by proposing suitable legislation on subjects such as the duty to report crimes. But I strongly believe that any attempt to reform Washington by reforming lawyers would be doomed to failure because it would be dealing with symptoms and only one symptom at that."

e. What if the lawyer were an army officer and could not resign before his or her tour of duty was over? Even if the government lawyer could resign, would it be ethical for an attorney to take information given in his or her capacity as a lawyer and use it against a former client/employer? [1]

---

1. Compare the strategy of one Mr. William M. Bennett, an attorney who worked on the El Paso litigation [Utah Public Service Commission v. El Paso Natural Gas Co., 395 U.S. 464, 89 S.Ct. 1860, 23 L.Ed.2d 474 (1969)] for the state of California. [Bennett] filed his own brief in the Supreme Court opposing Utah's motion to withdraw the appeal. Purporting to be a "consumer spokesman," he alleged that Utah was party to a purchased withdrawal. Bennett also alleged that California had not appealed the district court's decision because of a suspect agreement (which had not been publicly filed in California). See, Rotunda, The Public Interest Appellant: Limitations on the Right of Competent Parties to Settle Litigation Out of Court, 66 Nw.U.L.Rev. 199, 205–06 (1971). One of the petitions for rehearing alleged that Bennett had a retainer from an unsuccessful applicant for the pipeline. Id. at 206, n. 37. Was Bennett ethical in turning against his former employer, the state of California?

READINGS

In Re: **AMERICAN CONTINENTAL CORPORATION/LINCOLN SAVINGS AND LOAN SECURITIES LITIGATION.**

794 F.Supp. 1424 (D.Ariz.1992)

Richard M. Bilby, District Judge.

MEMORANDUM OPINION

* * *

These actions originate from the business dealings of Charles H. Keating, Jr. ("Keating"), former chairman of ACC. The claims at issue here were brought principally against professionals who provided services to ACC and/or Lincoln Savings.*

* * *

D. JONES, DAY, REAVIS & POGUE

* * * [Jones Day, a defendant in this action, moves for summary judgment.] Jones Day generally claims that it has not engaged in conduct for which it could be held liable because lawyers are obligated to keep their clients' confidence and to act in a ways [*sic.*] that do not discourage their clients from undergoing regulatory compliance reviews.

The record reveals the following facts concerning Jones Day's involvement with ACC and Keating.

Prior to joining Jones Day, defendant William Schilling was director of the FHLBB [Federal Home Loan Bank Board] Office of Examinations and Supervision. In that capacity, he was directly involved in the supervision of Lincoln Savings. During the summer of 1985, he wrote at least one memorandum and concurred in another, expressing serious regulatory concerns about numerous aspects of Lincoln's operations. For example, he wrote:

> Under new management, Lincoln has engaged in several serious regulatory violations. Some of these violations, such as the overvaluation of real estate and failure to comply with Memorandum R–41(b), are the same type of violations that have led to some of the worst failures in FSLIC's history.

Later in 1985, Schilling was hired by Jones Day to augment its expertise in thrift representation. On January 31, 1986, Schilling and Jones Day's Ron Kneipper flew to Phoenix to solicit ACC's business. ACC retained Jones Day to perform "a major internal audit of Lincoln's FHLBB compliance and a major project to help Lincoln deal with the FHLBB's direct investment regulations."

During the regulatory compliance audit, which Jones Day understood to be a pre-FHLBB examination compliance review, the law firm

---

* Ed. note. ACC was American Continental Corporation, the holding company that was dominated by Charles Keating and that owned Lincoln Savings and Loan as well as other companies. Jones, Day, Reavis & Pogue is a large, national law firm whose home office is in Cleveland.

found multiple regulatory violations. There is evidence that Jones Day knew that Lincoln had backdated files, destroyed appraisals, removed appraisals from files, told appraisers not to issue written reports when their oral valuations were too low, and violated affiliated transaction regulations. Jones Day found that Lincoln did no loan underwriting and no post-closure loan followup to ensure that Lincoln's interests were being protected. Jones Day learned Lincoln had multiple "loans" which were, in fact, joint ventures which violated FHLBB regulations, made real estate loans in violation of regulations, and backdated corporate resolutions which were not signed by corporate officers and did not reflect actual meetings. There is evidence that Jones Day may have tacitly consented to removal of harmful documents from Lincoln files. For example, one handwritten notation on a memorandum memorializing Jones Day's advice not to remove documents from files reads, "If something *is* devastating, consider it individually." (Emphasis in original).

There is evidence that Jones Day instructed ACC in how to rectify deficiencies so that they would not be apparent to FHLBB examiners. Jones Day attorneys, including Schilling, testified that they told ACC/Lincoln personnel to provide the Jones Day-generated "to do" lists only to the attorneys responsible for rectifying the deficiencies, and to destroy the lists so that FHLB–SF [Federal Home Loan Bank of San Francisco] would not find them in the files. For the same reason, Jones Day's regulatory compliance reports to ACC/Lincoln were oral. Jones Day paralegals testified that responsibilities for carrying out the "to do" lists were divided among Jones Day and ACC staff. Jones Day continued this work into the summer of 1986.

The evidence indicates that Jones Day may have been aware that ACC/Lincoln did not follow its compliance advice with respect to ongoing activities. There are material questions of fact concerning the procedures Jones Day used—if any—to ascertain whether their compliance advice was being heeded. The testimony suggests that Jones Day partners knew ACC/Lincoln personnel were preparing loan underwriting summaries contemporaneously with Jones Day's regulatory compliance review, even though the loan transactions had already been closed. Moreover, the evidence reveals that Jones Day attorneys participated in creating corporate resolutions to ratify forged and backdated corporate records.

* * *

The record indicates that the concept of selling ACC debentures in Lincoln savings branches may have originated at an April 9, 1986 real estate syndicate seminar given by Jones Day Defendant Ron Fein. There is evidence that Fein may have contributed to the detailed bond sales program outline, attending to details such as explaining how the sales would work, and insuring that the marketing table was far enough from the teller windows to distinguish between ACC and Lincoln Savings employees. The evidence indicates that Jones Day reviewed the debenture registration statement and prospectus, which is corroborated by

Jones Day's billing records. As a result, in January 1987, ACC was able to assure the California Department of Savings & Loan that:

> The process of structuring the bond sales program was reviewed by Kaye, Scholer and Jones Day to assure compliance not only with securities laws and regulations, but also with banking and FSLIC laws and regulations.

Moreover, there is evidence which suggests that political contributions were made on behalf of ACC, in exchange for ACC's consent that Jones Day could "bill liberally." * * * Jones Day set up an Arizona Political Action Committee ("PAC") specifically for the purpose of making a contribution to an Arizona gubernatorial candidate. The PAC was opened on September 4, 1986 and closed in December, 1986, after the contribution was made.

In June 1986, Jones Day solicited additional work from ACC. Jones Day attorney Caulkins wrote, in part:

> Rick Kneipper reports that ACC is very explicit that it does not care how much its legal services cost, as long as it gets the best. He states that Keating gave him an unsolicited $250,000 retainer to start the thrift work, and sent another similar check also unsolicited in two weeks. On the down side, he reports that he has never encountered a more demanding and difficult client,
>
> . . .
>
> It appears to Rick and to me that American Continental is made for us and we for them.

* * *

Jones Day contends that it may not be held liable for counseling its client. The line between maintaining a client's confidence and violating the securities law is brighter than Jones Day suggests, however. Attorneys must inform a client in a clear and direct manner when its conduct violates the law. If the client continues the objectionable activity, the lawyer must withdraw "if the representation will result in violation of the rules of professional conduct or other law." Ethical Rule 1.16. Under such circumstances, an attorney's ethical responsibilities do not conflict with the securities laws. An attorney may not continue to provide services to corporate clients when the attorney knows the client is engaged in a course of conduct designed to deceive others, and where it is obvious that the attorney's compliant legal services may be a substantial factor in permitting the deceit to continue.

* * *

An attorney who represents a corporation has a duty to act in the corporation's best interest when confronted by adverse interests of directors, officers, or corporate affiliates. It is not a defense that corporate representation often involves the distinct interests of affiliated entities. Attorneys are bound to act when those interests conflict.

There are genuine questions as to whether Jones Day should have sought independent representation for Lincoln.

Moreover, where a law firm believes the management of a corporate client is committing serious regulatory violations, the firm has an obligation to actively discuss the violative conduct, urge cessation of the activity, and withdraw from representation where the firm's legal services may contribute to the continuation of such conduct. Jones Day contends that it would have been futile to act on these fiduciary obligations because those controlling ACC/Lincoln would not have responded. Client wrongdoing, however, cannot negate an attorney's fiduciary duty. Moreover, the evidence reveals that attorney advice influenced ACC/Lincoln's conduct in a variety of ways. Accordingly, summary judgment * * * is denied.

———

SELECTED BIBLIOGRAPHY ON ISSUES IN CHAPTER V

Problem 17

Alferi, Impoverished Practices, 81 Georgetown L.J. 2567 (1993).

Ames, Formal Opinion 352: Professional Integrity and the Tax Audit Lottery, 1 Georgetown J.Legal Ethics 411 (1987).

Ashe, "Bad Mothers," "Good Lawyers," and "Legal Ethics", 81 Georgetown L.J. 2533 (1993).

Ayer, How to Think About Bankruptcy Ethics, 60 American Bankruptcy L.J. 355 (1986).

D. Binder & S. Price, Legal Interviewing and Counseling: A Client–Centered Approach (1977).

B. Bitker, ed., Professional Responsibility in Federal Tax Practice (1970).

Brown & Dauer, Professional Responsibility in Nonadversarial Lawyering: A Review of the Model Rules, 1982 A.B.F. Research J. 519 (1982).

Bundy & Elhouge, Knowledge About Legal Sanctions, 92 Michigan L.Rev. 261 (1993).

Burke, Duty of Confidentiality and Disclosing Corporate Misconduct, 36 Business Lawyer 239 (1981).

Burkhardt & Conover, The Ethical Duty to Consider Alternatives to Litigation, 19 Colorado Lawyer 249 (1990).

Cooper, The Avoidance Dynamic: A Tale of Tax Planning, Tax Ethics, and Tax Reform, 80 Columbia L.Rev. 1553 (1980).

Corneel, Ethical Guidelines for Tax Practice, 28 Tax L.Rev. 1 (1972).

Davie, Babes and Barristers: Legal Ethics and Lawyer–Facilitated Independent Adoptions, 12 Hofstra L.Rev. 933 (1984).

DiSalvo, The Fracture of Good Order: An Argument for Allowing Lawyers to Counsel the Civilly Disobedient, 17 Georgia L.Rev. 109 (1982).

Dotterer, Attorney–Client Confidentiality: The Ethics of Toxic Dumping Disclosure, 35 Wayne L.Rev. 1157 (1989).

Durst, The Tax Lawyer's Professional Responsibility, 39 U.Florida L.Rev. 1027 (1987).

Ethics and the Tax Lawyer, 38 Record of the Association of the Bar of the City of New York 218 (1983).

Fraley, Harwell, Russell, Ethics and the Sports Lawyer: A Comprehensive Approach, 13 J.Legal Profession 9 (1988).

Fried, Too High a Price for Truth: The Exception to the Attorney–Client Privilege for Contemplated Crimes and Frauds, 64 North Carolina L.Rev. 443 (1986).

Gaetke & Welling, Money Laundering and Lawyers, 43 Syracuse L.Rev. 1165 (1992).

Hazard, Dimensions of Ethical Responsibility: Relevant Others, 54 U.Pittsburgh L.Rev. 965 (1993).

Hazard, How Far May a Lawyer Go in Assisting a Client in Legally Wrongful Conduct?, 35 U.Miami L.Rev. 669 (1981).

Hazard, Rectification of Client Fraud: Death and Revival of a Professional Norm, 33 Emory L.J. 271 (1984).

Hazard, Lawyers and Client Fraud: They Still Don't Get It, 6 Georgetown J.Legal Ethics 701 (1993).

Hazard, Dimensions of Ethical Responsibility: Relevant Others, 54 U.Pittsburgh L.Rev. 965 (1993).

Heller, Legal Counseling in the Administrative State: How to Let the Client Decide, 103 Yale L.J. 2503 (1994).

Johnston, An Ethical Analysis of Common Estate Planning Practices—Is Good Business Bad Ethics?, 45 Ohio State L.J. 57 (1984).

Leubsdorf, Pluralizing the Client–Lawyer Relationship, 77 Cornell L.Rev. 825 (1992).

Neisser, Disclosing Adolescent Suicidal Impulses to Parents: Protecting the Child or the Confidence, 26 Indiana L.Rev. 433 (1993).

Parley, Post–Marital Agreements, 8 J.Amer.Acad.Matrimonial Lawyers 125 (1992).

Pizzimenti, Prohibiting Lawyers from Assisting in Unconscionable Transactions: Using an Overt Tool, 72 Marquette L.Rev. 151 (1989).

D. Rosenthal, Lawyer and Client: Who's in Charge? (1975).

Rotunda, The Notice of Withdrawal and the New Model Rules of Professional Conduct: Blowing the Whistle and Waving the Red Flag, 63 Oregon L.Rev. 455 (1984).

Rotunda, When the Client Lies: Unhelpful Guides from the A.B.A., 1 Corporation L.Rev. 34 (1978).

Sarat & Felstiner, Lawyers and Legal Consciousness: Law Talk in the Divorce Lawyer's Office, 98 Yale L.J. 1663 (1989).

Schneyer, Professionalism and Public Policy: The Case of House Counsel, 2 Georgetown J.Legal Ethics 449 (1988).

Shavell, Legal Advice About Contemplated Acts: The Decision to Obtain Advice, Its Social Desirability, and Protection of Confidentiality, 17 J.Legal Studies 123 (1988).

Simon, Ethical Discretion in Lawyering, 101 Harvard L.Rev. 1083 (1988).

Stuart, Child Abuse Reporting: A Challenge to Attorney–Client Confidentiality, 1 Georgetown J.Legal Ethics 243 (1987).

Thurman, Incest and Ethics: Confidentiality's Severest Test, 61 Denver L.J. 619 (1984).

Weiers, The Disciplinary Dilemma Confronting Attorneys Seeking to Counsel Civil Disobedients, 23 Duquesne L.Rev. 715 (1985).

B. Wolfman & Holden, Ethical Problems in Federal Tax Practice (2d ed. 1985).

Problem 18

Biernat, Corporate Practice: From the Model Code to the Model Rules to the States, 34 Saint Louis U.L.Rev. 27 (1989).

Conference, The Ethical Responsibilities of Corporate Lawyers, 33 Business Lawyer 1173 (1978).

Corporate Legal Ethics—An Empirical Study: The Model Rules, the Code of Professional Responsibility, and Counsel's Continuing Struggle Between Theory and Practice, 8 J.Corporation Law 601 (1983).

Ferrara & Steinberg, The Role of Inside Counsel in the Corporate Accountability Process, 4 Corporation L.Rev. 3 (1981).

Forrow, Corporate Law Department Lawyer: Counsel to the Entity, 34 Business Lawyer 1797 (1979).

Giesel, The Business Client is a Woman: The Effect of Women as In–House Counsel on Women in Law Firms and the Legal Profession, 72 Nebraska L.Rev. 760 (1993).

Gillers, Model Rule 1.13(c) Gives the Wrong Answer to the Question of Corporate Counsel Disclosure, 1 Georgetown J.Legal Ethics 289 (1987).

Glasser, Attorney's Conflicts of Interest in the Investment Company Industry, 6 U.Michigan J.L.Reform 58 (1972).

Higginbotham, "See No Evil, Hear No Evil, Speak No Evil"—Developing a Policy for Disclosure by Counsel to Public Corporations, 7 J.Corporation Law 285 (1982).

P. Hoffman, Lions in the Street (1973).

Hooker, Lawyers' Responses to Audit Inquiries and the Attorney–Client Privilege, 35 Business Lawyer 1021 (1980).

Kaplan, Some Ruminations on the Role of Counsel for a Corporation, 56 Notre Dame Lawyer 873 (1981).

Kaplow & Shavell, Private Versus Socially Optimal Provision of Ex Ante Legal Advice, 8 J.L. Economics & Organization 306 (1992).

Kershen, Ethical Issues for Corporate Counsel in Internal Investigations: A Problem Analyzed, 13 Oklahoma City U.L.Rev. 1 (1988).

Maupin, Environmental Law, The Corporate Lawyer and the Model Rules of Professional Conduct, 36 Business Lawyer 431 (1981).

McCall, The Corporation as Client: Problems, Perspectives, and Partial Solutions, 39 Hastings L.J. 623 (1988).

Miller & Warren, Conflicts of Interest and Ethical Issues for the Inside and Outside Counsel, 40 Business Lawyer 631 (1985).

Mitchell, Professional Responsibility and the Close Corporation: Toward a Realistic Ethic, 74 Cornell L.Rev. 466 (1989).

Newman, Legal Advice Toward Illegal Ends, 28 U.Richmond L.Rev. 287 (1994).

Note, Attorney Responses to Audit Letters: The Problem of Disclosing Loss Contingencies Arising From Litigation and Unasserted Claims, 51 N.Y.U. L.Rev. 838 (1976).

Note, Conflict of Interest for an Attorney Representing a Labor Union, 7 J.Legal Profession 203 (1982).

Note, Scope of Attorneys' Responses to Auditors' Requests for Information—The ABA and AICPA Compromise, 1976 U.Illinois L.Rev. 783.

Note, Scope of Lawyers' Responses to Auditors' Requests for Information (pts. 1–2), 30 Business Lawyer 513, 989 (1975).

Painter, The Moral Interdependence of Corporate Lawyers and Their Clients, 67 S.Calif.L.Rev. 507 (1994).

Paul, The Lawyer as a Tax Advisor, 25 Rocky Mountain L.Rev. 412 (1953).

Pope, Two Faces, Two Ethics: Labor Union Lawyers and the Emerging Doctrine of Entity Ethics, 68 Oregon L.Rev. 1 (1989).

Redmount, Client Counseling and the Regulation of Professional Conduct, 26 St. Louis U.L.J. 829 (1982).

Riger, Disqualifying Counsel in Corporate Representation–Eroding Standards in Changing Times, 34 U.Miami L.Rev. 995 (1980).

Riger, The Model Rules and Corporate Practice—New Ethics for a Competitive Era, 17 Connecticut L.Rev. 729 (1985).

Riskin, Toward New Standards for the Neutral Lawyer in Mediation, 26 Arizona L.Rev. 329 (1984).

Rotunda, Law, Lawyers and Managers, in C. Walton, ed., The Ethics of Corporate Conduct 127 (American Assembly 1977).

Slovak, The Ethics of Corporate Lawyers: A Sociological Approach, 1981 A.B.F. Research J. 753 (1981).

Symposium, Advisors to Management: Responsibilities and Liabilities of Lawyers and Accountants, 30 Business Lawyer 1 (Special Issue, March, 1975).

Vigil, Regulating In–House Counsel: A Catholicon or a Nostrum?, 77 Marquette L.Rev. 307 (1994).

Problem 19

Becker, Conducting Informal Discovery of a Party's Former Employees: Legal and Ethical Concerns and Constraints, 51 Maryland L.Rev. 239 (1992).

Cramton & Udell, State Ethics Rules and Federal Prosecutors: The Controversies Over the Anti–Contact and Subpoena Rules, 53 U.Pittsburgh L.Rev. 291 (1992).

Gallagher, Legal and Professional Responsibility of Corporate Counsel to Employees During an Internal Investigation for Corporate Misconduct, 6 Corporation L.Rev. 3 (1983).

Hacker & Rotunda, Ethical Restraints on Communications With Adverse Expert Witnesses, 5 Corporation L.Rev. 348 (1982).

Krulewitch, Ex Parte Communications With Corporate Parties: The Scope of the Limitations on Attorney Communications With One of Adverse Interest, 82 Northwestern U.L.Rev. 1274 (1988).

Note, Prosecutor's Dilemma: Can a Criminal Defendant Be Interviewed Outside the Presence of His Attorney?, 6 J.Legal Profession 347 (1981).

Schaefer, A Suggested Interpretation of DR 7–107(A)(1): The Employment Attorney's Perspective on Contacting Employees of an Adverse Business Organization, 18 Vermont L.Rev. 95 (1993).

Stuntz, Lawyers, Deception, and Evidence Gathering, 79 Virginia L.Rev. 1903 (1993).

Problem 20

Adams, The Proposed Model Rules of Professional Responsibility: Disclosure of Clients' Fraud in Negotiation, 16 U.C. Davis L.Rev. 419 (1983).

Brown, Financial Institution Lawyers as Quasi–Public Enforcers, 7 Georgetown J. Legal Ethics 637 (1994).

Burke, "Truth in Lawyering": An Essay on Lying and Deceit in the Practice of Law, 38 Arkansas L.Rev. 1 (1984).

Burton, Feminist Theory, Professional Ethics and Gender–Related Distinctions in Attorney Negotiating Styles, 1991 J.Dispute Resolution 199.

Combs, Understanding Kaye Scholer: The Autonomous Citizen, the Managed Subject and the Role of the Lawyer, 82 Calif.L.Rev. 663 (1994).

Condlin, Bargaining in the Dark: The Normative Incoherence of Lawyer Dispute Bargaining Role, 51 Maryland L.Rev. 1 (1992).

Davis, The Long–Term Implications of the Kaye Scholer Case for Law Firm Management—Risk Management Comes of Age, 35 S.Texas L.Rev. 677 (1994).

Guernsey, Truthfulness in Negotiation, 17 U.Richmond L.Rev. 99 (1982).

Hazard, The Lawyer's Obligation to be Trustworthy When Dealing with Opposing Parties, 33 South Carolina L.Rev. 181 (1981).

Hazard, Lawyer Liability in Third Party Situations: The Meaning of the Kaye Scholer Case, 26 Akron L.Rev. 395 (1993).

Kostant, When Zeal Boils Over: Disclosure Obligations and the Duty of Candor of Legal Counsel in Regulatory Proceedings After the Kaye Scholer Settlement, 25 Arizona State L.J. 487 (1993).

Lowenthal, The Bar's Failure to Require Truthful Bargaining by Lawyers, 2 Georgetown J.Legal Ethics 411 (1988).

McMunigal, Disclosure and Accuracy in the Guilty Plea Process, 40 Hastings L. J. 957 (1989).

Menkel–Meadow, Is Altruism Possible in Lawyering?, 8 Ga.State U.L.Rev. 385 (1992).

Odiaga, The Ethics of Judicial Discretion in Plea Bargaining, 2 Georgetown J.Legal Ethics 695 (1989).

Oh, Using Employment Testers to Detect Discrimination: An Ethical and Legal Analysis, 7 Georgetown J.Legal Ethics 473 (1993).

Pogoda, The Lawyer's Proper Role in the Examination of Financial Institutions: Defining the Duty to Disclose After Kaye, Scholer, 34 Santa Clara L.Rev. 135 (1993).

Schneyer, From Self–Regulation to Bar Corporatism: What the S & L Crisis Means for the Regulation of Lawyers, 35 S.Texas L.Rev. 639 (1994).

Shine, Deception and Lawyers: Away From a Dogmatic Principle and Toward a Moral Understanding of Deception, 64 Notre Dame L.Rev. 722 (Fall 1989).

Smiley, Professional Codes and Neutral Lawyering: An Emerging Standard Governing Nonrepresentational Attorney Mediation, 7 Geo.J. Legal Ethics 213 (1993).

Symposium, In the Matter of Kaye, Scholer, Fierman, Hays & Handler: A Symposium on Government Regulation, Lawyers' Ethics, and the Rule of Law, 66 S.California L.Rev. 985 (1993).

Weinstein, Attorney Liability in the Savings and Loan Crisis, 1993 U.Illinois L.Rev. 53.

Wetlaufer, The Ethics of Lying in Negotiations, 75 Iowa L.Rev. 1219 (1990).

White, Machiavelli and the Bar: Ethical Limits on Lying in Negotiation, 1980 A.B.F. Research J. 926.

Problem 21

Freeman, Opinion Letters and Professionalism, 1973 Duke L.J. 371.

Marson, Tax Shelter Opinions: Ethical Responsibilities of the Tax Attorney, 9 Ohio Northern L.Rev. 237 (1982).

Philipps, Its Not Easy Being Easy: Advising Tax Return Positions, 50 Washington & Lee L.Rev. 589 (1993).

Portuondo, Abusive Tax Shelters, Legal Malpractice, and Revised Formal Ethics Opinion 346: Does Revised 346 Enable Third Party Investors to Recover From Tax Attorneys Who Violate its Standards?, 61 Notre Dame L.Rev. 220 (1986).

Report of the State Bar of Arizona Corporate, Banking, and Business Law Section Subcommittee on Rendering Legal Opinions in Business Transactions, February 1, 1989, 21 Arizona State L.J. 563 (1989).

Sax, Lawyer Responsibility in Tax Shelter Opinions, 34 Tax Lawyer 5 (1980).

Problem 22

Block & Ferris, SEC Rule 2(e)—A New Standard for Ethical Conduct or an Unauthorized Web of Ambiguity? 11 Capital U.L.Rev. 501 (1982).

Clanton, Attorney Liability Under Rule 10b–5, 15 Creighton L.Rev. 1027 (1982).

Cramton, The Lawyer as Whistleblower: Confidentiality and the Government Lawyer, 5 Georgetown J.Legal Ethics 291 (1991).

D'Amore, Securities Attorneys' Affirmative Duty to Take Prompt Action to Have Clients Comply with Disclosure Requirements, 11 Seton Hall L.Rev. 838 (1981).

Dippel, Attorney Responsibility and Carter Under SEC Rule 2(e): The Powers That be and the Fear of the Flock, 36 Southwestern L.J. 897 (1982).

Fiflis, Choice of Federal or State Law for Attorneys' Professional Responsibility in Securities Matters, 56 N.Y.U. L.Rev. 1236 (1981).

Freedman, A Civil Libertarian Looks at Securities Regulation, 35 Ohio St. L.J. 280 (1974).

Goldberg, Ethical Dilemma: Attorney–Client Privilege vs. National Student Marketing Doctrine, 1 Securities Reg.L.J. 297 (1974).

Hacker & Rotunda, Liability for the Misuse of Nonpublic, Material Inside Information: The Duty to Convey and the Duty to Inquire, 1 Corporation L.Rev. 376 (1978).

Hacker & Rotunda, The Reliance on Counsel Defense in Securities Cases: Damage Actions vs. Injunctive Actions, 1 Corporation L.Rev. 159 (1978).

Hazard, The Liability of Attorneys Involved in the Preparation of Disclosure Statements, 1982 Institute on Securities Reg. 265.

Hazard, Lawyers and Client Fraud: They Still Don't Get It, 6 Georgetown J.Legal Ethics 701 (1993).

Kelleher, Scourging the Moneylenders From the Temple: The SEC, Rule 2(e) and the Lawyers, 17 San Diego L.Rev. 801 (1980).

Lorne, Corporate and Securities Adviser, The Public Interest and Professional Ethics, 76 Michigan L.Rev. 425 (1978).

Love & Fox, Letter to Professor Hazard: Maybe Now He'll Get It, 7 Georgetown J.Legal Ethics 145 (1993).

Note, Redefining the Attorney's Role in Abusive Tax Shelters, 37 Stanford L.Rev. 889 (1985).

Note, SEC Disciplinary Proceedings Against Attorneys Under Rule 2(e), 79 Michigan L.Rev. 1270 (1981).

Note, SEC Standard of Conduct for Lawyers: Comments on the SEC Rule Proposal, 37 Business Lawyer 915 (1982).

Patterson, The Limits of the Lawyer's Discretion and the Law of Legal Ethics: National Student Marketing Revisited, 1979 Duke L.J. 1251.

Rosenfeld, Between Rights and Consequences: A Philosophical Inquiry into the Foundation of Legal Ethics in the Changing World of Securities Regulation, 49 George Washington L.Rev. 462 (1981).

Rotunda, The Notice of Withdrawal and the New Model Rules of Professional Conduct: Blowing the Whistle and Waiving the Red Flag, 63 Oregon L.Rev. 455 (1984).

Sommer, The Emerging Responsibilities of the Securities Lawyer, [1973–1974, Transfer Binder] CCH Fed.Sec.L.Rep. ¶ 79,631 (1974).

Statement of Policy Adopted by American Bar Association Regarding Responsibilities and Liabilities of Lawyers in Advising with Respect to the Compliance by Clients with Laws Administered by the Securities and Exchange Commission, 31 Business Lawyer 544 (1975).

Subin, The Lawyer as Superego: Disclosure of Client Confidences to Prevent Harm, 70 Iowa L.Rev. 1091 (1985).

Treiman, Inter-lawyer Communication and the Prevention of Client Fraud: A Look Back at O.P.M, 34 U.C.L.A. L.Rev. 925 (1987).

Chapter VI

ETHICAL PROBLEMS IN LITIGATION

Civil and criminal litigation present the most dramatic problems of legal ethics—problems that have attracted a great deal of public attention. The lawyers who face these issues do not always think of themselves as litigators. Because the issues that any lawyer confronts ultimately may be resolved in a courtroom, many problems presented in this chapter may be faced whatever the nature of a lawyer's practice. As you analyze these problems ask yourself such questions as:

a. How far may an attorney go to suppress the truth in representing a client in litigation? How far *must* he or she go? May (must) the lawyer refrain from disclosing relevant information to the trier of fact, for example? May (must) the lawyer allow the client to offer perjured testimony to further the client's interest?

b. To what extent may (must) a lawyer adopt the client's values and objectives? Is the lawyer solely the client's advocate and never a judge of the client's position?

c. How is the role of the lawyer as litigator different from the role of the lawyer as counselor? May a lawyer defend what he or she could not recommend?

Remember as well that the reputation of a lawyer is his or her most important asset. A litigator may appear before the same judge or agency with some frequency. If hindsight shows that she was too clever by half in one case, she may develop a reputation that will haunt her and her clients in other cases. The extent to which a lawyer should take into consideration the effect on her future clients of the way she represents the present client is a recurring issue of professional responsibility.

PROBLEM 23

The Decision to File a Civil Suit

Your client is a producer of a large assortment of California wines. Many of its wines do not "travel well" from California to their destination and have a short bottle life. In order to enable the wines to travel better and maintain their quality for a longer period of time, your client uses a unique process that places a small amount of a chemical sub-

311

stance into each bottle. Recent testing of that substance suggests that when large amounts of the substance are consumed by rats, a statistically significant number of rats contract cancer of the throat. Under the so-called Delaney Amendment to the Food and Drug Act,[1] if the Food and Drug Administration determines that any substance consumed in any amount by man or animal causes cancer, the FDA must ban the substance.

Some reputable scientists fully support the very conservative approach taken by the Delaney Amendment; others do not. Your client tells you that it is imperative that the FDA delay banning his wines, because he believes he would likely go bankrupt if he could not sell the thousands of cases he has already shipped out. The Food & Drug laws do not provide for any compensation for your client, and the chances of Congress passing a private bill for your client are remote. Moreover, he tells you that the shelf life of his wine is only six months (that is, within six months, over 95% of the wine he has shipped will have been sold to consumers by the liquor stores and removed from the shelves). The new wines that he is producing will not contain substances that may be carcinogenic.

You plan to file suit attacking the factual basis for the FDA order in this case and the constitutionality of the Delaney Amendment. You know that court dockets are so crowded that such a suit is likely to delay the effectiveness of the FDA's order banning the wines. Several years ago, your circuit upheld the law against just such a constitutional attack.

QUESTIONS

1. What ethical standards govern whether or not it is proper to file the planned civil action in this case? Is the fact that the delay obtained by filing such a suit might serve to save the client from bankruptcy the only relevant concern?

a. Does Model Rule 3.1 clearly answer this question? How about DR 7–102(A)(1) & (2) and EC 7–4? Is it ever "obvious" that a position is taken "merely to harass or maliciously injure" the opponent? Is there any proposition of law that cannot be the subject of a good faith proposal for at least a change in the law?

b. Does Model Rule 3.2 establish yet another test? Is its key principle that a lawyer must "expedite" resolution of the matter, or that the lawyer must do so only when "consistent with the interests of the client"? Does the Comment to the rule help provide an answer?

c. May one never consider the benefits of delay which arise from filing a motion? Must the motion be justified only in terms of its probability of success? May the benefits of delay be considered if there

---

1. 21 U.S.C.A. § 348(c)(3)(A). It was   from soft drinks around 1970.
under this law that cyclamates were banned

is *some* possibility of success, i.e., the motion is not filed *solely* for purposes of delay? [2]

d.   If you *may* delay on behalf of your client, then *must* you delay? Are you required to use every tool in your bag to further your client's interest?   May you refuse to file the motion in order to protect your long-term relationship with the FDA, for example?   Suppose you conclude that if you pull your punches on this one, the FDA may be pleased and more likely to give the benefit of the doubt to your *other* clients, and to this one on other cases? [3]

2.   May you file suit here without verifying the state of the law and the client's version of the facts?   How much verification is required?

a.   Rule 11, Federal Rules of Civil Procedure, as amended in 1993, is not a traditional standard of professional discipline, but it provides the most important practical sanction if a lawyer fails to verify the factual basis of a representation made to a federal court.   It provides:

Rule 11.   Signing of Pleadings, Motions, and Other Papers; Representations to Court; Sanctions

(a) **Signature.**   Every pleading, written motion, and other paper shall be signed by at least one attorney of record in the attorney's individual name, or, if the party is not represented by an attorney, shall be signed by the party.   * * *

(b) **Representations to Court.**   By presenting to the court (whether by signing, filing, submitting, or later advocating) a pleading, written motion or other paper, an attorney or unrepresented party is certifying that to the best of the person's knowledge, information, and belief, formed after an inquiry reasonable under the circumstances,—

---

2.   In the case of In re True, III, 12 Collier Bankruptcy Cases 74 (D.Mass.1977) the bankruptcy court assessed costs and attorney fees against the bank and the law firm that filed on the bank's behalf an involuntary petition in bankruptcy against True.   The court concluded that the involuntary petition was groundless and used in bad faith as a collection device.   The court relied in large part on EC 7–4, DR 7–102(A)(2), and Rule 911 of the Rules of Bankruptcy, which is substantially identical to Rule 11, Fed.R.Civ.P.   The court noted that normally the attorney fees and costs would be levied against the party individually but "in cases such as this, the party's attorneys are at least as culpable as their client, and probably more so."   Id. at 77. See also, Overmyer v. Fidelity & Deposit Co. of Maryland, 554 F.2d 539 (2d Cir.1977) (appellant assessed double costs and $2,000 in attorney's fees for frivolous appeal); cf. Hibbert v. INS, 554 F.2d 17, 19 n. 1 (2d

Cir.1977);   Acevedo v. INS, 538 F.2d 918 (2d Cir.1976);   Nemeroff v. Abelson, 620 F.2d 339 (2d Cir.1980).

3.   One manual of trial practice states that the "duty of supporting the client's cause is sometimes so forcefully stated as to support the argument that as a trial lawyer you are obliged to assert every legal claim or defense available, except those you reject on tactical grounds relating to the immediate case.   But the aim of the trial system to achieve justice, the interests of future clients, and your legitimate interest in your own reputation and future effectiveness at the bar compel moderation of that extreme view."   R. Keeton, Trial Tactics and Methods § 1–3 (2d ed. 1973) (footnote omitted). See also, Rotunda, Book Review, 89 Harvard L.Rev. 622, 628–29 (1976).   Compare this view with EC 2–28, EC 7–7, EC 7–8, EC 7–9, and EC 7–10.   Which do you think is the better view?

(1) it is not being presented for any improper purpose, such as to harass or to cause unnecessary delay or needless increase in the cost of litigation;

(2) the claims, defenses, and other legal contentions therein are warranted by existing law or by a nonfrivolous argument for the extension, modification, or reversal of existing law or the establishment of new law;

(3) the allegations and other factual contentions have evidentiary support or, if specifically so identified, are likely to have evidentiary support after a reasonable opportunity for further investigation or discovery; and

(4) the denials of factual contentions are warranted on the evidence or, if specifically so identified, are reasonably based on a lack of information or belief.

(c) Sanctions. If, after notice and a reasonable opportunity to respond, the court determines that subdivision (b) has been violated, the court may, subject to the conditions stated below, impose an appropriate sanction upon the attorneys, law firms, or parties that have violated subdivision (b) or are responsible for the violation.

(1) How Initiated.

(A) By Motion. A motion for sanctions under this rule * * * shall not be filed with or presented to the court unless, within 21 days after service of the motion * * *, the challenged paper, claim, defense, contention, allegation, or denial is not withdrawn or appropriately corrected. If warranted, the court may award to the party prevailing on the motion the reasonable expenses and attorney's fees incurred in presenting or opposing the motion. Absent exceptional circumstances, a law firm shall be held jointly responsible for violations committed by its partners, associates, and employees.

(B) On Court's Initiative. On its own initiative, the court may enter an order describing the specific conduct that appears to violate subdivision (b) and directing an attorney, law firm, or party to show cause why it has not violated subdivision (b) with respect thereto.

(2) Nature of sanction: Limitations. A sanction imposed for violation of this rule shall be limited to what is sufficient to deter repetition of such conduct or comparable conduct by others similarly situated. Subject to the limitations in subparagraphs (A) and (B), the sanction may consist of, or include, directives of a nonmonetary nature, an order to pay a penalty into court, or, if imposed on motion and warranted for effective deterrence, an order directing payment to the movant of some or all of the reasonable attorneys' fees and other expenses incurred as a direct result of the violation.

* * *

Cf. Model Rule 3.1, Comment 2.[4]

b. Prior to its amendment in 1993, Rule 11 had a procrustean quality that neither gave lawyers a chance to correct a pleading prior to sanctions being imposed nor gave the trial court discretion not to impose a sanction. Cross & Cross Properties v. Everett Allied Co., 886 F.2d 497 (2d Cir.1989), for example, imposed Rule 11 sanctions for a single improper count in a complaint, although all other counts in the complaint were well pleaded, and Cooter & Gell v. Hartmarx Corp., 496 U.S. 384, 110 S.Ct. 2447, 110 L.Ed.2d 359 (1990), imposed sanctions even though the plaintiff withdrew the offending complaint.

In Garr v. U.S. Healthcare, 22 F.3d 1274 (3d Cir.1994), decided under former Rule 11, Lawyer A had filed a class action alleging that U.S. Healthcare had issued false and misleading statements about its financial health. Lawyers B & C read about the case and filed identical complaints, changing only the names of their clients and the number of shares owned. Lawyers B & C had only read the first complaint and seen that it seemed to be verified by a Wall Street Journal story. The Court held 2 to 1 that such a copycat filing violates Rule 11 *even if the complaint turns out to be meritorious.* Query?[5]

c. Does the current version of Rule 11 appropriately balance the competing interests of forcing lawyers to do their homework before they file a pleading or motion and not turning sanctions hearings into collateral litigation that ultimately delays justice in the underlying action? Should the Model Rules themselves be changed to incorporate any of the elements of Rule 11?

3. What obligation do you have to make witnesses available for trial and for deposition by the opposing party?

a. Assume that prior to any FDA hearing to determine whether or not to issue a ban against your client's wine additive, you knew that the

---

4. Consider also, 28 U.S.C.A. § 1927, which provides:

> Any attorney or other person * * * who so multiplies the proceedings in any case unreasonably and vexatiously may be required by the court to satisfy personally the excess costs, expenses, and attorneys' fees reasonably incurred because of such conduct.

5. Inevitably, when a rule change like this goes into effect, one of the first questions is whether the new provisions apply retroactively to cases filed before the rule's effective date. Knipe v. Skinner, 19 F.3d 72 (2d Cir.1994), had been a *Bivens* action alleging constitutional violations by officials of the FAA. The Court found the action had no basis in fact or law and thus Rule 11 sanctions were appropriate. The District Court was directed to apply the terms of old Rule 11 to find liability, but to have the discretion provided by amended Rule 11 as to the amount of the sanctions. But see, Silva v. Witschen, 19 F.3d 725 (1st Cir. 1994), where a remand to apply amended Rule 11 was held inappropriate; it would cause "inordinate delay and expense to innocent parties."

first and most important witness that the FDA would seek to call would be the chief research chemist for your client. The chemist prefers not to testify because his testimony would greatly damage his employer, your client. Would it be proper for you to recommend that the chemist be hospitalized for tests and possible surgery on his recently discovered knee injury that, while not life-threatening nor terribly painful, limits his workday? Would you be let off the ethical hook if the company doctor initiated the suggestion that the knee needs treatment? Is it merely a rationalization to say that by creating the delay you would eliminate the possibility that the zealously loyal chemist might commit perjury?

b. May you advise a witness who is not your client not to talk to the other party? Suppose that the witness does not want to "become involved." Do Model Rule 3.4(a) & (f) and DR 7–109(B) entirely answer the question?

In North Carolina State Bar v. Graves, 50 N.C.App. 450, 274 S.E.2d 396 (1981), the court upheld the discipline of an attorney who attempted to influence a witness (who was not his client) to refuse to testify or, in the alternative, to plead the Fifth Amendment. Indeed, although the witness had a constitutional right to plead the Fifth Amendment, the court held that it is still a criminal act for someone "with corrupt motive to induce a witness to exercise that privilege." See also United States v. Baker, 611 F.2d 964, 968 (4th Cir.1979).

In People v. Kenelly, 648 P.2d 1065 (Colo.1982), the Colorado courts suspended an attorney because he drew a contract under which his client settled a civil case against X, and, in exchange, agreed to evade a subpoena in X's upcoming criminal trial. Accord, In the Matter of Lutz, 101 Idaho 24, 607 P.2d 1078 (1980).

See also, Snyder v. State Bar, 18 Cal.3d 286, 133 Cal.Rptr. 864, 867, 555 P.2d 1104 (1976) (attorney disbarred, inter alia, for advising clients not to be available for depositions); Florida Bar v. Machin, 635 So.2d 938 (Fla.1994) (lawyer suspended for offering to establish a trust fund for the child of a murder victim if the victim's family agreed not to testify at the client's sentencing hearing). Cf. Taylor v. Commonwealth, 192 Ky. 410, 233 S.W. 895 (1921) (attorney disbarred when he was party to an arrangement under which a witness was paid to leave the jurisdiction and not return).

c. To cope with the knee problem, might you simply ask the FDA staff for a delay in the hearings? Remember, in six months the case will be moot as far as your client is concerned, although it would still be a real issue to the FDA and possibly other wine producers. Is the only ethical issue your motive for delaying the expected testimony of the research chemist? Consider Chevron Chemical Co. v. Deloitte & Touche, 501 N.W.2d 15 (Wis.1993), where the lawyer represented that a witness would be unavailable for six weeks due to surgery; in fact, he had hernia surgery and would have been available in less than a week. For this and other misconduct, a judgment against the defendant notwithstanding the verdict was imposed and the case remanded to assess damages.

4. Are the same answers about what is frivolous appropriate when one is selecting issues to raise on appeal?

a. Should it matter whether the appeal is of a criminal conviction instead of a verdict in a civil case? In Anders v. California, 386 U.S. 738, 87 S.Ct. 1396, 18 L.Ed.2d 493 (1967) the Court held that appointed counsel in a criminal case may not withdraw a nonfrivolous appeal.

Jones v. Barnes, 463 U.S. 745, 103 S.Ct. 3308, 77 L.Ed.2d 987 (1983), however, explained that there is no constitutional right to compel appointed counsel to press all nonfrivolous issues requested by the client "if counsel, as a matter of professional judgment, decides not to present those points." The majority noted that experienced counsel have long advocated "winnowing out weaker arguments on appeal and focusing on one central issue if possible, or at most on a few key issues," particularly because oral arguments are strictly limited and page limits on briefs are widely imposed. "For judges to second-guess reasonable professional judgments and impose on appointed counsel a duty to raise every 'colorable' claim suggested by client would disserve the very goal of vigorous and effective advocacy that underlies *Anders*." Justices Brennan and Marshall dissented and argued that because paying clients could "specify at the outset of their relationship with their attorneys what degree of control they wish to exercise * * *," poor clients should have the same right.

b. Both the Court and the dissent in *Barnes* cited Model Rule 1.2(a) and Defense Function Standard 4–5.2. Who has the better argument? Is a client usually competent to specify errors worthy of appeal? Is giving the client the sense that he or she is in control as important as the inherent force of the arguments raised? [6]

5. Should the appropriateness of delay in litigation vary depending on the type of legal proceeding involved?

a. Consider Rotunda, Law, Lawyers, and Managers, in C. Walton, ed., The Ethics of Corporate Conduct 142–43 (1977):

"[D]elay is a knife that cuts both ways. Some corporate lawyers have charged that environmentalists and other public-interest litigants have used delay to bog down the regulatory system, to prevent needed rate increases, to prohibit or delay power plant expansion, to obstruct programs for highway construction, and to delay or modify housing developments."

Is delay permissible when invoked in service of the public interest?

b. Should filing appeals and habeas corpus petitions for purposes of delay be a permissible strategy in a death penalty case, for example? Is it often the *only* strategy?

6. On sanctions for a frivolous civil appeal, see Cooter & Gell v. Hartmarx, 496 U.S. 384, 110 S.Ct. 2447, 110 L.Ed.2d 359 (1990), and Hilmon Co. (V.I.) Inc. v. Hyatt International, 899 F.2d 250 (3d Cir.1990).

c.   Does it trouble you that, under the assumptions in this problem, your delay will allow tainted wine to be sold *in the future?* That is, what you do here may actually expose consumers to danger instead of, say, allocating losses after your client has acted.

d.   Rather than seek delay, should you suggest that your client—before the FDA's expected order becomes effective—immediately sell his stock of tainted wine to a foreign wholesaler, assuming foreign law and scientific understanding are different and that the wine can be resold abroad? Will you sleep better knowing that only foreigners will have their cancer risk increased?

6.   What other sanctions might be appropriate for litigation misconduct?

a.   Chambers v. NASCO, Inc., 501 U.S. 32, 111 S.Ct. 2123, 115 L.Ed.2d 27 (1991) tested a federal court's inherent power to award attorneys' fees to a party whom the court concludes has been harassed by litigation. The Court found that Chambers had agreed to sell his television station to NASCO, but then changed his mind. He was found to have tried to prevent the sale by fraudulently trying to deprive the federal court of jurisdiction and by other tactics of "delay, oppression and harassment." Rule 11 would have allowed sanctions for frivolous pleadings, of which there were several, but not for the other wrongs. The Supreme Court held that a district judge has inherent power to manage the proceedings and may award attorneys' fees to sanction bad faith and oppressive conduct, even if it is not covered by Rule 11. The Chief Justice and Justices Kennedy, Scalia and Souter dissented, suggesting the Court had granted carte blanche to judges to sanction lawyers.

b.   University of Maryland at Baltimore v. Peat, Marwick, Main & Co., 996 F.2d 1534 (3d Cir.1993), involved state sanctions for filing an action in federal court. When an insurance company became insolvent, various cases were filed in Pennsylvania and certain lawyers were made subject to confidentiality orders by the state court. This action was filed in federal court, arguably in violation of those orders, and the state insurance commissioner moved for contempt sanctions in the state court. This Federal Court refused to enjoin the state proceedings. The Anti–Injunction Act allows a federal court to enjoin state proceedings where necessary to protect its jurisdiction or enforce its judgments, the Court said; it does not create "a safety net into which attorneys who find themselves in a predicament with a state court can simply jump."

c.   See also, Clomon v. Jackson, 988 F.2d 1314 (2d Cir.1993), sanctioning a lawyer under the Fair Debt Collections Act for allowing a client to send letters bearing a facsimile of the lawyer's signature to people who owed the client money. Where the lawyer had not investigated each case before the letters were sent, the practice was held to be deceptive.[7] But see, Green v. Hocking, 9 F.3d 18 (6th Cir.1993), saying

7.   See also, Fox v. Citicorp Credit Services Inc., 15 F.3d 1507 (9th Cir.1994), where a lawyer who did 80% of his work collecting debts was a "debt collector" with-that the FDCA was not intended to limit traditional litigation in this way.

d.   Finally, United States v. Eisen, 974 F.2d 246 (2d Cir.1992), provides an important reminder that a lawyer may be found guilty of criminal and tortious conduct—here, mail fraud and RICO violations—for allegedly professional activities.   The case was concededly extreme. The lawyers were accused of conspiring with private investigators and others in a scheme of contriving phony traffic accidents and then filing claims with insurance companies.   The opinion looked at several issues, but the bottom line was that Rule 11 and the Model Rules may be the least of a lawyer's worries in some cases.

PROBLEM 24

Litigation Tactics

Hugh Cohan, one of the most famous insurance defense lawyers in San Francisco, defends clients of many of the largest insurance companies in the United States.   His firm's office overlooks the bay and occupies an entire floor of the Transamerica building.   Yet despite his luxurious office and income to match, Cohan cuts a different figure in court.   He dresses in baggy tweed jackets with elbow patches, his shirts have badly frayed sleeves, and his unpolished shoes have very worn heels and soles.   While he is a dapper figure outside of the courtroom with his custom suits and handmade cigars, he justifies his shabby attire and country lawyer act in the halls of justice as an effort to win sympathy from the juries while defending insurance companies against large tort judgments.

Cohan confides to his young associates that they should avoid choosing younger jurors because of their "social worker, do-gooder mentality."   He also advises: "Try to pick a jury with racial and class differences;   by exploiting and encouraging dissension you create disunity;   a disunified jury rarely grants large awards."

In one lecture to new associates in his firm he explained:

"You have to use your ingenuity and use all the tricks of the trade to win for the defense in a large tort claim.   If you see that you can exploit an opposing witness' emotional weakness to make him seem uncertain about a fact, don't hesitate to do so even if the fact is true.   The client doesn't pay for justice.   It pays for victory."

Cohan always has an employee of the defendant company sit with him at the defense counsel table so that the defense can be personalized.

in the meaning of the Act.   Acts such as calling the debtors at night and improperly garnishing wages thus created civil liability of the lawyers to the non–client debtors.

In one case he used Jake Smith, the foreman of the plant where the fatal accident occurred. All during the trial, Smith dressed in working clothes and sat at the table. He was called as the defense's only witness. In Cohan's emotional closing argument he never mentioned the defendant company. He said, "I believe in the goodness of Jake Smith. He has a family and should not be required to pay the plaintiff anything." The jury found only nominal damages against the defense.

In another case that Cohan likes to brag about, he defended a manufacturing concern charged with the negligent death of the wife of a middle-aged worker. All during the trial Cohan had his attractive redheaded secretary sit in the courtroom. Then, according to plan, Cohan had this secretary—just before closing arguments, during a short break in the proceedings when the plaintiff's lawyer's back was turned—ask the plaintiff-widower the time; she smiled at his response, patted him on the head, and then left. The three older members of the jury looked with icy stares at the plaintiff and five hours later the jury rendered judgment for the defense.

Cohan justifies these and similar practices (he calls them "tricks") as necessary to counteract what he considers the unfair advantage of the plaintiff's lawyer in winning verdicts because of sympathy and other reasons not connected with the merits of the case.[1]

QUESTIONS

1. Which litigating "tricks" of Cohan's are proper, if any? Are some in a gray area? Are any clearly improper?

a. Should Cohan be subject to criticism for wearing different clothes in court than he wears to the office? Why or why not? Should regulation of Cohan's dress be the responsibility of the judges before whom he appears?

Courts sometimes do try to regulate the dress of lawyers who appear before them. In State v. Cherryhomes, 840 P.2d 1261 (N.M. App.1992), for example, the lawyer appeared in a dress shirt with a bandanna at his neck. A local court rule required that he wear a necktie. He argued that a bandanna was a form of tie, but he was fined for contempt. The Court of Appeals affirmed. A lawyer's dress is not a form of "speech", the court ruled, and the judge's interpretation of the local rule controlled. Do you agree?

b. Is there anything improper about Cohan's approach to jury selection? Does a lawyer have a duty to the justice system to pick only jurors who will be fair to both sides? See, e.g., Georgia v. McCollum, ___ U.S. ___, 112 S.Ct. 2348, 120 L.Ed.2d 33 (1992) (unconstitutional for either prosecutor or defense counsel to exercise peremptory challenges

1. This problem is adapted, with permission, from the discussion of a somewhat analogous situation in Ending Insult to Injury: No–Fault Insurance for Products and Services 4–6 (U. of Ill.Press, 1975) by Jeffrey O'Connell, drawing in turn from material originally appearing in The Wall Street Journal.

based on racial stereotypes); J.E.B. v. Alabama ex rel. T.B., 511 U.S. ___, 114 S.Ct. 1419, 128 L.Ed.2d 89 (1994) (same result re gender based challenges); United States v. Omoruyi, 7 F.3d 880 (9th Cir.1993) (improper for prosecutor to strike unmarried women in case involving "good looking" male defendant).

Should the result be different in a medical malpractice case if the defense lawyer exercises a peremptory challenge against a juror (a Jehovah's Witness or a Christian Scientist) for religious reasons? Assume that the lawyer believes that the juror may be prejudiced against the defendant medical doctor. See State v. Davis, 504 N.W.2d 767 (Minn.1993)(religiously–motivated peremptory challenge against Jehovah's Witness held constitutional).

c. When Cohan cross-examines a truthful witness, may he properly try to get that witness to express uncertainty about something Cohan knows to be true? Look at ABA Defense Standard 4–7.6, in the Standards Supplement. Compare DR 7–102(A)(1), DR 7–106(C)(2), and Rule 4.4. What understanding of "justice" would warrant Cohan's approach? Is Cohan right that the client is not paying for justice? If so, should that end the ethical discussion?

d. Is it proper for Cohan to have an employee sit at the counsel table instead of a company manager? Was it proper for Cohan to express his personal view that Jake Smith should not have to pay any judgment awarded to the plaintiff? Take a look at DR 7–106(C)(4) and Rule 3.4(e). Do they deal well with the facts presented here?

e. Were you offended by the incident where Cohan's secretary implied that she had a relationship with the plaintiff? What, if anything, made the incident ethically improper?

f. In deciding which of Cohan's "tricks" are unethical, should the test be a bright line or should it vary depending on whether a case is before a jury, for example? Would one argue that wearing shabby clothes during a settlement conference is improper? Is the test whether the lawyer's *motive* was to mislead? Is the test whether in a given case a juror or lawyer was in fact misled?

g. Need we worry about trial tactics at all? Is the point of the adversary system that a lawyer may rely on opposing counsel's guile to counterbalance his or her own?

2. What do you think of counsel's tactic in United States v. Thoreen, used as a Reading to this Problem?

a. Do you agree that counsel should have been held in contempt for substituting a person who resembled the defendant for the defendant at the counsel table? Was the court in fact benefitted by having the weakness of the identification testimony confirmed? Is it "truth" we should be interested in? Decorum?

Are those simply the wrong questions? Is the proper issue the honesty of the attorney's implicit representations to the Court?[2]

b. People v. Reichman, 819 P.2d 1035 (Colo.1991), involved a prosecutor using undercover investigators in the drug task force he had created. One investigator identified a lawyer as a possible drug user. He also said that his (the investigator's) cover might have been compromised. Thus, pursuant to a prearranged plan, the investigator was arrested for a fictitious crime and he hired the suspected lawyer to defend him. Charges were filed, the investigator was arraigned, and the trial judge knew nothing of the deception. The whole charade was to convince the lawyer that the investigator was really not a cop. Somehow, the Court found out the truth and was incensed. The prosecutor was publicly censured for engaging in fraud, deceit, and prejudicing the administration of justice.

c. Maryland Atty Grievance Commission v. Rohrback, 591 A.2d 488 (Md.1991), involved a client who told his lawyer that he had given a false name to the arresting officer. The court says that the lawyer was under no obligation to correct that prior misstatement. When the bondsman arrived, the lawyer gave him the client's real name, but the false name was again used at the bond hearing. That, says the court, was all right too because the client, not the lawyer, gave the false name. Where the lawyer went wrong was in using the false name with the pre-sentence investigator for whom the name was critical because the client was a repeat offender. Thus, the lawyer was suspended for 45 days.

Do you agree that the lawyer could stand silent earlier while his client continued to use a false name? Does Rule 3.3(a)(2) suggest the contrary?

d. In Resolution Trust Company v. Bright, 6 F.3d 336 (5th Cir. 1993), the District Judge disbarred two lawyers from practice in his Court for trying to get a witness to sign an affidavit that described how certain events had occurred. The witness had said she did not know all the things they wanted her to say and she refused to sign the affidavit. The Court of Appeals was not shocked by the lawyers' conduct. It held that there is no harm in trying to get a witness to see the case the lawyer's way. Evidence of undue pressure on the witness was lacking, so the disbarment order was reversed.

3. Suppose Plaintiff's cause of action against Defendant may, if true, also constitute a crime, e.g., theft, fraud, embezzlement. When, if ever, is it an acceptable tactic to use the threat of bringing criminal charges to aid your client in the civil case?

a. Look at DR 7–105. Until 1983, the issue was seen to be a matter for ethical regulation. Why do you suppose that it has no counterpart in the Model Rules?

---

2. By a 4 to 3 vote, the Illinois Supreme Court has followed *Thoreen* on similar facts. People v. Simac, 641 N.E.2d 416 (Ill.1994).

b.　Consider Kinnamon v. Staitman & Snyder, 66 Cal.App.3d 893, 136 Cal.Rptr. 321 (1977).　There, the lawyer in a debt collection matter sent a letter to the debtor saying the debtor had committed a crime by sending a rubber check and that criminal charges would be filed if she did not promptly make the check good.　The lawyer did not inform the debtor that fraudulent intent was an element of the charge.　The allegations that the threat was made with the intent of inflicting emotional distress and that severe distress resulted were held sufficient to state a cause of action against the attorney for the tort of intentional infliction of emotional distress.

Compare Decato's Case, 117 N.H. 885, 379 A.2d 825 (1977), an attorney discipline proceeding.　The lawyer's letter to the debtor said that unless the debtor explained why he had stopped payment on a check, the lawyer would consider filing a criminal complaint.　The Court found that the "mere mention of possibly filing criminal charges does not in itself suggest that the statement was made in an effort to gain leverage in a collection suit."　It could not be said that the criminal charges were threatened "solely" to gain an advantage in a civil case.

Can these two cases be distinguished?　Is it significant that one was a tort suit and the other a disciplinary matter? [3]

c.　MacDonald v. Musick, 425 F.2d 373, 375–76 (9th Cir.1970), cert. denied 400 U.S. 852, 91 S.Ct. 54, 27 L.Ed.2d 90 (1970), was a habeas corpus proceeding.　The Court found a violation of DR 7–105(A) when a prosecutor offered to dismiss criminal charges against the criminal defendant *if* that defendant would then agree that the police had probable cause for his arrest.　When the defendant refused to give up his possible civil suit against the police department, the prosecutor amended the criminal complaint to include an additional charge.　The Court held that the prosecutor violated DR 7–105(A), in part because of his special duties under DR 7–103(A).　Do you agree? [4]

d.　ABA Formal Opinion 92–363 (1992) revisited this issue.　Applying the Model Rules, the opinion said that a lawyer *may* use the

3. *Kinnamon* was later disapproved by the California Supreme Court in Silberg v. Anderson, 786 P.2d 365 (Cal.1990). A lawyer's statement in the course of litigation was said to be privileged.

4. Hoines v. Barney's Club, Inc., 28 Cal.3d 603, 170 Cal.Rptr. 42, 620 P.2d 628 (1980), distinguished *Musick* as involving "improper motivations" and "coercive tactics." "[T]he time-honored practice of discharging misdemeanants on condition of a release of civil liability [against third parties] or stipulation of probable cause for arrest, does not contravene public policy when the prosecutor acts in the interests of justice." The release of civil liability in exchange for dismissal of criminal charge is like a plea bargain. In this case the evidence showed that "the motivating con-

cerns for the release and dismissal were plaintiff's welfare as a future candidate for admission to the California State Bar, the state's lack of a keen interest in pursuing a jury trial on a misdemeanor charge [disturbing the peace] although there was probable cause therefor, and fairness to other concerned parties [the defendant club and the club's agents, who had made the arrest and] who had acted on such probable cause." The dissent relied on Prosecution Function Standard 3–3.9(b), (c), which lists various factors to guide the prosecutor's discretion, none of which relate to third party interests. Horne v. Pane, 514 F.Supp. 551 (S.D.N.Y.1981), agreed with the *Hoines* dissent and followed *Musick*.

possibility of bringing criminal charges in negotiations in a civil case if both the civil case and criminal violation are well founded in fact and law and the threat would not constitute extortion under state law. The lawyer may even agree not to file criminal charges as an element of settling a civil claim if that agreement would not violate some provision of law that required reporting of crimes. Is the ABA getting more realistic? Does the opinion simply represent a further decline in lawyers' ethical standards?

e. Does it follow that a lawyer should be permitted to threaten to file disciplinary charges against an opposing lawyer in order to induce agreement to settle a civil case? ABA Formal Opinion 94–383 (July 5, 1994) saw that as a different issue. Just as In re Himmel, 125 Ill.2d 531, 127 Ill.Dec. 708, 533 N.E.2d 790 (1988), cited in Problem 3 of these materials, held that a lawyer may not bargain away a duty to report a lawyer's disciplinary violation in order to get a better settlement for a client, the ABA Opinion says that a lawyer may not agree to fail to report any matter the lawyer is required to report by Model Rule 8.3(c). Even as to matters sufficiently minor as to not require reporting, a threat to report may possibly be "prejudicial to the administration of justice" because it might introduce extraneous calculations into the decision to settle. Do you agree?

4. Would it ever be an acceptable trial tactic for counsel for a defendant to agree, with the client's consent, not to fight vigorously?

In Daniel v. Penrod Drilling Co., 393 F.Supp. 1056 (E.D.La.1975), the court held that an agreement between the plaintiff and one defendant, not revealed to the jury or the other defendant, to dismiss one defendant at the end of the trial in exchange for the defendant's agreement to offer no resistance to the plaintiff's case, warrants a new trial. "Nor [is] the vice in the agreement eliminated by the last minute offer to disclose it to the jury" since the remaining defendant would not have sufficient opportunity to adapt its trial strategy. Even if such "Mary Carter" agreements were made known to the jury, "the agreement might in itself prejudice the defendant's case since the jurors might infer that all parties to the agreement believed that the nonagreeing defendant was the party really at fault. * * * " The court reasoned:

> "Courts are not merely arenas where games of counsel's skill are played. Even in football we do not tolerate point shaving." Id. at 1060.

Do you agree with the court's conclusion? With its analysis? The Texas Supreme Court recently reached the same result in Elbaor v. Smith, 845 S.W.2d 240 (Tex.1992) (Mary Carter agreements held to be against public policy and void).

5.   What is a lawyer's obligation upon receiving confidential information of the opponent?

a.   In Aerojet–General Corp. v. Transport Indemnity Insurance, 22 Cal.Rptr.2d 862 (Cal.App.1993), the firm read a confidential memo from defense counsel to the defendant's insurer giving the name of a witness the firm had not discovered. The memo had been inadvertently included in a packet of discovery documents. The trial court imposed monetary sanctions on the firm for failing to return the document unread, but the appellate court held that information about this witness was not privileged or work product under California law, and that in using the information, the firm did nothing wrong. Do you agree?

b.   ABA Formal Opinion 92–368 (November 10, 1992), on the other hand, argues that as a matter of ethical responsibility, a lawyer who gets misdirected material from an opponent should refrain from reading it, notify the sending lawyer, and return or destroy the material as the sending lawyer directs.

c.   Lipin v. Bender, 597 N.Y.S.2d 340 (App.Div.1993), was a more extreme case with a more extreme sanction. The Court dismissed the complaint to sanction a plaintiff who had stolen privileged documents that defense counsel had brought to a hearing. Plaintiff's counsel had then copied and used the stolen documents against the defendant.

d.   ABA Formal Opinion 94–382 (July 5, 1994), considered such cases of intentional but unauthorized disclosure, including cases of disclosure by whistleblowers or disgruntled employees. The Opinion relied in part on In re Shell Oil Refinery, 143 F.R.D. 105 (E.D.La.1992), where the Court had required the party receiving the materials not to make use of them, to identify and return them, and to have no further contact with the disclosing persons. However, the ABA Opinion suggests that there may be exceptions to that rule, such as where the materials should have been disclosed by the opponent in discovery but were not. Thus, the Opinion recommends the lawyer's—

> "(a) refraining from reviewing materials which are probably privileged or confidential, any further than is necessary to determine how appropriately to proceed; (b) notifying the adverse party of the party's lawyer that the receiving lawyer possesses the documents, (c) following the instructions of the adverse party's lawyer, or (d), in the case of a dispute, refraining from using the materials until a definitive resolution of the proper disposition of the materials is obtained from a court."

Do you agree that a lawyer following that process would satisfy her professional responsibility?

6.   Should courts attempt to require civility of litigators who appear before them?

a.   The efforts are now frequent and increasing. For example, Dondi Properties Corporation v. Commerce Savings & Loan Association, 121 F.R.D. 284 (N.D.Tex.1988)(en banc), promulgated a code of civility for civil litigation. The Texas Code is designed to end "unnecessary contention and sharp practices between lawyers".

b.   In Paramount Communications, Inc. v. QVC Network, Inc., 637 A.2d 34 (Del.1994), the Court criticized remarks of Texas lawyer Joseph Jamail towards opposing counsel during a deposition. The Court raised the issue sua sponte. Mr. Jamail, for example, instructed his witness not to answer a question, then said: "He's not going to answer that. Certify it. I'm going to shut it down if you don't go to your next question." The other lawyer said, "No. Joe, Joe". Mr. Jamail responded, "Don't 'Joe' me, asshole. You can ask some questions, but get off of that. I'm tired of you. You could gag a maggot off a meat wagon." The Court did not discipline Mr. Jamail, who was representing a witness in a deposition but did not otherwise appear in the case, was not a member of the Delaware bar, and was not admitted pro hac vice. However, the Court said that his conduct "relates to a serious issue of professionalism involving deposition practices in Delaware trial courts." Do you agree? [5]

c.   In Matter of Swan, 833 F.Supp. 794 (C.D.Cal.1993), sexist remarks in a letter subjected a lawyer to sanctions. A male criminal defense lawyer wrote a letter to the female Assistant U.S. Attorney with an attachment stating in large, bold type: "MALE LAWYERS PLAY BY THE RULES, DISCOVER TRUTH AND RESTORE ORDER. FEMALE LAWYERS ARE OUTSIDE THE LAW, CLOUD TRUTH AND DESTROY ORDER." The Court agreed that, standing alone, the statement could be said to be a political statement or a personal opinion. Interjected into an ongoing case, however, and targeted at opposing counsel, the remarks constituted an offense the court could sanction, albeit only by ordering an apology.

d.   Not everyone agrees that such conduct should be regulated. Some object to courtesy codes as serving no useful purpose, and indeed being potentially counterproductive. E.g., Brewer & Bickel, Etiquette of the Advocate?, Texas Lawyer 20, 21 (Mar. 21, 1994) (Clients "are bound to be adversely affected as they witness their lawyers tiptoeing toward compromise with opposing counsel as 'cooperatively' as possible. After all, if Rosa Parks were alive today, surely her lawyer could have gotten her a seat on the middle of the bus.") Do you agree that effective advocacy demands boorish behavior by lawyers?

---

5. Hall v. Clifton Precision, 150 F.R.D. 525 (E.D.Pa.1993), also involved deposition conduct. Plaintiff's counsel insisted that, while his client was being deposed by defense counsel, the plaintiff could confer with his counsel about his answers. The Court held that to be improper. A client may confer with counsel about whether a privilege can be asserted, but otherwise, the lawyer taking the deposition is entitled to the witness' answers uncorrupted by suggestions of counsel.

READINGS

UNITED STATES v. THOREEN

United States Court of Appeals, Ninth Circuit, 1981.
653 F.2d 1332, cert.denied 455 U.S. 938, 102 S.Ct. 1428, 71 L.Ed.2d 648 (1982).

EUGENE A. WRIGHT, Circuit Judge:

I. INTRODUCTION

The issue before us is whether an attorney may be found in criminal contempt for pursuing a course of aggressive advocacy while representing his client in a criminal proceeding such that, without the court's permission or knowledge, he substitutes someone for his client at counsel table with the intent to cause a misidentification, resulting in the misleading of the court, counsel, and witnesses; a delay while the government reopened its case to identify the defendant; and violation of a court order and custom.

We affirm the district court's finding of criminal contempt.   * * *

II. FACTS

By February 1980, Thoreen, an attorney, had practiced law for almost five years. He was a member of the bars of the State of Washington and of the Western District of Washington. He had made numerous court appearances and participated in one trial and several pretrial appearances before Judge Jack E. Tanner of the Western District of Washington.

In February 1980, he represented Sibbett, a commercial fisher, during Sibbett's nonjury trial before Judge Tanner for criminal contempt for three violations of a preliminary injunction against salmon fishing. In preparing for trial, Thoreen hoped that the government agent who had cited Sibbett could not identify him. He decided to test the witness's identification.

He placed next to him at counsel table Clark Mason, who resembled Sibbett and had Mason dressed in outdoor clothing—denims, heavy shoes, a plaid shirt, and a jacket-vest.

Sibbett wore a business suit, large round glasses, and sat behind the rail in a row normally reserved for the press.

Thoreen neither asked the court's permission for, nor notified it or government counsel of, the substitution.

On Thoreen's motion at the start of the trial, the court ordered all witnesses excluded from the courtroom. Mason remained at the counsel table.

Throughout the trial, Thoreen made and allowed to go uncorrected numerous misrepresentations. He gestured to Mason as though he was his client and gave Mason a yellow legal pad on which to take notes. The two conferred. Thoreen did not correct the court when it expressly referred to Mason as the defendant and caused the record to show identification of Mason as Sibbett.

328

ETHICAL PROBLEMS IN LITIGATION

Ch. 6

Because of the conduct, two government witnesses misidentified Mason as Sibbett. Following the government's case, Thoreen called Mason as a witness and disclosed the substitution. The court then called a recess.

When the trial resumed, the government reopened and recalled the government agent who had cited Sibbett for two of the violations. He identified Sibbett, who was convicted of all three violations.

On February 20, 1980, Thoreen was ordered to appear on February 27 and show cause why he should not be held in criminal contempt. At the hearing, Judge Tanner found him in criminal contempt. * * *

III. DISCUSSION * * *

B. CONTEMPT

Judge Tanner found Thoreen in criminal contempt for the substitution because it was imposed on the court and counsel without permission or prior knowledge; the claimed identification issue did not exist; it disrupted the trial; it deceived the court and frustrated its responsibility to administer justice; and it violated a court custom. He found Mason's presence in the courtroom after giving the order excluding witnesses another ground for contempt because Thoreen planned that Mason would testify when the misidentification occurred. Judge Tanner held also that Thoreen's conduct conflicted with DR 1–102(A)(4), DR 7–102(A)(6), and DR 7–106(C)(5) of the Washington Code of Professional Responsibility.

Thoreen's principal defense is that his conduct was a good faith tactic in aid of cross-examination and falls within the protected realm of zealous advocacy. He argues that as defense counsel he has no obligation to ascertain or present the truth and may seek to confuse witnesses with misleading questions, gestures, or appearances.

* * *

1. Zealous Advocacy

While we agree that defense counsel should represent his client vigorously, regardless of counsel's view of guilt or innocence, we conclude that Thoreen's conduct falls outside this protected behavior.

Vigorous advocacy by defense counsel may properly entail impeaching or confusing a witness, even if counsel thinks the witness is truthful, and refraining from presenting evidence even if he knows the truth. When we review this conduct and find that the line between vigorous advocacy and actual obstruction is close, our doubts should be resolved in favor of the former.

* * *

Thoreen's view of appropriate cross-examination, which encompasses his substitution, crossed over the line from zealous advocacy to actual obstruction because, as we discuss later, it impeded the court's search for truth, resulted in delays, and violated a court custom and rule. More-over, this conduct harms rather than enhances an attorney's effective-ness as an advocate.

It is fundamental that in relations with the court, defense counsel must be scrupulously candid and truthful in representa-tion of any matter before the court. This is not only a basic ethical requirement, but it is essential if the lawyer is to be effective in the role of advocate, for if the lawyer's reputation for veracity is suspect, he or she will lack the confidence of the court when it is needed most to the serve the client.

American Bar Association Standards for Criminal Justice, The Defense Function 4.9 (1980).

2. *Criminal Contempt*

18 U.S.C. § 401 (1976) provides

A court of the United States shall have power to punish by fine or imprisonment, at its discretion, such contempt of its authority, and none other, as

(1) *Misbehavior* of any person *in its presence* or so near thereto as to *obstruct the administration of justice*;

* * *

(3) *Disobedience* or resistance *to its* lawful writ, process, *order*, rule, decree, or command. (emphasis added)

* * *

The record supports Judge Tanner's conclusion that Thoreen's substitution was misbehavior that obstructed justice. It was inappropri-ate because it was done without consent, and violated a court custom to allow only counsel, parties, and others having the court's permission to sit forward of the rail. This conduct is deemed unprofessional and may subject an attorney to disciplinary measures in Washington. CPR DR 7–106(C)(5).

* * *

b. *Intent*

To be held in criminal contempt, the contemnor must have the requisite intent.

* * *

Good faith is a defense to a finding of intent, but it does not immunize all conduct undertaken by an attorney on behalf of a client. It requires only that a court allow an attorney great latitude in his pursuit of vigorous advocacy.

Thoreen admits he planned and intended the substitution, but defends by asserting that (1) it was a good faith effort to prove misidentification and attack the credibility of the government witnesses; (2) he never intended to misrepresent any facts to the court or to obstruct justice; and (3) he believed the court knew Sibbett's identity from the pretrial hearing.

The record shows that Sibbett's identification was not an issue, contradicting the need to attack credibility. The testimony about Sibbett's violations was thorough, credible, and not in conflict.

Thoreen's alleged belief that the court would remember Sibbett from a pretrial proceeding is unrealistic because that hearing took place several months earlier and Sibbett was but one of many persons cited for violating the salmon fishing injunction.

His alleged lack of intent to deceive the court or to obstruct justice is irrelevant. Section 401(1) does not require specific intent. It suffices that he should have been aware that his conduct exceeded reasonable limits and hindered the search for truth.

CONCLUSION

Thoreen's error in judgment was unfortunate. The court's ire and this criminal contempt conviction could have been avoided easily and the admirable goal of representing his client zealously preserved if only he had given the court and opposing counsel prior notice and sought the court's consent.[7]

Nonetheless, viewing the evidence in the light most favorable to the government, we find that there is sufficient evidence to find beyond a reasonable doubt that Thoreen violated 18 U.S.C. § 401(1) and (3). The district court's findings were not clearly erroneous. We AFFIRM the contempt conviction.   * * *

PROBLEM 25

Disclosure of Law or Facts Favorable to the Other Side

You have prepared your case fully, and you consider it a sure winner on the motion for summary judgment. However, hours before the argument on that motion, you discover several cases with dicta directly against you. Two of the cases have holdings that by analogy are against you. You conclude that the likelihood is great that the judge would rule against your client on the summary judgment motion if he knew of the cases you have discovered. Your opponent has not referred to these cases.

---

7. While finding Thoreen's tactic misleading and obstructive of justice, we acknowledge that certain variations are acceptable. If identification is at issue, an attorney could test a witness's credibility by notifying the court and counsel that it is and by seeking the court's permission to (1) seat two or more persons at counsel table without identifying the defendant; see Duke v. State, 260 Ind. 638, 298 N.E.2d 453 (1973); (2) have no one at counsel table; (3) hold an in-court lineup.

Now, you have come across a witness who can supply a *factual* piece of evidence harmful to your client's case. You conclude that if you make a motion for summary judgment you would win because opposing counsel has not been able to present an affidavit on a vital point. However your secretly-discovered witness could supply the essential link in the opposition's evidentiary chain. The witness has not been contacted by the opposing party, and you assume no one else knows of his existence.

In another case, you represent a convicted client who stands before the judge to be sentenced. The court clerk indicates to the court that the defendant has no record. The court thereupon says to the defendant—who stands silent—"Since you have no criminal record, I will only put you on probation." You know either by independent investigation or from what your client has told you that he in fact has a criminal record and the clerk's information is incorrect. The judge turns to you and says, "Anything to add, counsel?"

QUESTIONS

1. Must you cite all relevant cases to the court, even those not favorable to your position? What if the cases are from another jurisdiction?

a. Compare DR 7–106(B) with Rule 3.3(a)(3). May you simply put contrary cases in a footnote in your brief without in any way explaining their relevance? Consider EC 7–23.

b. In Katris v. Immigration and Naturalization Service, 562 F.2d 866, 869 (2d Cir.1977), the attorney for petitioner failed to cite a particular Second Circuit case and several cases from other circuits because, he said "these decisions were adverse to his position here and that he did not agree with them." The attorney had represented one of the parties in the adverse Second Circuit case. The court concluded the lawyer had been misleading the Court and taxed costs against the attorney personally.

c. ABA Informal Opinion 84–1505 (March 5, 1984), was a strong reaffirmation of the disclosure obligation. The questions posed concerned a plaintiff's lawyer who had successfully beaten the defendant's motion to dismiss in a case of first impression interpreting a recently enacted statute. Based on earlier analogous cases, the trial court's ruling had been correct. Later, however, during the pendency of the action, plaintiff's lawyer learned that an appellate court elsewhere in the state had recently interpreted the statute in a way that was arguably contrary to the trial court's ruling. He asked the ABA Standing Committee on Ethics and Professional Responsibility whether he was obliged to disclose the new appellate opinion to the trial court.

Even though one could have interpreted the appellate ruling in a way not "directly adverse to the position of the client," another reading was clearly adverse. The trial court would certainly be benefited in this case of first impression by having information about the appellate

332 ETHICAL PROBLEMS IN LITIGATION Ch. 6

decision, so the ABA Committee concluded that the plaintiff's lawyer had a duty to reveal the information to the court.

d. Would you be required to disclose the existence of an unfavorable law review article by a prominent professor? What if you had relied on an earlier article by the professor, who has now repudiated his views? If you cite the first article, must you cite the second?

e. How might the obligation imposed by the ethics rules relate to Rule 11 of the Federal Rules of Civil Procedure, discussed in Problem 23?

In Rodgers v. Lincoln Towing Service, Inc., 771 F.2d 194 (7th Cir.1985), the Seventh Circuit approved Rule 11 sanctions that the trial court had imposed, because the plaintiff's lawyer had insisted that a particular U.S. Supreme Court case was applicable "despite clear authority in this Circuit to the contrary." Counsel did not "even attempt to construct an argument regarding why" the case should apply. Counsel had "refused to recognize or to grapple with the established law of the Supreme Court and of this Circuit. * * * " Accord, DeSisto College, Inc. v. Line, 888 F.2d 755 (11th Cir.1989), cert. denied 495 U.S. 952, 110 S.Ct. 2219, 109 L.Ed.2d 544 (1990); Jorgenson v. Volusia County, 846 F.2d 1350 (11th Cir.1988) (counsel had argued the same point in an earlier case and lost but did not tell the trial court in this case).

In Golden Eagle Distributing Corp. v. Burroughs Corp., 801 F.2d 1531 (9th Cir.1986), on the other hand, the law firm had moved for summary judgment and the trial court had both denied the motion and, sua sponte, imposed sanctions against the firm. The judge, relying on Model Rule 3.3 and Comments 1 & 3, ruled that the firm's positions in its summary judgment motion papers were legally and factually supportable, but that the firm had engaged in misleading conduct because it "should have stated that a position it was taking was grounded in a 'good faith argument for the extension, modification, or reversal of existing law,' rather than implying that its position was warranted by existing law." The Ninth Circuit reversed. The language of Rule 11 does not require counsel to differentiate between a position supported by existing law and one that would extend it. It is "not always easy to decide whether an argument is based on established law or is an argument for the extension of existing law." In fact, whether "the case being litigated is or is not materially the same as earlier precedent is frequently the very issue which prompted the litigation in the first place."

2. Are fact issues to be treated differently? Must a lawyer reveal a witness when opposing counsel has not sought the witness out or asked questions in discovery that would lead to the witness.

a. Must you reveal the witness to the court anyway in order to further the search for truth?[1] *May* you reveal this witness to the court? Listen to Samuel Williston:

---

1. In a similar case, New York County Lawyers' Association Opinion No. 309 (1933) ruled, without discussion, that it is "not professionally improper" for the attor-

"The case was tried before Chief Justice Knowlton. I opened the case at some length and I also made the preliminary part of the final argument. The Chief Justice decided promptly in favor of [my client,] the defendant, and since the decision was upon the facts, there was no opportunity for the plaintiffs to carry the case further. The handsomely bound volumes of interrogatories were only useful as waste paper. The plaintiffs either did not have so full a file of their correspondence with the defendant as we did, or it had not been so carefully examined by their counsel, for we had letters in our file that would have been useful to them. They did not demand their production and we did not feel bound to disclose them. In the course of his remarks the Chief Justice stated as one reason for his decision a supposed fact which I knew to be unfounded. I had in front of me a letter that showed his error. Though I have no doubt of the propriety of my behavior in keeping silent, I was somewhat uncomfortable at the time.

"One of the troublesome ethical questions which a young trial lawyer is confronted with is the extent to which he is bound to disclose to the court facts which are injurious to his client's case. The answer is not doubtful. The lawyer must decide when he takes a case whether it is a suitable one for him to undertake and after this decision is made, he is not justified in turning against his client by exposing injurious evidence entrusted to him." [2]

Mr. Williston reports that he was "uncomfortable at the time" with his ethical decision. Are you satisfied that he was being "professional" in suppressing his discomfort?

b. Might modern civil practice rules relating to discovery impose a higher standard than that to which Mr. Williston was held? Federal Rule of Civil Procedure 26, as amended in 1993, for example, provides that:

(a) Required Disclosures; Methods to Discover Additional Matter

(1) Initial Disclosures. Except to the extent otherwise stipulated or directed by order or local rule, a party shall, without awaiting a discovery request, provide to other parties:

(A) the name and, if known, the address and telephone number of each individual likely to have discoverable information relevant to disputed facts alleged with particularity in the pleadings, identifying the subjects of the information;

---

ney not to volunteer this witness to the court.

2. S. Williston, Life and Law: An Autobiography 271–72 (1940).

(B) a copy of, of a description by category and location of, all documents, data compilations, and tangible things in the possession, custody, or control of the party that are relevant to disputed facts alleged with particularity in the pleadings;

(C) a computation of any category of damages claimed by the disclosing party, making available for inspection and copying as under Rule 34 the documents or other evidentiary material, not privileged or protected from disclosure, on which such computation is based, including materials bearing on the nature and extent of injuries suffered; and

(D) for inspection and copying as under Rule 34 any insurance agreement under which any person carrying on any insurance business may be liable to satisfy part or all of a judgment which may be entered in the action or to indemnify or reimburse for payments made to satisfy the judgment.

* * * A party shall make its initial disclosures based on the information then reasonably available to it and is not excused from making its disclosures because it has not fully completed its investigation of the case or because it challenges the sufficiency of another party's disclosures or because another party has not made its disclosures.

* * *

(e) Supplementation of Disclosures and Responses. A party who has made a disclosure under subdivision (a) or responded to a request for discovery with a disclosure or response is under a duty to supplement or correct the disclosure or response to include information thereafter acquired if ordered by the court or in the following circumstances:

(1) A party is under a duty to supplement at appropriate intervals its disclosures under subdivision (a) if the party learns that in some material respect the information disclosed is incomplete or incorrect and if the additional or corrective information has not otherwise been made known to the other parties during the discovery process or in writing. * * *

(2) A party is under a duty seasonably to amend a prior response to an interrogatory, request for production, or request for admission if the party learns that the response is in some material respect incomplete or incorrect and if the additional or corrective information has not otherwise been made known to the other parties during the discovery process or in writing.

* * *

If Federal Rule 26 were applicable in the circumstances of this problem, what would it compel you to do?

c. What should a lawyer do if the client is found to have lied in responding to a discovery request? Is Rule 3.3 controlling? May a lawyer reveal the truth if doing so will injure the client? These issues were addressed in ABA Formal Opinion 93–376 (1993). A lie in discovery is "perjury", the Committee said, and the requirements of both Model Rule 3.3(a)(2) & (4) control. As provided in Rule 3.3(b), the lawyer has an obligation to correct the record in spite of the usual operation of Model Rule 1.6. Do you agree?

d. Should "stonewalling" by a plaintiff in the face of defendant's discovery requests justify dismissal of the case? It did in Penthouse International, Limited v. Playboy Enterprises, Inc., 86 F.R.D. 396, 406–07 (S.D.N.Y.1980), affirmed 663 F.2d 371 (2d Cir.1981). But see, Taylor, Sleazy in Seattle, The American Lawyer, April 1994, p. 5 (describing failure to impose sanctions on firm that withheld a "smoking gun" document in spite of representation that all relevant documents had been produced).

e. Might sanctions better be directed at counsel than the client? They were in Litton Systems, Inc. v. AT & T, 700 F.2d 785 (2d Cir.1983). The court upheld the jury verdict for Litton but also upheld the trial court's finding that Litton's attorneys had engaged in a "pattern of intentional concealment of evidence" relating to certain documents. Thus, the 2d Circuit upheld the trial court's decision to deny Litton recovery of all costs and attorneys' fees to which it would otherwise be entitled. These fees had been expected to run "well into the eight figure range." 91 F.R.D. 574, 578 (S.D.N.Y.1981). See also Hilmon Co. (V.I.) Inc. v. Hyatt International, 899 F.2d 250 (3d Cir.1990) (lawyer a repeat offender).

f. Matter of Barrow, 278 S.C. 276, 294 S.E.2d 785 (1982), involved actual tampering with evidence. A law firm was representing a man who was injured when a CB antenna he was installing touched a power line. When the plaintiff's lawyer picked up the antenna he noticed a warning label on the mast. He "commented that he wished it were not there," so a friend of the plaintiff tore it off and the lawyer made no effort to preserve it. The law firm did not reveal what had happened until almost 18 months later. The state supreme court held that "it was incumbent upon [the attorney] to promptly inform the court and the defendants that relevant evidence had been materially altered." It characterized counsel's action as "appalling" but approved a sanction limited to public reprimand.

g. In Chilcutt v. United States, 4 F.3d 1313 (5th Cir.1993), cert. denied sub nom. Means v. Wortham, ___ U.S. ___, 115 S.Ct. 460, 130 L.Ed.2d 367 (1994), discovery abuse resulted in imposition of sanctions on government counsel. The lawyer argued that it was a violation of separation of powers for a federal judge to discipline an executive branch official, but the Court held that the Federal Rules of Civil Procedure override Justice Department regulations governing lawyers. The District Court could even bar the government's reimbursing the lawyer for a sanction imposed upon the lawyer personally.

In United States v. Horn, 29 F.3d 754 (1st Cir.1994), on the other hand, a federal prosecutor had surreptitiously obtained copies of documents being requested from a third party by the defense. The Court held that the conduct was clearly improper but that imposition of sanctions on the government would violate principles of sovereign immunity.

With which of these opinions do you agree?

3. How would Judge Frankel and Professor Freedman deal with facts contrary to a client's position?

a. The views of both are set out as a Reading to this Problem. From what philosophical premise is Judge Frankel arguing? Is it utilitarianism? Can you tell? In what philosophical approach does Professor Freedman ground his reply?

b. Do the Model Rules go farther in Judge Frankel's direction than the Code does? Look at Rule 3.3(a)(2) as reinforced by Rule 3.3(b). What facts, if any, would those provisions require you to disclose that the Code does not? Can one say that, regardless of the Code's position, tort and criminal law already require what Rule 3.3(a)(2) contemplates?

c. Assume that you are seeking a temporary restraining order. Your recently discovered witness has evidence adverse to your position. In the ex parte TRO proceeding, should you reveal the disadvantageous testimony to the court? Consider Rule 3.3(d). Why should the Rules create this distinct obligation?

4. How would you rationalize the distinction drawn in the Model Rules and Model Code between the duty of candor regarding adverse law and the duty of candor regarding adverse facts?

a. Is the following explanation persuasive to you?

"The first situation [nondisclosure of facts] falls within the obligation to represent the client fully within the law's framework. The second presents a question of a determination of the applicable law, and there is no obligation to the client to withhold knowledge of the applicable law. The obligation is to present the applicable law to the court. This, of course, is not to say that the lawyer need not do his best to distinguish, or even obtain an overruling of the prior law. The obligation is to represent the client fully in obtaining a determination of the law, but to extend it to a concealment of the law would be to distort our judicial process which relies upon stare decisis as a cornerstone. An allied question is whether or not the advocate is required to advance new theories, which may be controlling, on behalf of the other party to the lawsuit, as an aid to the court. I agree with those who say 'no'. This inaction does not mislead the court in deciding disputed points of law which are before the court. A contrary position involves an abandonment of the adversary system in regard to the decisional process."[3]

b. Is the distinction better grounded in the law of what constitutes privileged and confidential client information? That is, while one may correctly view disclosure of contrary legal authority as detrimental to the client, is it properly thought of as confidential information of the client?

5. Is the third item not disclosed to the court in this problem—the prior criminal record of your client—a factual matter or a legal matter, i.e., is it more analogous to the situation in Question 1 or Question 2?

a. Is it the duty of defense counsel to correct the court clerk who mistakenly informed the judge that the client had no previous record? Does the fact that this is a criminal case determine the result?

b. In ABA Formal Opinion 287 (1953), the Ethics Committee ruling on this question split three ways. The Committee included Henry S. Drinker, later author of *Legal Ethics*, and William B. Jones, later a district judge in the District of Columbia. The majority concluded:

"If the court asks the lawyer whether the clerk's statement is correct, the lawyer is not bound by fidelity to the client to tell the court what he knows to be an untruth, and should ask the court to excuse him from answering the question, and retire from the case, though this would doubtless put the court on further inquiry as to the truth.

"Even, however, if the court does not directly ask the lawyer this question, such an inquiry may well be implied from the circumstances, including the lawyer's previous relations with the court. The situation is analogous to that discussed in our Opinion 280 where counsel knows of an essential decision not cited by his opponent and where his silence might reasonably be regarded by the Court as an implied representation by him that he knew of no such authority. If, under all the circumstances, the lawyer believes that the court relies on him as corroborating the correctness of the statement by the clerk or by the client that the client has no criminal record, the lawyer's duty of candor and fairness to the court requires him, in our opinion, to advise the court not to rely on counsel's personal knowledge as to the facts of the client's record. * * * The indignation of the court * * * on learning that the lawyer had deliberately permitted him, where no privileged communication is involved, to rely on what the lawyer knew to be a misapprehension of the true facts, would be something that the lawyer could not appease on the basis of loyalty to the client. No client may demand or expect of his lawyer, in the furtherance of his

3. Thode, The Ethical Standard for the Advocate, 29 Ins. Counsel J. 33, 39–40 (1962) (footnotes omitted).

cause, disloyalty to the law whose minister he is (Canon 32) or 'any manner of fraud or chicane' (Canon 15).

"If the lawyer is quite clear that the court does not rely on him as corroborating, by his silence, the statement of the clerk or of his client, the lawyer is not, in our opinion, bound to speak out." [4]

The dissenting opinion argued that the lawyer may in no event "stand idly by in open court and permit the court to be deceived at a time when the lawyer knows that the court is relying upon an untrue statement."

If the lawyer does not speak up, and the court specifically asks the lawyer if the client has a criminal record, what should the lawyer do? Do you agree that the best course is to hem and haw? [5]

     c. ABA Formal Opinion 93–370 (February 5, 1993) addressed whether a Court should be able to ask a lawyer to be candid about the limits of the lawyer's settlement authority. The Opinion recognized encouragement of settlement discussions as an important part of modern trial management but concluded that a lawyer should not tell a judge the extent of settlement authority the client has given. Further, because such authority would be a material fact about which the lawyer could not lie if asked, a judge should not inquire into the authority. Should a lawyer tell the judge, "Don't ask me about that?" Or, "I am not permitted to answer that question?" The opinion is persuasive on the importance of protecting the confidentiality of client communications; it is less helpful as to how the lawyer is to deflect the judge's question gracefully.

6. If a court concludes that a lawyer has in fact deceived it, the sanctions can be severe.

     a. In Toledo Bar Association v. Fell, 51 Ohio St.2d 33, 364 N.E.2d 872 (1977), for example, the lawyer had filed a workers' compensation claim for permanent disability of his client, but before the hearing on the claim, his client died. The attorney did not volunteer this information to the Industrial Commission because he knew it routinely denied permanent disability claims in such cases. Assuming the claim was originally filed in good faith, what discipline, if any, is justified by this nondisclosure? The Ohio Supreme Court indefinitely suspended the attorney. Would you have done the same? [6]

---

4. ABA Formal Opinion 287 also considered what the lawyer should do if the lawyer knows that the client will lie about his or her previous record, or the lawyer discovers later that the client had lied. These issues are considered in Problem 29.

5. The ABA Committee on Ethics and Professional Responsibility again revisited this issue after adoption of the Model Rules and concluded that, on the assumption that the client has engaged in no fraud or perju-

ry, the ABA Committee "could offer no better guidance under the Model Rules" than that offered by the authors of Formal Opinion 287. ABA Formal Opinion 87–353 (1987). California Formal Opinion 1986–87 is to the same effect.

6. If this result sounds familiar, it may be because we looked at a similar answer in Problem 20 to the question of the duty to disclose adverse facts in negotiation.

b. In Office of Disciplinary Counsel v. Hazelkorn, 18 Ohio St.3d 297, 480 N.E.2d 1116 (1985), the defendant, whose real name was Foster, gave his name as Frantz when he was arrested. The lawyer knew that his client had given a false identity but represented him in the bond hearing as if his name were Frantz. If defendant had used his real name, the prosecutor and court would have realized that he had an extensive record; instead, they accepted a no-contest plea and sentenced him to a fine. When he failed to pay the fine, a contempt citation and then an arrest warrant were issued. He was arrested, and the judge learned of the original misinformation. When it was determined that the lawyer had known all along that his client was deceiving the court, the lawyer was indefinitely suspended from practice.

c. State v. Casby, 348 N.W.2d 736 (Minn.1984), upheld a criminal conviction of an attorney for misleading the court. Her client had stood accused of speeding and littering. Because he had also been driving after revocation of his license, when he was arrested, he identified himself using his brother's name. At his arraignment and pretrial hearing, he continued the deception. Later he plead guilty, still using the name of his brother. There was some issue whether the attorney knew the real name of her client, but the court found that she did.

The lawyer asserted that, even if she knew the client's name, she was precluded by the attorney-client privilege and the professional obligation to keep the client's secrets from disclosing the deception he was perpetrating on the court. The court held that the lawyer had gone far beyond *passively* protecting confidential information. She had undertaken plea negotiations and written letters in which she referred to her client using the brother's name. At minimum, she should have withdrawn, but the court went on to say that it believed she could and should properly have revealed her client's true identity.

d. Likewise, Virgin Islands Housing Authority v. David, 823 F.2d 764 (3d Cir.1987), reminds lawyers that they must state accurately what happened below when they make an argument on appeal. Tenant had clearly lost in the territorial court on the issue whether an administrative hearing had been denied Tenant before eviction. The Housing Authority had not appeared at the hearing in the District Court, however, and so was not in a position to correct the record when Tenant's lawyer flatly denied that any finding on the issue had been made below. Thus, the District Court had mistakenly reversed the judgment of eviction. The Third Circuit here both reversed the District Court and directed it to consider imposing sanctions on the tenant's lawyer for lying about the events in the territorial court.

READINGS

***

MARVIN E. FRANKEL,* THE SEARCH FOR
TRUTH: AN UMPIREAL VIEW

123 U.Pa.L.Rev. 1031 (1975).

* * * The advocate in the trial courtroom is not engaged much more than half the time—and then only coincidentally—in the search for truth. The advocate's prime loyalty is to his client, not to truth as such. All of us remember some stirring and defiant declarations by advocates of their heroic, selfless devotion to The Client—leaving the nation, all other men, and truth to fend for themselves. Recall Lord Brougham's familiar words:

> [A]n advocate, in the discharge of his duty, knows but one person in all the world, and that person is his client. To save that client by all means and expedients, and at all hazards and costs to other persons, and, among them, to himself, is his first and only duty; and in performing this duty he must not regard the alarm, the torments, the destruction which he may bring upon others. Separating the duty of a patriot from that of an advocate, he must go on reckless of consequences, though it should be his unhappy fate to involve his country in confusion.[13]

Neither the sentiment nor even the words sound archaic after a century and a half. They were invoked not longer than a few months ago by a thoughtful and humane scholar answering criticisms that efforts of counsel for President Nixon might "involve his country in confusion."[14] There are, I think, no comparable lyrics by lawyers to The Truth.

This is a topic on which our profession has practiced some self-deception. We proclaim to each other and to the world that the clash of adversaries is a powerful means for hammering out the truth. Sometimes, less guardedly, we say it is "best calculated to getting out all the facts * * *." That the adversary technique is useful within limits none will doubt. That it is "best" we should all doubt if we were able to be objective about the question. Despite our untested statements of self-congratulation, we know that others searching after facts—in history, geography, medicine, whatever—do not emulate our adversary system. We know that most countries of the world seek justice by different routes. What is much more to the point, we know that many of the

---

* Practicing Attorney. At the time this article was written, Mr. Frankel was United States District Judge, S.D.N.Y.

13. 2 Trial of Queen Caroline 8 (J. Nightingale ed. 1821).

14. Freedman, The President's Advocate and the Public Interest, N.Y.L.J., Mar.

27, 1974, at 1, col. 1. Dean Freedman went on to explain that the system contemplates an equally singleminded "advocate on the other side, and an impartial judge over both." Id. 7, col. 2.

rules and devices of adversary litigation as we conduct it are not geared for, but are often aptly suited to defeat, the development of the truth.

We are unlikely ever to know how effectively the adversary technique would work toward truth if that were the objective of the contestants. Employed by interested parties, the process often achieves truth only as a convenience, a byproduct, or an accidental approximation. The business of the advocate, simply stated, is to win if possible without violating the law. (The phrase "if possible" is meant to modify what precedes it, but the danger of slippage is well known.) His is not the search for truth as such. To put that thought more exactly, the truth and victory are mutually incompatible for some considerable percentage of the attorneys trying cases at any given time.

* * *

IV. SOME PROPOSALS

Having argued that we are too much committed to contentiousness as a good in itself and too little devoted to truth, I proceed to some prescriptions of a general nature for remedying these flaws. Simply stated, these prescriptions are that we should:

(1) modify (not abandon) the adversary ideal,

(2) make truth a paramount objective, and

(3) impose upon the contestants a duty to pursue that objective.

A. *Modifying the Adversary Ideal*

We should begin, as a concerted professional task, to question the premise that adversariness is ultimately and invariably good. For most of us trained in American law, the superiority of the adversary process over any other is too plain to doubt or examine. The certainty is shared by people who are in other respects widely separated on the ideological spectrum. The august Code of Professional Responsibility, as has been mentioned, proclaims, in order, the "Duty of the Lawyer to a Client," then the "Duty of the Lawyer to the Adversary System of Justice." There is no announced "Duty to the Truth" or "Duty to the Community." Public interest lawyers, while they otherwise test the law's bounds, profess a basic commitment "to the adversary system itself" as the means of giving "everyone affected by corporate and bureaucratic decisions * * * a voice in those decisions * * *."[57] We may note similarly the earnest and idealistic scholar who brought the fury of the (not necessarily consistent) establishment upon himself when he wrote, reflecting upon experience as devoted defense counsel for poor people, that as an advocate you must (a) try to destroy a witness "whom you know to be telling the truth," (b) "put a witness on the stand when you know he will commit perjury," and (c) "give your client legal advice when you

---

57. Halpern & Cunningham, Reflections on the New Public Interest Law, 59 Geo. L.J. 1095, 1109 (1971).

have reason to believe that the knowledge you give him will tempt him to commit perjury." [58] The "policies" he found to justify these views, included, as the first and most fundamental, the maintenance of "an adversary system based upon the presupposition that the most effective means of determining truth is to present to a judge and jury a clash between proponents of conflicting views."

* * *

B. *Making Truth the Paramount Objective*

We should consider whether the paramount commitment of counsel concerning matters of fact should be to the discovery of truth rather than to the advancement of the client's interest. This topic heading contains for me the most debatable and the least thoroughly considered of the thoughts offered here. It is a brief suggestion for a revolution, but with no apparatus of doctrine or program.

We should face the fact that the quality of "hired gun" is close to the heart and substance of the litigating lawyer's role. As is true always of the mercenary warrior, the litigator has not won the highest esteem for his scars and his service. Apart from our image, we have had to reckon for ourselves in the dark hours with the knowledge that "selling" our stories rather than striving for the truth cannot always seem, because it is not, such noble work as befits the practitioner of a learned profession. The struggle to win, with its powerful pressures to subordinate the love of truth, is often only incidentally, or coincidentally, if at all, a service to the public interest.

We have been bemused through the ages by the hardy (and somewhat appealing) notion that we are to serve rather than judge the client. Among the implications of this theme is the idea that lawyers are not to place themselves above others and that the client must be equipped to decide for himself whether or not he will follow the path of truth and justice. This means quite specifically, whether in Anatomy of a Murder[66] or in Dean Freedman's altruistic sense of commitment,[67] that the client must be armed for effective perjury as well as he would be if he were himself legally trained. To offer anything less is arrogant, elitist, and undemocratic.

---

58. Freedman, Professional Responsibility of the Criminal Defense Lawyer: The Three Hardest Questions, 64 Mich.L.Rev. 1469 (1966).

66. R. Traver, Anatomy of a Murder (1958). For those who did not read or have forgotten it, the novel, by a state supreme court justice, involved an eventually successful homicide defense of impaired mental capacity with the defendant supplying the requisite "facts" after having been told in advance by counsel what type of facts would constitute the defense.

67. See text accompanying note 58, supra. In M. Freedman, Lawyers' Ethics in an Adversary System, ch. 6, Dean Freedman reports a changed view on this last of his "three hardest questions." He would under some circumstances (including the case in Anatomy of a Murder) condemn the lawyer's supplying of the legal knowledge to promote perjury. Exploring whether the Dean's new position is workable would transcend even the wide leeway I arrogate in footnotes.

It is impossible to guess closely how prevalent this view may be as a practical matter. Nor am I clear to what degree, if any, received canons of legal ethics give it sanction. My submission is in any case that it is a crass and pernicious idea, unworthy of a public profession. It is true that legal training is a source of power, for evil as well as good, and that a wicked lawyer is capable of specially skilled wrongdoing. It is likewise true that a physician or pharmacist knows homicidal devices hidden from the rest of us. Our goals must include means for limiting the numbers of crooked and malevolent people trained in the vital professions. We may be certain, notwithstanding our best efforts, that some lawyers and judges will abuse their trust. But this is no reason to encourage or facilitate wrongdoing by everyone.

Professional standards that placed truth above the client's interests would raise more perplexing questions. The privilege for client's confidences might come in for reexamination and possible modification. We have all been trained to know without question that the privilege is indispensable for effective representation. The client must know his confidences are safe so that he can tell all and thus have fully knowledgeable advice. We may want to ask, nevertheless, whether it would be an excessive price for the client to be struck with the truth rather than having counsel allied with him for concealment and distortion. The full development of this thought is beyond my studies to date. Its implications may be unacceptable. I urge only that it is among the premises in need of examination.

If the lawyer is to be more truth-seeker than combatant, troublesome questions of economics and professional organization may demand early confrontation. How and why should the client pay for loyalties divided between himself and the truth? Will we not stultify the energies and resources of the advocate by demanding that he judge the honesty of his cause along the way? Can we preserve the heroic lawyer shielding his client against all the world—and not least against the State—while demanding that he honor a paramount commitment to the elusive and ambiguous truth? It is strongly arguable, in short, that a simplistic preference for the truth may not comport with more fundamental ideals—including notably the ideal that generally values individual freedom and dignity above order and efficiency in government.[68] Having stated such issues too broadly, I leave them in the hope that their refinement and study may seem worthy endeavors for the future.

C. *A Duty to Pursue the Truth*

The rules of professional responsibility should compel disclosures of material facts and forbid material omissions rather than merely pro-

68. Two previous Cardozo Lecturers have been among the line of careful thinkers cautioning against too single-minded a concern for truth. "While our adversary system of litigation may not prove to be the best means of ascertaining truth, its emphasis upon respect for human dignity at every step is not to be undermined lightly in a democratic state." Botein, The Future of the Judicial Process, 15 Record of N.Y.C.B.A. 152, 166 (1960). See also Shawcross, The Functions and Responsibilities of an Advocate. 13 Record of N.Y.C.B.A. 483, 498, 500 (1958).

scribe positive frauds. This final suggestion is meant to implement the broad and general proposition that precedes it. In an effort to be still more specific, I submit a draft of a new disciplinary rule that would supplement or in large measure displace existing disciplinary rule 7–102 of the Code of Professional Responsibility. The draft says:

(1) In his representation of a client, unless prevented from doing so by a privilege reasonably believed to apply, a lawyer shall:

(a) Report to the court and opposing counsel the existence of relevant evidence or witnesses where the lawyer does not intend to offer such evidence or witnesses.

(b) Prevent, or when prevention has proved unsuccessful, report to the court and opposing counsel the making of any untrue statement by client or witness or any omission to state a material fact necessary in order to make statements made, in the light of the circumstances under which they were made, not misleading.

(c) Question witnesses with a purpose and design to elicit the whole truth, including particularly supplementary and qualifying matters that render evidence already given more accurate, intelligible, or fair than it otherwise would be.

(2) In the construction and application of the rules in subdivision (1), a lawyer will be held to possess knowledge he actually has or, in the exercise of reasonable diligence, should have.

Key words in the draft, namely, in (1)(b), have been plagiarized, of course, from the Securities and Exchange Commission's rule 10b–5.[70] That should serve not only for respectability; it should also answer, at least to some extent, the complaint that the draft would impose impossibly stringent standards. The morals we have evolved for business clients cannot be deemed unattainable by the legal profession.

* * *

* * * A bar too tightly regulated, too conformist, too "governmental," is not acceptable to any of us. We speak often of lawyers as "officers of the court" and as "public" people. Yet our basic conception of the office is of one essentially private—private in political, economic, and ideological terms—congruent with a system of private ownership, enterprise, and competition, however modified the system has come to be. It is not necessary to recount here the contributions of a legal profession thus conceived to the creation and maintenance of a relatively free society. It *is* necessary to acknowledge those contributions and to consider squarely whether, or how much, they are endangered by proposed reforms.

70. 17 C.F.R. § 240.10b–5 (1974).

If we must choose between truth and liberty, the decision is not in doubt. If the choice seemed to me that clear and that stark, this essay would never have reached even the tentative form of its present submission. But I think the picture is quite unclear. I lean to the view that we can hope to preserve the benefits of a free, skeptical, contentious bar while paying a lesser price in trickery and obfuscation.

MONROE H. FREEDMAN,* JUDGE FRANKEL'S SEARCH FOR TRUTH
123 U.Pa.L.Rev. 1060 (1975).

The theme of Judge Marvin E. Frankel's Cardozo Lecture is that the adversary system rates truth too low among the values that institutions of justice are meant to serve. Accordingly, Judge Frankel takes up the challenging task of proposing how that system might be modified to raise the truth-seeking function to its rightful status in our hierarchy of values. His proposals, delivered with characteristic intellect, grace, and wit, are radical and, I believe, radically wrong.

Judge Frankel directs his criticism at the adversary system itself and at the lawyer as committed adversary. Challenging the idea that the adversary system is the best method for determining the truth, Judge Frankel asserts that "we know that others searching after facts— in history, geography, medicine, whatever—do not emulate our adversary system." I would question the accuracy of that proposition, at least in the breadth in which it is stated. Moreover, I think that to the extent that other disciplines do not follow a form of adversarial process, they suffer for it. * * * [T]he process of historical research and judgment on disputed issues of history is—indeed, must be—essentially adversarial. In medicine, of course, there is typically less partisanship than in historical research because there is less room for the play of political persuasion, and less room for personal interest and bias than in the typical automobile negligence case. Nevertheless, anyone about to make an important medical decision for oneself or one's family would be well advised to get a second opinion. And if the first opinion has come from a doctor who is generally inclined to perform radical surgery, the second opinion might well be solicited from a doctor who is generally skeptical about the desirability of surgery. According to one study, about nineteen percent of surgical operations are unnecessary. A bit more adversariness in the decisionmaking process might well have saved a gall bladder here or a uterus there. * * *

* * *

For my own part, I think it is essential that any evaluation of the truth-seeking function of a trial be done in the context of our system of

* Professor of Law, Hofstra University.

criminal justice[13] and, indeed, the nature of our society and form of government. We might begin, by way of contrast, with an understanding of the role of a criminal defense attorney in a totalitarian state. As expressed by law professors at the University of Havana, "the first job of a revolutionary lawyer is not to argue that his client is innocent, but rather to determine if his client is guilty and, if so, to seek the sanction which will best rehabilitate him." Similarly, a Bulgarian attorney began his defense in a treason trial by noting, "In a Socialist state there is no division of duty between the judge, prosecutor, and defense counsel. * * * The defense must assist the prosecution to find the objective truth in a case." In that case, the defense attorney ridiculed his client's defense, and the client was convicted and executed. Some time later the verdict was found to have been erroneous, and the defendant was "rehabilitated."

The emphasis in a free society is, of course, sharply different. Under our adversary system, the interests of the state are not absolute, or even paramount. The dignity of the individual is respected to the point that even when the citizen is known by the state to have committed a heinous offense, the individual is nevertheless accorded such rights as counsel, trial by jury, due process, and the privilege against self-incrimination. A trial is, in part, a search for truth; accordingly, those basic rights are most often characterized as procedural safeguards against error in the search for truth. We are concerned, however, with far more than a search for truth, and the constitutional rights that are provided by our system of justice serve independent values that may well outweigh the truth-seeking value, a fact made manifest when we realize that those rights, far from furthering the search for truth, may well impede it. What more effective way is there to expose a defendant's guilt than to require self-incrimination, at least to the extent of compelling the defendant to take the stand and respond to interrogation before the jury? The defendant, however, is presumed innocent, the burden is on the prosecution to prove guilt beyond a reasonable doubt, and even the guilty accused has an "absolute constitutional right to remain silent" and to put the government to its proof.

Thus, the defense lawyer's professional obligation may well be to advise the client to withhold the truth: "[A]ny lawyer worth his salt will tell the suspect in no uncertain terms to make no statement to police under any circumstances." Similarly, the defense lawyer is obligated to prevent the introduction of some evidence that may be wholly reliable, such as a murder weapon seized in violation of the fourth amendment or a truthful but involuntary confession. Justice White has observed that although law enforcement officials must be dedicated to "the ascertainment of the true facts * * * defense counsel has no comparable obligation to ascertain or present the truth. Our system assigns him a different mission. * * * [W]e * * * insist that he defend his client

---

13. Judge Frankel makes no apparent distinction in his article between criminal and civil cases, and several references in the article indicate clearly that his modifications of the system are intended to reach criminal as well as civil trials.

whether he is innocent or guilty." Such conduct by defense counsel does not constitute obstruction of justice. On the contrary, "as part of the duty imposed on the most honorable defense counsel, we countenance or require conduct which in many instances has little, if any, relation to the search for truth." Indeed, Justice Harlan noted that "the lawyer in fulfilling his professional responsibilities of necessity may become an obstacle to truthfinding," and Chief Justice Warren has recognized that when the criminal defense attorney successfully obstructs efforts by the government to elicit truthful evidence in ways that violate constitutional rights, the attorney is "exercising * * * good professional judgment. * * * He is merely carrying out what he is sworn to do under his oath— to protect to the extent of his ability the rights of his client. In fulfilling this responsibility the attorney plays a vital role in the administration of criminal justice under our Constitution."

    * * * By emphasizing that the adversary process has its foundations in respect for human dignity, I do not mean to deprecate the search for truth or to suggest that the adversary system is not concerned with it. On the contrary, truth is a basic value and the adversary system is one of the most efficient and fair methods designed for finding it. * * * Nevertheless, the point that I now emphasize is that in a society that respects the dignity of the individual, truth-seeking cannot be an absolute value, but may be subordinated to other ends, although that subordination may sometimes result in the distortion of the truth.

PROBLEM 26

Handling Physical Evidence

    Neil Hammer, a person whom you have never advised before, has come into your office, set a gun and a bag of money on your desk, and said, "I have just used this gun to rob a bank, and I killed a guard in the process. Help me; I don't want to get caught. What should I do?"

    Only yesterday, J.B. Wallace, president of the Wallace Corporation, came into your office. The Wall Street Journal had reported that the Justice Department is investigating a firm in Wallace's industry for possible price-fixing. A Wall Street Journal reporter had asked for an interview with Mr. Wallace about industry pricing practices and Mr. Wallace asked you to help him prepare for the interview. He told you that in order to help you evaluate any allegation involving him and price-fixing, you could listen to the secret tape recordings of all discussions in his office for the last three years. He keeps these tapes at his home and plans to use them to help write his memoirs. You have learned that the Department is about to file a criminal antitrust action against the corporation and perhaps Mr. Wallace personally.

QUESTIONS

1. May you take Hammer's gun for safekeeping?

a. Is the gun privileged from discovery if it is in the possession of the attorney? How does In re Ryder, in the Readings to this Problem, answer this question?

b. Compare State v. Olwell, 64 Wn.2d 828, 394 P.2d 681 (1964). Olwell was a lawyer who refused to honor a coroner's subpoena for the knife allegedly used in a murder by his client. He asserted both the attorney-client privilege and the client's privilege against self-incrimination. He was found in contempt and appealed. The court held:

> "The attorney should not be a depository for criminal evidence (such as a knife, other weapons, stolen property, etc.), which in itself has little, if any material value for the purposes of aiding counsel in the preparation of the defense of his client's case. Such evidence given the attorney during legal consultation for information purposes and used by the attorney in preparing the defense of his client's case, whether or not the case ever goes to trial, could clearly be withheld for a reasonable period of time. It follows that the attorney, after a reasonable period of time, should, as an officer of the court, on his own motion turn the same over to the prosecution.

> " * * * [T]he state [in order to protect the attorney-client privilege], when attempting to introduce such evidence at the trial, should take extreme precautions to make certain that the source of the evidence is not disclosed in the presence of the jury and prejudicial error is not committed." 394 P.2d at 684–85.

The court also found the self-incrimination privilege inapplicable because it must be asserted by the client alone. Is the decision consistent with *Ryder*? Does the procedure suggested by the court protect all the relevant interests?

c. Is your answer the same with respect to the bag of money? After all, the money belongs to the bank while the gun presumably belongs to Hammer. Consider In re January 1976 Grand Jury, 534 F.2d 719 (7th Cir.1976). The attorney refused to comply with a grand jury's subpoena duces tecum to turn over moneys received by him from clients suspected of bank robbery. The Court of Appeals affirmed the contempt order, and Judge Tone, joined by Judge Bauer, argued:

> "We must assume for purposes of this appeal that shortly after robbing a savings and loan association, the robbers delivered money stolen in the robbery to appellant. If that occurred, the money was delivered either for safekeeping, with or without appellant's knowledge that it was stolen, or as an attorney's fee.

"If it was the latter, the robbers voluntarily relinquished the money and with it any arguable claim that might have arisen from their possession or constructive possession. As Judge Pell points out, the payment of a fee is not a privileged communication. The money itself is non-testimonial and no plausible argument is left for resisting the subpoena.

"If the money was not given as a fee but for safekeeping, the delivery of the money was an act in furtherance of the crime, regardless of whether appellant knew it was stolen. The delivery of the money was not assertive conduct and therefore was not a privileged communication, and, as we just observed, the money itself is non-testimonial. The attorney is simply a witness to a criminal act. The fact that he is also a participant in the act, presumably without knowledge of its criminal quality, is irrelevant since he is not asserting his own privilege against self incrimination. There is no authority or reason, based on any constitutional provision or the attorney-client privilege, for shielding from judicial inquiry either the fruits of the robbery or the fact of the later criminal act of turning over the money to appellant. Accordingly, it is immaterial that in responding to the subpoena appellant will be making an assertion about who turned over the money and when.

"Finally, the proceedings have not yet reached the point at which we must decide whether, when the robbers have chosen to make appellant a witness to their crime, they may invoke the Sixth Amendment [right to effective assistance of counsel] to bar his eyewitness testimony at trial, although, for me, to ask that question is almost to answer it."

d. Morrell v. State, 575 P.2d 1200 (Alaska 1978), upheld the decision of the trial court to admit incriminating evidence of a kidnapping plan allegedly written by the defendant. The plan had been turned over to defense counsel by a friend of the defendant and defense counsel had then aided the friend in turning the evidence over to the police. Defense counsel thereupon withdrew from the case. After examining the cases discussed in the text the Alaska supreme court held at 575 P.2d at 1210–12:

"From the foregoing cases emerges the rule that a criminal defense attorney must turn over to the prosecution real evidence that the attorney obtains from his client. Further, if the evidence is obtained from a non-client third party who is not acting for the client, then the privilege to refuse to testify concerning the manner in which the evidence was obtained is inapplicable. * * *

* * *

"We believe that [defense counsel] would have been obligated to see that the evidence reached the prosecutor in this case even if he had obtained the evidence from Morrell. His obligation was even clearer because he acquired the evidence from [a third party], who made the decision to turn the evidence over to [defense counsel] without consulting Morrell and therefore was not acting as Morrell's agent.

"[Defense counsel] could have properly turned the evidence over to the police himself and would have been obliged to do so if [the third party] had refused to accept the return of the evidence.

"[Finally, while] statutes which address the concealing of evidence are generally construed to require an affirmative act of concealment in addition to the failure to disclose information to the authorities, taking possession of evidence from a non-client third party and holding the evidence in a place not accessible to investigating authorities would seem to fall within the statute's ambit. Thus, we have concluded that Cline breached no ethical obligation to his client which may have rendered his legal services to Morrell ineffective."

Do the earlier cases in this Problem support the Court's conclusion? Do you agree that defense counsel should sometimes be required to turn over evidence or provide testimony that will help to convict their clients?

2. Must you hold in confidence whatever you know about the gun? Was the client's statement to the lawyer linking the gun to the crime a privileged communication?

a. Consider the analysis in People v. Meredith, 29 Cal.3d 682, 175 Cal.Rptr. 612, 631 P.2d 46 (1981). The defendant had told his lawyer the location of the robbery-murder victim's wallet. The lawyer then had his investigator remove it. The Court held that the client's disclosure was privileged and telling the investigator the location did not destroy the privilege. On the other hand, removing the wallet did destroy it. When defense counsel removes or alters evidence, he necessarily deprives the prosecution of the opportunity to observe that evidence in its original condition or location. The lawyer's decision to remove evidence is therefore tactical; if he leaves the evidence where he discovered it, his observations derived from privileged communications are insulated from revelation. If he removes the evidence to examine or test it, "the original location and condition of that evidence loses the protection of the privilege." [1]

b. If you liked the result in *Meredith*, you will particularly like Clutchette v. Rushen, 770 F.2d 1469 (9th Cir.1985), cert. denied 475 U.S. 1088, 106 S.Ct. 1474, 89 L.Ed.2d 729 (1986). There, the defendant was accused of shooting a man in his car. The police were having a hard time proving their case until the defendant's wife voluntarily turned

---

1. The same result was reached in People v. Nash, 418 Mich. 196, 341 N.W.2d 439,   446–51 (1983).

over some receipts to them. She had been acting as an investigator for her husband's defense lawyer, and the lawyer had sent her to Los Angeles to get (and arguably to destroy) the receipts that showed that her husband had had the car reupholstered shortly after the murder. With the help of the receipts, the police found the former seat covers and matched the blood type to the victim's. The court held that the wife's surrender of the receipts was not a violation of the defendant's attorney-client privilege. If the attorney had not done anything to retrieve the receipts, he would not have had to tell the police about them. Having taken the receipts into his possession, however, through the wife-investigator, they were fair game for police discovery. Further, because the police made no overt act to get the receipts, there was even less reason to find a deprivation of Sixth Amendment rights.

c. Thereafter, in People v. Superior Court (Fairbank), 192 Cal. App.3d 32, 237 Cal.Rptr. 158 (1987), the court held that if a lawyer takes possession of stolen property, the lawyer must inform the court of the action. "The court, exercising care to shield privileged communications and defense strategies from prosecution view, must then take appropriate action to ensure that the prosecution has timely access to physical evidence possessed by the defense and timely information about alteration of any evidence." Nothing turns on whether the prosecution "needs" the evidence.[2]

3. What should you do—or advise Hammer to do—with the gun that you now know is an instrument of a crime?

a. Dean v. Dean, 607 So.2d 494 (Fla.App.1992), presented the privilege issue sharply. The husband in a domestic dispute had been the victim of a burglary. A lawyer with no connection to the dispute got a call from a prospective client saying he wanted to return the stolen goods. The lawyer told him to bring the goods to him, which he did (except for $35,000 in cash) and the lawyer turned the goods over to the police. The husband's lawyer then wanted to know who the burglar was, i.e., apparently whether the burglar had been hired by the wife, and the lawyer claimed the privilege. The Court held that the caller was a "client" for purposes of the privilege, the call was about a past crime, and public policy favored encouraging people to return stolen goods. Thus, the lawyer was not ordered to disclose the burglar's identity.

Do you agree with this result?[3] In our Problem, what if Hammer's fingerprints were on the gun? Should you advise Hammer to wipe off the fingerprints? Should you do so just to be safe before you send the

2. See also Commonwealth v. Stenhach, 356 Pa.Super. 5, 514 A.2d 114 (1986), leave to appeal denied 517 Pa. 589, 534 A.2d 769 (1987) (court affirms duty to turn over physical evidence but reverses criminal conviction of lawyers for failure to do so).

3. The good faith of an attorney who advises his client to invoke the Fifth Amendment in response to a subpoena in a civil case protects the lawyer from being held in contempt. Maness v. Meyers, 419 U.S. 449, 468, 95 S.Ct. 584, 596, 42 L.Ed.2d 574, 589 (1975). Should the same principle apply here?

gun to the police? If you did so, would it constitute an obstruction of justice? [4]

b. In United States v. Morales–Martinez, 672 F.Supp. 762 (D.Vt. 1987), an immigration lawyer had gotten changes in his client's terms of release when he showed the Magistrate a passport and visa bearing the client's name. It later was shown that the documents were forged. The court held that the attorney could be forced to tell where he got the passport. The information was not privileged because the source of the passport could not have been the client, and any discussions with the client about use of the passport would have been part of a crime or fraud and thus would not have been privileged either. Are you persuaded by the Court's reasoning?

4. Where is the line between concealing information and simply not disclosing it? How would you have acted in the following case?

a. A highly publicized news story reported:

"An Onondaga County grand jury this afternoon [February 7, 1975] cleared a lawyer, Frank H. Armani, of criminal wrongdoing in failing to disclose that his client in a murder case had told him where he had hidden two bodies.

* * *

"Mr. [Francois] Belge and Mr. Armani were lawyers for Robert Garrow, who was found guilty of murder after a trial in Hamilton County last summer.

"During the trial Mr. Belge revealed that he and Mr. Armani had discovered the two bodies after having been told of their whereabouts by Mr. Garrow, but that they did not tell authorities.

* * *

"Mr. Armani's attorney, Elliot A. Taikoff of New York City, said later that his client had been 'very troubled' over his role in the matter and had received advice from a 'very high-ranking judge in this state.' He refused to name the judge, but said he had testified before the grand jury." [5]

Was the grand jury's decision consistent with that of the *Ryder* court? Were the situations in fact analytically different?

b. In considering this case, N.Y. State Bar Committee on Professional Ethics, Opinion No. 479 (Mar. 6, 1978), held that "the lawyer was under an injunction not to disclose to the authorities his knowledge of

4. You may want to take a look at the definition of obstruction of justice in Question 5(a), infra.

5. New York Times, Feb. 8, 1975, p. 54, col. 5. See also, People v. Belge, 83 Misc.2d

186, 372 N.Y.S.2d 798, 803 (Cty.Ct.1975) (indictment on same facts dismissed on "grounds of a privileged communication and in the interests of justice * * * ").

the two prior murders, and was duty-bound not to reveal to the authorities the location of the bodies." The attorney also acted properly by using the information, with his client's consent, in engaging in plea bargaining, and in destroying photographs the lawyer took of the bodies and records the lawyer made of his conversation with the client.

Could the attorney ethically have destroyed the photographs if they had been taken by his client? If they were being subpoenaed?

c. Now suppose that one of the young women was not yet dead. Under the auspices of the Roscoe Pound–American Trial Lawyers Foundation, a special Commission prepared its own proposal called The American Lawyer's Code of Conduct.[6] The first version of the American Lawyer's Code provided in its Rule 1.6: "A lawyer may reveal a client's confidence when and to the extent that the lawyer reasonably believes that divulgence is necessary to prevent imminent danger to human life. The lawyer shall use all reasonable means to protect the client's interests that are consistent with preventing loss of life."

However, the Commission did *not* approve that version of Rule 1.6. It presented the factual situation in which Mr. Belge and Mr. Armani found themselves, but went on to assume that one of the women was not yet dead. The Commission applied its proposed Code to the *new* hypothetical as follows:

> [S]he is seriously injured and unable to help herself or to get help. The lawyer calls an ambulance for her, but takes care not to be personally identified. The lawyer has *committed a disciplinary violation*, if supplemental Rule 1.6 is not adopted as part of the Code.[7]

Do you agree that loyalty to the client requires this result? How would the ABA Model Rules deal with the same problem? What do you think is the right way of dealing with it?

5. Turning to your second client, Mr. Wallace, may you properly counsel him to destroy the incriminating tape recordings? Does it matter whether or not suit has already been filed? [8]

a. It has been held that a party may be charged with a "conspiracy to obstruct the due administration of justice in a proceeding which [is not pending but which] becomes pending in the future. * * *"[9] In

---

6. The proposal was intended to compete with the ABA Model Rules. You will find it included in the Standards Supplement; it provides interesting contrast to the Model Rules on several issues, but no state has yet adopted it in even significant part.

7. The American Lawyer's Code of Conduct, Illustrative Case 1(g) (Revised Draft, 1982) (emphasis added).

8. As you recognize, there is an important question presented whether you represent the corporation as an entity, the president of the corporation, or both, and whether or not representing both the president and the corporation would be a conflict of interest. That might be relevant to some of your answers here, but it is not the focus of this question.

9. United States v. Perlstein, 126 F.2d 789, 796 (3d Cir.1942), cert. denied 316 U.S. 678, 62 S.Ct. 1106, 86 L.Ed. 1752 (1942); see, also, e.g., In re Williams, 221

general, it is an obstruction of justice "to stifle, suppress or destroy evidence knowing that it *may* be wanted in a judicial proceeding or is being sought by investigating officers. * * * " [10] How should that construction of the law affect the lawyer's ethical responsibilities in a case like this?

  b. Assume that the Justice Department is not yet involved but that Mr. Wallace is afraid the Wall Street Journal reporter may come across information that indicates the secret taping device has been set up in the office. May you advise the president to destroy the tapes, using as your reason the embarrassment that would be caused if his business associates knew he had secretly taped and retained tapes of private conversations? [11] Compare DR 7–102(A)(3), EC 7–27 and Rule 3.4(a).

  c. After Mr. Wallace has told you of his taping system and you have listened to the relevant conversations, should you tell Mr. Wallace that the tapes are damaging and are likely to be subpoenaed by the government? May you tell Wallace this bad news if you privately expect him to destroy the incriminating material which has not yet been subpoenaed? Can you do anything about that? How does Rule 3.4(a) require you to act?

  d. To prevent Wallace from destroying the evidence, may you refuse to tell him that the material in the files is damaging? May you refuse to return the materials to him if you believe that he will then destroy them? Would you do this to protect Mr. Wallace? Would you do it to protect yourself?

  e. May you tell Mr. Wallace that if he destroys the tapes, he may well be involved in an obstruction of justice but that the next time he engages in a routine, regular housecleaning of the files he ought to destroy these tapes and any transcripts of them? Should the rule be that a client must keep all *incriminating* material even though businesses routinely dispose of countless other documents every day?

Minn. 554, 563–64, 23 N.W.2d 4, 9 (1946) (per curiam).

 10. R. Perkins, Criminal Law 499 (2d ed.1969) (emphasis added).

 11. Cf. Wall Street J., Apr. 7, 1975, at 7, col. 1–2 ("Official at ITT Unit Destroyed Letters After Journal Questioned Some Practices"):

"A retired official of International Telephone & Telegraph Corp. subsidiary disclosed in testimony before a Senate subcommittee that last summer, while he was still with the company, he destroyed certain letters in his file after the Wall Street Journal began questioning the unit's competitive practices.

" 'I was scared,' John James told the Senate subcommittee on Antitrust and Monopoly, which is investigating the effectiveness of voluntary industry standards. 'I have been associated with code and standard-making activities for many years, and this was the first time in all of that experience that I had anybody question the propriety of the way I conducted myself in connection with this type of work,' he said.

* * *

"After reviewing the testimony, an arm of the [American Society of Mechanical Engineers] came up with a conclusion that appears in the current issue of Mechanical Engineering. It commends Mr. James on this testimony and says the society's Professional Practice Committee 'finds no improper or unethical conduct in his action.' "

Would this conclusion have been the same if a lawyer had been the one who destroyed the letters?

f. Consider the following viewpoints of various lawyers, all discussed in K. Mann, Defending White Collar Crime (1985):

One lawyer:

> "My job is to keep the client out of jail. Some of my clients have ended up in jail not because of the crime for which they were being investigated, but because they lied, or burned documents, or altered them in the course of the investigation. So I tell them right off the bat that if they want to stay out of jail, let me know what's there, and keep hands off." (p. 121).

Another lawyer:

> "There are many cases in which one would surmise that documents summoned from the client existed at the time the summons was issued. My function in this procedure is a very limited one. I, of course, do not want the client convicted of [an] obstruction of justice charge, and I do warn him of the dire consequences of such a happening. But in the end it is the client's choice. I have no doubt that clients destroy documents. Have I ever known of such an occurrence? No. But you put two and two together. You couldn't convict anyone on such circumstantial evidence, but you can draw your own conclusion." (p. 110).

Yet another lawyer:

> "The person faced with the tragedy of a criminal prosecution should not be told by an attorney how to handle the evidence that can lead to a conviction. As long as the attorney does not involve himself directly, it is the client's choice." (Id.)

Which of this positions comes closest to your own?

6. Is a client's identity something that should be treated as confidential?

a. Would you expect it to be confidential in most cases? After all, if lawyers went around not telling courts and other lawyers whom they represented, the lawyers could get little done for the clients. As a result, the traditional rule has been that no privilege attaches to the fact that someone has consulted a lawyer or to the general subject of the representation.

b. On the other hand, might there be some situations in which the fact one had consulted a lawyer could itself be incriminating or embarrassing? Suppose you are a divorce lawyer. During an Internal Revenue Service audit of your tax records, for example, the investigator discovers a $25,000 cash deposit that you made into your client trust account marked "retainer". The client has not yet told his wife he is considering divorce. If the investigator asks you whose money it is, may you reply without asking the client's permission to do so? On similar facts, Baird v. Koerner, 279 F.2d 623 (9th Cir.1960), held that the attorney-client privilege can protect the client's identity against disclosure.

c.   In criminal cases, the *Baird* rule has come to be called in some cases the "last link" doctrine.   The courts have reasoned that if the fact of consultation would itself be sufficient to tie the client to a crime, the lawyer should not have to disclose the client's identity.   See, e.g., Matter of Grand Jury Proceeding, Cherney, 898 F.2d 565 (7th Cir.1990);   In re Grand Jury Proceedings 88–9(MIA), 899 F.2d 1039 (11th Cir.1990).[12]

d.   Baltes v. Doe I, 57 U.S.L.W. 2268 (Fla.Cir.Ct.1988) (No. CL–88–1145–AD), was a celebrated case in which a client told a lawyer that he had been the driver in a highly-publicized hit-and-run accident.   Without disclosing the client's identity, the lawyer tried to plea bargain on his behalf.   The victim's survivors filed a civil action against the unknown driver and tried to compel the lawyer to disclose his identity.   The trial court held that, under these circumstances, the client's identity was privileged.   The client ultimately turned himself in before the appeal was heard.

e.   Matter of Nackson, 114 N.J. 527, 555 A.2d 1101 (1989), considered whether an attorney may refuse to disclose the whereabouts of a client who jumped bail and consulted the lawyer about a fugitive warrant for his arrest.   The client wanted to return to the jurisdiction only if a plea agreement could be worked out in advance.   Citing *Baltes,* above, the court held that the privilege can protect against disclosure of client whereabouts, matrimonial cases being a common example.   The privilege is not absolute, the court said, but prosecutors must first use all other reasonable ways of learning the defendant's whereabouts.   Even then, before ordering disclosure, the lower court must balance the need to know against the client's right to confidentiality.

f.   Suppose you refuse to disclose the client's identity to the investigator and the IRS, in turn, asserts a claim against you for back taxes on the $25,000, asserting that it is unreported income.   Are you still obligated not to disclose the name of the client?   Must you go to jail before revealing the client's identity?   Compare Model Rule 1.6(b)(2) with DR 4–101(C)(4).   Do these rules adopt the position of two judges in People v. Kor, 129 Cal.App.2d 436, 447, 277 P.2d 94, 101 (1954), who stated that the attorney, rather than having testified, "should have chosen to go to jail and take his chances of release by a higher court"?   Is such self-sacrifice realistic?

g.   A new requirement, 26 U.S.C.A. § 60501, adopted as part of the war on drugs, requires cash transactions in excess of $10,000 to be reported to the Internal Revenue Service on its Form 8300.   On its face, the requirement applies to everyone, but lawyers have argued that

---

12.   See also, American Law Institute, Restatement of the Law (Third), The Law Governing Lawyers, § 119, Comment *g* (Tent.Draft No. 2, 1989): privileged character of client identity "cannot be dealt with categorically, but should be determined based on the extent to which the testimony or other information sought would result in revealing the content of a privileged communication."

transactions with them should be exempt from the requirement. So far, the I.R.S. considers lawyers subject to the law, but criminal defense lawyers complain that reporting will render Baird v. Koerner a nullity.

What do you think? One can argue that the reporting is "required by law" and thus, under DR 4–101(C)(2), that reporting presents no ethical problem. Is it that easy under Model Rule 1.6? Indeed, might this be the kind of case in which a lawyer should be obliged to assert the privilege no matter what the Model Rules and Model Code seem to permit as to disclosure?

READINGS

IN RE RICHARD R. RYDER

United States District Court, Eastern District of Virginia, 1967.
263 F.Supp. 360, aff'd per curiam 381 F.2d 713 (4th Cir.1967).

Before HOFFMAN, Chief Judge, and LEWIS and BUTZNER, Judges.

MEMORANDUM

PER CURIAM. This proceeding was instituted to determine whether Richard R. Ryder should be removed from the roll of attorneys qualified to practice before this court. Ryder was admitted to this bar in 1953. He formerly served five years as an Assistant United States Attorney. He has an active trial practice, including both civil and criminal cases.

* * * Ryder took possession of stolen money and a sawed-off shotgun, knowing that the money had been stolen and that the gun had been used in an armed robbery. He intended to retain this property pending his client's trial unless the government discovered it. He intended by his possession to destroy the chain of evidence that linked the contraband to his client and to prevent its use to establish his client's guilt.

On August 24, 1966 a man armed with a sawed-off shotgun robbed the Varina Branch of the Bank of Virginia of $7,583. Included in the currency taken were $10 bills known as "bait money," the serial numbers of which had been recorded.

On August 26, 1966 Charles Richard Cook rented safety deposit box 14 at a branch of the Richmond National Bank. Later in the day Cook was interviewed at his home by agents of the Federal Bureau of Investigation, who obtained $348 from him. Cook telephoned Ryder, who had represented him in civil litigation. Ryder came to the house and advised the agents that he represented Cook. He said that if Cook were not to be placed under arrest, he intended to take him to his office for an interview. The agents left. Cook insisted to Ryder that he had not robbed the bank. He told Ryder that he had won the money, which the agents had taken from him, in a crap game. At this time Ryder believed Cook.

Later that afternoon Ryder telephoned one of the agents and asked whether any of the bills obtained from Cook had been identified as a part of the money taken in the bank robbery. The agent told him that some bills had been identified. Ryder made inquiries about the number of bills taken and their denominations. The agent declined to give him specific information but indicated that several of the bills were recorded as bait money.

The next morning, Saturday, August 27, 1966, Ryder conferred with Cook again. He urged Cook to tell the truth, and Cook answered that a man, whose name he would not divulge, offered him $500 on the day of the robbery to put a package in a bank lockbox. Ryder did not believe this story. Ryder told Cook that if the government could trace the money in the box to him, it would be almost conclusive evidence of his guilt. He knew that Cook was under surveillance and he suspected that Cook might try to dispose of the money.

That afternoon Ryder telephoned a former officer of the Richmond Bar Association to discuss his course of action. He had known this attorney for many years and respected his judgment. The lawyer was at home and had no library available to him when Ryder telephoned. In their casual conversation Ryder told what he knew about the case, omitting names. * * *

The lawyers discussed and rejected alternatives, including having a third party get the money. At the conclusion of the conversation Ryder was advised "Don't do it surreptitiously and to be sure that you let your client know that it is going back to the rightful owners."

On Monday morning Ryder asked Cook to come by his office. He prepared a power of attorney, which Cook signed * * *.

Ryder did not follow the advice he had received on Saturday. He did not let his client know the money was going back to the rightful owners. He testified about his omission:

> "I prepared it myself and told Mr. Cook to sign it. In the power of attorney, I did not specifically say that Mr. Cook authorized me to deliver that money to the appropriate authorities at any time because for a number of reasons. One, in representing a man under these circumstances, you've got to keep the man's confidence, but I also put in that power of attorney that Mr. Cook authorized me to dispose of that money as I saw fit, and the reason for that being that I was going to turn the money over to the proper authorities at whatever time I deemed that it wouldn't hurt Mr. Cook."

Ryder took the power of attorney which Cook had signed to the Richmond National Bank. He rented box 13 in his name with his office address, presented the power of attorney, entered Cook's box, took both boxes into a booth, where he found a bag of money and a sawed-off shotgun in Cook's box. The box also contained miscellaneous items which are not pertinent to this proceeding. He transferred the contents of Cook's box to his own and returned the boxes to the vault. He left the bank, and neither he nor Cook returned.

Ryder testified that he had some slight hesitation about the propriety of what he was doing. Within a half-hour after he left the bank, he talked to a retired judge and distinguished professor of law. He told this person that he wanted to discuss something in confidence. Ryder then stated that he represented a man suspected of bank robbery. * * *

Ryder testified that he told about the shotgun. The judge also testified that Ryder certainly would not have been under the impression that he—the judge—thought that [Ryder] was guilty of unethical conduct.

The same day Ryder also talked with other prominent persons in Richmond—a judge of a court of record and an attorney for the Commonwealth. Again, he stated that what he intended to say was confidential. He related the circumstances and was advised that a lawyer could not receive the property and if he had received it he could not retain possession of it.

On September 7, 1966 Cook was indicted for robbing the Varina Branch of the Bank of Virginia. A bench warrant was issued and the next day Ryder represented Cook at a bond hearing. * * *

On September 12, 1966, F.B.I. agents procured search warrants for Cook's and Ryder's safety deposit boxes in the Richmond National Bank. They found Cook's box empty. In Ryder's box they discovered $5,920 of the $7,583 taken in the bank robbery and the sawed-off shotgun used in the robbery.

[On October 6, when a motion by Ryder was heard, the] court called to Ryder's attention papers pertaining to the search of the safety deposit boxes. Ryder moved for a continuance, stating that he intended to file a motion with respect to the seizure of the contents of the lockbox.

On October 14, 1966 the three judges of this court removed Ryder as an attorney for Cook; suspended him from practice before the court until further order; referred the matter to the United States Attorney, who was requested to file charges within five days; set the matter for hearing November 11, 1966; and granted Ryder leave to move for vacation or modification of its order pending hearing.

* * *

At the outset, we reject the suggestion that Ryder did not know the money which he transferred from Cook's box to his was stolen. We find that on August 29 when Ryder opened Cook's box and saw a bag of money and a sawed-off shotgun, he then knew Cook was involved in the bank robbery and that the money was stolen. The evidence clearly establishes this. Ryder knew that the man who had robbed the bank used a sawed-off shotgun. He disbelieved Cook's story about the source of the money in the lockbox. He knew that some of the bills in Cook's possession were bait money.

* * *

We reject the argument that Ryder's conduct was no more than the exercise of the attorney-client privilege.

* * *

It was Ryder, not his client, who took the initiative in transferring the incriminating possession of the stolen money and the shotgun from Cook. Ryder's conduct went far beyond the receipt and retention of a confidential communication from his client. Counsel for Ryder conceded, at the time of argument, that the acts of Ryder were not within the attorney-client privilege.

* * *

We conclude that Ryder violated Canons 15 and 32 [of the ABA Canons of Ethics of 1908, as adopted and amended in Virginia]. His conduct is not sanctioned by Canons 5 or 37. * * *

The money in Cook's box belonged to the Bank of Virginia. The law did not authorize Cook to conceal this money or withhold it from the bank. His larceny was a continuing offense. Cook had no title or property interest in the money that he lawfully could pass to Ryder. * * * No canon of ethics or law permitted to Ryder to conceal from the Bank of Virginia its money to gain his client's acquittal.

Cook's possession of the sawed-off shotgun was illegal. 26 U.S.C. § 5851. Ryder could not lawfully receive the gun from Cook to assist Cook to avoid conviction of robbery. Cook had never mentioned the shotgun to Ryder. When Ryder discovered it in Cook's box, he took possession of it to hinder the government in the prosecution of its case, and he intended not to reveal it pending trial unless the government discovered it and a court compelled its production. No statute or canon of ethics authorized Ryder to take possession of the gun for this purpose.

* * *

In helping Cook to conceal the shotgun and stolen money, Ryder acted without the bounds of law. He allowed the office of attorney to be used in violation of law. The scheme which he devised was a deceptive, legalistic subterfuge—rightfully denounced by the canon as chicane.

Ryder also violated Canon 32. He rendered Cook a service involving deception and disloyalty to the law. He intended that his actions should remove from Cook exclusive possession of stolen money, and thus destroy an evidentiary presumption. His service in taking possession of the shotgun and money, with the intention of retaining them until after the trial, unless discovered by the government, merits the "stern and just condemnation" the canon prescribes.

Ryder's testimony that he intended to have the court rule on the admissibility of the evidence and the extent of the lawyer-client privilege does not afford justification for his action. He intended to do this only if the government discovered the shotgun and stolen money in his lockbox. If the government did not discover it, he had no intention of submitting any legal question about it to the court. If there were no discovery, he would continue to conceal the shotgun and money for Cook's benefit pending trial.

Ryder's action is not justified because he thought he was acting in the best interests of his client. To allow the individual lawyer's belief to determine the standards of professional conduct will in time reduce the ethics of the profession to the practices of the most unscrupulous. Moreover, Ryder knew that the law against concealing stolen property and the law forbidding receipt and possession of a sawed-off shotgun contain no exemptions for a lawyer who takes possession with the intent of protecting a criminal from the consequences of his crime.   * * *

We find it difficult to accept the argument that Ryder's action is excusable because if the government found Cook's box, Ryder's would easily be found, and if the government failed to find both Cook's and Ryder's boxes, no more harm would be done than if the agents failed to find only Cook's. Cook's concealment of the items in his box cannot be cited to excuse Ryder. Cook's conduct is not the measure of Ryder's ethics. The conduct of a lawyer should be above reproach. Concealment of the stolen money and the sawed-off shotgun to secure Cook's acquittal was wrong whether the property was in Cook's or Ryder's possession.

There is much to be said, however, for mitigation of the discipline to be imposed. Ryder intended to return the bank's money after his client was tried. He consulted reputable persons before and after he placed the property in his lockbox, although he did not precisely follow their advice. Were it not for these facts, we would deem proper his permanent exclusion from practice before this court. In view of the mitigating circumstances, he will be suspended from practice in this court for eighteen months * * *.

PROBLEM 27

The Client Who Intends to Commit Perjury

William Smith is a defendant in a robbery prosecution. Smith is also one of the many criminal defendants represented by M. Maynard Hawley. Smith said to Hawley that he would like to be called as a witness in order to present an alibi defense. After Hawley reminded him that he had never mentioned an alibi defense before, Smith said that his girl friend had agreed now to lie for him and testify that he was at her house at the time of the robbery. Smith told Hawley that he would like to take the stand to confirm his girl friend's story.

Hawley told Smith, "I cannot be a party to any perjurious testimony." Smith retorted: "I have a right to take the stand and testify," but Hawley was reluctant to let Smith do so. Smith assured Hawley: "The last thing I would want you to do is to be unethical. Put me on the stand; I will have to tell the truth."

Hawley put Smith on the stand. Contrary to Smith's earlier pledge, he lied.

QUESTIONS

1. If Hawley "knows" that Smith will commit perjury, what should he do?

a. Does an attorney ever "know" that a witness will commit perjury? When the Code talks about "knowing" something, does it mean "know pragmatically" or "know absolutely"? You may remember that related questions were presented by the lawyer's duty to report another lawyer's "known" misconduct considered in Problem 3.

b. In preparing Smith's testimony, if Smith tells Hawley a story that appears untruthful, may Hawley explain to him the weaknesses that the prosecutor would see in his story? If Smith then revises his story to eliminate these weaknesses, may Hawley counsel him as to whether the new story is more plausible? May Hawley advise him that the new story would be even more plausible if Smith would change it slightly again? Would Hawley in effect be advising his client as to the best method of committing perjury?

2. May the lawyer simply refuse to call Smith's girl friend, whom he knows will commit perjury?

a. The general rule is clear: Lawyers have a duty not to suborn perjury and the sanctions for ignoring the rule are severe.

In Louisiana State Bar Association v. Thierry, 366 So.2d 1305 (La.1978), a grand jury indicted Thierry (a lawyer) for having Henry Joshua testify falsely as an alibi witness for Thierry's client in a robbery prosecution. Thierry was found guilty of suborning the perjury of Joshua and sentenced to three years. Thierry's main defense "appears to be that in his enthusiasm he acted zealously in the interest of his client as well as out of naivete or ignorance * * *." He argued that "a more experienced lawyer would perhaps have considered the impropriety of his conduct and 'have seen [it] as a stop sign,' but respondent demonstrated a 'lack of caution.'" The state Supreme Court ordered Thierry disbarred. "So basic to the criminal justice system of this country is the sanctity of the oath of witnesses and the integrity of lawyers that these principles cannot be unknown to or violated by, the least learned or experienced in the profession of law."

In re Friedman, 76 Ill.2d 392, 30 Ill.Dec. 288, 392 N.E.2d 1333 (1979), was a case where false testimony was introduced in the name of justice. The respondent, an attorney in the criminal division of the

Cook County State's Attorney office, learned that the defense lawyer solicited a police officer to commit perjury. The respondent instructed the officer to agree in order to apprehend the briber. After the officer testified falsely under oath that a witness was unavailable, the defense lawyer gave the officer $50, and the state indicted the defense lawyer for bribery. Although the assistant State's Attorney allowed the false testimony to be introduced solely for the purpose of developing evidence to be used in a subsequent prosecution, a disciplinary action was brought against him. Two of the justices found a violation of DR 7–102(A)(4), (6), & DR 7–109(B): "The integrity of the courtroom is so vital to the health of our legal system that no violation of that integrity, no matter what its motivation, can be condoned or ignored." These Justices refused to impose any sanctions, however, because respondent had acted without the guidance of settled opinion, and because of the belief of many lawyers that respondent's conduct in the circumstances of this case was proper. Two of the justices went further and found the respondent guilty of prejudicing the administration of justice. Two justices found that the respondent did not violate any ethical proscriptions at all. What do you think?

b.　Look at Model Rules 3.3(a)(4) and 3.3(c) and DR 7–102(A)(4). Do they totally end discussion of proper behavior in a problem such as this? Look at Professor Freedman's article in the Readings to this Problem. Do you agree with him? Compare Chief Justice Burger's analysis in Nix v. Whiteside, also in the Readings. Cf. DR 7–102(B)(2).

c.　Look at ABA Defense Function Standard 4–5.2(b) in the Standards Supplement. Does it help the analysis to define the question of what witnesses to call as "strategic and tactical" and thus within the "exclusive province" of the lawyer?

d.　People v. Schultheis, 638 P.2d 8 (Colo.1981), examined the procedures a lawyer should follow when confronted with a client who insists that the lawyer call an alibi witness who will testify perjuriously. The Court stated bluntly:

> "A lawyer who presents a witness knowing that the witness intends to commit perjury thereby engages in the subornation of perjury. We will not permit the truth-finding process to be deflected by the presentation of false evidence by an officer of the court. Therefore, we hold that a lawyer may not offer testimony of a witness which he knows is false, fraudulent, or perjured."

The court said further that if the lawyer cannot persuade the client to stop insisting that false testimony be offered, the lawyer should request permission to withdraw based on an irreconcilable conflict. This motion should not elaborate further. If the trial court denies the motion to withdraw, the lawyer must continue to represent the defendant but still not offer the false testimony of the witness. Because of the possibility of post conviction challenges the lawyer "should proceed with a request for a record out of the presence of the trial judge and the prosecutor if the court denies the motion to withdraw.''

e. In Tibbs v. United States, 628 A.2d 638 (D.C.App.1993), the defendant had been convicted of armed robbery. He said the victim had identified the wrong man. At his first trial (which ended in a hung jury), his wife had provided him with an alibi. At the second trial, his lawyer did not call her; the wife had told the lawyer before the second trial that she would not testify because ''her testimony [at the first trial] was not true and [the defendant] knew this.'' The defendant said that the failure to call her was ineffective assistance of counsel, but the Court held that a lawyer may not call a witness who would testify falsely and thus that ''as a matter of law'' the failure to do so cannot be ineffective assistance.

f. United States v. Shaffer Equipment Co., 11 F.3d 450 (4th Cir. 1993), was interesting because a government witness was the one doing the lying. The suit was to recover clean-up costs at a hazardous waste site, and the EPA's on–site coordinator lied to the Court about his academic and professional record. When government lawyers learned of the lie, they obstructed efforts of the defendant to get at the true facts. The District Court dismissed the case against the defendant to sanction the government for its conduct, but the Fourth Circuit vacated the judgment. In a careful opinion on the ethical and sanction issues, the Court of Appeals agreed there had been a serious violation of Model Rule 3.3, but it found that sanctions other than outright dismissal of the case had been inadequately explored.

3. Does a criminal defendant have a constitutional right to take the stand in his or her own defense? Notice that the Supreme Court assumed but did not decide the matter in Nix v. Whiteside.

a. In United States v. Curtis, 742 F.2d 1070 (7th Cir.1984), cert. denied 475 U.S. 1064, 106 S.Ct. 1374, 89 L.Ed.2d 600 (1986), the defendant told his counsel that he planned to testify that he was in Chicago on the day of the crime when in fact he had earlier admitted to the lawyer that he had not been there. Under those circumstances, the court held, it did not deny the defendant's constitutional right to testify in his own behalf when counsel kept him off the stand. Defense counsel may not deny his client the right to testify truthfully, but one does not have a constitutional right to commit perjury, the court said. The court explicitly held that it was not passing on the conformity of counsel's conduct to professional standards.

b. Contrast United States v. Butts, 630 F.Supp. 1145 (D.Me.1986). Defendant was convicted of possession of a stolen credit card. He wanted to testify in his own defense, but his lawyer refused to let him do so. The refusal was based, not on a fear that he would lie, but rather on a concern that his defense was implausible and that he could be impeached on the basis of his prior convictions. The judge said that even though Nix v. Whiteside did not hold that a defendant always has a constitutional right to testify in his own behalf, the right to testify is so basic that when a lawyer denies the right based on other than a fear of perjury, the failure to give the defendant a right to testify was a denial of the effective assistance of counsel.

c.   In United States v. Teague, 953 F.2d 1525 (11th Cir.1992) (en banc), the defense lawyer had advised the client not to testify and he had taken the advice. The court says that the decision whether or not to testify is for the defendant to make, but the lawyer's professional advice on the question is part of the effective assistance of counsel, not a denial of it.[1]   In a companion case, however, Nichols v. Butler, 953 F.2d 1550 (11th Cir.1992) (en banc), the Court found ineffective assistance of counsel where the lawyer threatened to withdraw in the middle of trial if the defendant elected to testify. This was said to constitute coercion not to testify. Do you agree? Look at Nix v. Whiteside; isn't that almost exactly the conduct the Supreme Court approved in *Nix*?

4.   When Smith took the stand and broke his promise to be truthful, what should Hawley have done? Should Hawley have tried to withdraw from the representation in the middle of the trial?

a.   Did the ABA Code of Professional Responsibility provide helpful guidance on this point? Look at DR 7–102(B)(1), for example? Does Model Rule 3.3, and particularly Comment 11 on Perjury by a Criminal Defendant, now resolve all outstanding ambiguities?

b.   United States v. Scott, 909 F.2d 488 (11th Cir.1990), showed how a trial court should *not* proceed. When the lawyer moved to withdraw, the judge told the defendant that if he were to have counsel, he would have to agree not to testify; otherwise, he would have to proceed pro se. He chose the pro se alternative and the Court of Appeals reversed the conviction. It recognized that the proper way of dealing with client perjury was unclear, but it relied on the alleged lack of evidence here that the defendant would have lied if he were represented. Basically, it said the trial judge's approach of requiring the defendant to act pro se from the outset solved a problem that might not have arisen.

c.   In United States v. Litchfield, 959 F.2d 1514 (10th Cir.1992), on the other hand, defense counsel held an ex parte conference with the judge during the trial. He told the judge that he had advised the client he should testify but the lawyer now feared the client would not be truthful. The judge told the lawyer it was for the jury to decide what was true and untrue, so the trial went on normally, the defendant took the stand, and he was convicted. The Court of Appeals held that the

---

1.   Many cases have tended not to grant defendants new trials where their lawyers decided to keep them off the witness stand, sometimes without regard to whether the defendant understood that the decision whether or not to testify was his to make. See, e.g., Ortega v. O'Leary, 843 F.2d 258 (7th Cir.1988), cert. denied 488 U.S. 841, 109 S.Ct. 110, 102 L.Ed.2d 85 (1988); United States v. Rantz, 862 F.2d 808 (10th Cir.1988), cert. denied 498 U.S. 1089, 109 S.Ct. 1554, 103 L.Ed.2d 857 (1989); United States v. Edwards, 897 F.2d 445 (9th Cir. 1990).

lawyer's alerting the judge about his concerns, by itself, did not deny the defendant effective assistance of counsel.

5. Look at Rule 3.3(b) of the Washington D.C. Rules of Professional Conduct in the Standards Supplement. Could a lawyer follow its recommendations with confidence?

a. The D.C. Rule provides that a lawyer whose client is lying should allow the client to testify in a narrative fashion. That approach was once Proposed Standard 4–7.7 of the ABA Standards Relating to the Defense Function. It has long been controversial. What do you suppose is the argument in favor of the approach?

b. Lowery v. Cardwell, 575 F.2d 727 (9th Cir.1978), approved the narrative testimony suggested in Proposed Standard 4–7.7 but found it inapplicable to a trial where the judge is the fact finder. In the midst of a trial, the Court went on, if defense counsel is surprised by a client's perjury, counsel need not withdraw because that course is not feasible. Instead, the lawyer should not "advance" the perjury. Judge Hufstedler, concurring, said: "No matter how commendable may have been counsel's motives, his interest in saving himself from potential violation of the canons was adverse to his client, and the end product was his abandonment of a diligent defense." Id. at 732. See also, Matter of Goodwin, 279 S.C. 274, 305 S.E.2d 578 (1983); State v. Robinson, 290 N.C. 56, 224 S.E.2d 174 (1976).

c. State v. Fosnight, 235 Kan. 52, 679 P.2d 174 (1984), on the other hand, was another case in which defense counsel chose the ABA Proposed Defense Standards' approach to his client's intention to testify falsely. He requested permission to withdraw; the trial court refused. Before the jury, he asked the client whether he wished to "tell the court some things today" and then stood aside while the defendant told his story. The court held that the attorney's actions were not grounds for reversal. The request to withdraw was made in chambers during a natural break in the proceeding; it did not itself call the jury's attention to any problem. The use of narrative testimony was similarly not prejudicial. The court distinguished Lowery v. Cardwell, on the ground that that was a bench trial and there the defense counsel had affirmatively told the judge of the intention of his client to testify falsely.

d. The lawyer in United States v. Long, 857 F.2d 436 (8th Cir. 1988), asked to approach the bench at the close of the government's case. He told the judge that he was concerned about the truth of what his client might testify. The lawyer told the court that he had advised his client not to take the stand and he offered to withdraw. The trial judge then told the defendant that he could testify on his own behalf but that his lawyer could not assist him to testify falsely. The judge said that the defendant could give narrative testimony but that if he lied, his lawyer "may have other obligations at that point". The client did not testify and he was convicted.

The Eighth Circuit (the court which had been reversed in Nix v. Whiteside) held there were three key distinctions that made this case different from *Nix.* There, the court found that the client would have testified falsely; here the lawyer only believed that he would. There must be "a firm, factual basis" for the belief before the lawyer may raise a red flag. Second, in *Nix,* the client did testify and simply did so truthfully; here the client did not testify at all. Third, here the lawyer told the trial judge about his concerns, while in *Nix* there was no discussion beyond that between lawyer and client. Thus *Nix* did not control this case. An evidentiary hearing was required, the court said, to see whether prejudice arising from the lawyer's action amounted to ineffective assistance of counsel.

     e. In People v. Gadson, 24 Cal.Rptr.2d 219 (Cal.App.1993), the defendant was convicted and now complained that his lawyer *did* let him and his alibi witnesses testify contrary to the lawyer's advice. The lawyer had told the Court that the lawyer could not examine the witnesses himself but that the defendant was prepared to do so. The Court warned the defendant against this plan, but the defendant wanted to go forward. Two witnesses (who were already in prison) testified they had acted alone. They could not, however, explain why the defendant's fingerprints were also found at the crime scene, so he was convicted as well. On appeal, he argued that making him examine the witnesses denied him counsel for that period of the trial. The Court concluded that there is no good way to handle situations like this, that the way chosen was not improper, that it was clearly understood by the defendant, and the defendant must live with his choice.[2]

     f. After the adoption of the Model Rules and the Supreme Court's decision in Nix v. Whiteside, the ABA Standing Committee on Ethics and Professional Responsibility issued Formal Opinion 87–353 (1987). The opinion reviewed and superseded Formal Opinion 287 (1953) (discussed in Problem 25), and Formal Opinion 341 (1975). The Committee wrote:

> "It is now mandatory * * * for a lawyer, who knows the client has committed perjury, to disclose this knowledge to the tribunal if the lawyer cannot persuade the client to rectify the perjury.
>
> " * * * Rule 3.3(a)(2) and (4) complement each other. While (a)(4), itself, does not expressly require disclosure by the lawyer to the tribunal of the client's false testimony after the lawyer has offered it and learns of its falsity, such disclosure will be the only 'reasonable remedial [measure]' the lawyer will be able to take if the client is unwilling to rectify the perjury. The Comment to Rule 3.3 states that disclosure of the client's perjury to the tribunal would be required of the lawyer by (a)(4) in this situation.

---

2. Most states have not decided which way to jump on these issues. For example, D.C.Bar Ethics Rule 3.3(b) approves the use of narrative testimony, while Florida Bar rule 3.3(4) prohibits all false testimony whether or not in a narrative form.

"Although Rule 3.3(a)(2), unlike 3.3(a)(4), does not specifically refer to perjury or false evidence, it would require an
irrational reading of the language: 'a criminal or fraudulent act
by the client,' to exclude false testimony by the client."

Turning then to the situation of the criminal defendant who *intends*
to lie, the Committee concluded that the lawyer could not call that client
as a witness. The Committee continued:

"[I]f the lawyer does not offer the client's testimony, and,
on inquiry by the court into whether the client has been fully
advised as to the client's right to testify, the client states a
desire to testify, but is being prevented by the lawyer from
testifying, the lawyer may have no other choice than to disclose
to the court the client's intention to testify falsely."

The authorities considered by the Committee are contained in the
Readings to this Problem and in the Standards Supplement. Do you
agree with the Committee's interpretation of those authorities?

6. Should the lawyer be permitted simply to put the lying client on the stand and examine the client in the ordinary manner?

a. Monroe Freedman was one of the reporters for the Proposed
American Lawyer's Code of Conduct (Rev.Draft, 1982), prepared under
the auspices of the Roscoe Pound–American Trial Lawyers Foundation
and contained in the Standards Supplement. This Code proposed to
solve the problem of client perjury by protecting client confidences
completely. Consider Illustrative Case 1(j) from the proposed American
Lawyer's Code:

A lawyer learns from a client during the trial of a civil or
criminal case that the client intends to give testimony that the
lawyer knows to be false. The lawyer reasonably believes that a
request for leave to withdraw would be denied and/or would be
understood by the judge and by opposing counsel as an indication that the testimony is false. The lawyer does not seek leave
to withdraw, presents the client's testimony in the ordinary
manner, and refers to it in summation as evidence of the case.
The lawyer has not committed a disciplinary violation.

Consider also Illustrative Case 3(e):

A lawyer is conducting the defense of a criminal prosecution.
The judge calls the lawyer to the bench and asks her whether
the defendant is guilty. The lawyer knows that the defendant
is guilty, and reasonably believes that an equivocal answer will
be taken by the judge as an admission of guilt. The lawyer
assures the judge that the defendant is innocent. The lawyer
has not committed a disciplinary violation.

Compare Illustrative Case 3(f):

> The same facts as in 3(e), but the lawyer replies to the judge, "I'm sorry, your Honor, but it would be improper for me to answer that question." The lawyer has committed a disciplinary violation.

b.   See also the National Association of Criminal Defense Lawyers' Formal Opinion 92–2 on this subject. It stresses the lawyer's relationship of trust with the client as a basis for dissuading the client from testifying falsely. But, failing that, it urges examining the client in the normal way and arguing the perjured story to the jury. The thoughtful opinion is published in The Champion, March 1993, p. 23. The opinion is, of course, contrary to Model Rule 3.3(b) and Comments 9–12.

c.   Are you satisfied with these solutions to the problems? Is there any argument after Nix v. Whiteside that such an approach is constitutionally required? Does Professor Friedman's article in the Readings to this Problem convince you that the Supreme Court was wrong in *Nix*?

READINGS

MONROE H. FREEDMAN,* PERJURY: THE LAWYER'S TRILEMMA

1 Litigation 26 (No. 1, Winter 1975).

Is it ever proper for a lawyer to present perjured testimony?

One's instinctive response is in the negative. On analysis, however, it becomes apparent that the question is exceedingly perplexing. In at least one situation, that of the criminal defense lawyer, my own answer is in the affirmative.

At the outset, we should dispose of some common question-begging responses. The attorney, we are told, is an officer of the court participating in a search for truth. Those propositions, however, merely serve to state the problem in different words: As an officer of the court, participating in a search for truth, what is the attorney obligated to do when faced with perjured testimony? That question cannot be answered properly without an appreciation of the fact that the attorney functions in an adversary system of justice which imposes three conflicting obligations upon the advocate. The difficulties presented by these obligations are particularly acute in the criminal defense area because of the presumption of innocence, the burden on the state to prove its case

* When this article was written the author was Dean and Professor of Law at Hofstra University School of Law and Chairman of the Ethics Advisory Committee of the District of Columbia Bar. This article has been adapted from Chapter 3 from Lawyers' Ethics in an Adversary System, by Monroe H. Freedman, Copyright 1975, by the Bobbs–Merrill Company, Inc. All rights reserved. Reprinted by permission.

beyond reasonable doubt, and the right to put the prosecution to its proof.

First, the ABA Standards Relating to the Defense Function requires the lawyer to determine all relevant facts known to the accused, because "counsel cannot properly perform their duties without knowing the truth." The lawyer who is ignorant of any potentially relevant fact "incapacitates himself to serve his client effectively," because "an adequate defense cannot be framed if the lawyer does not know what is likely to develop at trial."

Second, the lawyer must hold in strictest confidence the disclosures made by the client in the course of the professional relationship. The Standards admonish that "nothing is more fundamental to the lawyer-client relationship than the establishment of trust and confidence," and that the "first duty" of an attorney is "to keep the secrets of his clients." If this were not so, the client would not feel free to confide fully, and the lawyer would not be able to fulfill the obligation to ascertain all relevant facts. Accordingly, counsel is required to establish a relationship of trust and confidence, to explain the necessity of full disclosure of all facts, and to explain to the client the obligation of confidentiality which makes privileged the accused's disclosures.

Third, Canon 22 of the Canons of Professional Ethics tells us that the lawyer is an officer of the court, and his or her conduct before the court "should be characterized by candor."

Defining the Trilemma

As soon as one begins to think about those responsibilities, it becomes apparent that the conscientious attorney is faced with what we may call a trilemma—that is, the lawyer is required to know everything, to keep it in confidence, and to reveal it to the court.

* * *

Misleading First Reading

Where the lawyer has foreknowledge of perjury, * * * the Code appears, at first reading, to be unambiguous. According to DR 7–102(A)(4), a lawyer must not "knowingly use perjured testimony or false evidence." The difficulty, however, is that the Code does not indicate how the lawyer is to go about fulfilling that obligation. What if the lawyer advises the client that perjury is unlawful and, perhaps, bad tactics as well, but the client nevertheless insists upon taking the stand and committing perjury? What steps, specifically, should the lawyer take? Just how difficult it is to answer that question becomes apparent if we review the relationship between lawyer and client as it develops, and consider the contexts in which the decision to commit perjury may arise.

If we recognize that professional responsibility requires that an advocate have full knowledge of every pertinent fact, then the lawyer must seek the truth from the client, not shun it. That means that the attorney will have to dig and pry and cajole, and, even then, the lawyer will not be successful without convincing the client that full disclosure to the lawyer will never result in prejudice to the client by any word or action of the attorney. That is particularly true in the case of the indigent criminal defendant, who meets the lawyer for the first time in the cell block or the rotunda of the jail. The client did not choose the lawyer, who comes as a stranger sent by the judge and who therefore appears to be part of the system that is attempting to punish the defendant. It is no easy task to persuade such a client to talk freely without fear of harm.

However, the inclination to mislead one's lawyer is not restricted to the indigent or even to the criminal defendant. Randolph Paul has observed a similar phenomenon among a wealthier class in a far more congenial atmosphere. The tax advisor, notes Mr. Paul, will sometimes have to "dynamite the facts of his case out of the unwilling witnesses on his own side—witnesses who are nervous, witnesses who are confused about their own interest, witnesses who try to be too smart for their own good, and witnesses who subconsciously do not want to understand what has happened despite the fact that they must if they are to testify coherently." Mr. Paul goes on to explain that the truth can be obtained only by persuading the client that it would be a violation of a sacred obligation for the lawyer ever to reveal a client's confidence. Of course, once the lawyer has thus persuaded the client of the obligation of confidentiality, that obligation must be respected scrupulously.

Illustrating the Trilemma

Assume the following situation. Your client has been falsely accused of a robbery committed at 16th and P Streets at 11:00 p. m. He reveals to you that he was at 15th and P Streets at 10:55 that evening, but that he was walking east, away from the scene of the crime, and that by 11:00 p. m., he was six blocks away. At the trial, there are two prosecution witnesses. The first mistakenly, but with some degree of persuasiveness, identifies your client as the criminal. The second prosecution witness is an elderly woman who is somewhat nervous and who wears glasses. She testifies truthfully and accurately that she saw your client at 15th and P Streets at 10:55 p. m. She has corroborated the erroneous testimony of the first witness and made conviction extremely likely.

The client then insists upon taking the stand in his own defense, not only to deny the erroneous evidence identifying him as the criminal, but also to deny the truthful, but highly damaging, testimony of the corroborating witness who placed him one block away from the intersection five minutes prior to the crime. Of course, if he tells the truth and thus verifies the corroborating witness, the jury will be more inclined to accept the inaccurate testimony of the principal witness, who specifically identified him as the criminal.

In my opinion, the attorney's obligation in such a situation would be to advise the client that the proposed testimony is unlawful, but to proceed in the normal fashion in presenting the testimony and arguing the case to the jury if the client makes the decision to go forward. Any other course would be a betrayal of the assurances of confidentiality given by the attorney to induce the client to reveal everything, however damaging it might appear.

A frequent objection to the position that the attorney must go along with the client's decision to commit perjury is that the lawyer would be guilty of subornation of perjury. Subornation, however, consists of willfully procuring perjury, which is not the case when the attorney indicates to the client that the client's proposed course of conduct would be unlawful, but then accepts the client's decision. Beyond that, there is a point of view which has been expressed to me by a number of experienced attorneys, that the criminal defendant has a "right to tell his story." What that suggests is that it is simply too much to expect of a human being, caught up in the criminal process and facing loss of liberty and the horrors of imprisonment, not to attempt to lie to avoid that penalty. For that reason, criminal defendants in most European countries do not testify under oath, but simply "tell their stories." It is also noteworthy that subsequent perjury prosecutions against criminal defendants in this country are extremely rare, being used almost exclusively in cases in which the prosecutor's motive is questionable.

Collateral Witnesses

The discussion thus far has focused only on the lawyer's obligation when the perjury is presented by the client. Some authorities indicate a distinction between perjury by the criminal defendant who has a right to take the stand, and perjury by collateral witnesses. I agree that there is an important distinction, and that the case involving collateral witnesses is not at all as clear as that involving the client alone. In one criminal case, however, a new trial was ordered when the trial court discovered that the defendant's attorney had refused to put on the defendant's mother and sister because he was concerned about perjury.* Certainly a spouse or parent would be acting under the same human compulsion as a defendant, and I find it difficult to imagine myself denouncing my client's spouse or parent as a perjurer, and, thereby, denouncing my client as well. I do not know, however, how much wider that circle of close identity might be drawn.

The most obvious way to avoid the ethical difficulty of the trilemma is for the lawyer to withdraw from the case, at least if there is sufficient time before trial for the client to retain another attorney. The client will then go to the nearest law office, realizing that the obligation of confidentiality is not what it has been represented to be and withhold incriminating information or the fact of guilt from the new attorney.

---

* [Ed. note] Prof. Freedman has indicated in his book on legal ethics that his citation for this case is a newspaper article. M. Freedman, Lawyers' Ethics in an Adversary System, 32 & 41, n. 18 (Bobbs–Merrill, 1975).

And, of course, in a substantial number of cases, the courts will not permit counsel to withdraw.

In terms of professional ethics, the practice of withdrawing from a case under such circumstances is difficult to defend, since the identical perjured testimony will ultimately be presented. Moreover, the new attorney will be ignorant of the perjury and therefore will be in no position to attempt to discourage the client from presenting it. Only the original attorney, who knows the truth, has that opportunity but loses it in the very act of evading the ethical problem.

* * *

Since there are actually three obligations that create the difficulty—the third being the attorney's duty to learn all the facts—there is, of course, another way to resolve the difficulty. That is, by "selective ignorance." The attorney can make it clear to the client from the outset that the attorney does not want to hear an admission of guilt or incriminating information from the client. According to the Standards, that tactic is "most egregious" and constitutes "professional improprie-ty." On a practical level, it also puts an unreasonable burden on the unsophisticated client to select what to tell and what to hold back, and it can seriously impair the attorney's effectiveness in counseling the client and in trying the case.

The question remains: What should the lawyer do when faced with the client's insistence upon taking the stand and committing perjury? It is in response to that question in criminal cases that the Standards [Proposed Standard 4–7.7] present a most extraordinary solution, which, to my knowledge, has never been advocated by anyone other than Chief Justice Burger (who served as chairman in preparing the Standards): If the lawyer knows that the client intends to commit perjury, the lawyer "must confine his examination to identifying the witness as the defen-dant and permitting him to make his statement." The lawyer "may not engage in direct examination of the defendant * * * in the conventional manner" and, moreover, "may not later * * * recite or rely upon the false testimony in his closing argument."

It is difficult to imagine a more unprofessional and irresponsible proposal. The first objection is a purely practical one: The prosecutor might well object to testimony from the defendant in narrative form rather than in the conventional manner, because it would give the prosecutor no opportunity to object to inadmissible evidence prior to the jury's hearing it. The Standards provide no guidance as to what the defense attorney should do if the objection is sustained.

The Jury's Assumptions

More importantly, experienced trial attorneys have often noted that jurors assume that the defendant's lawyer knows the truth about the case, and that the jury will frequently judge the defendant by drawing inferences from the attorney's conduct in the case. There is, of course, only one inference that can be drawn if the defendant's own attorney turns his or her back on the defendant at the most critical point in the trial, and then, in closing argument, sums up the case with no reference whatsoever to the fact that the defendant has testified or to the evidence presented in that testimony. Ironically, the Standards reject any solution that would involve informing the judge, but then propose a solution that, as a practical matter, succeeds in informing not only the judge but the jury as well.

It would appear that the ABA Standards have chosen to resolve the trilemma by maintaining the requirements of complete knowledge and of candor to the court, and sacrificing confidentiality. Interestingly, however, that may not in fact be the case. I say that because the Standards fail to answer a critically important question: Should the client be told about the obligation the Standards seek to impose on the attorney? That is, the Standards ignore the issue of whether the lawyer should say to the client at the outset of their relationship, "I think it's only fair that I warn you: If you should tell me anything incriminating and subsequently decide to deny the incriminating facts at trial, I would not be able to examine you in the ordinary manner or to argue your untrue testimony to the jury." The Canadian Bar Association, for example, takes an extremely hard line against the presentation of perjury by the client, but it also explicitly requires that the client be put on notice of that fact. Obviously, any other course would be a gross betrayal of the client's trust, since everything else said by the attorney in attempting to obtain complete information about the case would indicate to the client that no information thus obtained would be used to the client's disadvantage.

On the other hand, the inevitable result of the position taken by the Canadian Bar Association would be to caution the client not to be completely candid with the attorney. That, of course, returns us to resolving the trilemma by maintaining confidentiality and candor, but sacrificing complete knowledge—a solution which, as we have already seen, is denounced in criminal cases by the Standards as "unscrupulous," "most egregious," and "professional impropriety."

Thus, the Standards, by failing to face up to the question of whether to put the client on notice, take us out of the trilemma by one door only to lead us back by another.

Earlier we noted that the Code of Professional Responsibility appears to be unambiguous in proscribing the known use of perjured testimony, but that the Code does not indicate how the lawyer is to go about fulfilling that obligation. Analysis of the various alternatives that have been suggested shows that none of them is wholly satisfactory, and that some are impractical and violate basic rights of the client. In addition, the ABA Standards rely upon unsupported assertions of what lawyers "universally" think and do. It is therefore relevant and important to consider the actual practices of attorneys faced with the ethical issue in their daily work.

A survey conducted among lawyers in the District of Columbia is extremely revealing. The overall conclusion is that "less than five percent of practicing attorneys queried consistently acted in a manner the legal profession claims that members of the Bar act, and, under the new Code of Professional Responsibility, demands that they act." Specifically, when asked what to do when the client indicates an intention to commit perjury, ninety-five percent of the attorneys responding indicated that they would call the defendant and ninety percent stated that they would question the witness in the normal fashion.

That rather gross discrepancy between published standards and professional action is perhaps best explained by attorneys' reactions to being asked to participate in the survey. Virtually all of the attorneys personally interviewed refused to make an on-the-record statement, although without exception they eagerly cooperated and were willing to participate in an anonymous interview.

Senior partners of two of Washington's most prestigious law firms, after refusing to allow the circulation of the questionnaire among the firm's members, permitted personal interviews on the condition that neither their names, names of the other members in the firm interviewed, nor the name of their firm would be published. Both attorneys, after apologizing for their insistence upon anonymity, explained that many of the local judges with whom they dealt daily would not look favorably upon their true views about the role of the defense attorney in a criminal case, especially if aired publicly. Their reason for not complying with the ABA's rules relating to the presentation of perjury was that those standards would compromise their role as advocates in an adversary system.

* * * I continue to stand with those lawyers who hold that the lawyer's obligation of confidentiality does not permit him to disclose the facts he has learned from his client which form the basis for his conclusion that the client intends to perjure himself. What that means—necessarily, it seems to me—is that, at least the criminal defense attorney, however unwillingly in terms of personal morality, has a professional responsibility as an advocate in an adversary system to examine the perjurious client in the ordinary way and to argue to the jury, as evidence in the case, the testimony presented by the defendant.

NIX v. WHITESIDE

Supreme Court of the United States, 1986.
475 U.S. 157, 106 S.Ct. 988, 89 L.Ed.2d 123.

Chief Justice BURGER delivered the opinion of the Court.

We granted certiorari to decide whether the Sixth Amendment right of a criminal defendant to assistance of counsel is violated when an attorney refuses to cooperate with the defendant in presenting perjured testimony at his trial.

Whiteside was convicted of second degree murder by a jury verdict which was affirmed by the Iowa courts. The killing took place on February 8, 1977 in Cedar Rapids, Iowa. Whiteside and two others went to one Calvin Love's apartment late that night, seeking marihuana. Love was in bed when Whiteside and his companions arrived; an argument between Whiteside and Love over the marihuana ensued. At one point, Love directed his girlfriend to get his "piece," and at another point got up, then returned to his bed. According to Whiteside's testimony, Love then started to reach under his pillow and moved toward Whiteside. Whiteside stabbed Love in the chest, inflicting a fatal wound.

Whiteside was charged with murder, and when counsel was appointed he objected to the lawyer initially appointed, claiming that he felt uncomfortable with a lawyer who had formerly been a prosecutor. Gary L. Robinson was then appointed and immediately began an investigation. Whiteside gave him a statement that he had stabbed Love as the latter "was pulling a pistol from underneath the pillow on the bed." Upon questioning by Robinson, however, Whiteside indicated that he had not actually seen a gun, but that he was convinced that Love had a gun. No pistol was found on the premises; shortly after the police search following the stabbing, which had revealed no weapon, the victim's family had removed all of the victim's possessions from the apartment. Robinson interviewed Whiteside's companions who were present during the stabbing and none had seen a gun during the incident. Robinson advised Whiteside that the existence of a gun was not necessary to establish the claim of self defense, and that only a reasonable belief that the victim had a gun nearby was necessary even though no gun was actually present.

Until shortly before trial, Whiteside consistently stated to Robinson that he had not actually seen a gun, but that he was convinced that Love had a gun in his hand. About a week before trial, during preparation for direct examination, Whiteside for the first time told Robinson and his associate Donna Paulsen that he had seen something "metallic" in Love's hand. When asked about this, Whiteside responded that

> "[I]n Howard Cook's case there was a gun. If I don't say I saw a gun I'm dead."

Robinson told Whiteside that such testimony would be perjury and repeated that it was not necessary to prove that a gun was available but only that Whiteside reasonably believed that he was in danger. On Whiteside's insisting that he would testify that he saw "something metallic" Robinson told him, according to Robinson's testimony,

> "[W]e could not allow him to [testify falsely] because that would be perjury, and as officers of the court we would be suborning perjury if we allowed him to do it; * * * I advised him that if he did do that it would be my duty to advise the Court of what he was doing and that I felt he was committing perjury; also, that

I probably would be allowed to attempt to impeach that particular testimony."

Robinson also indicated he would seek to withdraw from the representation if Whiteside insisted on committing perjury.

Whiteside testified in his own defense at trial and stated that he "knew" that Love had a gun and that he believed Love was reaching for a gun and he had acted swiftly in self defense. On cross examination, he admitted that he had not actually seen a gun in Love's hand. Robinson presented evidence that Love had been seen with a sawed-off shotgun on other occasions, that the police search of the apartment may have been careless, and that the victim's family had removed everything from the apartment shortly after the crime. Robinson presented this evidence to show a basis for Whiteside's asserted fear that Love had a gun.

The jury returned a verdict of second-degree murder and Whiteside moved for a new trial, claiming that he had been deprived of a fair trial by Robinson's admonitions not to state that he saw a gun or "something metallic." The trial court held a hearing, heard testimony by Whiteside and Robinson, and denied the motion. The trial court made specific findings that the facts were as related by Robinson.

The Supreme Court of Iowa affirmed respondent's conviction. That court held that the right to have counsel present all appropriate defenses does not extend to using perjury, and that an attorney's duty to a client does not extend to assisting a client in committing perjury. Relying on DR 7–102(A)(4) of the Iowa Code of Professional Responsibility for Lawyers, which expressly prohibits an attorney from using perjured testimony, and Iowa Code § 721.2 (now Iowa Code § 720.3 (1985)), which criminalizes subornation of perjury, the Iowa court concluded that not only were Robinson's actions permissible, but were required. The court commended "both Mr. Robinson and Ms. Paulsen for the high ethical manner in which this matter was handled."

Whiteside then petitioned for a writ of habeas corpus in the United States District Court for the Southern District of Iowa. In that petition Whiteside alleged that he had been denied effective assistance of counsel and of his right to present a defense by Robinson's refusal to allow him to testify as he had proposed. The District Court denied the writ. Accepting the State trial court's factual finding that Whiteside's intended testimony would have been perjurious, it concluded that there could be no grounds for habeas relief since there is no constitutional right to present a perjured defense.

The United States Court of Appeals for the Eighth Circuit reversed and directed that the writ of habeas corpus be granted. The Court of Appeals accepted the findings of the trial judge, affirmed by the Iowa Supreme Court, that trial counsel believed with good cause that Whiteside would testify falsely and acknowledged that under *Harris v. New York,* 401 U.S. 222, 91 S.Ct. 643, 28 L.Ed.2d 1 (1971), a criminal defendant's privilege to testify in his own behalf does not include a right to commit perjury. Nevertheless, the court reasoned that an intent to commit perjury, communicated to counsel, does not alter a defendant's right to effective assistance of counsel and that Robinson's admonition to Whiteside that he would inform the court of Whiteside's perjury constituted a threat to violate the attorney's duty to preserve client confidences. According to the Court of Appeals, this threatened violation of client confidences breached the standards of effective representation set down in *Strickland v. Washington,* 466 U.S. 668, 104 S.Ct. 2052, 80 L.Ed.2d 674 (1984). The court also concluded that *Strickland* 's prejudice requirement was satisfied by an implication of prejudice from the conflict between Robinson's duty of loyalty to his client and his ethical duties. * * *

[W]e reverse.

The right of an accused to testify in his defense is of relatively recent origin. Until the latter part of the preceding century, criminal defendants in this country, as at common law, were considered to be disqualified from giving sworn testimony at their own trial by reason of their interest as a party to the case. * * *

By the end of the 19th century, however, the disqualification was finally abolished by statute in most states and in the federal courts. Although this Court has never explicitly held that a criminal defendant has a due process right to testify in his own behalf, cases in several Circuits have so held and the right has long been assumed. We have also suggested that such a right exists as a corollary to the Fifth Amendment privilege against compelled testimony.

In *Strickland v. Washington,* we held that to obtain relief by way of federal habeas corpus on a claim of a deprivation of effective assistance of counsel under the Sixth Amendment, the movant must establish both serious attorney error and prejudice. [W]e acknowledged that the Sixth Amendment does not require any particular response by counsel to a problem that may arise. Rather, the Sixth Amendment inquiry is into whether the attorney's conduct was "reasonably effective." To counteract the natural tendency to fault an unsuccessful defense, a court reviewing a claim of ineffective assistance must "indulge a strong presumption that counsel's conduct falls within the wide range of reasonable professional assistance." In giving shape to the perimeters of this range of reasonable professional assistance, *Strickland* mandates that

> "Prevailing norms of practice as reflected in American Bar Association Standards and the like, * * * are guides to determining what is reasonable, but they are only guides."

Under the *Strickland* standard, breach of an ethical standard does not necessarily make out a denial of the Sixth Amendment guarantee of assistance of counsel. When examining attorney conduct, a court must be careful not to narrow the wide range of conduct acceptable under the Sixth Amendment so restrictively as to constitutionalize particular standards of professional conduct and thereby intrude into the State's proper authority to define and apply the standards of professional conduct applicable to those it admits to practice in its courts. In some future case challenging attorney conduct in the course of a state court trial, we may need to define with greater precision the weight to be given to recognized canons of ethics, the standards established by the State in statutes or professional codes, and the Sixth Amendment, in defining the proper scope and limits on that conduct. Here we need not face that question, since virtually all of the sources speak with one voice. * * *

In *Strickland,* we recognized counsel's duty of loyalty and his "overarching duty to advocate the defendant's cause." Plainly, that duty is limited to legitimate, lawful conduct compatible with the very nature of a trial as a search for truth. Although counsel must take all reasonable lawful means to attain the objectives of the client, counsel is precluded from taking steps or in any way assisting the client in presenting false evidence or otherwise violating the law. This principle has consistently been recognized in most unequivocal terms by expositors of the norms of professional conduct since the first Canons of Professional Ethics were adopted by the American Bar Association in 1908. The 1908 Canon 32 provided:

> "No client, corporate or individual, however powerful, nor any cause, civil or political, however important, is entitled to receive nor should any lawyer render any service or advice involving disloyalty to the law whose ministers we are, or * * * corruption of any person or persons exercising a public office or private trust, or deception or betrayal of the public. * * * "

Of course, this Canon did no more than articulate centuries of accepted standards of conduct. Similarly, Canon 37, adopted in 1928, explicitly acknowledges as an exception to the attorney's duty of confidentiality a client's announced intention to commit a crime. * * *

These principles have been carried through to contemporary codifications of an attorney's professional responsibility. Disciplinary Rule 7–102[(A)(4), (7)] of the Model Code of Professional Responsibility * * * This provision has been adopted by Iowa, and is binding on all lawyers who appear in its courts. The more recent Model Rules of Professional Conduct (1983) similarly admonish attorneys to obey all laws in the course of representing a client:

"*RULE 1.2*　Scope of Representation

. . .

> "(d) A lawyer shall not counsel a client to engage, or assist a client, in conduct that the lawyer knows is criminal or fraudulent. * * * "

Both the Model Code of Professional Conduct and the Model Rules of Professional Conduct also adopt the specific exception from the attorney-client privilege for disclosure of perjury that his client intends to commit or has committed. DR 4–101(C)(3) (intention of client to commit a crime); Rule 3.3 (lawyer has duty to disclose falsity of evidence even if disclosure compromises client confidences). Indeed, both the Model

Code and the Model Rules do not merely *authorize* disclosure by counsel of client perjury; they *require* such disclosure. See Rule 3.3(a)(4); DR 7–102(B)(1).

These standards confirm that the legal profession has accepted that an attorney's ethical duty to advance the interests of his client is limited by an equally solemn duty to comply with the law and standards of professional conduct; it specifically ensures that the client may not use false evidence. This special duty of an attorney to prevent and disclose frauds upon the court derives from the recognition that perjury is as much a crime as tampering with witnesses or jurors by way of promises and threats, and undermines the administration of justice.

* * * An attorney who aids false testimony by questioning a witness when perjurious responses can be anticipated risks prosecution for subornation of perjury under Iowa Code § 720.3 (1985).

It is universally agreed that at a minimum the attorney's first duty when confronted with a proposal for perjurious testimony is to attempt to dissuade the client from the unlawful course of conduct. A statement directly in point is found in the Commentary to the Model Rules of Professional Conduct under the heading "False Evidence":

> "When false evidence is offered by the client, however, a conflict may arise between the lawyer's duty to keep the client's revelations confidential and the duty of candor to the court. Upon ascertaining that material evidence is false, the lawyer *should seek to persuade the client that the evidence should not be offered* or, if it has been offered, that its false character should immediately be disclosed." Model Rules of Professional Conduct, Rule 3.3, Comment [5] (1983) (emphasis added).

The Commentary thus also suggests that an attorney's revelation of his client's perjury to the court is a professionally responsible and acceptable response to the conduct of a client who has actually given perjured testimony. Similarly, the Model Rules and the commentary, as well as the Code of Professional Responsibility adopted in Iowa expressly permit withdrawal from representation as an appropriate response of an attorney when the client threatens to commit perjury. Model Rules of Professional Conduct, Rule 1.16(a)(1), Rule 1.6, Comment [14, 15] (1983); Code of Professional Responsibility, DR 2–110(B), (C) (1980). Withdrawal of counsel when this situation arises at trial gives rise to many difficult questions including possible mistrial and claims of double jeopardy.[6]

---

6. In the evolution of the contemporary standards promulgated by the American Bar Association, an early draft reflects a compromise suggesting that when the disclosure of intended perjury is made during the course of trial, when withdrawal of counsel would raise difficult questions of a mistrial holding, counsel had the option to let the defendant take the stand but decline to affirmatively assist the presentation of perjury by traditional direct examination. Instead, counsel would stand mute while the defendant undertook to present the false version in narrative form in his own words unaided by any direct examination. This conduct was thought to be a signal at least to the presiding judge that the attorney considered the testimony to be false

The essence of the brief *amicus* of the American Bar Association reviewing practices long accepted by ethical lawyers, is that under no circumstance may a lawyer either advocate or passively tolerate a client's giving false testimony. This, of course, is consistent with the governance of trial conduct in what we have long called "a search for truth." The suggestion sometimes made that "a lawyer must believe his client not judge him" in no sense means a lawyer can honorably be a party to or in any way give aid to presenting known perjury.

Considering Robinson's representation of respondent in light of these accepted norms of professional conduct, we discern no failure to adhere to reasonable professional standards that would in any sense make out a deprivation of the Sixth Amendment right to counsel. Whether Robinson's conduct is seen as a successful attempt to dissuade his client from committing the crime of perjury, or whether seen as a "threat" to withdraw from representation and disclose the illegal scheme, Robinson's representation of Whiteside falls well within accepted standards of professional conduct and the range of reasonable professional conduct acceptable under *Strickland*.

The Court of Appeals assumed for the purpose of the decision that Whiteside would have given false testimony had counsel not intervened; its opinion states: "[W]e presume that appellant would have testified falsely. * * * Counsel's actions prevented [Whiteside] from testifying falsely. We hold that counsel's action deprived appellant of due process and effective assistance of counsel." * * *

The Court of Appeals' holding that Robinson's "action deprived [Whiteside] of due process and effective assistance of counsel" is not supported by the record since Robinson's action, at most, deprived Whiteside of his contemplated perjury. * * *

Whatever the scope of a constitutional right to testify, it is elementary that such a right does not extend to testifying *falsely*. * * * In *Harris* [*v. New York*,] we held the defendant could be impeached by prior contrary statements which had been ruled inadmissible under *Miranda v. Arizona*, 384 U.S. 436, 86 S.Ct. 1602, 16 L.Ed.2d 694 (1966). *Harris* and other cases make it crystal clear that there is no right whatever—constitutional or otherwise—for a defendant to use false evidence.

The paucity of authority on the subject of any such "right" may be explained by the fact that such a notion has never been responsibly

and was seeking to disassociate himself from that course. Additionally, counsel would not be permitted to discuss the known false testimony in closing arguments. See ABA Standards for Criminal Justice, 4–7.7 (2d ed. 1980). Most courts treating the subject rejected this approach and insisted on a more rigorous standard, see, e.g., *United States v. Curtis*, 742 F.2d 1070 (CA7 1984); *McKissick v. United States*, 379 F.2d 754 (CA5 1967), aff'd after remand, 398 F.2d 342 (CA5 1968); *Dodd v. Florida Bar*, 118 So.2d 17, 19 (Fla.1960).

The Eighth Circuit in this case and the Ninth Circuit have expressed approval of the "free narrative" standards. *Whiteside v. Scurr*, 744 F.2d 1323, 1331 (CA8 1984); *Lowery v. Cardwell*, 575 F.2d 727 (CA9 1978).

The Rule finally promulgated in the current Model Rules of Professional Conduct rejects any participation or passive role whatever by counsel in allowing perjury to be presented without challenge.

advanced; the right to counsel includes no right to have a lawyer who will cooperate with planned perjury. A lawyer who would so cooperate would be at risk of prosecution for suborning perjury, and disciplinary proceedings, including suspension or disbarment.

Robinson's admonitions to his client can in no sense be said to have forced respondent into an *impermissible* choice between his right to counsel and his right to testify as he proposed for there was no *permissible* choice to testify falsely. For defense counsel to take steps to persuade a criminal defendant to testify truthfully, or to withdraw, deprives the defendant of neither his right to counsel nor the right to testify truthfully. * * * The crime of perjury in this setting is indistinguishable in substance from the crime of threatening or tampering with a witness or a juror. A defendant who informed his counsel that he was arranging to bribe or threaten witnesses or members of the jury would have no "right" to insist on counsel's assistance or silence. Counsel would not be limited to advising against that conduct. An attorney's duty of confidentiality, which totally covers the client's admission of guilt, does not extend to a client's announced plans to engage in future criminal conduct. * * * We hold that, as a matter of law, counsel's conduct complained of here cannot establish the prejudice required for relief under the second strand of the *Strickland* inquiry. * * * If a "conflict" between a client's proposal and counsel's ethical obligation gives rise to a presumption that counsel's assistance was prejudicially ineffective, every guilty criminal's conviction would be suspect if the defendant had sought to obtain an acquittal by illegal means. Can anyone doubt what practices and problems would be spawned by such a rule and what volumes of litigation it would generate?

Whiteside's attorney treated Whiteside's proposed perjury in accord with professional standards, and since Whiteside's truthful testimony could not have prejudiced the result of his trial, the Court of Appeals was in error to direct the issuance of a writ of habeas corpus and must be reversed.

Reversed.

Justice BRENNAN, concurring in the judgment. * * *

Unfortunately, the Court seems unable to resist the temptation of sharing with the legal community its vision of ethical conduct. But let there be no mistake: the Court's essay regarding what constitutes the correct response to a criminal client's suggestion that he will perjure himself is pure discourse without force of law. As Justice BLACKMUN observes, *that* issue is a thorny one, but it is not an issue presented by this case. Lawyers, judges, bar associations, students and others should understand that the problem has not now been "decided." * * *

Justice BLACKMUN, with whom Justice BRENNAN, Justice MARSHALL, and Justice STEVENS join, concurring in the judgment.

How a defense attorney ought to act when faced with a client who intends to commit perjury at trial has long been a controversial issue.

But I do not believe that a federal habeas corpus case challenging a state criminal conviction is an appropriate vehicle for attempting to resolve this thorny problem.   When a defendant argues that he was denied effective assistance of counsel because his lawyer dissuaded him from committing perjury, the only question properly presented to this Court is whether the lawyer's actions deprived the defendant of the fair trial which the Sixth Amendment is meant to guarantee.   Since I believe that the respondent in this case suffered no injury justifying federal habeas relief, I concur in the Court's judgment.   * * *

It is no doubt true that juries sometimes have acquitted defendants who should have been convicted, and sometimes have based their decisions to acquit on the testimony of defendants who lied on the witness stand.   It is also true that the Double Jeopardy Clause bars the reprosecution of such acquitted defendants, although on occasion they can be prosecuted for perjury.   But the privilege every criminal defendant has to testify in his own defense "cannot be construed to include the right to commit perjury."   * * *

In addition, the lawyer's interest in not presenting perjured testimony was entirely consistent with Whiteside's best interest.   If Whiteside had lied on the stand, he would have risked a future perjury prosecution.   Moreover, his testimony would have been contradicted by the testimony of other eyewitnesses and by the fact that no gun was ever found.   In light of that impeachment, the jury might have concluded that Whiteside lied as well about his lack of premeditation and thus might have convicted him of first-degree murder.   And if the judge believed that Whiteside had lied, he could have taken Whiteside's perjury into account in setting the sentence.   In the face of these dangers, an attorney could reasonably conclude that dissuading his client from committing perjury was in the client's best interest and comported with standards of professional responsibility.   * * *

Whether an attorney's response to what he sees as a client's plan to commit perjury violates a defendant's Sixth Amendment rights may depend on many factors: how certain the attorney is that the proposed testimony is false, the stage of the proceedings at which the attorney discovers the plan, or the ways in which the attorney may be able to dissuade his client, to name just three.   The complex interaction of factors, which is likely to vary from case to case, makes inappropriate a blanket rule that defense attorneys must reveal, or threaten to reveal, a client's anticipated perjury to the court.   Except in the rarest of cases, attorneys who adopt "the role of the judge or jury to determine the facts," *United States ex rel. Wilcox v. Johnson,* 555 F.2d 115, 122 (CA3 1977), pose a danger of depriving their clients of the zealous and loyal advocacy required by the Sixth Amendment.[8]

8. A comparison of this case with *Wilcox* is illustrative.   Here, Robinson testified in detail to the factors that led him to conclude that respondent's assertion he had seen a gun was false.   The Iowa Supreme Court found "good cause" and "strong support" for Robinson's conclusion.   Moreover, Robinson gave credence to those parts of

I therefore am troubled by the Court's implicit adoption of a set of standards of professional responsibility for attorneys in state criminal proceedings. The States, of course, do have a compelling interest in the integrity of their criminal trials that can justify regulating the length to which an attorney may go in seeking his client's acquittal. But the American Bar Association's implicit suggestion in its brief *amicus curiae* that the Court find that the Association's Model Rules of Professional Conduct should govern an attorney's responsibilities is addressed to the wrong audience. It is for the States to decide how attorneys should conduct themselves in state criminal proceedings, and this Court's responsibility extends only to ensuring that the restrictions a State enacts do not infringe a defendant's federal constitutional rights. * * *

Justice STEVENS, concurring in the judgment.

[B]eneath the surface of this case there are areas of uncertainty that cannot be resolved today. A lawyer's certainty that a change in his client's recollection is a harbinger of intended perjury—as well as judicial review of such apparent certainty—should be tempered by the realization that, after reflection, the most honest witness may recall (or sincerely believe he recalls) details that he previously overlooked. Similarly, the post-trial review of a lawyer's pre-trial threat to expose perjury that had not yet been committed—and, indeed, may have been prevented by the threat—is by no means the same as review of the way in which such a threat may actually have been carried out. Thus, one can be convinced—as I am—that this lawyer's actions were a proper way to provide his client with effective representation without confronting the much more difficult questions of what a lawyer must, should, or may do after his client has given testimony that the lawyer does not believe. The answer to such questions may well be colored by the particular circumstances attending the actual event and its aftermath. * * *

PROBLEM 28

The Verdict That May Be Tainted

Marian Talley represented the defendant in a products liability case in which the jury returned an unexpectedly large verdict against her client. After the verdict, Talley sought to determine what had gone wrong. She visited one juror at his home. He was completely cooperative and said, "Most of us initially voted to find no liability, or at least to set a much lower damage figure. One juror held out, however, and we

Whiteside's account which, although he found them implausible and unsubstantiated, were not clearly false. By contrast, in *Wilcox,* where defense counsel actually informed the judge that she believed her client intended to lie and where her threat to withdraw in the middle of the trial led the defendant not to take the stand at all, the Court of Appeals found "no evidence on the record of this case indicating that Mr. Wilcox intended to perjure himself," and characterized counsel's beliefs as "private conjectures about the guilt or innocence of [her] client."

finally came around to his position. He later confided to me that he worked for a competitor of your client and would be paid handsomely for making the verdict come out as it did."

Talley was angered by this explanation of the verdict and she asked the former juror to put the story in an affidavit. The juror said that he would prefer not to do so, but he told Talley where the supposed payoff was to be made. The juror threatened to deny everything if he were ever asked about the incident in court. At that point Talley activated a secret tape recording device that she always carried with her for occasions in which she needed to preserve what was said in a conversation. Talley skillfully got the former juror to repeat most of the story, and Talley left satisfied that she had gotten the information on the tape.

Using the information supplied by the former juror, Talley went to the place established for the payoff and saw a fat envelope handed to the allegedly dishonest juror by an executive of the juror's employer. She has moved for a new trial and plans to authenticate the tape recording of the former juror's disclosures and testify about her own observations of the payoff at the hearing on her motion.

QUESTIONS

1. Did Talley act ethically in visiting the juror and investigating the jury's deliberative process?

a. Do the restrictions on contact of jurors depend on whether the case is civil or criminal? Look at Model Rule 3.5 and DR 7–108. Is it important here that Talley did not contact any jurors until the close of the trial?

b. Now that Talley knows that the juror violated his oath, what should she do? Note that Rule 606(b) of the Federal Rules of Evidence provides that "a juror may testify on the question whether extraneous prejudicial information was improperly brought to the jury's attention or whether any outside influence was improperly brought to bear upon any juror." Does Talley have a professional obligation to bring the juror's allegation to the attention of the trial judge?

2. Does the diversity within modern society mean that jury dynamics and the characteristics of individual jurors must be of greater concern than ever to a trial lawyer?

a. Consider:

"In an unusual post-trial move, the lawyer for Eric Menendez invited seven sympathetic female jurors to her office where they told reporters on Saturday that a battle between men and women on Mr. Menendez's jury doomed the chances for a verdict.[1]

* * *

1. In case anyone is unfamiliar with this case, Eric and Lyle Menendez were accused of killing their parents in order to inherit a substantial fortune. The killing was ulti-

" 'It was hostile in there,' said one juror * * *. 'There were insults, sexual comments. * * *

"Another juror * * * said, 'We were called ignorant asses and empty headed and "those women." We had one juror who would put on his sunglasses and be balancing his checkbook and cutting out coupons when the women were talking.'

* * *

"A vote on the first day of deliberations indicated the jury was split, the female jurors said, with six women for manslaughter convictions and six men for first-degree murder. Ultimately, five men voted for first-degree murder, one for second-degree. The women voted for voluntary manslaughter." [2]

b. If a lawyer reasonably believes that racial, ethnic, or other factors could similarly affect jury deliberations, should the lawyer be permitted to interview potential jurors *before* the trial?

c. Should a lawyer be permitted to have the jury list before trial and to have private investigators do background checks on potential jurors? Should prosecutors have the information as well as defense counsel; should they be able to use police officers to investigate the jurors? What might we worry about if jurors are subject to such scrutiny?

d. Given the Supreme Court's limitations on the use of peremptory challenges to strike jurors based on general categories of race and sex,[3] do lawyers need more freedom to investigate so as to be able to challenge for cause and to defend their peremptory strikes? Or, should judges give lawyers less information in order to limit the lawyers' ability to exclude jurors for reasons that do not relate to their impartiality?

e. Might giving lawyers less information also tend to protect the privacy of jurors? In the O.J. Simpson case, jurors being considered for selection to decide the murder charges against a former football hero accused of killing his ex-wife and her friend were forced to answer a questionnaire over 50 pages in length about their religion, political attitudes, and life experiences. Should we be concerned about intruding into the jurors' personal lives? Is such intrusion inevitably necessary in order to guarantee a defendant a fair trial?

3.   How should Talley be able to preserve accurate evidence of what was said? Was it professionally responsible for her to

mately admitted, but they claimed self-defense, asserting that they had been molested by their father for many years and were afraid he would kill them to prevent their disclosing his acts.

2. New York Times, Jan. 13, 1994, Sec. A. p. 13, col. 1.

3. Georgia v. McCollum, ___ U.S. ___, 112 S.Ct. 2348, 120 L.Ed.2d 33 (1992) (un-

constitutional for either prosecutor or defense counsel to exercise peremptory challenges based on racial stereotypes); J.E.B. v. Alabama ex rel. T.B., ___ U.S. ___, 114 S.Ct. 1419, 128 L.Ed.2d 89 (1994) (same result re gender–based challenges). Some of these issues were seen earlier in Problem 24.

tape record the conversation when it became clear that the juror would not commit his testimony to paper or repeat it to any other person?

a. Talley's secret recording may not have been a violation of state civil or criminal law. It was not a violation of federal law. Section 2511 of the Omnibus Crime Control and Safe Streets Act of 1968, 18 U.S.C.A. § 2511(2)(d), reads:

> "It shall not be unlawful under this Chapter for a person not acting under color of law to intercept a wire or oral communication where such person is a party to the communication * * * unless such communication is intercepted for the purpose of committing any criminal or tortious act * * * [or] any other injurious act."

See also, United States v. White, 401 U.S. 745, 91 S.Ct. 1122, 28 L.Ed.2d 453 (1971), holding that Sections 2510–2520 of the Omnibus Crime Control Act permit a participant to record a conversation secretly.

A minority of states depart from federal law and require the consent of all parties before a conversation is recorded. FCC regulations are applicable only if telephones are used; these require that there be an automatic tone warning device furnished, installed, and maintained by the telephone company before telephone conversations may be recorded. Failure of a person to use this device is not criminal, although it can subject one to loss of phone service. The law of evidence has been held not to prohibit the introduction of tapes obtained in violation of these FCC tariffs. Battaglia v. United States, 349 F.2d 556 (9th Cir.1965), cert. denied 382 U.S. 955, 86 S.Ct. 430, 15 L.Ed.2d 360 (1965).[4]

b. However, ABA Formal Opinion 337 (1974) concluded as to the conduct of lawyers:

> "With the exception noted in the last paragraph, the Committee concludes that no lawyer should record any conversation whether by tapes or other electronic device, without the consent or prior knowledge of all parties to the conversation.

> "There may be extraordinary circumstances in which the Attorney General of the United States or the principal prosecuting attorney of a state or local government or law enforcement attorneys or officers acting under the direction of the Attorney General or such principal prosecuting attorneys might ethically make and use secret recordings if acting within strict statutory limitations conforming to constitutional requirements. This opinion does not address such exceptions which would necessar-

---

4. Whether or not a crime has been committed, however, there may be a violation of Model Rule 8.4(c) and DR 1–102(A)(4) if circumstances indicate the lawyer deceived the person into believing there would be no taping. For example, in Committee on Professional Ethics v. Mollman, 488 N.W.2d 168 (Iowa 1992), the lawyer had agreed to wear a concealed microphone to a meeting with his drug client in exchange for leniency in his own prosecution for drug possession. The Court held that for the lawyer to mislead his client in this way justified a 30-day suspension.

ily require examination on a case by case basis. It should be stressed, however, that the mere fact that secret recordation in a particular instance is not illegal will not necessarily render the conduct of a public law enforcement officer in making such a recording ethical."

Was the ABA Committee realistic in its conclusion? Would you support a similar broad prohibition by the ethics committee of your state? Why should private attorneys (especially in criminal cases) be placed under stricter ethical standards than the prosecutor?

c. The Association of the Bar of the City of New York has partly rejected ABA Formal Opinion No. 337 and held that because prosecutors may surreptitiously record a conversation by placing a tape recorder on one of the parties to the conversation with only the consent of that party, criminal defense lawyers should be able to record their conversations with witnesses as well. Recording of conversations with the lawyer's own clients and recording in commercial or civil contexts remains prohibited. See A.B.C.N.Y. Inquiry No. 80–95 (1982).

The New York State Bar Association added that a lawyer should be able to respond to a question initiated by a client and advise that client that the client may surreptitiously record a conversation where that recording is lawful. Counsel may not do the recording, however. Opinion No. 515 (1979). Does such a distinction make sense to you?

d. Whatever the answer where the recording is legal, if the tape recording violated state law punishable as a misdemeanor, would Talley's conduct also make her subject to professional discipline? Look at Model Rule 4.4 and DR 1–102.

e. How else might a court deal with an attorney who engaged in secret tape recording? See, e.g., Parrott v. Wilson, 707 F.2d 1262 (11th Cir.1983), cert. denied 464 U.S. 936, 104 S.Ct. 344, 78 L.Ed.2d 311 (1983), holding that any alleged work product privilege involving clandestine tape recordings of witnesses was lost because such secret taping violated the attorney's ethical standards even though neither federal nor the relevant state law prohibited taping. Thus, the tapes had to be produced for discovery. Does this seem to you to be a sensible compromise? An arbitrary result?

4. Is any ethical problem presented if Talley testifies at the hearing on her motion for a new trial?

a. Look at Model Rule 3.7 and DR 5–101(B) & 5–102. For whose protection were the ethical restrictions on the lawyer's acting as a witness intended? A pro se litigant (even though a lawyer) can both represent himself and testify, so how can one argue that the two roles are inherently inconsistent?

b. If one argues that a jury might not be able to distinguish between a lawyer's argument and her testimony, does that mean the rule ought not apply when the advocate testifies in a bench trial? A hearing on a motion for new trial?

c. Are there any justifications for applying the rule when the lawyer-witness is not herself the advocate but other members of her firm are trial counsel? Is Model Rule 3.7(b) more realistic than the Model Code was on this issue?

d. Does the lawyer-as-witness rule apply only to lawyers or also to employees of a law firm? Ohio State Bar Informal Opinion 87–7 (1987) considered whether the testimony of a paralegal employee of a corporation triggers the rule and disqualifies the general counsel's office from representing the corporation in the case. The opinion says no. The practical problem that could arise would be a charge that the paralegal employee is biased, but that charge could be made about any corporate employee. See also In re American Cable Publications, Inc., 768 F.2d 1194 (10th Cir.1985) (conceding that the literal language of DR 5–101(B) and DR 5–102(A) would disqualify the lawyer, but holding that the rules should not be so construed when the lawyer-witness is also a party).[5]

5. When is the lawyer required to be disqualified? Is it at the moment the lawyer is put on a witness list? Is it at some earlier time?

a. In Comden v. Superior Court, 20 Cal.3d 906, 145 Cal.Rptr. 9, 576 P.2d 971 (1978), cert. denied 439 U.S. 981, 99 S.Ct. 568, 58 L.Ed.2d 652 (1978), the California Supreme Court upheld a trial court decision disqualifying a lawyer who could testify as to what was said in certain meetings involving the litigants.[6] The plaintiffs argued that the disqualification order was premature because later discovery might make the attorney's testimony unnecessary. However, the court concluded that withdrawal is required whenever the attorney "ought" to testify. Contra, e.g., Connell v. Clairol, Inc., 440 F.Supp. 17, 18 n. 1 (N.D.Ga.1977) (the attorney's testimony must be "in fact, genuinely needed.").

b. If an attorney is disqualified from representing a client because the attorney will be a witness and the client then hires another law firm to handle the litigation, may the lawyer/witness help prepare the new lawyers? Why or why not? What interests are in fact served by the lawyer as witness rule?

6. How much "substantial hardship" should be required to trigger the exception to the lawyer-as-witness rule?

a. In Comden v. Superior Court, above, plaintiff argued that disqualification of the firm created a substantial hardship because of the

5. State v. Johnson, 702 S.W.2d 65 (Mo. 1985) (en banc), also refused to disqualify an entire prosecutor's office although one of the assistant prosecutors (who had been a police officer) was a witness who had been involved in the arrest of the defendant. The court concluded that the attorney-witness rule was directed more at protecting the attorney-witness' client than at protecting the other side. Further, it distinguished the prosecutor's office from a private firm on the ground that there was no shared financial interest among the members. Is the attorney-witness rule really grounded in financial interest? Protection of the client? Note that Model Rule 3.7(b) would avoid this problem.

6. The court relied on then existing California Rules of Professional Conduct, Rule 2–111(A)(4), which closely paralleled DR 5–101(B) and 5–102.

distinctive value of the services of the law firm. The lawyer argued that although some of his work product could be transferred to new counsel, his "impressions and rapport with the people involved" could not be transferred. The court rejected these arguments and held that loss of expertise, interviews, research, and preliminary discussions of trial strategy do not constitute substantial hardship. Do you agree? Is that view consistent with ABA Formal Opinion 339 (1974), set forth as Reading to this Problem?

b. California responded to *Comden* by amending its Rule 2–111(A)(4) to allow a lawyer to let the client decide how to balance the need for the lawyer against the possible problems created by the dual role. A lawyer could be both advocate and witness if the client consented in writing after being fully advised and after having had a reasonable opportunity to seek the advice of independent counsel. Does the new Rule go too far in allowing the client to be the one deciding the issue? See present California Rule 5–210.

———

READINGS

———

ABA FORMAL OPINION 339 (NOVEMBER 16, 1974)

This committee continues to receive inquiries as to whether a law firm (or a lawyer) should withdraw as trial counsel when a lawyer in the firm (or the lawyer) ought to testify on behalf of the client.   * * *

The circumstances which may lead to deciding whether withdrawal is required or whether duty to the client requires the lawyer or firm to continue as advocate despite the necessity for the testimony are, of course, extremely varied. Necessarily the answer in each instance will depend upon the attending facts.

* * *

The four exceptions, from DR 5–101(B), permit testimony (1) relating solely to an uncontested matter; (2) relating solely to a matter of formality and there is no reason to believe that substantial evidence will be offered in opposition to the testimony; (3) relating solely to the nature and value of legal services rendered in the case by the lawyer or his firm to the client; and (4) "as to any matter, if refusal [to continue as trial counsel] would work a substantial hardship on the client because of the distinctive value of the lawyer or his firm as counsel in the particular case."

Circumstances within exceptions (1) through (3) will usually be easily identifiable and should not present a difficult problem.

It is the sanctioning of the lawyer's testifying "as to any matter," under the conditions described in (4) above, which has generated most of the inquiries to the committee, and the purpose of which perhaps needs exposition.

Ethical Considerations 5–9 and 5–10 make clear that the principal ethical objections to a lawyer's testifying for his client as to contested issues are that the client's case will, to that extent, be presented through testimony of an obviously interested witness who is subject to impeachment on that account; and that the advocate is put in the position of arguing his own credibility or that of a lawyer in his firm.

In some situations, the practice may also handicap opposing counsel in challenging the credibility of the lawyer-witness. See EC 5–9.

The fact that a witness may be interested, even financially, in the outcome of the case does not necessarily mean that he will testify falsely or will color or slant his testimony to favor the party with whom his interest rests. But given a choice between two or more witnesses competent to testify as to contested issues, and other factors being equal, a client's cause is best served by having the testimony from the witness not subject to impeachment for interest in the outcome of the trial.

Because a trial advocate clearly possesses such an interest, his testimony, or that of a lawyer in his firm, is properly subject to inquiry based on such interest, perhaps including elements of his fee arrangement in some instances. Thus, the weight and credibility of testimony needed by the client may be discounted, and in some cases the effect will be detrimental to the client's cause.

Accordingly, the code generally requires that a lawyer who ought to be a witness for the client should fulfill that function and should not diminish the value of his prospective testimony by also being the client's trial advocate. The client's need for the testimony from a disinterested source and the client's entitlement to an advocate whose effectiveness cannot be impaired because of his advocate having been a witness as to contested issues are the foundation of DR 5–102(A) and DR 5–102(B).

Despite these considerations, exceptional situations may arise when these disadvantages to the client would clearly be outweighed by the real hardship to the client of being compelled to retain other counsel in the particular case. For example, where a complex suit has been in preparation over a long period of time and a development which could not be anticipated makes the lawyer's testimony essential, it would be manifestly unfair to the client to be compelled to seek new trial counsel at substantial additional expense and perhaps to have to seek a delay of the trial. Similarly, a long or extensive professional relationship with a client may have afforded a lawyer or a firm such an extraordinary familiarity with the client's affairs that the value to the client of representation by that lawyer or firm in a trial involving those matters would clearly outweigh the disadvantages of having the lawyer or a lawyer in the firm testify to some disputed and significant issue. By the same criterion, a lawyer having knowledge of misconduct of a juror during the trial of a case is not required to withdraw as counsel in the proceedings in order to testify as to facts of which he has knowledge.

Although not all-inclusive, such situations serve to illustrate the intent of DR 5–101(B)(4).[1]

Under the code the critical question is whether the distinctive and particular value to the client of that lawyer or that law firm as trial counsel in that particular case is so great that withdrawal would work a substantial personal or financial hardship upon the client. The most serious and extensive consideration should be given, with the client's informed participation, of the possibility and practicality of engaging other counsel to try the case so that the client may have the lawyer's necessary testimony without the risk of less effective representation resulting from his own counsel being both witness and advocate. If withdrawal, under the circumstances, would clearly work such a hardship on the client, the lawyer or firm should continue as counsel despite the necessity for such testimony.

The lawyer or firm concluding under this standard to continue as counsel should advise the court and opposing counsel immediately that he or a lawyer in his firm intends to testify and the nature of the testimony.

A lawyer may be confronted with the question of whether to *accept* employment as trial counsel when he then knows or it is obvious that he or a lawyer in his firm ought to be called as a witness either on behalf of the client or by an adverse party. The answer to the ethical question is found in DR 5–101(B) and is, in general, the same as when the question first arises after representation has been undertaken.

* * *

In the opinion of the committee, however, a lawyer or firm offered employment when it is known or obvious that he or a lawyer in the firm ought to be called as a witness by an opposing party has critical additional determinations to make. It will be infrequent, if ever, that a lawyer is called by an adversary for testimony within DR 5–101(B)(1), (2), or (3). We thus consider the circumstances in which a lawyer may properly accept employment knowing that he or a lawyer in his firm ought to be called as a witness by an adversary or other party for testimony as to other matters.

In the committee's opinion, if it can be anticipated that the lawyer's testimony will be adverse to the client, there will be very few situations in which accepting employment as trial counsel could be justified under the controlling standard of DR 5–101(B)(4). Because there are degrees of "adverse" evidence, however, we are not prepared to hold that it would *never* be ethically permissible, but we note that with such employment the lawyer also accepts a heavy responsibility. The most skilled advocate cannot always accurately assess the impact of any testimony upon the trier of facts and the prejudice likely to result from the

---

1. For a discussion of diverse opinions reached under Canon 19 of the former Canons of Professional Ethics, see Sutton, The Testifying Advocate, 41 Texas L.Rev. 477 (1963).

prospect of unfavorable testimony being elicited from a party's trial advocate must be carefully considered with the client. In this connection, the lawyer must, of course, consider carefully the effect on the client's cause of fulfilling his obligation as a witness to testify truthfully while honoring his correlative duty to maintain inviolate the client's secrets and confidences.

Any doubt about the answer to the ethical question, whether it arises when employment is tendered or after representation has been undertaken, should be resolved in favor of the lawyer's testifying and against his becoming or continuing as counsel. Ethical Consideration 5–10.

PROBLEM 29

The Crusading Prosecutor

"Clean Gene" White is the crusading young State's Attorney of Springfield County, the home of the state legislature. He says he sees a public interest (and his detractors say a personal political benefit) in uncovering what he publicly has called a "lot of skeletons under the beds of some state legislators." Gene has started a "special prosecutions" branch of his office that is charged with discovering the misdeeds of legislators. Each week, on Monday, Gene holds a press conference to assert his belief in ethics, report on indictments just issued, allude to possible indictments, and answer questions put to him by the reporters covering his office.

Newspapers have begun to report rumors and rumors of rumors as to which persons are likely to be indicted; Gene has denied publicly that he or anyone in his office is responsible for the leaks and has said that he "denounces the rumor mill."

The special unit is responsible thus far for successfully prosecuting three cases: one consisting of forty-six unpaid parking tickets by the chairman of the motor vehicle committee (a "callous breach of the public trust," according to Gene); a second for failure to report a sale of race track stock on a legislator's ethics form; and a third against a House committee chairman for taking a $5,000 bribe to kill a bill.

Though his office normally exercises discretion not to prosecute persons found with minor amounts of marijuana, the office recently indicted a state official found with one marijuana cigarette in his car. This particular legislator is widely suspected of being in league with organized crime, although no admissible evidence has ever been found to support such a charge. Gene privately told one of his assistants to follow this legislator in an effort to uncover some wrongdoing. When the assistant reported the discovery of the marijuana cigarette, Gene said: "Prosecute. I know we normally don't in such cases, but I want to make it hot for this fellow."

QUESTIONS

1.   Has Gene violated any ethical rules by holding his weekly press conferences?   In the manner in which he has conducted those press conferences?

a.   Canon 20 of the Canons of Professional Ethics (1908), in the Standards Supplement, provided:

> Newspaper publications by a lawyer as to a pending or anticipated litigation * * * [g]enerally * * * are to be condemned.   * * * An ex parte reference to the facts should not go beyond quotation from the record and papers on file in the court; but even in extreme cases it is better to avoid any ex parte statement.

Did the Model Code permit more pre-trial publicity than this Canon? Do you prefer the greater liberality of DR 7–107?

b.   Was DR 7–107 itself too limited?   The Seventh Circuit so held. In Chicago Council of Lawyers v. Bauer, 522 F.2d 242, 249–50 (7th Cir.1975), cert. denied sub nom. Cunningham v. Chicago Council of Lawyers, 427 U.S. 912, 96 S.Ct. 3201, 49 L.Ed.2d 1204 (1976), the court said:

> "We are of the view that the rubric used in the rules under consideration, that lawyers' comments about pending or imminent litigation must be proscribed 'if there is a reasonable likelihood that such dissemination will interfere with a fair trial or otherwise prejudice the due administration of justice' is overbroad and therefore does not meet constitutional standards. Instead, we think a narrower and more restrictive standard * * * should apply: Only those comments that pose a 'serious and imminent threat' of interference with the fair administration of justice can be constitutionally proscribed." [1]

c.   Should the rules on pre-trial publicity in civil cases differ from those in criminal cases?   The Court in Chicago Council of Lawyers v. Bauer, said yes:

> " * * * [W]e should recognize that although we rightfully place a prime value on providing a system of impartial justice to settle civil disputes, we require even a greater insularity against the possibility of interference with fairness in criminal cases. Perhaps this is symbolically reflected in the Sixth Amendment's requirement of an 'impartial jury' in criminal cases whereas the Seventh Amendment guarantees only 'trial by jury' in civil cases.   The point to be made is that the mere invocation of the phrase 'fair trial' does not as readily justify a restriction on

---

1.   The court also ruled that comments (under DR 7–107(E)) during the period between completion of trial and sentencing could "never be deemed a serious and imminent threat of interference with the fair administration of justice" and thus that the prohibition of comments "reasonably likely to affect the imposition of sentence" was invalid.

speech when we are referring to civil trials." 522 F.2d at 257–58.

The Fourth Circuit, in Hirschkop v. Snead, 594 F.2d 356 (4th Cir.1979) (per curiam), went further. It upheld the constitutionality of Virginia DR 7–107 as applied to *criminal jury* trials, but invalidated it as applied to other litigation, such as bench trials, presentencing hearings, disciplinary proceedings before a judge, civil cases, and matters pending before administrative agencies.

d. Should different rules apply to prosecutors than to defense counsel? In re Axelrod, 150 Vt. 136, 549 A.2d 653 (1988), read DR 7–107(A) as intended to apply only to prosecutors. The court noted that DR 7–107(B), (C), & (D) all speak of lawyers "associated with the prosecution or defense" of a criminal case while (A) refers only to lawyers "associated with the investigation" of such a case. Do you believe rules as to pre–trial publicity should draw this distinction?

2. Is Model Rule 3.6 more permissive than the earlier rules? Does it track the *Bauer* test? Is even it constitutional?

a. Gentile v. Nevada State Bar, 501 U.S. 1030, 111 S.Ct. 2720, 115 L.Ed.2d 888 (1991), was the first Supreme Court case in many years to test the rules on pre-trial statements to the press. Drugs had disappeared from a safe deposit box rented by undercover police officers. Gentile's client was charged with taking them. Gentile held a press conference on the day of the arraignment at which he said that a police officer had likely taken the drugs and that his client was being used as a scapegoat by the police. His client was acquitted and the Nevada State Bar charged Gentile with creating a "substantial likelihood of material prejudice" by influencing the potential jury pool against the state. The Nevada Supreme Court affirmed a private reprimand.

The U.S. Supreme Court reversed in opinions authored by Chief Justice Rehnquist and Justice Kennedy. The Chief Justice persuaded a slim majority (White, O'Connor, Scalia & Souter) that lawyers' speech may be regulated by less than a "clear and present danger" standard, and that the "substantial likelihood of material prejudice" standard used by Nevada balanced relevant interests permissibly.

Justice Kennedy persuaded an equally slim majority (Marshall, Blackmun, Stevens & O'Connor), however, that the specific Nevada rule was void for vagueness. The rule permitted a lawyer to announce the "general nature of the defense" but only to do so "without elaboration". That, said the Kennedy majority, was too vague to let Gentile know what he could and could not say. Instead of creating a safe harbor, Rule 3.6(c) created a "trap for the wary as well as the unwary." It seems fair to suggest that after *Gentile* we know little more than before about the *proper* way to write rules in this area.

b. In United States v. Bingham, 769 F.Supp. 1039 (N.D.Ill.1991), a District Judge ordered the U.S. Attorney to consider prosecuting defense counsel who, on the eve of jury selection in a case involving street gangs, gave television interviews criticizing the judge for planning to empanel an "anonymous jury", i.e., not reporting their names. The judge considered this statement to be a serious and imminent threat to the administration of justice and subject to discipline in spite of *Gentile*. Do you agree? If the lawyer had objected to the anonymous jury in open court, could he then have repeated the objection to the media? See Model Rule 3.6(c)(2) ("state without elaboration * * * information contained in a public record").

c. Assuming that some restrictions on pre-trial comment may be constitutional, on whom should such restrictions be imposed? Is the public interest served by news stories about lawsuits filed by public interest groups, for example? Are some lawsuits filed more for the publicity they will generate than for the actual result expected at trial? Should that practice be discouraged? Remember Federal Rule 11, discussed in Problem 23.

d. Do the Model Code and Model Rules recognize a different public disclosure interest in cases involving alleged public corruption? Look at the press release issued by the Watergate Special Prosecutor which is set forth as a Reading to this problem? When Archibald Cox moved to prevent the Senate Watergate Committee from granting testimonial immunity from prosecution to John Dean and Jeb Stuart Magruder on the grounds that their testimony in public would create prejudicial pre-trial publicity, Judge Sirica denied the motion and stated, inter alia:

> "It is apparent as well that a committee's legislative purpose may legitimately include the publication of information." [2]

It was the official position of the Senate Watergate Committee that:

> "the public had a right to know. * * * The full import of the hearings could only be achieved by observing the witnesses and hearing their testimony.

> " * * * The committee believes that its position has proven correct and its public hearings awakened the public to the perils posed by the Watergate affair to the integrity of the electoral process and our democratic form of government.

> "Perhaps proof of the impact of the committee's hearings is found in the unprecedented public response to the firing of Special Prosecutor Cox on October 20, 1973. On that weekend alone, a half million telegrams came to the Congress. Hundreds of thousands of telegrams flowed in during the following days. The overwhelming sentiment of these telegrams was in opposition to the President's action. It is doubtful that public sentiment would have been so aroused by the President's action had the public not been sensitized to the issues involved through the

---

2. In re Application of United States Senate Select Committee on Presidential Campaign Activities, 361 F.Supp. 1270, 1281–82 (D.D.C.1973).

committee's hearings." [3]

e. Buckley v. Fitzsimmons, ___ U.S. ___, 113 S.Ct. 2606, 125 L.Ed.2d 209 (1993), was a damage suit against a prosecutor for allegedly fabricating evidence of defendant's guilt and for announcing the defendant's arrest at a press conference that arguably prejudiced the later trial. The defendant spent about three years in jail and went through one mistrial before a third party confessed to the crime and the defendant was released. The Seventh Circuit held the conduct of the prosecutor subject to an absolute privilege because it was all part of normal preparation of a case. The Supreme Court instead applied a "functional test" looking to the function being performed rather than the role of the actor. "Comments to the media have no functional tie to the judicial process", the Court said. In some cases, such comments may serve an important public function, but that is not enough to cloak them in the absolute immunity that applies to statements made in the course of a trial.

f. May the lawyer for the state legislator in this Problem advise the legislator that publicity may help his cause? For example, publicity adverse to White's special unit may deter the vigor of that unit's prosecution. Look again at Model Rule 3.6 and DR 7–107. May the legislator himself call a press conference to give his side of the story? If the legislator does give a press conference, may the lawyer answer questions that reporters pose and that relate to the upcoming trial?

g. United States v. Cutler, 6 F.3d 67 (2d Cir.1993), involved John Gotti's lawyer, Bruce Cutler, who was quoted in several news stories commenting on the lack of merit of the government's case, all in apparent violation of a gag order imposed by the trial judge in the case. When charged with violation of the order, Cutler sought the notes of all the reporters who had quoted him, including their notes of statements made by others than Cutler. The Court held that Cutler was entitled to notes relating to his own statements, including portions of televised interviews that were not used, but that he was not entitled to notes of the reporters' conversations with government officials or others.

h. From what you see on television these days, do lawyers seem to be following even the current rules? Look at Model Rule 3.6(c).

"(c) * * * [A] lawyer may make a statement that a reasonable lawyer would believe is required to protect a client from the substantial undue prejudicial effect of recent publicity not initi-

---

3. The Final Report of the Select Committee on Presidential Campaign Activities, United States Senate, Report No. 93–981, 93d Cong., 2d Sess. (June, 1974) at xxxi–xxxii.

That a committee claims a need for publicity does not mean that types of publicity may not be distinguished. The Select Committee ruled for its public sessions:

"The committee followed a practice not typical of certain congressional hearings.

It refrained from calling a witness in public session that it knew would refuse to testify on the assertion of the fifth amendment privilege against self-incrimination. * * * This policy was instituted * * * on the belief that no legislative purpose would be served by public exhibition of witnesses who claimed the privilege." Id. at xxxi.

ated by the lawyer or the lawyer's client. A statement made pursuant to this paragraph shall be limited to such information as is necessary to mitigate the recent adverse publicity."

Does this rule provide defense counsel with a necessary defense against leaks from prosecutors and police officers? Why is Model Rule 3.8(e) not sufficient protection? Do Model Rules 3.6(c) and 3.8(e) threaten to turn pre-trial proceedings into successive rounds of public statements by defense counsel and motions for sanctions against prosecutors?

3.   What ethical standards, if any, should govern the prosecutor's decision whether and what to charge?

a.   May a prosecutor file a charge that he or she does not believe can be proved beyond a reasonable doubt? See DR 7–103 and Rule 3.8. Do you believe that the Code and Model Rules are too lenient on this point? Should it be relevant that filing a serious charge may let the prosecutor more successfully work out a plea bargain to a reduced charge? Which way should that fact cut?

b.   In United States v. Goodwin, 457 U.S. 368, 102 S.Ct. 2485, 73 L.Ed.2d 74 (1982), the government had originally filed several misdemeanor charges against the defendant, but after he asked for a jury trial, an indictment was obtained including a felony count. The defendant alleged prosecutorial vindictiveness and retaliatory intent that he argued should void the conviction. The Supreme Court disagreed. "Just as a prosecutor may forego legitimate charges * * *, a prosecutor may file additional charges if an initial expectation that a defendant would plead guilty to lesser charges proves unfounded." Thus no presumption of vindictiveness was appropriate and no actual vindictiveness was found in the circumstances of the case. The Court cited Bordenkircher v. Hayes, 434 U.S. 357, 98 S.Ct. 663, 54 L.Ed.2d 604 (1978) (prosecutor, without violating due process, may threaten defendant with more severe charges, to which he is plainly subject, if defendant does not plead guilty to lesser charges).

c.   How much exculpatory information should the prosecutor be required to give the grand jury in seeking an indictment? In United States v. Williams, 504 U.S. 36, 112 S.Ct. 1735, 118 L.Ed.2d 352 (1992), the defendant was charged with giving willfully false financial statements to a bank in order to get a large loan. At the time the indictment was obtained, the prosecutor allegedly had exculpatory information in his possession that he did not reveal to the grand jury. The Supreme Court rejected a claim that the indictment thus should have been dismissed. A grand jury sits to determine whether there is enough evidence to charge, Justice Scalia wrote for the Court; it does not sit to weigh conflicting evidence. Justices Stevens, Blackmun, O'Connor and Thomas dissented.

Even assuming that the Constitution does not require disclosure, what should the prosecutor's ethical duty be? Should the prosecutor who has exculpatory evidence be deemed to have probable cause to charge within the meaning of Model Rule 3.8? Can the prosecutor properly ignore portions of the evidence in his or her possession in making that determination?

d. What should the state's attorney's obligation be when she believes the police are lying? In People v. Berrios, 28 N.Y.2d 361, 321 N.Y.S.2d 884, 270 N.E.2d 709 (1971), the New York County District Attorney joined the defense in an effort to have the New York Court of Appeals shift the burden of proof to the state when the police alleged—in reply to a motion to suppress contraband drugs—that the defendant had abandoned the drugs. The district attorney had become very concerned that the police seemed to have a consistent story that the drugs had been abandoned. The New York court rejected the joint request, quoting then Judge Warren Burger in Bush v. United States, 375 F.2d 602, 604 (D.C.Cir.1967):

> "[I]t would be a dismal reflection on society to say that when the guardians of its security are called to testify in court under oath, their testimony must be viewed with suspicion."

Do you agree that the prosecutor should rely on Judge Burger's analysis and put the problem out of mind? [4]

e. Should a prosecutor be able to accept a plea to a reduced charge even though the prosecutor personally believes that the defendant is not guilty of the offense? How about accepting the plea when she believes the defendant is guilty but that the jury might acquit, thus hurting the prosecutor's batting average? See ABA Prosecution Standard § 3–3.9.[5]

f. May a prosecutor negotiate the defendant's agreement to perform charitable work for a certain time in exchange for dropping all charges, i.e., could the prosecutor pretend the defendant was not guilty if the negotiated disposition conforms to rough justice? Cf. ABA Prosecution Function Standards § 3–3.8.

g. Should the victim properly have any role in a prosecutor's decision to be lenient? Office of State Attorney v. Parrotino, 628 So.2d 1097 (Fla.1993), was a suit against the prosecuting attorney's office for failing to obtain an order that would have effectively restrained a violent man who later killed his girl friend. The problem of domestic abuse is a serious one, and the Court did not take it lightly, but it concluded that this was the kind of case where prosecutors must have absolute immunity lest they be sued every time a tragedy occurs.

4. What other "leverage" should be available to a prosecutor? Should a prosecutor be permitted to subpoena office rec-

4. Is Judge Burger's view here consistent with that which he took writing for the Court in Nix v. Whiteside, discussed in Problem 27?

5. For a discussion of the prosecutor and selective prosecution, prejudgment of credibility, and conflict of interest in the light of the ABA Standards Relating to the Prosecution Function, see Uviller, The Virtuous Prosecutor in Quest of an Ethical Standard: Guidance from the ABA, 71 Michigan L.Rev. 1145 (1973). For a different view, see Freedman, The Professional Responsibility of the Prosecuting Attorney, 55 Georgetown L.J. 1030 (1967).

ords of lawyers known to do criminal defense work, for example?

a. Should lawyers have any more right than non–lawyers to resist a subpoena?[6] Two lawyers who specialize in the defense of white collar criminal cases have argued that government subpoenas of attorneys are a serious interference with the attorney-client relationship and should not be issued without prior judicial approval:

> "Regardless of the type of information sought, * * * an attorney-subpoena has an obvious, unavoidable, and substantial impact on the attorney-client relationship. The fragile relationship of trust, built upon the understanding that what is said to the attorney is confidential and that the attorney's sole function is to serve as a zealous advocate for the client within the bounds of the law, is seriously strained whenever the government even attempts to have the attorney act as a witness against his client. As a practical matter, most clients simply do not understand the fine distinctions the courts have drawn between what is a privileged communication and what is not. [A client may] hold back critical information for fear that a future subpoena might be enforced. Nor can the client be absolutely sure that the attorney has actually invoked the privilege in response to all of the substantive questions asked in the secrecy of the grand jury room. The attorney, too, may decide to skimp on eliciting certain information from the client for fear he may have to divulge it in the future. * * * [O]nce the subpoena is served on the attorney, the attorney's own philosophical, emotional and financial concerns may color his professional judgment. Any advice he gives in this situation, whether it be to fight, to comply, or to compromise, may reasonably be seen by the client, or by others, as having been affected by those concerns. The resulting peril to the attorney-client relationship, and to the adversary system, is apparent.

> * * *

> "Finally, and perhaps most importantly, by using the subpoena the prosecutor can effectively exercise a veto power over the defendant's choice of counsel. Disciplinary Rule 5–102(B) of the Code of Professional Responsibility requires that an attorney withdraw from a case if 'it is apparent that [the attorney's] testimony is or may be prejudicial to his client.' The unrestrained power to issue a grand jury or trial subpoena, therefore, may substantially skew the adversary system—defen-

---

6. Lawyers should understand that, contrary to the wishful thinking of some, neither the work product doctrine, the attorney client privilege, nor the Constitution absolutely prohibits a police search of a lawyer's office if there is probable cause to believe that the lawyer may be aiding in commission of a crime. See, e.g., Law Offices of Bernard D. Morley, P. C. v. MacFarlane, 647 P.2d 1215 (Colo.1982); Bloom, The Law Office Search: An Emerging Problem and Some Suggested Solutions, 69 Georgetown L.J. 1 (1980).

dant's counsel serves at the pleasure of the prosecution.
* * *"

Rudolph & Maher, The Attorney Subpoena: You Are Hereby Command-
ed to Betray Your Client, 1 Crim. Justice 15 (Spring 1986).

b.   In Government of Virgin Islands v. Zepp, 748 F.2d 125 (3d
Cir.1984), defense counsel faced potential criminal liability on the same
charges for which defendant was tried; defense counsel was also a
prosecution witness.   The defendant was convicted for possession of
cocaine and destruction of evidence.   Defense counsel, in order to avoid
being called as a witness and thereby being disqualified, had *stipulated*
that he (who was *alone with the defendant* in her house at a time when
the toilet was heard to flush several times) did not personally flush any
toilets; subsequently the cocaine giving rise to the prosecution was
discovered in the house's septic tank.   The appellate court reversed the
conviction and concluded: "Trial counsel's interest in testifying [via the
stipulation] on his own behalf impaired the exercise of independent
professional judgment on behalf of the client," because "[p]lastic bags of
cocaine do not fall off of trees into septic tanks."   Does this case support
the proposition that there is a need for special rules governing attorney
subpoenas?   Does it confirm that a lawyer should be automatically
disqualified from acting in a case in which the lawyer is a potential co-
defendant?

c.   The defendant in In re Grand Jury Subpoena Served Upon Doe,
781 F.2d 238 (2d Cir.1986) (en banc), cert. denied sub nom. Roe v.
United States, 475 U.S. 1108, 106 S.Ct. 1515, 89 L.Ed.2d 914 (1986),
asserted that if his attorney were required to testify before the grand
jury, the attorney would be disqualified from representing him in the
later criminal case.   The Government was investigating the "Colombo
organized crime family and a faction of that enterprise known as the
'Anthony Colombo crew.'"   The grand jury sought "to determine
whether Colombo paid for, or otherwise arranged for, the legal representation of members of his crew.   Evidence of such benefactor payments
made to [Attorney] Slotnick might establish Colombo as the head of 'an
enterprise' as that term is defined in the Racketeer Influenced and
Corrupt Organizations Act (RICO)," 18 U.S.C.A. § 1961(4).   The government had not attempted to show a compelling or reasonable "need"
for the lawyer's information.   In fact, it expressly asserted that there
was no requirement that it demonstrate need (i.e., that it could not
obtain the information from alternative sources).

The *en banc* Court agreed and held that in the "preindictment
context" a requirement of such a showing of need "would unjustifiably
impede the grand jury process."   The possibility that the lawyer's
testimony would disqualify him from later representing the defendant
under the lawyer/witness rule was not sufficient to change the result.
The majority said: "Before disqualification can ever be contemplated,
the attorney's testimony must incriminate his client; the grand jury
must indict; the government must go forward with the prosecution of

the indictment; and ultimately, the attorney must be advised that he will be called as a trial witness against his client." After all, the attorney's grand jury testimony "may be exculpatory or neutral," or be otherwise inadmissible, or come within one of the exceptions to DR 5–102(B) or Model Rule 3.7. "The pretrial stage, not the grand jury stage, is the appropriate time to balance Colombo's interest in his right to counsel against the public interest in obtaining benefactor payment information, should the issue of disqualification arise."

Do you agree?

d.   On October 1, 1985, the Massachusetts Supreme Judicial Court adopted a new disciplinary rule, Prosecution Function 15, which states:

> It is unprofessional conduct for a prosecutor to subpoena an attorney to a grand jury without prior judicial approval in circumstances where the prosecutor seeks to compel the attorney-witness to provide evidence concerning a person who is represented by the attorney-witness.

The Massachusetts rule was upheld against a challenge under the Supremacy Clause (as applied to federal prosecutors) in United States v. Klubock, 639 F.Supp. 117 (D.Mass.1986), affirmed by an equally divided court 832 F.2d 649 (1st Cir.1987) (en banc).[7]

In 1990, the ABA adopted the Massachusetts idea as Rule 3.8(f) of the Model Rules. Is the rule likely to reduce the likelihood that the problems feared by defendants and defense counsel will arise? Does your answer depend on the standard that will be used by trial judges in deciding whether a subpoena should issue?[8]

e.   In re Grand Jury Proceedings, 13 F.3d 1293 (9th Cir.1994), for example, was a proceeding to force a lawyer to testify before a grand jury about what fees he had been paid by a particular client, the amount of any trust funds held by the lawyer for that client, and what the lawyer knew about the client's lifestyle, spending habits and sources of income. The Court upheld the order. The lawyer's 5th Amendment rights were not at issue, it said, the facts did not relate to privileged information, and any 6th Amendment challenge was premature. A contempt finding was thus affirmed.

---

7. Federal prosecutors have chafed under the rule, however, and in Almond v. U.S. District Ct., 852 F.Supp. 78 (D.N.H. 1994), a Court has held that Model Rule 3.8(f) requiring advance judicial approval of federal grand jury subpoenas for lawyers' records is invalid even when adopted by the local federal court because it invades the power of grand jury.

8. Cf. United States v. Mittelman, 999 F.2d 440 (9th Cir.1993), that involved a motion to suppress evidence seized in the search of a lawyer's office. The affidavit for the search warrant said the office was believed to contain evidence of conspiracy to commit bankruptcy fraud. The lawyer was subsequently charged with that crime along with the client. The Court found the search had exceeded the terms of the warrant, but said only evidence seized in "flagrant disregard" of those terms would be suppressed.

5. Significant other issues for criminal defense lawyers arise from issues relating to their fees.

a. With the enactment of the Comprehensive Forfeiture Act of 1984, amending the Continuing Criminal Enterprise Statute (CCE), 21 U.S.C.A. §§ 848–853, and the Racketeer Influenced and Corrupt Organization Act (RICO), 18 U.S.C.A. §§ 1961–1968, title to income or property derived directly or indirectly from various criminal activities is subject to forfeiture at the time the defendant committed the illegal acts. This "relation back" doctrine lets the government argue that even property that is now in the hands of a third party can be seized by the government.

Neither RICO nor CCE expressly mentions (or exempts) attorneys' fees. In a typical scenario, an indictment will allege that the defendant received 95% or more of his income as profits from narcotics trafficking, and that these assets are subject to forfeiture. The Government also then will serve notice to defendant's retained counsel that fees paid or promised to be paid are subject to forfeiture if the defendant is convicted. The Government then will claim that the attorney can retain fees already paid only if he establishes, in a post trial hearing, that "he is a bona fide purchaser for value of such property who at the time of purchase was reasonably without cause to believe that the property was subject to forfeiture." 18 U.S.C.A. § 1963(c), 21 U.S.C.A. § 853(c). The Government warning to the attorney that the fees are subject to forfeiture is designed to assure that the lawyer cannot establish that.

If the Government discovers the name of your client and then serves notice to you that your retainer may have been generated by the client's illegal activities (e.g., drug dealing), and therefore may be subject to forfeiture, are you put in an ethical quandary? How should you respond?

b. Some commentators argue that applying RICO and CCE forfeiture provisions to moneys paid to a defendant's retained counsel violate constitutional and ethical commands. Public defenders are "overwhelmed" and often have neither the staff nor experience necessary to handle a complex RICO or drug case. The forfeiture potential, it has also been argued, "creates a prohibited contingency fee"—see DR 2–106(C) and Model Rule 1.5(d)(2)—but the "compelling objection" is that to "hold that a defendant may be deprived of the assets necessary to defend himself against criminal charges before those charges are proved is obnoxious to basic notions of due process as well as to the presumption of innocence." [9]

c. Other commentators have supported the forfeiture statutes. The purpose of forfeiture is "to separate convicted criminals from the economic power bases essential to continuation of their unlawful activities." The defendant who is indigent has only a right to appointed counsel, not to retained counsel of his choice; defendants whose assets are subject to forfeiture are no worse off. "An attorney's decision not to

---

9. Taylor & Strafer, Attorney Fee Forfeiture: Can It Be Justified? No. 1 Crim. Justice 9, 43 (Spring, 1986).

represent a defendant whose assets are threatened with forfeiture seems constitutionally indistinguishable from his decision not to represent a defendant whose assets have been seized as contraband or subjected to an IRS levy, or a defendant who has no assets at all." The lawyer has no ethical duty "to preserve forfeitable assets as a fee," though he does have a duty to "serve his client loyally." [10]

Another commentator noted: "[S]uppose a defendant is accused of stealing a car and pays a lawyer to defend against that charge by giving the car to the lawyer. Few would argue that the lawyer has a worthy claim to the car if the defendant is convicted and the jury finds that the car the lawyer received is the one that was stolen. Even fewer would champion the lawyer's right to keep the car if the lawyer had reason to know it was stolen. Suggest, however, that a lawyer who receives money generated by drug dealing or racketeering, is not entitled to keep that money for defending the drug dealer or racketeer, and an acrimonious debate ensues." Lawyers claim that they "must be immune from the hazards that others face when transacting business with drug dealers and racketeers." [11]

d. Lower courts had split on this issue. Most had interpreted the statutes to exempt attorneys fees, assuming that the payment was not a fraud or sham designed to protect illegal activities of the client. The Supreme Court resolved the issue in United States v. Monsanto, 491 U.S. 600, 109 S.Ct. 2657, 105 L.Ed.2d 512 (1989). The Second Circuit had said that a pre-trial order may not freeze the defendant's assets intended to be paid as attorneys' fees, but by a 5 to 4 vote, the Supreme Court reversed. Writing for the majority, Justice White found first that the statutory language was "clear and unambiguous". All property of a defendant was subject to forfeiture; the statute did not say "crime does not pay, except for attorney's fees".

Caplin & Drysdale v. United States, 491 U.S. 617, 109 S.Ct. 2646, 105 L.Ed.2d 528 (1989), then considered whether forfeiture of the defendant's assets under such a statute was constitutional. The same majority (White, Rehnquist, O'Connor, Scalia & Kennedy) held that it was. The Sixth Amendment does not give "impecunious defendants" the right to "choose their own counsel"; it only gives them the right to be "adequately represented by attorneys appointed by the courts". Further, the government has a valid interest in getting the forfeited assets back to their rightful owners or having them go into a fund for law enforcement use. Any Fifth Amendment due process concern must await an instance of actual deprivation, e.g., a plea to a non-forfeiture offense induced by a lawyer interested only in preserving his fee.

---

10. Brickey, Forfeiture of Attorneys' Fees: The Impact of RICO and CCE Forfeitures on the Right to Counsel, 72 Virginia L.Rev. 493 (1986). In addition, Professor Brickey notes that the Justice Department's internal guidelines require the Government to describe with particularity the specific assets subject to forfeiture before they are transferred. Id. at 537–38. See U.S.Atty.Manual, § 9–111.530, reprinted in 38 Criminal L.Rep. 3001, 3006 (Oct. 2, 1985).

11. Landers, Attorney Fee Forfeiture: Can It Be Justified? Yes, 1 Crim.Justice 8, 10 (Spring 1986).

Justice Blackmun, for himself and Justices Brennan, Marshall & Stevens, found no express statutory language requiring forfeiture of attorney's fees and urged a reading that would permit district courts latitude not to order it. On the constitutional issues, the dissenters asserted, "When the Government insists upon the right to choose the defendant's counsel for him * * * counsel is too readily perceived as the Government's agent rather than his own." The effectiveness of our "equal and adversarial" system is thus at risk because the power to seek disclosure gives the prosecutor a powerful club. This will, the dissenters predict, "decimate the private criminal-defense bar". Thus, they called on Congress to rewrite the statute and reverse the Court's construction of it.

e. Yet another problem for criminal defense lawyers is presented by 18 U.S.C.A. § 1957, adopted as part of the Anti–Drug Abuse Act of 1986, which provides:

(a) Whoever * * * knowingly engages or attempts to engage in a monetary transaction in criminally derived property of a value greater than $10,000 and [which] is derived from [a broad range of] specified unlawful activity, shall be [guilty of a felony].

* * *

(c) In a prosecution for an offense under this section, the Government is not required to prove the defendant knew that the offense from which the criminally derived property was derived was specified unlawful activity.

Given the breadth of this language, can an attorney ever safely take money from a client as suggested in this problem? Is receipt of any legal fee over $10,000 potentially a felony? The Justice Department reportedly has promised to use this statute against attorneys only sparingly and only after approval from Washington. Is that assurance likely to cause criminal defense lawyers to feel secure against abuse of prosecutorial discretion?

f. In addition, IRS Form 8300 requires lawyers to file Form 8300 reporting cash transactions in excess of $10,000 even when the payments are made by clients. The nominal purpose, of course, is to see that taxes are paid on the money. The broader purpose is to find out who is trying to conceal the fact they have hired lawyers. The IRS has announced that it will prosecute lawyer's failures to file the Form. Do you believe the information is privileged?

In United States v. Ritchie, 15 F.3d 592 (6th Cir.1994), the lawyers moved to quash subpoenas asking the names of clients who had made cash payments to the firm in excess of $10,000. The lawyer had reported the three payments but not the name of the client or the nature of the legal services. He said that gave the IRS enough information to determine his own tax liability, and nothing else was relevant to legitimate IRS concern. Consistent with the majority of cases on the issues, however, the Court found no violation of the 5th or 6th Amendment, the attorney-client privilege, or due process, and refused to quash the subpoena.

Are you troubled by this result?

6. Does a prosecutor have any obligation to worry about fairness in deciding how much leverage to use against a criminal defendant? Can one simply say the "war on crime" must be fought with any and all available weapons?

a.   Consider one prosecutor's advice on concealing motives:

"The voir dire is multi-purposed.   In addition to selecting a sympathetic jury, you have a secondary purpose, that of endearing yourself and exhibiting your 'impartiality' and your objectivity to the jury.

"That is not a difficult task because you are on the side of right, you are on the side of the angels.   The defense is defending a guilty man.

"Although your true purpose is to convict the guilty man who sits at the defense table, and to go for the jugular as viciously and rapidly as possible, do not allow the jury to perceive your attempt.   Hide your claws.   You must never forget your goal is total annihilation." [12]

This prosecutor has also opined:

"Man's greatest experience is the act of lovemaking.

"I sometimes wonder, if the moment when the jury foreman rises to utter those sweet words of verdict—'We the jury find the defendant guilty as charged'—is not as satisfactory an experience." [13]

Is such enthusiasm in a prosecutor admirable?   Is it a sign of a society based on law and order?   Is it quite a different sign?

b.   Freeport–McMoRan Oil & Gas Co. v. F.E.R.C., 962 F.2d 45 (D.C.Cir.1992), is authority for the idea that government lawyers have a special duty to be fair in litigation.   The government knew certain orders had been superseded, but instead of conceding the point, it made the plaintiff challenge them in court.   Do you agree as a lawyer that Courts should condemn such conduct?   Do you believe as a taxpayer and citizen that the government should press every advantage?

---

12. Quoted in Frankel, The Adversary Judge, 53 Tex.L.Rev. 465, 471 (1976) (footnote omitted).

13. Id.

READINGS

PRESS RELEASE

WATERGATE SPECIAL PROSECUTION FORCE
1425 K Street, N.W.
Washington, D.C. 20005

FOR IMMEDIATE RELEASE MARCH 1, 1974

THE FOLLOWING INDICTMENT WAS HANDED DOWN BY A FEDERAL GRAND JURY IN WASHINGTON TODAY:

NAMES:

Charles Colson, 42, McLean, Virginia

John Ehrlichman, 48, Seattle, Washington

Harry R. Haldeman, 47, Los Angeles, California

Robert C. Mardian, 50, Phoenix, Arizona

John Mitchell, 60, New York, New York

Kenneth W. Parkinson, 46, Washington, D.C.

Gordon Strachan, 30, Salt Lake City, Utah

CHARGES:

All defendants were charged with one count of conspiracy (Title 18, USC, § 371).

The following defendants were indicted on additional charges:

MITCHELL: One count of violation of 18, USC, § 1503 (Obstruction of Justice), two counts of violation of 18, USC, § 1623 (Making false declaration to Grand Jury or Court), one count of violation of 18, USC, § 1621 (Perjury) and one count of violation of 18, USC, § 1001 (Making false statement to agents of the Federal Bureau of Investigation).

EHRLICHMAN: One count of violation of 18, USC, § 1503 (Obstruction of Justice), one count of violation of 18, USC, § 1001 (Making false statement to agents of the Federal Bureau of Investigation) and two counts of violation of 18, USC, § 1623 (Making false declaration to Grand Jury or Court).

HALDEMAN: One count of violation of 18, USC, § 1503 (Obstruction of Justice), three counts of violation of 18, USC, § 1621 (Perjury).

STRACHAN: One count of violation of 18, USC, § 1503 (Obstruction of Justice), one count of violation of 18, USC, § 1623 (Making false declaration to Grand Jury or Court).

PENALTIES:

§ 371. Conspiracy. Carries a maximum penalty of five years imprisonment or fine of $5,000, or both. § 1503. Obstruction of

Justice. Carries a maximum penalty of five years imprisonment or a fine of $5,000, or both.

§ 1001. Making false statement to agents of the Federal Bureau of Investigation. Carries a maximum penalty of five years imprisonment or a fine of $10,000, or both.

§ 1621. Perjury. Carries a maximum penalty of five years imprisonment or a fine of $2,000, or both.

§ 1623. Making false declaration to Grand Jury or Court. Carries a maximum penalty of five years imprisonment or a fine of $10,000, or both.

A COPY OF THE INDICTMENT AND COPIES OF THE APPROPRIATE STATUTES ARE ATTACHED TO THIS FACT SHEET.

THE INDICTMENT WAS HANDED DOWN BY THE GRAND JURY IMPANELLED JUNE 5, 1972.

PROBLEM 30

The Duty to See Justice Done

Hamilton York was hired to represent a workers' compensation insurance carrier in the defense of a compensation claim brought by a woman who had been sexually assaulted in the course of her duties as a hotel night clerk. As a direct result of the assault, the woman suffered severe psychological shock that disabled her and prevented her from obtaining and holding gainful employment.

In the course of defending the substantial claim for compensation, the attorney was furnished psychological reports indicating that the claimant said she had been assaulted by "a Black man." The psychologist concluded that, as a result of her experience, whenever she encountered an African–American male, she became extremely fearful and withdrew into herself. Indeed, her psychological problems were such that if she even encountered a dark-skinned man walking down the street, she became terrified and would turn around and run. Further, she was unable to distinguish one African–American man from another. She considered all such men to be her attacker and this psychological situation had existed since the time of the attack.

In connection with the investigation of the facts underlying this compensation claim, York also learned that the victim had identified the first African–American she had seen in the lineup. At his criminal trial, the defendant asserted an alibi that had been supported by two corroborating witnesses. However, the testimony of the victim had been so compelling that the jury apparently believed her. The defendant was convicted and sentenced to a life term in the penitentiary.

Some of this information, at least as to the general nature of the victim's disability, was available to both the prosecution and defense at the time of the criminal trial, but not to the extent it was developed later in the course of the workers' compensation negotiations. The psychologists' reports were furnished by the claimant's attorney to York with an explicit demand that their contents be revealed only to persons involved in settling the claim. The claim will soon be settled without a trial and the reports will not become a matter of public record.

York has never handled a criminal case in his professional career, and the facts he finds himself facing in this instance are the closest he has ever come to the criminal justice system. He believes an innocent man may be in the penitentiary for the rest of his life unless he acts, but the man is not his client and he does not know how to proceed.

QUESTIONS

1. To whom does York, the workers' compensation attorney, owe duties in this situation? What kinds of duties?

a. Does York owe at least a duty of confidentiality and a duty of loyalty to his client, the insurance company? Is the company's consent required before York may reveal what he has learned that makes him believe there was an unjust conviction in the criminal case? Does DR 4–101(B)(3) impose such an obligation? How about Rule 1.6(a)?

b. If the client withholds consent out of a fear that it will upset the settlement negotiations in the workers' compensation case, should that end the analysis of York's obligations? Are there some decisions that a lawyer simply must take as final?

c. Does York have any duty to the rape victim not to make her psychiatric studies public? Does DR 1–102(A)(5) apply? How about Model Rule 4.4? What is the source, if any, of York's obligation to the victim? Is her lawyer's demand that the reports not be shown to others controlling here? Should York feel a moral obligation not to further injure a person who has been severely traumatized?

d. Does York have any duty to the court that tried the case? Look at DR 7–102(B)(2). Are its requirements limited to revealing fraud in the case York is now handling? Is what is involved here "fraud" at all?

Look at Model Rule 3.3(a). Does it apply only to lawyers actually appearing before the Court in a pending case? Model Rule 3.3 is a disciplinary provision, of course, so one might expect it to be relatively narrow, but does it suggest a moral obligation to the Court to disclose information necessary to prevent an unjust result?

e. Does York have any duty under the Model Code or Model Rules to the wrongly-convicted man? Does any section even come close to creating such a duty? Does the absence of any affirmative duty to him, however, suggest there is anything wrong with York's assuming an obligation to help him? Put another way, might lawyers too often see discipline rules as *ceilings* on their conduct rather than *floors*?

2. How do you believe York should respond to this situation?

a. How would an act utilitarian respond? You may want to look again at Chapter 1. Clearly, freedom would make the innocent man happier here, but would it increase the disquiet of the citizens who would know the guilty party is still loose in the community? Would it reduce the happiness of the victim whose secret is out, the police officers who investigated the case, and the like? Does even asking these questions suggest the difficulty of using act utilitarianism to get morally satisfactory answers?

b. How about a rule utilitarian's analysis? Would it produce more net happiness in the world to preserve victims' secrets or to convict only the truly guilty? Can one give general answers to such questions? Are they at least questions that are easier to discuss than the situation–specific questions of act utilitarians?

c. Where would a rights analysis lead you? Did the accused man have a right not to be convicted of a crime he did not commit? Did he have only the right to a fair trial? Did he have a fair trial if the victim's inaccurate testimony was used, however innocently at the time, by the prosecution?

d. Where does a duty analysis come out? From what would York's duty to the accused man arise? Does every person have a moral duty to see justice done? Is that duty greater for lawyers than for citizens generally?

e. Professor David Luban proposes four principles to restrict the lawyer's "standard conception" of the duty to act as a partisan. They are restrictions:

"(1) on modes of practice that inflict morally unjustifiable damage on other people, especially innocent people;

"(2) on deceit, i.e., actions that obscure truths or that lure people into doing business under misapprehensions, even if these are legally permissible;

"(3) on manipulations of morally defensible law to achieve outcomes that negate its generality or violate its spirit; and, in general,

"(4) on the pursuit of substantively unjust results." [1]

What, if any, useful directions would Professor Luban's principles provide in this case?

f. Where would the "ethic of care" lead a lawyer? That view could be understood to say that a lawyer should focus less on individual players and their rights and instead try to minimize hurt in the situation. Could the lawyer fail to act on behalf of the incarcerated person here? Would you want to know whether the assault victim's name could

1. D. Luban, Lawyers and Justice: An Ethical Study 157 (1988).

be protected against disclosure in the media, for example? Once one says that an entire context must be considered, may so many uncertainties be presented that the lawyer may become paralyzed into inaction?

g. Is there a deeper issue than individual justice here? Should it be relevant to York that the innocent man is an African–American? Is our judicial system still inherently more likely to believe the testimony of a white victim than an African–American accused? Is the convicted man likely to have fewer persons coming to his defense than he would if he were white? Should that affect York's decision to pursue justice in the man's case?

h. Could York simply argue: "I know I have a duty to the innocent man because I could sleep soundly if I helped him and couldn't sleep at all if I did not." Is such an answer too ad hoc to be useful? Too unsophisticated to take seriously? Does it ignore too many obligations the lawyer owes to persons other than the innocent man? Does it instead rely on principles deeper than words can form?

3. Who, if anyone, would have an obligation to listen to York?

a. How about the prosecutor? Do the obligations of DR 7–103 or Model Rule 3.8 extend beyond the end of a case? Does anything in the A.B.A. Standards Relating to the Prosecution Function, other than Standard 3–1.1(c), create a higher duty?

b. How about defense counsel? How long does the "zealous representation" obligation of DR 7–101 continue? Look at Standard 4–8.5 of the A.B.A. Standards Relating to the Defense Function? Does it suggest that former counsel, either trial or appellate, would have a duty to act?

c. Does the trial judge have a duty higher than the prosecutor or defense counsel's? Does the judge have any duty at all?

d. Suppose no one listened. Might you try to interest Oprah? Geraldo? Hard Copy? The question is a serious one. Have the news media become the "court of last resort" in the United States today?

Is that a positive development? Would a televised account of this story likely protect the assault victim, for example? Remember that she did not intentionally lie about what happened and her welfare and privacy are surely appropriate for the lawyer's moral concern.

4. Look at *Spaulding v. Zimmerman,* set forth as a Reading to this Problem. Are the issues there the same?

a. Were you struck by the court's simultaneous findings there of (1) nondisclosure sufficient to reopen the settlement and (2) a lack of "ethical or legal obligation" to reveal the plaintiff's life-threatening condition to him? Are the findings consistent?

b. Did it bother you that the court there expressed so little sensitivity to the danger in which the plaintiff had been left? If the plaintiff had died, would the defense lawyers have borne any legal or moral responsibility for his death?

c.   What would you have done as the lawyer in *Spaulding*?   Might you have tried to work out an agreement to disclose the condition so long as the information could not be used against your client, for example? Do you suppose that would have been realistically possible in the context of negotiating a settlement?

d.   If you had been counsel for the plaintiff and defense counsel had promised "life-saving information" in exchange for a waiver of rights, would you have accepted the offer?   Is genuine concern for the welfare of a non-client so rare among lawyers today that you would suspect a trick?

5.   Is it hard to believe you would ever face issues such as those in this Problem?

a.   Suppose you learn that in spite of the fact that you recently defeated a pollution charge against your client, it does indeed sometimes discharge toxic chemicals into a stream from which a nearby city gets its water supply?   Would you go to the E.P.A.?   Would you go back to Court and confess error?   Would you confront the client?   Does your answer depend at all on how much the client pays in fees?   On whether you have already made partner at your firm?

b.   Suppose you have learned that the client whom you have just helped to defeat a charge of child molestation is indeed a pedophile. Suppose you learn he has just become a camp director without revealing the earlier charge and certainly not the reality of his condition?   Could or would you do anything?

c.   Would you just try to forget what you now know and reason that trials are never perfect?   Would you see whether there are any openings in medical school or seek some other career confronting you with less stress-producing questions?

READINGS

SPAULDING v. ZIMMERMAN

Supreme Court of Minnesota, 1962.
263 Minn. 346, 116 N.W.2d 704.

THOMAS GALLAGHER, Justice.

Appeal from an order of the District Court of Douglas County vacating and setting aside a prior order of such court * * * approving a settlement made on behalf of David Spaulding, * * * at which time he was a minor.   * * *

The prior action was brought against defendants by Theodore Spaulding, as father and natural guardian of David Spaulding, for injuries sustained by David in an automobile accident. * * *

* * *

After the accident, David's injuries were diagnosed by his family physician, Dr. James H. Cain, as a severe crushing injury of the chest with multiple rib fractures; a severe cerebral concussion, probably with petechial hemorrhages of the brain; and bilateral fractures of the clavicles. At Dr. Cain's suggestion, on January 3, 1957, David was examined by Dr. John F. Pohl, an orthopedic specialist, who made X-ray studies of his chest. * * * Nothing in [Dr. Pohl's] report indicated the aorta aneurysm with which David was then suffering. On March 1, 1957, at the suggestion of Dr. Pohl, David was examined from a neurological viewpoint by Dr. Paul S. Blake, and in the report of this examination there was no finding of the aorta aneurysm.

In the meantime, on February 22, 1957, at defendants' request, David was examined by Dr. Hewitt Hannah, a neurologist. On February 26, 1957, the latter reported to Messrs. Field, Arveson, & Donoho, attorneys for defendant John Zimmerman, as follows:

> "The one feature of the case which bothers me more than any other part of the case is the fact that this boy of 20 years of age has an aneurysm, which means a dilatation of the aorta and the arch of the aorta. Whether this came out of this accident I cannot say with any degree of certainty and I have discussed it with the Roentgenologist and a couple of Internists. * * * Of course an aneurysm or dilatation of the aorta in a boy of this age is a serious matter as far as his life. This aneurysm may dilate further and it might rupture with further dilatation and this would cause his death.

> "It would be interesting also to know whether the X-ray of his lungs, taken immediately following the accident, shows this dilatation or not. If it was not present immediately following the accident and is now present, then we could be sure that it came out of the accident."

* * *

The case was called for trial on March 4, 1957, at which time the respective parties and their counsel possessed such information as to David's physical condition as was revealed to them by their respective medical examiners as above described. It is thus apparent that neither David nor his father, the nominal plaintiff in the prior action, was then aware that David was suffering the aorta aneurysm but on the contrary believed that he was recovering from the injuries sustained in the accident.

On the following day an agreement for settlement was reached wherein, in consideration of the payment of $6,500, David and his father agreed to settle in full for all claims arising out of the accident.

Richard S. Roberts, counsel for David, thereafter presented to the court a petition for approval of the settlement * * *.

Early in 1959, David was required by the army reserve, of which he was a member, to have a physical checkup. For this, he again engaged the services of Dr. Cain. In this checkup, the latter discovered the aorta aneurysm. He then reexamined the X rays which had been taken shortly after the accident and at this time discovered that they disclosed the beginning of the process which produced the aneurysm. He promptly sent David to Dr. Jerome Grismer for an examination and opinion. The latter confirmed the finding of the aorta aneurysm and recommended immediate surgery therefor. This was performed by him at Mount Sinai Hospital in Minneapolis on March 10, 1959.

Shortly thereafter, David having attained his majority, instituted the present action for additional damages done to the more serious injuries including the aorta aneurysm which he alleges proximately resulted from the accident. * * *

* * *

* * * [I]t is clear that in the instant case the court did not abuse its discretion in setting aside the settlement which it had approved on plaintiff's behalf while he was still a minor. It is undisputed that neither he nor his counsel nor his medical attendants were aware that at the time settlement was made he was suffering from an aorta aneurysm which may have resulted from the accident. The seriousness of this disability is indicated by Dr. Hannah's report indicating the imminent danger of death therefrom. This was known by counsel for both defendants but was not disclosed to the court at the time it was petitioned to approve the settlement. While no canon of ethics or legal obligation may have required them to inform the plaintiff or his counsel with respect thereto, or to advise the court therein, it did become obvious to them at the time that the settlement then made did not contemplate or take into consideration the disability described. This fact opened the way for the court to later exercise its discretion in vacating the settlement and under the circumstances described we cannot say that there was any abuse of discretion on the part of the court in so doing. * * *

Affirmed.

SELECTED BIBLIOGRAPHY ON ISSUES IN CHAPTER VI

Problem 23

S. Burbank, Rule 11 in Transition. The Report of the Third Circuit Task Force on Federal Rule of Civil Procedure 11 (Am. Judicature Society, 1989).

Cann, Frivolous Lawsuits—The Lawyer's Duty to Say "No.", 52 U.Colorado L.Rev. 367 (1981).

Comment, Financial Penalties Imposed Directly Against Counsel Without Resort to the Contempt Power, 26 U.C.L.A. L.Rev. 855 (1979).

Comment, Sanctions Imposed by Courts on Attorneys Who Abuse the Judicial Process, 44 U.Chicago L.Rev. 619 (1977).

Edelstein, The Ethics of Dilatory Motion Practice: Time for Change, 44 Fordham L.Rev. 1069 (1976).

C. Ellington, A Study of Sanctions for Discovery Abuse (1979).

Hayden, Reconsidering the Litigator's Absolute Privilege to Defame, 54 Ohio.St.L.J. 985 (1993).

S. Kassin, An Empirical Study of Rule 11 Sanctions (Fed.Jud.Ctr. 1985).

Nelken, Sanctions Under Amended Federal Rule 11—Some "Chilling" Problems in the Struggle Between Compensation and Punishment, 74 Georgetown L.J. 1313 (1986).

Parness, Groundless Pleadings and Certifying Attorneys in the Federal Courts, 1985 Utah L. Rev. 325.

Parness, Fines Under the New Federal Civil Rule 11: The New Monetary Sanctions for the "Stop and Think Again" Rule, 1993 B.Y.U. L.Rev. 879.

Parness, Disciplinary Referrals Under New Federal Civil Rule 11, 61 Tennessee L.Rev. 37 (1993).

Peeples, Litigant Responsibility: Federal Rule of Civil Procedure 11 and Its Application, 27 Boston College L.Rev. 385 (1986).

Polinsky & Rubinfeld, Sanctioning Frivolous Suits: An Economic Analysis, 82 Georgetown L.J. 397 (1993).

Risinger, Honesty in Pleading and Its Enforcement: Some "Striking" Problems with Federal Rule of Civil Procedure 11, 61 Minnesota L.Rev. 1 (1976).

Shaneyfelt, Courts Are no Place for Fun and Frivolity: A Warning to Vexatious Litigants and Over-Zealous Attorneys, 20 Willamette L.Rev. 441 (1984).

Symposium, Amended Rule 11 of the Federal Rules of Civil Procedure, 54 Fordham L.Rev. 20 (1985).

Zeisel, Court Delay Caused by the Bar?, 54 A.B.A.J. 886 (1968).

Problem 24

Ahrens, Advocacy Ideals and the Representation of Children, 35 U.Florida Law Rev. 464 (1983).

Alschuler, Courtroom Misconduct by Prosecutors and Trial Judges, 50 Texas L.Rev. 629 (1972).

Alschuler, The Search for Truth Continued, the Privilege Retained: A Response to Judge Frankel, 54 U.Colorado L.Rev. 67 (1982).

Baldini, Overzealousness, 3 Georgetown J.Legal Ethics 81 (1989).

Carlson, Competency and Professionalism in Modern Litigation: The Role of the Law Schools, 23 Georgia L.Rev. 689 (1989).

Carrington, The Right to Zealous Counsel, 1979 Duke L.J. 1291.

Chernoff & Schaffer, Defending the Mentally Ill: Ethical Quicksand, 10 Am.Criminal 505 (1972).

Flynn, On "Borrowed Wits": A Proposed Rule for Attorney Depositions, 93 Columbia L.Rev. 1956 (1993).

Fried, The Lawyer as Friend: The Moral Foundations of the Lawyer–Client Relation, 85 Yale L.J. 1060 (1976).

Gaetke, Lawyers as Officers of the Court, 42 Vanderbilt L.Rev. 39 (1989).

Garth, From Civil Litigation to Private Justice: Legal Practice At War With the Profession and Its Values, 59 Brooklyn L.Rev. 931 (1993).

Gedicks, Justice or Mercy? A Personal Note on Defending the Guilty, 13 J.Legal Profession 139 (1988).

Gerber, Victory vs. Truth: The Adversary System and its Ethics, 19 Arizona State L.J. 3 (1987).

Gilson & Mnookin, Disputing Through Agents: Cooperation and Conflict Between Lawyers in Litigation, 94 Columbia L.Rev. 509 (1994).

Kaufman, A Commentary on Pepper's "The Lawyer's Amoral Ethical Role", 1986 A.B.F.Research J. 651 (1986).

Landon, Clients, Colleagues, and Community: The Shaping of Zealous Advocacy in Country Law Practice, 1985 A.B.F. Research J. 81.

Landsberg, Policing Attorneys: Exclusion of Unethically Obtained Evidence, 53 U.Chicago L.Rev. 1399 (1986).

Landsman, Decline of the Adversary System and the Changing Role of the Advocate in that System, 18 San Diego L.Rev. 251 (1981).

E. Loftus, Witness for the Defense (1992).

Luban, The Lysistratian Prerogative: A Response to Stephen Pepper, 1986 A.B.F. Research J. 637 (1986).

Martineau, The Attorney as Officer of the Court: Time to Take the Gown Off the Bar, 35 S.Carolina L. Rev. 541 (1984).

Mashburn, Professionalism as Class Ideology: Civility Codes and Bar Hierarchy, 28 Valparaiso U.L.Rev. 657 (1994).

Medina, Ethical Concerns in Civil Appellate Advocacy, 43 Southwestern L.J. 677 (1989).

D. Mellinkoff, The Conscience of a Lawyer (1973).

Meyer, Unringing the Bell: Enforcing Model Rule 3.4(e) as an Alternative to Trial Reversal for Attorneys' Improper Argument, 11 J.Legal Profession 187 (1986).

Pepper, A Lawyer's Amoral Ethical Role: A Defense, a Problem, and Some Possibilities, 1986 A.B.F. Research J. 613 (1986).

Robinson, Redefining the Advocate's Role: A Contract Theory of Legal Ethics, 3 W.New England L.Rev. 409 (1981).

See, An Essay on Legal Ethics and the Search for Truth, 3 Georgetown J.Legal Ethics 323 (1989).

Selinger, Perry Mason Perspective and Others: A Critique of Reductionist Thinking About the Ethics of Untruthful Practices by Lawyers for "Innocent" Defendants, 6 Hofstra L.Rev. 631 (1978).

Selinger, The "Law" on Lawyer Efforts to Discredit Truthful Testimony, 46 Oklahoma Law Review 99 (1993).

Shaffer, Serving the Guilty, 26 Loyola L.Rev. 71 (1980).

Shaffer, The Unique, Novel, and Unsound Adversary Ethic, 41 Vanderbilt L.Rev. 697 (1988).

Symposium, Professionalism in the Practice of Law: A Symposium on Civility and Judicial Ethics in the 1990s, 28 Valparaiso U.L.Rev. 513–741 (1994).

Underwood, Adversary Ethics: More Dirty Tricks, 6 American Journal of Trial Advocacy 265 (1982).

Underwood, Curbing Litigation Abuses: Judicial Control of Adversary Ethics—The Model Rules of Professional Conduct and Proposed Amendments to the Rules of Civil Procedure, 56 St. John's L.Rev. 625 (1982).

R. Underwood & W. Fortune, Trial Ethics (1988).

Problem 25

Freedman, Arguing the Law in an Adversary System, 16 Georgia L.Rev. 833 (1982).

Greenwalt, Silence as a Moral and Constitutional Right, 23 William and Mary L.Rev. 15 (1981).

Hazard, Arguing the Law: The Advocate's Duty and Opportunity, 16 Georgia L.Rev. 821 (1982).

Smith & Metzloff, The Attorney as Advocate: "Arguing the Law", 16 Georgia L.Rev. 841 (1982).

Uviller, Zeal & Frivolity: The Ethical Duty of the Appellate Advocate to tell the Truth About the Law, 6 Hofstra L.Rev. 729 (1978).

Weinstein, Ethical Dilemmas in Mass Tort Litigation, 88 Northwestern U.L.Rev. 469 (1994).

White, The Ethics of Argument: Plato's Gorgias and the Modern Lawyer, 50 U.Chicago L.Rev. 849 (1983).

Problem 26

Freedman, Where the Bodies are Buried: The Adversary System and the Obligation of Confidentiality, 10 Criminal L.Bull. 979 (1974).

Graffeo, Ethics, Law, and Loyalty: The Attorney's Duty to Turn Over Incriminating Physical Evidence, 32 Stanford L.Rev. 977 (1980).

Hill, Judicial Activism and the Destruction of Evidence: Reconsidering Traditional Responses to Evidence Destruction in Civil Proceedings, 23 Land and Water L.Rev. 209 (1988).

Imwinkelried, A New Antidote for an Opponent's Pretrial Discovery Misconduct: Treating the Misconduct at Trial as an Admission by Conduct of the Weakness of the Opponent's Case, 1993 B.Y.U. L.Rev. 793 (1993).

Lefstein, Incriminating Physical Evidence, the Defense Attorney's Dilemma, and the Need for Rules, 64 N.Carolina L.Rev. 897 (1986).

Martin, Incriminating Criminal Evidence: Practical Solutions, 15 Pacific L.J. 807 (1984).

Note, Disclosure of Incriminating Physical Evidence Received From a Client: The Defense Attorney's Dilemma, 52 U.Colorado L.Rev. 419 (1981).

Note, Right of a Criminal Defense Attorney to Withhold Physical Evidence Received from His Client, 38 U.Chicago L.Rev. 211 (1970).

Note, An Attorney in Possession of Evidence Incriminating His Client, 25 Washington & Lee L.Rev. 133 (1968).

Note, The Emerging Deterrence Orientation in the Imposition of Discovery Sanctions, 91 Harvard L.Rev. 1033 (1978).

Note, Professional Responsibility and In re Ryder: Can an Attorney Serve Two Masters, 54 Virginia L.Rev. 145 (1968).

Oesterle, A Private Litigant's Remedies for an Opponent's Inappropriate Destruction of Relevant Documents, 61 Texas L.Rev. 1185 (1983).

Rosenberg & King, Curbing Discovery Abuse in Civil Litigation: Enough is Enough, 1981 B.Y.U. L.Rev. 579.

Rosenberg, The Federal Civil Rules After Half A Century, 36 Maine L.Rev. 243 (1984).

Trahan, A First Step Toward Resolution of the Physical Evidence Dilemma, 48 Louisiana L.Rev. 1019 (1988).

Problem 27

S. Bok, Lying: Moral Choice in Public and Private Life (1978).

Bress, Professional Ethics in Criminal Trials: A View of Defense Counsel's Responsibility, 64 Michigan L.Rev. 1493 (1966).

Bright, Counsel for the Poor: The Death Sentence Not for the Worst Crime But for the Worst Lawyer, 103 Yale L.J. 1835 (1994).

Burke, Truth in Lawyering: An Essay on Lying and Deceit in the Practice of Law, 38 Arkansas L.Rev. 1 (1984).

Curtis, The Ethics of Advocacy, 4 Stanford L.Rev. 3 (1951).

Dash, The Emerging Role and Function of the Criminal Defense Lawyer, 47 N.Carolina L.Rev. 598 (1969).

Erickson, The Perjurious Defendant: A Proposed Solution to the Defense Lawyer's Conflicting Ethical Obligations to the Court and to His Client, 59 Denver L.J. 75 (1981).

Frankel, The Search for Truth Continued: More Disclosure, Less Privilege, 54 U.Colorado L.Rev. 51 (1982).

M. Freedman, Lawyers' Ethics in an Adversary System (1975).

Freedman, The Aftermath of Nix v. Whiteside: Slamming the Lid on Pandora's Box, 23 Criminal L.Bull. 25 (1987).

Freedman, Professional Responsibility of the Criminal Defense Lawyer: The Three Hardest Questions, 64 Michigan L.Rev. 1469 (1966).

Goldberg, Heaven Help the Lawyer for a Civil Liar, 2 Georgetown J. Legal Ethics 885 (1989).

Gottlieb, Pinocchio for the Defense, 14 Florida St.U.L.Rev. 891 (1987).

Green, Lethal Fiction: The Meaning of "Counsel" in the Sixth Amendment, 78 Iowa L.Rev. 433 (1993).

Harvey, Responding to the Criminal Defense Client Who Insists on the Presentation of Perjuring Nonparty Witnesses: The *Schultheis* Solution, 68 Iowa L.Rev. 359 (1983).

Heffernan, The Moral Accountability of Advocates, 61 Notre Dame L.Rev. 36 (1986).

Helms, Client Perjury and Effective Assistance of Counsel, 11 Oklahoma City U.L.Rev. 817 (1986).

Lawry, Lying, Confidentiality and the Adversary System of Justice, 1977 Utah L.Rev. 653.

Lefstein, Criminal Defendant Who Proposes Perjury: Rethinking the Defense Lawyer's Dilemma, 6 Hofstra L.Rev. 665 (1978).

Lehman, The Pursuit of a Client's Interest, 77 Michigan L.Rev. 1078 (1979).

Luban, Are Criminal Defendants Different?, 61 Michigan L.Rev. 1729 (1993).

MacCarthy & Mejia, The Perjurious Client Question: Putting Criminal Defense Lawyers Between a Rock and a Hard Place, 74 J.Criminal L. & Criminology 1197 (1984).

Marschall, Who Should Decide the Appropriate Response to the Criminal Defendant Who Proposes or Commits Perjury: A Comparison of the North Carolina Rules of Professional Conduct and the American Bar Association's Model Rules of Professional Conduct, 17 North Carolina Central L.J. 157 (1988).

Mitchell, The Ethics of the Criminal Defense Attorney—New Answers to Old Questions, 32 Stanford L.Rev. 293 (1980).

Morrow, Perjured Alibi Testimony: The Defense Attorney's Conflicting Duties, 48 Missouri L.Rev. 257 (1983).

Mounts, Public Defender Programs, Professional Responsibility, and Competent Representation, 1982 Wisconsin L.Rev. 473 (1982).

O'Brien, Removing the Client Perjury Skeleton From the Defense Counsel's Closet, 22 New England L.Rev. 675 (1988).

Polster, Dilemma of the Perjurious Defendant: Resolution, Not Avoidance, 28 Case Western Res.L.Rev. 3 (1977).

Pye, The Role of Counsel in the Suppression of Truth, 1978 Duke L.J. 921.

Rich, The Role of Lawyers: Beyond Advocacy, 1980 B.Y.U. L.Rev. 767 (1980).

Rieger, Client Perjury: A Proposed Resolution of the Constitutional and Ethical Issues, 70 Minnesota L.Rev. 121 (1985).

Rotunda, When the Client Lies: Unhelpful Guides From the ABA, 1 Corporation L.Rev. 34 (1978).

Rotunda, Book Review of Freedman's Lawyers' Ethics in an Adversary System, 89 Harvard L.Rev. 62 (1976).

Rotunda, Client Fraud: Blowing the Whistle, Other Options, 24 Trial Magazine 92 (Nov., 1988).

Rotunda, The Litigator's Professional Responsibility, 25 Trial Magazine 98 (March, 1989).

Rotunda, The Notice of Withdrawal and the New Model Rules of Professional Conduct: Blowing the Whistle and Waving the Red Flag, 63 Oregon L.Rev. 455 (1984).

Saltzburg, Lawyers, Clients, and the Adversary System, 37 Mercer L.Rev. 647 (1986).

Sampson, Client Perjury: Truth, Autonomy, and the Criminal Defense Lawyer, 9 Am.J.Criminal L. 387 (1981).

Schwartz, The Zeal of the Civil Advocate, 1983 A.B.F. Research J. 543 (1983).

Silver, Truth, Justice, and the American Way: The Case Against the Client Perjury Rules, 47 Vanderbilt L.Rev. 339 (1994).

Simon, The Ethics of Criminal Defense, 91 Michigan L.Rev. 1703 (1993).

Subin, Is This Lie Necessary? Further Reflections on the Right to Present a False Defense, 1 Georgetown J.Legal Ethics 689 (1988).

Thode, The Ethical Standard for the Advocate, 39 Texas L.Rev. 575 (1961).

Underwood, False Witness: A Lawyer's History of the Law of Perjury, 10 Arizona J.Inter. & Compar.L. 215 (1993).

Wolfram, Client Perjury, 50 S.California L.Rev. 809 (1977).

Problem 28

Abramovsky, Surreptitious Recording of Witnesses in Criminal Cases: A Quest for Truth or a Violation of Law and Ethics?, 57 Tulane L.Rev. 1 (1982).

Campbell, Jury Secrecy and Impeachment of Jury Verdicts—Part II, 9 Criminal L.J. 187 (1985).

Enker, The Rationale of the Rule that Forbids a Lawyer To Be Advocate and Witness in the Same Case, 1977 A.B.F. Research J. 455.

Jablonski, The Advocate–Witness Rule: Let's Call it the Way We See it, 52 Albany L.Rev. 531 (1988).

Lewis, The Ethical Dilemma of the Testifying Advocate: Fact or Fancy?, 19 Houston L.Rev. 75 (1981).

Lynch, Application of the Advocate–Witness Rule, 1982 Southern Illinois U. L.J. 291 (1982).

Note, Advocate–Witness Rule: If Z, then X, But Why?, 52 N.Y.U.L.Rev. 1365 (1977).

Smith, Model Rule 4.2: Ethical Restrictions on Communications with Former Employees, 15 Employee Relations L.J. 239 (1989).

Wise, The Attorney–Witness Rule in Patent Infringement Litigation, 68 Journal of the Patent and Trademark Office Society 294 (1986).

Wydick, Trial Counsel as Witness: The Code and the Model Rules, 15 U.California (Davis) L.Rev. 651 (1982).

Problem 29

Berkowitz–Caballero, In the Aftermath of *Gentile*: Reconsidering the Efficacy of Trial Publicity Rules, 68 N.Y.U. L.Rev. 494 (1993).

Berman, The Attorney/Client Privilege and the IRS: Assessing the Currency Transaction Reporting Regulations, 77 Illinois Bar J. 530 (1989).

Bresler, Seeking Justice, Seeking Election, and Seeking the Death Penalty: The Ethics of Prosecutorial Candidates' Campaigning on Capital Convictions, 7 Georgetown J.Legal Ethics 941 (1994).

Brickey, Forfeiture of Attorney's Fees: The Impact of RICO and CCE Forfeitures on the Right to Counsel, 72 Virginia L.Rev. 493 (1986).

Erlinder & Thomas, Prohibiting Prosecutorial Vindictiveness While Protecting Prosecutorial Discretion: Toward a Principled Resolution of a Due Process Dilemma, 76 J.Crim.L. & Criminology 341 (1985).

Cross, Prosecutorial Vindictiveness: An Examination of Divergent Lower Court Standards and a Proposed Framework for Analysis, 34 Vanderbilt L.Rev. 431 (1981).

Day, The Supreme Court's Attack on Attorneys' Freedom of Expression: The *Gentile v. State Bar of Nevada* Decision, 43 Case Western Res. L.Rev. 1347 (1993).

Dubin, The Case of the Missing Evidence: Why Prosecutors and Defense Lawyers are Judged by Different Standards, 15 Student Lawyer 8(2) (1987).

Edwards, Professional Responsibilities of the Federal Prosecutor, 17 U. Richmond L.Rev. 511 (1983).

Fisher, "Just the Facts Ma'am": Lying and the Omission of Exculpatory Evidence in Police Reports, 28 N.England L.Rev. 1 (1993).

Freedman, The Professional Responsibility of the Prosecuting Attorney, 55 Georgetown L.J. 1030 (1967).

Freedman & Starwood, Prior Restraints on Freedom of Expression by Defendants and Defense Attorneys, 29 Stanford L.Rev. 607 (1977).

Goldberg, Publication Rights Agreements in Sensational Criminal Cases: A Response to the Problem, 68 Cornell L.Rev. 686 (1983).

Goode, Identity, Fees, and the Attorney–Client Privilege, 59 George Washington L.Rev. 307 (1991).

Hacker & Rotunda, Restrictions on Agency and Congressional Subpoenas Issued for an Improper Purpose, 4 Corporation L.Rev. 74 (1981).

Hassett, A Jury's Pre–Trial Knowledge in Historical Perspective: The Distinction Between Pre–Trial Information and "Prejudicial" Publicity, 43 Law & Contemp.Prob. 155 (1980).

Hoye, Silencing the Advocates or Policing the Profession? Ethical Limitations on the First Amendment Rights of Attorneys, 38 Drake L.Rev. 31 (1989).

Jackson, The Federal Prosecutor, 24 J.American Judicature Soc'y 18 (1940).

Jorstad, Litigation Ethics: A Niebuhrian View of the Adversarial Legal System, 99 Yale L.J. 1089 (1990).

Kaplan, The Prosecutorial Discretion—A Comment, 60 Northwestern U.L.Rev. 174 (1965).

Lynch, The Lawyer as Informer, 1986 Duke L.J. 491 (1986).

Note, A Constitutional Assessment of Court Rules Restricting Lawyer Comment on Pending Litigation, 65 Cornell L.Rev. 1106 (1980).

Note, A Critical Appraisal of the Justice Dept. Guidelines for Grand Jury Subpoenas Issued to Defense Attorneys, 1986 Duke L.J. 145.

Note, Actions Against Prosecutors Who Suppress or Falsify Evidence, 47 Texas L.Rev. 642 (1969).

Note, Against Forfeiture of Attorney's Fees Under RICO: Protecting the Constitutional Rights of Criminal Defendants, 61 N.Y.U. L.Rev. 124 (1986).

Note, Attorney Fee Forfeiture, 86 Columbia L.Rev. 1021 (1986).

Note, Attorney "Gag" Rules: Reconciling the First Amendment and the Right to a Fair Trial, 1976 U.Illinois L.Forum 763.

Note, Grand Jury Subpoena of a Target's Attorney: The Need for a Preliminary Showing, 20 Georgia L.Rev. 747 (1986).

Note, Grand Jury Proceedings: The Prosecutor, the Trial Judge, and Undue Influence, 39 U.Chicago L.Rev. 761 (1972).

Note, Prejudicial Publicity in Trials of Public Officials, 85 Yale L.J. 123 (1975).

Note, The Prosecutor's Duty to Disclose to Defendants Pleading Guilty, 99 Harvard L.Rev. 1004 (1986).

Note, The Prosecutor's Duty to Disclose Unrequested Impeachment Evidence: The Fifth Circuit's Approach, 61 Washington U.L.Q. 163 (1983).

Note, Publication Rights Agreements in Sensational Criminal Cases: A Response to the Problem, 68 Cornell L.Rev. 686 (1983).

Podgor & Weiner, Prosecutorial Misconduct: Alive and Well, and Living in Indiana?, 3 Georgetown J. Legal Ethics 657 (1990).

Robertson, Criminal Procedure—After United States v. Klubock: Can Massachusetts' New Ethical Rule Curb the Practice of Subpoenaing the Attorneys of Grand Jury Targets?, 11 Western New England L.Rev. 283 (1989).

Rotondo, A Constitutional Assessment of Court Rules Restricting Lawyer Comment on Pending Litigation, 65 Cornell L.Rev. 1106 (1980).

Rotunda, Racist Speech and Attorney Discipline, 6 The Professional Lawyer 1 (ABA No. 6, 1995).

Rotunda, Can You Say That?, 30 Trial Magazine 18 (Dec.1994).

Sanders, Government Attorneys and the Ethical Rules: Good Souls in Limbo, 7 B.Y.U. J.Public L. 39 (1992).

Sperber, Publication Rights Fee Contracts Between Attorneys and Criminal Defendants: Waiving the Right to Conflict–Free Counsel, 17 University of San Francisco L.Rev. 549 (1983).

Steele, Unethical Prosecutors and Inadequate Discipline, 38 Southwestern L.J. 965 (1984).

Stern & Hoffman, Privileged Informers: The Attorney Subpoena Problem and a Proposal for Reform, 136 U.Pennsylvania L.Rev. 1783 (1988).

Swift, Model Rule 3.6: An Unconstitutional Regulation of Defense Attorney Trial Publicity, 64 Boston U.L.Rev. 1003 (1984).

Turlington, Socrates's Courtroom Ethics, 59 A.B.A. J. 505 (1973).

Uviller, The Virtuous Prosecutor in Quest of an Ethical Standard: Guidance from the ABA, 71 Michigan L.Rev. 1145 (1973).

Zacharias, A Critical Look at Rules Governing Grand Jury Subpoenas of Attorneys, 76 Minnesota L.Rev. 917 (1992).

Zacharias, Specificity in Professional Codes: Theory, Practice, and the Paradigm of Prosecutorial Ethics, 69 Notre Dame L.Rev. 223 (1993).

Zwerling, Federal Grand Juries v. Attorney Independence and the Attorney–Client Privilege, 27 Hastings L.J. 1263 (1976).

Chapter VII

THE DELIVERY OF LEGAL SERVICES

In the final version of the ABA Model Code (1981), Ethical Consideration 2–2, reflected the hesitancy with which the bar approached legal advertising: "Preparation of advertisements * * * and participation in seminars, lectures, and civic programs should be motivated by a desire to educate the public to an awareness of legal needs and to provide information relevant to the selection of the most appropriate counsel rather than to obtain publicity for particular lawyers. The problems of advertising on television require special consideration, due to the style, cost, and transitory nature of such media."

Model Rule 7.2, Comment 1, exhibits a very different attitude: "To assist the public in obtaining legal services, lawyers should be allowed to make known their services not only through reputation but also through organized information campaigns in the form of advertising."

In recent years lawyers have talked more opening and frankly of "marketing" legal services, increasing client demand for services, and seeking new clients. In addition, they have talked of "one-stop shopping" and the integrating of legal services with a variety of ancillary activities including investment banking, lobbying and real estate development.

As you examine the problems and materials in this chapter, ask yourself such questions as:

a. Is law becoming a "commercial" activity? Is that inevitable? Desirable for lawyers? Desirable for clients? Does such a change make law less of a "profession"? Is there a difference between practicing a "profession" and being in a "trade or business"?

b. What role are the federal courts—as distinguished from the state supreme courts—playing in transforming the profession? At whose expense are the rules being changed?

c. What is the nature of a law firm today? How does it come into being? How does it break up? What are the duties of its members to each other?

d. How can legal services be made widely available? Should lawyers be required to volunteer their services to persons unable to pay for assistance? Should lawyers be given an incentive to bring cases in the public interest by requiring losing defendants to pay the plaintiffs' legal fees? What alternatives to traditional law partnerships might better provide legal services to persons not now receiving them?

PROBLEM 31

Professional Advertising

Jerry Harrold has just moved to a new community. He has published the following quarter-page advertisement in the local newspaper:

Introducing

JERRY HARROLD

Doctor of Law

Hi—

    I'm Jerry Harrold and I'm a lawyer. I'm 34 years old and a native of this state. I was born in Rushville and have practiced law for the past six years in Capital City. I went to State Law School, was a member of the moot court team, and served my country for three years as a Judge Advocate in the Army. My doctor's degree in law is the professional degree a lawyer normally earns. I don't claim to be the best lawyer in the state, but some of my former clients have agreed to act as references. I'll be glad to supply their names to you so that you can check me out yourself.

    I am unusual in one respect. I charge clients a flat rate of $65 per hour, win or lose, big case or small. That lets me cover my expenses and have a decent income, but most of my clients have found that it saves them a great deal in legal fees, particularly in routine matters like real estate and probate for which many lawyers charge a percentage of the sum involved in the transaction.

    I look forward to meeting you soon.

                                   Jerry

425 Center Street
Suite 518
Lewistown, Michigan 40608
332–4816

QUESTIONS

1. Is Harrold's advertisement constitutionally protected?

a. What, if anything, is it inherently proper to say in an advertisement after Bates v. State Bar of Arizona, found in the Readings to this Problem? Does Jerry's ad deal with subjects that could constitutionally be limited?

b. Could professional discipline of Jerry survive the four–part test of constitutionality applied in Zauderer v. Office of Disciplinary Counsel, also a Reading to this Problem? Look at those four elements: "Commercial speech that is [1] not false or deceptive and [2] does not concern unlawful activities * * * may be restricted [3] only in the service of a substantial governmental interest, and [4] only through means that directly advance that interest." Can you posit a "substantial governmental interest" in limiting what Jerry has said here? [1]

c. Do you agree with the Court in *Bates* that advertising has no impact on lawyer professionalism? How about on the public perception of lawyer professionalism?

d. Would it serve a "substantial governmental interest" to require that a lawyer's advertising be "dignified"? [2] How would you define "dignity" in the context of lawyer advertising? After *Zauderer*, is there any room left for such a requirement?

e. Could Jerry constitutionally be disciplined if portions of his advertisement (e.g., his fee arrangement) were printed in all capital letters, or in bold print? What if the advertisement included his picture?

f. May a state require that disclaimers be included with certain kinds of statements? Is the rule that, in general, a state may require more information in lawyer advertising, but not less? Do you agree with the Court in *Zauderer* that even requiring a disclaimer might "chill" protected speech under some circumstances?

2. How does Harrold's advertisement fare under the ABA Model Code, as revised after Bates? How about under the Model Rules?

a. Look at the list of things that DR 2–101(B) said an ad may

---

1. The Court was relying on Central Hudson Gas & Electric Corp. v. Public Service Commission, 447 U.S. 557, 100 S.Ct. 2343, 65 L.Ed.2d 341 (1980). *Central Hudson* invalidated a state regulation that completely banned a utility from advertising that promoted the use of electricity. Although the electric utility had a monopoly over the sale of electricity in its service area, the Court said consumers still had an interest in receiving its message. The state said the advertising ban served the interest of energy conservation but made no show-

ing that a more limited restriction on the content of promotional advertising would not adequately serve the state's interest; for example, the state could have required that advertisements include information about the relative efficiency and expense of the services it offered.

2. A pre-*Zauderer* opinion defending such a requirement is Spencer v. Honorable Justices of Supreme Ct. of Pennsylvania, 579 F.Supp. 880 (E.D.Pa.1984), aff'd 760 F.2d 281 (3d Cir.1985).

contain. Has Jerry gone beyond what is permitted by that list?[3] Is being a member of the moot court team, for example, something a lawyer could advertise?

b. Under Model Rules 7.1 and 7.2, notice that lawyer advertising is presumptively valid. Has Jerry violated any of the prohibitions in the Model Rules?

c. If Jerry is also a certified public accountant, should he be permitted to so indicate in Martindale–Hubbell, the Yellow Pages, a newspaper advertisement, and his professional card?

Ibanez v. Florida Board of Accountancy, ___ U.S. ___, 114 S.Ct. 2084, 129 L.Ed.2d 118 (1994), involved a lawyer who was also a CPA and CFP (certified financial planner). She wanted to use both designations in her yellow pages advertising as a lawyer, and on her business card and stationery. The Florida Board of Accountancy (not The Florida Bar) reprimanded her for engaging in "false, deceptive and misleading advertising." Justice Ginsburg, writing for the Court, found the State's position "entirely insubstantial" and reversed the order of sanction. Justice O'Connor and Chief Justice Rehnquist, however, raised concerns that the designations might be inherently misleading; they would have approved use of the well-known CPA designation but not the less-known CFP.

d. Should a lawyer be entitled to make claims as to her quality? Her won-lost record?

Matter of Zang, 154 Ariz. 134, 741 P.2d 267 (1987), cert. denied 484 U.S. 1067, 108 S.Ct. 1030, 98 L.Ed.2d 994 (1988), illustrated that lawyers can be disciplined if their advertising is truly misleading. Two lawyers claimed to have "a personal injury law firm" with the capability to discover facts "essential to victory in the courtroom." Each of their advertisements showed Mr. Zang arguing before a jury. In fact, Mr. Zang had very little trial experience and "scrupulously avoided" taking a case to trial. If a trial were necessary, he would refer the case to another firm. He personally had never tried a personal injury case, and he conceded in the discipline proceeding that he did not feel competent to try one. He argued that the advertisements did not say that the lawyers were good at trial; they only said the lawyers were good at *preparing for* trial. The Court rejected the argument and suspended the lawyers for 30 days.

Later, in People v. Morse, 25 Cal.Rptr.2d 816 (Cal.App.1993), a lawyer was assessed over $800,000 in civil penalties and restitution for making misleading claims about his ability to help homeowners file homestead exemptions.

---

3. Notice that until relatively quite recently, the law of attorney advertising did not change much: the list in DR 2–101(B) was derived from the old ABA Canons of Professional Ethics, Canon 37 ("Advertising, Direct or Indirect"), in the Standards Supplement.

3. May Harrold put his advertisement on television?

a. Could Jerry stand before the camera himself and recite the information in his "letter"? Should he be permitted to hire a famous television personality to endorse him? Why or why not?

b. Should there be any limit on the context in which advertising may be placed? Might an attorney buy an ad on reruns of "L.A. Law" if she wanted to emphasize her sophisticated, tough trial style, or "Entertainment Tonight" if she wanted to emphasize her interest in high-profile cases?

c. Should a lawyer be able to buy time on "Oprah" and say, "Taken enough from your husband? Come to my office for an understanding ear and a quick divorce"? Cf. California Attorney General Opinion No. CR 77–65 (1978), asserting the invalidity of a statute seeking to regulate advertising of divorce services.

d. Issues surrounding television advertising have become more interesting since Committee on Professional Ethics v. Humphrey, 377 N.W.2d 643 (Iowa 1985). The Iowa Supreme Court adopted strict limitations on television advertising, forbidding background sounds, visible displays, more than a single nondramatic voice, and any self-laudatory statements. After *Zauderer,* the U.S. Supreme Court remanded *Humphrey,* which had upheld the Iowa rules.

On remand, the Iowa Supreme Court, by a 5 to 3 vote, again upheld the rules. As the Iowa court saw the problem, "Both sight and sound are immediate and can be elusive because, for the listener or viewer at least, in a flash they are gone without a trace. Lost is the opportunity accorded to the reader of printed advertisements to pause, to restudy, and to thoughtfully consider." 377 N.W.2d at 646. When an appeal from this decision was again taken to the U.S. Supreme Court, the Court surprised almost everyone by dismissing the appeal for lack of a substantial federal question. 475 U.S. 1114, 106 S.Ct. 1626, 90 L.Ed.2d 174 (1986).

e. In The Florida Bar: Petition to Amend the Rules—Advertising Issues, 571 So.2d 451 (Fla.1990), Florida also approved broad restrictive rules on lawyer advertising. Among the prohibitions are the use of celebrity voices, background sounds other than instrumental music, dramatizations, and testimonials. Further, media spots must carry a legend saying "The hiring of a lawyer * * * should not be based solely on advertisements."

In 1994, Texas lawyers adopted new requirements that include (1) explaining how contingent fees will be calculated, (2) revealing if the case will be referred to another lawyer, and (3) omitting addresses of branch offices unless a lawyer will be there at least 3 days a week or unless the ad specifies what hours the lawyer will be there.

The California Assembly also proposed in 1994 imposing new restrictions on television advertising by that state's lawyers, among them, (1) there must be only one voice on the ad and it must be that of a lawyer in the firm, (2) a legend must be shown saying "The filing of a claim or suit solely to coerce a settlement or to harass another could be illegal * * * ", and (3) a legend must say "The * * * choice of a lawyer * * * should not be based solely upon advertisements or self–proclaimed expertise."

Do you think any of these rules will survive constitutional scrutiny? If they are upheld in future cases, they can be expected to be the basis for comparable rules in other states.

4. May a law firm practice under a trade name, e.g. the Main Street Law Factory?

a. Compare Model Rule 7.5(a) with DR 2–102(B). Is there any limit on names that can be selected? Is the "Winning Team" a misleading name? If not, may it constitutionally be banned? Cf. Friedman v. Rogers, 440 U.S. 1, 99 S.Ct. 887, 59 L.Ed.2d 100 (1979), holding that a statute forbidding optometrists from practicing under a trade name does not violate the First Amendment.

b. If the state allows a law firm to practice under the names of partners who died long ago, e.g., Cravath, Swaine & Moore, may it forbid practicing under names of lawyers licensed in other states? See Model Rule 7.5(b) and DR 2–102(B) & (D). In reviewing an opinion of its Professional Ethics Committee, the New Jersey Supreme Court upheld forbidding Jacoby & Meyers (a national organization of "legal clinics") from advertising in the state because neither Leonard Jacoby nor Stephen Meyers was personally admitted in New Jersey. See On Petition for Review of Opinion 475, 89 N.J. 74, 444 A.2d 1092 (1982). Should such a limitation on advertising survive constitutional challenge?

5. Should lawyers be permitted to advertise complete fee information?

a. Compare DR 2–101(B)(20)–(25) with Model Rules 7.1 and 7.2. Is there a danger that fee information might be misleading? For example, might factors underlying the fee in a particular case be difficult to explain in a general announcement? Might lawyers be forced into billing based on schedules, formulas or percentages? Are these concerns serious enough to justify prohibiting Jerry Harrold from publicizing his $65 per hour rate?

b. Should a lawyer be permitted to advertise "discount" services to certain groups, say, a 20% discount on wills for persons over 65? Why or why not? A public reprimand for such a pricing policy was imposed in Kentucky Bar Association v. Gangwish, 630 S.W.2d 66 (Ky.1982).

c. May clients be offered a coupon for a free chicken dinner with every office visit? Cf. Talsky v. Department of Registration and Education, 68 Ill.2d 579, 12 Ill.Dec. 550, 370 N.E.2d 173 (1977), cert. denied 439 U.S. 820, 99 S.Ct. 84, 58 L.Ed.2d 111 (1978) (chiropractor disciplined for making such an offer).

d. Attorney Ken Hur of Madison, Wisconsin, advertised that he would give a free 10–speed bicycle to any of his clients whose drunk driving case he lost. Would you have subjected him to professional discipline? See Bar Leader, Nov./Dec. 1978, p. 7.

6. What kinds of lawyers benefit from being able to advertise?

a. Are small firms and young lawyers given a competitive boost because they can make themselves known? Are large firms with big budgets growing at the expense of smaller economic units? Notice the majority and dissent's analysis of these issues in *Bates* in the Readings to this Problem. Which has proved more correct?

b. Do restrictions on advertising tend to keep lawyers' fees low? Do fees have to rise to cover the cost of advertising? Might fees come down as advertising permits comparative shopping? Should such consequences affect your judgment about the value of advertising to consumers of legal services?

c. Might one predict that the lawyers who advertise most will be the ones who tend to make the most "profit" on each case, i.e., the ones who have the biggest spread between their fees and their costs? Is that confirmed by the kinds of lawyers you see doing the most advertising today? Keep these questions in mind as you think about the economics of contingent fees that you saw in Problem 7.

7. Should the organized bar be subject to ethical restrictions on its own advertising?

a. Do the Rules prohibit a bar association, for example, from using advertising to convince the public of a need for legal services in general? Should they do so? Is the same possibility of misleading lay people present?

b. Are the economic consequences of competitive advertising different from those of institutional advertising by bar associations?

READINGS

One Vision of Legal Advertising

Reprinted with permission from the *Journal of the Academy of Florida Trial Lawyers*, December, 1974. Adapted from a drawing by Dale Morgan of the Orlando Bar.

[B2798]

AN INTRODUCTORY NOTE TO THE *BATES* DECISION

For many years the organized bar, and state courts in their regulation of lawyers, forbade most types of attorney advertising. Canon 27 of the ABA Canons of Professional Ethics (1908) declared simply: "It is unprofessional to solicit professional employment by circulars, advertisements, through touters or by personal communications or interviews not warranted by personal relations."

In the mid–1970s, concern about lawyer self-touting increased. Justice Powell presided over a panel at the August 1976 "Bicentennial" A.B.A. Annual Meeting at which British speakers reported their longstanding opposition to professional advertising, and former Solicitor General Erwin Griswold argued:

The restriction on advertising * * * is deeply embedded in a profession with ancient roots, but it has no direct competitive effect. The client is wholly free to make inquiries, and the members of the profession are unrestrained in their responses. The client can always ask in advance what the lawyer's qualifications are, and what the fee will be. He can make similar inquiries of other lawyers, and there are many lawyers. The client is then wholly free to choose the one he wants.

Nevertheless, two developments supported undercutting the prohibition of lawyer advertising. First were the "commercial speech" cases, which had found a First Amendment right to engage in truthful advertising, at least where there was an apparent public interest in having the information available. Second was the developing belief that the general public lacks important information about the nature and cost of legal services, which in turn affects the ability and willingness of people to use those services.*

BATES v. STATE BAR OF ARIZONA
Supreme Court of the United States, 1977.
433 U.S. 350, 97 S.Ct. 2691, 53 L.Ed.2d 810.

Justice BLACKMUN delivered the opinion of the Court.

* * *

I

Appellants John R. Bates and Van O'Steen are attorneys licensed to practice law in the State of Arizona. As such, they are members of the appellee, the State Bar of Arizona. After admission to the bar in 1972, appellants worked as attorneys with the Maricopa County Legal Aid Society.

In March 1974, appellants left the Society and opened a law office, which they call a "legal clinic," in Phoenix. Their aim was to provide legal services at modest fees to persons of moderate income who did not qualify for governmental legal aid. In order to achieve this end, they would accept only routine matters, such as uncontested divorces, uncontested adoptions, simple personal bankruptcies, and changes of name, for which costs could be kept down by extensive use of paralegals, automatic typewriting equipment, and standardized forms and office procedures. More complicated cases, such as contested divorces, would not be accepted. Because appellants set their prices so as to have a relatively low return on each case they handled, they depended on substantial volume.

After conducting their practice in this manner for two years, appellants concluded that their practice and clinical concept could not survive unless the availability of legal services at low costs was advertised and in particular, fees were advertised. Consequently in order to generate the necessary flow of business, that is, "to attract clients," appellants on February 22, 1976, placed an advertisement (reproduced in the Appendix) in the *Arizona Republic*, a daily newspaper of general circulation in the Phoenix metropolitan area. As may be seen, the advertisement

----

* An interesting earlier study on this issue was Federal Trade Commission, Improving Consumer Access to Legal Services (1984). See also, Benham, The Effect of Advertising on the Price of Eyeglasses, 15 J.Law & Econ. 337 (1972).

stated that appellants were offering "legal services at very reasonable fees," and listed their fees for certain services.

Appellants concede that the advertisement constituted a clear violation of Disciplinary Rule 2–101(B), embodied in Rule 29(a) of the Supreme Court of Arizona.

[Bates and O'Steen were suspended from the practice of law for one week each, the weeks to run consecutively. The result was affirmed, and the challenge to the advertising ban rejected by the Arizona Supreme Court.]

II.　THE SHERMAN ACT

* * *

In *Goldfarb* * we held that § 1 of the Sherman Act was violated by the publication of a minimum-fee schedule by a county bar association and by its enforcement by the State Bar. * * * Both bar associations argued that their activity was shielded by the state-action exemption. This Court concluded that the action was not protected, * * * "because it cannot fairly be said that the State of Virginia through its Supreme Court Rules required the anticompetitive activities of either respondent." In the instant case, by contrast, the challenged restraint is the affirmative command of the Arizona Supreme Court * * *. That Court is the ultimate body wielding the State's power over the practice of law, * * * and, thus, the restraint is "compelled by direction of the State acting as a sovereign."

* * *

III.　THE FIRST AMENDMENT

A

Last Term, in Virginia Pharmacy Bd. v. Virginia Consumer Council, 425 U.S. 748, 96 S.Ct. 1817, 48 L.Ed.2d 346 (1976), the Court considered the validity under the First Amendment of a Virginia statute declaring that a pharmacist was guilty of "unprofessional conduct" if he advertised prescription drug prices. * * * We recognized that the pharmacist who desired to advertise did not wish to report any particularly newsworthy fact or to comment on any cultural, philosophical, or political subject; his desired communication was characterized simply: " 'I will sell you the X prescription drug at the Y price.' " Nonetheless, we held that commercial speech of that kind was entitled to the protection of the First Amendment.

* * *

* [Ed. note] The Court was referring to Goldfarb v. Virginia State Bar, 421 U.S. 773, 95 S.Ct. 2004, 44 L.Ed.2d 572 (1975), set forth as a Reading to Problem 7.

B

* * *

The heart of the dispute before us today is whether lawyers also may constitutionally advertise the *prices* at which certain routine services will be performed. Numerous justifications are proffered for the restriction of such price advertising. We consider each in turn:

1. **The Adverse Effect on Professionalism.** * * * [W]e find the postulated connection between advertising and the erosion of true professionalism to be severely strained. At its core, the argument presumes that attorneys must conceal from themselves and from their clients the real-life fact that lawyers earn their livelihood at the bar. We suspect that few attorneys engage in such self-deception. And rare is the client, moreover, even one of the modest means, who enlists the aid of an attorney with the expectation that his services will be rendered free of charge. In fact, the American Bar Association advises that an attorney should reach "a clear agreement with his client as to the basis of the fee charges to be made," and that this is to be done "[a]s soon as feasible after a lawyer has been employed." [EC 2–19] If the commercial basis of the relationship is to be promptly disclosed on ethical grounds, once the client is in the office, it seems inconsistent to condemn the candid revelation of the same information before he arrives at that office.

Moreover, the assertion that advertising will diminish the attorney's reputation in the community is open to question. Bankers and engineers advertise, and yet these professions are not regarded as undignified. In fact, it has been suggested that the failure of lawyers to advertise creates public disillusionment with the profession. The absence of advertising may be seen to reflect the profession's failure to reach out and serve the community: studies reveal that many persons do not obtain counsel even when they perceive a need because of the feared price of services[22] or because of an inability to locate a competent attorney.[23] Indeed, cynicism with regard to the profession may be created by the fact that it long has publicly eschewed advertising, while

---

22. * * * P. Murphy & S. Walkowski, Compilation of Reference Materials on Prepaid Legal Services 2–3 (1973) (summarizing study in which 514 of 1,040 respondents gave expected cost as reason for not using a lawyer's services despite a perceived need). There are indications that fear of cost is unrealistic. See Petition of the Board of Governors of the District of Columbia Bar * * *, reprinted in the Brief of the United States as *Amicus Curiae*, App. B, 10a, 24a–25a (reporting study in which middle class consumers over-estimated lawyers' fees by 91% for the drawing of a simple will, 340% for reading and advising on a 2–page installment sales contract, and 123% for 30 minutes of consultation). See also F. Marks, R. Hallauer, R. Clifton, The Shreveport Plan: An Experiment in the Delivery of Legal Services 50–52 (1974).

23. The preliminary release of some of the results of a survey conducted by the ABA Special Committee to Survey Legal Needs in collaboration with the American Bar Foundation reveals that 48.7% strongly agreed and another 30.2% slightly agreed with the statement that people do not go to lawyers because they have no way of knowing which lawyers are competent to handle their particular problems. 3 Alternatives: Legal Services & the Public, January 1976, 15. See B. Curran & F. Spalding, The Legal Needs of the Public 96 (Preliminary Report 1974) (an earlier report concerning the same survey). Although advertising by itself is not adequate to deal with this problem completely, it can provide some of the information that a consumer needs to make an intelligent selection.

condoning the actions of the attorney who structures his social or civic associations so as to provide contacts with potential clients.

* * * Since the belief that lawyers are somehow "above" trade has become an anachronism, the historical foundation for the advertising restraint has crumbled.

2. **The Inherently Misleading Nature of Attorney Advertising.** * * *

We are not persuaded that restrained professional advertising by lawyers inevitably will be misleading. Although many services performed by attorneys are indeed unique, it is doubtful that any attorney would or could advertise fixed prices for services of that type.[25] The only services that lend themselves to advertising are the routine ones: the uncontested divorce, the simple adoption, the uncontested personal bankruptcy, the change of name, and the like—the very services advertised by appellants.[26] Although the precise service demanded in each task may vary slightly, and although legal services are not fungible, these facts do not make advertising misleading so long as the attorney does the necessary work at the advertised price.[27] The argument that legal services are so unique that fixed rates cannot meaningfully be established is refuted by the record in this case: the appellee State Bar itself sponsors a Legal Services Program in which the participating attorneys agree to perform services like those advertised by the appellants at standardized rates. Indeed, until the decision of this Court in *Goldfarb* * * * the Maricopa County Bar Association apparently had a schedule of suggested minimum fees for standard legal tasks. We thus find of little force the assertion that advertising is misleading because of an inherent lack of standardization in legal services.

The second component of the argument—that advertising ignores the diagnostic role—fares little better. It is unlikely that many people go to an attorney merely to ascertain if they have a clean bill of legal health. Rather, attorneys are likely to be employed to perform specific tasks. Although the client may not know the detail involved in perform-

---

25. See Morgan, The Evolving Concept of Professional Responsibility, 90 Harv. L.Rev. 702, 741 (1977); Note, Advertising, Solicitation and the Profession's Duty to Make Legal Counsel Available, 81 Yale L.J. 1181, 1203 (1972). Economic considerations suggest that advertising is a more significant force in the marketing of inexpensive and frequently used goods and services with mass markets, than in the marketing of unique products or services.

26. Moreover, we see nothing that is misleading in the advertisement of the cost of an initial half-hour consultation. The American Bar Association's Code of Professional Responsibility, DR 2–102(A)(6) (1976) permits the disclosure of such fee

information in the classified section of a telephone directory. If the information is not misleading when published in a telephone directory, it is difficult to see why it becomes misleading when published in a newspaper.

27. One commentator has observed that "a moment's reflection reveals that the same argument can be made for barbers; rarely are two haircuts identical, but that does not mean that barbers cannot quote a standard price. Lawyers perform countless relatively standardized services which vary somewhat in complexity but not so much as to make each job utterly unique." Morgan, supra, at 714.

ing the task, he no doubt is able to identify the service he desires at the level of generality to which advertising lends itself.

The third component is not without merit: advertising does not provide a complete foundation on which to select an attorney. But it seems peculiar to deny the consumer, on the ground that the information is incomplete, at least some of the relevant information needed to reach an informed decision. The alternative—the prohibition of advertising—serves only to restrict the information that flows to consumers. Moreover, the argument assumes that the public is not sophisticated enough to realize the limitations of advertising, and that the public is better kept in ignorance than trusted with correct but incomplete information. We suspect the argument rests on an underestimation of the public. In any event, we view as dubious any justification that is based on the benefits of public ignorance. Although, of course, the bar retains the power to correct omissions that have the effect of presenting an inaccurate picture, the preferred remedy is more disclosure, rather than less. If the naiveté of the public will cause advertising by attorneys to be misleading, then it is the bar's role to assure that the populace is sufficiently informed as to enable it to place advertising in its proper perspective.

3. **The Adverse Effect on the Administration of Justice.** Advertising is said to have the undesirable effect of stirring up litigation. * * * But advertising by attorneys is not an unmitigated source of harm to the administration of justice. It may offer great benefits. Although advertising might increase the use of the judicial machinery, we cannot accept the notion that it is always better for a person to suffer a wrong silently than to redress it by legal action. As the bar acknowledges, "the middle 70% of our population is not being reached or served adequately by the legal profession." [33] Among the reasons for this underutilization is fear of the cost, and an inability to locate a suitable lawyer. See nn. 22 and 23, supra. Advertising can help to solve this acknowledged problem: advertising is the traditional mechanism in a free-market economy for a supplier to inform a potential purchaser of the availability and terms of exchange. The disciplinary rule at issue likely has served to burden access to legal services, particularly for the not-quite-poor and the unknowledgeable. A rule allowing restrained advertising would be in accord with the bar's obligation to "facilitate the process of intelligent selection of lawyers, and to assist in making legal services fully available." [EC 2–1]

4. **The Undesirable Economic Effects of Advertising.** It is claimed that advertising will increase the overhead costs of the profession, and that these costs then will be passed along to consumers in the form of increased fees. Moreover, it is claimed that the additional cost of practice will create a substantial entry barrier, deterring or preventing

---

33. The ABA survey discussed in n. 23 indicates that 35.8% of the adult population has never visited an attorney and another 27.9% has visited an attorney only once. 3 Alternatives, supra, n. 23, at 12. Appellee concedes the existence of the problem, but argues that advertising offers an unfortunate solution.

young attorneys from penetrating the market and entrenching the position of the bar's established members.

These two arguments seem dubious at best. Neither distinguishes lawyers from others, and neither appears relevant to the First Amendment. The ban on advertising serves to increase the difficulty of discovering the lowest-cost seller of acceptable ability. As a result, to this extent attorneys are isolated from competition, and the incentive to price competitively is reduced. Although it is true that the effect of advertising on the price of services has not been demonstrated, there is revealing evidence with regard to products; where consumers have the benefit of price advertising, retail prices often are dramatically lower than they would be without advertising.[34] It is entirely possible that advertising will serve to reduce, not advance, the cost of legal services to the consumer.

The entry barrier argument is equally unpersuasive. In the absence of advertising, an attorney must rely on his contacts with the community to generate a flow of business. In view of the time necessary to develop such contacts, the ban in fact serves to perpetuate the market position of established attorneys. Consideration of entry-barrier problems would urge that advertising be allowed so as to aid the new competitor in penetrating the market.

5. **The Adverse Effect of Advertising on the Quality of Service.** It is argued that the attorney may advertise a given "package" of service at a set price, and will be inclined to provide, by indiscriminate use, the standard package regardless of whether it fits the client's needs.

Restraints on advertising, however, are an ineffective way of deterring shoddy work. An attorney who is inclined to cut quality will do so regardless of the rule on advertising. And the advertisement of a standardized fee does not necessarily mean that the services offered are undesirably standardized. Indeed, the assertion that an attorney who advertises a standard fee will cut quality is substantially undermined by the fixed fee schedule of appellee's own prepaid Legal Services Program. Even if advertising leads to the creation of "legal clinics" like that of appellants'—clinics that emphasize standardized procedures for routine problems—it is possible that such clinics will improve service by reducing the likelihood of error.

6. **The Difficulties of Enforcement.** Finally, it is argued that the wholesale restriction is justified by the problems of enforcement if any other course is taken. Because the public lacks sophistication in legal matters, it may be particularly susceptible to misleading or deceptive advertising by lawyers. After-the-fact action by the consumer lured by such advertising may not provide a realistic restraint because of the

---

34. See Benham, The Effect of Advertising on the Price of Eyeglasses, 15 J.Law & Econ. 337 (1972); Cady, Restricted Advertising & Competition: The Case of Retail Drugs (1976). See also Virginia Pharmacy Board v. Virginia Consumer Council, 425 U.S., at 754, and n. 11, 96 S.Ct., at 1821 (noting variation in drug prices of up to 1200% in one city).

inability of the layman to assess whether the service he has received meets professional standards. Thus, the vigilance of a regulatory agency will be required. But because of the numerous purveyors of services, the overseeing of advertising will be burdensome.

It is at least somewhat incongruous for the opponents of advertising to extol the virtues and altruism of the legal profession at one point, and, at another, to assert that its members will seize the opportunity to mislead and distort. We suspect that, with advertising, most lawyers will behave as they always have: they will abide by their solemn oaths to uphold the integrity and honor of their profession and of the legal system. For every attorney who overreaches through advertising, there will be thousands of others who will be candid and honest and straight-forward. And, of course, it will be in the latters' interest, as in other cases of misconduct at the bar, to assist in weeding out those few who abuse their trust.

In sum, we are not persuaded that any of the proffered justifications rises to the level of an acceptable reason for the suppression of all advertising by attorneys.

C

[The Court held that restrictions on professional advertising were not appropriate for invocation of the "overbreadth" doctrine but it found that the advertisement at issue here was not so misleading as to be properly regulatable.]

IV

In holding that advertising by attorneys may not be subjected to blanket suppression, and that the advertisement at issue is protected, we, of course, do not hold that advertising by attorneys may not be regulated in any way. We mention some of the clearly permissible limitations on advertising not foreclosed by our holding.

Advertising that is false, deceptive, or misleading of course is subject to restraint. See Virginia Pharmacy Board v. Virginia Citizens Council. Since the advertiser knows his product and has a commercial interest in its dissemination, we have little worry that regulation to assure truthful-ness will discourage protected speech. Id. And any concern that strict requirements for truthfulness will undesirably inhibit spontaneity seems inapplicable because commercial speech generally is calculated. Indeed, the public and private benefits from commercial speech derive from confidence in its accuracy and reliability. Thus, the leeway for untruth-ful or misleading expression that has been allowed in other contexts has little force in the commercial arena. In fact, because the public lacks sophistication concerning legal services, misstatements that might be overlooked or deemed unimportant in other advertising may be found quite inappropriate in legal advertising. For example, advertising claims as to the quality of services—a matter we do not address today—are not susceptible to measurement or verification; accordingly, such claims may be so likely to be misleading as to warrant restriction. Similar objections might justify restraints on in-person solicitation. We do not foreclose the possibility that some limited supplementation, by way of warning or disclaimer or the like, might be required of even an advertisement of the kind ruled upon today so as to assure that the consumer is not mislead. In sum, we recognize that many of the problems in defining the boundary between deceptive and nondeceptive advertising remain to be resolved, and we expect that the bar will have a special role to play in assuring that advertising by attorneys flows both freely and cleanly.

As with other varieties of speech, it follows as well that there may be reasonable restrictions on the time, place, and manner of advertising. * * * Advertising concerning transactions that are themselves illegal obviously may be suppressed. * * * And the special problems of advertising on the electronic broadcast media will warrant special consideration. * * *

The constitutional issue in this case is only whether the State may prevent the publication in a newspaper of appellants' truthful advertisement concerning the availability and terms of routine legal services. We rule simply that the flow of such information may not be restrained, and we therefore hold the present application of the disciplinary rule against appellants to be violative of the First Amendment.

The judgment of the Supreme Court of Arizona is therefore affirmed in part and reversed in part.

It is so ordered.

APPENDIX

Justice POWELL, with whom Justice STEWART joins, concurring in part and dissenting in part.

* * *

Although I disagree strongly with the Court's holding as to price advertisements of undefined—and I believe undefinable—routine legal services, there are reservations in its opinion worthy of emphasis since they may serve to narrow its ultimate reach. First, the Court notes that it has not addressed "the peculiar problems associated with advertisements containing claims as to the *quality* of legal services." There are inherent questions of quality in almost any type of price advertising by lawyers, and I do not view appellants' advertisement as entirely free from quality implications. * * *

Second, as in *Virginia Pharmacy*, the Court again notes that there may be reasonable restrictions on the time, place, and manner of commercial price advertising. In my view, such restrictions should have a significantly broader reach with respect to professional services than as to standardized products. This Court long has recognized the important state interests in the regulation of professional advertising. * * * Although the opinion today finds these interests insufficient to justify prohibition of all price advertising, the state interests recognized in these cases should be weighed carefully in any future consideration of time, place and manner restrictions.[12]

Finally, the Court's opinion does not "foreclose the possibility that some limited supplementation, by way of warning or disclaimer or the like, might be required of even an advertisement of the kind ruled upon today so as to assure that the consumer is not misled." I view this as at least some recognition of the potential for deception inherent in fixed price advertising of specific legal services. This recognition, though ambiguous in light of other statements in the opinion, may be viewed as encouragement to those who believe—as I do—that if we are to have price advertisement of legal services, the public interest will require the most particularized regulation. * * *

[The opinions of Chief Justice Burger and Justice Rehnquist are omitted. Both joined Part II of the Court's opinion on the effect of the Sherman Act. The Chief Justice's opinion was similar to Justice Powell's. Justice Rehnquist adhered to his position in *Virginia Pharmacy* that commercial speech is not protected by the First Amendment.]

ZAUDERER v. OFFICE OF DISCIPLINARY COUNSEL

Supreme Court of the United States, 1985.
471 U.S. 626, 105 S.Ct. 2265, 85 L.Ed.2d 652.

Justice WHITE delivered the opinion of the Court: * * *

I

Appellant is an attorney practicing in Columbus, Ohio. * * *

* * * In the spring of 1982, appellant placed an advertisement in 36 Ohio newspapers publicizing his willingness to represent women who

12. The Court speaks specifically only of newspaper advertising, but it is clear that today's decision cannot be confined on a principled basis to price advertisements in newspapers. No distinction can be drawn between newspapers and a rather broad spectrum of other means, for example, magazines, signs in buses and subways, posters, handbills, and mail circulations. But questions remain open as to time, place, and manner restrictions affecting other media, such as radio and television.

had suffered injuries resulting from their use of a contraceptive device known as the Dalkon Shield Intrauterine Device. The advertisement featured a line drawing of the Dalkon Shield accompanied by the question, "DID YOU USE THIS IUD?" The advertisement then related the following information:

> "The Dalkon Shield Interuterine [sic] Device is alleged to have caused serious pelvic infections resulting in hospitalizations, tubal damage, infertility, and hysterectomies. It is also alleged to have caused unplanned pregnancies ending in abortions, miscarriages, septic abortions, tubal or ectopic pregnancies, and full-term deliveries. If you or a friend have had a similar experience do not assume it is too late to take legal action against the Shield's manufacturer. Our law firm is presently representing women on such cases. The cases are handled on a contingent fee basis of the amount recovered. If there is no recovery, no legal fees are owed by our clients."

The ad concluded with the name of appellant's law firm, its address, and a phone number that the reader might call for "free information."

The advertisement was successful in attracting clients: appellant received well over 200 inquiries regarding the advertisement, and he initiated lawsuits on behalf of 106 of the women who contacted him as a result of the advertisement. The ad, however, also aroused the interest of the Office of Disciplinary Counsel. On July 29, 1982, the Office filed a complaint against appellant charging him with a number of disciplinary violations arising out of * * * [the] Dalkon Shield advertisement.

* * *

The complaint * * * alleged that the advertisement violated DR 2–101(B)(15), which provides that any advertisement that mentions contingent-fee rates must "disclos[e] whether percentages are computed before or after deduction of court costs and expenses," and that the ad's failure to inform clients that they would be liable for costs (as opposed to legal fees) even if their claims were unsuccessful rendered the advertisement "deceptive" in violation of DR 2–101(A). The * * * Office of Disciplinary Counsel stipulated that the [other] information and advice regarding Dalkon Shield litigation was not false, fraudulent, misleading or deceptive and that the drawing was an accurate representation of the Dalkon Shield.

* * *

The Supreme Court of Ohio * * * adopted the Board's findings that appellant's advertisements had violated the Disciplinary Rules specified by the hearing panel [and] concluded that appellant's conduct warranted a public reprimand. * * *

* * *

II

Our general approach to restrictions on commercial speech is * * * by now well settled. The States and the Federal Government are free to prevent the dissemination of commercial speech that is false, deceptive, or misleading, see Friedman v. Rogers, 440 U.S. 1, 59 L.Ed.2d 100, 99 S.Ct. 887 (1979), or that proposes an illegal transaction, see Pittsburgh Press Co. v. Human Relations Comm'n, 413 U.S. 376, 37 L.Ed.2d 669, 93 S.Ct. 2553 (1973). Commercial speech that is not false or deceptive and does not concern unlawful activities, however, may be restricted only in the service of a substantial governmental interest, and only through means that directly advance that interest. Central Hudson Gas & Electric, [447 U.S. 557, 566], 65 L.Ed.2d 341, 100 S.Ct. 2343.

III

* * *

Because appellant's statements regarding the Dalkon Shield were not false or deceptive, our decisions impose on the State the burden of establishing that prohibiting the use of such statements to solicit or obtain legal business directly advances a substantial governmental interest.

* * * Although some sensitive souls may have found appellant's advertisement in poor taste, it can hardly be said to have invaded the privacy of those who read it. More significantly, appellant's advertisement—and print advertising generally—poses much less risk of over-reaching or undue influence. Print advertising may convey information and ideas more or less effectively, but in most cases, it will lack the coercive force of the personal presence of a trained advocate. In addition, a printed advertisement, unlike a personal encounter initiated by an attorney, is not likely to involve pressure on the potential client for an immediate yes-or-no answer to the offer of representation. Thus, a printed advertisement is a means of conveying information about legal services that is more conducive to reflection and the exercise of choice on the part of the consumer than is personal solicitation by an attorney. Accordingly, the substantial interests that justified the ban on in-person solicitation upheld in *Ohralik* * cannot justify the discipline imposed on appellant for the content of his advertisement.

Nor does the traditional justification for restraints on solicitation— the fear that lawyers will "stir up litigation"—justify the restriction imposed in this case. * * * That our citizens have access to their civil courts is not an evil to be regretted; rather, it is an attribute of our system of justice in which we ought to take pride. The State is not entitled to interfere with that access by denying its citizens accurate information about their legal rights. Accordingly, it is not sufficient justification for the discipline imposed on appellant that his truthful and

* Ed. note: The *Ohralik* case is set out as a reading to Problem 32, infra.

nondeceptive advertising had a tendency to or did in fact encourage others to file lawsuits.

* * *

We need not * * * address the theoretical question whether a prophylactic rule is ever permissible in this area, for we do not believe that the State has presented a convincing case for its argument that the rule before us is necessary to the achievement of a substantial governmental interest. The State's contention that the problem of distinguishing deceptive and nondeceptive legal advertising is different in kind from the problems presented by advertising generally is unpersuasive.

* * *

IV

The application of DR 2–101(B)'s restriction on illustrations in advertising by lawyers to appellant's advertisement fails for much the same reasons as does the application of the self-recommendation and solicitation rules. The use of illustrations or pictures in advertisements serves important communicative functions: it attracts the attention of the audience to the advertiser's message, and it may also serve to impart information directly. Accordingly, commercial illustrations are entitled to the First Amendment protections afforded verbal commercial speech: restrictions on the use of visual media of expression in advertising must survive scrutiny under the *Central Hudson* test. * * *

The text of DR 2–101(B) strongly suggests that the purpose of the restriction on the use of illustrations is to ensure that attorneys advertise "in a dignified manner." There is, of course, no suggestion that the illustration actually used by appellant was undignified; thus, it is difficult to see how the application of the rule to appellant in this case directly advances the State's interest in preserving the dignity of attorneys. More fundamentally, although the State undoubtedly has a substantial interest in ensuring that its attorneys behave with dignity and decorum in the courtroom, we are unsure that the State's desire that attorneys maintain their dignity in their communications with the public is an interest substantial enough to justify the abridgment of their First Amendment rights. Even if that were the case, we are unpersuaded that undignified behavior would tend to recur so often as to warrant a prophylactic rule. As we held in Carey v. Population Services International, 431 U.S. 678 (1977), the mere possibility that some members of the population might find advertising embarrassing or offensive cannot justify suppressing it. The same must hold true for advertising that some members of the bar might find beneath their dignity.

In its arguments before this Court, the State has asserted that the restriction on illustrations serves a somewhat different purpose, akin to that supposedly served by the prohibition on the offering of legal advice in advertising. The use of illustrations in advertising by attorneys, the State suggests, creates unacceptable risks that the public will be misled, manipulated, or confused. Abuses associated with the visual content of advertising are particularly difficult to police, because the advertiser is skilled in subtle uses of illustrations to play on the emotions of his audience and convey false impressions. Because illustrations may produce their effects by operating on a subconscious level, the State argues, it will be difficult for the State to point to any particular illustration and prove that it is misleading or manipulative. Thus, once again, the State's argument is that its purposes can only be served through a prophylactic rule.

We are not convinced. The State's arguments amount to little more than unsupported assertions: nowhere does the State cite any evidence or authority of any kind for its contention that the potential abuses associated with the use of illustrations in attorneys' advertising cannot be combatted by any means short of a blanket ban. * * *

* * *

V

Appellant contends that assessing the validity of the Ohio Supreme Court's decision to discipline him for his failure to include in the Dalkon Shield advertisement the information that clients might be liable for significant litigation costs even if their lawsuits were unsuccessful entails precisely the same inquiry as determining the validity of the restrictions on advertising content discussed above. * * *

Appellant, however, overlooks material differences between disclosure requirements and outright prohibitions on speech. In requiring attorneys who advertise their willingness to represent clients on a contingent-fee basis to state that the client may have to bear certain expenses even if he loses, Ohio has not attempted to prevent attorneys from conveying information to the public; it has only required them to provide somewhat more information than they might otherwise be inclined to present. * * *

We do not suggest that disclosure requirements do not implicate the advertiser's First Amendment rights at all. We recognize that unjustified or unduly burdensome disclosure requirements might offend the First Amendment by chilling protected commercial speech. But we hold that an advertiser's rights are adequately protected as long as disclosure requirements are reasonably related to the State's interest in preventing deception of consumers.

The State's application to appellant of the requirement that an attorney advertising his availability on a contingent fee basis disclose that clients will have to pay costs even if their lawsuits are unsuccessful (assuming that to be the case) easily passes muster under this standard. * * *

* * *

VII

The Supreme Court of Ohio issued a public reprimand * * * . That judgment is affirmed to the extent that it is based on appellant's advertisement involving * * * the omission of information regarding his contingent fee arrangements in his Dalkon Shield advertisement. But insofar as the reprimand was based on appellant's use of an illustration in his advertisement * * * and his offer of legal advice in his advertisement * * * , the judgment is reversed.

Justice POWELL took no part in the decision of this case.

Justice O'CONNOR, with whom THE CHIEF JUSTICE [BURGER] and Justice REHNQUIST join, concurring in part and dissenting in part.

* * *

In my view, state regulation of professional advice in advertisements is qualitatively different from regulation of claims concerning commercial goods and merchandise, and is entitled to greater deference than the majority's analysis would permit. In its prior decisions, the Court was better able to perceive both the importance of state regulation of professional conduct, and the distinction between professional services and standardized consumer products. See, e.g., Goldfarb v. Virginia State Bar. The States understandably require more of attorneys than of others engaged in commerce. Lawyers are *professionals,* and as such they have greater obligations. * * * The legal profession has in the past been distinguished and well served by a code of ethics which imposes certain standards beyond those prevailing in the marketplace and by a duty to place professional responsibility above pecuniary gain. While some assert that we have left the era of professionalism in the practice of law, substantial state interests underlie many of the provisions of the state codes of ethics, and justify more stringent standards than apply to the public at large.

* * *

[The opinion of Justice BRENNAN, with whom Justice MARSHALL joined, concurring in part and dissenting in part, is omitted].

PROBLEM 32

Solicitation of Legal Business

The President has signed a major new tax reform package into law. You have asked your secretary to get you the names of every client for whom your firm has drafted a will in the last two decades. You have sent each a personal letter saying, "The new Tax Reform Act has changed the way we now must think about estate planning, both to provide lifetime income for you and to provide for your loved ones after you're gone. Why don't you stop in soon and have a routine legal checkup? It will put your mind at ease."

New solid waste disposal regulations have also just been issued by your state EPA. It has occurred to you that there are probably many businesses in town that could benefit from advice about the impact of the new regulations. Thus, you have sent invitations to clients and non-clients alike for a free "seminar" about the regulations that you will conduct at a local hotel. Refreshments will be served, and you plan to have plenty of copies of your firm's color brochure available for distribution. That way, those in attendance will know where to turn when they need advice on environmental problems in the future.

At the end of last week, an airline crash in your state killed 125 people and permanently injured 15 others. You placed an advertisement in the local newspaper where the accident happened to try to attract some of the victims or their estates as clients. That has not produced any results, so you plan to visit potential plaintiffs at home. You plan to leave a copy of your newspaper ad, saying only: "It's up to you to decide whether or not you want a lawyer, but if you do, I am available."

QUESTIONS

1. Does the letter to your clients proposing a "legal checkup" present any ethical problems?

a. Does the fact that the addressees are clients or former clients make the ethical issues in contacting them less or more difficult? Are your fiduciary duties to such current or recent clients greater than your duties to strangers?

b. Might such a contact be in the clients' interests? Indeed, might you have a continuing duty to keep abreast of changes in the law that affect their interests? At least as to clients for whom you have periodically done estate planning, might you even be charged with malpractice if you failed to warn about changes in the law as potentially significant as the Tax Reform Act?

c. A 1958 study of the ABA Special Committee on the Economics of Law Practice recommended trying to get all one's clients back to the office periodically for a "routine legal checkup" as a way of raising lawyers' incomes more nearly to the incomes of doctors. Should such a concern for the lawyer's income be improper in evaluating advertising for, and solicitation of, clients? Can such issues ever be wholly ignored?

2. Is it proper for a lawyer to give seminars and print color brochures extolling the law firm's virtues?

a. Should it be improper where the lawyer's unquestioned motive is to bring more business to the law firm. The report of the A.B.A. Commission on Professionalism[1] pointed out that for the average 10 member firm to have enough left after expenses that each member will

---

1. " * * * In the Spirit of Public Service:" A Blueprint for the Rekindling of   Lawyer Professionalism (Aug. 1986).

receive an income of $40,000 to $50,000 per year, the firm must gross about $1 million in revenues for the year. To gross $1 million requires that approximately $20,000 be billed and collected each week. That is for a small firm and a relatively small income per lawyer; is it any wonder, then, that the pressures to generate new business are so great in law firms today?

b.   Having said that, must one say that there should be no limits on the techniques a lawyer may use to generate new business? What does Model Rule 7.3 say about the use of seminars to get new clients? What did DR 2–103(A) and DR 2–104(A) say about use of the technique? If no one is coerced to attend such a seminar, why should anyone (except perhaps a competing lawyer) complain?

c.   May your law firm write to real estate agents asking the agents to recommend your law firm to their customers? Here the New York Court of Appeals drew the line. The lawyer might have an incentive to find good title so as to assure that the referring agent got his fee, the court said. The interest in preventing such conflicts of interests should permit regulation of letters to the agents. Greene v. Grievance Committee, 54 N.Y.2d 118, 444 N.Y.S.2d 883, 429 N.E.2d 390 (1981). Compare DR 2–103(C).

Do you agree? Is it the letter that should be the subject of discipline? Would the later conflict of interest be so hard to prove that the bar must have a prophylactic rule? Cf. Allison v. Louisiana State Bar Association, 362 So.2d 489 (La.1978) (prohibits letters to employers soliciting establishment of prepaid legal service plans). See also Rule 7.3(d) and DR 2–103(D)(4)(b).

d.   May a lawyer make public speeches about the law and legal problems? Is the analysis of proper motives in EC 2–2 to 2–5 still relevant? May a lawyer represent a person who comes for advice after attending one of these lectures? Can you see any reasons for being troubled by such representation? Is a different question presented when the lawyer distributes his or her business card at such a lecture? Why?

e.   May a church announce that a lawyer (not named) will be available on certain evenings at the church to help members draft their wills? The lawyer's regular fee would be paid as a donation to the church and the members would be encouraged but not required to remember the church in their wills. In holding the practice improper, the ABA committee relied primarily on DR 2–103(B).[2] Do you agree that this section is controlling? Are any other sections relevant?

3.   As for the plane crash, at what point does protected "advertising" become prohibited "in-person solicitation"?

a.   At what point did attorney Ohralik cross the line from propriety to impropriety in the case set forth in the Readings to this Problem? Do you agree with Justice Marshall that we cannot paint with too broad a

---

2. ABA Informal Opinion 1288 (June 17, 1974).

brush, i.e., that lawyers such as Ohralik may actually give valuable information to potential clients?

b.   Is the Court's concern that the lawyer will be too intimidating in acquiring the clients?   Is the situation improved if the firm sends "investigators" to the victims' homes to leave the attorney's business cards and encourage signing of retainers.[3]

c.   Should we be concerned about the possible "stirring up" of litigation?   Should a lawyer be able to mail brochures saying, "Women who have used Dalkon Shield may be entitled to compensation" to persons who had read news accounts of medical problems allegedly associated with this contraceptive device?   Matter of Discipline of Appert, 315 N.W.2d 204 (Minn.1981), held that the brochures were protected under *Bates* although it refused to give the attorneys "accolades for their conduct."   After *Zauderer,* included as a Reading to the preceding problem, can the concern about stirring up litigation—which used to be called "barratry"—constitutionally be used as a basis for lawyer discipline?

d.   The circumstances in which lawyers will engage in face–to–face solicitation of accident victims continue to amaze.   In The Florida Bar v. Weinstein, 624 So.2d 261 (Fla.1993), for example, the lawyer solicited a brain injury victim who was still in the hospital.   In Texas State Bar v. Kilpatrick, 874 S.W.2d 656 (Tex.1994), the lawyer waited until the brain–damage victim had been transported to a nursing home, but otherwise the solicitation—and the disbarment sanction—were the same.

e.   The Supreme Court considered a related problem in Edenfield v. Fane, 507 U.S. ___, 113 S.Ct. 1792, 123 L.Ed.2d 543 (1993), where Florida had tried to regulate CPAs' personal solicitation of business clients.   The plaintiff sued for the right to make unsolicited calls to such clients and to arrange appointments to explain his expertise and lower fees.   The State said that the rule against such contacts was designed both to protect consumers of accounting services against overreaching and to assure the independence of financial audits.   In an opinion by Justice Kennedy, the Court found the state interests "substantial in the abstract" but found that business clients were able to protect themselves against overreaching.   Further, the concern about a lack of audit independence was said to be greater where businesses could *not* turn to newcomers like Fane because then the incumbent firm could get too close to management.

The state expressly relied on *Ohralik,* and the Court expressly distinguished it.   The *Ohralik* "holding was narrow and depended upon certain 'unique features of in-person solicitation by lawyers' that were present in the circumstances of that case."   CPAs, the Court observed,

---

3.   Several courts have suspended attorneys who used such non-lawyer agents. Koden v. United States Department of Justice, 564 F.2d 228 (7th Cir.1977), and Goldman v. State Bar, 20 Cal.3d 130, 141 Cal. Rptr. 447, 570 P.2d 463 (1977) (both decided before *Ohralik* and *Primus*), and In re Arnoff, 22 Cal.3d 740, 150 Cal.Rptr. 479, 586 P.2d 960 (1978), and In re Teichner, 75 Ill.2d 88, 25 Ill.Dec. 609, 387 N.E.2d 265 (1979) (both decided later).

are not "trained in the art of persuasion" and the clients being solicited "are sophisticated and experienced business executives who understand well the services that a CPA offers."

4. Instead of going to their homes, may the lawyer send a telegram to each surviving spouse of a victim and offer to represent the spouse in a claim for damages?

a. This kind of contact has come to be called "targeted direct mail". Should it be seen as more like constitutionally-protected advertising or more like unprotected solicitation? Matter of Von Wiegen, 63 N.Y.2d 163, 481 N.Y.S.2d 40, 470 N.E.2d 838 (1984), applied the advertising characterization on the ground that, like advertising, targeted direct mail gives the recipient time to reflect about—or indeed to ignore—the offer of services.

b. In Shapero v. Kentucky Bar Association, 486 U.S. 466, 108 S.Ct. 1916, 100 L.Ed.2d 475 (1988), the lawyer had applied to the state Attorney General's Advertising Commission for approval of a letter he planned to send to persons he believed had had foreclosure suits filed against them. The Commission did not find the letter false or misleading, but it ruled that a letter sent only to persons who were believed to need the lawyer's services did not constitute constitutionally protected advertising. The Kentucky Supreme Court affirmed.

A divided U.S. Supreme Court reversed, holding that free speech guarantees do not allow states to prohibit lawyers categorically from soliciting legal business for pecuniary gain by sending truthful and nondeceptive letters to potential clients known to face particular problems. The lawyer clearly could have mailed his letter widely throughout the public, the Court said, citing the then existing version of Rule 7.3. Surely, the majority then said, there is nothing about the constitutionality of advertising that requires that the method chosen be inefficient. As for *Ohralik*-type concerns about "overwhelming" the targets of the letters, the Court said that whether or not the letters were overwhelming had nothing to do with how randomly they were sent. Furthermore, no form of written communication presents the dangers of overreaching that *Ohralik* illustrated. The fact that targeted direct mail could be the subject of abuses or mistakes did not justify a complete ban.

Perhaps most interesting was the dissent of Justice O'Connor, joined by Chief Justice Rehnquist and Justice Scalia, for it showed their continuing willingness to reconsider all of the attorney advertising cases. Justice O'Connor said that she "agree[d] with the Court that the reasoning in *Zauderer* supports the conclusion reached today. That decision, however, was itself the culmination of a line of cases built on defective premises and flawed reasoning." The entire analytical framework, she argued, "should be reexamined." [4]

c. The ABA responded to *Shapero* with the current version of Model Rule 7.3. Florida tried to go farther and prohibit all targeted

---

4. Justice O'Connor reasserted this position in Edenfield v. Fane, discussed above.

direct mail within 30 days of an accident. McHenry v. The Florida Bar, 808 F.Supp. 1543 (M.D.Fla.1992), aff'd 21 F.2d 1038 (11th Cir.1994), found that limit unconstitutional, and the Supreme Court agreed to resolve the issue, ___ U.S. ___, 115 S.Ct. 42, 129 L.Ed.2d 937 (1994).[5]

d. Norris v. Alabama State Bar, 582 So.2d 1034 (Ala.1991), is one of those cases that proves truth is stranger than a hypothetical. A young child had died after being left in a closed van in the hot sun by a day care center. Someone called the lawyer's office and told the receptionist that the family was "broke" and too poor to buy flowers for the funeral. The lawyer sent a wreath to the funeral home with his firm brochure attached and a letter inviting the family to contact him if he could be of any help. Somehow the story of his gesture got into the news. The Alabama Supreme Court acknowledged that DR 2–103 "could be drafted better" but said that the lawyer showed "indifference to the purpose and spirit of the rule." The Court rejected his reference to *Shapero* and suspended him for two years.

Do you agree that sending a wreath is qualitatively different from sending a letter to the family offering legal services? Arguably, the family could always throw the letter away; by custom, however, sending the wreath requires the family to send a thank-you note. Should that distinction or any other, however, make sending the wreath a disciplinable act? Was the problem that the wreath did not bear the legend, "Advertising Material"? See Rule 7.3

e. In Matter of Anis, 599 A.2d 1265 (N.J.1992), the court publicly reprimanded a lawyer for sending a letter to the father of a victim of the Lockerbie, Scotland air crash. The letter was not high pressure; it expressed condolences to the family and invited them to contact the lawyer. The court, however, found the condolences "hollow" and the letter misleading. Indeed, it said, the lawyer "could only have deepened the family's suffering." In an opinion replete with references to lawyers' low public image, the Court said the sanction was for "conduct that is patently offensive to the common sensibilities of the community because it intrudes upon the private grief of victims * * * and solicits representation of them at a moment of their extreme vulnerability."

---

5. Moore v. Morales, 843 F.Supp. 1124 (S.D.Tex.1994) held amendments to the Texas barratry statute and the Uniform Traffic Act unconstitutional. The first provisions prohibited a lawyer's sending any solicitation of employment to a potential client within 30 days of an accident, criminal arrest, or filing of a civil suit. The second denied lawyers access to auto accident reports until 180 days after the accident. The State's expert testified that people may be in shock for 6 to 8 weeks after a traumatic event and thus may be unable to make a sound decision about counsel. The Court found instead that both amendments were simply intended to cut down constitutionally–protected direct mail solicitation by lawyers.

But see, DeSalvo v. State, 624 So.2d 897 (La.1993), upholding such a law against a challenge that it violated lawyers' First Amendment right to seek clients. See also, Lanphere & Urbaniak v. Colorado, 21 F.3d 1508 (10th Cir.), cert. denied ___ U.S. ___, 115 S.Ct. 638, 130 L.Ed.2d 544 (1994), holding that a statute prohibiting release of criminal defendants' names to prospective lawyers is constitutional as a protection of defendants' privacy.

Again, do you agree? Are you convinced the lawyers in the case did something morally wrong? Was their conduct cruel and selfish? Professional and caring? Was the conduct distinguishable from that in *Shapero*?

f.   Interestingly, one of the most active proponents of restrictions on solicitation is the Association of Trial Lawyers of America (ATLA). Under its new Code, an ATLA member's agrees: (1) not to solicit a potential client unless the client contacts the lawyer first, (2) not to go to the scene of an event that causes injury, and (3) not to initiate television comment about an event within 10 days of the event unless the member foregoes all financial return from those injured in the event. The FTC has found that these provisions do not constitute an unlawful restraint of trade.

5. If solicitation in the Ohralik sense is proved, what should be the sanction or remedy?

a.   Should the possible remedies include disqualification of the attorney from proceeding with the representation, for example? Cf. Lefrak v. Arabian American Oil Co., 527 F.2d 1136 (2d Cir.1975) (no prejudice to defendant from plaintiff's lawyer's acts of solicitation which that justify denying plaintiff's desire to keep the firm as its counsel).

b.   Even if the client wishes to retain the soliciting lawyer, should disqualification be ordered as a deterrent to the practice of solicitation generally? Cf., Rubin v. Green, 847 P.2d 1044 (Cal.1993) (solicitation of plaintiff is not an actionable tort against the party being sued).

6. Under Ohralik and Primus, is solicitation of cases that the attorney will handle at no fee always constitutionally protected?

a.   Should it be unconstitutional to prohibit soliciting cases testing legal questions of broad social importance? Must both social importance and no fee be present or is either one enough for the solicitation to be protected?

b.   Is the constitutional distinction in *Primus* based on a requirement that to find a lawyer guilty of solicitation the state must show that the lawyer actually has overreached the potential client? Was there an actual finding that Ohralik had unduly pressured his clients? Look at when and how Carol McClintock indicated that she wanted Ohralik to represent her.

c.   Do you agree with Justice Rehnquist that public interest firms may have their own agendas in some cases and thus that their clients' interests may be more at risk of compromise than the clients know? Even if Justice Rehnquist is right, are prohibitions on solicitation the right way to deal with the problem?

d.   Are you as troubled as Justice Rehnquist about knowing when a *Primus*-type situation is presented? Will you or he be persuaded when a plaintiff's lawyer asserts that obtaining large damage verdicts is a "political" act?

READINGS

OHRALIK v. OHIO STATE BAR ASSOCIATION

Supreme Court of the United States, 1978.
436 U.S. 447, 98 S.Ct. 1912, 56 L.Ed.2d 444.

Justice POWELL delivered the opinion of the Court.

In Bates v. State Bar of Arizona, this Court held that truthful advertising of "routine" legal services is protected by the First and Fourteenth Amendments against blanket prohibition by a State. The Court expressly reserved the question of the permissible scope of regulation of "in-person solicitation of clients—at the hospital room or the accident site, or in any other situation that breeds undue influence—by attorneys or their agents or 'runners'." Today we answer part of the question so reserved, and hold that the Bar—acting with state authorization—constitutionally may discipline a lawyer for soliciting clients in person, for pecuniary gain, under circumstances likely to pose dangers that the State has a right to prevent.

I

Appellant, a member of the Ohio Bar, lives in Montville, Ohio. Until recently he practiced law in Montville and Cleveland. On February 13, 1974, while picking up his mail at the Montville Post Office, appellant learned from the postmaster's brother about an automobile accident that had taken place on February 2 in which Carol McClintock, a young woman with whom appellant was casually acquainted, had been injured. Appellant made a telephone call to Ms. McClintock's parents, who informed him that their daughter was in the hospital. Appellant suggested that he might visit Carol in the hospital. Mrs. McClintock assented to the idea, but requested that appellant first stop by at her home.

During appellant's visit with the McClintocks, they explained that their daughter had been driving the family automobile on a local road when she was hit by an uninsured motorist. Both Carol and her passenger, Wanda Lou Holbert, were injured and hospitalized. In response to the McClintocks' expression of apprehension that they might be sued by Holbert, appellant explained that Ohio's guest statute would preclude such a suit. When appellant suggested to the McClintocks that they hire a lawyer, Mrs. McClintock retorted that such a decision would be up to Carol, who was 18 years old and would be the beneficiary of a successful claim.

Appellant proceeded to the hospital, where he found Carol lying in traction in her room. After a brief conversation about her condition, appellant told Carol he would represent her and asked her to sign an agreement. Carol said she would have to discuss the matter with her parents. She did not sign the agreement, but asked appellant to have her parents come to see her. Appellant also attempted to see Wanda Lou Holbert, but learned that she had just been released from the hospital. He then departed for another visit with the McClintocks.

On his way appellant detoured to the scene of the accident, where he took a set of photographs. He also picked up a tape recorder, which he concealed under his raincoat before arriving at the McClintocks' residence. Once there, he re-examined their automobile insurance policy, discussed with them the law applicable to passengers, and explained the consequences of the fact that the driver who struck Carol's car was an uninsured motorist. Appellant discovered that the McClintocks' insurance policy would provide benefits of up to $12,500 each for Carol and Wanda Lou under an uninsured motorist clause. Mrs. McClintock acknowledged that both Carol and Wanda Lou could sue for their injuries, but recounted to appellant that "Wanda swore up and down she would not do it." The McClintocks also told appellant that Carol had phoned to say that appellant could "go ahead" with her representation. Two days later appellant returned to Carol's hospital room to have her sign a contract, which provided that he would receive one-third of her recovery.

In the meantime, appellant obtained Wanda Lou's name and address from the McClintocks after telling them he wanted to ask her some questions about the accident. He then visited Wanda Lou at her home, without having been invited. He again concealed his tape recorder and recorded most of the conversation with Wanda Lou. After a brief, unproductive inquiry about the facts of the accident, appellant told Wanda Lou that he was representing Carol and that he had a "little tip" for Wanda Lou: the McClintocks' insurance policy contained an uninsured motorist clause which might provide her with a recovery of up to $12,500. The young woman, who was 18 years of age and not a high school graduate at the time, replied to appellant's query about whether she was going to file a claim by stating that she really did not understand what was going on. Appellant offered to represent her, also, for a contingent fee of one-third of any recovery, and Wanda Lou stated "O. K."[4]

Wanda's mother attempted to repudiate her daughter's oral assent the following day, when appellant called on the telephone to speak to Wanda. Mrs. Holbert informed appellant that she and her daughter did not want to sue anyone or to have appellant represent them, and that if they decided to sue they would consult their own lawyer. Appellant

---

4.   * * In explaining the contingency fee arrangement, appellant told Wanda Lou that his representation would not "cost [her] anything" because she would receive two-thirds of the recovery if appellant were successful in representing her but would not "have to pay [him] anything" otherwise.

insisted that Wanda had entered into a binding agreement. A month later Wanda confirmed in writing that she wanted neither to sue nor to be represented by appellant. She requested that appellant notify the insurance company that he was not her lawyer, as the company would not release a check to her until he did so. Carol also eventually discharged appellant. Although another lawyer represented her in concluding a settlement with the insurance company, she paid appellant one-third of her recovery [6] in settlement of his lawsuit against her for breach of contract.

Both Carol McClintock and Wanda Lou Holbert filed complaints against appellant with the Grievance Committee * * *. * * * After a hearing, the Board found that appellant had violated Disciplinary Rules DR 2–103(A) and 2–104(A) of the Ohio Code of Professional Responsibility. * * * The Supreme Court of Ohio adopted the findings of the Board, reiterated that appellant's conduct was not constitutionally protected, and increased the sanction of a public reprimand recommended by the Board to indefinite suspension. * * *

II

The solicitation of business by a lawyer through direct, in-person communication with the prospective client has long been viewed as inconsistent with the profession's ideal of the attorney-client relationship and as posing a significant potential for harm to the prospective client. It has been proscribed by the organized Bar for many years.[11] * * * The balance struck in *Bates* does not predetermine the outcome in this case. * * *

A

Appellant contends that his solicitation of the two young women as clients is indistinguishable, for purposes of constitutional analysis, from the advertisement in *Bates*. * * * But in-person solicitation of professional employment by a lawyer does not stand on a par with truthful advertising about the availability and terms of routine legal services, let alone with forms of speech more traditionally within the concern of the First Amendment.

* * *

In-person solicitation by a lawyer of remunerative employment is a business transaction in which speech is an essential but subordinate component. While this does not remove the speech from the protection of the First Amendment, as was held in *Bates* and *Virginia Pharmacy*, it lowers the level of appropriate judicial scrutiny.

* * * Unlike a public advertisement, which simply provides information and leaves the recipient free to act upon it or not, in-person

---

6. Carol recovered the full $12,500 and paid appellant $4,166.66. She testified that she paid the second lawyer $900 as compensation for his services.

11. An informal ban on solicitation, like that on advertising, historically was linked to the goals of preventing barratry, champerty, and maintenance. * * *

solicitation may exert pressure and often demands an immediate response, without providing an opportunity for comparison or reflection. The aim and effect of in-person solicitation may be to provide a one-sided presentation and to encourage speedy and perhaps uninformed decisionmaking; there is no opportunity for intervention or counter-education by agencies of the Bar, supervisory authorities, or persons close to the solicited individual. The admonition that "the fitting remedy for evil counsels is good ones" is of little value when the circumstances provide no opportunity for any remedy at all. In-person solicitation is as likely as not to discourage persons needing counsel from engaging in a critical comparison of the "availability, nature, and prices" of legal services, cf. *Bates*; it actually may disserve the individual and societal interest, identified in *Bates*, in facilitating "informed and reliable decisionmaking."

* * * [N]either of the disciplinary rules here at issue prohibited appellant from communicating information to these young women about their legal rights and the prospects of obtaining a monetary recovery, or from recommending that they obtain counsel. DR 2–104(A) merely prohibited him from using the information as bait with which to obtain an agreement to represent them for a fee. * * *

Appellant does not contend, and on the facts of this case could not contend, that his approaches to the two young women involved political expression or an exercise of associational freedom, "employ[ing] constitutionally privileged means of expression to secure constitutionally guaranteed civil rights." NAACP v. Button, 371 U.S. 415 (1963); see In re Primus. Nor can he compare his solicitation to the mutual assistance in asserting legal rights that was at issue in United Transportation Union v. Michigan Bar, 401 U.S. 576 (1971); Mine Workers v. Illinois Bar Assn., 389 U.S. 217 (1967); and Railroad Trainmen v. Virginia Bar, 377 U.S. 1 (1964).[16] A lawyer's procurement of remunerative employment is a subject only marginally affected with First Amendment concerns. It falls within the State's proper sphere of economic and professional regulation. While entitled to some constitutional protection, appellant's conduct is subject to regulation in furtherance of important state interests.

B

The state interests implicated in this case are particularly strong. In addition to its general interest in protecting consumers and regulating

---

16. * * In recognizing the importance of the State's interest in regulating solicitation of paying clients by lawyers, we are not unmindful of the problem of the related practice, described in Railroad Trainmen, of the solicitation of releases of liability by claims agents or adjusters of prospective defendants or their insurers. Such solicitations frequently occur prior to the employment of counsel by the injured person and during circumstances posing many of the dangers of overreaching we address in this case. Where lay agents or adjusters are involved, these practices for the most part fall outside the scope of regulation by the organized Bar; but releases or settlements so obtained are viewed critically by the courts. See, e.g., Florkiewicz v. Gonzalez, 38 Ill.App.3d 115, 347 N.E.2d 401 (1976); Cady v. Mitchell, 208 Pa.Super. 16, 220 A.2d 373 (1966).

commercial transactions, the State bears a special responsibility for maintaining standards among members of the licensed professions. * * *

As is true with respect to advertising, see *Bates*, it appears that the ban on solicitation by lawyers originated as a rule of professional etiquette rather than as a strictly ethical rule. * * * But the fact that the original motivation behind the ban on solicitation today might be considered an insufficient justification for its perpetuation does not detract from the force of the other interests the ban continues to serve. * * *

The substantive evils of solicitation have been stated over the years in sweeping terms: stirring up litigation, assertion of fraudulent claims, debasing the legal profession, and potential harm to the solicited client in the form of overreaching, overcharging, underrepresentation, and misrepresentation.

We need not discuss or evaluate each of these interests in detail as appellant has conceded that the State has a legitimate and indeed "compelling" interest in preventing those aspects of solicitation that involve fraud, undue influence, intimidation, overreaching, and other forms of "vexatious conduct." * * *

III

Appellant's concession that strong state interests justify regulation to prevent the evils he enumerates would end this case but for his insistence that none of those evils was found to be present in his acts of solicitation. * * * But appellant errs in assuming that the constitutional validity of the judgment below depends on proof that his conduct constituted actual overreaching or inflicted some specific injury on Wanda Holbert or Carol McClintock. * * * Appellant's argument misconceives the nature of the State's interest. The rules prohibiting solicitation are prophylactic measures whose objective is the prevention of harm before it occurs. The rules were applied in this case to discipline a lawyer for soliciting employment for pecuniary gain under circumstances likely to result in the adverse consequences the State seeks to avert. In such a situation, which is inherently conducive to overreaching and other forms of misconduct, the State has a strong interest in adopting and enforcing rules of conduct designed to protect the public from harmful solicitation by lawyers whom it has licensed.

The State's perception of the potential for harm in circumstances such as those presented in this case is well-founded. The detrimental aspects of face-to-face selling even of ordinary consumer products have been recognized and addressed by the Federal Trade Commission, and it hardly need be said that the potential for overreaching is significantly greater when a lawyer, a professional trained in the art of persuasion, personally solicits an unsophisticated, injured, or distressed lay person.[24]

---

24. Most lay persons are unfamiliar with the law, with how legal services normally are procured, and with typical arrangements between lawyer and client. To

Such an individual may place his or her trust in a lawyer, regardless of the latter's qualifications or the individual's actual need for legal representation, simply in response to persuasion under circumstances conducive to uninformed acquiescence. Although it is argued that personal solicitation is valuable because it may apprise a victim of misfortune of his or her legal rights, the very plight of that person not only makes him or her more vulnerable to influence but also may make advice all the more intrusive. Thus, under these adverse conditions the overtures of an uninvited lawyer may distress the solicited individual simply because of their obtrusiveness and the invasion of the individual's privacy, even when no other harm materializes. Under such circumstances, it is not unreasonable for the State to presume that in-person solicitation by lawyers more often than not will be injurious to the person solicited.

The efficacy of the State's effort to prevent such harm to prospective clients would be substantially diminished if, having proved a solicitation in circumstances like those of this case, the State were required in addition to prove actual injury. Unlike the advertising in *Bates*, in-person solicitation is not visible or otherwise open to public scrutiny. Often there is no witness other than the lawyer and the lay person whom he has solicited, rendering it difficult or impossible to obtain reliable proof of what actually took place. This would be especially true if the lay person were so distressed at the time of the solicitation that he or she could not recall specific details at a later date. If appellant's view were sustained, in-person solicitation would be virtually immune to effective oversight and regulation by the State or by the legal profession, in contravention of the State's strong interest in regulating members of the Bar in an effective, objective, and self-enforcing manner. It therefore is not unreasonable, or violative of the Constitution, for a State to respond with what in effect is a prophylactic rule.

On the basis of the undisputed facts of record, we conclude that the disciplinary rules constitutionally could be applied to appellant. * * *

Accordingly, the judgment of the Supreme Court of Ohio is

Affirmed.

IN RE PRIMUS

Supreme Court of the United States, 1978.
436 U.S. 412, 98 S.Ct. 1893, 56 L.Ed.2d 417.

Justice POWELL delivered the opinion of the Court.

We consider on this appeal whether a State may punish a member of its Bar who, seeking to further political and ideological goals through

----

be sure, the same might be said about the lay person who seeks out a lawyer for the first time. But the critical distinction is that in the latter situation the prospective client has made an initial choice of a lawyer at least for purposes of a consultation; has chosen the time to seek legal advice; has had a prior opportunity to confer with family, friends, or a public or private referral agency; and has chosen whether to consult with the lawyer alone or accompanied.

associational activity, including litigation, advises a lay person of her legal rights and discloses in a subsequent letter that free legal assistance is available from a nonprofit organization with which the lawyer and her associates are affiliated. Appellant, a member of the Bar of South Carolina, received a public reprimand for writing such a letter. * * *

I

Appellant, Edna Smith Primus, is a lawyer practicing in Columbia, S.C. During the period in question, she was associated with the "Carolina Community Law Firm," and an officer of and cooperating lawyer with the Columbia branch of the American Civil Liberties Union (ACLU). She received no compensation for her work on behalf of the ACLU, but was paid a retainer as a legal consultant for the South Carolina Council on Human Relations (Council), a nonprofit organization with offices in Columbia.

During the summer of 1973, local and national newspapers reported that pregnant mothers on public assistance in Aiken County, S.C. were being sterilized or threatened with sterilization as a condition of the continued receipt of medical assistance under the "Medicaid" program. Concerned by this development, Gary Allen, an Aiken businessman and officer of a local organization serving indigents, called the Council requesting that one of its representatives come to Aiken to address some of the women who had been sterilized. At the Council's behest, appellant, who had not known Allen previously, called him and arranged a meeting in his office in July 1973. Among those attending was Mary Etta Williams, who had been sterilized by Dr. Clovis H. Pierce after the birth of her third child. Williams and her grandmother attended the meeting because Allen, an old family friend, had invited them and because Williams wanted "[t]o see what it was all about * * *." At the meeting, appellant advised those present, including Williams and the other women who had been sterilized by Dr. Pierce, of their legal rights and suggested the possibility of a lawsuit.

Early in August 1973 the ACLU informed appellant that it was willing to provide representation for Aiken mothers who had been sterilized. Appellant testified that after being advised by Allen that Williams wished to institute suit against Dr. Pierce, she decided to inform Williams of the ACLU's offer of free legal representation. Shortly after receiving appellant's letter dated August 30, 1973 [6]—the center-

---

6. Written on the stationery of the Carolina Community Law Firm, the letter stated:

"August 30, 1973
"Mrs. Marietta Williams
347 Sumter Street
Aiken, South Carolina 29801

"Dear Mrs. Williams:

"You will probably remember me from talking with you at Mr. Allen's office in July about the sterilization performed on you. The American Civil Liberties Union would like to file a lawsuit on your behalf for money against the doctor who performed the operation. We will be coming

piece of this litigation—Williams visited Dr. Pierce to discuss the progress of her third child who was ill. At the doctor's office, she encountered his lawyer and at the latter's request signed a release of liability in the doctor's favor. Williams showed appellant's letter to the doctor and his lawyer, and they retained a copy. She then called appellant from the doctor's office and announced her intention not to sue. There was no further communication between appellant and Williams.

On October 9, 1974, the Secretary of the Board of Commissioners on Grievances and Discipline of the Supreme Court of South Carolina (Board) filed a formal complaint with the Board, charging that appellant had engaged in "solicitation in violation of the Canons of Ethics" by sending the August 30, 1973 letter to Williams. * * *

After a hearing on January 9, 1976, the full Board * * * administered a private reprimand. On March 17, 1977, the Supreme Court of South Carolina * * * increased the sanction, *sua sponte*, to a public reprimand.

* * * We now reverse.

II

This appeal concerns the tension between contending values of considerable moment to the legal profession and to society. * * *

The States enjoy broad power to regulate "the practice of professions within their boundaries," * * *. For example, we decide today in *Ohralik* that the States may vindicate legitimate regulatory interests through proscription, in certain circumstances, of in-person solicitation by lawyers who seek to communicate purely commercial offers of legal assistance to lay persons.

Unlike the situation in *Ohralik*, however, appellant's act of solicitation took the form of a letter to a woman with whom appellant had discussed the possibility of seeking redress for an allegedly unconstitutional sterilization. This was not in-person solicitation for pecuniary gain. Appellant was communicating an offer of free assistance by attorneys associated with the ACLU, not an offer predicated on entitle-

to Aiken in the near future and would like to explain what is involved so you can understand what is going on.

"Now I have a question to ask of you. Would you object to talking to a women's magazine about the situation in Aiken? The magazine is doing a feature story on the whole sterilization problem and wants to talk to you and others in South Carolina. If you don't mind doing this, call me *collect* at 254–8151 on Friday before 5:00, if you receive this letter in time. Or call me on Tuesday morning (after Labor Day) *collect*.

"I want to assure you that this interview is being done to show what is happening to women against their wishes,

and is not being done to harm you in any way. But I want you to decide, so call me collect, and let me know of your decision. This practice must stop.

"About the lawsuit, if you are interested, let me know, and I'll let you know when we will come down to talk to you about it. We will be coming to talk to Mrs. Waters at the same time; she has already asked the American Civil Liberties Union to file a suit on her behalf.

"Sincerely,

s/ Edna Smith

Edna Smith

Attorney-at-law"

ment to a share of any monetary recovery. And her actions were undertaken to express personal political beliefs and to advance the civil-liberties objectives of the ACLU, rather than to derive financial gain. The question presented in this case is whether, in light of the values protected by the First and Fourteenth Amendments, these differences materially affect the scope of state regulation of the conduct of lawyers.

III

In NAACP v. Button, supra, the * * * solicitation of prospective litigants,[14] many of whom were not members of the NAACP or the Conference, for the purpose of furthering the civil-rights objectives of the organization and its members was held to come within the right "to engage in association for the advancement of beliefs and ideas."

* * *

Subsequent decisions have interpreted *Button* as establishing the principle that "collective activity undertaken to obtain meaningful access to the courts is a fundamental right within the protection of the First Amendment." * * * Without denying the power of the State to take measures to correct the substantive evils of undue influence, over-reaching, misrepresentation, invasion of privacy, conflict of interest, and lay interference that potentially are present in solicitation of prospective clients by lawyers, this Court has required that "broad rules framed to protect the public and to preserve respect for the administration of justice" must not work a significant impairment of "the value of associational freedoms."

IV

* * * The Supreme Court of South Carolina * * * rejected appellant's First Amendment defenses by distinguishing *Button* from the case before it. Whereas the NAACP in that case was primarily a "political" organization that used "litigation as an adjunct to the overriding political aims of the organization," the ACLU "has as one of its primary purposes, the rendition of legal services." The court also intimated that the ACLU's policy of requesting an award of counsel fees indicated that

---

14. The *Button* Court described the solicitation activities of NAACP members and attorneys in the following terms:

"Typically a local NAACP branch will invite a member of the legal staff to explain to a meeting of parents and children the legal steps necessary to achieve desegregation. The staff member will bring printed forms to the meeting authorizing him, and other NAACP or [NAACP Legal] Defense Fund attorneys of his designation, to represent the signers in legal proceedings to achieve desegregation. On occasion, blank forms have been signed by litigants, upon the understand-ing that a member or members of the legal staff, with or without assistance from other NAACP lawyers, or from the Defense Fund, would handle the case. It is usual after obtaining authorizations, for the staff attorney to bring into the case the other staff members in the area where suit is to be brought, and some-times to bring in lawyers from the national organization or the Defense Fund. In effect, then, the prospective litigant retains not so much a particular attorney as the 'firm' of NAACP and Defense Fund lawyers. * * *"

the organization might "benefit financially in the event of successful prosecution of the suit for money damages."

Although the disciplinary panel did not permit full factual development of the aims and practices of the ACLU, the record does not support the state court's effort to draw a meaningful distinction between the ACLU and the NAACP. From all that appears, the ACLU and its local chapters, much like the NAACP and its local affiliates in *Button*, "engage * * * in extensive educational and lobbying activities" and "also devote * * * much of [their] funds and energies to an extensive program of assisting certain kinds of litigation on behalf of [their] declared purposes." * * * For the ACLU, as for the NAACP, "litigation is not a technique of resolving private differences"; it is "a form of political expression" and "political association."

* * *

Contrary to appellee's suggestion, the ACLU's policy of requesting an award of counsel fees does not take this case outside the protection of *Button*. Although the Court in *Button* did not consider whether the NAACP seeks counsel fees, such requests are often made both by that organization and by the NAACP Legal Defense Fund, Inc. In any event, in a case of this kind there are differences between counsel fees awarded by a court and traditional fee-paying arrangements which militate against a presumption that ACLU sponsorship of litigation is motivated by considerations of pecuniary gain rather than by its widely recognized goal of vindicating civil liberties. Counsel fees are awarded in the discretion of the court; awards are not drawn from the plaintiff's recovery, and are usually premised on a successful outcome; and the amounts awarded often may not correspond to fees generally obtainable in private litigation. Moreover, under prevailing law during the events in question, an award of counsel fees in federal litigation was available only in limited circumstances. And even if there had been an award during the period in question, it would have gone to the central fund of the ACLU.[24] Although such benefit to the organization may increase with the maintenance of successful litigation, the same situation obtains with voluntary contributions and foundations support, which also may arise with ACLU victories in important areas of the law. That possibility, standing alone, offers no basis for equating the work of lawyers associated with the ACLU or the NAACP with that of a group that exists for the primary purpose of financial gain through the recovery of counsel fees.

24. Appellant informs us that the ACLU policy then in effect provided that cooperating lawyers associated with the ACLU or with an affiliate could not receive an award of counsel fees for services rendered in an ACLU-sponsored litigation.

This policy was changed in 1977 to permit local experimentation with the sharing of court-awarded fees between state affiliates and cooperating attorneys. The South Carolina chapter has not exercised that option. We express no opinion whether our analysis in this case would be different had the latter policy been in effect during the period in question.

* * *

Appellant's letter of August 30, 1973 to Mrs. Williams thus comes within the generous zone of First Amendment protection reserved for associational freedoms. * * *

V

* * *

* * * Because of the danger of censorship through selective enforcement of broad prohibitions, and "[b]ecause First Amendment freedoms need breathing space to survive, government may regulate in [this] area only with narrow specificity." *Button*.

A

The disciplinary rules in question sweep broadly. * * * [T]he disciplinary rules in question permit punishment for mere solicitation unaccompanied by proof of any of the substantive evils that appellee maintains were present in this case. In sum, the rules in their present form have a distinct potential for dampening the kind of "cooperative activity that would make advocacy of litigation meaningful," *Button*, as well as for permitting discretionary enforcement against unpopular causes.

B

* * *

* * * The approach we adopt today in *Ohralik*, that the State may proscribe in-person solicitation for pecuniary gain under circumstances likely to result in adverse consequences, cannot be applied to appellant's activity on behalf of the ACLU. Although a showing of potential danger may suffice in the former context, appellant may not be disciplined unless her activity in fact involved the type of misconduct at which South Carolina's broad prohibition is said to be directed.

The record does not support appellee's contention that undue influence, overreaching, misrepresentation, or invasion of privacy actually occurred in this case. Appellant's letter of August 30, 1973, followed up the earlier meeting—one concededly protected by the First and Fourteenth Amendments—by notifying Williams that the ACLU would be interested in supporting possible litigation. The letter imparted additional information material to making an informed decision about whether to authorize litigation, and permitted Williams an opportunity, which she exercised, for arriving at a deliberate decision. The letter was not facially misleading; indeed, it offered "to explain what is involved so you can understand what is going on." The transmittal of this letter— as contrasted with in-person solicitation—involved no appreciable invasion of privacy; nor did it afford any significant opportunity for over-reaching or coercion. Moreover, the fact that there was a written communication lessens substantially the difficulty of policing solicitation practices that do offend valid rules of professional conduct. See *Ohralik*.

The manner of solicitation in this case certainly was no more likely to cause harmful consequences than the activity considered in *Button*, see n. 14, supra.

Nor does the record permit a finding of a serious likelihood of conflict of interest or injurious lay interference with the attorney-client relationship. Admittedly, there is some potential for such conflict or interference whenever a lay organization supports any litigation. That potential was present in *Button*, in the NAACP's solicitation of nonmembers and its disavowal of any relief short of full integration. But the Court found that potential insufficient in the absence of proof of a "serious danger" of conflict of interest, or of organizational interference with the actual conduct of the litigation. * * *

[C]onsiderations of undue commercialization of the legal profession are of marginal force where, as here, a nonprofit organization offers its services free of charge to individuals who may be in need of legal assistance and may lack the financial means and sophistication necessary to tap alternative sources of such aid.[31]

At bottom, the case against appellant rests on the proposition that a State may regulate in a prophylactic fashion all solicitation activities of lawyers because there may be some potential for overreaching, conflict of interest, or other substantive evils whenever a lawyer gives unsolicited advice and communicates an offer of representation to a layman. Under certain circumstances, that approach is appropriate in the case of speech that simply "propose[s] a commercial transaction," Pittsburgh Press Co. v. Human Relations Comm'n, 413 U.S. 376, 385, 93 S.Ct. 2553, 3558, 37 L.Ed.2d 669 (1973). See *Ohralik*. In the context of political expression and association, however, a State must regulate with significantly greater precision.[32]

---

31. *Button* makes clear that "regulations which reflect hostility to stirring up litigation have been aimed chiefly at those who urge recourse to the courts for private gain, serving no public interest," and that "[o]bjection to the intervention of a lay intermediary * * * also derives from the element of pecuniary gain." In recognition of the overarching obligation of the lawyer to serve the community, see Canon 2 of the ABA Code of Professional Responsibility, the ethical rules of the legal profession traditionally have recognized an exception from any general ban on solicitation for offers of representation, without charge, extended to individuals who may be unable to obtain legal assistance on their own. See, e.g., In re Ades, 6 F.Supp. 467, 475–476 (Md.1934); Gunnels v. Atlanta Bar Assn., 191 Ga. 366, 12 S.E.2d 602 (1940); American Bar Association, Committee on Professional Ethics and Grievances, Formal Opinion 148, at 416–419 (1935).

32. Normally the purpose or motive of the speaker is not central to First Amendment protection, but it does bear on the distinction between conduct that is "an associational aspect of 'expression' " Emerson, Freedom of Association and Freedom of Expression, 74 Yale L.J. 1, 26 (1964), and other activity subject to plenary regulation by government. * * * As shown above, appellant's speech—as part of associational activity—was expression intended to advance "beliefs and ideas." In *Ohralik*, the lawyer was not engaged in associational activity for the advancement of beliefs and ideas; his purpose was the advancement of his own commercial interests. The line, based in part on the motive of the speaker and the character of the expressive activity, will not always be easy to draw, cf. Virginia Pharmacy Board v. Virginia Consumer Council, 425 U.S. 748, 787–788, 96 S.Ct. 1817, 1838, 48 L.Ed.2d 246 (1976) (Rehnquist, J., dissenting), but that is no reason for avoiding the undertaking.

VI

The State is free to fashion reasonable restrictions with respect to the time, place and manner of solicitation by members of its Bar. See *Bates, Virginia Pharmacy*, and cases cited therein. The State's special interest in regulating members of a profession it licenses, and who serve as officers of its courts, amply justifies the application of narrowly drawn rules to proscribe solicitation that in fact is misleading, overbearing, or involves other features of deception or improper influence.[33] A State also may forbid in-person solicitation for pecuniary gain under circumstances likely to result in these evils. See *Ohralik*. And a State may insist that lawyers not solicit on behalf of lay organizations that exert control over the actual conduct of any ensuing litigation. See *Button* (White, J., concurring in part and dissenting in part). Accordingly, nothing in this opinion should be read to foreclose carefully tailored regulation that does not abridge unnecessarily the associational freedom of nonprofit organizations, or their members, having characteristics like those of the NAACP or the ACLU.

* * * The judgment of the Supreme Court of South Carolina is

Reversed.

[Justice Brennan took no part in the decision of either case. Justice Blackmun wrote a short concurring opinion in *Primus* expressing reservations about Part VI of the Court's opinion.]

Justice MARSHALL, concurring in part and concurring in the judgments [in both *Ohralik* and *Primus*].

* * *

What is objectionable about Ohralik's behavior here is not so much that he solicited business for himself, but rather the circumstances in which he performed that solicitation and the means by which he accomplished it. Appropriately, the Court's actual holding in *Ohralik* is a limited one: that the solicitation of business, under circumstances—such as those found in this record—presenting substantial dangers of harm to society or the client independent of the solicitation itself, may constitutionally be prohibited by the State. In this much of the Court's opinion in *Ohralik*, I join fully.

The facts in *Primus*, 268 S.C. 259, 233 S.E.2d 301, by contrast, show a "solicitation" of employment in accordance with the highest standards of the legal profession. Appellant in this case was acting not for her own pecuniary benefit, but to promote what she perceived to be the legal rights of persons not likely to appreciate or to be able to vindicate their own rights. * * *

---

33. We have no occasion here to delineate the precise contours of permissible state regulation. Thus, for example, a different situation might be presented if an innocent or merely negligent misstatement were made by a lawyer on behalf of an organization engaged in furthering associational or political interests.

In light of this long tradition of public interest representation by lawyer volunteers, I share my Brother Blackmun's concern with respect to Part VI of the Court's opinion, and believe that the Court has engaged in unnecessary and unfortunate *dicta* therein. * * * I find particularly troubling the Court's dictum that "a State may insist that lawyers not solicit on behalf of lay organizations that exert control over the actual conduct of any ensuing litigation." This proposition is by no means self-evident, has never been the actual holding of this Court, and is not put in issue by the facts presently before us. Thus * * * I cannot join in the first paragraph of Part VI.

Our holdings today deal only with situations at opposite poles of the problem of attorney solicitation. * * * A large number of situations falling between the poles represented by the instant facts will doubtless occur. In considering the wisdom and constitutionality of rules directed at such intermediate situations our fellow members of the Bench and Bar must be guided not only by today's decisions, but also by our decision last Term in Bates v. State Bar of Arizona. * * * In that context we rejected many of the general justifications for rules applicable to one intermediate situation not directly addressed by the Court today—the commercial but otherwise "benign" solicitation of clients by an attorney.[3]

* * * Just as the persons who suffer most from lack of knowledge about lawyers' availability belong to the less privileged classes of society, so the disciplinary rules against solicitation fall most heavily on those attorneys engaged in a single practitioner or small partnership form of practice—attorneys who typically earn less than their fellow practitioners in larger, corporate-oriented firms. Indeed, some scholars have suggested that the rules against solicitation were developed by the professional bar to keep recently immigrated lawyers, who gravitated toward the smaller, personal injury practice, from effective entry into the profession. See J. Auerbach, Unequal Justice 42–62, 126–129 (1976). In light of this history, I am less inclined than the majority appears to be to weigh favorably in the balance of the State's interests here the longevity of the ban on attorney solicitation. * * *

Justice REHNQUIST, dissenting [in *Primus*].

* * *

In distinguishing between Primus' protected solicitation and Ohralik's unprotected solicitation, the Court lamely declares, "We have not discarded the 'commonsense' distinction between speech proposing a commercial transaction, which occurs in an area traditionally subject to government regulation, and other varieties of speech." Yet to the extent that this "commonsense" distinction focuses on the content of the

---

3. By "benign" commercial solicitation, I mean solicitation by advice and information that is truthful and that is presented in a noncoercive, nondeceitful and dignified manner to a potential client who is emo-tionally and physically capable of making a rational decision either to accept or reject the representation with respect to a legal claim or matter that is not frivolous. * * *

speech, it is at least suspect under many of this Court's First Amendment cases, and to the extent it focuses upon the motive of the speaker, it is subject to manipulation by clever practitioners. If Albert Ohralik, like Edna Primus, viewed litigation "not [as] a technique of resolving private differences," but as "a form of political expression" and "political association," for all that appears he would be restored to his right to practice. And we may be sure that the next lawyer in Ohralik's shoes who is disciplined for similar conduct will come here cloaked in the prescribed mantle of "political association" to assure that insurance companies do not take unfair advantage of policyholders. * * *

I do not believe that any State will be able to determine with confidence the area in which it may regulate prophylactically and the area in which it may regulate only upon a specific showing of harm. Despite the Court's assertion to the contrary, at [*Primus*]n. 32, the difficulty of drawing distinctions on the basis of the content of the speech or the motive of the speaker *is* a valid reason for avoiding the undertaking where a more objective standard is readily available. I believe that constitutional inquiry must focus on the character of the conduct which the State seeks to regulate, and not on the motives of the individual lawyers or the nature of the particular litigation involved. The State is empowered to discipline for conduct which it deems detrimental to the public interest unless foreclosed from doing so by our cases construing the First and Fourteenth Amendments.

* * *

* * * I cannot agree that a State must prove such harmful consequences in each case simply because an organization such as the ACLU or the NAACP is involved.

I cannot share the Court's confidence that the danger of such consequences is minimized simply because a lawyer proceeds from political conviction rather than for pecuniary gain. A State may reasonably fear that a lawyer's desire to resolve "substantial civil liberties questions," may occasionally take precedence over his duty to advance the interests of his client. It is even more reasonable to fear that a lawyer in such circumstances will be inclined to pursue both culpable and blameless defendants to the last ditch in order to achieve his ideological goals. Although individual litigants, including the ACLU, may be free to use the courts for such purposes, South Carolina is likewise free to restrict the activities of the members of its Bar who attempt to persuade them to do so.

I can only conclude that the discipline imposed upon Primus does not violate the Constitution, and I would affirm the judgment of the Supreme Court of South Carolina.*

---

* These cases are discussed and their implications assessed in 3 R. Rotunda & J. Nowak, Treatise on Constitutional Law § 20.31 (2d ed, 1991), and Nowak & Rotun-

PROBLEM 33

The Ethics of Referral to a Specialist

Hector Ramirez has represented the Peron family for several years in minor matters for which he has charged minimal fees. Joseph Peron was recently seriously injured when a telephone company truck went out of control and into a schoolyard. The Peron family wants to file suit and has come to Ramirez for help.

Ramirez realizes that he is a competent attorney and could handle this case without obvious errors. However, he also knows that he is not experienced in personal injury work, that the medical evidence necessary to prove the case correctly will be complex and that he may not be able to cross-examine the defense doctors effectively. Ramirez can see, on the other hand, that the fee this case would justify would be the largest he has ever earned and would support him while he did other, less-remunerative work.

Ramirez knows further that Joe Castro is a very successful "Certified Trial Specialist." He is experienced at handling personal injury cases and will take the Peron case very seriously. Best of all, Castro has offered to pay Ramirez one-third of his own one-third fee, or $10,000, whichever is less, as a "finder's fee" for sending the case to him. If Ramirez prefers, he and Castro will "jointly" handle the case on the same financial basis. Ramirez also has met another personal injury lawyer who might do an even better job than Castro but who is so ethical that he would be shocked at being asked to share his fee with Ramirez.

QUESTIONS

1. Does Ramirez have an ethical obligation to recommend that the Peron family seek a more experienced lawyer?

a. Did the Code require any more than "competent" work by an attorney? Look at DR 6–101(A)(1). What is connoted by the term "competent"? Is it the same as "average"? Does it include all performance that is not "incompetent"?

b. The Model Rules make competence their first priority; look at Rule 1.1. Is the attempt to define competence there any more helpful? [1]

da, Constitutional Law (4th ed. 1992), at § 16.31.

1. California used to define "failing to act competently" in part as follows:

"A member of the State Bar shall not wilfully or habitually

(1) Perform legal services for a client or clients if he knows or reasonably should know that he does not possess the learning and skill ordinarily possessed by

lawyers in good standing who perform, but do not specialize in, similar services practicing in the same or similar locality and under similar circumstances unless he associates or, where appropriate, professionally consults another lawyer who he reasonably believes does possess the requisite learning and skill; * * * "

Rule 6–101, Rules of Professional Conduct of the State Bar of California, later

2. Joe Castro is a "Certified Trial Specialist." What does that designation mean to you? What do you suppose it means to a potential lay client?

a. Model Rule 7.4 and DR 2–105 were drafted when most states traditionally recognized no "specialities" except perhaps patent, trademark, and admiralty law; those were simply designations permitted by accidents of history. States that did recognize specialities most often imitated California's plan. The California Supreme Court adopted the plan in 1971 and put it into operation on an experimental basis in 1973. Because California is such a large state, with most lawyers located in two of the larger metropolitan areas, it is more complex than other plans. All these plans have been modified over the years to adapt to Supreme Court decisions in the advertising area and to meet other changing circumstances. In 1975, Richard Zehnle of the American Bar Foundation described the California plan as follows:

> A nine-member California Board of Legal Specialization administers the plan with the assistance of nine-member advisory commissions for each approved area of specialization. The California plan has begun with three fields of specialization: (1) criminal law; (2) workmen's compensation; (3) taxation. * * * [A] candidate for specialization must meet the following requirements: (1) at least five years of law practice; (2) substantial involvement in the field of specialization for a reasonable period of time before certification (minimum standards are specified for each field); (3) special educational experience in the field (specifically, a board-approved program of advanced study); (4) successful performance on a written examination.
>
> Certification is for five years, after which recertification is required. There are three requirements for recertification: (1) 10 years of law practice; (2) substantial involvement in the area of specialization during the period of certification; (3) special education experience in the area of specialization during the period of certification. If a lawyer fails to meet the requirements [of continuing legal education], he may be entitled to take a written examination.[2]

b. Should every area of law practice be a potential specialty or only those requiring unusual training and experience? Should only especially complex areas of law—e.g., bankruptcy and tax—be recognized as specialties? Should the test be whether people tend to limit their activities to the area, e.g., might trial practice be a specialty so defined?

c. "Certifying" specialists refers to designating certain people as having special skills and experience in an area; "licensing" specialists would mean that only the specialist could practice in an area. Might you favor one of these systems of specialization over the other?

amended. See present California Rule 3– **2.** Richard F. Zehnle, Specialization in
110 in the Standards Supplement.   the Legal Profession 5–11 (1975).

d.   Is any additional public protection provided by licensing specialists? Would the distinction have economic significance for the lawyers involved? Do you agree with the concerns about both certification and licensing expressed in the Mindes article in the Readings?

e.   Should specialists be permitted to practice *only* their specialty? If a lawyer is a patent specialist, for example, might the public need protection against his or her planning an estate? Would such an approach excessively compartmentalize the practice of law?

3. May lawyers claim that persons with specialty designations perform at a higher level of skill than would the average lawyer?

a.   Do lawyers have a First Amendment right to say that they are better than other lawyers? Think back to the *Bates* case in the Readings to Problem 31. Look at Model Rule 7.1(c), and read the *R.M.J.* and *Peel* decisions in the Readings to this Problem. Should there be a constitutional distinction between what an individual may assert in advertising, what an association of specialists may assert, and what the organized bar generally may say in urging lay people to seek legal counsel?

b.   Under what conditions may a lawyer say that she is certified as a specialist? Look at Model Rule 7.4(c) & (d). Was the Model Code equally receptive to the speciality claim? The language you see in Rule 7.4 has been amended to be consistent with *Peel.*[3]

c.   What terms short of the label "specialty" may a lawyer use to describe his or her practice? May she say that her "practice is limited to" real estate law, for example, if in fact she will only take matters in that area? What public interest is served by preventing a lawyer from informing the public that his or her practice is "limited" if in fact it is? After *Bates*, *R.M.J.* and *Peel*, may any limit on such a representation be imposed? May any qualification or disclaimer be required?

d.   If a lawyer is presented with an award by a bona fide bar organization (e.g., the "Crystal Gavel" awarded by the State Bar Civil Practice Section for "outstanding contributions to the law of Civil Practice in 1994") should the lawyer be permitted to advertise that fact? If a lawyer belongs to the American Law Institute, or some other bona fide, prestigious private lawyers' group, may the lawyer note that on a business card? May the lawyer so distinguish herself from other lawyers even though the state does not recognize or certify specialities?

e.   May a lawyer say that she is "experienced" in a field of law, or has "15 years experience"? What does the term "experience" mean in this context? See, e.g., N.Y. State Bar Association Committee on Professional Ethics Opinion No. 487 (July 15, 1978), asserting that a representation of "experience" without "further qualification implies that the

3. In the aftermath of *Peel*, the American Bar Association has undertaken to "accredit" private organizations to certify specialists. The ABA's authority to accredit or not accredit organization seems entirely self-granted, but state courts may welcome the ABA's relatively independent review of certification standards.

lawyer's experience over the stated period has been frequent rather than merely occasional, and substantial as distinguished from casual." Is that a good definition of what a lawyer should be understood to mean after *Peel*?

f.   Only a bare majority of the Court in *Peel* upheld Peel's constitutional right to have his letterhead state that he is certified as a civil trial specialist, and even this majority was unable to muster a majority opinion.   Do you think that the dissenters will be able to create a majority to put limits on *Bates* itself now that Justices Brennan, Blackmun, and Marshall have left the Court?   Does the unanimous *R.M.J.* opinion suggest that *Bates* will survive changes in the Supreme Court membership?

g.   If the state allows a lawyer to claim that he or she is a specialist in a particular area of law, should the courts impose a higher standard of performance for determining malpractice liability?   Cf. Wright v. Williams, 47 Cal.App.3d 802, 121 Cal.Rptr. 194 (1975) (specialist held to higher duty of care).

4.   Is there anything improper about Castro's paying or Ramirez' accepting a "finder's fee" in a case such as this?

a.   What did the Model Code say about that in DR 2–107(A)? Would prohibiting such payments tend to discourage less experienced lawyers from sending clients to more experienced ones?   Might allowing the payments tend to corrupt the judgment of the referring lawyer as to who the best qualified person is to handle the case?

b.   In a rebuttal to an American Trial Lawyers Association proposal defending use of above-the-table referral fees, the editors of a legal newspaper argued that the proposal "amounts to saying that a lawyer should be bribed to act ethically.   For it happens to be the unambiguous rule * * * that lawyers not competent to handle cases should not handle them."   The editorial continued, "if a lawyer can afford to forgo some percentage of his fee in favor of a lawyer who does no work on the case, then that lawyer * * * is charging too much."   National Law Journal, Feb. 5, 1979, p. 18, col. 1.   Can you suggest any responses to these arguments?

c.   The traditional rules against referral fees have tended to create traps for the unwary.

In ACLU/Eastern Missouri Fund v. Miller, 803 S.W.2d 592 (Mo. 1991), for example, Miller was an ACLU staff attorney who agreed that any attorney's fees recovered in actions he filed would be turned over to the ACLU.   On behalf of two clients, Miller and a volunteer lawyer pursued and won a civil rights action against the city of St. Louis.   The court awarded Miller fees totalling $8090, but by this time he had resigned from the ACLU.   He refused to turn the fee over to the organization, asserting that to do so would violate the Missouri counterpart of DR 3–102 and Model Rule 5.4(a).   Over a strong dissent that this was basically conversion of funds that belonged to the ACLU, a majority of the Court agreed with Miller. A lawyer may make a voluntary donation of the fees to the organization, of course, but he may not make a binding contract to do so.

Do you agree? Would any significant principle of ethical conduct be violated by requiring Miller to keep the promise he made to the ACLU? The ABA Standing Committee on Ethics and Professional Responsibility did not believe any such principle existed and in its Formal Opinion 93–374 (1993), it rejected this reading of Model Rule 5.4(a).

c. Should Ramirez be able to act as an "agent" for the Peron family in finding a lawyer, i.e. could he perform the function attorneys often perform in negotiating contracts for athletes? Would it be proper for Ramirez to interview tort lawyers, get "bids" on their taking the Peron child's case, and help the family decide which lawyer to retain? Under the Model Rules, could he be paid by the hour for this service? Could his pay be contingent on the amount recovered? Should it matter whether the Peron family paid Ramirez' fee or whether the winning lawyer paid it?

d. Could the ethical issues be avoided if Ramirez "associated" with Castro in handling the case? Do you agree that association is so different from "referral" that the Code properly made the distinction crucial? Would Ramirez retain significant obligations in an association that he could avoid by referral? Is the fee allocation in an association relationship likely to be different in amount from a "finder's fee"?

e. Notice that neither the Model Rules nor the Model Code regulate distribution of legal fees within the same law firm. Should they do so? Should one think of referral fees as small practitioners' way of (1) securing access to specialists (something that big firms can do internally), and (2) getting rewarded for bringing in business (something that "rainmakers" in the big firms do without thinking)? Is that too cynical a way to think about ethical principles?

5. Do the Model Rules improve on the Model Code's approach to referral fees?

a. Look at Rule 1.5(e), and Comment 4. What is "joint responsibility for the representation?" Does it imply assumption of malpractice liability? Why is that thought to be an important requirement? Is it analogous to what happens in a law firm? [4]

b. In order to make the referral proper, should the client have to be told what percentage of the fee the referring lawyer will receive? Does a client of the usual law firm know the intra–firm division of the fee?

c. Should the provisions of Model Rule 1.5(e) be controlling in a civil suit by one lawyer against the other? In Kaplan v. Pavalon &

4. Note that Rule 1.5(e) is not radical. It harkens back to an earlier era. Canon 34 of the ABA Canons of Professional Ethics, in the Standards Supplement stated simply: "No division of fees for legal services is proper, except with another lawyer, based upon a division of services *or* responsibility." (emphasis added).

Gifford, 12 F.3d 87 (7th Cir.1993), an agreement to divide fees was found to be unenforceable unless it was made in accord with the state's version of Rule 1.5(e). Even though that rule only purports to create a disciplinary standard, the lawyer who orally promised to pay a referral fee could avoid a contract that did not comply with Rule 1.5(e).

Do you agree? Weren't the requirements of Rule 1.5(e) drafted primarily for the protection of clients? Indeed, if you had been trying to protect lawyers from each other, would you have drafted Rule 1.5(e) the same way?

d. Is there any rationale for limiting payment of referral fees only to lawyers, assuming that the client does not object? Even Canon 34 required that the division of legal fees be with another lawyer, but is there any reason to prohibit payment to a labor union, for example, for referral of a member's case? How about to a doctor? The police officer who carries the lawyer's cards while investigating traffic accidents? [5]

6. Are the issues of this problem likely to be presented whenever a lawyer tries a case in another state?

a. Do state laws requiring the employment of "local counsel" to "assist" the out-of-state lawyer by sitting at the counsel table tend to further the protection of clients? Might they tend to make the court process run more smoothly?

b. What should local counsel be paid for their efforts? Should that fee be paid by the client in addition to or as part of the fee contracted to be paid to the out-of-state attorney? See EC 3–9.

7. What would you advise Ramirez to do in the circumstances of this problem?

a. Does he have any alternatives that we have not mentioned here? Could he avoid all referral fee problems by saying to Castro, for example, "I'll send you this big case if you'll refer some good clients my way"?

b. Could he serve an important function by remaining involved in the case as co-counsel or even by acting as lead counsel and hiring help for the trial itself? Do we sometimes overemphasize trial experience given that only 5% or so of cases go to trial? Might these clients' confidence in Ramirez and his desire to see them well served be among

---

5. The prohibition apparently derives from the practice of "ambulance chasers" finding injured persons and then selling their cases to attorneys. The bar has traditionally condemned this method of acquiring cases, but consider the several opinions in In re Cohn, 10 Ill.2d 186, 139 N.E.2d 301 (1956). Justice Bristow, for example, was unwilling to be wholly critical, saying: "Today, insurance companies' * * * claims agents * * * try by fair means to obtain the lowest possible settlement for injured plaintiffs. * * * It is a veritable scramble between the claim agent and the 'chaser' to see which one can reach an injured claimant first. The net result of a timely arrival of the solicitor is that the claimant will eventually receive an amount that a court and jury deems adequate and just." 10 Ill.2d at 195, 139 N.E.2d at 305–06. On the other hand, in his book, The Injury Industry (1971), Professor Jeffrey O'Connell argues that fees for referring cases contribute to the excessive cost of processing accident claims.

the most important factors in assuring that the Perons will get a satisfactory resolution of their case?

READINGS

MINDES,[1] LAWYER SPECIALTY CERTIFICATION: THE MONOPOLY GAME

61 A.B.A. Journal 42 (1975).

Further movement toward specialization in the legal profession is inevitable. To the extent that it is brought about by the need of clients for better and more efficient services, it is unexceptionable. However, specialization has been followed by a growing campaign by a number of specialists for regulation.

* * *

Generalizations from the medical experience to law are difficult to make safely. Unlike lawyers, American physicians always have been allowed to indicate publicly that they practice in a specialized area, the rationalization being that this was a self-imposed limitation and thus a narrower claim to competence than that of a general practitioner. This was not changed with the advent of certifying boards for various specialty areas. On the other hand, certification of specialists in the legal profession, combined with exclusive permission to indicate the specialty publicly, would be considerably more monopolistic than the parallel development in medicine.

* * *

Board-certified specialists are gaining in income and prestige at the expense of others mainly because of their advantages in getting hospital staff positions and privileges. Restrictions on the right to practice in a hospital are particularly harmful to general practitioners, many of whom have no access to hospital facilities, although they may have the option of surrendering control of a case to a staff specialist. The departmental organization of modern hospitals also adds doubt as to the status of previously admitted general practitioners. This, together with the substantially increased importance of hospitals in medical treatment and training, has gotten the message across to medical students, who almost all opt for specialization.

* * *

---

1. The late Mr. Mindes was Adjunct Associate Professor, I.I.T.—Chicago/Kent College of Law.

Certified public accountancy offers another view of the consequences of certification.

* * *

The profession started, of course, by grandfathering in existing practitioners, and benefited substantially from the federal income tax amendment. But the major competitive breakthroughs came when those who determined the type of accountant to be hired were not the same persons to pay for the work, thereby rendering considerations of cost secondary. Meetings with the American Institute of Accountants led the New York Stock Exchange early in 1933 to require C.P.A. audits for all listing applications. Next, the Securities Act of 1933 required C.P.A.-verified balance sheets for all issuers of registered securities. There followed a substantial number of regulatory and statutory pre-scriptions, federal, state, and private, and in 1957 the American Federa-tion of Labor–Congress of Industrial Organizations began requiring C.P.A. audits of member unions.

In the private economic sector, banks more and more tended to insist on C.P.A. audits; corporate lawyers in business deals began to require certification. What better way to avoid business difficulties and hazards, including exposure to criticism, than to hire accountants who were pre-evaluated by certification?

* * *

The success of certified groups in achieving greater and greater control of their occupational territories might be attributed to competi-tive advantage through selling better services. But control is achieved by anticompetitive devices, and success is often unrelated to either the quality of their services or the need for them. We have, for example, an over elaboration of accounting detail that serves neither uniformity of rules nor adequate disclosure, and there are systems that are unrelated to actual management needs. In medicine we see bizarre examples, such as unnecessary operations, psycho-surgery, heroic measures to maintain comatose terminal life, and a wasteful overqualification of specialists for much of their work. Indeed a central tendency of a profession is to exercise as much control as possible, to the exclusion of outside influ-ences, over the decisions that determine when and what kind of services are necessary and how much they will cost.

* * *

In the later stages of this process, the organized specialty will view its differences from other portions of the bar, and particularly from general practitioners, as considerably more important than its similari-ties. The specialty group will have completely convinced themselves, despite the fact that most of them were grandfathered in, that no one else has the judgment, wisdom, and skill to perform the simplest service within their domain. Of course, their mission and public responsibility will compel them to protect the public against uncertified practitioners.

The main impact of certification on the bar comes from the fact that the choice of attorneys is so subjective that any self-protecting public or private bureaucrat will tend to use certification as a criterion rather than to take the chance of allowing—or making—an independent judgment. Thus certification does succeed, but at severe cost to the public, as well as to the excluded generalist or the lawyer who wishes to switch fields. First, as entry to the field is restricted, the price goes up, and many persons cannot afford the services. Second, the tendencies to differentiate the law and practice in the certified field and to overcomplicate and overextend tasks will be exacerbated. A final cost is that needed reforms, which change the way in which legal practice is structured, will become less likely since custom will be more strongly protected by the new, more homogeneous, professional groups.

* * *

This is not to argue against the honesty, good faith, character, or intentions of the proponents of certification. The point is that certification is a basic restructuring of relationships that leads individuals and groups to behave in ways that bring about other consequences that are different from those for which it is advocated and adopted. That a change in structure often has these consequences should be a surprise to lawyers no more than to sociologists. But in this instance for most legal practitioners the deal is comparable to some land transactions between American settlers and the Indian tribes. The Indians thought they were granting concurrent hunting rights and later were surprised to find that they had sold title in fee simple.

IN RE R.M.J.

Supreme Court of the United States, 1982.
455 U.S. 191, 102 S.Ct. 929, 71 L.Ed.2d 64.

Justice POWELL delivered the opinion of the Court.

* * *

I

As with many of the states, until the decision in *Bates,* Missouri placed an absolute prohibition on advertising by lawyers. After the Court's invalidation of just such a prohibition in *Bates*, the Committee on Professional Ethics and Responsibility of the Supreme Court of Missouri revised that court's Rule 4 regulating lawyer advertising. The Committee sought to "strike a midpoint between prohibition and unlimited advertising," and the revised regulation of advertising, adopted with slight modification by the State Supreme Court, represents a compromise. Lawyer advertising is permitted, but it is restricted to certain categories of information, and in some instances, to certain specified language.

* * *

* * * [T]he Advisory Committee [charged with enforcing Missouri Rule 4—the lawyer advertising rule] has issued an addendum to the Rule providing that if the lawyer chooses to list areas of practice in his advertisement, he must do so in one of two prescribed ways. He may list one of three general descriptive terms specified in the Rule— "General Civil Practice," "General Criminal Practice," or "General Civil and Criminal Practice." Alternatively, he may use one or more of a list of twenty-three areas of practice, including, for example, "Tort Law," "Family Law," and "Probate and Trust Law." He may not list both a general term and specific subheadings, nor may he deviate from the precise wording stated in the rule. He may not indicate that his practice is "limited" to the listed areas and he must include a particular disclaimer of certification of expertise following any listing of specific areas of practice.

* * *

II

* * *

The advertisements at issue in this litigation appeared in January, February, and August of 1978, and included information that was not expressly permitted by Rule 4. They included the information that appellant was licensed in Missouri and Illinois. They contained, in large capital letters, a statement that appellant was "Admitted to Practice Before the United States Supreme Court." And they included a listing of areas of practice that deviated from the language prescribed by the Advisory Committee—e.g., "personal injury" and "real estate" instead of "tort law" and "property law"—and that included several areas of law without analogue in the list of areas prepared by the Advisory Committee—e.g., "contract," "zoning & land use," "communication," "pension & profit sharing plans." In addition, and with the exception of the advertisement appearing in August, 1978, appellant failed to include the required disclaimer of certification of expertise after the listing of areas of practice.

On November 19, 1979, the Advisory Committee filed an information in the Supreme Court of Missouri charging appellant with unprofessional conduct. * * * In a disbarment proceeding, the Supreme Court of Missouri upheld the constitutionality of DR 2–101 of Rule 4 and issued a private reprimand. * * *

III

* * *

Commercial speech doctrine, in the context of advertising for professional services, may be summarized generally as follows: Truthful advertising related to lawful activities is entitled to the protections of the First Amendment. But when the particular content or method of the advertising suggests that it is inherently misleading or when experience has proven that in fact such advertising is subject to abuse, the states may impose appropriate restrictions. Misleading advertising may be prohibited entirely. But the states may not place an absolute prohibition on certain types of potentially misleading information, e.g., a listing of areas of practice, if the information also may be presented in a way that is not deceptive. * * *

IV

* * *

* * * The Advisory Committee does not argue that appellant's listing was misleading. The use of the words "real estate" instead of "property" could scarcely mislead the public. Similarly, the listing of areas such as "contracts" or "securities," that are not found on the Advisory Committee's list in any form, presents no apparent danger of deception. Indeed, as Chief Justice Bardgett explained in dissent, in certain respects appellant's listing is more informative than that provided in the addendum. Because the listing published by the appellant has not been shown to be misleading, and because the Advisory Committee suggests no substantial interest promoted by the restriction, we conclude that this portion of Rule 4 is an invalid restriction upon speech as applied to appellant's advertisements.

* * *

Accordingly, the judgment of the Supreme Court of Missouri is *Reversed.*

———

PEEL v. ATTORNEY REGISTRATION AND DISCIPLINARY COMMISSION

Supreme Court of the United States, 1990.
496 U.S. 91, 110 S.Ct. 2281, 110 L.Ed.2d 83.

Justice STEVENS announced the judgment of the Court and delivered an opinion in which Justice BRENNAN, Justice BLACKMUN, and Justice KENNEDY join.

The Illinois Supreme Court publicly censured petitioner because his letterhead states that he is certified as a civil trial specialist by the National Board of Trial Advocacy. We granted certiorari to consider whether the statement on his letterhead is protected by the First Amendment.

This case comes to us against a background of growing interest in lawyer certification programs. In the 1973 Sonnett Memorial Lecture, then Chief Justice Warren E. Burger advanced the proposition that specialized training and certification of trial advocates is essential to the American system of justice. That proposition was endorsed by a number of groups of lawyers who were instrumental in establishing the National Board of Trial Advocacy (NBTA) in 1977.

Since then, NBTA has developed a set of standards and procedures for periodic certification of lawyers with experience and competence in trial work. Those standards, which have been approved by a board of judges, scholars, and practitioners, are objective and demanding. They require specified experience as lead counsel in both jury and nonjury trials, participation in approved programs of continuing legal education, a demonstration of writing skills, and the successful completion of a day-long examination. Certification expires in five years unless the lawyer again demonstrates his or her continuing qualification.

* * *

Petitioner practices law in Edwardsville, Illinois. He was licensed to practice in Illinois in 1968, in Arizona in 1979, and in Missouri in 1981. He has served as president of the Madison County Bar Association, and has been active in both national and state bar association work. He has tried to verdict over 100 jury trials and over 300 nonjury trials, and has participated in hundreds of other litigated matters that were settled. NBTA issued petitioner a "Certificate in Civil Trial Advocacy" in 1981, renewed it in 1986, and listed him in its 1985 Directory of "Certified Specialists and Board Members."

Since 1983 petitioner's professional letterhead has contained a statement referring to his NBTA certification and to the three States in which he is licensed. It appears as follows:

> "Gary E. Peel
>
> Certified Civil Trial Specialist
>
> By the National Board of Trial Advocacy
>
> Licensed: Illinois, Missouri, Arizona"

In 1987, the Administrator of the Attorney Registration and Disciplinary Commission of Illinois (Commission) filed a complaint alleging that petitioner, by use of this letterhead, was publicly holding himself out as a certified legal specialist in violation of Rule 2–105(a)(3) of the Illinois Code of Professional Responsibility. That Rule provides:

> "A lawyer or law firm may specify or designate any area or field of law in which he or its partners concentrates or limits his or its practice. Except as set forth in Rule 2–105(a), no lawyer may hold himself out as 'certified' or a 'specialist.' "[8]

The complaint also alleged violations of Rule 2–101(b), which requires that a lawyer's public "communication shall contain all information necessary to make the communication not misleading and shall not contain any false or misleading statement or otherwise operate to

---

8. Disciplinary Rule 2–105(a)(3) (1988). The exceptions are for patent, trademark, and admiralty lawyers. * * *

deceive," and of Rule 1–102(a)(1), which generally subjects a lawyer to discipline for violation of any Rule of the Code of Professional Responsibility.

* * * In this case we must consider whether petitioner's statement was misleading and, even if it was not, whether the potentially misleading character of such statements creates a state interest sufficiently substantial to justify a categorical ban on their use.

The facts stated on petitioner's letterhead are true and verifiable. It is undisputed that NBTA has certified petitioner as a civil trial specialist and that three States have licensed him to practice law. There is no contention that any potential client or person was actually misled or deceived by petitioner's stationery. * * *

In evaluating petitioner's claim of certification, the Illinois Supreme Court focused not on its facial accuracy, but on its implied claim "as to the quality of [petitioner's] legal services," and concluded that such a qualitative claim "might be so likely to mislead as to warrant restriction." This analysis confuses the distinction between statements of opinion or quality and statements of objective facts that may support an inference of quality. A lawyer's certification by NBTA is a verifiable fact, as are the predicate requirements for that certification. Measures of trial experience and hours of continuing education, like information about what schools the lawyer attended or his or her bar activities, are facts about a lawyer's training and practice. A claim of certification is not an unverifiable opinion of the ultimate quality of a lawyer's work or a promise of success, but is simply a fact, albeit one with multiple predicates, from which a consumer may or may not draw an inference of the likely quality of an attorney's work in a given area of practice.

We must assume that some consumers will infer from petitioner's statement that his qualifications in the area of civil trial advocacy exceed the general qualifications for admission to a state bar. Thus if the certification had been issued by an organization that had made no inquiry into petitioner's fitness, or by one that issued certificates indiscriminately for a price, the statement, even if true, could be misleading. In this case, there is no evidence that a claim of NBTA certification suggests any greater degree of professional qualification than reasonably may be inferred from an evaluation of its rigorous requirements. Much like a trademark, the strength of a certification is measured by the quality of the organization for which it stands. * * *

Nor can we agree with the Illinois Supreme Court's somewhat contradictory fears that juxtaposition of the references to being "certified" as a "specialist" with the identification of the three States in which petitioner is "licensed" conveys, on the one hand, the impression that NBTA had the authority to grant those licenses and, on the other, that the NBTA certification was the product of official state action. The separate character of the two references is plain from their texts * * *. There has been no finding that any person has associated certification with governmental action—state or federal—and there is no basis for belief that petitioner's representation generally would be so construed.

We are satisfied that the consuming public understands that licenses—to drive cars, to operate radio stations, to sell liquor—are issued by governmental authorities and that a host of certificates—to commend job performance, to convey an educational degree, to commemorate a solo flight or a hole in one—are issued by private organizations. The dictionary definition of "certificate," from which the Illinois Supreme Court quoted only excerpts, comports with this common understanding:

> "[A] document issued by a *school*, a state agency, *or a professional organization* certifying that one has satisfactorily *completed a course of studies, has passed a qualifying examination, or has* attained professional standing in a given field and may officially practice or hold a position in that field." Webster's Third New International Dictionary 367 (1986 ed.) (emphasis added to portions omitted from 126 Ill.2d, at 405, 128 Ill.Dec., at 539, 534 N.E.2d, at 984).

* * * The Federal Trade Commission, which has a long history of reviewing claims of deceptive advertising, fortifies this conclusion with its observation that "one can readily think of numerous other claims of specialty—from 'air conditioning specialist' in the realm of home repairs to 'foreign car specialist' in the realm of automotive repairs—that cast doubt on the notion that the public would automatically mistake a claim of specialization for a claim of formal recognition by the State." * * *

Even if petitioner's letterhead is not actually misleading, the Commission defends Illinois' categorical prohibition against lawyers' claims of being "certified" or a "specialist" on the assertion that these statements are potentially misleading. * * * We may assume that statements of "certification" as a "specialist," even though truthful, may not be understood fully by some readers. However, such statements pose no greater potential of misleading consumers than advertising admission to "Practice before: The United States Supreme Court," In re R.M.J., of exploiting the audience of a targeted letter, Shapero v. Kentucky Bar Assn., 486 U.S. 466, 108 S.Ct. 1916, 100 L.Ed.2d 475 (1988), or of confusing a reader with an accurate illustration, Zauderer v. Office of Disciplinary Counsel. In this case, as in those, we conclude that the particular State rule restricting lawyers' advertising is "broader than reasonably necessary to prevent the 'perceived evil.'" * * *

* * *

* * * We do not ignore the possibility that some unscrupulous attorneys may hold themselves out a certified specialists when there is no qualified organization to stand behind that certification. A lawyer's truthful statement that "XYZ Board" has "certified" him as a "specialist in admiralty law" would not necessarily be entitled to First Amendment protection if the certification was a sham. States can require an attorney who advertises "XYZ certification" to demonstrate that such

certification is available to all lawyers who meet objective and consistently applied standards relevant to practice in a particular area of the law.[17]
* * *

Petitioner's letterhead was neither actually nor inherently misleading. There is no dispute about the bona fides and the relevance of NBTA certification. The Commissioner's concern about the possibility of deception in hypothetical cases is not sufficient to rebut the constitutional presumption favoring disclosure over concealment. Disclosure of information such as that on petitioner's letterhead both serves the public interest and encourages the development and utilization of meritorious certification programs for attorneys. As the public censure of petitioner for violating Rule 2–105(a)(3) violates the First Amendment, the judgment of the Illinois Supreme Court is reversed and the case is remanded for proceedings not inconsistent with this opinion.

Justice MARSHALL, with whom Justice BRENNAN joins, concurring in the judgment.

Petitioner's letterhead is neither actually nor inherently misleading. I therefore concur in the plurality's holding that Illinois may not prohibit petitioner from holding himself out as a civil trial specialist certified by the National Board of Trial Advocacy. I believe, though, that petitioner's letterhead statement is potentially misleading. Accordingly, I would hold that Illinois may enact regulations other than a total ban to ensure that the public is not misled by such representations. Because Illinois' present regulation is unconstitutional as applied to petitioner, however, the judgment of the Illinois Supreme Court must be reversed and the case remanded for further proceedings.

* * * The name "National Board of Trial Advocacy" could created the misimpression that the NBTA is an agency of the Federal Government. Although most lawyers undoubtedly know that the Federal Government does not regulate lawyers, most nonlawyers probably do not; thus, the word "National" in the NBTA's name does not dispel the potential implication that the NBTA is a governmental agency. Furthermore, the juxtaposition on petitioner's letterhead of the phrase "Certified Civil Trial Specialist By the National Board of Trial Advocacy" with "Licensed: Illinois, Missouri, Arizona" could lead even lawyers to believe that the NBTA, though not a governmental agency, is somehow sanctioned by the States listed on the letterhead. * * *

Justice WHITE, dissenting.

* * * [T]here are five Justices who believe that this particular letterhead is unprotected: Justice O'CONNOR, THE CHIEF JUSTICE, and Justice SCALIA believe the letterhead is inherently misleading and hence would uphold Rule 2–105(a)(3); at least two of us—Justice MAR-

---

17. It is not necessary here—as it also was not in *In re R.M.J.*—to consider when a State might impose some disclosure requirements, rather than a total prohibition, in order to minimize the possibility that a reader will misunderstand the significance of a statement of fact that is protected by the First Amendment. [footnote repositioned]

SHALL and myself—find it potentially misleading and would permit the State to ban such letterheads but only if they are not accompanied by disclaimers appropriate to avoid the danger. This letterhead does not carry such a disclaimer. The upshot is that while the State may not apply its flat ban to any and all claims of certification by attorneys, particularly those carrying disclaimers, the State should be allowed to apply its Rule to the letterhead in its present form and forbid its circulation. That leads me to affirm, rather than to reverse, the judgment below. * * *

Justice O'CONNOR, with whom Chief Justice REHNQUIST and Justice SCALIA join, dissenting.

This case provides yet another example of the difficulties raised by rote application of the commercial speech doctrine in the context of state regulation of professional standards for attorneys. Nothing in our prior cases in this area mandates that we strike down the state regulation at issue here, which is designed to ensure a reliable and ethical profession. Failure to accord States considerable latitude in this area embroils this Court in the micromanagement of the State's inherent authority to police the ethical standards of the profession within its borders. * * *

PROBLEM 34

Responsibilities of Lawyers to Others in Their Firm

Several years ago, Bill Bright and Larry Learned started the firm of Bright and Learned. It prospered and now has grown to 125 lawyers, of whom only 6 are women. Four of the women are associates; two are partners. All of the women have been assigned to work in the field of estate administration.

The women view the firm as singularly unenlightened. None of the women has been allowed to move into the litigation section of the firm, and many of the firm's partnership meetings are held in the all-male Thomas Jefferson Club. Just before Christmas the women associates organized a committee to present their objections and proposals for reform to the firm's partners.

These negotiations proved unsuccessful, and the female associates have decided to leave the firm and start a new one. They feel that they can persuade the two female partners to leave with them. The female partners generate a disproportionate share of the income of Bright & Learned. They could provide not only the necessary financing and experience needed for a new firm but also bring with them most of their important clients. The women associates also believe that they can bring with them at least some of the clients for whom they have worked during the past several years. The women have asked you for advice as to how to proceed.

QUESTIONS

1.   Do legal ethics deal with the interrelationships of lawyers in a law firm?

a.   The Model Code contained no counterpart to Model Rule 5.2 and no direct counterparts to Rules 5.1 and 5.3.   Do these Model Rules constitute an improvement over the Code?   Do the Rules merely codify what was already a lawyer's responsibility in light of the fact that lawyers have always had fiduciary duties to their clients?

b.   Do Bill Bright and Larry Learned have obligations under Model Rules 5.1, 5.2, and 5.3 to make sure that their associates, paralegals, secretaries and staff engage in conduct that is consistent with the ethical responsibilities of lawyers in the firm?   If Bright, for example, makes no efforts to instruct new associates and paralegals on the need to keep client confidences, even if it happily turns out that no associates or paralegals divulge client confidences, could Bright be held to have violated the Model Rules?

c.   If Bright puts in place a reasonable training program about the need to keep client confidences, and buttresses that program with periodic reminders, yet one of the paralegals divulges a confidence, should Bright be subject to discipline under Rule 5.3?   Could the firm still be subject to malpractice liability?

2.   Did Bright & Learned treat its women partners and associates "ethically"?   Do principles of legal ethics deal with how members of a law firm should treat each other?

a.   Should the bar have ethical standards on such questions?   May lawyers be presumed to be sufficiently good bargainers that they can take care of themselves?

b.   Should a law firm incur legal liability for failing to give a new associate a job assignment discussed in the interview?   The question might seem facetious, but Stewart v. Jackson & Nash, 976 F.2d 86 (2d Cir.1992), upheld a new associate's cause of action for fraud where the firm had falsely asserted that it had a large environmental case and was building an environmental law department.

c.   Should all law firm partners have a right to be treated equally?   Quite the opposite is true at most firms.   Law firms are sometimes said to categorize partners as "finders", "minders" and "grinders"; that is, some lawyers primarily bring in clients, others manage and supervise cases, while still others do most of the detail work in cases.   Often, firms distinguish sharply among these groups in terms of pay, the "finders" typically commanding the highest share of firm profits.   "Minders" or "grinders," even those who are called "partners" today, sometimes work on a salary and may have no equity interest in the firm.

d.   Should these relationships be subject to ethical rules?   Is the number of possible permutations of relationships so great that rules could not encompass them? Is anyone other than the lawyers in the firm affected by the arrangements? Should those lawyers be presumed to be capable of practicing in some other setting if they are unhappy? Might one argue that in the present employment market for lawyers, that assumption is increasingly open to question?

e. Should a retired law partner have a cause of action against his former law firm's management committee for acts of negligence that caused the firm to dissolve, resulting in the termination of his retirement benefits? In Bane v. Ferguson, 890 F.2d 11 (7th Cir.1989), the court said no. A partner of a firm has a fiduciary duty to his partners, but none to his former partners. Judge Posner acknowledged that "[w]e are sorry about the financial blow" to the plaintiff, who was 72 years old when he retired and apparently had no source of income other than the pension (now lost) of less than $28,000 per year, plus social security. However, the former partner should have protected himself through contract; "people should be encouraged to protect themselves through voluntary transactions rather than to look to tort law to repair the consequences of their improvidence."

Do you agree that expecting trust among law partners is "improvident"?

3. Regardless of what the Model Rules and Model Code provide, cases have held that some relationships within law firms may be governed by federal law.

a. Lucido v. Cravath, Swaine & Moore, 425 F.Supp. 123 (S.D.N.Y. 1977), for example, held that an associate may sue his law firm under Title VII of the Civil Rights Act of 1964 for discrimination on the basis of religion (Catholic) and national origin (Italian). Lucido alleged that he was subjected to discrimination with respect to work assignments, training, rotation and outside work appointments, and that he was denied promotion to partnership for the same unlawful reasons. Plaintiff's charges were found to state a cause of action.

b. In Hishon v. King & Spalding, 467 U.S. 69, 104 S.Ct. 2229, 81 L.Ed.2d 59 (1984), a unanimous Supreme Court held that Title VII prohibits a law firm from discriminating on the basis of sex, race, religion, or national origin in deciding which associates to promote to partner. Even if elevation to partnership is a change in status from employee to employer, consideration for partnership is still a term, condition, or privilege of employment. Plaintiff's claim of sex discrimination thus stated a cause of action.[1]

---

1. There is a difference, of course, between alleging sex discrimination and proving it. In Ezold v. Wolf, Block, Schorr and Solis–Cohen, 983 F.2d 509 (3d Cir.1992), the plaintiff alleged she had been denied partnership because of her sex. The court examined in great detail both her evaluations and those of males who made partner. The District Court ruled for the plaintiff in a detailed and interesting opinion, but the Court of Appeals reversed, apparently concluding that the firm reasonably thought that the plaintiff was not capable of handling complex corporate matters. At minimum, the case illustrates that creating a civil right cause of action is a far cry from granting relief.

c.   In Plessinger v. Castleman & Haskell, 838 F.Supp. 448 (N.D.Cal. 1993), a fired associate sued his firm for age discrimination and the firm's client (Allstate Insurance) for tortious interference with business relations.   The complaint alleged that Allstate had ordered the firm to fire him because it wanted younger lawyers working on its cases. Allstate asserted that it had an absolute right to counsel of its choice and thus that the claim must be dismissed.   This Court disagreed, saying that otherwise clients could demand that no women work on its cases, for example, or no African–Americans.   Allstate's motion to dismiss was denied.

d.   How should the Americans with Disabilities Act affect law firms?   May a firm refuse to hire or promote a lawyer with AIDS?   May it fire a lawyer whose alcoholism affects his work performance?   See Barnhart v. Pickrel, Schaeffer & Ebling Co., L.P.A., 12 F.3d 1382 (6th Cir.1993) (evidence of impaired performance sufficient to justify dismissal);   Doe   v.   Kohn   Nast   &   Graf,   P.C.,   862   F.Supp.   1310 (E.D.Pa.1994)(lawyer fired when he was discovered to be HIV positive has cause of action under the ADA).

e.   What do you think is likely to be the effect of these decisions? As a practical matter, are people who want to become partners in a law firm likely to sue the present partners?   On the other hand, might the existence of these precedents tend to increase the cost of treating lawyers unfairly and thus perhaps reduce the incidence of unfair treatment?

f.   How should women deal with sexual harassment in a law firm? The ways of dealing with it are only now evolving in many places, but one study indicates that 73% of large law firms have formal, written policies for dealing with such incidents.   See Sex and the Firms: A Progress Report, National L.J., Dec. 20, 1993, p. 1.

g.   Should violation of federal antidiscrimination law also constitute a basis for state professional discipline?   Action on rule changes to address questions of employment discrimination has been significant. The California Supreme Court has adopted a new Rule 2–400, for example, that forbids discrimination on the basis of race, sex, national origin, sexual orientation, religion, age or disability.   For a description of similar developments, see ABA/BNA Lawyers' Manual of Professional Conduct, 10 Current Reports 30 (1994).

h.   Various groups have been urging the ABA House of Delegates to amend Rule 8.4 to make lawyers subject to discipline if they engage in conduct or use words that evidence prejudice on the basis of various categories (such as race, sex, sexual preference, and socio–economic status), whether or not the law makes such discrimination illegal. Others object to a discipline rule but think that the ABA House of Delegates should pass a Resolution telling lawyers that they should not use certain words or engage in certain discriminatory conduct.   Opponents have voiced concerns based on the First Amendment to the extent that the prohibitions relate to speech.

4. Should special rules apply to termination of a lawyer who works for a corporate legal office?

a. In Herbster v. North American Company for Life and Health Insurance, 150 Ill.App.3d 21, 103 Ill.Dec. 322, 501 N.E.2d 343 (2d Dist.1986), cert. denied 484 U.S. 850, 108 S.Ct. 150, 98 L.Ed.2d 105 (1987), the chief legal officer of North American alleged he was fired because he had refused to destroy or remove documents that tended to show the company's fraud in its sale of flexible annuities. The documents were subject to discovery orders issued by a federal court in Alabama.

The Illinois appellate court assumed that this allegation was true but still held the employee had no recourse for his discharge. Although the Court conceded that "at will" employees can sue for retaliatory discharge if the discharge contravenes a clearly mandated public policy, it said lawyers are different because a client always has the right to substitute counsel for any reason. The Court concluded that if any rule required a client to justify its dismissal of a lawyer, that would destroy the special bond between client and lawyer.

Do you agree? Is saying that one may fire a lawyer for no reason the same as saying that one may fire a lawyer for the wrong reason?

b. In Balla v. Gambro, Inc., 584 N.E.2d 104 (Ill.1991), the Illinois Supreme Court approved the *Herbster* approach. The Court argued that the lawyer was ethically *required* to report the employer's wrongdoing; to say the employer cannot fire him for doing so would impose the cost of ethical compliance on the client instead of the lawyer. Further, once the lawyer *did* report on the client, there would be no relationship of trust and the Court said that it would be perverse to keep lawyer and client yoked together.

Ironically, the Illinois Supreme Court in *Balla* was persuaded by the decision of the Minnesota Appellate Court in Nordling v. Northern States Power Co., 465 N.W.2d 81 (Minn.App.1991), that also had barred a suit for retaliatory discharge. However, the *Nordling* decision was itself later disavowed by the Minnesota Supreme Court, 478 N.W.2d 498 (Minn.1991), at least insofar as it rested on a special exception for attorneys from the usual protections granted an employee against arbitrary termination.

See also, General Dynamics v. Superior Court, 876 P.2d 487 (Cal. 1994), upholding the cause of action for wrongful discharge by in-house counsel who claimed that mandatory ethical norms found in the California Rules of Professional Conduct conflicted with illegitimate demands of the employer.

c. Which approach do you find more convincing? Remember that the remedy in such cases need *not* be injunctive relief, i.e., the lawyer need not get the job back. The remedy could be damages, and in the case of a corporate lawyer with pension rights, the damages could be substantial.[2]

d. In any event, there is certainly no reason to treat an *associate's* discharge by a *law firm* for reporting an ethical violation as discharge by a *client*. In Wieder v. Skala, 609 N.E.2d 105 (N.Y.1992), the New York Court of Appeals treated the ethics rules as part of the implied contract that the lawyer had with his law firm and found his suit for wrongful discharge stated a cause of action for breach of contract.

5. Did Bright & Learned even use good business judgment in its treatment of its women partners and associates in this Problem?

a. Notice that the two female partners here generate a "disproportionate share of the income of Bright & Learned." If these partners were treated with more respect and entitled to a larger "draw" (i.e., share of the partnership profits), the partners would presumably be less likely to leave. See, e.g., Gilson & Mnookin, Sharing Among the Human Capitalists: An Economic Inquiry into the Corporate Law Firm and How Partners Split Profits, 37 Stanford L.Rev. 313 (1985).

b. If clients follow the women associates to the new firm, can the lawyers be said to have "stolen" an asset of Bright & Learned? Does it matter whether the clients originally came to Bright & Learned because of the firm's, not the women's, reputation? Is it relevant whether the clients now consider the individual women, not the firm, as their lawyers?[3]

c. May the women here call each client to seek to persuade the clients to consult them at the new firm? Former Canon 7 provided that, "Efforts, direct or indirect, in any way to encroach upon the business of another lawyer, are unworthy of those who should be brethren at the Bar; * * *." Do you agree? Is this spirit preserved in the Code or Model Rules? Does this mean that if a client asks the lawyer why she is leaving she may not give an honest or responsive answer?

d. In a well-publicized case, associates in a law office decided to form their own firm. Before leaving, they told 400 clients on whose cases they were working of their plans. Some clients received phone calls; others were contacted in person. Forms were then mailed to the clients which they could use to terminate the present firm and retain the

2. Oregon State Bar Ethics Committee Opinion 1994–136 (1994) added that a lawyer allegedly terminated for failure to file a patent claim for his employer on an invention made by the employer's customer may reveal his employer's secrets insofar as necessary to establish his wrongful discharge claim.

3. Cf. Koehler v. Wales, 16 Wn.App. 304, 556 P.2d 233 (1976), where the court allowed attorneys to agree that one lawyer would handle another's cases while the latter was out of the country, with the fee division largely based on work performed. However the court refused to allow the absent lawyer to collect damages for "business interference" when some of her clients stayed with the "interim" lawyer after the absent lawyer's return. "[W]e decline to recognize," the court said, "that plaintiff had any proprietary interest in her former law practice and the trial court was correct in restricting the recovery to the contractual percentage." 556 P.2d at 238.

new one as their counsel.   The old firm filed suit to enjoin the associates from "contacting and/or communicating with" persons who were its clients except "in accordance with the requirements of DR 2–102."   If you were the trial court, would you have entered the injunction?

The injunction was entered, but the Superior Court reversed. Adler, Barish, Daniels, Levin & Creskoff v. Epstein, 252 Pa.Super. 553, 382 A.2d 1226 (1977).   The communication was "not false, misleading or coercive," the court reasoned, citing *Bates* as to the importance of a free flow of information about the availability of legal services.   Further, while the first firm had expected additional fee generating business from these clients, "because the law permits a client to seek and re-seek counsel of his choice, any expectation that a client would remain constant * * * is unrealistic."   Finally, the court believed the clients would be best served by permitting contacts from the associates.   "Having one's file transferred to a new associate" as proposed by the existing firm "will undoubtedly engender additional cost and time to the client." Balancing the interests at stake in the issue, the court held the associates' contacts not to be tortious.

The Pennsylvania Supreme Court disagreed, 482 Pa. 416, 393 A.2d 1175 (1978).   Its first expressed concern was for the clients.   The associates

> "were actively attempting to induce the clients to change law firms in the middle of their active cases.   Appellees' concern for their line of credit and the success of their new law firm gave them an immediate, personally created financial interest in the clients' decisions.   In this atmosphere, appellees' contacts posed too great a risk that clients would not have the opportunity to make a careful, informed decision."

The court's other concern was for the nature of relationships within law firms.   The court reasoned that the associates'

> "contacts were possible because Adler Barish partners trusted appellees with the high responsibility of developing its clients' cases.   From this position of trust and responsibility, appellees were able to gain knowledge of the details, and status, of each case to which appellees had been assigned.   In the atmosphere surrounding appellees' departure, appellees' contacts unduly suggested a course of action for Adler Barish clients and unfairly prejudiced Adler Barish.   No public interest is served in condoning use of confidential information which has these effects.   Clients too easily may suffer in the end."

Thus, the injunction was reinstated.

With which opinion do you agree?   Which one is more nearly true to *Bates, Ohralik* and *Primus?*   Does this case demonstrate that the principles which the U.S. Supreme Court has tried to establish will not always be easy to apply?

e.   What is the professionally proper way for a lawyer to inform a client that he or she is changing firms?   May professional announcement cards be sent?   What information may be included?   See DR 2–102(A)(2).   Compare ABA Informal Opinion No. 1457 (April 29, 1980), which authorized sending the following letter:

"Dear [Client]:

"Effective [date], I became the resident partner in this city of the *XYZ* law firm, having withdrawn from the *ABC* law firm. My decision should not be construed as adversely reflecting in any way on my former firm.   It is simply one of those things that sometimes happens in business and professional life.

"I want to be sure that there is no disadvantage to you, as the client, from my move.   The decision as to how the matters I have worked on for you are handled and who handles them in the future will be completely yours, and whatever you decide will be determinative."

The ABA Committee made clear that—

"This opinion is limited to the facts presented: (a) the notice is mailed; (b) the notice is sent only to persons with whom the lawyer had an active lawyer-client relationship immediately before the change in the lawyer's professional association; (c) the notice is clearly related to open and pending matters for which the lawyer had direct professional responsibility to the client immediately before the change; (d) the notice is sent promptly after the change; (e) the notice does not urge the client to sever relationship with the lawyer's former firm and does not recommend the lawyer's employment (although it indicates the lawyer's willingness to continue his responsibility for the matters); (f) the notice makes clear that the client has the right to decide who will complete or continue the matters; and (g) the notice is brief, dignified, and not disparaging of the lawyer's former firm." [4]

Should *all* of the elements noted by the ABA Committee have to be present for the communication to be proper?   Which, if any, might be unnecessary?

f.   In re Smith, 843 P.2d 449 (Ore.1992), shows what can happen when the lawyer is not candid and accurate in contacts with the clients. The lawyer had each new law firm client sign letters retaining him individually.   When he opened his new firm, he sent them letters implying nothing material had changed.   For the misrepresentations involved in his conduct, the lawyer was suspended for four months.

g.   See also, Meehan v. Shaughnessy, 404 Mass. 419, 535 N.E.2d 1255 (1989), which cited ABA Informal Opinion 1457 as a "general

4. Excerpted from Recent Ethics Opinions, as updated 1981, copyright American   Bar Association.

guideline" for what attorneys should tell clients. In this case, two partners left to open a new office and sued for fees due from their old partners, who counter-sued them for violation of fiduciary obligations and tortious interference with relations with clients. The two partners had decided in July to leave the firm at the end of December and had recruited four others to join them. During the summer and fall, they worked on getting office space and financing, and they kept up their caseload at the firm rather than letting people who would stay at the firm become familiar with the cases. During this period, they expressly denied plans to leave. They eventually gave the old firm 30 days notice, immediately called clients, and were able to get 142 out of 350 active cases shifted to the new firm. The court began by reminding lawyers that law partners owe fiduciary obligations to each other. The departing partners "used speed and preemptive" tactics and abused "their position of trust and confidence" in the firm. Then it remanded to let the old firm show its economic harm from the loss of clients, and it imposed on the departing lawyers the burden to prove that the clients would have come anyway had the lawyers acted properly.

h. Is the rule that Courts adopt as to the right to "grab" clients when leaving a firm likely to affect how lawyers are treated while at the firm? If the law did less to restrain partners who left firms and tried to take their clients with them, might a law firm have an incentive to treat its lawyers more humanely to try to prevent such departures? Professor Hillman has noted:

> "That some lawyers prosper from grabbing [business and leaving] while others suffer is likely evidence of market forces at work. A significant factor underlying the growth of grabbing and leaving is the inability of many firms to develop a method of compensation acceptable to their more mobile partners. Because there is now a market for lawyers who can carry a substantial "portfolio' of clients to another firm, these lawyers have something to auction. Viewed from this perspective, the solution to the problem of grabbing may lie more in the modification of business practices, particularly those pertaining to compensation, than in law reform.

> "A laissez faire approach to the machinations of law partners is not without its drawbacks, however. One of the more important problems is that a hands off attitude fails to address the interests and values advanced in a more stable environment for law firms. An atmosphere conducive to grabbing encourages the hoarding of clients by lawyers within the same firm. At least a modicum of cooperation is required to maximize the value of a firm to both its lawyers and clients. Furthermore, firms need some sense of confidence concerning the client base in order, as businesses, to engage in long-term planning and commitments in such areas as hiring and promotion of associates and support staff * * *.

"It may be that another kind of market—a market for stable law firms—already exists and may develop further over time. * * * Those firms presently enjoying relative stability of membership are well positioned to capture gains in an environment of instability."

R. W. Hillman, Law Firm Breakups: The Law and Ethics of Grabbing and Leaving 143–45 (1990)(footnotes omitted).

6. Would any ethical problem have been presented if the women associates had bought their portion of the law practice from Bright & Learned?

a. Quoting a New York County opinion, ABA Formal Opinion 266 (1945) asserts: "Clients are not merchandise. Lawyers are not tradesmen. They have nothing to sell but personal service. An attempt, therefore, to barter in clients, would appear to be inconsistent with the best concepts of our professional status." Does that end the matter? Can you come up with reasons other than "professional status" to criticize sale of a practice?

b. What sound reasons would there be for restricting a lawyer's right to sell case files? Whose interests would be protected by such restrictions? Would the ethical problems be less if the firm gave, not sold, files to the departing women? What interests of the clients are at stake in either case?

c. Look at Model Rule 1.17; was there anything comparable in the Model Code? Are its terms applicable to this problem?

d. Does Rule 1.17 only apply to sale of a firm to a stranger? Is Bright & Learned's practice being sold as a whole? Must the whole firm's practice be sold or just the practice of particular lawyers? Because the women partners and associates have been a part of Bright & Learned, are the rules on sale of files different? Should they be?[5]

e. What would be the proper way for lawyers to handle the termination of a retiring lawyer's practice? Could the retiring lawyer properly recommend that his clients come to the lawyer who had bought his practice? Look at Rule 7.2(c) and DR 2–103(B). See also, Association of the Bar of the City of New York Formal Opinion 1993–1 (1993) (retired lawyer may assign accounts receivable to another lawyer).

f. Do the Code and Model Rules treat the sale of a deceased lawyer's practice differently than sale of the practice of a lawyer who is retiring? Look at Model Rule 5.4(a) and DR 3–102(A). ABA Formal Opinion 92–369 (1992) recommended that lawyers, particularly solo practitioners, have a plan as to who will take over their files if they should die unexpectedly. The Opinion advises the successor lawyer to

5. Do you agree that, as Model Rule 1.17 provides, a purchasing lawyer should be able to drop any client who is unwilling to pay the purchaser's higher fees? What does that proviso do to the basic requirement that the practice be sold as a whole, i.e., that the purchaser may not take the best cases and leave the other clients unprotected?

preserve each client's property and files until each client can decide whom to retain as a new lawyer.

7. Is the way to handle departures from a firm something that should be thought through in advance and dealt with in the firm's partnership agreement? What should such an agreement provide? Are there things that it may not provide?

a. What would be the relevance of a covenant not to compete in the firm partnership agreement requiring its former partners and associates not to practice law in the same community for a period of one year after leaving the firm? Is such an agreement permissible under DR 2–108(A)? See also Rule 5.6(a).

b. D.C. Bar Ethics Committee, Opinion 194 (1988), examined a law firm's employment contract providing that if the lawyer went into practice competitive with the firm within a year of leaving the firm, the lawyer would lose rights to half of the unearned fees to which he would otherwise be entitled. The Opinion condemned the arrangement as improperly limiting both the client's right to choose counsel freely and the lawyer's right to practice law.

c. Even if it is "unethical," is the covenant not to compete, to which the women had freely agreed, "morally" binding on them? Knowing the situation presented in this problem, how would you as a lawyer react to the "ethics" or "morals" of the respective parties' actions?

d. Today, these issues often arise in litigation over what partnership agreements say the rights of a departing partner are.

Denburg v. Parker Chapin Flattau & Klimpl, 624 N.E.2d 995 (N.Y. 1993), involved a provision requiring that if a withdrawing partner practiced in the private sector, he or she had to pay the firm 12.5% of the greater of the profits allocated to the partner in the preceding two years or the billings to the firm's former clients who followed the lawyer to the new firm. The firm said that the provision was to protect the firm against partners leaving just as the firm had contracted for larger space. The Court noted, however, that only lawyers who went into competition with the firm had to pay, and citing Cohen v. Lord, Day & Lord, 550 N.E.2d 410 (N.Y.1989), it held the clause unenforceable.[6]

In Howard v. Babcock, 863 P.2d 150 (Cal.1993), on the other hand, the firm's partnership agreement provided that a partner who withdrew and engaged in the same kind of practice in the same county would be entitled to his capital interest in the firm but to none of the share in the next 12 months' receipts of the firm to which he would have been entitled but for the competition. The Court said that California has a public policy in favor of competition and that not every non-competition agreement will be upheld. But the Court adopted the reasoning of

---

6. ABA Ethics Opinion 94–381 (1994) dealt with a narrow issue. A corporation wanted to require lawyers in its in-house legal department to sign an agreement never to take cases against the corporation, even those that were unrelated to work the lawyer did for the corporation. The Ethics Committee said that such a prohibition would be too broad and would violate Model Rule 5.6(a).

Haight, Brown & Bonesteel v. Superior Court, 285 Cal.Rptr. 845 (Cal. App.1991), and said the decision to practice in competition with one's former partners does not have to be costless; instead, a rule of reason will be applied. Firms have a legitimate interest in loyalty of their members, and it does not violate public policy to put reasonable limits on the absolute freedom of lawyers to practice somewhere else. In dissent, Justice Kennard accused the majority of putting the interest of law firms ahead of the interest of their clients. The remaining partners have no "moral entitlement to protection from competition," he said. The withdrawing partner may have left because of the "unwillingness by nonproductive partners to fairly share income with productive partners, associates, and other personnel in the law firm."

Which of these approaches makes more sense to you?

PROBLEM 35

The Duty to Work for No Compensation

The State Bar of Georgia, to which all the state's lawyers are required to belong,[1] has proposed a requirement that each lawyer in the state devote a minimum of 100 hours per year to uncompensated legal assistance in legal aid clinics to be established by the bar. The attorney's time would be scheduled insofar as possible to suit his or her convenience, and no attorney would be required to take an individual case in which there was a conflict of interest. An attorney could begin a case at the legal aid office but credit work done on the case in his or her own office against the 100 hours.

Not pursuant to any formal plan, J.R. Wright was appointed by the court to represent a defendant in a murder case after the defendant refused representation by the public defender. The statutory compensation in such a case is a maximum of $750. Wright believed his client was guilty, but the defendant protested his innocence and the case ultimately required 300 hours of the attorney's time. Wright sued the state for a fee of $30,000 based on his regular hourly fee of $100 per hour. The state's defense was, in part, that the work was part of the inherent duty of an attorney.

---

1. As described in this problem, the State Bar of Georgia is an "integrated" or "unified" bar, as discussed in the introduction to Chapter II. In Lathrop v. Donohue, 367 U.S. 820, 81 S.Ct. 1826, 6 L.Ed.2d 1191 (1961), the Court, with no majority opinion, upheld such a bar against an attack based on freedom of association but reserved the question of impairment of free speech. Citing Abood v. Detroit Board of Education, 431 U.S. 209, 97 S.Ct. 1782, 52 L.Ed.2d 261 (1977), the Supreme Court held in Keller v. State Bar of California, 496 U.S. 1, 110 S.Ct. 2228, 110 L.Ed.2d 1 (1990), that the integrated State Bar of California may not constitutionally use compulsory dues to finance political and ideological causes that the petitioners opposed. The State Bar may use compulsory dues to finance regulation of the legal profession or improve the quality of legal services (for example, to propose ethical codes or discipline Bar members), but not, for example, to endorse gun control or nuclear freeze initiatives.

The State Bar also has a proposal before it to establish a Lawyer Referral Service at which an individual may get a one-half hour consultation with an attorney for an established fee of $25. Any attorney who takes a case upon referral by the agency agrees to charge no more than $75 per hour for the first 10 hours of work involved.

QUESTIONS

1. Do lawyers have a moral obligation to provide some legal services free or at a reduced fee?

a. The Joint Committee on Professional Responsibility of the ABA and the AALS concluded in 1958:

"The moral position of the advocate is here at stake. Partisan advocacy finds its justification in the contribution it makes to a sound and informed disposition of controversies. Where this contribution is lacking, the partisan position permitted to the advocate loses its reason for being. The legal profession has, therefore, a clear moral obligation to see to it that those already handicapped do not suffer the cumulative disadvantage of being without proper legal representation, for it is obvious that adjudication can neither be effective nor fair where only one side is represented by counsel.

"In discharging this obligation, the legal profession can help to bring about a better understanding of the role of the advocate in our system of government. Popular misconceptions of the advocate's function disappear when the lawyer pleads without a fee, and the true value of his service to society is immediately perceived. The insight thus obtained by the public promotes a deeper understanding of the work of the legal profession as a whole.

"The obligation to provide legal services for those actually caught up in litigation carries with it the obligation to make preventive legal advice accessible to all. It is among those unaccustomed to business affairs and fearful of the ways of the law that such advice is often most needed. If it is not received in time, the most valiant and skillful representation in court may come too late." [2]

b. Do you agree that members of the bar have this "moral obligation"? Is the obligation reflected in the Code and Model Rules? Look at Model Rule 6.1 as amended in 1993 to make the pro bono obligation specific, i.e., 50 hours per year.

c. Does Rule 6.1 impose a legal requirement? Why should a rule be specific if it is not to be made mandatory? Where does the 1977 A.B.A. Report on the lawyer's public interest obligation, set forth as a Reading to this Problem, fit into the picture today?

---

2. 44 A.B.A.J. 1159, 1216 (1958).

d. Does the existence of the Legal Services Corporation[3] and other organizations delivering legal services to the poor affect the moral obligation of lawyers generally? Is the duty to work without fee made more pressing by the reductions in federal funding of the Legal Services Corporation? An analysis of questions presented is provided in A.B.A. Formal Opinion 347 (1981), set forth as a Reading to this Problem. Do you believe the opinion adequately deals with the problem of cases the legal aid office cannot take on? Will indigent clients likely go on their own to private counsel or should a referral service be provided?

e. Should legal services lawyers have a continuing personal responsibility to clients even if funding ends? Do the Model Code and Model Rules permit a lawyer to withdraw from representation if the client cannot continue to pay the bills? Is your conclusion about the lawyer's moral obligation principled, pragmatic, or both?

2. Does a state court have the legal authority to compel an attorney to represent clients without compensation?

a. From what source does that authority derive? Is the duty to take cases without compensation inherent in being a lawyer? Is the same duty inherent in being a plumber, a funeral director, or some other licensed "professional"? Consider the position of Raymond Marks set out in the Readings to this Problem. Do you agree with his analysis?

b. On whom should the obligation fall? Only young lawyers? Should lawyers not in practice have the obligation? How about lawyers employed by the government? Law teachers? What does the ABA Report, infra, propose?

3. Should there be a greater or different obligation to take criminal cases without compensation than to take civil cases?

a. What is the analytic basis of that distinction, if any? Do cases holding that the Constitution guarantees each defendant a right to counsel necessarily imply that attorneys must bear the cost of such representation? Some lawyers have not taken low pay in assigned cases without protest. *In re* Hunoval, 294 N.C. 740, 247 S.E.2d 230 (1977), concerned an appointed attorney who had seen his client convicted and sentenced to death. The conviction was affirmed by the state Supreme Court, but a stay of execution was granted for the attorney to seek certiorari before the U.S. Supreme Court. At that point, the attorney refused to file the petition for certiorari until the state paid him more money. In the face of this impasse, the attorney was removed from the case but the court was not sympathetic. It both suspended the attorney from practice in the state's appellate courts and barred him from receiving appointments in criminal cases for one year.[4]

3. The Corporation was created by The Legal Services Corporation Act of 1974, 88 Stat. 378, 42 U.S.C.A. § 2996a–k et seq.

4. See also, State v. Richardson, 230 Kan. 23, 631 P.2d 221 (1981) (lawyer suspended indefinitely for failing to take steps to represent defendant for whom he was

c. On the other hand, some attorneys have had greater success protesting, in a more professionally responsible way, low pay in assigned cases.

In State *ex rel.* Stephan v. Smith, 242 Kan. 336, 747 P.2d 816 (1987), the Kansas Supreme Court held that attorneys' professional services are property rights that may not be put to public use without just compensation. It further relied on the Equal Protection clause to conclude that the burden of being appointed counsel may not be imposed involuntarily on some attorneys and not others.[5]

DeLisio v. Alaska Superior Court, 740 P.2d 437 (Alaska 1987), reversed the contempt conviction of lawyer who refused to accept a trial court's order to serve as uncompensated appointed counsel. The attorney should receive "just compensation," it said, defined as the rate reflecting compensation received by the average competent attorney operating on the open market. See also, State v. Lynch, 796 P.2d 1150 (Okla.1990) (inherent powers used to order that lawyers who represent indigent defendants be paid at the same rate that the state pays assistant district attorneys; system put into place immediately for capital cases, and effective in 1992 for all other cases).[6]

d. Should appointed counsel in a criminal case be excused from acting where the defendant's conduct puts him in an "untenable ethical position"? In Chaleff v. Superior Court, 69 Cal.App.3d 721, 138 Cal. Rptr. 735 (1977), a deputy public defender asked to be relieved as "advisory counsel," inter alia, because the defendant's alleged self-destructive urge caused him to reject the lawyer's suggestions of defenses. Should the lawyer be relieved? The appellate court said yes, citing a rule comparable to DR 2–110 and noting that, "while the attorney's duty is to his client, he cannot be placed in the position where discharging that duty impinges upon his ethical responsibilities as a member of the bar."

e. Should appointed counsel be excused if he asserts he is incompetent? United States v. Wendy, 575 F.2d 1025 (2d Cir.1978), holds that he should. A tax lawyer who had never tried a case "civil or criminal, state or federal" was held not guilty of contempt for refusing to accept assignment to defend a felony tax case carrying a potential five year

appointed counsel); F.T.C. v. Superior Court Trial Lawyers Ass'n, 493 U.S. 411, 110 S.Ct. 768, 107 L.Ed.2d 851 (1990) (concerted action to withhold services until compensation raised violates antitrust laws).

5. In Williamson v. Vardeman, 674 F.2d 1211 (8th Cir.1982), a state rule that denied reimbursement of litigation expenses, as distinguished from attorney's fees, was held unconstitutional.

6. Compare, e.g., People v. Sanders, 58 Ill.2d 196, 317 N.E.2d 552 (1974) (court need not award fees above statutory maximum of $250 in capital case; attorneys had spent 463 hours preparing and trying the case), with People ex rel. Conn v. Randolph, 35 Ill.2d 24, 219 N.E.2d 337 (1966) (reimbursement in excess of statutory maximum allowed because the statute cannot constitutionally be applied to a case where the attorney must assume a staggering financial burden in defending the case).

prison term. Do you agree? If the lawyer had accepted the assignment and had proved incompetent, could he have been held liable to the client for malpractice? See Ferri v. Ackerman, 444 U.S. 193, 100 S.Ct. 402, 62 L.Ed.2d 355 (1979), holding that he could be.

4. Even though most appointments are made in criminal cases, should courts have the power to appoint counsel to serve indigents in civil cases?

a. Several courts have held unconstitutional statutes that required attorneys to serve as counsel, without compensation, in civil cases. E.g., Bedford v. Salt Lake County, 22 Utah 2d 12, 447 P.2d 193 (1968). Cf. State ex rel. Scott v. Roper, 688 S.W.2d 757 (Mo.1985)(en banc)(court refuses to appoint counsel for indigent prisoner). See also, Knox County Council v. State, 217 Ind. 493, 29 N.E.2d 405, 412 (1940) (dictum).

b. Yet some courts are moving in the opposite direction.

Ex parte Dibble, 279 S.C. 592, 310 S.E.2d 440 (App.1983), was a case in which a prisoner brought civil actions complaining of conditions in the state penitentiary. The trial judge had appointed two lawyers to represent the prisoners in those actions. The Court of Appeals recognized that this was not a traditional criminal case, but it refused to hold that requiring representation without compensation was a violation of the attorney's constitutional rights. Citing ECs 2–25 and 2–29, the Court noted that lawyers are an "integral and necessary part" of the justice system, and concluded that courts have "the inherent power" to appoint lawyers "to serve without compensation where it appears reasonably necessary for the court to do justice."

The court noted that law is a profession, and said that "the chief end of a profession is public service." The case was remanded, however, for a determination by the trial court that (1) the clients in fact required free counsel, (2) no other lawyers were willing to take the case pro bono, and (3) such assignments would be distributed fairly among the bar and not fall on a limited group of lawyers. The court raised, but did not reach, the question whether courts also have inherent power to order that lawyers be compensated from public funds.

c. Yarbrough v. Superior Court of Napa County, 39 Cal.3d 197, 216 Cal.Rptr. 425, 702 P.2d 583 (1985), involved court appointment of a lawyer to defend a prisoner in a civil suit brought against him for the wrongful death of his murder victim. The facts were very close to the ones for which he had been originally convicted, and the question was whether the defendant could have appointed counsel to defend him in this civil matter as well.

The court held that the trial court should consider the inmate's indigency, whether an adverse judgment would affect the prisoner's present or future property rights (i.e., does the indigent have a reasonable likelihood of acquiring property subject to judgment), whether counsel would be helpful in the circumstances of the case before it, and whether the cause of action could be abated until the prisoner is released "and therefore better able to make his own arrangements." The Court did not reach the issues of what to do if the attorney is unwilling to be appointed and whether the court can provide compensation to the attorney.

Chief Justice Rose Bird dissented. "As with any other working person, lawyers should be properly compensated for their time and effort," she said. She criticized the majority for avoiding this issue, and went on: "No one would dare suggest courts have the authority to order a doctor, dentist or any other professional to provide free services, while at the same time telling them they must personally pay their own overhead charges for that time. No crystal ball is necessary to foresee the public outrage which would erupt if we ordered grocery store owners to give indigents two months of free groceries or automobile dealers to give them two months of free cars. Lawyers in our society are entitled to no greater privileges than the butcher, the baker and the candlestick-maker; but they certainly are entitled to no less."

d. Federal law provides that in a civil case the "court may request an attorney to represent any [person claiming *in forma pauperis* status] unable to employ counsel * * *." 28 U.S.C.A. § 1915(d). In Mallard v. United States District Court, 490 U.S. 296, 109 S.Ct. 1814, 104 L.Ed.2d 318 (1989), the Court held (5 to 4) that § 1915(d) does *not* authorize federal courts to impose compulsory assignments of attorneys in civil cases, here an action brought by inmates against prison guards under 42 U.S.C.A. § 1983. The statute only authorizes courts to "request", i.e., ask a lawyer to serve voluntarily as appointed counsel. In a footnote, the Court said that it did "not reach the question whether the federal courts have inherent authority to order attorneys to represent litigants without pay * * *." Justice Kennedy, concurring, noted that lawyers, "like all those who practice a profession, have obligations to their calling which exceed their obligations to the State. [I]t is precisely because our duties go beyond what the law demands that ours remains a noble profession." Justice Stevens, Marshall, Blackmun & O'Connor dissented, believing the statute made the moral obligation compulsory.[7]

e. Scott v. Tyson Foods, Inc., 943 F.2d 17 (8th Cir.1991), was an employment discrimination case in which the employee asked that counsel be appointed for him. Citing *Mallard*, the District Court said that it lacked power to do so in a civil case, but the Eighth Circuit disagreed. There is a special provision in Title VII for appointment of counsel, the Court said, and the District Court must appoint counsel for Mr. Scott.[8]

---

7. In Tabron v. Grace, 6 F.3d 147 (3d Cir.1993), a District Court was held to have authority to appoint a lawyer to act for a prisoner in a 28 U.S.C.A. § 1983 action against prison officials for failing to protect him against assault by other prisoners.

8. National Association of Radiation Survivors v. Derwinski, 778 F.Supp. 1096

(N.D.Cal.1991), reexamined a related statutory anomaly, the $10 ceiling on attorney's fees for cases brought by veterans against the V.A. The limitation purports not to require pro bono service, but if a veteran is to be represented at all, the lawyer effectively has to be a volunteer. In a lengthy opinion, Judge Patel held that—at least in

5. May the State Bar in this Problem, as a way of raising funds for providing counsel to indigent clients, require lawyers to deposit client trust funds that are small in amount or held only for a short time, in an interest bearing account with the interest going to the Bar and not the client?

a. Voluntary IOLTA (Interest on Lawyer Trust Accounts) programs are in existence in most jurisdictions today. Client consent is rarely required or sought. May a lawyer properly participate in such a program? The ABA said yes in Formal Opinion 348 set forth in the Readings to this Problem.

b. Lawyers would probably not be willing to participate in such programs if their clients explicitly objected. It is thought that "this sense of client acquiescence to program participation" removes any argument that bar is unconstitutionally "taking" the client's property without just compensation. Cone v. State Bar of Florida, 819 F.2d 1002 (11th Cir.1987), cert.denied 484 U.S. 917, 108 S.Ct. 268, 98 L.Ed.2d 225 (1987) (upholding constitutionality of Florida's Interest on Lawyers' Trust Accounts (IOLTA) program). Do you agree? Do we accept acquiescence as consent in conflicts cases, for example?

Cone was a test case on behalf of clients whose small amounts of earned interest were arguably expropriated for support of legal aid programs by IOLTA. The court held that no client has a property right to have her lawyer have an interest bearing trust account. Thus, the plan took nothing belonging to the client and the program was upheld.[9] Do you agree that a fiduciary, say a trustee, who holds assets of a beneficiary, has no obligation to invest the assets?

c. But compare, Webb's Fabulous Pharmacies, Inc. v. Beckwith, 449 U.S. 155, 101 S.Ct. 446, 66 L.Ed.2d 358 (1980), where Justice Blackmun, for a unanimous Court, invalidated a Florida statute that provided that the county may take for itself the interest accruing on an interpleader fund deposited in the county court. The Court rejected the rationale that the funds deposited were considered to be "public money" from the date of deposit until it left the account: "A State, by *ipse dixit*, may not transform private property into public property without compensation, even for the limited duration of the deposit in court. This is the very kind of thing that the Takings Clause of the Fifth Amendment was meant to prevent." 449 U.S. at 164, 101 S.Ct. at 452.

Have lawyers created a special exception for themselves from normal fiduciary standards to divert their clients' money to fund services that

cases alleging service-connected death or disability—the $10 limitation is unconstitutional. Walters v. National Association of Radiation Survivors, 473 U.S. 305, 105 S.Ct. 3180, 87 L.Ed.2d 220 (1985), however, was clearly to the contrary, and *Derwinski* was rev'd, 994 F.2d 583 (9th Cir.1993).

9. See also, Washington Legal Foundation v. Massachusetts Bar Foundation, 993 F.2d 962 (1st Cir.1993), reaching the same result, and IRS Revenue Ruling 87–2 saying that the sums on deposit in an IOLTA program are not taxable to the client or the lawyer.

lawyers would otherwise be morally obligated to provide without compensation?

READINGS

F. RAYMOND MARKS ET AL.,* THE LAWYER, THE PUBLIC AND PROFESSIONAL RESPONSIBILITY
Pages 288–92 (1972).

The grant of a monopoly license to practice law is based on three assumptions: (1) There is a socially useful function for the lawyer to perform; (2) the lawyer is a professional person who will perform that function; and (3) his performance as a professional person will be regulated by himself and more formally by the profession as a whole. In view of the practices of the American legal profession, only the first assumption seems warranted. We have seen too little evidence of professional as opposed to trade performance by the individual lawyer and no evidence of serious professional self-regulation toward diverting the profession to the pursuit of the common good—the public interest.

* * *

Given the function that the lawyer has to perform—structuring the conflicts of society so that they are capable of peaceful resolution—we feel that even without a monopoly grant of power the legal profession is a public utility. The law is a calling which by definition deals with public interest, not self-interest. The monopoly grant simply makes the need for regulation by self or state more urgent.

In many ways the legal profession is like that sensitive area of the field of radio and television in which licensees control access to public discussion. In the communications field, the announced public policy— the Communications Act—requires that a commitment be made when a license is granted, that the licensee affirmatively undertake to "operate its license in the public interest." The licensee has a duty to so operate, and the licensee's discharge of that duty is reviewed when a license is renewed. The question is faced directly:

> At what level of public responsibility must the licensee operate to retain the license?

The review is in terms of public interest. There have not been satisfactory answers to the question, but at least the question is directly put. And the duty of each licensee—each outlet—is perceived.

---

* When the authors wrote this book, they were attorneys with the American Bar Foundation.

The license for the practice of law is perpetual; regulation is illusory, and the question is *never* put:

> At what level of public interest *must* the lawyer operate as a condition of retaining his license?

The issue of the right to practice has never been put in terms of what a lawyer's *duty* is.

There are no disciplinary procedures for the lawyer who refuses to take a case; there is only the suggestion that it would be nice if he would. The absence of controls over the lawyer with respect to what he turns away is socially dangerous. It is more dangerous than the risk involved in drafting or socializing a percentage of a lawyer's time. The latter would be a drastic step but less drastic than socializing all of a lawyer's time. To some this will be a shocking notion. But why?

* * *

A draft of lawyers is not outrageous when one considers that we draft children from the ages of six to sixteen so that they can acquire the skills of good citizens. This is compulsory education. We draft into the military—and at the risk of their lives—men from the ages of eighteen to twenty-six who may have no particular qualifications for the draft other than citizenship. The military draft is supported on the premise that the country's security is involved. Yet when one examines the policies of our country, arrived at without hearing from all, and then sees the lawyers, who possess unique skills for arriving at balanced social policy, exempting themselves from their professional duty or being exempted by others, why *would* a draft for lawyers be outrageous?

If a draft is not acceptable, what about a tax on the lawyer's time? Perhaps a set of penalties could be assessed through the tax structure on those lawyers who are unable to certify that they have operated their licenses with balanced programming for the public good.

We do not think it likely that these drastic measures will be taken. But we think that they should be taken if the profession is unwilling to regulate itself. We are talking about professional regulation that is real, not the myth of self-regulation. Perhaps one of the reasons for the exemption of the legal profession from the external—state—regulation imposed on other public utilities is that it appears to be self-regulated. Lawyers are skilled in rhetoric. They have given the appearance of self-regulation. Even when making public interest responses they have often managed to make what is vocation look like voluntarism and what is duty look like grace—at least to the casual observer. * * *

A.B.A. SPECIAL COMMITTEE ON PUBLIC INTEREST PRACTICE, IMPLEMENTING THE LAWYER'S PUBLIC INTEREST OBLIGATION

1–7 (June, 1977).

In August, 1975, in Montreal, the American Bar Association House of Delegates confirmed "the basic responsibility of each lawyer engaged in the practice of law to provide public interest legal services" without fee, or at a substantially reduced fee, in one or more of the following areas: poverty law, civil rights law, public rights law, charitable organization representation, and administration of justice.

The five areas were defined as follows:

1. **Poverty Law:** Legal services in civil and criminal matters of importance to a client who does not have the financial resources to compensate counsel.

2. **Civil Rights [including Civil Liberties] Law:** Legal representation involving a right of an individual which society has a special interest in protecting.

3. **Public Rights Law:** Legal representation involving an important right belonging to a significant segment of the public.

4. **Charitable Organization Representation:** Legal service to charitable, religious, civic, governmental and educational institutions in matters in furtherance of their organizational purpose, where the payment of customary legal fees would significantly deplete the organization's economic resources or would be otherwise inappropriate.

5. **Administration of Justice:** Activity, whether under bar association auspices or otherwise, which is designed to increase the availability of legal services, or otherwise improve the administration of justice.

* * *

Our Special Committee has been studying this subject since 1973 and is prepared, we believe, to make some informed suggestions. Accordingly, we offer the following report and initial recommendations.

* * *

We suggest * * * that the ABA encourage each state and local bar association to adopt *specific guidelines* for members of the bar who wish to budget their public interest legal service. * * *

* * *

In this connection, it is important to note that a practicing lawyer may spend from 1,000 to 2,000 hours or more each year on billable client matters (as distinguished from non-client matters such as law firm administration, continuing legal education, bar association activity, and professional writing and speaking). Without focusing on this wide range of legal practice, some commentators have urged every lawyer to budget a flat 5% of client-related time for public interest legal service, yielding 50 to 100 hours per year; others have called for 10% of a lawyer's time, or 100 to 200 hours per year. Still others have suggested that a more realistic and manageable approach would be for the bar to settle on a fixed minimum number of hours, without reference to the time a lawyer spends on fee-producing matters.[2] Whatever approach is selected, it is clear that lawyers are being asked with increasing frequency to commit from two to five weeks of their professional time each year to such service.

Various considerations, of course, including the economics of law practice in each community, will inevitably influence a determination as to whether such suggestions are realistic for the bar to adopt in a particular locality. * * *

The principal point, however, should not be lost: publication of quantitative public interest legal service guidelines by the organized bar, coupled with the professional responsibility of each lawyer to budget and carry through such a commitment, should be part of the process of implementing the 1975 resolution at the local level. For many years, other organizations, such as public charities and religious denominations, have developed equitable formulas to guide their contributors. We believe that the bar should become involved, similarly, in helping every lawyer measure the "basic responsibility" to provide public interest legal service. * * *

A. Meeting the Responsibility Collectively Through a Law Firm

The bar will want to consider whether it is appropriate for lawyers practicing in firms to fulfill their responsibility collectively by contributing, as a firm, the number of hours which all the lawyers, taken together, should provide. Our Committee believes that this approach would be appropriate.

B. Making Financial Contributions in Lieu of Providing Time

In our Committee's judgment, the professional responsibility to contribute public interest legal service is inherently an obligation to contribute one's time—one's abilities. Given the breadth of the 1975 definition, few lawyers, if any, can responsibly argue that they are unable to make a useful, personal contribution.

2. It is important to note that legislators have taken an interest in this subject, at least in California, where Assembly Bill No. 4050 was introduced—and defeated—in 1976, to require every active member of the bar to provide "not less than 40 hours per year" of "professional services without fee, or at a substantially reduced fee." More recently, Ralph J. Gampell, President of the California State Bar, proposed that lawyers, doctors, and dentists be required by state law to contribute, free of charge, 40 hours of professional service each year (or one-half day per month). San Jose Mercury, Nov. 29, 1976, at 26, col. 1.

With this said, we recognize that some lawyers will protest that they lack the necessary competence or efficiency to provide the kinds of public interest legal service most frequently required in their community. Others will rightly point out that existing referral systems rarely yield public interest clients who need their particular expertise. Still others will correctly remind us that legal aid programs, civil rights litigation efforts, and public interest law firms in general cannot exist without regular financial support from the private bar. Accordingly, we suggest that in developing public interest guidelines, state and local bar associations consider including a formula whereby lawyers, under certain circumstances, can meet the suggested minimum standard of hours—in whole or in part—by making an equivalent financial contribution to one or more legal assistance organizations.

C.   The Responsibility of Lawyers Who Practice for the Government, or as Corporate House Counsel, or in Other Private Enterprises

The basic responsibility to provide public interest legal service is not limited to lawyers engaged in private practice; it extends to members of the bar "engaged in the practice of law" for other private organizations (both profit and nonprofit), as well as for governmental agencies. In keeping with this commitment, lawyers from corporate law departments volunteer their time to legal services programs in a number of communities. Recently, moreover, the Legal Services Corporation announced guidelines authorizing *pro bono publico* services by staff attorneys at LSC headquarters.[3]

Obviously, special considerations are involved in creating opportunities for lawyers to provide public interest legal service while employed by government, or by a wide range of private enterprises. The organized bar, therefore, should work with such attorneys and their employers to achieve feasible guidelines permitting contributions of service equivalent to those suggested for lawyers in private practice.

D.   Essential Record Keeping; Public Interest Statistical Surveys by the Bar

It will be difficult to budget the responsibility for public interest legal service unless a lawyer regularly maintains time records. Accordingly, for those who do keep time records, we suggest that the record keeping system be adjusted, as necessary, to include public interest legal service as defined in the 1975 resolution.

Uniform record keeping not only will help every lawyer know whether he or she is meeting the responsibility, as established locally, but also will facilitate appropriate statistical surveys by the bar, on an anonymous basis, to determine the average levels of public interest legal

---

3. Memorandum of December 29, 1976, from Thomas Ehrlich, LSC President, to All Staff. See regulation governing "uncompensated outside practice" by federally funded legal services program attorneys, 41 Fed.Reg. 18512 (1976) (to be codified in 45 C.F.R. § 1604.5), as corrected with reference to effective date in 41 Fed.Reg. 19110 (1976).

service by lawyers in various communities. Surveys are an appropriate and desirable way to assist members of the bar in determining how their contributions compare with those of other lawyers and to help evaluate the extent to which governmental and other resources are necessary to supplement the professional contributions of the bar in meeting the need for public interest legal services.

A.B.A. FORMAL OPINION 347 (DECEMBER 1, 1981)

* * *

The dilemma now faced by legal services lawyers throughout the country is caused by the knowledge that substantial cuts in financial support may soon occur, coupled with uncertainty over the extent of the cuts. Should a local office begin limiting the legal services offered before the extent of lost funding is known? * * *

* * *

Although there is no ethical mandate to decline new work in the face of an uncertain future, the legal services lawyer must nonetheless prepare for possible interruption of legal services in ongoing matters. When the likelihood of significantly reduced staffing exists, adequate preparation includes these measures:

1. Notice of the risk of disrupted services must immediately be given to existing clients and to any new clients accepted. * * *

2. A stringent system of priorities must be established for handling pending matters and accepting new clients. * * *

3. Every reasonable effort should be made to arrange for alternate funding or, failing that, for substitution of lawyers to handle pending matters. * * *

When a lawyer leaves the staff of a legal services office, it is not presumed that clients will continue to be represented by the departing lawyer. A.B.A. Informal Opinion 1428 (1979) says that a legal services office should be considered as a firm retained by the client, and that the primary responsibility for handling the caseload of a departing legal services lawyer devolves upon the office as a whole, rather than upon a lawyer who leaves. The question therefore is what course should be followed when the remaining salaried legal services lawyers cannot competently handle legal matters pending in the office because of an overwhelming crush of cases?

Under these circumstances, it is our view that the lawyers remaining in the legal services office must, with limited exceptions, decline new legal matters and must continue representation in pending matters only to the extent that the duty of competent, nonneglectful representation can be fulfilled.

* * *

* * * A.B.A. Informal Opinion 1428 (1979), discussed above, which does not consider the problem of substantial loss of funding throughout the entire legal services program, has been interpreted by some as implying that total responsibility for pending matters may fall upon the "last attorney out the door" when a legal services office is closed.

The committee does not subscribe to that view. Rather, the committee believes that the model code should be construed to permit liberal withdrawal from pending matters when a legal services lawyer no longer receives a salary and the office is closed because of lost funding. * * *

* * *

* * * The specter of tens of thousands of indigent clients with pending matters suddenly cast adrift in our legal system without benefit of counsel is a threat to the fair and orderly administration of justice on a national scale. The problem of reduced funding of legal services offices is a problem for all lawyers, not merely for those who have been employed by the legal services offices or who have volunteered their time to serve as members of the boards of directors of those offices. The legal profession has a clear responsibility to respond by helping to obtain funds for existing legal services programs and by providing free legal services to indigent clients who would be served by legal services offices were funding available.

* * *

If local procedures permit court appointment of substitute counsel for indigent clients in civil matters, the response exhorted by the model code is again pointed: "When a lawyer is appointed by a court or requested by a bar association to undertake representation of a person unable to obtain counsel, whether for financial or other reasons, he should not seek to be excused from undertaking the representation except for compelling reasons." EC 2–29.

———

ABA FORMAL OPINION 348 (JULY 23, 1982) *

* * *

Historically, client funds entrusted to lawyers in the United States have been placed in non-interest-bearing bank checking accounts maintained by the lawyers separate from their own funds. Typically these funds are held temporarily for use in a particular transaction in behalf of the client and must be readily available for this purpose. Because of the impracticability of establishing a separate account for each client, all client funds generally are commingled in the lawyer's trust account. Since it also is impracticable to calculate interest on each client's funds when commingled with the funds of other clients, the lawyer's trust

* Reprinted with permission of the American Bar Association.

account is left uninvested. For years, clients have accepted this practice, apparently recognizing that the earnings potential of their funds in relation to the administrative costs would not justify investing the funds. As a consequence, the depository institutions have had the use of the funds without payment of any interest. Occasionally, a client's funds are deposited in a separate account at interest for the benefit of the client where the amount and expected holding period make it obvious that the interest earned will exceed the administrative costs of placing the funds at interest for the client.

* * * [N]othing in the Model Code prohibits a lawyer from placing clients' funds in interest-bearing accounts so long as the other requirements of DR 9–102 are met. [However, in] addition to expenses created by the notification, record keeping and accounting requirements of DR 9–102(B), lawyers may incur other costs in attempting to place clients' funds at interest. Income tax filings may be necessary to enable the client to report the interest earned on the funds, and bank handling fees may further reduce the potential return. It is evident, therefore, that in many—if not most—instances, the accounting and administrative costs, plus any bank charges, will more than offset the potential gains to the client. Thus, while no ethical rule proscribes placing client funds at interest for the benefit of an individual client, administrative costs and practical considerations often will make it self-defeating for the lawyer to attempt to obtain interest on small sums or even on large amounts of clients' funds held for short periods of time.

In apparent recognition of these practical difficulties, the Model Code does not specify that a lawyer has the duty to invest clients' nominal or short-term funds entrusted to the lawyer. The thrust of DR 9–102 is that lawyers must neither misuse a client's funds nor impede their prompt delivery. The focus is on safekeeping, accounting and delivery, and not on investment of the funds.

The law of agency and trusts governs when a lawyer has a fiduciary duty to invest a client's funds. A trustee may be liable for lost earnings on funds left with the trustee for investment and kept uninvested for an unreasonably long time. Where, however, circumstances show that the trustee "was not under a duty to invest trust money but merely to safeguard it, he is not liable for interest because of this failure to invest." * * *

[T]he notification, recordkeeping and payment requirements [of DR 9–102] apply to the interest generated by a separate bank account established by a lawyer for an individual client, because that interest, when posted to the client's account, becomes funds of the client. * * *

* * * The Committee perceives no intention by the drafters of the Model Code to relax in any manner the long-standing restrictions on a lawyer's [own] use of client funds. Moreover, retention of interest earned on clients' funds inevitably would create a conflict between the financial interests of the lawyer and those of the client, requiring client consent after full disclosure (DR 5–104).

For these reasons, the opinion of the Committee is that the Model Code does not permit the lawyer to use interest earned on client funds to defray the lawyer's own operating expenses without the specific and informed consent of the client. * * *

Successful programs using the interest on lawyers' trust accounts for law-related public service projects in Canadian provinces and several British Commonwealth countries have inspired bar groups in the United States to consider the creation of similar programs. Several recent developments have caused the use of this untapped resource to become desirable and feasible. The availability of public funds for law-related public service uses, such as legal services for the indigent, has been reduced. The Internal Revenue Service has ruled that income generated under the circumstances of one program is not taxable to the client. * * * As a consequence, Florida has a program authorized by supreme court rule, California and Maryland have legislated programs, and numerous other states are in various stages of developing similar programs.

The programs being implemented vary in detail but have certain elements in common. All strive to have the pooled funds generate income for remittance to tax-exempt organizations where it will be applied to underwrite law-related public service activities. Under most plans, participation is at the option of the lawyer. Included are funds nominal in amount or to be held for a short period of time; all other funds are outside the scope of the programs. The decision as to what funds will be included is left to the sound discretion of the lawyer to whom the funds are entrusted, and the lawyers' reasonable exercise of discretion often is protected by either judicial or legislative statement. Prior client consent is not required. Notice to clients also is not required but is encouraged where practicable. The funds are placed in interest-bearing accounts in conventionally insured depository institutions and can be withdrawn on request. The banks are directed to remit earnings net of handling charges to a designated receiving entity, usually a bar foundation or similar tax-exempt organization, and to report account activity periodically to both the organization and the participating lawyer. The tax-exempt organizations generally segregate and strictly account for the funds, and apply them as directed by governing boards to law-related uses compatible with section 501(c)(3) of the Internal Revenue Code. * * *

The Model Code does not establish whether it is ethically permissible for lawyers to participate in these programs. In the opinion of the Committee, however, the rationale for the ethical acceptability of these programs is the same as the premise for acceptability in constitutional law and tax law. The client has no right under the circumstances to require the payment of any interest on the funds to himself or herself because the amount of interest which the funds could earn is likely to be less than the appropriate charges for administering the earnings. The practical effect of implementing these programs is to shift a part of the economic benefit from depository institutions to tax-exempt organizations. There is no economic injury to any client. The program creates income where there was none before. For these reasons, the interest is not client funds in the ethical sense any more than the interest is client property in the constitutional sense or client income in the tax law sense. * * *

For several reasons, participation in these programs differs significantly from the lawyer's use of interest earned on clients' funds to defray the lawyer's own operating expenses, a practice which, as noted above, is prohibited by the Model Code unless the client consents after full disclosure.

First, retention by a lawyer of interest earned on clients' funds inevitably places the lawyer's own financial interests in conflict with those of the client. * * * In contrast, a state-authorized program, by requiring payment of the interest to tax-exempt organizations not selected by the lawyer, poses no conflict between the financial interest of the client and that of the lawyer.

Second, the state-authorized programs are subject to public scrutiny and accountability. Precise standards for use of interest earned on lawyer trust accounts are set by state legislatures and state supreme courts. As circumstances may warrant, the programs may be altered by law. Any direct use by a lawyer of interest on clients' funds, on the other hand, would be virtually unsupervised and in most states, subject to public review only on complaint of a client.

Third, lawyer participation in these programs involves no commingling of funds belonging to the client and the lawyer. Since all the interest is payable to the charitable organization, interest earned on the account is not even arguably the lawyer's property. In contrast, the lawyer's personal retention of interest on client trust funds would lead inevitably to some commingling, could lead to disputes between the lawyer and client, and might subject the account to claims made by the lawyer's creditors.

The Model Code also imposes no duty to obtain prior consent or to notify clients of the application of their funds in the programs described above. Although keeping the client informed about the program is laudatory, here, as a practical matter, the client's funds cannot be placed at interest for the benefit of the individual client. Therefore, the lawyer has no ethical responsibility to advise the client that the interest earned will be used towards funding law-related public service projects. Furthermore, it is ethically proper without the client's consent to allow the application of a portion of the earnings on these funds to reasonable bank charges, as distinguished from the law firm's own expenses, for performing the additional computerization, transfer and reporting called for in the programs.

* * * The Committee finds no conflict with the principle of careful stewardship when a lawyer participates in the state-authorized programs described. Canon 8 of the Model Code says "[a] lawyer should assist in improving the legal system." This standard of conduct is advanced when a lawyer participates in a program which puts idle funds to law-related public uses. Moreover, by focusing attention on the earnings potential of lawyer trust accounts, these programs have the added benefit of encouraging lawyers to earn interest for clients on trust funds where the expected interest is more than the cost of administering the account.

PROBLEM 36

Problems in Class Action Representation

You know that landlords' failure to pay interest on tenants' damage deposits has cost tenants, in the aggregate, large sums of money each year. You believe that this practice is unconscionable and illegal. You want to stop it by requiring the landlords to pay their tenants interest on the deposits at the average prime rate for the term of the lease. You have put an advertisement in the local newspaper asking any tenant who is interested in filing a suit against his landlord on this basis to come to you for free legal assistance. Three persons come to your office, and you pick the most attractive and articulate one. You are thinking of filing a class action in the name of this individual and all other tenants similarly situated, but as of now you have not done so and have simply written to your client's landlord threatening suit.

QUESTIONS

1. Is it proper to use publicity to find a representative client for a class action suit?

a. To what extent may you seek out members of the class in order to advise them of their legal rights and persuade them not to opt out of the class? Look at Model Rule 7.3, Comment 6, and DR 2–104(A)(5). See also, Coles v. Marsh, 560 F.2d 186, 189 (3d Cir.1977), cert. denied 434 U.S. 985, 98 S.Ct. 611, 54 L.Ed.2d 479 (1977): "We hold * * * that [under the Federal Rules of Civil Procedure] the district court lacked power to impose any restraint on communication for the purpose of preventing the recruitment of additional parties plaintiff or of the solicitation of financial or other support to maintain the action."

b. The Supreme Court quoted from *Coles* with approval in Gulf Oil Co. v. Bernard, 452 U.S. 89, 101 S.Ct. 2193, 68 L.Ed.2d 693 (1981). Gulf Oil, pursuant to an agreement with the EEOC, sent notices to alleged victims of racial and gender discrimination offering back-pay in exchange for signed releases of all claims based on discrimination. Respondents then filed a class action on behalf of all present and former employees who had been subject to discrimination. Gulf moved for an order limiting communications between the named class action plaintiffs and their counsel to prospective or actual class members. The district court granted the order but the Supreme Court reversed, holding that the order violated Rule 23 and raised questions involving serious restraints on expression in violation of the First Amendment:

"The order interfered with their [the class representatives'] efforts to inform potential class members of the existence of this lawsuit, and may have been particularly injurious * * * because the employees at that time were being pressed to decide whether to accept a back-pay offer from Gulf that required them to sign a full release of all liability for discriminatory acts. In addition, the order made it more difficult for respondents, as the class representatives, to obtain information about the merits of the case from the persons they sought to represent.

"Because of these potential problems, an order limiting communications between parties and potential class members should be based on a clear record and specific findings that reflect a weighing of the need for a limitation and the potential interference with the rights of the parties. * * * In addition, such a weighing—identifying the potential abuses being addressed—should result in a carefully drawn order that limits speech as little as possible, consistent with the rights of the parties under the circumstances. * * * [T]he mere possibility of abuses does not justify routine adoption of a communications ban that interferes with the formation of a class or the prosecution of a class action in accordance with the Rules." 452 U.S. at 101–04, 101 S.Ct. at 2200–02, 68 L.Ed.2d at 703–05.

Is this holding consistent with the Supreme Court's earlier decisions, In re Primus, 436 U.S. 412, 98 S.Ct. 1893, 56 L.Ed.2d 417 (1978)(upholding solicitation of pro bono cases), and Shapero v. Kentucky Bar Association, 486 U.S. 466, 108 S.Ct. 1916, 100 L.Ed.2d 475 (1988)(upholding direct mail advertising/solicitation), both discussed in Problem 32?

c.   Compare Resnick v. American Dental Association, 95 F.R.D. 372, 376–78 (N.D.Ill.1982), ordering *defense* counsel, in a class action charging employment discrimination, not to communicate with *plaintiff* class action members because of DR 7–104(A). Cf. Model Rule 4.2. *Resnick* held that *Gulf Oil* does not protect communications by opposing counsel to class members. *Gulf Oil* itself, in fact, stated in dictum that DR 7–104 is an example of a "properly impose[d]" restraint on communication. 452 U.S. at 104 n. 21, 101 S.Ct. at 2202 n. 21, 68 L.Ed.2d at 705 n. 21. See also, In re Federal Skywalk Cases (Hyatt Regency Hotel Disaster), 97 F.R.D. 370 (W.D.Mo.1983) (defense counsel who had unauthorized contact with plaintiff class members violated DR 7–104 and would be held in contempt).

d.   In Kleiner v. First National Bank of Atlanta, 751 F.2d 1193 (11th Cir.1985), the Court both imposed a $50,000 fine on a defense lawyer who violated the Court's order not to contact class members and disqualified the lead trial counsel for the defense, 102 F.R.D. 754 (N.D.Ga.1983). The Court of Appeals affirmed, relying on Ohralik v. Ohio State Bar, set forth as a Reading to Problem 32, supra. The defense effort to urge potential plaintiffs to opt out of the class was said to be "inherently conducive to overreaching and duress." Do you agree?

2. Does Federal Rule of Civil Procedure 23(a)(4) impose an ethical obligation on the attorney in the selection of plaintiffs?

a. Rule 23(a)(4) provides, inter alia, that a prerequisite of a class action is that "the representative parties will fairly and adequately protect the interests of the class." Should that requirement be considered more than merely a procedural rule for the guidance of the court?

b. May a government lawyer act as counsel for a class of employees of which he (counsel) is a member? Does the situation present a conflict of interests? More than one conflict?

Bachman v. Pertschuk, 437 F.Supp. 973 (D.D.C.1977), found two serious conflicts—the attorney versus his employer and the attorney versus other members of the class with interests differing from his own. First, the lawyer's representation, the court concluded, violates DR 5–103: "a member of the class, desirous of personal gain, should not also act as attorney for that class." Second, the representation also violated DR 5–101(B) because, as a member of the class, the lawyer might be called upon to be a witness. The court concluded:

> "[The attorney] is a present employee seeking relief as a member of a class consisting of persons who are presently employed, were denied employment, or were discharged. Whenever an attorney's personal interest as a class member is limited to the interest of those persons presently employed, the possibility exists that he may favor a settlement which gives preference to the interests of such persons over those denied employment by or discharged from the FTC. Furthermore, he may devote a disproportionate amount of time preparing for trial on the issues relevant to the subgroup to which he belongs. Thus, the varying interests of the class represented coupled with the difficulty of viewing one's own limited interest in the context of the interests of the entire class require that Mr. Ramadhan be disqualified as attorney for the class because he may not adequately be able to 'protect the interests of the [entire] class.' Fed.R.Civ.P. 23(a)(4)." 437 F.Supp. at 977.

3. Must a lawyer advise a named plaintiff of the difficulties and limitations inherent in the class action if one is filed?

a. Assume that the class action will be governed by a rule like Federal Rule 23. Subsection (e) of that rule provides that a class action "shall not be dismissed or compromised without the approval of the court. * * *" Should you specifically warn your client that if you file as a class action, it will no longer be in his discretion when to settle out of court and on what terms?

b. Assume that the client you have picked—when told of the difficulties of a class action for damages—decides that he wants you to file suit only in his individual capacity. May you "fire" your client and pick another? Is a class action filed for the benefit of the named client, you the lawyer, or the class? Does the rhetoric fit the reality in all cases?

c. Suppose the landlord whom you have chosen to sue is a major property owner in the community. He offers to settle the case for five times the actual damages of your client or a total of $125, if your client refrains from filing the class action. May you permit your client to settle on that basis? May you ethically refuse to do so? Note that since you have not yet filed the class action, Rule 23(e), quoted above, has not yet formally come into play.

d. Now assume that you have filed a class action on behalf of unemployed Black construction workers seeking to require the city to institute an affirmative action program for its construction work on a massive subway project. The city officials are anxious to settle but they have developed a strong animosity towards the named plaintiff in the class action. The city proposes to settle, offers a reasonable affirmative action program for all construction workers, but informs you orally that it will never employ the particular named plaintiff. You realize that the plan will greatly benefit the class of minority construction workers, but that nowhere does the plan obligate the city to hire the named plaintiff. As counsel to the entire class, may you—must you—urge acceptance of the plan? What, if anything, should or must you tell the named plaintiff? [1]

4. Suppose your class action suit turns out to require a large amount of professional survey work and your named client has no funds with which to pay for it. The requirement of notice to the members of the class may also be expensive. May you advance the funds necessary to meet the expenses of litigation?

a. Suppose that you can clearly see that the litigation expenses will be recoverable only out of the proceeds of recovery (if any) against the landlord? Compare DR 5–103(B) with Rule 1.8(e). Would your answer differ if the suit were not a class action?

Rand v. Monsanto Co., 926 F.2d 596 (7th Cir.1991), was a purported securities class action, but the District Court denied class certification because the small shareholder named plaintiff refused to be personally liable for all costs of litigation. The District Court held that this violated the local rule counterpart to DR 5–103(B). Judge Easterbrook, for the Court of Appeals, held that DR 5–103(B) is "long in the tooth", a "relic of the rules against champerty and barratry", and inconsistent

---

1. Consider, Parker v. Anderson, 667 F.2d 1204, 1211 (5th Cir.1982). Class counsel informed the trial judge of opposition to the settlement by some named plaintiffs. "The courts have recognized that the duty owed by class counsel is to the entire class and is not dependent on the special desires of the named plaintiffs. * * * [T]he named plaintiffs should not be permitted to hold the absentee class hostage by refusing to assent to an otherwise fair and adequate settlement in order to secure their individual demands."

with Federal Rule 23. The matter was remanded to see if the named plaintiff was otherwise an appropriate class representative.

b. May you pay your client's living expenses during the pendency of the action? The traditional answer has been no, but the law on this point may be changing.

The American Law Institute Annual Meeting in May 1991 tentatively approved § 48 of the Restatement of the Law, Third, The Law Governing Lawyers which provides that a lawyer may pay a client's living expenses during the pendency of litigation if delay otherwise might cause a settlement to be based on financial hardship rather than the merits. Repayment by the client may be contingent on success of the litigation. The provision will be qualified by saying that the arrangement may not be made prior to representation, i.e., as an element of competition in recruiting clients.

c. If your case also needs the aid of an expert witness and your clients are too poor to hire one, may you hire the expert witness and make his or her fee contingent on the outcome of the case? The constitutionality of DR 7–109(C), proscribing the payment of contingent fees to expert witnesses, was attacked in Person v. Association of the Bar of the City of New York, 554 F.2d 534 (2d Cir.1977), cert. denied 434 U.S. 924, 98 S.Ct. 403, 54 L.Ed.2d 282 (1977). The district court struck down the rule but the Court of Appeals reversed reasoning:

> "States have a compelling interest in regulating the conduct of professionals who practice within their borders. The interest in regulating lawyers is especially great because lawyers are essential for the functioning of the administration of justice. Goldfarb v. Virginia State Bar (1975). * * *

> "Person * * * points out that cross-examination would reveal whatever financial stake a witness has in the outcome of litigation. He notes that experts often have ongoing business relationships with the parties who retain them and therefore, in an indirect sense, frequently have a stake in the outcome of litigation although their fee is not contingent and thus not covered by DR 7–109(C). Other experts, although retained on a 'fixed fee' basis, often do not expect to receive payment unless the party for whom they testify is successful. These are factors which may indicate the desirability of legislative change, but they do not constitute sufficient grounds for invalidating the current canon or rule.

> "New York Disciplinary Rule 7–109(C) does not affect a fundamental right nor create a suspect classification. We hold that it has a sufficient rational basis to withstand a constitutional challenge under the equal protection and due process clauses of the fourteenth amendment." 554 F.2d at 538–39.

Are the policies behind DR 7–109(C) persuasive to you? Cf. Model Rule 3.4(b) and Comment 3.

5.   What fee should a lawyer receive for prevailing in a class action case?

a.   Most non-class action cases in this country follow what is often called the American Rule: all parties in litigation bear their own costs and attorneys' fees.   However, courts have "inherent" power to award attorney fees in certain classes of cases.   A typical example is the common fund doctrine: when the plaintiff's class action creates a fund of money to be distributed to members of the class, the court may allow court costs, other expenses, and counsel fees to be paid out of the fund on the theory that those who have benefitted from the fund should pay for the legal services rendered.   At other times, Congress by statute may require the losing party to pay the winner's legal fees, for example, where the plaintiff is treated as a private attorney general vindicating public rights.   The lawyer is said to have conferred a benefit upon the public, even if that benefit is not monetary.

b.   Congress has authorized attorneys' fees in civil rights cases. Section 1988 of title 42 provides that "the court, in its discretion, may allow the prevailing party, other than the United States, a reasonable attorney's fee as part of the costs" in "any action or proceeding" to enforce various civil rights laws (42 U.S.C.A. §§ 1981, 1982, 1983, 1985, 1986;   20 U.S.C.A. § 1681 et seq.;   and 42 U.S.C.A. § 20004 et seq.)

c.   In determining attorneys fees under § 1988, the Supreme Court has said that the "most useful starting point" is to take the "number of hours reasonably expended on the litigation multiplied by a reasonable hourly rate." [2]   In determining what the reasonable hourly rate is, the court should use the "prevailing market rates in the relevant community, regardless of whether plaintiff is represented by private or nonprofit counsel." [3]   This figure is often called the lodestar.

d.   Courts, in a few instances, increase or decrease the lodestar by use of a multiplier.   Courts may reduce the fee if the success obtained, "however significant, is limited in comparison to the scope of the litigation as a whole." [4]   An upward adjustment should exist only for those "rare" cases where the success was "exceptional." [5]   Neither the novelty nor complexity of the issues should justify an upward adjustment because both will be reflected in the number of hours expended.   Similarly, the experience and quality of the attorneys should already be reflected in the hourly rate.

Thus, in Pennsylvania v. Delaware Valley Citizens' Council for Clean Air, 483 U.S. 711, 107 S.Ct. 3078, 97 L.Ed.2d 585 (1987), the Court refused to allow a "risk multiplier" to be used to increase the

---

2.   Hensley v. Eckerhart, 461 U.S. 424, 433, 103 S.Ct. 1933, 1939, 76 L.Ed.2d 40 (1983).

3.   Blum v. Stenson, 465 U.S. 886, 895, 104 S.Ct. 1541, 1547, 79 L.Ed.2d 891 (1984).

4.   Hensley v. Eckerhart, 461 U.S. at 433, 103 S.Ct. at 1939. See generally, 3 R.

Rotunda & J. Nowak, Treatise on Constitutional Law: Substance and Procedure § 19.36 (2d ed. 1992).

5.   Blum v. Stenson, 465 U.S. at 894, 104 S.Ct. at 1547.

lodestar. That is, plaintiff's attorney should not be awarded separate, increased compensation above the lodestar amount for assuming the risk of not being paid at all. There was no majority opinion. Justice White, joined by Chief Justice Rehnquist and Justices Powell and Scalia, concluded that the statute should not be construed to permit enhancement of a reasonable lodestar fee. Further, if the statute should be so construed, an enhancement was inappropriate in this case because there was no finding that without risk-enhancement plaintiff was so poor that it would have faced substantial difficulty in finding counsel. The justices also pointed out that granting a risk multiplier would mean that the lawyer would be paid more for bringing weak cases than strong ones, which would encourage the filing of weak cases. Justice O'Connor, concurred in part, but said that she would be willing to allow a risk multiplier if a plaintiff could identify a class of cases where the market compensates for contingency. Justices Blackmun, Brennan, Marshall, and Stevens, dissented.[6]

e.　Swedish Hospital Corp. v. Shalala, 1 F.3d 1261 (D.C.Cir.1993), went on to examine the recurring question of when fees should be set as a percentage of the "common fund" recovery and when the lodestar method should be used. The class action had recovered $27.8 million for a group of hospitals. The Court found a percentage fee was appropriate. It set the percentage at 20% and applied it only to the amount of the recovery for which the lawyers efforts had been responsible. That sum was $10 million, so the fee was set at $2 million.

f.　The lack of doctrinal consistency in this area is illustrated by In re Washington Public Power Supply System Securities Litigation, 19 F.3d 1291 (9th Cir.1994). Again, the class action produced a common fund, but the District Court used the lodestar approach where the sum recovered was very large. That approach was held to be proper, but the Court of Appeals said the Court should have augmented the lodestar with a risk multiplier, presumably so that the actual fee determined would reward the large recovery after all.

6.　Attorneys' fee cases raise special conflict of interest issues.　What should a court (or Congress) do to encourage settlements, provide for reasonable, but not excessive, attorney fees, and reduce conflicts?

a.　In Evans v. Jeff D., 475 U.S. 717, 106 S.Ct. 1531, 89 L.Ed.2d 747 (1986), the Court held that a judge in a class action may approve a class settlement even if it is conditioned on the waiver of attorney's fees that were authorized by statute. In *Evans,* plaintiffs filed a class action to improve conditions of institutionalized handicapped children in Idaho. As part of the settlement agreement, the plaintiffs' lawyers (a public interest law firm) stipulated they would waive attorneys' fees, but only if

---

6. See also, City of Burlington v. Dague, 505 U.S. ___, 112 S.Ct. 2638, 120 L.Ed.2d 449 (1992). Under the Clean Water Act and Solid Waste Disposal Acts, a federal court may not enhance the lodestar because of the contingency. To increase the fee if the plaintiff is successful would be redundant, the Court said. Attorney's fees are only available at all under the statutes if the client is successful.

the court approved. The Ninth Circuit recognized the strong principle in favor of settlements but said that the defendants could not force the plaintiffs to waive statutory attorneys' fees. The district court, said the Ninth Circuit, should have determined what reasonable fees should be in a case like this.

In a 6 to 3 opinion written by Justice Stevens, the Supreme Court reversed. It held that the question "derives ultimately from the Fees Act rather than from the strictures of professional ethics." As the Court reasoned, the attorney "had no *ethical* obligation to seek a statutory fee award. His ethical duty was to serve his clients loyally and competently. Since the proposal to settle on the merits was more favorable than the probable outcome of the trial, [the attorneys'] decision to recommend acceptance was consistent with the highest standards of our profession. The district court, therefore, correctly concluded that approval of the settlement involved no breach of ethics in this case." (emphasis in original)

Justices Brennan, Marshall and Blackmun, in dissent, suggested that the Court's result would likely lead to fewer civil rights actions being brought because of the lawyers' uncertainty of getting their fees. Do you agree?

b. Earlier bar opinions had said that it is unethical for defense counsel to submit a settlement offer to the plaintiff conditioned on an agreement to waive or limit attorneys fees. E.g., D.C. Bar Ethics Opinion 147 (Jan. 22, 1985); Committee on Professional and Judicial Ethics of the New York City Bar Association, Opinion No. 80–94 ("Defense Counsel * * * are in a uniquely favorable position when they condition settlement on the waiver of the statutory fee: they make a demand for a benefit which the plaintiff's lawyer cannot resist as a matter of ethics and which the plaintiff will not resist due to lack of interest."); Grievance Commission of Board of Overseers of the Bar of Maine, Advisory Opinion No. 17 (1983). Should *Jeff D.* supersede the ethical judgment of these committees? Does *Jeff D.* address the ethical obligations of defense counsel at all?

c. *Jeff D.* recognized that it is the party's right to waive, settle, or negotiate his or her eligibility for fees from the losing party. Thus in Blanchard v. Bergeron, 489 U.S. 87, 109 S.Ct. 939, 103 L.Ed.2d 67 (1989), the Court unanimously held that under 42 U.S.C.A. § 1988, authorizing fee shifting, if the plaintiff negotiates a contingent fee with the lawyer, that agreement does not impose an automatic ceiling on the amount that can be allowed under § 1988; the court should instead look to the lodestar.

Later, in Venegas v. Mitchell, 495 U.S. 82, 110 S.Ct. 1679, 109 L.Ed.2d 74 (1990), plaintiff and attorney entered into a contingent fee contract that provided that the attorney would receive 40% of the gross amount of recovery, and that any court awarded fee would be applied, dollar for dollar, to offset the contingent fee. A unanimous Court held that § 1988 does not prevent a lawyer from collecting a reasonable contingent fee even if it *exceeds* the statutory fee award. "[N]either *Blanchard* nor any other of our cases has indicated that § 1988, by it own force, protects plaintiffs from having to pay what they have contracted to pay, even though their contractual liability is greater than the statutory award that they may collect from losing opponents." Section 1988 "controls what the losing defendant must pay, not what the prevailing plaintiff must pay his lawyer."

d. In light of *Blanchard* and *Venegas,* is it important for class action lawyers to arrange for fees by contract and not rely exclusively on a later court award?

7. Finally, fee shifting statutes raise questions of proportionality. If a successful plaintiff can shift the fee to defendant, should there be any concern that cases will be brought in which the plaintiff's lawyer has a greater interest in the outcome of the case than the plaintiff does?

a. In Riverside v. Rivera, 477 U.S. 561, 106 S.Ct. 2686, 91 L.Ed.2d 466 (1986), the Supreme Court considered whether attorneys' fees in a civil rights action must be "proportional" to the amount recovered. In this case, two lawyers recovered $33,350 in damages for a family in a suit against the police department. Their fee award was $245,456. In a 5 to 4 decision with no majority opinion, the Supreme Court upheld the fee. For the plurality it was sufficient that the District Court had found that the case served the public interest and that the hours invested were not inflated.

The dissent cast doubt on the high hourly rate claimed by two attorneys only briefly out of law school and questioned whether lawyers should be encouraged to expend time so far beyond a case's economic value. A plaintiff in a *Rivera* situation is in a better economic position than ordinary plaintiffs who could not economically pay their own lawyer nearly a quarter of a million dollars to prosecute a case worth less than $35,000. But Justice Brennan's plurality opinion responded: "Because damage awards do not reflect fully the public benefit advanced by civil rights litigation, Congress did not intend for fees in civil rights cases, unlike most private law cases, to depend on obtaining substantial monetary relief." Civil rights plaintiffs seek to vindicate rights that should not be valued solely in economic terms.

Who had the better of the argument?[7] Why? Is the underlying reality that *many* class actions seem to be brought more for the benefit of the lawyers than the clients?

b. A prime purpose of fee shifting statutes is to make the prevailing party eligible to collect attorney's fees from the defendant. The fact

---

7. See also, Ramirez v. Sturdevant, 26 Cal.Rptr.2d 554 (Cal.App. 1994), where the client had been terminated by her employer, and the lawyer had agreed to a ⅓ contingent fee. In a supplemental fee agreement entered into when an adverse ruling required an appeal, the client agreed to let the lawyer negotiate the fee directly with the employer. The final settlement was $150,000 to the client and $215,000 for the lawyer. The Court remanded for an inquiry into whether the disparate awards were the result of the lawyer not working hard enough for the client.

that plaintiff can afford to pay for his own attorney, or that he is represented free of charge by a nonprofit group, does not preclude the prevailing plaintiff from collecting attorneys' fees. Blum v. Stenson, 465 U.S. 886, 894–95, 104 S.Ct. 1541, 1547, 79 L.Ed.2d 891 (1984). Does that make sense to you?[8] What justifies such a result?

c. If the potential class action defendant promises to pay the client $5000, which is much more than the individual claim is worth, and to pay you an extremely generous fee of $125,000 on the condition that you not bring any other actions against the defendant, may you agree? The object, of course, would be to require lawyers for any future claimants to educate themselves from scratch about the case. If your client wants to accept the offer, must you agree?

Model Rule 5.6(b) and DR 2–108(B) forbid you to accept such an offer. What rationale justifies those rules? Do the rules require you to sacrifice the interests of a present client to protect the interests of hypothetical future clients? Do the rules ordinarily require subverting the interests of today's clients? ABA Formal Opinion 93–371 (1993) tries to justify and explain the required result.

PROBLEM 37

Group Legal Service Plans

The Building Trades Council of your area has negotiated a master contract with the local contractors' association. One element of the agreement is prepaid legal insurance. As a fringe benefit for employees, the employers have agreed to pay sufficient sums to the Council to create a Fund that will pay union members' legal fees whenever they (1) are sued, (2) are charged with a criminal offense, (3) buy or sell a house, (4) draft a will or codicil, (5) adopt a child, (6) obtain a divorce, or (7) need tax advice.

Union members are to apply to the Fund whenever they need legal help and the Fund manager is to assign them a lawyer from the list of "approved" attorneys. To be an "approved" attorney, the lawyer must first become an "honorary member" of the Building Trades Council. To do so, he or she must pay a sum equivalent to the average dues of the union members, although none of the benefits provided active union members are provided to honorary members.

Jerry McManus, a bricklayer, wants to buy a house, but he has had difficulty securing a mortgage. He has been assigned to Mary Anderson,

---

8. See also, Fogerty v. Fantasy, Inc., ___ U.S. ___, 114 S.Ct. 1023, 127 L.Ed.2d 455 (1994), where the defendant had prevailed in a copyright infringement action, but the lower courts had declined to award attorney's fees. They reasoned that while suc- cessful plaintiffs should routinely get fee awards, defendants should only get them when the suit was filed in bad faith. The Supreme Court held here that the Copy- right Act gives an equal claim to fees to lawyers for both plaintiffs and defendants.

an "approved" attorney. Jerry has objected vehemently. "I don't want no woman for my lawyer," Jerry told his union business agent. "Besides, she represented my wife in my divorce last year. She bled me dry and I don't trust her." The Fund manager has refused even to discuss the matter with Jerry. "If you don't want the lawyer you're given," a sign on his door reads, "go out and hire your own, at your own expense." The Fund will not even assign Jerry another lawyer in the plan.

Unhappy with the response of the prepaid plan, Jerry has visited the National Home Buyers Rights Organization (NHBRO), a nonprofit association that is interested in Jerry's case and will arrange free counsel for Jerry. The NHBRO believes that the banks are reluctant to give Jerry a mortgage because of the area where he plans to buy the house. Jerry is white, but many of the houses in the area are owned by African–Americans and NHBRO believes that the banks may be illegally "redlining." Jerry is assigned to Andrew Adams, a lawyer for NHBRO, who advises Jerry that the NHBRO will take Jerry's case and help him secure a mortgage, search the title, and handle the closing, but only if Jerry will lend his name to a broad-based attack on bank lending practices. Jerry responds: "I just want to get a mortgage and buy a house." Adams candidly advises Jerry that NHBRO's practice of using cases like Jerry's to make "new law" means that sometimes parties will lose cases that they might have won if a narrower legal theory had been asserted. In this case, it will probably mean that the closing on Jerry's house will be delayed. "But we all must make sacrifices for the greater good," says Adams. "And if you don't like our conditions, we don't have to accept you as a client."

QUESTIONS

1. Turn first to the Model Code. What was its approach to the phenomenon of group legal services?

a. Look at DR 2–103(D). Did its attitude seem to be one of enthusiasm? Resignation? Suspicion?

b. Why was there such concern about such plans, the legal equivalent of Health Maintenance Organizations ("HMO's")? Was it fear of competition (e.g., unions steering clients to preferred lawyers, a group of clients for whom lawyers outside the plan cannot compete)?

c. Given modern changes in advertising and solicitation rules, is there anything left of such concerns? The Readings may give you a partial sense of the long struggle behind the Code's present provisions.[1]

d. Is there a counterpart to the extensive requirements of DR 2–103(D) in the Model Rules? Look at Rule 5.4(c), Rule 7.2(c) & Comment 6, and Rule 7.3(d) & Comment 8. Are ethical standards lower under the

---

1. An argument can be made that P.L. 93–406, the Employment Retirement Income Security Act of 1974, 88 Stat. 829 (1974), preempts the Code and other state law at least with respect to provision of legal services as an employee benefit. See ABA Consortium on Legal Services and the Public, Alternatives, Dec. 1974, p. 1.

Model Rules? Does the long battle between the organized bar and potential deliverers of group service seem to be nearing an end?

2. Should it be proper for an attorney to become an "honorary member" of the Building Trades Council?

a. Is there any basis for questioning the practice? Would it matter if the "dues" were expressed as a percentage of the legal fees collected?

b. May the Building Trades Council require lawyers assigned under the plan to charge the Fund according to a prescribed fee schedule? How would that differ, if at all, from the situation presented in *Goldfarb*? [2]

c. Are you getting rights in a closed panel legal services plan every time you obtain auto insurance? Under most policies, does the insurance company promise to select and pay for a lawyer to defend you and also to pay any judgments within policy limits if you are found liable? Does DR 2–103(D)(4)(a) recognize the insurance arrangement? Why should the Code say, as a matter of ethics, it is necessary that the insurance company bear ultimate liability?

3. Should a professionally proper plan be required to have an "opt-out" provision allowing a client to reject one attorney and be assigned another? Why might plan proponents resist such a feature?

a. If the lawyer has what would otherwise be a prohibited conflict of interest, may it be ignored when a "Plan" is involved? Is it enough to say that Jerry can always hire his own attorney?

b. Should Jerry's prejudice against women be entitled to any weight in evaluating the propriety of the Plan's requirement that Mary represent him? What weight should be given to his prejudice against a lawyer who "bled [him] dry" in a suit last year? [3]

c. Does an indigent criminal defendant have to be represented by the public defender if the latter has a conflict of interest? What if the defendant has a personality conflict with the lawyer assigned to him? Should the need for an opt-out feature in a group legal services plan be judged by the same standard that we apply in such "right to counsel" settings?

4. Now assume that McManus, with help from a lawyer who is not a part of the Building Trades Council Legal Insurance Plan, sues his former wife Joan to get back property that he says belongs to him. Assume that Joan is herself entitled to representation by this same Building Trades Council Plan. May the

---

2. Cf. B.N.A. Antitrust & Trade Reg. Rep. No. 677, Aug. 20, 1974, at D–1 (Request for Business Review Letter and Justice Dept. Response re California Lawyers Service).

3. Cf. Grievance Committee of Bar of Hartford County v. Rottner, 152 Conn. 59, 65, 203 A.2d 82, 84 (1964): If a client "is sued and his own home attached by his own attorney, [representing someone else in another case] * * *, all feeling of loyalty is necessarily destroyed, and the profession is exposed to the charge that it is only interested in money." Is *Rottner* distinguishable?

Plan's attorney, Mary Anderson, defend Joan against the suit filed by McManus?

a. May Anderson, an attorney with a prepaid legal services plan, ever represent one person who is entitled to benefits against another person entitled to benefits?[4] May the Fund's charter provide that it alone (or its counsel alone) has the discretion to determine whom to represent in such cases?

b. Should it matter that the suit filed by Jerry in this question is not something for which he is entitled to legal services under the Plan? Remember that he is only entitled to the Fund's legal help for his mortgage problem.

c. Must Anderson have Jerry's consent to represent Joan here? If Anderson may not represent Joan, should the Fund be obligated to pay another lawyer to furnish representation to Joan? Is paying another lawyer enough; are Jerry and Joan both clients of the Fund or of Anderson personally?

d. Similar issues arose in Board of Education of City of New York v. Nyquist, 590 F.2d 1241 (2d Cir.1979). There, three male physical education teachers were represented by the General Counsel of the New York State United Teachers (NYSUT) in a suit alleging that maintenance of separate seniority lists for male and female physical education teachers is illegal. Female teachers, who were also members of NYSUT, would be disadvantaged if the men prevailed. Thus they sought to disqualify the men's counsel. The District Court's disqualification order was reversed by the Second Circuit. Judge Feinberg wrote:

> "The district court disqualified Mr. Sandner because a 'layman's faith would be severely troubled' by the fact that 'the female teachers are paying, in part, for their opponents' legal expenses.' There is no claim, however, that Mr. Sandner feels any sense of loyalty to the women that would undermine his representation of the men. Nor is there evidence that his representation of the men is anything less than vigorous. There is also no claim that the men have gained an unfair advantage through any access to privileged information about the women. * * *

> "We agree that there is at least some possibility that Mr. Sandner's representation of the men has the appearance of impropriety, because of the large number of union members involved and the public importance of the civil rights issue at the heart of the dispute. But in any event, we think that disqualification was inappropriate. We believe that when there is no claim that the trial will be tainted, appearance of impropriety is simply too slender a reed on which to rest a disqualifi-

---

4. You remember from Problem 10, of course, that a lawyer ordinarily may not represent a client against a current client of the lawyer even in an entirely unrelated matter.

cation order except in the rarest cases. This is particularly true where, as in this case, the appearance of impropriety is not very clear."

Judge Mansfield, concurring, found no "appearance of impropriety:"

"[A]n organization financed with dues received from all members may properly take a position that benefits some members at the expense of others, provided it acts reasonably, in good faith and without hostility or arbitrary discrimination. If it is proper for the organization to do so, there is no impropriety in its counsel doing likewise, subject to the same conditions.

* * *

"It could be argued that the NYSUT legal services plan vests its counsel with too wide a discretion to determine what members' claims are meritorious or job-related in an intra-organizational dispute, or that the plan poses too great a risk of erroneous, invidious, fraudulent or discriminatory decisions by its counsel in such matters. If so, the remedy rests in the hands of NYSUT's members who have the power to change or modify its legal services plan. In addition, of course, they would be entitled to seek relief from the court upon a showing that NYSUT's counsel had abused his powers or acted in bad faith or for reasons unconnected with the merits of the cause which he chose to advance."

Do you agree with this result? Is one of these opinions more persuasive to you than the other?

5. May Andrew Adams agree to manage a case according to the interests of the NHBRO rather than exclusively according to the interests of the particular clients to whom he is assigned?

a. Look at DR 5–107(B) and Rule 5.4(c). Do you agree with their approach to this issue? Might a poor person's private interest ever conflict with the public interest?

b. Is the same point being made in Rule 1.8(f), whose Code counterpart is DR 5–107(A)? Should anything turn on whether the public interest group is paying the lawyer a fee?

c. If the client agrees to any restrictions or conditions on the representation, are DR 5–107(A),(B) and Rules 1.8(f) & 5.4(c) applicable? Once the client consents, can we say it is the client and not the third party payor for the legal services who is presumed to be specifying the objectives of the representations?

d. Is it important for the lawyer to verify that the client understands the basis of the representation? How can the client's understanding be confirmed with certainty? May the lawyer be guilty of malpractice if the client does not understand? Cf. ABA Formal Opinion 334 (Aug. 10, 1974), excerpted in the Readings to this Problem.

e. Consider the following description of conflicting interests faced by lawyers, some of whose clients want integrated schools and others of whose clients focus more on the inherent quality of the schools attended by African–Americans, whether or not the schools are integrated:

"The *Code* approach, urging the lawyer to 'constantly guard against erosion of his professional freedom' [110] and requiring that he 'decline to accept direction of his professional judgment from any layman,' [111] is simply the wrong answer to the right question in civil rights offices where basic organizational policies such as the goals of school desegregation are often designed by lawyers and then adopted by the board or other leadership group. The NAACP's reliance on litigation requires that lawyers play a major role in basic policy decisions. Admonitions that the lawyer make no important decisions without consulting the client [112] and that the client be fully informed of all relevant considerations[113] are, of course, appropriate. But they are difficult to enforce in the context of complex, long term school desegregation litigation where the original plaintiffs may have left the system and the members of the class whose interests are at stake are numerous, generally uninformed, and, if aware of the issues, divided in their views.

* * *

"It is essential that lawyers 'lawyer' and not attempt to lead clients and class. Commitment renders restraint more, not less, difficult, and the inability of black clients to pay handsome fees for legal services can cause their lawyers, unconsciously perhaps, to adopt an attitude of 'we know what's best' in determining legal strategy. Unfortunately, clients are all too willing to turn everything over to the lawyers. In school cases perhaps more than in any other civil rights field, the attorney must be more than a litigator. The willingness to innovate, organize, and negotiate—and the ability to perform each with skill and persistence—are of crucial importance. In this process of overall representation, the apparent—and sometimes real—conflicts of interest between lawyer and client can be resolved.

"Finally, commitment to an integrated society should not be allowed to interfere with the ability to represent effectively parents who favor education-oriented remedies. Those civil rights lawyers, regardless of race, whose commitment to integration is buoyed by doubts about the effectiveness of predominantly black schools should reconsider seriously the propriety of representing blacks, at least in those school cases involving heavily minority districts."

110. [EC 5–23.]   **112.** EC 7–7.

111. EC 5–24.   **113.** EC 7–8.

Bell, Serving Two Masters: Integration Ideals and Client Interests in School Desegregation Litigation, 85 Yale L.J. 470, 504, 512 (1976).

Conceding that the problems outlined are difficult, are there practical ways they might be resolved? Could a committee of plaintiffs be elected, for example, whom the lawyers could consult? Would even the members of such a committee necessarily agree? Might its decisions potentially undercut the purpose of the suit?

6. Will prepaid and group legal services be the financial salvation of the bar, i.e., will they make more funds available for payment of legal fees and create additional consumers of legal services?

a. Should there be any ethical objection to lawyers establishing and promoting a plan under which persons pay a sum each year to become entitled to free or discounted fees for legal services rendered by the lawyers? Would such a plan in effect be prepaid legal services? Could lawyers place advertisements in newspapers announcing the plan and seeking subscribers? Look at Rule 7.3(d) and DR 2–103(D)(4)(b). Do you agree with the policy underlying these rules?

b. If a law firm wishes to organize itself so as to provide group legal services at a fixed rate, may it write letters to employers in the area offering to provide such an arrangement as a fringe benefit for employees? May it write letters to employees and unions encouraging them to demand such a benefit in upcoming contract talks? Is such direct mail solicitation now constitutionally protected after Shapero v. Kentucky Bar Association, 486 U.S. 466, 108 S.Ct. 1916, 100 L.Ed.2d 475 (1988), discussed in Problem 32, supra?

c. For many years, there has been relative slow growth in the number of prepaid legal plans. One development, however, has been the creation of "individual access" plans under which members pay a certain fee every month which usually grants them unlimited telephone consultation with "access" attorneys and then the right to deal with "referral" attorneys for more complex problems at a lower than normal hourly fee.

Montgomery Ward, for example, introduced an individual access plan in 1985. In 1989, a customer paying just $6.75 a month (which could be charged to a credit card) would receive unlimited telephone consultation with an attorney, "who will write letters and make phone calls on the client's behalf. The plan also offers a laundry list of free services, including a 'simple' will, document review of up to six pages and a 24–hour emergency bail service." For referral work, the plan provided discounted contingency fees and guaranteed maximum rates of $50 per hour.

"Every day of the week except Sunday, telemarketers call residents in 25 states, where regulations expressly permit telemarketing by non-lawyers." By early 1989, Montgomery Ward had a 2000–lawyer network in place for its prepaid individual access plan. Hyatt Legal Services, Amway Corp., and other companies are marketing their own prepaid individual access plans. Hyatt's plan has over 100,000 members. To check up on possibly incompetent or dishonest lawyers, most plans rely on customer complaints and questionnaires. The general counsel of one prepaid plan stated: "The winners in this are clearly lawyers. This is probably the most positive economic movements for lawyers with the exception of the M[ergers] & A[cquisitions] craze in New York." The plans put "money in the lawyer's pockets they would not have because people would not have used them." Galen, Prepaid Plans a Boon for the Bar, National L.J., Jan. 30, 1989, at p.1, 32–35.

Do you agree? Will group legal services mean the end of the solo practitioner?

READINGS

BROTHERHOOD OF RAILROAD TRAINMEN v. VIRGINIA EX REL. VA. STATE BAR

Supreme Court of the United States, 1964.
377 U.S. 1, 84 S.Ct. 1113, 12 L.Ed.2d 89.

Justice BLACK delivered the opinion of the Court.

The Virginia State Bar brought this suit * * * to enjoin [defendants] from carrying on activities which, the Bar charged, constituted the solicitation of legal business and the unauthorized practice of law in Virginia. It was conceded that in order to assist the prosecution of claims by injured railroad workers or by the families of workers killed on the job the Brotherhood maintains in Virginia and throughout the country a Department of Legal Counsel which recommends to Brotherhood members and their families the names of lawyers whom the Brotherhood believes to be honest and competent. Finding that the Brotherhood's plan resulted in "channeling all, or substantially all," the workers' claims to lawyers chosen by the Department of Legal Counsel, the court issued an injunction against the Brotherhood's carrying out its plan in Virginia.

* * *

* * * The result of the plan, the Brotherhood admits, is to channel legal employment to the particular lawyers approved by the Brotherhood as legally and morally competent to handle injury claims for members and their families. It is the injunction against this particular practice which the Brotherhood, on behalf of its members, contends denies them rights guaranteed by the First and Fourteenth Amendments. We agree with this contention.

It cannot be seriously doubted that the First Amendment's guarantees of free speech, petition and assembly give railroad workers the right to gather together for the lawful purpose of helping and advising one another in asserting the rights Congress gave them in the Safety Appliance Act and the Federal Employers' Liability Act, statutory rights which would be vain and futile if the workers could not talk together freely as to the best course to follow. The right of members to consult with each other in a fraternal organization necessarily includes the right to select a spokesman from their number who could be expected to give the wisest counsel. That is the role played by the members who carry out the legal aid program. And the right of the workers personally or through a special department of their Brotherhood to advise concerning the need for legal assistance—and, most importantly, what lawyer a member could confidently rely on—is an inseparable part of this constitutionally guaranteed right to assist and advise each other.

* * *

Only last Term we had occasion to consider an earlier attempt by Virginia to enjoin the National Association for the Advancement of Colored People from advising prospective litigants to seek the assistance of particular attorneys. In fact, in that case, unlike this one, the attorneys were actually employed by the association which recommended them, and recommendations were made even to nonmembers. NAACP v. Button, [371 U.S. 415, 83 S.Ct. 328, 9 L.Ed.2d 405 (1963)]. We held that "although the petitioner has amply shown that its activities fall within the First Amendment's protections, the State has failed to advance any substantial regulatory interest, in the form of substantive evils flowing from petitioner's activities, which can justify the broad prohibitions which it has imposed." In the present case the State again has failed to show any appreciable public interest in preventing the Brotherhood from carrying out its plan to recommend the lawyers it selects to represent injured workers. The Brotherhood's activities fall just as clearly within the protection of the First Amendment. And the Constitution protects the associational rights of the members of the union precisely as it does those of the NAACP.

* * *

Justice CLARK, whom Justice HARLAN joins, dissenting.

By its decision today the Court overthrows state regulation of the legal profession and relegates the practice of law to the level of a commercial enterprise. The Court permits a labor union—contrary to state law—to engage in the unauthorized practice of soliciting personal injury cases from among its membership on behalf of 16 regional attorneys whom its president has placed on the union's approved list. Local officials of the union call on each member suffering an injury and seek to secure employment of these approved attorneys in the prosecution of claims for damages arising therefrom. Moreover the union, through its president, not only controls the appointment and dismissal of the approved attorney but also has considerable influence over his fees and often controls the disposition of cases. Furthermore, from 1930 to at least 1959, the union had required these approved attorneys to pay to it a portion of their fees, usually 25%. Such an arrangement may even now be in effect through the ruse of reimbursement for investigatory services rendered by the union. This state of affairs degrades the profession, proselytes the approved attorneys to certain required attitudes and contravenes both the accepted ethics of the profession and the statutory and judicial rules of acceptable conduct. * * * *

ALAN B. MORRISON,** BAR ETHICS: BARRIER TO THE CONSUMER

Trial Magazine, March–April 1975, Page 14.

* * * [C]rimes against consumers are increasingly being perpetrated under the guise of "professional ethics," with the latest evidence being the American Bar Association's treatment of group legal service plans.

In the face of four Supreme Court decisions which held that under the First Amendment consumers of legal services have the absolute right to organize as they please in order to retain counsel of their choice under terms of their choice [United Transportation Union v. State Bar of Michigan, 401 U.S. 576 (1971); United Mine Workers v. Illinois State Bar Ass'n, 389 U.S. 217 (1967); Brotherhood of R.R. Trainmen v. Virginia State Bar, 377 U.S. 1 (1964); and NAACP v. Button, 371 U.S. 415 (1963)], the ABA has erected significant new barriers for consumers in an attempt to control the operation of group legal service plans in a way that is financially most profitable for the bar. * * *

The largest affront to the consumer interest is the prohibition of closed panel legal service plans. Under such plans a group engages a law firm (or hires staff attorneys) to take on all the work covered by the plan, much the way that a medical clinic or group health plan works. While the individual's choice of attorneys is limited to those employed by the plan, this method of delivery provides significant opportunities for

* Editors' Note: Justice Stewart took no part in the disposition of this case. Following this case the Court, in United Mine Workers of America v. Illinois State Bar Ass'n, 389 U.S. 217, 88 S.Ct. 353, 19 L.Ed.2d 426 (1967), reversed the state court and upheld as constitutionally protected the practice of the United Mine Workers in employing a licensed attorney on a salaried basis to represent any of its members who wished to prosecute workmen's compensation claims before the Illinois Industrial Commission. Next, in United Transp. Union v. State Bar of Michigan, 401 U.S. 576, 91 S.Ct. 1076, 28 L.Ed.2d 339 (1971), the Union recommended selected attorneys to its members and their families in connection with suits for damages under the Federal Employers' Liability Act; it secured a commitment from those attorneys that the maximum fee charged would not exceed 25% of the recovery, and it recommended Chicago lawyers to represent Michigan claimants. The Court again reversed the state court, found the practice constitutionally protected, and concluded that the "common thread running through our decisions in NAACP v. Button, Trainmen, and United Mine Workers is that collective activity undertaken to obtain meaningful access to the courts is a fundamental right within the protection of the First Amendment."

** Mr. Morrison was Director of Litigation, Ralph Nader's Public Citizen Organization.

cost savings which are simply unavailable under the traditional means of providing legal services. The ABA now prohibits such plans, unless there is an option for each member to obtain an attorney of his choice outside the plan *and* to have the plan pay that attorney at least the reasonable cost to the group had the member used retained counsel.*

The effect of such an opt-out requirement is to undermine one of the principal benefits of the closed panel—the ability to control costs by setting limits on the costs of attorney's services. This results from the fact that the plan will have no way of knowing how many beneficiaries will exercise the right to opt-out and thus it will be virtually impossible to calculate the cost of such a provision to the plan. There may be consumer groups who would prefer a plan with that opt-out feature, and they should be permitted to include such a provision in their agreement. But that does not mean that other groups who decide that they prefer a pure closed panel plan should have the option thrust on them by the bar.

The requirement for an opt-out provision may lead many groups to select an open panel plan, which is precisely what the bar wants. Under such a plan, the member may select any attorney to perform the work, but the opportunities for quality control and cost reduction are lost by having that element of choice, an element largely irrelevant to most individuals who have neither information about attorneys nor the means to evaluate them. For those who wish to pay for the right to select an attorney, the open panel plan is fine, but it should not be forced upon the unwilling by the bar, whose members will profit more than with the use of closed panels.

HOWARD C. SORENSON,** BAR ETHICS: GUARDIAN OF THE PROFESSION

Trial Magazine, March–April 1975, Page 15.

The scheme of having a lay intermediary introduced into the attorney-client relationship is at the heart of the hazards associated with group legal services. In all closed panel plans a * * * lay intermediary can * * * effectively challenge the lawyer's professional judgment. This position of influence comes about because the lay intermediary—not the client—hires and pays the lawyer. Left unchecked, the lay intermediary's role introduces commercialism and conflicts of interest into the attorney-client relationship.

* * *

Under some proposals, groups of organizations such as labor unions, credit unions, farm organizations, corporations, banks and chambers of

---

* Editors' note: The section referred to was the predecessor to DR 2–103(D)(4)(e). See also, DR 2–103(D)(4)(a).

** The late Mr. Sorenson practiced law in Chicago.

commerce could deliver legal services and benefits to their employees, members, or depositors. Unrestricted, these groups are placed in a position where they dominate the delivery, the rendition, and the exercise of judgment necessary to legal services. No longer is the attorney the dominant figure in upholding the rule of law. The lay intermediary becomes a significant factor, threatening the quality of service and the existence of the vast majority of small firms dependent upon middle income clientele.

Quite possibly, the untoward effect will be the reduced availability of legal services to neighborhoods and country towns, which surveys show need legal services the most. * * * Change in our traditional delivery system must not do violence to the basic tenets that the legal profession stands upon. It is in the public interest that we as a profession promote and preserve the integrity, competence, confidentiality, and independence of judgment within our ranks. * * *

ABA FORMAL OPINION 334 (AUGUST 10, 1974)

* * *

2. Independence of Judgment

Canon 5 requires a lawyer to exercise independent professional judgment on behalf of a client. To what extent may a governing board prescribe organizational rules and regulations or operational methods of a legal services office to limit or restrict the activities of lawyers acting on behalf of clients of the office without placing those lawyers in violation of the duty to exercise their independent judgment in legal matters? DR 5–107(B).

We hold that the activities on behalf of clients of the staff of lawyers of a legal services office may be limited or restricted only to the extent necessary to allocate fairly and reasonably the resources of the office and establish proper priorities in the interest of making maximum legal services available to the indigent, and then only to an extent and in a manner consistent with the requirements of the Code of Professional Responsibility.

A. Broad Policy Matters. The committee previously attempted answers to the problems presented in this area in Formal Opinion 324 and Informal Opinions 1232 and 1252.[6] Formal Opinion 324 states that:

" * * * [T]he governing board of a legal aid society has a moral and ethical obligation to the community to determine such broad policy matters as the financial and similar criteria of persons eligible to participate in the legal aid program, selection of the various services which the society will make available to

----

6. These holdings were based primarily upon DR 2–103(D)(1) and 5–107(B), along with EC 5–24, but the Committee also cited EC 2–25, 2–27, 2–28, 5–1, 5–21, and 5–23.

such persons, setting priorities in the allocation of available resources and manpower and determining the types or kinds of cases staff attorneys may undertake to handle and the type of clients they may represent."

B.   Case–by–Case Supervision.   The committee further held in Formal Opinion 324 that there should be no interference with the lawyer-client relationship by the directors of a legal aid society after a case has been assigned to a staff lawyer and that the board should set broad guidelines respecting the categories or kinds of cases that may be undertaken rather than act on a case-by-case, client-by-client basis.

The above holdings still appear to the committee to be sound and fully supported by the sections of the Code of Professional Responsibility.

* * *

C.   Class Actions.   If a staff attorney has undertaken to represent a client in a particular matter and the full representation of that client (aside from any collateral objective such as law reform) requires the filing of a class action in order to assert his rights effectively, then any limitation upon the right to do so would be unethical.   Of course, in the case of any proposed class action it is the individual client who must make the decision to expand the suit into a class action after a full explanation of all of the foreseeable consequences.   However, if the purpose of expanding the suit to a class action is not solely to protect the rights of the individual client, or a group of similarly situated clients, but primarily to obtain law reform, and law reform, as such, is not one of the authorized purposes of the legal services office, the case cannot be expanded to a class action unless the authorized purposes are changed to include law reform.   * * *

A governing board may legitimately exercise control by establishing priorities as to the categories or kinds of cases which the office will undertake.   It is possible that, in order to achieve the goal of maximizing legal services, services to individuals may be limited in order to use the program's resources to accomplish law reform in connection with particular legal subject matter.   The subject matter priorities must be based on a consideration of the needs of the client community and the resources available to the program.   They may not be based on considerations such as the identity of the prospective adverse parties or the nature of the remedy ("class action") sought to be employed.

D.   Advisory Committees to Governing Boards.   * * * [I]f an Advisory Committee consisted entirely of lawyers, if it had no power to veto the bringing of a suit but was advisory only, and if the requirement of prior consultation did not in practice result in interference with the staff's ability to use its own independent professional judgment as to whether an action should be filed, there would appear to be no harm in requiring such consultation.   But if such a requirement did in fact result in interference with the exercise of the staff's independent judgment, it would be improper.

The members of the Advisory Committee should not be given confidences or secrets of the client, for there is no lawyer-client relationship between the client and the Advisory Committee or any member of it. * * *

E. Supervision by Senior Staff Lawyer. * * * [A]n indigent person who seeks assistance from a legal services office has a lawyer-client relationship with its staff of lawyers which is the same as any other client who retains a law firm to represent him. It is the firm, not the individual lawyer, who is retained. In fact, several different lawyers may work upon different aspects of one case, and certainly it is to be expected that the lawyers will consult with each other upon various questions where they may seek or be able to give assistance. Staff lawyers of a legal services office are subject to the direction of and control of senior lawyers, the chief lawyer, or the executive director (if a lawyer), as the case may be, just as associates of any law firm are subject to the direction and control of their seniors. Such internal communication and control is not only permissible but salutary. It is only control of the staff lawyer's judgment by an external source that is improper.

* * *

G. Legislative Activity. Informal Opinion 1252 * * * does not hold that a lawyer employed by a legal services office may not engage in law reform or seek to secure the passage of legislation. In fact, it says specifically that "any lawyer, whether he drafted legislation for a client or not, may of course as a citizen, gratuitously engage in activities of a political nature in support of it."

What the opinion does hold is that the governing body of a legal aid society may broadly limit the categories of legal services its lawyers may undertake for a client, and that in doing so it may, but need not, exclude such categories as political activity and lobbying. There are three important qualifications inherent in this statement. First, in the absence of such affirmative action by the board, no such limitation exists. Second, the action of the board must be a broad limitation upon the scope of services established prior to the acceptance by the staff lawyer of representation of any particular client, and preferably made known to its public and staff in advance like any other limitation on the scope of legal services offered. Once representation has been accepted under DR 5–107(B) and DR 7–101 nothing can be permitted to interfere with that representation to the full extent permitted by law and the disciplinary rules, including of course legislative activity.

* * *

It has been suggested that even the limitations upon the activities of a legal services office permitted by Formal Opinion 324 are improper because, while a private law office may limit its activities in any way it pleases, as the services which it does not furnish will be available elsewhere, the indigent have nowhere else to turn and therefore any limitation upon the services available at a legal services office amounts to a deprivation of those services. The Code of Professional Responsibility does not ban such limitations. As a practical matter, the resources of a legal services office are always limited, and some allocation of them upon a basis of priorities must be made if they are to be effectively utilized. As long as this is done fairly and reasonably with the objective of making maximum legal services available, within the limits of available resources, it is not improper.

It has been urged that there are certain rights of indigent clients which can only be asserted through legislative means. There can be no limitation on the availability of the staff lawyer to give advice in connection with such legislative means. DR 5–107(B).

Finally, limitations upon the activities of a legal services office which stem from motives inconsistent with the basic tenet set out in EC 5–1 are always improper. As a general proposition it may be stated that the obligation of the bar to make legal services available to the indigent requires that no such limitations should be imposed upon a legal services office and no staff lawyer should subject himself to such limitations. Whether or not such reprehensible motives are present must necessarily be determined upon the facts of each individual case.

PROBLEM 38

The Unauthorized Practice of Law

Victor Dowd is an attorney who believes that persons of even relatively modest means should plan their estates better than they do. He also believes that many people are afraid of the expense of estate planning by present methods of private law practice.

A local insurance agency offers to refer its clients to him for preparation of a basic will. He agrees to draft a basic will and any other necessary simple documents for a fee of $225. The fee will be paid to him directly by the insurance agency as part of the $399 fee it charges for "complete financial planning services."

Victor knows that skills other than legal training are helpful in the process of estate planning. He proposes to start a planning company of his own in cooperation with some accountants and insurance agents. His corporation plans to sell a complete package service consisting of planning before death and estate administration after. All participants plan to bill at an hourly rate, no matter which type of specialty is involved. They propose to advertise the service with television commercials that say, "We've all got to go sometime. We might as well do it right."

In order to make estate planning available to persons with small estates, Victor's corporation proposes to publish do-it-yourself kits both for planning and administration. They plan to sell these kits only in states for which they have been fully verified as to legal accuracy. The forms and instructions are to be carefully prepared and there is no reason to question the ability of an ordinarily intelligent person to follow them step by step and handle a completely routine case.

QUESTIONS

1. Will anyone be engaged in the unauthorized practice of law under these facts?

a. Do any of Dowd's activities raise problems under either Rule 5.5 or DR 3–101?[1] Does EC 3–5 give you guidance as to what constitutes the "practice of law"?

b. State Unauthorized Practice of Law Committee v. Paul Mason & Associates, 159 B.R. 773 (N.D.Tex.1993), was a charge of "unauthorized practice of law" brought against a "creditors bankruptcy service" that did clerical work necessary to get creditors' claims on file in bankruptcy cases around Texas. A lawyer's fee for such work would have exceeded the amount of most of the claims. The group handled no disputed claims. This Court held the case was controlled by Sperry v. Florida Bar, 373 U.S. 379 (1963), where the Supreme Court held that states may not regulate who can engage in a wholly-federal patent practice. Here, all the bankruptcy proceedings were federal, so summary judgment was granted for the respondent.

c. Are you troubled that Dowd is to be paid by the insurance agency here? Should that be interpreted as an attempt by the agency to "practice law"? May an attorney be paid other than directly by his or her client? Compare Rule 1.8(f) and DR 5–107.[2]

d. Is the case posed here significantly different from the system of prepaid legal insurance discussed in Problem 37? Would it satisfy all concerns about the arrangement if Dowd disclosed to the client how Dowd was getting paid?

e. If an individual may represent herself *pro se*, should a corporate officer who is not a lawyer be entitled to represent her corporation in court? Should the answer turn on whether the corporation is large or small? Whether the amount in controversy is large or small? What policies are served by allowing a sole proprietor of an unincorporated business to appear *pro se* but denying the 100% owner of a corporation

1. Lawline v. American Bar Association, 956 F.2d 1378 (7th Cir.1992), was a suit by an association of lawyers, paralegals, and lay people who had organized a service that proposed to answer legal questions from the public over the phone. It also planned to make referrals to legal aid and to lawyers who would charge reduced fees. The suit challenged the constitutionality of DR 3–101 and DR 3–103 on their face, and in effect, Model Rules 5.4(b) and 5.5(b) as well. The Court dismissed the action. The cited rules were all rationally related to the goal of "safeguard[ing] the public, maintain[ing] the integrity of the profession, and protect[ing] the administration of justice from reproach."

2. See also, Association of the Bar of the City of New York, Formal Opinion 1994–6 (1994), upholding a similar plan so long as the fee paid to the bank or insurance company for the lawyer's work did not exceed the sum passed on to the lawyer.

the same right to so appear? Regardless of the policies served, corporations are usually forced to hire lawyers. See, e.g., Merco Construction Engineers, Inc. v. Municipal Court, 21 Cal.3d 724, 147 Cal.Rptr. 631, 581 P.2d 636 (1978)(statute designed to reverse this rule held unconstitutional).

2. Will Dowd's sale of do-it-yourself kits in states in which Dowd is not admitted to practice constitute the unauthorized practice of law in those states?

a. Should it?[3] Are people likely to be misled by the kits into believing they have had all the legal advice that they need?

b. Can a lay person tell whether he or she has a "completely routine case" for which the kit would be adequate?[4]

People v. Macy, 789 P.2d 188 (Colo.1990), was an example of vigorous prosecution of a lawyer much like the one in this problem. The lawyer reviewed a package of living trust forms for Taylor, a non-lawyer, knowing that Taylor planned to sell them to other lay people. For so assisting the unauthorized practice of law, the Court suspended the lawyer from practice for two years.

Matter of Pearce, 806 P.2d 21 (Mont.1990), involved a lawyer who ran a business selling prepackaged estate plans. Indeed, sometimes the clients dealt only with a salesperson and never met the lawyer. For thus threatening traditional forms of practice, the Court disbarred Mr. Pearce. Do you agree that such a severe sanction should have been imposed?

3. Should a licensed attorney who is a full-time employee of an insurance company be permitted to represent one of the company's insureds as counsel of record in an action brought by a third party for a claim covered by the terms of the policy?

a. Gardner v. North Carolina State Bar, 316 N.C. 285, 341 S.E.2d 517 (1986), said no. Nor may the attorney appear as counsel of record for the insured in the prosecution of a subrogation claim for property damage. North Carolina law (like the law of many states) bans corporations (states typically exclude professional legal corporations) from performing legal services for another. "Since a corporation cannot practice law directly, it cannot do so indirectly by employing lawyers to practice for it."[5]

---

3. See, e.g., Matter of New York County Lawyers' Association v. Dacey, 21 N.Y.2d 694, 287 N.Y.S.2d 422, 234 N.E.2d 459 (1967), reversing on the dissenting opinion at 28 A.D.2d 161, 171, 283 N.Y.S.2d 984, 996 (1967); State v. Winder, 42 A.D.2d 1039, 348 N.Y.S.2d 270 (1973).

4. Where the lay advisor has gone beyond writing books and has started giving specific, personalized legal advice, unauthorized practice has been found. E.g., People v. Divorce Associated & Publishing Limited, 95 Misc.2d 340, 407 N.Y.S.2d 142 (1978); Matter of Estate of Margow, 77 N.J. 316, 390 A.2d 591 (1978); Florida Bar v. Brower, 402 So.2d 1171 (Fla.1981).

5. An economic result of this prohibition of corporations practicing law is that it "can forestall attempts to form the capital structures necessary to make law practice a true consumer product for a mass market. It also prevents competition from banks, insurance companies, title insurance companies and other potential competitors.

b. In re Allstate Insurance Co., 722 S.W.2d 947 (Mo.1987) (en banc), however, went the other way. It specifically refused to follow *Gardner* and concluded that the insurance company may either hire independent lawyers or use its own employee-lawyers instead. "An insurer has a very substantial interest in litigation involving its insured, and is entitled to retain counsel of its own choosing to protect its interest." If the insurer can hire an independent contractor it can act through its employee. Any danger of conflict of interest is minimized because the insurance company uses its employee-lawyers "only when there is no question of coverage, and when the claim is within policy limits."

Do you agree? Should *Allstate* be seen as the wave of the future, or simply an aberrant decision?

4. Does the giving of legal advice by law students in a legal clinic constitute the unauthorized practice of law?

a. How about representation of the client in court? In People v. Perez, 82 Cal.App.3d 89, 147 Cal.Rptr. 34 (1978), a California Court of Appeals startled almost everyone by holding student representation to be improper unauthorized practice. The California Supreme Court reversed, 24 Cal.3d 133, 155 Cal.Rptr. 176, 594 P.2d 1 (1979), and later formally approved State Bar Rules Relating to Practical Training of Law Students.

b. Should a law clerk, not part of a student program, be permitted to appear in court on behalf of his or her employer? People v. Alexander, 53 Ill.App.2d 299, 202 N.E.2d 841 (1st Dist.1964), upheld the practice, but only for answering calendar calls.

5. Will Dowd's estate planning corporation violate the Rule 5.4(b) and DR 3–103 prohibition against forming "a partnership with a nonlawyer"?

a. Will the business involve Dowd in "dividing fees with a non-lawyer" under Rule 5.4(a) and DR 3–102? Does Dowd's package plan differ significantly from the operation of a bank trust department?

b. Will the attorney-client privilege be available when the client talks to non-lawyers in Dowd's company? Will it be available when the lawyer is doing work that non-lawyers are also doing? Is this a matter for concern?

c. May conflicts of interest be created by or inherent in such a situation? Can a lawyer be expected to give impartial advice on estate planning when one of his or her associates is an insurance agent?

d. What is the problem with forming a partnership with a non-lawyer? Could Dowd ethically hire the non-lawyers (accountants, insurance agents, money managers, business consultants, etc.) and make

The prohibition presented a momentary embarrassment when, for tax reasons, it made economic sense for a lawyers to practice in the corporate form. That was gotten around by obtaining state legislation permitting lawyers to form 'professional corporations.' " Charles W. Wolfram, Modern Legal Ethics 840 (1986).

them employees of the partnership? Could he ethically include his nonlawyer employees in a profit-sharing plan? See Rule 5.4(a)(3); DR 1–102(A)(3).

e. Does the fact it is unethical for Dowd to enter into a fee sharing agreement with a non-lawyer mean the agreement itself is unenforceable? Atkins v. Tinning, 865 S.W.2d 533 (Tex.App.1993), says no; the contract question and the ethical issue are distinct.

6. Another form of the above issues is raised when lawyers seek to take non-lawyers into their partnership to perform tasks helpful to their clients, e.g., lobbying or economic analysis.

a. District of Columbia Court of Appeals Rule 5.4 provides:

(b) A lawyer may practice law in a partnership or other form of organization in which a financial interest is held or managerial authority is exercised by an individual nonlawyer who performs professional services which assist the organization in providing legal services to clients, but only if:

(1) The partnership or organization has as its sole purpose providing legal services to clients;

(2) All persons having such managerial authority or holding a financial interest undertake to abide by these rules of professional conduct;

(3) The lawyers who have a financial interest or managerial authority in the partnership or organization undertake to be responsible for the nonlawyer participants to the same extent as if nonlawyer participants were lawyers under Rule 5.1;

(4) The foregoing conditions are set forth in writing.

Comment 5 to this Rule explains that nonlawyer participants "ought not to be confused with nonlawyer assistants under Rule 5.3. Nonlawyer participants are persons having managerial authority or financial interests in organizations which provide legal services."

Comment 8 adds that the Rule "does not permit an individual or entity to acquire all or any part of the ownership of a law practice organization for investment or other purposes" because "such an investor would not be an individual performing professional services within the law firm or other organization".

b. What do you think of this rule? Does it go too far in reducing restrictions on nonlawyer participation in law firm management? Not far enough? The North Dakota Supreme Court rejected a similar proposal in 1987.

c. Under this rule, if the District of Columbia disbars a lawyer who is a partner in a firm, may that lawyer continue to work on matters as a non-lawyer partner? For example, if Lawyer Alpha engages in lobbying activities, and later is disbarred for bribery of an official, may Alpha continue to perform his lobbying activities for clients as a nonlawyer partner?

7. Could Dowd overcome all ethical problems by having his law firm form a wholly-owned subsidiary corporation to deliver the ancillary, not-traditionally-legal services?

a. Such subsidiaries or law firm "affiliates" are becoming more common today as law firms have gone into the publishing business, financial consulting, and even forms of investment banking. Are these positive developments or do they constitute a threat to the independence and professionalism of lawyers? The debate as to whether law firms should be able to operate non-law entities has become more heated over the years.

b. Washington, D.C. firms initially founded about three-quarters of the first wave of law firm affiliates. A partner in Arnold & Porter explained a typical reason for creating the subsidiary: the firm wished to hire a departing government official who was not a lawyer; this official would be hired to engage in lobbying activities for clients but "[w]e would have to call him or her a paralegal."

c. An early draft of the Model Rules recommended that non-lawyers be permitted to form partnerships with lawyers if there would be no interference with the lawyers' independent professional judgment or with the lawyer-client relationship, client confidentiality would be maintained, and advising and fee arrangements did not violate the Rules governing lawyers.

During the ABA floor debates an ABA delegate asked: "Does this rule mean Sears & Roebuck will be able to open a law office?" Professor Geoffrey C. Hazard, Jr., the Reporter for the Model Rules, answered "Yes." The proposal failed. See, Jensen, Ethics Row Looms on [Law Firm] Affiliates, Nat'l L. J., Feb. 20, 1989, at 1, 28. Compare, e.g., Silas, Diversification, 72 A.B.A.J., May 1986, at 17, with A.B.A. Commission on Professionalism, "In the Spirit of Public Service:" A Blueprint for the Rekindling of Lawyer Professionalism 30–31 (Aug.1986).

d. The arguments in favor of such affiliates seem to be four-fold. First, they make the law firm more convenient for the client. When the client has a problem that requires the services of several professionals, as is often the case, it is beneficial and useful for the client be able to engage in one-stop shopping. Second, the law firm wishes to give the non-lawyer professionals the status and titles that they deserve. Third, these entities are perhaps not as constrained in the manner of calculating fees as lawyers may be. Fourth, having the affiliates may retain existing clients, bring in new clients, and thus offer new sources of revenue.

e. The arguments against creating such affiliates are both ethical and pragmatic. Ethically, a lawyer who advises a client in dealings with the lawyer's affiliate may not have the independent judgment needed to give sound advice, such as the advice to fire the affiliate. Also, such arrangements inevitably involve the lawyer in business transactions with the client, raising separate problems under Rule 1.8(a) and DR 5–104(A).

Pragmatically, law firms must be concerned, first, about the partners' being jointly and severally liable for the acts of the affiliates, ranging from simple negligence to dishonesty of the nonlawyers. When the affiliate is making large sums of money by brokering substantial transactions, the potential exposure to malpractice may look small by comparison, but liability can be enormous.

Second, there is a risk that the affiliate will expand the number of situations disqualifying the law firm, i.e., the affiliate may work on behalf of a client who has an interest that conflicts with a different client of the law firm.

Third, to the extent that law firms become one-stop shopping centers instead of dispensers of a unique service, there is a danger that lawyers will lose their power of self-regulation and that the state supreme courts, which usually claim an inherent power to regulate the practice of law, will lose that claim of authority. Finally, if a law firm is allowed to set up a non-lawyer affiliate, a non-lawyer entity might be allowed to set up a law firm subsidiary. The fear of becoming a Sears, Roebuck employee seems to haunt many lawyers.

8. Do you think that ancillary businesses owned by lawyers should be governed principally by Rule 1.8(a) and DR 5–104(A), or should lawyer-owned businesses properly be subject to a special rule?

a. Take a look at Model Rule 5.7 and its Comments. A similar Rule was adopted in 1992, repealed in 1993, and the present version was adopted in 1994.

b. What will constitute "law-related services" within the meaning of the rule? Why is "financial planning" a law-related service, for example? Is the test whether a service is one that some lawyers might offer to some clients? By that definition, is every service performed by a lawyer potentially law-related?

c. What is the significance of calling something "law-related"? Is a lawyer's title insurance business subject to different in-person solicitation rules than would govern sale of the usual insurance policy, for example? What is the rationale for holding lawyers to a more restrictive standard?

d. Is there any reason not to call every service a lawyer provides a legal service? Could a lawyer be guilty of legal malpractice for negligence in legislative lobbying? May a lawyer do environmental consulting for someone that could disadvantage another of the lawyer's clients without the consent of that other client?

e. Is there any ethical restriction on a lawyer's owning a business that is not ancillary to the practice of law? May two lawyers in a law partnership buy a restaurant, for example? May they take clients to dine there without the restaurant's becoming law-related?

9. Do you agree that most unauthorized practice rules are anticompetitive?

a. Look at the excerpt from the Morgan article set forth as a Reading to this Problem. If the rules are anticompetitive, are the economic costs due to the lessened competition justified by other considerations? [6]

b. Many other countries function quite well with virtually no rules governing the unauthorized practice of law. In France, for example, anyone—without any restrictions of citizenship, residency, or even training—can offer legal advice. Unregulated advisors include law departments of banks that offer below cost legal service in order to attract business, the law department of accounting firms, telephone services that offer legal advice, and so forth. Such unregulated advisors are not subject to any regulations, except that they may not hold themselves out to be a member of one of the regulated professions, such as a "conseil juridique" (legal advisor). The legal advisors are one of the regulated professions of law and can render any form of legal advice and appear before some lower courts. Only an "avocat" is allowed to appear before higher courts. The French Government is reexamining (and perhaps will liberalize even more) the regulation of the legal professions in light of the major European integration that began in 1992. See, Mission D'Etude Sur L'Europe et Les Professions Du Droit: Rapport (Juin 1989).

c. The Treaty of Rome, which created what is now the European Community that is moving toward to political, economic, and legal integration, seeks to remove obstacles to the free movement of capital, persons, and services among the member states. Under the Treaty, a qualified EC lawyer may provide legal services in another member state either by visiting on an occasional basis or by setting up a permanent office. He or she may provide this legal service using the qualifications of his or her original home ("home title"), or by obtaining additional qualifications, as an "integrated lawyer" from the place where he or she is setting up the permanent office. If the lawyer is using only home qualifications and is not an integrated lawyer, then the lawyer cannot undertake activities "specifically reserved to full members of the local legal profession." In the United Kingdom, activities specifically reserved to the local legal profession or an integrated lawyer are confined "to appearing in court on his own and to undertaking probate and convey-

---

6. See also Christensen, The Unauthorized Practice of Law: Do Good Fences Really Make Good Neighbors—or Even Good Sense?, 1980 A.B.F.Res.J. 159, 216:

"Ultimately, the legal profession's traditional unauthorized practice position rests upon either of two serious doubts—or perhaps on both. Lawyers either lack confidence in themselves to meet free and open competition, or they lack faith in the intelligence of the public and in the ability of citizens to determine their lives for themselves. Neither doubt is justified. If we lawyers are the splendid fellows that we claim to be—and, though the claim is immodest, it may even be at least partly true—then we have nothing to fear from open competition. And if the citizen is competent to do important things like govern himself, then surely he is capable of deciding from whom he will purchase legal services. The time has come to let the public choose."

ancing work." A lawyer from one country in the European Community relying on his or her home title while practicing in another country in the EC may give legal advice, "including advice in local law." Toulmin, Legal Practice in Europe, International Financial Law Review, August, 1989.

Compare DR 3–101(B) and Model Rule 5.5(a). Do we have something to learn from the new "United States of Europe"?[7]

10. Should it be the responsibility of the state disciplinary system to discipline lawyers for unauthorized practice?

See former ABA Standards for Lawyer Discipline and Disability Proceedings § 3.17 (1979). Proposed § 3.17—*not* adopted by the ABA House of Delegates—had said:

> "The functions of the agency should be limited to matters concerning lawyer discipline and disability. The agency should not perform other functions, for example, admitting lawyers to practice, prohibiting the unauthorized practice of law, rendering advisory ethics opinions or administering the client security fund."

The commentary to this proposed section noted that "[n]othing should be done which might subject the agency's responsibility to ensure compliance with the profession's high ethical standards to the accusation that it is a mere subterfuge for eliminating competitors."

Do you believe that the proposed commentary accurately describes the role of unauthorized practice rules?

READINGS

MORGAN,* THE EVOLVING CONCEPT OF PROFESSIONAL RESPONSIBILITY
90 Harv.L.Rev. 702, 707–712 (1977).**

Perhaps the clearest example of a Code standard which operates primarily for the benefit of lawyers is the prohibition of the "unauthorized practice of law" reinforced by Disciplinary Rule (DR) 3–101(A). Ostensibly designed to ensure that clients are served only by persons of

---

7. The United States may be moving closer to the European model. In response to foreign pressure, and the pressure of American lawyers who want to open access to legal markets abroad, the Court of Appeals of the State of New York has amended its rules for licensing foreign legal consultants. The new rules allow foreign lawyers to form partnerships with New York lawyers. *See,* In the Matter of the Amendments of the Rules of the Court of Appeals for the Licensing of Legal Consultants, 603 N.Y.S.2d 20–117 (Nov. 17, 1993, effective Dec. 8, 1993), amending 22 N.Y.C.R.R. Part 421.

* At the time this article was written the author was Professor of Law, University of Illinois.

** Copyright © 1977 by the Harvard Law Review Association.

integrity and competence,[15] the unauthorized practice rules have histori-cally been used to suppress competition by lay persons seeking to perform services at less cost than those provided by members of the Bar. While the variety of competitors confronted by the Bar has been broad, five or six major areas continue to be the primary source of controversy: debt collection,[16] preparation of real estate contracts,[17] sale of kits or forms for divorce[18] or probate,[19] tax counseling,[20] and appearance before specialized administrative agencies.[21] Certainly, lawyers may have some-thing to contribute in each of these fields; indeed, it can even be argued that most lawyers perform many tasks in these areas better than most nonlawyers. But the important question is not whether lawyers have something to contribute, but, rather, what justification there is for wholly excluding the alternative services which could be provided by nonlawyers.

The interest of individual clients clearly cannot justify the blanket prohibition on unauthorized practice. For client protection to be the basis for giving lawyers the *exclusive* right to perform given tasks, one would have to conclude that a client could not reasonably choose to have those tasks performed by a nonlawyer. Even the Code itself is unwilling to go so far. While the Code supports the necessity for lawyers by pointing to the "complex nature of our legal system" [22] and emphasizing the desirability of a "personal relationship" with someone having "a disciplined, analytic approach to legal problems, and a firm ethical commitment," [23] Ethical Consideration (EC) 3–7 concedes that a layman may choose to represent himself. * * *

15. EC 3–1. See generally Marden, The American Bar & Unauthorized Practice, 33 Unauth.Prac.News 1 (1967).

16. See, e.g., J.H. Marshall & Associates Inc. v. Burleson, 313 A.2d 587 (D.C.App. 1973); State ex rel. State Bar of Wis. v. Bonded Collections, Inc., 36 Wis.2d 643, 154 N.W.2d 250 (1967); In re Incorporated Consultants, 6 Ohio Misc. 143, 216 N.E.2d 912 (Com.Pl.1965).

17. See, e.g., Cape May County Bar Ass'n v. Ludlam, 45 N.J. 121, 211 A.2d 780 (1965); State Bar of Arizona v. Arizona Land Title & Trust Co., 90 Ariz. 76, 366 P.2d 1 (1961); Keyes Co. v. Dade County Bar Ass'n, 46 So.2d 605 (Fla.1950).

18. Compare Florida Bar v. Stupica, 300 So.2d 683 (Fla.1974), with Oregon State Bar v. Gilchrist, 272 Or. 552, 538 P.2d 913 (1975), and State v. Winder, 42 A.D.2d 1039, 348 N.Y.S.2d 270 (4th Dept. 1973).

19. Compare New York County Lawyers Ass'n v. Dacey, 21 N.Y.2d 694, 287 N.Y.S.2d 422, 234 N.E.2d 459 (1967), with Palmer v. Unauthorized Practice Com. of State Bar, 438 S.W.2d 374 (Tex.Civ.App.1969). See also National Conference of Lawyers &

C.P.A.s, Statement of Principles in Estate Planning, 40 Unauth.Prac.News 47 (1976).

20. See, e.g., Matter of Bereu, 273 App. Div. 524, 78 N.Y.S.2d 209 (1st Dept. 1948); Lowell Bar Ass'n v. Loeb, 315 Mass. 176, 52 N.E.2d 27 (1943); New York State Bar Ass'n, Unlawful Practice of Law Committee Advisory Opinion No. 28 (1975), reprinted at 40 Unauth.Prac.News 59 (1976).

21. In Sperry v. Florida ex rel. Florida Bar, 373 U.S. 379, 83 S.Ct. 1322, 10 L.Ed.2d 428 (1963), the Supreme Court held that the Patent Office could authorize the giving of patent advice and practice before the agency by persons not licensed to practice law in any state. State courts have been more restrictive as regards practice before state agencies. See, e.g., State ex rel. State Bar of Wis. v. Keller, 21 Wis.2d 100, 123 N.W.2d 905 (1963); Denver Bar Ass'n v. Public Utilities Comm'n, 154 Colo. 273, 391 P.2d 467 (1964); New York State Bar Ass'n, Unlawful Practice of Law Com-mittee Advisory Opinion No. 27 (1975), re-printed at 40 Unauth.Prac. News 52 (1976).

22. EC 3–1.

23. EC 3–2.

Once one agrees that a layman can choose self-representation, it becomes difficult to argue that he should be unable to seek counsel on legal issues from a nonlawyer.[24] A lawyer occupies many roles, including those of personal advisor, guardian, informal mediator, negotiator and litigator. In the specific fields of controversy about unauthorized practice mentioned earlier, it is clear that lawyers are overtrained for many required activities. In each role and each field, there are problems of correspondence, document management and psychological judgment as to which lay experience may be as important as intellectual training. In such situations, it seems entirely reasonable to expect that many lay persons would perform "legal services" at a level of quality equal to or exceeding that of many lawyers.

Moreover, even in areas where—because of the need to apply several statutes to a complicated set of facts, for example—the lawyer might provide more sophisticated counsel, a client might still reasonably seek lay assistance. If a lawyer would provide forty or fifty per cent better service than a lay person, for example, it would nonetheless be reasonable for the client to prefer the lay advisor's counsel if the lawyer's fee was fifty or sixty per cent higher. Even conceding that professional services are hard to evaluate and thus that qualitative distinctions between types of advisors would be hard for a lay client to make, the choices would not be significantly different from the ones the client now has to make among lawyers of widely differing ability and experience.[25]

While it is impossible to predict accurately the actual prices competitors of lawyers could or would charge if the limits on unauthorized practice were broken down, it is reasonable to suppose that the savings

---

24. The Supreme Court has held that where a state does not provide licensed legal advisors to assist inmates in the preparation of petitions for post-conviction relief, it may not deprive prisoners of the legal advice and assistance of fellow inmates. Johnson v. Avery, 393 U.S. 483, 89 S.Ct. 747, 21 L.Ed.2d 718 (1969). In Procunier v. Martinez, 416 U.S. 396, 94 S.Ct. 1800, 40 L.Ed.2d 224 (1974) [overruled in part, on other grounds, Thornburgh v. Abbott, 490 U.S. 401, 109 S.Ct. 1874, 104 L.Ed.2d 459 (1989)], the Court similarly struck down a prison regulation limiting attorneys' use of lay and law student investigators. However, the assertion that all litigants in federal court have a general constitutional right to be represented by lay persons has recently been rejected in a series of suits consolidated as Turner v. American Bar Ass'n, 407 F.Supp. 451 (N.D.Tex. 1975), affirmed sub nom., Pilla v. American Bar Ass'n, 542 F.2d 56 (8th Cir.1976).

25. One sometimes hears it argued that requiring a lawyer serves the client's interest by guaranteeing that someone would be subject to professional discipline if the client were victimized. See ABA Comm. on Professional Ethics, Opinions, No. 316 (1967). See generally EC 3–6. However, one way to assess the purpose of a given Code provision is to ask whether some other approach could have served the client's interest equally well, albeit at the expense of the lawyers' interests. In the case of the unauthorized practice rule, for example, the law could provide that all persons purporting to act for others in law-related fields will be held to the same standard of demonstrated competence and integrity as attorneys. The requirement would be enforced, not by a one-time licensing examination or bar association grievance committee, but through appropriate suits for malpractice. Indeed, this is the result the courts have already reached in cases where lay persons have purported to give legal advice and have later been sued for malpractice. See, e.g., Latson v. Eaton, 341 P.2d 247 (Okl. 1959); Biakanja v. Irving, 49 Cal.2d 647, 320 P.2d 16 (1958); cf. Monahan v. Devinny, 223 App.Div. 547, 229 N.Y.S. 60 (3d Dept. 1928) (practicing medicine without a license).

to clients would be significant. Part of the savings would come in the form of lower charges for routine services. The time of a lawyer is valuable, both because of high training costs and the demand for lawyer services to which the unauthorized practice rules contribute. Even the time of a paralegal assistant, billed by an attorney, can be inflated by this artificial scarcity.[26] A more competitive market for law-related services would almost inevitably bring down fees. At the same time, relaxation of the unauthorized practice rules might allow society to reallocate some of the resources currently being directed towards legal education. Over 100,000 law students have been enrolled in ABA-approved law schools each year since 1972.[27] If one conservatively projects the annual cost of each student, including income foregone, at $10,000 [28] that is an annual national investment of over $1,000,000,000 in legal training. Of course a large part of this cost would be incurred even without the rules as to unauthorized practice, since many people will want legal training even if they cannot have a monopoly of certain work. Even so, to the extent that individuals who wish to represent tenants in disputes with landlords or to serve as consumer credit advisors or real estate developers could do so without full legal training in the traditional sense, the national investment might be substantially decreased without a corresponding loss in the social benefits obtained.

However, while the unauthorized practice rules clearly *impose* social and individual costs, an argument can be made that leaving the limited area of judicial dispute resolution to lawyers might tend to reduce the total cost of resolving such disputes. First, if lawyers' training could be counted upon to allow cases in which lawyers appear to be resolved more quickly than cases presented by lay advocates, then total costs of litigation could be reduced. For example, assume that lay advocates acting for each side would charge $200 per day and take eight days to try a case. Assume lawyers would charge each side $400 per day but try the case in five days. Assume further that court time costs $1,000 per day, the whole of which is assumed by the public. All else equal, parties acting in their own interest would prefer lay advocates because they would charge their clients $1,600 each, compared to $2,000 each for

---

26. In theory, of course, this should not be so. If the number of paralegal personnel were infinitely expandable and clients had perfect information, the effect on prices to consumers of legal services would be the same as a comparable expansion in the number of lawyers. The ability of attorneys to inflate the price of paralegal services is greatly affected by restrictions on advertising and limitations on appearances in court by persons not admitted to the bar.

27. White, Legal Education: A Time of Change, 62 A.B.A.J. 355, 356 (1976). In 1975, the figure was 116,991, and while the rate of increase in law school attendance is declining, the absolute number of students seems destined to remain high.

28. This calculation is obviously hard to make with precision. A good attempt to do so is Ahart, Economic Observations on the Decision to Attend Law School, 27 J. Legal Educ. 93, 99 (1975). Mr. Ahart estimates the cost to students of tuition, books and transportation at between $500 and $3,000 per year. Salary foregone is estimated at $900 per month, or about $8,000 per nine month year. Further, since even schools charging high tuition often rely on endowment income to meet some operating costs, the real cost of educating a law student is understated by Mr. Ahart's figures.

lawyers. However, the total cost, including court time, of the lay advocates' trial would be $11,200 and the lawyers' $9,000. In such a case, unauthorized practice rules would require litigants to go against their personal interests and adopt the course involving the lower total cost.

Second, it might be that attorneys can resolve a great many matters without trial because the field of attorneys is sufficiently small that two attorneys familiar with one another can often quickly reach a fair settlement of a case. These cost-reducing benefits of having a lawyer's representation, however, might well be tied to *both* sides being so represented: if either side was represented by a nonlawyer, the probability of a speedy, informal resolution would be reduced. Without the unauthorized practice rules, a litigant could not be sure that his opponent would in fact hire a lawyer, and thus his own incentive to do so would be lessened. The result might well be more litigation and less settlement, at a greater cost to all.

Whether these theoretical public benefits from unauthorized practice rules are ever realized would require much more detailed factual analysis,[29] although the rest of the Code seems to tolerate or require so much complexity and delay in litigation that any of the benefits produced would likely be largely eroded. But in any event, the scope of the "practice of law" which would be necessary to achieve such benefits would be small indeed compared to the broad and ambiguous definition currently adopted by the Code. "Functionally," the Code announces, "the practice of law relates to the rendition of services for others that call for the professional judgment of a lawyer." An attorney must be consulted whenever "professional legal judgment is required." To the bewildered reader looking for guidance, the Code suggests only that the "essence" of professional legal judgment is the "educated ability to relate the general body and philosophy of law to a specific legal problem."[30] Indeed, not only does this latter formulation fail to accommodate the public interests involved, but the ambiguity itself creates a "chilling effect" on potential competition because of the penalties associated with overstepping the lines.[31] Because the ambiguity tends to expand the scope of the lawyers' monopoly, it seems fair to view it as further confirmation of the fact that the prohibition of unauthorized practice is primarily for the benefit of lawyers.

---

29. Some suggestions for areas of fruitful research are contained in Ehrlich & Schwartz, Reducing the Costs of Legal Services: Possible Approaches by the Federal Government, A Report to the Subcommittee on Representation of Citizen Interests, U.S. Senate Committee on the Judiciary, 93d Cong., 2d Sess. (1974).

30. EC 3–5.

31. In some states, the unauthorized practice of law is a misdemeanor, e.g., West's Ann.Cal.Bus. & Prof.Code § 6126; in some others it is a criminal contempt of court, e.g., Ill.—S.H.A. ch. 13, § 1; N.Y.—McKinney's Judiciary Law § 750(B).

SELECTED BIBLIOGRAPHY ON ISSUES IN CHAPTER VII

Problem 31

L. Andrews, Birth of a Salesman: Lawyer Advertising and Solicitation (1980).

Brown, The Quiet Revolution in the American Law Profession: Remarks Before the Commission on Professionalism of the American Bar Association, 14 Fordham Urban L.J. 855 (1986).

DeGraw & Burton, Lawyer Discipline and "Disclosure Advertising": Towards a New Ethos, 72 N.Car.L.Rev. 351 (1994).

Devine, Letting the Market Control Advertising by Lawyers: A Suggested Remedy for the Misled Client, 31 Buffalo L.Rev. 351 (1982).

Hazard, Pearce & Stempel, Why Lawyers Should Be Allowed to Advertise: A Market Analysis of Legal Services, 58 N.Y.U.L.Rev. 1084 (1983).

Makar, Advertising Legal Services: The Case for Quality and Self-laudatory Claims, 37 University of Florida L.Rev. 969 (1985).

McChesney, Commercial Speech in the Professions: The Supreme Court's Unanswered Questions and Questionable Answers, 134 U.Pa. L.Rev. 45 (1985).

Muris & McChesney, Advertising and the Price and Quality of Legal Services: The Case for Legal Clinics, 1979 A.B.F. Research J. 179.

Note, Advertising Legal Services, The Case for Quality and Self–Laudatory Claims, 37 U.Fla.L.Rev. 969 (1985).

Note, Advertising, Solicitation and the Profession's Duty to Make Legal Counsel Available, 81 Yale L.J. 1181 (1972).

Rotunda, The Commercial Speech Doctrine in the Supreme Court, 1976 U.Ill.L. Forum 1080.

Rotunda, The First Amendment Now Protects Commercial Speech, 10 The Center Magazine: A Publication of the Center for the Study of Democratic Institutions 32 (May/June 1977).

Singsen, Competition in Personal Legal Services, 2 Georgetown Journal of Legal Ethics 21 (1988).

Problem 32

American Bar Association, Lawyers' Economic Problems and Some Bar Association Solutions (1959).

Daly, In–Person Solicitation by Public Interest Law Firms: A Look at the A.B.A. Code Provisions in Light of Primus and Ohralik, 49 Geo. Wash.L.Rev. 309 (1981).

Drecksel, Targeted, Direct-mail Solicitation by Lawyers: How Can States Protect Their Residents From Overreaching and Deceptive Solicitation?, 1989 Utah L.Rev. 521 (1989).

Freedman, Access to the Legal System: The Professional Responsibility to Chase Ambulances, in M.H. Freedman, Lawyers' Ethics in an Adversary System (1975).

Graham, Professional Responsibility—an Economic Analysis of Shapero v. Kentucky Bar Association: Is There Any Possibility of Overreaching in a Targeted, Direct Mail Solicitation?, 14 Journal of Corporation Law 809 (1989).

Mauro, Constitutional Regulation of "Targeted Direct–Mail Solicitation" by Attorneys After Shapero—a Proposed Rule of Conduct, 34 Villanova L.Rev. 281 (1989).

Note, Benign Solicitation of Clients by Attorneys, 54 Wash.L.Rev. 671 (1979).

Pulaski, In–Person Solicitation and the First Amendment: Was Ohralik Wrongly Decided, 1979 Ariz.St.L.J. 23.

Steele, Ethical Considerations for Catastrophe Litigators, 55 Journal of Air Law and Commerce 123 (1989).

Whitman, Direct Mail Advertising by Attorneys, 20 New Mexico L.Rev. 87 (1990).

Problem 33

R. Zehnle, Specialization in the Legal Profession (1975).

Problem 34

Arndt & Bull, The Impact of the Family and Medical Leave Act of 1993 on the Legal Profession, 3 UCLA Women's L.J. 77 (1993).

Carson, Under New Mismanagement: The Problem of Non–Lawyer Equity Partnership in Law Firms, 7 Geo.J. Legal Ethics 593 (1994).

Draper, Enforcing Lawyers' Covenants Not to Compete, 69 Washington L.Rev. 161 (1994).

Ethical Dilemmas in a Professional Business; The Case of the Successful, Obnoxious, Alcoholic Lateral Partner, and Other People Problems at Cruel & Short, 11 American Lawyer, pp. S30–42 (1989).

Franck, MRPC 5.1: Responsibilities of Partners and Other Supervisory Lawyers, 67 Michigan Bar J. 1086 (1988).

Galanter & Palay, The Many Futures of the Big Law Firm, 45 S.Carolina L. Rev. 905 (1994).

Gillers, Protecting Lawyers Who Just Say No, 5 Georgia St. U. L. Rev. 1 (1988).

Gross, Ethical Problems of Law Firm Associates, 26 William and Mary L.Rev. 259 (1985).

Heinz, Ethics and the Megafirm—III, 16 Loyola University of Chicago L.J. 496 (1985).

R. Hillman, Law Firm Breakups: The Law and Ethics of Grabbing and Leaving (1990).

Hillman, Law Firms and Their Partners: The Law and Ethics of Grabbing and Leaving, 67 Texas L.Rev. 1 (1988).

Hillman, The Law Firm as Jurassic Park: Comments on Howard v. Babcock, 27 U.C.Davis L.Rev. 533 (1994).

Hurley, In Search of the New Paradigm: Total Quality Management in the Law Firm—A Case Study, 43 Emory L.J. 521 (1994).

Jarvis, A Question of Ethics: The "Good" Associate's Duty to Report a "Bad" Partner, 62 Florida Bar J. 61 (1988).

Kalish, Covenants Not to Compete and the Legal Profession, 29 St. Louis U.L.J. 423 (1985).

Lambert, An Academic Visit to the Modern Law Firm: Considering a Theory of Promotion–Driven Growth, 90 Michigan L.Rev. 1719 (1992).

Levinson, Book Review of Ewing, "Do It My Way or You're Fired," 36 Vand.L.Rev. 847 (1983).

Levinson, Independent Law Firms that Practice Law Only: Society's Need, the Legal Profession's Responsibility, 51 Ohio St. L. J. 229 (1990).

Levinson, To a Young Lawyer: Thoughts on Disobedience, 50 Missouri L.Rev. 483 (1985).

McKim, The Lawyer Track: The Case for Humanizing the Career Within a Large Firm, 55 Ohio St.L.J. 167 (1994).

Miller, Preventing Misconduct By Promoting the Ethics of Attorneys' Supervisory Duties, 70 Notre Dame L.Rev. 259 (1994).

Mindes, Proliferation, Specialization and Certification: The Splitting of the Bar, 11 U.Toledo L.Rev. 273 (1980).

Minkus, Sale of a Law Practice: Toward a Professionally Responsible Approach, 12 Golden Gate U.L.Rev. 353 (1982).

Nelson, The Changing Structure of Opportunity: Recruitment and Careers in Large Law Firms, 1983 A.B.F. Research J. 109.

Note, Regulating Multistate Law Firms, 32 Stan.L.Rev. 1211 (1980).

Note, Unionization of Law Firms, 46 Fordham L.Rev. 1008 (1978).

Note, Winding Up Dissolved Law Partnerships: The No–Compensation Rule and Client Choice, 73 Calif.L.Rev. 1597 (1985).

Paas, Professional Corporations and Attorney–Shareholders: The Decline of Limited Liability, 11 Journal of Corporation Law 371 (1986).

Quick, Ethical Rules Prohibiting Discrimination by Lawyers: The Legal Profession's Response to Discrimination on the Rise, 7 Notre Dame Journal of Law, Ethics & Public Policy 5 (1993).

Schneyer, Policymaking and the Perils of Professionalism: The ABA's Ancillary Business Debate as a Case Study, 35 Arizona L.Rev. 363 (1993).

Schoenwald, Model Rule 1.17 and the Ethical Sale of Law Practices: A Critical Analysis, 7 Georgetown J.Legal Ethics 395 (1993).

Symposium On the Law Firm as a Social Institution, 37 Stanford L.Rev. 271 (1985).

Tate, Lawyer Ethics and the Corporate Employee: Is the Employee Owed More Protection Than the Model Rules Provide?, 23 Indiana L. Rev. 1 (1990).

Terry, Ethical Pitfalls and Malpractice Consequences of Law Firm Breakups, 61 Temple L. Rev. 1055 (1988).

Twitchell, The Ethical Dilemmas of Lawyers on Teams, 72 Minnesota L.Rev. 697 (1988).

Wilbur, Wrongful Discharge of Attorneys: A Cause of Action to Further Professional Responsibility, 92 Dickinson L.Rev. 777 (1988).

<h3 style="text-align:center">Problem 35</h3>

Abel, Law Without Politics: Legal Aid Under Advanced Capitalism, 32 U.C.L.A.L.Rev. 474 (1985).

Abrogast, Revitalizing Public Interest Lawyering in the 1990s: The Story of One Effort to Address the Problem of Homelessness, 34 Howard L.J. 91 (1991).

Brakel, Fee Legal Services for the Poor–Staffed Office Versus Judicare; The Client's Evaluation, 1973 Wis.L.Rev. 532.

Breger, Disqualification for Conflicts of Interest and the Legal Aid Attorney, 62 B.U.L.Rev. 1115 (1982).

Bretz, Why Mandatory Pro Bono is a Bad Idea, 3 Georgetown Journal of Legal Ethics 623 (1990).

L. Brickman & D. Eakeley, A Lawyer at a Price People Can Afford (1974).

Brickman, Of Arterial Passageways Through the Legal Process: The Right of Universal Access to Courts and Lawyering Services, 48 N.Y.U.L.Rev. 595 (1973).

Buchanan & Trubek, Resistances and Possibilities: A Critical and Practical Look at Public Interest Lawyering, 19 N.Y.U. Rev.L. & Social Change 687 (1992).

Cahn & Cahn, The War on Poverty: A Civilian Perspective, 73 Yale L.J. 1317 (1964).

Cappelletti & Garth, Access to Justice: The Newest Wave in the World–Wide Movement to Make Rights Effective, 27 Buffalo L.Rev. 181 (1978).

Cappelletti, Garth & Trocker, Access to Justice: Variations and Continuity of a World–Wide Movement, 46 Rabels Zeitschrift 664 (1982).

E. Cheatham, A Lawyer When Needed (1963).

Christensen, The Lawyer's Pro Bono Publico Responsibility, 1981 A.B.F. Research J. 1 (1981).

Christensen, Regulating Group Legal Services: Who Is Being Protected— Against What—and Why?, 11 Ariz.L.Rev. 229 (1969).

Coombs, Your Money or Your Life: A Modest Proposal for Mandatory Pro Bono Services, 3 Boston U.Pub.Interest L.J. 215 (1993).

Cramton, Delivery of Legal Services to Ordinary Americans, 44 Case Western Res.L.Rev. 531 (1994).

Ehrlich, Giving Low Income Americans Minimum Access to legal Services, 64 A.B.A.J. 696 (1978).

Eldred & Schoenherr, The Lawyer's Duty of Public Service: More than Charity?, 96 W. Virginia L.Rev. 367 (1993–94).

Frankel, Proposal: A National Legal Service, 45 S. Carolina L. Rev. 887 (1994).

Goldberger, The Right to Counsel in Political Cases: The Bar's Failure, 43 Law & Contemp.Prob. 321 (1979).

Hill & Calvocoressi, The Corporate Counsel and Pro Bono Service, 42 The Business Lawyer 675 (1987).

Levinson, Making Society's Legal System Accessible to Society: The Lawyer's Role and Its Implications, 41 Vanderbilt L.Rev. 789 (1988).

Luban, The Noblesse Oblige Tradition in the Practice of Law, 41 Vanderbilt L.Rev. 717 (1988).

F.R. Marks, K. Leswing, & B.A. Fortinsky, The Lawyer, The Public and Professional Responsibility (1972).

Note, In Defense of an Embattled Mode of Advocacy: An Analysis and Justification of Public Interest Practice, 90 Yale L.J. 1436 (1981).

Note, Structuring the Public Service Efforts of Private Law Firms, 84 Harv.L.Rev. 410 (1970).

W. Pfenningstorf, Legal Expense Insurance: The European Experience in Financing Legal Services (1976).

Rosenfeld, Mandatory Pro Bono: Historical and Constitutional Perspectives, 2 Cardozo L.Rev. 255 (1981).

Schulhofer & Friedman, Rethinking Indigent Defense: Promoting Effective Representation Through Consumer Sovereignty and Freedom of Choice for All Criminal Defendants, 31 Amer.Crim.L.Rev. 73 (1993).

Shapiro, The Enigma of the Lawyer's Duty to Serve, 55 N.Y.U.L.Rev. 735 (1980).

Smith, A Mandatory Pro Bono Service Standard—Its Time Has Come, 35 University of Miami L.Rev. 727 (1981).

Smith, The Limits of Compulsory Professionalism: How the Unified Bar Harms the Legal Profession, 22 Florida State U.L.Rev. 35 (1994).

Spencer, Mandatory Public Service for Attorneys: A Proposal for the Future, 2 Southwestern U.L.Rev. 493 (1981).

Symposium, The Practice of Law in the Public Interest, 13 Ariz.L.Rev. 797 (1971).

Torres & Stansky, In Support of a Mandatory Public Service Obligation, 29 Emory L.J. 997 (1980).

Tudzin, Pro Bono Work: Should it be Mandatory or Voluntary?, 12 Journal of the Legal Profession 103 (1987).

Uelmen, Converting Retained Lawyers Into Appointed Lawyers: The Ethical and Tactical Implications, 27 Santa Clara L.Rev. 1 (1987).

Problem 36

Bell, Serving Two Masters: Integration Ideals and Clients Interests in School Desegregation Litigation, 85 Yale L.J. 470 (1976).

Dawson, Lawyers and Involuntary Clients: Attorney Fees from Funds, 87 Harv.L.Rev. 1597 (1974).

Ellmann, Client–Centeredness Multiplied: Individual Autonomy and Collective Mobilization in Public Interest Lawyers Representation of Groups, 78 Virginia L.Rev. 1103 (1992).

Gabaldon, Free Riders and the Greedy Gadfly: Examining Aspects of Shareholder Litigation as an Exercise in Integrating Ethical Regulation and Laws of General Applicability, 73 Minnesota Law Rev. 425 (1988).

Hylton, Fee Shifting and Incentives to Comply With the Law, 46 Vanderbilt L.Rev. 1069 (1993).

Krent, Explaining One–Way Fee Shifting, 79 Va.L.Rev. 2039 (1993).

Lynk, The Courts and the Plaintiffs' Bar: Awarding the Attorney's Fee in Class–Action Litigation, 23 J.Legal Studies 185 (1994).

Macey & Miller, The Plaintiffs' Attorney's Role in Class Action and Derivative Litigation, 58 U.Chi.L.Rev. 1 (1991).

Nickles & Adams, Tracing Proceeds to Attorneys' Pockets (and the Dilemma of Paying for Bankruptcy), 78 Minnesota L.Rev. 1079 (1994).

Rabin, Lawyers for Social Change: Perspectives on Public Interest Law, 28 Stan.L.Rev. 207 (1976).

Rhode, Class Conflicts in Class Actions, 34 Stan.L.Rev. 1183 (1982).

Silver, Unloading the Lodestar: Toward a New Fee Award Procedure, 70 Texas L.Rev. 865 (1992).

Sisk, A Primer on Awards of Attorney's Fees Against the Federal Government, 25 Ariz.St. L.J. 733 (1993).

Symposium, Court–Awarded Attorneys' Fees, 14 N.Y.U.Rev. Law & Social Change 473 (1986).

Underwood, Legal Ethics and Class Actions: Problems, Tactics and Judicial Responses, 71 Kentucky L.J. 787 (1983).

Weisbrod, Ed., Public Interest Law: An Economic and Institutional Analysis (1978).

Problem 37

Bartosic & Bernstein, Group Legal Services as a Fringe Benefit: Lawyers for Forgotten Clients Through Collective Bargaining, 59 Va.L.Rev. 410 (1973).

B. Christensen, Lawyers for People of Moderate Means (1970).

Cole & Greenberger, Staff Attorneys vs. Judicare: A Cost Analysis, 50 J. Urban L. 705 (1973).

Getman, Critique of the Report of the Shreveport Experiment, 3 J. Legal Studies 487 (1974).

Hallauer, Shreveport Experiment in Prepaid Legal Services, 2 J. Legal Studies 223 (1973).

F.R. Marks, R.P. Hallauer & R.R. Clifton, The Shreveport Plan: An Experiment in the Delivery of Legal Services (1974).

Meeks, Antitrust Aspects of Prepaid Legal Services Plans, 1976 A.B.F. Research J. 855.

Moss, Prepaid Plans Face Hurdles (includes a related glossary), 74 A.B.A.J. 38 (1988).

Stolz, Insurance for Legal Services: A Preliminary Study of Feasibility, 35 U.Chi.L.Rev. 417 (1968).

Zander, Judicare or Staff? A British View, 64 A.B.A.J. 1436 (1978).

Problem 38

Andrews, Nonlawyers in the Business of Law: Does the One Who Has the Gold Really Make the Rules?, 40 Hastings L.J. 577 (1989).

Brakel & Loh, Regulating the Multistate Practice of Law, 50 Wash.L.Rev. 699 (1975).

Christensen, The Unauthorized Practice of Law: Do Good Fences Really Make Good Neighbors—Or Even Good Sense, 1980 A.B.F. Research J. 159.

Gilbert & Lempert, The Nonlawyer Partner: Moderate Proposals Deserve a Chance, 2 Georgetown Journal of Legal Ethics 383 (1988).

Haskell, Issues in Paralegalism: Education, Certification, Licensing, Unauthorized Practice, 15 Ga.L.Rev. 631 (1981).

Lytton, Crossing State Lines to Practice Law: The Poverty Lawyer and Interstate Practice, 20 Am.U.L.Rev. 7 (1970).

Michelman, Guiding the Invisible Hand: The Consumer Protection Function of Unauthorized Practice Regulation, 12 Pepperdine L.Rev. 1 (1984).

Nielsen, Legalizing Nonlawyer Proprietorship in the Legal Clinic Industry: Reform in the Public Interest, 9 Hofstra L.Rev. 625 (1981).

Note, Legal Paraprofessionals and Unauthorized Practice, 8 Harv.Civ.Rts.—Civ.Lib.L.Rev. 104 (1973).

Note, Trust Companies and the Practice of Law, 68 U.Pennsylvania L.Rev. 356 (1920).

Note, The Unauthorized Practice of Law and Pro Se Divorces: An Empirical Analysis, 86 Yale L.J. 104 (1976).

Rhode, Policing the Professional Monopoly: A Constitutional and Empirical Analysis of Unauthorized Practice Prohibitions, 34 Stanford L.Rev. 1 (1981).

Chapter VIII

THE ETHICAL CONDUCT OF JUDGES

Not all lawyers will be judges. But almost all lawyers will appear before them and public and professional confidence in the integrity of the judiciary is close to the heart of the respect for law. Judicial ethics thus is of central importance to any lawyer, whether or not he or she aspires to be on the bench.

By this time it should be clear to you that ethical standards do not draw simplistic lines between honest persons and crooks. The Model Code of Judicial Conduct is no exception. Indeed many of its principles are based heavily on an important but amorphous concern about the "appearance of impropriety."

As you work through these materials, then, ask yourself questions such as:

a. Which of the principles of judicial ethics are designed to help assure "correct" or at least disinterested decisions?

b. Which principles are primarily designed to prevent judges from abusing the unusual influence they have over lawyers and in the community?

c. To what extent would some of the current Code be unnecessary if judges were appointed everywhere and not elected?

d. How do issues of judicial misconduct reach official attention and what is the duty of lawyers in that process?

e. Are any aspects of the Code unnecessarily restrictive on judges? Might any tend to discourage able people from seeking judicial office?

PROBLEM 39

Financial Grounds for Disqualification

Harold Baxter and Martin Anderson met in law school and have been good friends ever since. Baxter has now become a state trial judge and Anderson practices in the same city. Recently, Baxter sought to buy a new house, but the required down payment was higher than he had expected. Anderson, who was attorney for the bank from which Baxter planned to borrow, personally lent Baxter $5,000 evidenced by a demand note that Anderson assured Baxter would not be "called under any conditions I can foresee." Judge Baxter then got his mortgage from the bank.

Anderson is now representing the same bank, which is the plaintiff in a hotly-contested case that has been assigned to Judge Baxter. The case involves a close question of lien priorities and both sides expect the case to go to the state supreme court. Judge Baxter orally informed defense counsel about the loans in an early pre–trial conference and asked, "Do you have any problems with my presiding in this case?" Defense counsel, who frequently appears before Judge Baxter, replied, "No, sir."

Judge Baxter's niece, Marilyn, is 19 and lives with the Baxters while going to college. She has some money of her own that she has invested. She owns 10 shares, a ¹⁄₁₀₀,₀₀₀ interest, in the insurance company that is defendant in the lien priorities case before Judge Baxter. The Judge does not know of her interest. "I don't ask my relatives about their business dealings nor tell them about mine," he says.

Judge Baxter's daughter is a partner doing federal tax work in a local law firm. Another partner in the firm will represent the defendant in a personal injury suit scheduled to be tried before Judge Baxter. Judge Baxter has taken no steps either to recuse himself from the matter or to determine whether either party believes he should do so.

QUESTIONS

1. Was it improper for Anderson to lend money to Judge Baxter? Was it improper for Baxter to accept the loan?

a. Look at Model Rules 3.5(a) and 8.4(f) and Model Code DR 7–110(A). Unfortunately, loans and gifts to judges are more than hypothetical.

In re Corboy, 124 Ill.2d 29, 124 Ill.Dec. 6, 528 N.E.2d 694 (1988)(per curiam), involved six lawyers who gave checks for $1000 each to a state judge. Each of the lawyers testified they considered the checks to be a gift or loan to the judge's mother to pay the mother's hospital bills. The checks were deposited in the judge's checking account. The funds were not used to pay the hospital bills, which were covered by insurance. The Court rejected the argument that the moneys given to the judge were "ordinary social hospitality" under what is now Canon 4D(5)(c) of the ABA Model Code of Judicial Conduct (1990). The transactions were "a far cry from the social dinners, gratuitous rides, birthday recognitions and gifts of books or flowers, which might be genuine instances of social hospitality * * *." Surprisingly, the Court refused to censure any of the attorneys (including prominent lawyers such as Philip Corboy and William James Harte) because "They acted without the guidance of precedent or settled opinion, and there was, apparently, considerable belief among members of the bar that they acted properly." Do you agree?

In re Alexander, 585 N.E.2d 70 (Ill.1991), involved a Chicago lawyer who had grown up in the same neighborhood with a Judge but did not practice before him. The lawyer apparently got a call from the judge who said he badly needed money to pay his condominium fees, so the lawyer loaned the judge $11,000. That in itself might arguably not have raised questions, but the judge then appointed the lawyer a guardian ad litem in a case and awarded him a $1355 fee. The apparent quid pro quo led to the lawyer's 6 month suspension from practice.

In Lisi v. Several Attorneys, 596 A.2d 313 (R.I.1991), over twenty-one lawyers received calls from a judge at various times, all saying that he desperately needed money. Some of the lawyers had appeared before the judge in Family Court but several had not. All lent him the money he requested. There were no reported quid pro quos but some lawyers were in a position to have received favorable treatment. The judge resigned; four of the lawyers were suspended for a year and seventeen received public reprimands.

b. Are similar problems presented if Judge Baxter got his home mortgage from a financial institution that may regularly appear before him? Look generally at Canon 4D of the ABA Model Code of Judicial Conduct, and particularly at Canon 4D(5)(e) & (f). Do you agree that borrowing from a bank should be treated differently from borrowing from an attorney? Why?

2. What interests give a judge a financial interest in the subject matter of litigation over which the judge is presiding?

a. Look at Canon 3E(1)(c) and the definition of "economic interest" in the Terminology section of the ABA Model Code of Judicial Conduct (1990). By contrast, in the 1972 version of the ABA Model Code of Judicial Conduct, "financial interest" was defined as any interest "however small". Which version do you prefer?

Should a judge be disqualified from hearing a case involving I.B.M. if he or she owns just one share of I.B.M. stock? Will determining when an interest is "de minimis" intrude on the privacy of the judge? What may seem like a large amount to one judge may be de minimis to a very rich judge, and the Reporter's Notes to the 1972 Judicial Code indicate that for that reason, the ABA in 1972 adopted an absolute prohibition that it thought would be mitigated by the waiver provisions of Canon 3F, discussed below.[1]

---

1. Notice that questions as to disqualification of a federal judge are governed by 28 U.S.C.A. §§ 144, 455, also reprinted in the Standards Supplement. In re Virginia Electric & Power Co., 539 F.2d 357 (4th Cir.1976), extensively analyzes both 28 U.S.C.A. § 455 and former Canon 3C (now Canon 3E). The Court of Appeals concluded that a Federal District Judge was not disqualified from hearing a damage suit filed by the public utility of which he was a ratepayer. The judge was held to have no financial (i.e. "ownership") * * * interest under former Canon 3C(1)(c) [now Canon 3E(1)(c)], but he did have an "other interest" within the meaning of that section. Nevertheless, the interest was found so speculative and remote that the trial judge was not compelled to recuse himself.

b.   Should a judge be permitted to buy the bonds of a governmental entity that is within the judge's jurisdiction? Is it important whether issues relating to such bonds are likely to come before the judge, as distinguished from issues relating to the governmental entity generally?

The issue was presented in Matter of Fuchsberg, 426 N.Y.S.2d 639 (N.Y.Ct.Jud.1978), where a judge of the New York Court of Appeals was formally censured for his transactions in New York City bonds while cases affecting the value of those bonds were before the New York courts, including the Court of Appeals. Should it be a defense for the judge that ownership of such bonds in troubled times might seem a sign of loyalty by a public official?

c.   Should a judge be able to rule on a challenge to the judge's own pay? In 1976, some 44 federal judges filed a lawsuit arguing that failure to grant cost-of-living pay increases to the judges constituted an unconstitutional reduction of their salaries. The Court of Claims held that under the "rule of necessity", its judges need not recuse themselves and could hear the case. The claim was then denied. Atkins v. United States, 214 Ct.Cl. 186, 556 F.2d 1028 (1977) (per curiam), cert. denied 434 U.S. 1009, 98 S.Ct. 718, 54 L.Ed.2d 751 (1978).

Despite failing to win their first lawsuit in the Court of Claims or Supreme Court, some judges filed new suits in federal district courts. The Supreme Court heard the appeal and decided that the "rule of necessity" allowed the lower courts and the Supreme Court to hear the case, notwithstanding the ABA Code of Judicial Conduct and 28 U.S.C.A. § 455. The Court then decided that for two of the four years in question Congress had unconstitutionally diminished the salaries of Article III Judges and Justices. United States v. Will, 449 U.S. 200, 101 S.Ct. 471, 66 L.Ed.2d 392 (1980).

3. How does the Code of Judicial Conduct provide that a waiver of disqualification is to be handled? Did Judge Baxter take the proper steps here?

a.   May the waiver be made orally on the record in the manner defense counsel did here? Look at Canon 3F. Should the lawyers be permitted to waive a disqualifying circumstance on behalf of their clients? Are you satisfied that the procedure specified in the Code of Judicial Conduct will guarantee anonymity to an objector?

b.   Should it be significant that the case before Judge Baxter is almost certain to go to the Supreme Court? Does that mean that whatever Judge Baxter decides will not make much difference anyway?

4. What obligation does Judge Baxter have to know his niece's financial holdings? Would it matter if she were 17 and were his daughter?

a.   Should a judge be able to take an "I don't ask" attitude about his or her relatives' financial affairs? Look carefully at Canons 3E(2) and 3E(1)(c) & (d). If Judge Baxter knew of the niece's holdings, what would he have been obliged to do in this case? [2]

b. Note that placing the judge's assets (or his family's assets) in a blind trust does not satisfy the Code of Judicial Conduct. Should it do so? Why or why not?

c. Should a judge be able to "cure" a financial conflict brought on by investments of a relative?

Union Carbide Corporation v. United States Cutting Service, Inc., 782 F.2d 710 (7th Cir.1986), involved an effort to disqualify a judge based on her spouse's holdings. During the discovery period in an antitrust class action, Judge Susan Getzendanner got married. Her husband had a self-managed retirement account which contained stock in IBM and Kodak. At the time, there was no list of class members. When the judge disclosed her husband's holdings in her annual financial disclosure statements, the defendant moved to disqualify her because it knew that IBM and Kodak had bought products from the defendant. Instead, the judge immediately ceased ruling on motions in the case while her husband sold his interest in the two companies.

The Court of Appeals upheld that procedure. After the sale, the judge's husband no longer had an interest in the stock, the court reasoned. The court also rejected the defendant's argument that a reasonable person might conclude that the judge "might be sore at Union Carbide" because her husband, in selling the stock, had to pay $900 in brokerage fees and give up potential appreciation in the value of the stock. But, said the majority, "we do not mean to endorse sale as a cure for disqualification in all cases." The dissent by Judge Flaum suggested that nothing in 28 U.S.C.A. § 455(b)(4)—which corresponds to Canon 3E(1)(c)—permitted a judge to "cure" a disqualifying situation in this way. "Congress desired to rid the statute of flexibility where financial interests are concerned." Note that Canon 3F, like Judge Flaum, also does not recognize such a "cure". After this case, however, Congress added 28 U.S.C.A. § 455(f), which largely codified the Seventh Circuit ruling for the federal courts.

5. Should the fact that Judge Baxter's daughter practices federal tax law in a local firm require the judge to recuse himself whenever his daughter's firm enters an appearance in a case?

a. Does Canon 3E(1)(d) provide an unambiguous answer? Should the answer be the same in a large city with many available judges as in a small town with no other judges within 50 miles?

---

2. You can find out the financial holdings of a federal judge and his or her close relatives. See P.L. 95–521, Title III, Judicial Personnel Financial Disclosure Requirements § 305, in the Standards Supplement. The Fifth Circuit has summarily rejected a challenge to these disclosure requirements. Duplantier v. United States, 606 F.2d 654 (5th Cir.1979), cert. denied 449 U.S. 1076, 101 S.Ct. 854, 66 L.Ed.2d 798 (1981).

b. Should it matter whether the firm has taken the case on a contingent fee? Is the proportion of the fee to be shared with the daughter relevant? Suppose the daughter became "of counsel" to the firm, i.e., she did not automatically share all fees?

c. How is the judge to determine whether his daughter has a "more than a de minimis interest" which will be "substantially affected" by the outcome of a case? May he call his daughter on the telephone? Must he hold a hearing? [3]

d. Might Canon 3E(1)(d)(ii) serve to facilitate forum shopping? In McCuin v. Texas Power & Light Co., 714 F.2d 1255, 1263–66 (5th Cir.1983), the court observed that a litigant should not be able to obtain a new judge "by the simple expedient of finding one of the judge's relatives who is willing to act as counsel." If counsel was chosen "solely or primarily for the purpose of disqualifying the judge," the judge may disqualify counsel instead. The court admitted that "a litigant's motives for selecting a lawyer are not ordinarily subject to judicial scrutiny." However, "a contrary ruling would permit unscrupulous litigants and lawyers to thwart our system of judicial administration."

e. The United States Supreme Court now has confronted this issue. Several Justices have spouses, children or other relatives who practice law and whose law firms may work on matters that will come before the Court. On November 1, 1993, seven Justices [4] announced that, absent "some special factor", they would not recuse themselves solely because a relative of theirs had personally worked on a matter at an earlier stage before it reached the Supreme Court. One "special factor" might be that the relative had been "lead counsel below" because then the outcome of the case "might reasonably be thought capable of enhancing or damaging his or her professional reputation." 112 S.Ct. at CX (Dec. 1, 1993) (unbound). See also, 80 A.B.A.J. 18 (Feb. 1994). Further, if the relative is a law firm partner, recusal will be required unless the relative's firm gives "written assurance that income from Supreme Court litigation is, on a permanent basis, excluded from our relative's partnership shares." 112 S.Ct. at CXI.

Do you agree that the Justices have appropriately balanced the competing interests in establishing these standards? Were they properly concerned that recusing themselves in any more cases might create opportunities for " 'strategizing' recusals, that is, selecting law firms with an eye to producing the recusal of particular Justices." Id. at CX.

---

3. One federal case that read 28 U.S.C.A. § 455(a) and (b)(5) very broadly to disqualify the judge whenever anyone in his brother's firm appeared before him in virtually any matter was SCA Services, Inc. v. Morgan, 557 F.2d 110 (7th Cir.1977).

4. Only Justice Blackmun who was about to retire, and Justice Souter, a bachelor, did not sign the statement. 112 S.Ct. at CIX (1993).

6.   Should recusal be required when counsel for one of the parties is the judge's former law clerk?

a.   What should be the rule when someone from the judge's former firm appears before the judge?   Look at Canon 3E(1)(b);   see also, e.g., National Auto Brokers Corp. v. General Motors Corp., 572 F.2d 953 (2d Cir.1978) (recusal not required unless the specific case was in the firm when the judge was a lawyer there).

b.   Is the judge-clerk relationship likely to have been more close or less than the judge's relationship with his or her law partners?   See Smith v. Pepsico, Inc., 434 F.Supp. 524 (S.D.Fla.1977) (judge need not recuse himself where the clerkship ended over a year before).   Compare, Wall v. Coleman, 393 F.Supp. 826 (S.D.Ga.1975) (recusal required where former law clerk is a party to the case).

7.   What happens when the judge leaves the bench and seeks to form a relationship with new partners?

Pepsico, Inc. v. McMillen, 764 F.2d 458 (7th Cir.1985), involved a judge who had become eligible to take senior status.   He contacted a "head hunter" who agreed to contact Chicago firms to see if any would want the judge to become affiliated with them.   Inadvertently, and contrary to the judge's instructions, the head hunter contacted firms representing both the plaintiff and defendant in a pending antitrust case.   Neither expressed an interest in hiring the judge, although the plaintiff's firm left the matter a bit more open than did the other.   The judge did not go to work for either firm.   Defendants sought a writ of mandamus to disqualify the judge.   The Court of Appeals was careful to stress that there was no intentional impropriety committed in the case, but it ordered the judge disqualified to avoid any "appearance of partiality" in the matter before him.

a.   The case raises the issue of how judges may ever accomplish a transition back to practice given the likelihood that almost all the major firms in a given area are likely to be counsel, or potentially counsel, in cases before the judge.   Cf. Model Rule 1.11(c)(2).

b.   How might the judge in *Pepsico* have avoided disqualification?   Look at the Commentary following Canon 3E(1).

PROBLEM 40

The Judge Identified With a Strong Policy Position

Marlene Miller was one of the founders of the Lawyers' Committee for the Equal Rights Amendment (the "Committee") a group that continues to lobby for the addition of an ERA to the state Constitution. This particular proposed amendment would explicitly guarantee women a state constitutional right to an abortion.   The "Committee" also intervenes from time to time in federal litigation aimed at redressing discrimination against women.

Ms. Miller has now been appointed to the Supreme Court of her state.   Her interest in the rights of women remains unabated.   She has continued as a director of the "Committee" (which is organized as a not-for-profit corporation) and attends meetings as often as her schedule will allow.

The "Committee" has asked Justice Miller to be its lead-off witness when the issue comes before the legislature this spring. She has agreed, and has also agreed to be the featured speaker at a "brown bag" lunch to be held in a park across the street from the State Capitol. There are plans to solicit cash donations to the Committee from those who attend Justice Miller's speech.

Troubled by the level of her judicial salary, Justice Miller has decided to continue teaching part-time at a local law school. She continues to be known for the strong positions she takes in class on unsettled points of law. She even encouraged the law review to devote a student note to one of her favorite issues, and she acted as faculty advisor to the student writing the note. When the question came before Justice Miller in court, she wrote the Court's majority opinion and relied heavily on the "outstanding analysis" in the student note. She did not disclose the history of the note to either counsel or her colleagues because she thought it irrelevant.

In areas with which she is less familiar, Justice Miller has asked certain of her colleagues at the law school to write drafts of her opinions in important cases. The drafts are polished with the famous Miller flair, and she signs them as her own, but the ideas were developed by experts. Again, Justice Miller has not disclosed the source of her opinions.

QUESTIONS

1. Should Justice Miller disqualify herself in all cases dealing with equal rights for women?

a. Do Canons 2B and 3E provide an answer or only suggest more questions? Do you agree with Chief Justice Rehnquist's approach to policy bias set forth in the Readings to this Problem? Will his attempt to distinguish "bias" from "favoritism" help Justice Miller know what she should do? Is he right, however, that any thoughtful person old enough to become a judge is likely to have well formed views on many questions of public policy.

b. Is it useful to ask how the judge's views on a question were formed? Might we apply something like the "extrajudicial source doctrine" to say that views formed in the course of trying a case should never be disqualifying?

That was the issue presented in Liteky v. United States, ___ U.S. ___, 114 S.Ct. 1147, 127 L.Ed.2d 474 (1994). There, three defendants were to be tried for spilling human blood on walls and objects at Fort Benning, Georgia. The judge assigned to preside at their trial had tried and convicted one of the defendants, Father Bourgeois, for similar conduct eight years earlier. During that first trial, the judge had repeatedly admonished the defense to limit its evidence and argument to the issues in the case, not the motivations for the protest. On the basis of those admonitions, it was alleged that the judge's "impartiality might reasonably be questioned" and that 28 U.S.C.A. § 455(a) required his recusal. The judge refused to recuse himself, and the defendants were convicted.

Justice Scalia, writing for five justices, observed that a "judge who presides at a trial may, upon completion of the evidence, be exceedingly ill disposed towards the defendant, who has been shown to be a thoroughly reprehensible person. But the judge is not thereby recusable for bias or prejudice, since his knowledge and the opinion it produced were properly and necessarily acquired in the course of the proceedings, and are indeed sometimes (as in a bench trial) necessary to completion of the judge's task."

However, extrajudicial sources are "not the *exclusive* reason a predisposition can be wrongful or inappropriate." A point of view can also constitute "bias or prejudice" even if it comes from a judicial source, if "it is so extreme as to display clear inability to render fair judgment." Thus, the fact that a source is extrajudicial should only be a *"factor "* in determining whether a judge's recusal is required.

Summarizing, Justice Scalia wrote that judicial rulings alone almost never constitute valid basis for a disqualification motion; "they are proper grounds for appeal, not recusal." And, "opinions formed by the judge on the basis of facts introduced or events occurring in the course of the current proceedings, or of prior proceedings, do not constitute a basis for a bias or partiality motion unless they display a deep–seated favoritism or antagonism that would make a fair judgment impossible." Clearly, "expressions of impatience, dissatisfaction, annoyance, and even anger" such as shown by this judge at the first trial, do not constitute bias.[1]

c. A change of judge was allowed just two years before *Liteky*, however, in Haines v. Liggett Group, 975 F.2d 81 (3d Cir.1992). Judge Lee Sarokin had conducted the trial of, and was assigned to retry, the nation's major cigarette companies who stood accused of producing a product that caused cancer. In an opinion from the bench he said: "Who are these persons who knowingly and secretly decide to put the buying public at risk solely for the purpose of making profits? * * * The tobacco industry may be the king of concealment and disinformation."

The Court of Appeals concluded that these words raised at least a question as to Judge Sarokin's impartiality and ordered a change of judge. Should a Court reach the same result on these facts after *Liteky*?

---

1. Justice Kennedy wrote a concurring opinion for himself and Justices Blackmun, Stevens and Souter. They found the Court's "impossibility of fair judgment" standard objectively different from the "impartiality might reasonably be questioned" standard of 28 U.S.C.A. § 455(a). They believed the first might be a fair reading of § 455(b)(1), but that Congress intended § 455(a) to reach those cases in which there was an appearance of partiality. Justice Kennedy agreed that in this case, however, the Judge's prior conduct did not require recusal under either standard.

Was this what Justice Scalia had in mind in leaving open the possibility that even some statements made in the course of judicial proceedings would show that a judge's "fair judgment [is] impossible"?

d. If you were Justice Miller, would you now know whether you should sit when issues concerning women's rights were presented? What would your answer be?

e. Would your answer be the same in cases in which the Committee appears as a party or amicus curiae? Look at Canon 3E(1)(a) & (b). How long after leaving the Committee should Justice Miller have to wait before it is proper for her to hear cases in which the Committee appears?

2. Is the concern about Justice Miller's possible bias any different than the concern one might have about possible bias of Judge Baxter in Problem 39? Sometimes the line between financial grounds for disqualification and policy-preference grounds is finer than one might think.

a. In Aetna Life Insurance Co. v. Lavoie, 475 U.S. 813, 106 S.Ct. 1580, 89 L.Ed.2d 823 (1986), appellees had submitted a health insurance claim to Aetna, which paid about half of the amount requested. It had failed to pay the rest, about $1,375, on the ground that the length of the hospitalization was unnecessary. Appellant sought punitive damages for the alleged bad faith refusal to pay the claim, and the jury awarded $3.5 million in punitive damages. The Alabama Supreme Court affirmed (5 to 4) in an opinion written by Justice Embry.

While the case was pending before the Alabama Supreme Court, Justice Embry had himself filed two actions against other insurance companies making similar allegations and seeking punitive damages. The U.S. Supreme Court held that "only in the most extreme of cases would disqualification [for bias or prejudice] be constitutionally required, and appellant's arguments [based on the judge's general hostility toward insurance companies] here fall well below that level." However the Court held that much more than Justice Embry's general hostility was at stake here. This was the first case in which the Alabama Supreme Court clearly established the right of action which Justice Embry was seeking to rely upon in his own simultaneous litigation. As the Supreme Court found, "Justice Embry's opinion for the Alabama Supreme Court had the clear and immediate effect of enhancing both the legal status and the settlement value of his own case * * *. We hold simply that when Justice Embry made that judgment, he acted as 'a judge in his own case.'" Three justices concurred but specially made the point that they would have found Justice Embry's participation improper even if his had not been the deciding vote in the case and even if he had not written the majority opinion.

b. In Liljeberg v. Health Services Acquisition Corp., 486 U.S. 847, 108 S.Ct. 2194, 100 L.Ed.2d 855 (1988), after a bench trial about who owned a hospital corporation, the loser discovered that the trial judge was a Trustee of Loyola University. During the time that the case was pending, the ultimate winner, Liljeberg, was negotiating with Loyola to buy some land for a hospital and prevailing in the litigation was central to Liljeberg's ability to buy Loyola's land. The trial judge ruled for Liljeberg, which thereby benefitted Loyola. Health Services then moved to vacate the judgment, alleging that the trial judge should have disqualified himself under § 455(a). At a hearing to determine what the trial judge knew, he testified that he knew about the land dealings before the case was filed, but that he had forgotten all about them during the pendency of the matter. He learned again of Loyola's interest after his decision, but before the expiration of the 10 days in which the loser could move for a new trial. Even then, the judge did not recuse himself or tell the parties what he knew.

The Court of Appeals reversed the judgement in favor of Liljeberg in the underlying case and the Supreme Court affirmed. The majority held that "[s]cienter is not an element of a violation of § 455(a)." While the trial judge could not have disqualified himself over something about which he was unaware, he was "called upon to rectify an oversight and to take the steps necessary to maintain public confidence in the impartiality of the judiciary." Moreover, while § 455 does not, on its own, authorize the reopening of closed litigation, "Congress has wisely delegated to the judiciary the task of fashioning the remedies that will best serve the purpose of the litigation." The Court recognized that while harmless error could justify failing to reverse a judgment in some cases, in this instance the appearance of impropriety required reversal of the judgment because there was "ample basis in the record for concluding that an objective observer would have questioned" the trial judge's impartiality. Moreover, the trial judge's failure to stay informed of his fiduciary interest in Loyola University "may well constitute a separate violation of § 455. See § 455(c)."

Chief Justice Rehnquist, joined by Justices White & Scalia, dissented and would have ruled that § 455(a) required an "actual knowledge" standard. Justice O'Connor agreed and would have remanded to determine whether "extraordinary circumstances" justified a reversal of the underlying case. Is Liteky v. United States, supra, more consistent with the views of these dissenters than the views of the *Liljeberg* majority?

3. Does Justice Miller's elevation to the Supreme Court require her to cease her present role in the "Committee"?

a. The purpose of the Committee is to achieve law reform in the area of gender discrimination. Is it thus dedicated to the "improvement of the law" within the meaning of Canon 4C(3)? Is it a "civic organization" not conducted for profit? If the Committee is not an organization described in Canon 4C(3), may the Judge still remain a member?

b. If the Committee is frequently involved in litigation that may come before her court, must she withdraw from membership in the Committee? If she must, does that mean that no judge should be a member of the ACLU or the NAACP, because such groups are frequently involved in litigation? May Justice Miller remain a member because she is a *state* judge while the Committee primarily intervenes in litigation in the *federal* courts?

c. May Justice Miller remain a director of the Committee? Could she be a university trustee? Would it be important whether the university is public or private? See Canon 4C(2) & (3) and related Commentary.

4. What kinds of things may Justice Miller personally do on behalf of equal rights for women now that she is on the Court?

a. May Justice Miller testify about the Equal Rights Amendment? Look at Canon 4C(1). What should she answer if someone asks her how the ERA would apply in particular hypothetical cases?

b. Is it proper for Justice Miller to speak at a public rally? Consider Canons 4A, 4B, and 4C(3)(b). Does it matter whether contributions are solicited?

5. May a judge act as a part-time law professor?

a. Look at Canon 4B. May he or she normally practice part-time? Should a distinction be drawn between the two activities?

b. Should a judge be obliged not to take positions in class on unsettled questions of law? Could those opinions be a basis for disqualifying the judge in later cases? Would you as an advocate before the judge believe you should know the opinions he or she has expressed?

c. May the judge write articles on issues that may come before her? See Canon 4A and 4B. Is it better or worse to encourage students to write the articles? Is the degree of intellectual independence of the law review editors relevant to your answer? Could an ethical rule be made to turn on something that variable?[2]

6. Is anything wrong with a judge having experts write his or her opinions?

a. Is such a practice different from having law clerks write the opinions? Does the Code permit both? Look at Canon 3B(7)(b).

---

2. Cf. B. Murphy, The Brandeis/Frankfurter Connection: The Secret Political Activities of Two Supreme Court Justices (1982), documenting how Frankfurter and Brandeis "found it impossible to curb their political zeal after their appointment to the bench." While Frankfurter was a law professor, Justice Brandeis enlisted him "as his paid political lobbyist and lieutenant." They "placed a network of disciples in positions of influence and labored diligently for the enactment of their desired programs." The "adroit use of the politically skillful Frankfurter as an intermediary enabled Brandeis to keep his considerable political endeavors hidden from the public." Frankfurter became the clearing house through which the justice's ideas were passed on to a variety of liberal publications, particularly the *New Republic*. "Frankfurter was instructed by Brandeis to propose those ideas that he liked under his own name at future meetings of *The New Republic*'s board of editors." Thus "Brandeis began to prepare the climate of public opinion for his reform programs [by educating] the editorial board on his views so that the whole slant of the journal would favor his philosophy." Brandeis' letters to Frankfurter were redrafted and published in *The New Republic* as unsigned articles and covered such issues as the 1924 Immigration Act, the McNary–Haugen bill on agriculture surplus, and Coolidge's silence on Teapot Dome. Id. at 9–10, 89–91.

Should the judge be required to disclose who was consulted in the decision of a case?

b. In Collins v. SEC, 532 F.2d 584 (8th Cir.1976), the Court reported:

> "The Administrative Office of the United States Courts authorized the appointment of Professor Roger B. Upson, Associate Dean of the University of Minnesota College of Business Administration, to serve as a contract consultant in the office of the Circuit Executive. His duties as a contract consultant were to assist the Court in understanding the record in this case and to prepare reports and memoranda for this Court in connection with that function. Dean Upson's report was filed with the Clerk of this Court and copies thereof were submitted to the parties. The parties have been given an opportunity to respond. Dean Upson's consulting fees were paid by the Administrative Office."

532 F.2d at 605, n. 40.

The Supreme Court specifically commented on the practice.

> "We note that after receiving briefs and hearing oral argument, the Court of Appeals—over the objection of the Commission, Cristiana and du Pont—undertook the unique appellate procedure of employing a university professor to assist the court in understanding the record in this case and to prepare reports and memoranda for the court. Thus, the reports relied upon by that court included a variety of data and economic observations which had not been examined and tested by the traditional methods of the adversary process. We are not cited to any statute, rule, or decision authorizing the procedure employed by the Court of Appeals. Cf. Fed. Rule App.Proc. 16."

E. I. du Pont de Nemours & Co. v. Collins, 432 U.S. 46, 57, 97 S.Ct. 2229, 2235, 53 L.Ed.2d 100 (1977).

Does the Supreme Court's surprise cast doubt or create limits on the scope of Canon 3B(7)? Should it be relevant that Dean Upson was not a law professor? In 1992, the Judicial Conference of the United States adopted a Code of Conduct for United States Judges patterned loosely on the 1990 version of the ABA Model Code of Judicial Conduct. Canon 3A(4) of that Code is similar to the present Canon 3B(7). See Code of Conduct for United States Judges, 150 F.R.D. 307 (Sept. 22, 1992).

c. A case presenting the issue even more directly is Matter of Fuchsberg, 426 N.Y.S.2d 639 (N.Y.Ct.Jud.1978). The evidence showed that a judge of the New York Court of Appeals had consulted with law professors in at least 12 cases. In some, telephone conversations were held about developments in particular areas of the law. In others, the judge sent the briefs to a professor and asked for a draft opinion, substantial portions of which he used in his own opinion. In at least one case the judge sent a draft opinion from another judge to a professor for comments. Do any of these acts violate Canon 3B(7)? Is it revealing that neither the judge nor any of the professors knew of former Canon 3A(4), now Canon 3B(7)? The Court's opinion concludes that his behavior "properly subjects [Judge Fuchsberg] to censure and disapproval" but not to removal from office. 426 N.Y.S.2d at 649.

READINGS

HON. WILLIAM H. REHNQUIST, SENSE AND NONSENSE ABOUT JUDICIAL ETHICS

28 Record of Assoc. of the Bar of the City of New York 694, 708–713 (1973).

Though the Canons of Ethics are extraordinarily detailed and specific about what shall constitute a "financial interest," they have virtually nothing to say about what constitutes "bias." The Canons state that:

> "A judge should disqualify himself in a proceeding in which his impartiality might reasonably be questioned * * *."

and thereafter set forth specific examples of required disqualification. The first is the case of a personal bias or prejudice concerning a party, or personal knowledge of disputed evidentiary facts; the second is where the judge has served as a lawyer in the matter in controversy, or a partner of the judge's has served as an attorney in the controversy. The illustrative examples are not, in my opinion, open to any serious question, and I shall say a few words only as to my understanding of the meaning of "impartiality" over and above the illustrative examples. One of the definitions of Webster's Third New International Dictionary of "impartiality" is "freedom from bias or favoritism"; one of the definitions of "bias" in that same volume is "an inclination of temperament or outlook." In that broad definition of "bias," one can scarcely escape the conclusion that all judges, to a greater or lesser extent, are biased. What can explain five to four or four to three decisions of appellate courts by judges all sworn to faithfully uphold the same laws and the same Constitution, other than a difference in attitude or outlook, which leads to the ascription of different meanings to the same words of a statute or of a constitutional provision? The late Justice Black was, in this sense of the word, "biased" in favor of a literal construction of the First Amendment to the United States Constitution, and made no bones about saying so. But it cannot be this sort of "bias" which would disqualify a judge, else it would be the rare case in which a quorum of a court could be mustered for decision.

I would suggest that the true distinction is between the concept of attitude or outlook, which is not disqualifying, and the concept of "favoritism," which is disqualifying. Favoritism to me means a tendency or inclination to treat a particular litigant more or less generously than a different litigant raising the identical legal issue.

Let me here comment briefly about a ground for disqualification which is found neither in the Canons of Ethics nor in section 455, but nonetheless appears to have acquired some substance if only through repetition. It is apparently thought by some that if a judge has spoken publicly on an issue which later comes before him as a judge, he ought to disqualify himself from sitting in the case. I have never heard it stated in any detail why this should be a ground of disqualification, though it must be grounded in some notion of "bias." It seems to me that the answers to this contention are numerous and convincing.

If what is sought to be avoided is any publicly expressed notion of how the judge might vote on a particular issue, the best evidence of his propensities would presumably be previous opinions on the same question or a related question which he has either authored or concurred in as a judge; and yet no one has ever advanced this as a ground for disqualification. Even if the concept be limited to statements made prior to assuming the bench, enforcement of such a rule would scarcely guarantee that the judge's mind would be a *tabula rasa*, even if such were thought desirable; it would merely separate those who might have advanced professional opinions publicly from those who advanced them privately. It is unlikely that a judge prior to his appointment to the bench will have expressed an opinion as to how a particular law suit ought to be decided unless he is counsel for one of the parties, and disqualified from hearing the case as a judge for that reason. But it is not at all unlikely that a member of the bar, whether in the teaching profession, in private practice, or in government service, may have had occasion to comment and give his views as to the merits of a particular constitutional or statutory issue, rather than as to the outcome of a particular law suit.

Disqualification for this reason would have the double disadvantage of denying to courts the services of members who have been active in the public arena prior to taking the bench, and presumably of denying these services for an indefinite period of time on the particular issue. For if what we are talking about is disqualification because of an expressed view on a constitutional or statutory issue, rather than on the outcome of a particular law suit, there is no logical terminating point for disqualification short of a judge's leaving the bench. There may be good reasons for discouraging extrajudicial statements on the part of sitting judges with respect to issues that may come before them, but if so it seems to me they should be articulated in the form of a separate standard of conduct, rather than tied in to judicial disqualification. But there surely is no reason to make participation in public discussions of current legal issues prior to taking the bench a liability when one becomes a judge.

Even more far afield from any established norm of judicial disqualification is the notion that a sitting judge may not properly engage in private conversations at a social event about matters of general interest, even those with legal overtones, without fear of some sort of professional damnation or the prospect of having to disqualify himself if a case involving some aspect of this general issue should ever come before him. I was sitting with a group of people whom I didn't know very well at a dinner party in Washington this summer, during the time the Watergate hearings were being televised daily. Not long after we sat down, the subject turned, as it doubtless did at most other dinner parties in Washington that evening, to the subject of Watergate and what the various diners thought of the various witnesses. In the midst of the discussion, one of the speakers turned to me and said: "Wait a minute. We probably shouldn't be talking about this in front of you, because it will probably come to the Supreme Court eventually."

I thanked him for his consideration, but added that if listening to this conversation were to render me damaged goods for the purpose of adjudication, it was at most harmless error in view of the damage I had already sustained by being exposed to the daily newspapers and television news programs.

In conclusion, let me reiterate, if any of the foregoing remarks can have raised any doubt whatever about it, that I stand four-square, along with every other thinking person, against any sort of judicial corruption or any conduct on the part of judges which could lead reasonable people to conclude that they are behaving corruptly. I concur just as quickly with the notion that no judge should sit in judgment in a case which might substantially affect his own financial interests or in which he might reasonably be thought to be partial to one of the parties.

But I do find troubling what seems to be a general current of opinion among spokesmen from both within and without our profession, spokesmen with the best of motives, to treat judicial disqualification for interest or bias as a matter of personal honor, such that the more ready a judge is to disqualify himself, the higher shall be his standing on the list compiled by that descendant of Abou Ben Adhem who specializes in judges. Once we depart from the area of corruption, or reasonable grounds to suspect corruption, I believe a strong case may be made for the proposition that the decision as to disqualification in a particular instance ought, like so many other questions, to be decided by weighing the relevant factors on the appropriate legal scale. The factors favoring disqualification are familiar to us all; the factors which weigh against disqualification are less well advertised.

Judicial disqualification at the trial court level, and often at the appellate court level where the appellate court does not sit *en banc* can result in docketing and scheduling problems which, while no one would say they outweigh a moral imperative on the other side, ought not to be lightly disregarded. Judicial disqualification at the appellate level has the added disadvantage of causing the decision of the case to be made by less than a full complement of the court charged with responsibility for the decision. If we recognize that the standards, both of the statute and of the Canons, pertaining to disqualification for interest and for bias are themselves based on the desire to avoid the appearance of impropriety on the part of a judge, there is no need to throw into the scales, as an additional standard over and above those addressed to disqualification, a desire to "avoid the appearance of impropriety."

During my sixteen years of the private practice of law, the judge who was the most "sensitive" to the "appearance of impropriety" of any I knew sat in a court of general jurisdiction in the state where I practiced. He was so "sensitive" to the appearance of impropriety that if he had so much as shaken hands at a large political gathering with one of the litigants who appeared before him, he would summarily disqualify himself. The principal result of this "sensitivity" on his part, so far as I could see, was that at least one working day a week he was able to reach the first tee of the golf course before eleven o'clock in the morning, or else get home and do some of those odd jobs which escape the attention of all of us on the weekends.

Judge Learned Hand, in his classic opinion for the Court of Appeals for this circuit in Gregoire v. Biddle, 177 F.2d 579, observed that denying immunity to a class of public officials

"would dampen the ardor of all but the most resolute, or the most irresponsible, in the unflinching discharge of their duties."

I do not think our profession will be well served by the creation of a climate of professional opinion in which the kudos invariably go to the judge who is quickest to disqualify himself, for such a climate could easily bring about a situation in which, to use Judge Hand's words, only "the most resolute or the most irresponsible" judges would sit in cases in which they ought to sit. Far more important than unanimity as to particular standards of disqualification is the recognition that outside of the area of corruption or reasonable suspicion of improper motives, disqualification is an issue to be decided by rational application of the governing standards to the facts of the case in a lawyer-like way. Such recognition is fully consistent with the most stringent condemnation of any conduct smacking of improper motivation, and with the avoidance of the appearance of impropriety; and it will aid the maintenance of other values essential to sound judicial administration which may be impaired by overly frequent resort to disqualification.

PROBLEM 41

The Judge as a Political Candidate

J. R. Kraft, a local lawyer, was a declared candidate for a vacancy on the trial court at a recent election. Shortly before the primary, the following advertisement appeared in the newspaper in his judicial district:

J. R. KRAFT

(A Working Man's Son)

— The Next Best Thing to Being a Judge Yourself —

I, J. R. Kraft, am a local boy. My Dad died when I was eight, and I worked in a foundry for ten years to earn enough money to go to law school. I have never lost a jury trial in all my time in practice and I have never been a member of a political party. If elected, I will do my best to stop inflation, give the benefit of the doubt to any working man who comes before me, and throw the book at every weirdo and pervert I can find.

Permissiveness is the issue in this campaign. My opponent stupidly gave bail to a 45-year-old low-life who everybody knew had raped a 12-year-old child, but then he slapped a $500 fine on a working man who had been laid off. You can count on me never to do those things!

VOTE FOR J. R. KRAFT

[C2592]

To most people's surprise, Kraft won the primary. To everyone's surprise, the "non-politician" became a party stalwart. He made the rounds of political meetings and gave a five-minute speech at each about how good it was for a working man's son to be on the ticket with the likes of Governor Ford, Senator Barker, and Mayor Black. He called upon "all working people" to support the entire ticket "from the top down to little me at the bottom."

At several meetings, listeners called him aside and pressed $1, $5, $10 or even $20 into his hand to help him meet his campaign expenses. He turned most of the money over to his campaign committee, but he used $189.95 of it to buy a second suit.

Kraft's style appealed to the voters. He won the general election as well and became a judge. He still had some campaign expenses left unpaid, so two weeks after the election he asked his campaign committee to solicit members of the bar to make up the deficit.

After Kraft was on the bench for less than a year, he presided over a major murder trial, which the defense won after Kraft approved unusual jury instructions. Ellen Embers, the State's Attorney, was quite upset. She had no right of appeal, of course, so she called a press conference and said: "Judge Kraft is the most biased, incompetent judge that I have ever seen. He ruled against the people throughout the recent murder trial, and he alone is responsible for letting a maniacal killer out to prey on the citizens of this county."

Two weeks later, State's Attorney Embers issued a statement from her office. "The rumors around the court house have been intense the past several weeks that Judge Kraft tilts his decisions toward Anthony Roberts, the city's leading slum landlord and a regular litigant before Judge Kraft, because Roberts is a major contributor to Kraft's election campaign. I have filed a grievance with the Judicial Inquiry Board to have Judge Kraft investigated and, if the rumors are true, to have him removed from the bench."

In the meantime, one of Kraft's close friends, who was also a major contributor to Kraft's campaign, is now on trial for perjury and bribery in connection with allegedly corrupt labor practices. His defense is that he engaged in an innocent, if careless, oversight. He has asked Judge Kraft to be a character witness. Kraft, who would disqualify himself anyway if the case came before him, said: "Of course, but it would be better if you would subpoena me."

QUESTIONS

1. By what standard is Kraft's advertisement to be judged?

a. Should it matter that Kraft was not yet a judge at the time the advertisement was run? Look at Model Rule 8.2(b) and Model Code DR 8–103.

b. Under the Code of Judicial Conduct, could the content of this advertisement subject Kraft to discipline? Look at Canon 5A(3)(a) & (d). If the advertisement had been extolling the lawyer's credentials for sheriff, would it have violated ethical standards to make these charges and promises? Should the standard be different when the lawyer is running for judge?

c. Does the First Amendment draw any such distinction? Courts are looking more carefully on the restrictions imposed on judicial campaign speech.

In Buckley v. Illinois Judicial Inquiry Board, 997 F.2d 224 (7th Cir.1993), for example, the Seventh Circuit declared unconstitutional, on first amendment grounds, a state judicial rule providing, in part, that "a candidate, including an incumbent judge, for a judicial office filled by election or retention ... should not make pledges or promises of conduct in office other than the faithful and impartial performance of the duties of the office; announce his views on disputed legal or political issues...." In this case, one of the plaintiffs was an appellate judge whose campaign literature accurately stated that he had "never written an opinion reversing a rape conviction."

The court said that the Illinois "pledges or promises" clause is not "limited to pledges or promises to rule a particular way.... The 'announce' clause is not limited to declarations as to how the candidate intends to rule in particular cases or classes of case. . . . [H]e cannot, for example, pledge himself to be a strict constructionist, or for that matter a legal realist. He cannot promise a better shake for indigent litigants or harried employers. He cannot criticize Roe v. Wade." [1]

d. In an Illinois judicial election, the Chicago Council of Lawyers—a group representing an important segment of the Bar—wrote:

> "Judge Elward * * * is *a person of substantial intellectual ability who works hard,* but reports from many lawyers also indicate clearly that he has a terrible judicial temperament characterized by extreme rigidity, unreasonable demands and positions, and closed-mindedness. His efforts *to achieve worthy objectives—such as avoiding delays in the court process* attributable to dilatory lawyers—have in several cases been vitiated by the rigidity and excessive zeal with which he has attempted to pursue them. Because of his clear lack of judicial temperament, the Council concludes that he should not be retained as a judge." (emphasis added).

With the judge's approval, a "Citizens Committee" published an advertisement before the election in certain suburban newspapers and the Chicago Sun Times. The advertisements quoted from an editorial which had appeared in the Chicago Tribune, a statement by a former president of the Chicago Bar Association, and continued:

> " * * * a person of substantial intellectual ability who works hard * * * to achieve worthy objectives—such as avoiding delays in the court process.

"CHICAGO COUNCIL OF LAWYERS"

Judge Elward was retained in office and a complaint was filed against him for publishing an advertisement that was "materially misleading." The Courts Commission, a panel of judges established to consider judicial discipline, disagreed:

> "We find analogous the test which has been applied in determining whether in the light of the circumstances under which they were made, omissions to state a material fact in a registration statement, filed with the Securities and Exchange Commission, were misleading. The rule applied is that 'the adequacy of disclosure of material information must be evaluated by a consideration of the "total mix" of all information conveyed or available to the investors [voters].' "

The Commission found that several unrelated news stories and editorials had appeared which were critical of Judge Elward and that

---

1. The court noted that the Illinois Rule was broader than ABA Model Judicial Code Canon 5A(3)(d)(ii), and admitted that its opinion created "undoubted tension" with another circuit, Stretton v. Disciplinary Board, 944 F.2d 137 (3d Cir.1991), which had upheld a similar rule. *Stretton,* said the court, "is distinguishable, although precariously."

several had accurately reported the Chicago Council of Lawyers evaluation. The Commission concluded:

> "Measured against this 'total mix,' we conclude that the respondent, in the use of excerpts from the Council's statements, did not create the false impression that the Council had recommended him for retention or that he had significant Bar Association support.

> " * * * Canon 7 of the Code of Judicial Conduct adopted by the American Bar Association, recognize[s] that a judge seeking retention may find himself confronted with the necessity of mounting a campaign. On this record, we hold that the use of the advertisements in the manner alleged in the Complaint did not constitute conduct that was prejudicial to the administration of justice or that brought the judicial office into disrepute. The Complaint is, accordingly, dismissed."

In re Circuit Judge Paul F. Elward, Case No. 77, Illinois Courts Commission 1 (1977).

Do you agree with this result? Was Judge Elward's advertisement misleading? Is that the proper issue; whether or not it was misleading, did its use show Judge Elward to be dishonest or unfit? Is the S.E.C. analogy apt? Would a person charged with misstatements in a registration statement be heard to defend that the investor could have put together the true picture from stories in the *Wall Street Journal*?[2]

2. May a judicial candidate run as part of a party team?

a. What limits are there on the political activities in which a judge may engage? Compare Canons 5A(1), 5B(2), 5C(1) and 5C(3).

b. May he or she make speeches on behalf of candidates for nonjudicial public office? See Canon 5A(1)(b).

c. How about contribute money to a political party or other candidates? See Canon 5C(1)(a).

d. If Judge Kraft now wanted to run for Congress, would he be required to resign from the bench first? Look at Canon 5A(2). Do you agree that he should be required to do so?

3. How may a judge running for election solicit and receive campaign contributions?

a. May a judge accept cash contributions pressed into his or her palm as Kraft did here? Look at Canon 5C(2). May a judge be told who his or her big contributors are? Might state ethics legislation supersede the Code on this issue in your state?

b. Do campaign contributions from lawyers raise questions of propriety? The multi-billion dollar Pennzoil Co. v. Texaco, Inc., 481 U.S. 1, 107 S.Ct. 1519, 95 L.Ed.2d 1 (1987), case was litigated primarily in the

2. For a good debate about this case, compare Cohn, Judicial Discipline in Illinois—a Commentary on the Judge Elward Decision, 59 Chi.Bar Rec. 200 (1978), with Reuben and Ring, Judges Have Rights Too, Id. at 220.

Texas state courts. The trial judge received a $10,000 contribution from Pennzoil's chief trial lawyer "[w]ithin days of being assigned the Pennzoil case", a sum the trial judge described as "princely." Wall Street Journal, Nov. 4, 1987, at 1, 20, col. 2. In the three and one-half years prior to their decision in *Pennzoil*, all nine members of the Texas Supreme Court, consistent with Texas law, "openly accepted campaign contributions from lawyers with cases pending before them." Forbes, Sept. 7, 1987, at 8.

c. Why should these gifts be distinguished from any other gifts made to a judge? Do you believe the judge will consider them different? Which is he or she most likely to "appreciate"? [3]

d. May a judge's campaign committee solicit funds from lawyers *after* the election when the winner is known? See Canon 5C(2). Do you agree with the position the ABA Model Code of Judicial Conduct takes on this question? What arguments would one make in support of the position?

e. Would a "merit system" of judicial selection remove all ethical issues from the selection process? Might the "political activity" take other forms? Could a governor's aide properly question a prospective judge about his or her attitudes on bail for "low-lifes," for example? Look at Canon 5B(2). Should it be proper for an attorney to work in a Senator's election campaign in the hope of being rewarded with a judicial appointment?

4. Does State's Attorney Embers have an obligation to move for disciplinary action against Judge Kraft?

a. Look at Model Rule 8.3(b) and Model Code EC 8–5. If another judge knew that Embers' charges were true, would that judge have an obligation to report Judge Kraft? See Canon 3D(1).

b. Should a lawyer be more limited in publicly announcing the filing of charges against a judge than if the charges had been filed against another public official? Is there a public interest in preserving confidence in the judiciary that may distinguish these from ordinary cases? Does the argument cut the other way, i.e., that confidence is instilled by aggressively rooting out corruption? See, e.g., Justices of Appellate Div. v. Erdmann, 33 N.Y.2d 559, 347 N.Y.S.2d 441, 301 N.E.2d 426 (1973), excerpted in the Readings to this Problem.

c. Does the question turn, in part, on the way judicial discipline is handled in your state? In Illinois, for example, the state constitution provides that "All proceedings of the [Judicial Inquiry] Board shall be confidential except the filing of a complaint with the Courts Commission." Art. 6, sec. 15(c). See the Braithwaite article excerpted below in the Readings.

---

3. An interesting alternative method of funding campaigns was reported in White, New Approach to Financing Judicial Campaigns, 59 A.B.A.J. 1429 (1973). In Dade County, Florida, a fund has been established to which lawyers may make contributions. The fund is then distributed pro rata to all judicial candidates rated "qualified" in a poll of the attorneys. Cf. ABA Informal Opinion 1281 (Aug. 8, 1973).

d. Baugh v. Judicial Inquiry & Review Commission, 907 F.2d 440 (4th Cir.1990), tested the constitutionality of a state statute prohibiting a complainant from announcing the filing of a complaint with the Judicial Inquiry Commission. The court agreed that the rule was "viewpoint–neutral", but said the rule was not "content-neutral", i.e., it related to what was said and not to the time, place and manner of speech. Thus, the case was remanded to make a record and to determine whether a compelling state interest justified the restriction. See also, Doe v. Florida Judicial Qualifications Commission, 748 F.Supp. 1520 (S.D.Fla.1990) (holding a disclosure restriction unconstitutional).

5. Should a lawyer be subject to discipline for making critical remarks about a judge at a press conference as described in this problem?

a. In re Holtzman, 577 N.E.2d 30 (N.Y.1991), was a celebrated case involving a district attorney who publicly released a letter charging a trial judge with misconduct during a sexual assault trial. The D.A. had been told, and alleged in her letter, that the Judge had made the complainant get down on the floor and in effect reenact the crime before the jury. It was found that this allegation was not in fact true. The Court rejected a N.Y. Times v. Sullivan standard and upheld issuance of a letter of reprimand.

b. U.S. District Court for E.D. Washington v. Sandlin, 12 F.3d 861 (9th Cir.1993), affirmed an order suspending a lawyer from practice before the District Court for falsely charging that the District Judge had ordered important passages deleted from the transcript of a recusal hearing. The statements were made in a judicial hearing on the lawyer's charges and also in a statement to an Assistant U.S. Attorney that led to FBI scientific tests and a Grand Jury investigation that both cleared the judge. The Court agreed that Rule 8.2(a) does not prohibit all criticism of judges, but it refused to create an "actual malice" standard to replace the "known to be false or made with reckless disregard as to its truth or falsity" language of the rule. The test must be "what the reasonable attorney, considered in light of all his professional functions, would do in the same or similar circumstances." Applying this standard to the facts, the six month suspension was affirmed.

c. Should your answers to questions regarding criticism of judges be affected by whether or not judges are elected in your state? Cf. DR 8–102(A) and EC 8–6. Does the public have an interest in knowing about the integrity of the judges who stand for election? Would it matter how long it was until these judges next had to face the voters? On the other hand, are elected judges particularly exposed to unjust vilification and unusually limited in the propriety of their responding to criticism? Should it be the judges with life tenure whom lawyers are most free to criticize?

d. If a judge were as reckless as Embers in her comments about a fellow judge, could the judge be similarly sanctioned? See Canon 3D(3).

Is the short answer that both lawyers and judges should communicate with the disciplinary authorities and not go public?

6. Would State's Attorney Embers be subject to any form of discipline if she made her remarks about Judge Kraft to the judge's face or in a letter to the judge?

a.   In re Snyder, 472 U.S. 634, 105 S.Ct. 2874, 86 L.Ed.2d 504 (1985), involved a lawyer appointed to handle a case under the Criminal Justice Act.   He submitted a claim for fees that was returned with a request for additional information.   Because the lawyer had technical problems with his computer software, he did not provide the information in the form requested by the Chief Judge.   The lawyer did provide a supplemental application, which the secretary to the Chief Judge again returned.   Finally, the lawyer wrote the Judge's secretary complaining of the "extreme gymnastics" required of him to get paid "puny amounts," which allegedly did not even cover overhead.   He wrote that he was "extremely disgusted" by the Eighth Circuit's treatment and he asked to be taken off the list of counsel willing to accept appointment. For these "disrespectful remarks," and because he refused to apologize "for what I consider to be telling the truth, albeit in harsh terms," the lawyer was suspended from practice before the federal courts for six months, 734 F.2d 334 (8th Cir.1984).

A unanimous Supreme Court reversed.   One intemperate letter does not justify such a sanction, the Court said.   The Court did not reach the first amendment issue but rather relied on its interpretation of Federal Rule of Appellate Procedure 46, which authorizes a court to suspend or disbar an attorney "guilty of conduct unbecoming a member of the bar of the court * * *."   The Supreme Court noted that the lawyer's criticisms of the administration of the Criminal Justice Act had merit (a point the Eighth Circuit had conceded) and that such criticism cannot be a cause for discipline or suspension.   The Circuit Court's testy opinion on remand is at 770 F.2d 743 (8th Cir.1985).

b.   Morrissey v. Commonwealth, 428 S.E.2d 503 (Va.1993), involved a prosecutor's effort to protect his assistants against what he considered to be a judge's high-handed conduct.   The judge had refused to approve a plea agreement and had publicly called the assistant prosecutor "lazy". The Commonwealth Attorney then wrote to the judge, saying: "In the future, should you have any criticism of this Office or [one of my assistants], you are directed to set up an appointment with [my deputy] so that you can voice your complaints in a more professional manner. * * * [I]f that behavior ever, ever happens again, I will not be so kind as to merely draft you a letter of indignation."

The Virginia Supreme Court affirmed the prosecutor's conviction for contempt of court.   Even if the letter were not threatening violence but were only threatening to report the judge to the disciplinary commission, the letter was intimidating and thus "calculated to embarrass, hinder or obstruct the court in the administration of justice."   Do you agree?

7. May Judge Kraft be a character witness for his close friend? Should it matter whether he is subpoenaed?

a. One state bar committee proposed that Canon 2B should read:

"He should not appear as a character witness unless he appears pursuant to compulsory process of law * * * and unless the judge or other official presiding in the proceeding determines that his testimony is needed to protect the constitutional rights of a party or to provide a fair hearing." [4]

b. Do you see the reason for the different language? Would such an approach make the subpoena more than a formality? Do you agree with the proposed change?

READINGS

JUSTICES OF APPELLATE DIVISION v. ERDMANN
New York Court of Appeals, 1973.
33 N.Y.2d 559, 347 N.Y.S.2d 441, 301 N.E.2d 426.

PER CURIAM. Without more, isolated instances of disrespect for the law, Judges and courts expressed by vulgar and insulting words or other incivility, uttered, written, or committed outside the precincts of a court are not subject to professional discipline. Nor is the matter substantially altered if there is hyperbole expressed in the impoverished vocabulary of the street. On this view, no constitutional issue of privileged expression is involved in the conduct ascribed to appellant.

Perhaps persistent or general courses of conduct, even if parading as criticism, which are degrading to the law, the Bar, and the courts, and are irrelevant or grossly excessive, would present a different issue. No such issue is presented now.

* * *

Accordingly, the order of the Appellate Division should be reversed and the petition dismissed.

BURKE, Judge (dissenting). This appeal involves an order of the Appellate Division, Third Department, which decided, with two Justices dissenting, that the appellant was guilty of professional misconduct and censured him.

The charge was based on statements and language used in an article entitled "I Have Nothing To Do With Justice", which appeared in the March 12, 1971 issue of Life magazine. Lawyer Erdmann said of and concerning the courts within the First Judicial Department: "There are

---

4. Report and Recommendations of the Joint Illinois State Bar Ass'n–Chicago Bar   Ass'n Committee on Rules of Judicial Conduct, April, 1974, at p. 5.

so few trial judges who just judge, who rule on questions of law, and leave guilt or innocence to the jury. And Appellate Division judges aren't any better. They're the whores who became madams. I would like to [be a judge] just to see if I could be the kind of judge I think a judge should be. But the only way you can get it is to be in politics or buy it—and I don't even know the going price."

* * *

The article in Life magazine containing the vulgar and insulting language as far as Erdmann is concerned is not protected by the First and Fourteenth Amendments of the United States Constitution and Article I of the New York State Constitution. The article, as well as the remarks, violate restrictions placed on attorneys which they impliedly assume when they accept admission to the Bar. * * *

Returning to the First Amendment argument, it is only necessary to cite Bradley v. Fisher, 13 Wall. (80 U.S.) 335, 20 L.Ed. 646 wherein the Supreme Court of the United States summed up the distinction between the ordinary citizen and the member of an honorable profession. The court stated (p. 355) that: "[Attorneys] take upon themselves, when they are admitted to the bar, * * * not merely to be obedient to the Constitution and laws, but to maintain at all times the respect due to courts of justice and judicial officers. This obligation is not discharged by merely observing the rules of courteous demeanor in open court, but it includes abstaining out of court from all insulting language and offensive conduct toward the judges personally for their judicial acts. 'In matter collateral to official duty,' said Chief Justice Gibson in the case of *Austin and others,* 'the judge is on the level with the members of the bar as he is with his fellow-citizens, his title to distinction and respect resting on no other foundation than his virtues and qualities as a man. But it is nevertheless evident that professional fidelity may be violated by acts which fall without the lines of professional functions, and which may have been performed out of the pale of the court.' "

* * *

On this issue, the Second Circuit Court of Appeals said (Erdmann v. Stevens, 458 F.2d 1205, 1210) in denying the appellant's application for a preliminary injunction: "The issue before us is not merely the constitutionality of a state court's action in a suit between third parties but its application of standards established by it for observance by its own officers." To require civility of a lawyer is not arbitrary or a violation of his constitutional rights. Children are repeatedly reprimanded for incivility. Does this amount to an abrogation of Federally protected rights? The Appellate Divisions have been allowed wide discretion in the establishment and application of standards of professional conduct to be observed by its officers. "Only thus has the level of conduct for [lawyers] been kept at a level higher than that trodden by the crowd" (Meinhard v. Salmon, 249 N.Y. 458, 464, 164 N.E. 545, 546).

* * *

Accordingly, the order of the Appellate Division should be affirmed.
GABRIELLI, Judge (dissenting).

* * *

Second, it matters not whether the instances of disrespect for the administration of justice by the use of vulgar and insulting words or other acts of incivility, are uttered or committed outside the courtroom. The standard of conduct must remain unchanged even when the lawyer departs from the courtroom.

Third, appellant's statement was made with the knowledge that it would be published in a weekly magazine, having a Nationwide and foreign circulation of several million copies. In that sense, his utterance may not be characterized as one of those "isolated instances of disrespect for law, Judges and courts". Since his conduct was a designed and calculated act we are required, as a practical matter, to equate his act as intending to have been uttered the innumerable times represented by the copies sold and distributed, not only at newsstands, but by individual subscriptions as well as placement in public and school libraries, for millions to read.

However one may desire to parochialize this statement or, in fact, to now defensively limit its application, a fair reading of it leads to the inescapable conclusion that the vulgarity of Erdmann's undocumented and baseless charges that "Appellate Division judges aren't any better. They're the whores who became madams." was directed to all such Judges, wherever located.

His conduct may well be characterized as morally and ethically reprehensible; and his widely published statement, couched in such scandalous terms, is bound to have the effect of bringing discredit upon the administration of justice amongst the citizenry, an act which ought not be permitted.

WILLIAM T. BRAITHWAITE,* WHO JUDGES THE JUDGES? 161–165 (1971).

* * * [W]e may say that the general problem of judicial misconduct includes a range of particular problems, from occasional corruption and major felonies at one extreme to tardiness and discourtesy at the other. To be effective, a removal-discipline procedure should be able to deal with all these problems; that is, it should be capable of a range of dispositions, from informal admonition to formal public censure to termination of service. The procedure should, as well, be capable of operating reasonably expeditiously and with minimum cost and public spectacle.

* Mr. Braithwaite's study was sponsored by the American Bar Foundation.

Although it is sometimes necessary (and sometimes unavoidable) that a trial of misconduct charges be public—for example, when the charges have been publicly made and are apparently well founded—there is in most cases nothing to be gained, and respect for the judiciary to be lost, by having a public proceeding. It is reasonable to assume that once the charges and evidence are privately made known to them, most judges who are accused of misconduct serious enough to warrant initiating a proceeding to remove them will prefer to resign or retire. After the charges become public, the judge has less to lose by contesting them to the finish. From this research, it does appear to be the fact that cases of serious misconduct are more often resolved by the judge's voluntary resignation or retirement than by his removal after a public trial. The research also found that in most cases where the sanction imposed is discipline rather than removal, it is done confidentially (and often informally) rather than publicly.

The argument for confidentiality is even stronger in the case of disability. We learned * * * that the legal community finds it unacceptable to deal with the problem of disability by means of formal, public, adversary proceedings. The disability retirement procedures that were studied differ in their degree of formality, but all are administrative much more than adversary and are if not legally confidential, at least private as a matter of actual practice.

Maintaining confidentiality, at least in preliminary proceedings, serves several purposes. First, in those cases where termination of service is warranted, it allows the judge to avoid the time, expense, and spectacle of a public trial by resigning or retiring, a convenient and desirable disposition from the agency's point of view also. It also facilitates discipline for "minor" misconduct not serious enough to warrant termination of the judge's service. Publicizing incidents of minor misconduct serves no purpose in most cases, and contrition and cooperation from the judge are more likely if he is not made needlessly to suffer a public recitation of his professional or personal failings.

Confidentiality also protects judges from groundless accusations. Based upon the findings of this research, it is estimated that about two-thirds of the complaints received by removal-retirement agencies in the five states studied are prima facie trivial, do not raise an issue within the agency's jurisdiction, or are found after preliminary investigation to be without merit. Many complaints come from losing litigants and jail-house lawyers. A removal-retirement agency may arguably be serving a therapeutic function by providing these people a means to express their dissatisfaction with the court system. It need not also provide a means for them to defame honest judges.

Finally, confidentiality may also help protect lawyer-complainants. This research found that some lawyers who appear in court frequently, while they are in a good position to know firsthand about disability and some kinds of misconduct, are reluctant to report it because they believe (whether justifiably is not the point) that if they do, their clients' interests will suffer. A practice of keeping complainants' identity confidential can help allay this anxiety, although there will of course be cases where confidentiality is impossible to maintain, such as a case eventuating in a formal hearing at which the complainant must be called as witness. But particularly in cases that do not involve formal hearings, the agency can often protect a complainant's identity by the procedural device of treating the case as one initiated on its own motion rather than by external complaint.

* * *

* * * No complaint should ever be simply ignored; even those that are prima facie trivial or foolish from the staff's point of view should be acknowledged with a letter explaining why the agency cannot act. California's Commission on Judicial Qualifications follows this practice of acknowledging all complaints but goes a step further in public relations by publishing a brief annual report summarizing the Commission's activities. The report does not identify the judges who were the subject of complaints, but states the number of complaints received and investigations conducted and the number of judges who resigned or retired during Commission investigation. Provided it is discreet in substance and language, such a report can help to create public confidence that the agency is carrying out its responsibilities and will conscientiously consider every complaint submitted.

PROBLEM 42

The Overly Active Federal Judge

Lowell M. Richardson is the Chief Judge of the District of Massachusetts, a position reached by being senior judge in point of federal service. Seven other judges are in the district.

L. M. Richardson is known behind his back as "Loud Mouth" because of the way he interjects himself in trials. His long experience on the bench has given him what he believes to be an unfailing sense of who is telling the truth. If a witness appears to be lying, Richardson will interrupt to question the witness himself. If a skilled attorney is making an apparently honest witness look bad, Richardson will call a recess.

Judge Richardson can be particularly insensitive in dealing with female lawyers. He typically uses the title "Mr." when addressing male lawyers, while he usually calls female lawyers by their first name. He told one female lawyer who appeared before him: "With a pretty young lady like you in the courtroom, I wonder if the jury will pay any attention to me."

Judge Richardson is well known for his colorful opinions invalidating state laws regulating allegedly obscene song lyrics. Playboy magazine has solicited an article from him on this topic. At the present time, no cases involving this issue are before him. He has also accepted an invitation to play in a celebrity golf tournament designed to raise money to help the homeless.

Judge Richardson is 65 years of age. Recently he was stopped by Cambridge police for travelling 70 miles per hour in a residential zone. He was incoherent and chemical tests showed him to be intoxicated. His companion, a 28-year-old dancer in a local "nude review," attempted to flee when the car was stopped. The story has received front-page newspaper coverage in the Boston area and the dancer has appeared on several television programs to detail her experiences with Judge Richardson. She explained that she met Judge Richardson through a mutual friend at a dinner at the Owl Club, an athletic club to which the Judge belongs. Owl Club membership is open only to white males. The Judge and his wife of 42 years have been unavailable for comment.

QUESTIONS

1. How much should Judge Richardson insert himself into a trial?

a. Look at Canon 3B(4). Does Judge Richardson seem to comply with its requirements? Look at the stories of the "active" judges described by Professor Alschuler in the Readings to this Problem. What protection should a litigant and lawyer have from such abuse? Cf. Canon 3E(1).

b. The late Judge Charles Wyzanski once contended that the judge's role should depend on the nature of the case, with the judge generally passive in tort cases, more active in commercial cases (because he is more likely to have a specialized knowledge) and passive in criminal cases until the point of sentencing.[1] Later, Judge Wyzanski had changed his view. As reported by Judge Frankel, Wyzanski became "confessedly more activist today than [he] was a quarter of a century ago."[2] Frankel himself has admitted:

> "Introspecting, I think I have usually put my penetrating questions to witnesses I thought were lying, exaggerating, or obscuring the facts. Less frequently, I have intruded to rescue a witness from questions that seemed unfairly to put the testimony in a bad light or to confuse its import. * * * [But within] the confines of the adversary framework, the trial judge probably serves best as relatively passive moderator."[3]

c. Judges are not always entitled to be king or queen in their courtroom. In Frankel v. Roberts, 567 N.Y.S.2d 1018 (App.Div. 1991), the judge had sought to prevent Legal Aid lawyers from wearing pins

---

1. Wyzanski, A Trial Judge's Freedom and Responsibility, 65 Harv.L.Rev. 1281, 1283–93 (1952).

2. Frankel, The Search for Truth: An Umpireal View, 123 U.Pa.L.Rev. 1031, 1045 (1975).

3. Id. at 1043.

stating "Ready to Strike". He said he believed it would make the lawyers' clients nervous. On appeal, the Court recognized a judge's interest in courtroom decorum, but said it did not justify forbidding unobtrusive forms of free expression.

d.   Should judges be permitted more latitude to be creative when they are engaged in settlement discussions?   DDI Seamless Cylinder International, Inc. v. General Fire Extinguisher Corp., 14 F.3d 1163 (7th Cir.1994), was a case in which the parties agreed to have their civil dispute arbitrated by the federal magistrate who was handling settlement efforts. The parties agreed that the initial arbitration would be held before a third party and that the magistrate would resolve any issues on which the parties continued to disagree. That was done and the magistrate issued a "judgment" ordering the defendant to pay about $125,000. The defendant then asserted that federal magistrates may not moonlight as arbitrators, a point with which the Seventh Circuit agreed. However, the Court construed what happened as an agreement by the parties to find an abbreviated, informal way to have the magistrate act within his judicial capacity. Furthermore, by calling the arrangement "arbitration," the parties were found to have agreed not to appeal the result of the process, and the Court found no basis for setting aside that agreement. The case may one day be an historical footnote, but it just might suggest that there may be some creative, simplified ways to get binding results short of full trial or full agreement in cases brought in federal courts.

2.   Are the judge's sexist remarks a basis for discipline?

a.   How should Judge Richardson address attorneys who appear before him?   Look at Canon 3B(5), and the Commentary following Canon 4A.

b.   Consider the following situation, as reported in the American Bar Association Journal. A 27 year old female lawyer from a large, prestigious Chicago law firm, appeared before Illinois Circuit Court Judge Arthur Cieslik for a pre-trial conference. The judge said: "I am going to hear the young lady's case first. They say I'm a male chauvinist. I don't think that ladies should be lawyers. I believe that you belong at home raising a family. Ladies do not belong down here. Are you married?" "Yes," she replied. "What does your husband think about you working here?" The lawyer was concerned because she feared judicial reprisal against her client's interests. The judge later said, in defense of his actions: "I don't think I did anything wrong." He said: "I have a way of kidding around but some women take on the status of prima donnas and misconstrue what is being done. She said I should call her counsel, not young lady. It's nonsense. If she were 10 or 12 years older, she'd like to be called young lady." [4]

4.   See Blodgett, "I Don't Think That   Dec. 1, 1986, at 48.
Ladies Should be Lawyers," A.B.A. Journal,

c. In Disciplinary Counsel v. Campbell, 623 N.E.2d 24 (Ohio 1993), a judge received a one-year suspension as a lawyer (and presumably lost his judgeship) for offensive sexual remarks and touching. He told new female prosecutors, for example, that their success in cases before him would depend on their becoming his lover. The Ohio Supreme Court observed that conduct that would be reprehensible in any context is even more so when engaged in by someone with the authority of a judge. See also, Matter of Brooks, 436 S.E.2d 493 (Ga.1993), where another judge found guilty of sexual battery was required to resign as a judge and disciplined as a lawyer.

d. Judges are required to see that neither their staff nor lawyers appearing before them manifest bias or prejudice based on race, sex, religion, national origin, disability, age, sexual orientation or socioeconomic status. See Canons 3B(5) & (6), the related Commentary, and Canon 3C(2). In August, 1986, the ABA House of Delegates approved a resolution that recommended that judicial education programs for state and federal judges include "a separate course on the role of the judge in keeping a courtroom free from sex and race bias, and that relevant courses include a discussion of sexual and racial stereotypes that may affect judicial decisions." [5]

3. Is it wrong for a judge to cultivate or enjoy publicity?

a. Should a judge like Judge Richardson, who is not subject to popular election, try to avoid the public eye? If Judge Richardson were a state judge in a state where judges were chosen by popular election, would it be all right for the judge to call attention to himself?

b. Was it proper for Judge Richardson to accept the Playboy invitation? Is Canon 2A relevant here? Canon 4B?

c. May Judge Richardson play in the celebrity golf tournament? Would your answer be different if the event had no charitable purpose? Should it be significant whether the charity frequently finds itself in litigation? See Canon 4C(3)(b) and the Commentary accompanying it.

d. A clothing store in the small town where a trial judge lived had a wall on which hung pictures of famous local citizens who wore neckties sold at the store. The judge agreed to have his picture hung on the wall of the store as well, and for doing so, the store gave him a free necktie. Ohio Supreme Court Opinion 87–42 (1987) held that it is unseemly for a judge to further a private business in this way. Presumably, now the judge either will pay for his neckties or wear open-neck shirts under his robe. Do you feel better knowing that judicial ethics were enforced in this situation?

5. ABA Journal, Dec. 1, 1986, at 49.

4. Do the Judge's arrest for drunk driving and his affair with the young woman constitute professional offenses?

a.   Look at Canons 1 & 2A; are they inevitably only sanctimonious and unenforceable? Is there any basis for believing Judge Richardson's effectiveness as a judge may be impaired?

b.   Should a judge's open and notorious adulterous relationship be a basis for disciplinary action? No, the Pennsylvania Supreme Court has ruled. Matter of Dalessandro, 483 Pa. 431, 397 A.2d 743 (1979). One dissenter maintained, however, that the Code of Judicial Conduct does not limit itself to the judge's activities when he is "clothed in a robe." Does the test for "appearance of impropriety" proposed in the Commentary following Canon 2A support the majority or the dissent?

c.   Would a uniform retirement age for judges be desirable? Would it be constitutional? Such a statutorily imposed mandatory retirement age for state judges has been upheld. Gregory v. Ashcroft, 501 U.S. 452, 111 S.Ct. 2395, 115 L.Ed.2d 410 (1991).

5. Is it proper for Judge Richardson to belong to a private club that only admits white males to membership?

a.   Look at Canon 2C and the accompanying Commentary. Do you think the language is too vague? Too strict? There is presently nothing in the Model Rules or Model Code which restricts *lawyers* from joining clubs which exclude persons from membership because of race, religion, or sex. Should judges be subject to different standards?

b.   In August of 1990 the U.S. Senate Judiciary Committee passed a nonbinding resolution declaring that it is "inappropriate" for nominees to the federal bench or to posts in the Justice Department to belong to clubs that discriminate on the basis of race, color, religion, sex, disability, or national origin. The resolution provided that Senators should consider such continued membership "an important factor" in evaluating nominees, but nominees are excused from this requirement if they "are actively engaged in bona fide efforts to eliminate the discriminatory practices" in the clubs to which they belong. The resolution also states: "So as to promote a consistent policy on this issue, any Senator belonging to such a club should resign." What do you think of this resolution?

6.   Should judges be subject to private remedies brought by offended lawyers or litigants?

a.   Pulliam v. Allen, 466 U.S. 522, 104 S.Ct. 1970, 80 L.Ed.2d 565 (1984), involved a suit for injunction alleging that a state magistrate's practice of imposing bail on persons arrested for non-jailable offenses was unconstitutional. The federal court agreed, issued an injunction against the magistrate, and charged her with the plaintiff's attorney's fees which amounted to $7,038, plus $653.09 costs. The magistrate asserted that judicial immunity barred the payment of the fees, but the Supreme Court disagreed. Judicial immunity does not extend to injunctive proceedings, the Court said, and therefore a judge would be liable for fees incident to the injunction.[6]

---

6. Judges may legitimately be concerned that they will have to buy malpractice in-   surance against the costs of defending such actions and against the potential awards

b. Forrester v. White, 484 U.S. 219, 108 S.Ct. 538, 98 L.Ed.2d 555 (1988), considered a state judge's potential liability under Title VII when he fired his female probation officer. The lower courts had held that the decision to fire a close associate of the judge in whom the judge must have confidence is protected by an absolute immunity. The Supreme Court reversed. Judicial immunity is a steadily eroding concept, the Court said, and there is no reason to continue it for administrative decisions such as this one which do not relate directly to deciding cases. See also, Guercio v. Brody, 814 F.2d 1115 (6th Cir.1987) (bankruptcy judge's firing secretary, allegedly because she exposed corruption in the court, was not a "judicial act"; thus, there was no absolute immunity.)

c. In Mireles v. Waco, 502 U.S. 9, 112 S.Ct. 286, 116 L.Ed.2d 9 (1991) (per curiam), on the other hand, a public defender had sued a state judge (and two police officers) for damages in federal court, alleging that the judge requested and authorized the police to use excessive force to bring the attorney into the judge's courtroom. The Court held that judicial immunity is not overcome by allegations of bad faith, malice, or corruption. Unless the state judge acts in the absence of jurisdiction or not in a judicial capacity, there is at least no federal liability. Justice Stevens dissented, arguing that "[o]rdering a battery has no relation to a function normally performed by a judge." [7]

7. Is it important in this problem that Richardson is a federal judge?

a. We saw in Problem 41 that states have processes by which to remove their judges. In addition to impeachment and removal by the state legislature, in many states a judicial conduct commission can hear complaints against judges and provide for suitable discipline, ranging from private censure to suspension to removal from office.

b. Can federal judges likewise be disciplined for misconduct? Could Congress constitutionally create a panel of federal judges to impose discipline on other federal judges? Should a Constitutional Amendment be adopted to provide for a fixed term of office for federal judges? Periodic reconfirmation by the Senate?

Consider the comments of the ABA Joint Committee on Professional Discipline:

> The federal judicial system should have an appropriate structure for the discipline of federal judges. This can be accomplished through: (1) limited inherent power of the United

that may be made against them in spite of their immunity from damage actions. After *Pulliam,* the number of judges buying malpractice insurance has increased, though in only a small number of cases have there been judgments or settlements in favor of plaintiffs suing judges for damages. See generally, Judicial Immunity Insurance Available, 23 Judges Journal 2 (Summer, 1984); Plotkin & Mazoral, Judicial Malpractice: Pulliam Is Not the Answer, 20 Trial 24 (Dec. 1984).

7. Justices Scalia and Kennedy also dissented, objecting to the majority's summary reversal. Whether or not the majority is correct, they said, "if we are to decide this case, we should not do so without briefing and oral argument."

States Supreme Court; (2) a constitutional amendment; or (3) a congressional act.

With regard to the first alternative, the United States Supreme Court does not have any constitutional authority to remove a judge from office but it may by administrative order provide procedures for the investigation and the discipline by reprimand and declination to assign cases. This authority is derived from the court's inherent power. The United States Supreme Court also after investigation and due process may recommend impeachment of a judge to the Congress of the United States. It is, however, doubtful the court would ever take this action. The view that the United States Supreme Court has the inherent power to discipline the federal judiciary is not widely accepted * * *. Justices Douglas and Black, in a dissent, reflected what may well be a majority opinion of the United States Supreme Court when they stated:

> "An independent judiciary is one of this nation's outstanding characteristics. Once a federal judge is confirmed by the Senate and takes his oath, he is independent of every other judge. He commonly works with other federal judges who are likewise sovereign. But neither one alone nor any number banded together can act as censor and place sanctions on him. Under the Constitution the only leverage that can be asserted against him is impeachment * * *.

> "It is time that an end be put to these efforts of federal judges to ride herd on other federal judges. This is a form of 'hazing' having no place under the Constitution. Federal judges are entitled, like other people, to the full freedom of the First Amendment. If they break a law, they can be prosecuted. If they become corrupt or sit in cases in which they have a personal or family stake, they can be impeached by Congress. But I search the Constitution in vain for any power of surveillance that other federal judges have over those aberrations * * *." Chandler v. Judicial Council of Tenth Circuit of the United States (Douglas dissenting), 398 U.S. 74, 136–37, 140, 90 S.Ct. 1648, 1680, 26 L.Ed.2d 100, 137, 138 (1970), reh. denied 399 U.S. 937, 90 S.Ct. 2248, 26 L.Ed.2d 809.[8]

The court, however, has stated in a matter involving the discipline of an attorney:

> "[T]he courts ought not to hesitate * * * to protect themselves from scandal and contempt and the public from prejudice, by removing grossly improper persons from par-

---

8. Ed. Note: In *Chandler* the 10th Circuit Judicial Council refused to assign any cases to a federal judge because of its belief that Judge Chandler was "unable, or un- willing, to discharge his duties efficiently" and the Supreme Court, for procedural reasons, did not reverse the 10th Circuit order.

ticipation in the administration of the law." Ex Parte Wall, 107 U.S. (17 Otto) 265, 288, 2 S.Ct. 569, 589, 27 L.Ed. 552, 561 (1883).

Some writers have gone further and stated that the United States Supreme Court, as part of its implied and inherent powers, has the right to discipline as well as remove federal judges. See Burke Shartel, Federal Judges—Appointment, Supervision, and Removal—Some Possibilities Under the Constitution, 28 Mich.L.Rev. 723 (1930).

We suggest that the United States Supreme Court consider an appropriate disciplinary structure within its inherent powers to discipline the federal judiciary. Such a structure should provide an accessible means to receive and process complaints from the public and the legal profession in accordance with these standards.

The second alternative for a federal judicial discipline is the adoption of a constitutional amendment similar to that in effect in nineteen states. The necessary action to obtain a constitutional disciplinary provision for the federal judiciary would be a cumbersome process which would take years to accomplish.

The third alternative is the establishment of a disciplinary structure for the federal judiciary by congressional act. There have been and there are now before Congress, congressional acts which would establish such a disciplinary structure. Such a congressional act is subject to possible constitutional attack on the authority of Congress to define "good behavior" for the judicial branch. See Powell v. McCormack, 395 U.S. 486, 89 S.Ct. 1944, 23 L.Ed.2d 491 (1969), which spells out the powers of Congress to expel one of its own members. We know, however, that the Federal Judicial Conference has approved in principle this approach.

ABA Standards Relating to Judicial Discipline and Disability Retirement, Part 10 (1977).

c. Congress has now enacted a law creating the Judicial Council of each circuit as the body to hear complaints against federal judges. See 28 U.S.C.A. § 372, reprinted in the Standards Supplement. A Code of Conduct for Federal judges has now been promulgated. The format and much of the text is similar to the 1990 ABA Model Code of Judicial Conduct, but the ABA Code does not directly apply to Federal judges. The text of the new Code is published at 150 F.R.D. 307 (1992).

d. Gardiner v. A.H. Robins Co., Inc., 747 F.2d 1180 (8th Cir.1984), involved an effort to control the allegedly intemperate statements of a federal judge. Judge Miles Lord of Minnesota, in approving a settlement of some tort actions arising out of the use of the Dalkon Shield, had read a "speech" to officers of the defendant condemning them for violating "every ethical precept to which every doctor under your supervision must pledge." The prejudicial statements were struck from the record by the Eighth Circuit, but the defendants asked the Judicial Council of the Eighth Circuit to consider disciplinary action. The Judicial Council held that the remedy in the reported opinion had been sufficient, and it dismissed the disciplinary complaint as moot. Shortly thereafter, Judge Lord retired.

e. In October of 1986, Federal District Judge Harry Claiborne of Nevada had become the first judge in approximately a half century to be impeached by the House and removed by the Senate after he was convicted in Federal court of income tax evasion. Since then, Congress has also impeached Judge Walter Nixon who was convicted of perjury but refused to resign. See Nixon v. United States, ___ U.S. ___, 113 S.Ct. 732, 122 L.Ed.2d 1 (1993) (form of impeachment trial is a matter for the Senate and not subject to judicial review).

f. Finally, Matter of Certain Complaints Under Investigation, 783 F.2d 1488 (11th Cir.1986), involved the Judicial Council of the Eleventh Circuit's investigation of Judge Alcee Hastings of Florida. The Council was investigating allegations of several violations of the Code of Judicial Conduct, including a charge that Judge Hastings conspired to obtain a bribe. The investigating committee of the Judicial Council issued subpoenas to the judge and several of his staff members which were sought to be enforced in this proceeding. In this opinion, a three judge court, made up entirely of judges from outside the Eleventh Circuit, rejected the argument that only Congress has jurisdiction by way of an impeachment proceeding. It enforced the subpoenas, even in the face of the further allegation that the communications between a judge and his staff should be privileged.

Subsequently, Hastings v. Judicial Conference of the United States, 829 F.2d 91 (D.D.Cir. 1987), upheld the constitutionality of the federal judicial discipline system. The court also upheld the propriety of referring the Hastings matter to the House of Representatives for possible impeachment even though Hastings had been acquitted in a criminal trial of accepting the alleged bribe. Hastings claimed that the charges levied against him were false and racially motivated, but the House voted to impeach and the Senate voted to remove him from office. In October, 1989, Hastings became the first judge impeached and removed from office on the basis of charges for which he had earlier been acquitted, and in November, 1992, he was elected a member of the House of Representatives that had impeached him.

See generally, Rotunda, Impeachment Showdown: Congress vs. Judges, Legal Times, Nov. 1, 1993, p. 37.

––––––––

READINGS

ALBERT W. ALSCHULER,* COURTROOM MISCONDUCT
BY PROSECUTORS AND TRIAL JUDGES

50 Texas Law Review 629, 677–685 (1972).

II. The Trial Judge

The quality of our judges is the quality of our justice.

Leflar, The Quality of Judges, 35 Ind.L.J. 289, 305 (1960).

A. Introduction: The Trial Judge as Traffic Cop

An effective traffic policeman must sometimes be an aggressive, "take-charge kind of guy." When a motorist attempts an illegal left-hand turn in heavy traffic and then disobeys an order to drive straight ahead, the situation does not call for a sensitive understanding of the motorist's social circumstances. Instead, it usually requires an immediate, forceful, and intimidating response—perhaps by an officer whose lip is even stronger than the motorist's. A certain amount of authoritarianism seems to come with the policeman's uniform and badge.

The nature of a trial judge's job is, of course, essentially different. In theory at least, a trial judge should rarely be called upon to act in a crisis situation. He should act after the fact to resolve carefully focused disputes that have not yielded to private settlement. Because both parties to each case are usually convinced of the soundness of their positions, the trial judge's task is frequently difficult. It requires ample time, an atmosphere of careful deliberation, and the maintenance of what Mr. Justice Sutherland called "the calm spirit of regulated justice."

Nevertheless, over the course of the last half-century, this nation seems to have done its best to divert its trial judges from their naturally reflective role and to convert them into traffic policemen. At least we have placed most of our judges at very busy intersections. In 1964, the three judges of Atlanta's Municipal Court resolved over 70,000 cases. The following year, a single judge sitting in Detroit's Early Sessions Division disposed of more than 20,000 cases. In 1968, New York City's criminal courts took on 480,000 new cases, and they ended the year with 520,000 cases still unresolved. In many urban jurisdictions, criminal caseloads have doubled within a single decade.

* * *

Many trial judges seem to have become as preoccupied with "moving" cases as traffic policemen are with moving vehicles. Moreover, the techniques that they have come to employ are not entirely dissimilar.

* At the time this was written, the author was Professor of Law, University of Colorado.

Justice Mitchell D. Schweitzer of the New York Supreme Court apparently expressed the philosophy of many trial judges when he said:

> "In this job, one can do as much work as he wants to do. He can sit back and listen patiently to every matter that is brought before him. If he does that, he has done the job that a judge is paid to do. But if every judge took that attitude, the courts would be backed-up for twenty years. Some of us therefore take a more active part."

The general change in judicial attitudes can be seen, not only in the trial courts themselves, but in appellate opinions concerning courtroom conduct by trial judges. During the late nineteenth and early twentieth centuries, appellate courts generally attempted to promote a truly antiseptic atmosphere in America's trial courts. In 1899, for example, a New York court reversed a criminal conviction because the trial judge had instructed an evasive defendant to "answer the question and stop quibbling." Similarly, in North Carolina in 1917, a judge told a criminal defendant to answer a question without "dodging." The defense attorney objected, and the trial judge both apologized and instructed the jury to disregard his remark. The North Carolina Supreme Court nevertheless found the use of the word "dodging" so offensive that it reversed the defendant's conviction. In 1967, by contrast, a Michigan court found no error when a trial judge, without significant provocation, told a defendant under cross-examination to "shut up."

* * *

Although the relative formalism of the early cases would probably have disappeared in any event, today's overwhelming caseloads have undoubtedly played a significant part in altering the trial judge's role. Unlike a traffic policeman whose tasks are eased by the fact that motorists invariably share his interest in promoting the smooth flow of traffic, a trial judge must confront some lawyers and litigants who would not be at all distressed to see the flow of cases come to a halt. Perhaps even more than traffic policemen, judges must be alert for illegal turns.

When criminal proceedings are delayed, tempers cool, memories fade, witnesses are worn down by repeated court appearances, and other witnesses disappear. Accordingly, criminal defendants—at least those who are able to secure their release on bond—usually attempt to postpone their trials for as long as they can. Delay is also useful to defense attorneys who have encountered difficulty in collecting their fees, and the techniques, both honest and dishonest, for postponing the day of trial are many.

In an effort to improve their position in guilty-plea negotiations, defense attorneys commonly employ tactics whose primary function is simply to threaten the trial court's time. An attorney may, for example, file a series of frivolous pre-trial motions hoping that a prosecutor will offer sentencing concessions to avoid the burden of a hearing. Other defense maneuvers are used, not for their stated purposes, but to bring cases before judges who are considered favorable to the defense.   * * *

Many judges therefore believe that lawyers and litigants—particularly those on the defense side of criminal cases—will take advantage of our inundated court systems if the judges do not exercise a firm control. These judges may conclude, with some justification, that only an authoritarian attitude can bring a measure of order out of the chaos of America's criminal courts.

Our society has, of course, learned that authoritarian police attitudes cannot easily be confined to the situations in which they are appropriate. Similarly, when a trial judge adopts a forceful, "take-charge" attitude toward defense maneuvers in criminal cases, he may be unlikely to abandon that attitude when it becomes manifestly inappropriate. In that way, the administrative crisis confronting our courts has undoubtedly intensified the likelihood of courtroom misconduct by trial judges.

The pressures of the caseload not only encourage litigants to abuse the system and judges to react to this threat; in addition, the rapid flow of cases tends to dehumanize the criminal process. Cases come to represent numbers rather than people, and authoritarian judicial behavior becomes more likely. Judge Tim C. Murphy explains, "You sit there day after day and you hear the same problems and the same excuses. You find yourself becoming impatient or losing interest." In his 1956 Holmes Lecture at the Harvard Law School, Justice Walter V. Schaefer wrote, "Someone once wisely said that the basic trouble with judges is not that they are incompetent or venal beyond other men; it is just that they get used to it."

Of course judicial misconduct cannot be attributed entirely to the chaotic atmosphere that prevails today in urban courts. In relatively unpressured rural courts, there are many judges who, in Professor Herman Schwartz's phrase, "daily prove the truth of Acton's dictum." Professor Schwartz's portrait of a common species of American trial judge may be a bit overdrawn, but no trial lawyer will fail to recognize the figure that it portrays: "Glaring down from their elevated perches, insulting, abrupt, rude, sarcastic, patronizing, intimidating, vindictive, insisting on not merely respect but also abject servility—such judges are frequently encountered in American trial courts, particularly the lowest criminal and juvenile courts which account for most of our criminal business."

A local magazine for the District of Columbia, The Washingtonian, recently investigated the performance of trial judges in and around that city. Its report provided frequent and striking illustrations of judicial misconduct.   * * *

In suburban Maryland, the reporter investigated the courtroom behavior of Judge William B. Bowie, whose approach to life and to judging was illustrated by a remark that he made in court about certain black defendants: "If they want to live like animals, let them stay in a pen somewhere."

In the District of Columbia, The Washingtonian focused largely on the Court of General Sessions. In the courtroom of Judge Edward A. Beard, two defendants were awaiting trial on a narcotics charge when one of them fell asleep. Judge Beard promptly sentenced both defendants to thirty days' imprisonment for contempt of court.

"But I'm all right," the non-offending defendant said. "Why me?"

"You are guilty by association," the judge replied. "Get them out of here."

* * *

These examples are extreme. Nevertheless, similar incidents have occurred throughout the nation. Judges have, for example, asked defense attorneys whether they were not taught better in their first year of law school, referred to their behavior as "shyster stuff," called their cross-examination of prosecution witnesses "just ridiculous," and characterized them as "troublesome, like a school boy." Judges have similarly referred to defendants as drifters, as bamboozlers, as black cats in a white Buick, and as Sing Sing graduates. As recently as 1960 and 1963, moreover, judges told juries that they might consider racial factors in reaching their verdicts.

* * *

Courtroom misconduct by prosecutors may merit special condemnation because of the influence that prosecutors commonly have with juries, but juries are undoubtedly even more attentive to the views and prejudices of trial judges. As the Iowa Supreme Court recently remarked, a trial judge's behavior "may influence the jury more than the evidence." Moreover, if prosecutorial misconduct hinders rehabilitative efforts and encourages defendants to believe that the courts are stacked against them, if it promotes disrespect for the law by the public in general and by minority groups in particular, judicial misconduct surely has an even more harmful effect on the attitudes of various constituencies toward our system of justice. Trial judges are, however, even less subject to effective corrective measures than prosecutors.

One can imagine a vignette in which a trial judge and a defense attorney exchange obscenities with one another during a trial. Because provocation by the trial judge ordinarily is not a defense to a charge of contempt of court, the defense attorney might well be imprisoned as a result of this incident. The trial judge, however (who is commonly called "a symbol of experience, wisdom and impartiality"), could in many jurisdictions not be disciplined at all. For some observers, the "Chicago Eight" trial has already dramatized this paradox. Professor Herman Schwartz, notes, "Abbie Hoffman may go to jail for five years, but Julius Hoffman went to Florida with a stop at the White House for breakfast * * *."

BIBLIOGRAPHY ON ISSUES IN CHAPTER VIII

Problem 39

Franck, "A Judge Shall Avoid Impropriety and the Appearance of Impropriety in All of the Judge's Activities.", 69 Michigan Bar J. 234 (1990).

Holland, The Code of Judicial Conduct and the Model Rules of Professional Conduct: A Comparison of Ethical Codes for Judges and Lawyers, 2 Georgetown J.Legal Ethics 725 (1989).

Kaufman, Judicial Ethics: The Less–Often Asked Questions, 64 Washington L.Rev. 851 (1989).

Lubet, Regulation of Judges' Business and Financial Activities, 37 Emory L.J. 1 (1988).

Lubet, Judicial Ethics and Private Lives, 79 Northwestern U.L.Rev. 983 (1984).

Lubet, The Search for Analysis in Judicial Ethics or Easy Cases Doesn't Make Much Law, 66 Nebraska L.Rev. 430 (1987).

Markey, The Delicate Dichotomies of Judicial Ethics, 101 F.R.D. 373 (1984).

McFadden, Hors d'oeuvres and Ethics: Social Relations of Judges and Lawyers, 77 Illinois Bar J. 358(7) (1989).

Shaman, Bias on the Bench: Judicial Conflict of Interest, 3 Georgetown J.Legal Ethics 245 (1989).

Swan, Protecting the Appearance of Judicial Impartiality in the Face of Law Clerk Employment Negotiations, 62 Washington L.Rev. 813 (1987).

Van Noy, The Appearance of Fairness Doctrine: A Conflict in Values, 61 Washington L.Rev. 533 (1986).

Wald, Some Thoughts on Judging as Gleaned From One Hundred Years of the Harvard Law Review and Other Great Books, 100 Harvard L.Rev. 887 (1987).

Problem 40

Leslie W. Abramson, Judicial Disqualification Under Canon 3 of the Code of Judicial Conduct (2d ed.1992).

Abramson, Specifying Grounds for Judicial Disqualification in Federal Courts, 72 Nebraska L.Rev. 1046 (1993).

Abramson, Deciding Recusal Motions: Who Judges the Judges?, 28 Valparaiso U.L.Rev. 543 (1994).

Bartels, Peremptory Challenges to Federal Judges: A Judge's View, 68 A.B.A.J. 449 (1982).

Benefiel, Off–the–Bench Restrictions on Judges: Ambiguity in Search of an Answer, 20 Loyola U.(Chicago) L.J. 903 (1989).

Carlisle, Service on Board of MADD (Mothers Against Drunk Drivers), 57 Florida Bar J. 653 (1983).

Carter, The Religiously Devout Judge, 64 Notre Dame L.Rev. 932 (1989).

Copple, From the Cloister to the Street: Judicial Ethics and Public Expression, 64 Denver U.L.Rev. 549 (1988).

Goldstein, Fundraising by Judges: Ethical Restrictions on Assisting Civic, Charitable and Other Organizations, 70 Judicature 26 (1986).

Steven Lubet, Beyond Reproach: Ethical Restrictions on the Extrajudicial Activities of State and Federal Judges (1984).

Lubet, Ex Parte Communications: An Issue in Judicial Conduct, 74 Judicature 96 (Aug.-Sept.1990).

Middleton, Hunger and Ethics: No Conflict in Judge's Case, 69 A.B.A.J. 573 (1983).

Nathanson, The Extra–Judicial Activities of Supreme Court Justices: Where Should the Line be Drawn?, 78 Northwestern U.L.Rev. 494 (1983).

Note, Justice Rehnquist's Decision to Participate in Laird v. Tatum, 73 Columbia L.Rev. 106 (1973).

Ross, Extrajudicial Speech: Charting the Boundaries of Propriety, 2 Georgetown J.Legal Ethics 589 (1989).

Problem 41

Alfini & Brooks, Ethical Constraints on Judicial Election Campaigns: A Review and Critique of Canon 7, 77 Kentucky L.J. 671 (1989).

Burke, Code of Judicial Conduct Canon 7B(1)(c): Toward the Proper Regulation of Judicial Speech, 7 Georgetown J.Legal Ethics 181 (1993).

Gary, Ethical Conduct in a Judicial Campaign: Is Campaigning an Ethical Activity?, 57 Washington L.Rev. 119 (1981).

Lubet, Professor Polonius Advises Judge Laertes: Rules, Good Taste and the Scope of Public Comment, 2 Georgetown J.Legal Ethics 665 (1989).

McFadden, Electing Justice: The Law and Ethics of Judicial Election Campaigns (1990).

Molley, Restrictions on Attorney Criticism of the Judiciary: A Denial of First Amendment Rights, 56 Notre Dame Lawyer 489 (1981).

Riccardi, Code of Judicial Conduct Canon 7B(1)(c): An Unconstitutional Restriction on Freedom of Speech, 7 Georgetown J.Legal Ethics 153 (1993).

Smoler & Stokinger, The Ethical Dilemma of Campaigning for Judicial Office: A Proposed Solution, 14 Fordham Urban Law J. 353 (1986).

Problem 42

Abramson, Specifying Grounds for Judicial Disqualification in Federal Courts, 72 Nebraska L.Rev. 1046 (1993).

Alfini, Doing Justice in a Bureaucracy: The Need to Reconcile Contemporary Judicial Roles in Light of Ethical and Administrative Imperatives, 54 Missouri L.Rev. 323 (1989).

Austern, Legal and Judicial Ethics and the Supreme Court, 22 Trial 22(2) (1986).

Bell, Private Clubs and Public Judges: A Nonsubstantive Debate About Symbols, 59 Texas L.Rev. 733 (1981).

W. Braithwaite, Who Judges the Judges (1971).

Burbank, Alternative Career Resolution: An Essay on The Removal of Federal Judges, 76 Kentucky L.Rev. 643 (1987–1988).

Forer, When Should Judges be Whistle Blowers? Ethical Obligations of the Judiciary to the Public, 27 Judges Journal 4(8) (1988).

Frankel, The Adversary Judge, 54 Texas L.Rev. 465 (1976).

Fretz, Peeples & Wicker, Ethics for Judges (1982).

Gaffney, The Importance of Dissent and the Imperative of Judicial Civility, 28 Valparaiso U.L.Rev. 583 (1994).

Gardiner, Preventing Judicial Misconduct: Defining the Role of Conduct Organizations, 70 Judicature 113 (1986).

Hall, Federal Circuit Judicial Councils: A Legislative History and Revisions Needed, 11 Georgia State U.L.Rev. 1 (1994).

Hastie, Judicial Role and Judicial Image, 121 U.Pennsylvania L.Rev. 947 (1973).

Kastenmeier & Remington, Judicial Discipline: A Legislative Perspective, 76 Kentucky L.J. 763 (1987–1988).

Keyt, Reconciling the Need for Confidentiality in Judicial Disciplinary Proceedings with the First Amendment: A Justification–Based Analysis, 7 Georgetown J. Legal Ethics 959 (1994).

Kirkland, Constitution and the Tenure of Federal Judges: Some Notes from History, 36 U.Chicago L.Rev. 665 (1969).

Leitch, Judicial Disqualification in the Federal Courts: A Proposal to Conform Statutory Provisions to Underlying Policies, 67 Iowa L.Rev. 525 (1982).

Marcus, Who Should Discipline Federal Judges, and How?, 149 F.R.D. 375 (1993).

Markey, A Need for Continuing Education in Judicial Ethics, 28 Valparaiso U.L.Rev. 647 (1994).

McConnell, Reflections on the Senate's Role in the Judicial Impeachment Process and Proposals for Change, 76 Kentucky L.J. 739 (1987–88).

Peterson, The Role of the Executive Branch in the Discipline and Removal of Federal Judges, 1993 U. Illinois L.Rev. 809 (1993).

Rotunda, An Essay on the Constitutional Parameters of Federal Impeachment, 76 Kentucky L.Rev. 707 (1987–88).

Rotunda, The Combination of Functions in Administrative Actions: An Examination of European Alternatives, 40 Fordham L.Rev. 101 (1971).

Sahl, Secret Discipline in the Federal Courts: Democratic Values and Judicial Integrity At Stake, 70 Notre Dame L.Rev. 193 (1994).

Schafram, Documenting Gender Bias in the Courts: The Task Force Approach, 70 Judicature 280 (1987).

Shaman, State Judicial Conduct Organizations, 76 Kentucky L.J. 811 (1987–1988).

J. Shaman, S. Lubet & J. Alfini, Judicial Conduct and Ethics (1990).

Stoltz, Disciplining Federal Judges: Is Impeachment Hopeless, 57 California L.Rev. 659 (1969).

Symposium, On the Code of Judicial Conduct, 1972 Utah L.Rev. 333.

Symposium, Disciplining the Federal Judiciary, 142 U.Pennsylvania L.Rev. 1 (1993).

Thode, The Code of Judicial Conduct: The First Five Years in the Courts, 1977 Utah L.Rev. 395.

Traynor, Who Can Best Judge the Judges, 53 Virginia L.Rev. 1266 (1967).

INDEX

References are to Pages

599

†